Henry James

a reference guide
1975–1987

A
Reference
Guide
to
Literature

Henry James

a reference guide
1975–1987

JUDITH E. FUNSTON

G.K. HALL &CO.
70 LINCOLN STREET, BOSTON, MASS.

First published 1991
by G.K. Hall & Co.
70 Lincoln Street
Boston, Massachusetts 02111

10 9 8 7 6 5 4 3 2

Library of Congress Cataloging-in-Publication Data

Funston, Judith E.
    Henry James, 1975-1987 : a reference guide / Judith E. Funston.
        p.   cm.
    Includes indexes.
    ISBN 0-8161-8953-6
    1. James, Henry, 1843-1916 – Bibliography.
I. Title. II. Series.
Z8447.F85   1991
[PS2123]
016.813'4 – dc20   90-48856
                                                     CIP

The paper used in this publication meets the minimum requirements of
American National Standard for Information Sciences – Permanence of
Paper for Printed Library Materials. ANSI Z39.48-1984.   ∞™
MANUFACTURED IN THE UNITED STATES OF AMERICA

Contents

The Author

After completing her Ph.D in American literature in 1982, Judith Funston accepted an administrative position in the Multidisciplinary Program at Michigan State University and published numerous articles on Henry James, Edith Wharton, and other American authors. Currently, she is assistant professor of American literature at Potsdam College, State University of New York, and is working on a book-length study of Edith Wharton's travel essays.

Preface

This Reference Guide, the fourth on Henry James published by G.K. Hall (see Taylor 1982.144, McColgan 1979.90, and Scura 1979.134) is an annotated bibliography of criticism published during the years 1975 to 1987. Included in this listing of over 2,300 items are books, chapters of books, Ph.D. dissertations, articles (primarily though not exclusively from professional journals), introductions to reprints of James's works, reviews of adaptations of James's work, and selected book reviews. As a rule, reviews of secondary works have been omitted, but I have annotated reviews of Edel's biography of James and the four volumes of James's letters – such reviews often offer insight on James's life and work as well as on the man who has done so much to advance James studies.

In addition to the book reviews, items omitted from this Reference Guide include M.A. theses, passing mentions, instructor's guides, and nonprint material. As much as I would like to claim that this Guide is all-inclusive, I cannot – the amount of published work on James is monumental. My hope is that I have listed all significant work on James that has appeared during the years 1975 to 1987.

The purpose of G.K. Hall's Reference Guides is to provide enough information on the listed items to enable the reader to judge whether or not the item merits closer reading and to locate that item. To these ends, then, the citation is as accurate as possible and the annotation is descriptive, not evaluative. To summarize an item, book, or article in a few sentences does considerable violence to the author's carefully wrought argument; again, my purpose here is to give the reader enough of a sense of each item to judge whether or not it merits tracking down. I have summarized, paraphrased, or quoted directly in the annotations. Occasionally I have noted minor points, in addition to the major, in cases I thought interesting or amusing – of course, this is a personal judgment. Excellent evaluative remarks on many items can be found in the annual bibliographical essays published in American Literary Scholarship and Henry James Review.

Items preceded by an asterisk designate those I have been unable to locate; these include books and articles unobtainable through interlibrary loan or items whose original citation contained an error. For all these unverified items I have included the source of my citation. Otherwise, I have personally examined all the items included in this Reference Guide.

For my citations I have drawn on a range of sources. For the most part these include the standard bibliographies: Abstracts of English Studies; American Literary Scholarship: An Annual; Annual Bibliography of English Language and Literature; Arts and Humanities Citation Index; British Humanities Index; Dissertation Abstracts International; Essay and General Literature Index; Henry James: A Bibliography of Criticism, 1975-1981 (1983.32); Humanities Index; MLA International Bibliography; and Year's Work in English Studies. Database searches by BRS Information Technologies (Latham, New York) and DIALOG Information Services (MLA Bibliography Database) supplied citations as well. Professional journals – particularly American Literature, Journal of Modern Literature, Modern Fiction Studies, Studies in Short Fiction, and Henry James Review – have also provided useful bibliographical lists. Notices of my project placed in these journals yielded additional citations from scholars whose work had not appeared in the standard bibliographies. Finally, luck, serendipity, and hunch played a part in locating additional items.

I have tried to make this Reference Guide as comprehensive as possible. It is my hope that this volume not only shows the wide range of James criticism but also makes it accessible to the reader.

Acknowledgments

Henry James, 1975-1987: A Reference Guide is the result of the assistance, support, and good will of many. Michigan State University awarded me two All-University Research Grants for supplies, database searches, translation, and typing. Michigan State University Libraries provided me with invaluable assistance: in particular, thanks to Clifford Haka and Janice Clark for a quiet place to work; the librarians of General Reference and Social Science and Humanities Reference; and above all, the staff of Document Delivery, who processed hundreds of interlibrary loan requests cheerfully and expeditiously.

Many scholars generously sent me information and offprints: Paul B. Armstrong, Richard Hall, Clair Hughes, Jennifer Jordan-Henley, James J. Kirschke, Brita Lindberg-Seyersted, Darshan Singh Maini, Rayburn S. Moore, William J. Scheick, Elizabeth Steele, Adeline R. Tintner, and Austin M. Wright. Teiko Takamatsu, Yoko Okuda, Paula Koppisch, Paul Fontana, and Carl Goldschmidt assisted with translations. William Marx, Karen Hall, Cathy N. Davidson, and Linda Wagner-Martin provided additional support; special thanks to Henriette Campagne, my editor at G.K. Hall, for her patience and flexibility.

Last, but certainly not least, my gratitude to Liz Bartels, who was undaunted by the Herculean task of typing the manuscript. That our friendship survived this project says much about her forbearance with me!

Introduction

On 23 May 1975, Henry James was "honored, in a way" by students and faculty of the University of Chicago at The Bakery, a Chicago restaurant. After regaling themselves on Victorian fare–oeufs frou frou, goose liver mousse with toast points, haddock in sorrel sauce, gateau allard, champagne, Stilton, and port–the diners, albeit irreverently, paid homage to "the man who spawned a still thriving cottage industry in the groves of academe" (1975.34).

Irreverence aside, this volume testifies to the vitality of that "industry": it is the fourth *Reference Guide* on James published by G.K. Hall, thus providing a comprehensive annotated bibliography of criticism on James from 1866 to 1987. Taylor covers the years 1866 to 1916 (1982.144); McColgan, 1917 to 1959 (1979.90); and Scura, 1960 to 1974 (1979.134). This volume, covering fewer years than any of the previous, contains over 2,300 items and indicates that interest in James and his work continues to flourish.

James died in 1916, deeply disappointed by his native land: his hope that the New York Edition of his novels and tales would gain him a wider readership in America was never realized, and he was troubled by America's refusal to enter the Great War, prompting him to reject his American citizenship for British. Yet his prediction to William Dean Howells in 1888 that "someday all my buried prose will kick off its various tombstones"–even such "curious" works as *The Bostonians* and *The Sacred Fount*–has come true, and especially so during the years 1975 to 1987. Indeed, it is safe to say that during no other period since James's death has there been such an outpouring of primary and secondary texts.

Leon Edel, truly the dean of James studies, dominates the work of the years covered in this volume. Three of the four volumes of James's letters, published by the Belknap Press of Harvard University Press, appeared during this time (1975.31, 1980.47, and 1984.47; the first volume was published in 1974). Although these volumes contain only a fraction of James's correspondence (during his lifetime James wrote over 15,000 letters, approximately a fifteenth of which have now appeared in print) and Edel's editing has provoked some criticism, the four volumes of letters give the general reader and the scholar an unprecedented glimpse of James's growth from youthful "passionate pilgrim" to venerated "cher Maître." This personal portrait is complemented by *The Complete Notebooks of Henry James*, edited by Edel and Lyall H. Powers (1987.33). Although this volume duplicates the material in Matthiessen's and Murdock's 1961 edition – specifically the nine notebooks and sketches for *The Ambassadors* and *The Sense of the Past* – Edel and Powers's volume contains James's pocket diaries, dictations, miscellaneous notes, and the fragment of a tale, "Hugh Merrow," in which a childless couple asks an artist to paint a portrait of the child they can never have. This volume gives, as a result, a very detailed picture of James the artist as well as a fascinating look at the daily, often intimate, life of the Master. And finally, Edel brings both man and artist together in *Henry James: A Life* (1985.38), a one-volume revision of his five-volume biography of James. In keeping with the times, in which candor about intimate matters is possible and expected, Edel is much more explicit about James's "homo-eroticism" and its relation to his art than he was in the five-volume version.

The indefatigable Adeline Tintner renders yet another portrait of James: her relentless detective work illuminates the nature of James's creative process. Her scholarship reveals how James appropriated and "rewrote" the work of many writers and painters and how he transformed contemporary figures, events, and artifacts into his own art. Her many essays, frequently illustrated and always well written, have been revised, expanded, and gathered into a series of volumes issued by the UMI Research Press: *The Museum World of Henry James* (1986.151); *The Book World of Henry James* (1987.122); and *The Pop World of Henry James* (1989). Tintner's three books show the extent to which James realized his own description of the artist's mind in his 1884 essay, "The Art of Fiction": "an immense sensibility, a kind of huge spider-web of the finest silken threads . . . catching every air-borne particle in its tissue." Moreover, these volumes are indispensable to understanding hundreds of allusions and contemporary references in James's fiction.

In addition to Edel's and Tintner's major contributions to James scholarship, the Library of America has reissued James's early novels, from *Watch and Ward* (1871) to *The Princess Casamassima* (1886), as well as much of his criticism. Two volumes include James's essays on American, British, and continental writers; *Hawthorne* (1879); and the New York Edition prefaces. The easy availability of James's criticism is enhanced by two major studies of James's literary criticism: Daugherty's *The Literary Criticism of Henry James* (1981.36) and Jones's *James the Critic* (1985.72).

James studies were also greatly advanced by the creation of the Henry James Society in 1979. Its journal, the *Henry James Review*, under the editorship of Daniel Mark Fogel, is a significant resource as well as a respected forum for scholars. In addition to articles of exceptional quality, the *Review* publishes annual bibliographical essays and special issues [a Leon Edel issue, volume 3, no. 3 (Spring 1982)], and an issue devoted to *The Portrait of a Lady* [volume 7, nos. 2-3 (Winter-Spring 1986)]. The *Review* has also carried useful reference material, including an "artsography" (a bibliography of adaptations of James's fiction in dance, film, opera, radio, television, and spoken word recordings) (1981.101) and a subject index to the New York Edition prefaces (1985.75). The years 1975 to 1987 have occasioned an incredible variety of significant publications that further our understanding of James and his work.

Besides the primary material, Edel's biography of James, and Tintner's source studies, an exciting array of criticism has appeared in print during these thirteen years, ranging from the frivolous to the sublime – from "Lucullan fetes" to detailed studies of James's relationship to major literary figures and movements. James's fiction is illuminated by such theoretical approaches as structuralism, semiotics, deconstruction, psychoanalysis, and feminist criticism; John Carlos Rowe surveys and analyzes modern critical theories in *The Theoretical Dimensions of Henry James* (1984.171). For the most part, however, the scholarship is dominated by "traditional" concerns: sources, biography, influences, themes, narrative technique, and imagery. One of the most fruitful areas of investigation has been influence studies on James as well as his impact on contemporaries and successors. Hawthorne remains the most significant figure, with several full-length works, including Babiiha's *The James-Hawthorne Relation: Bibliographical Essays* (1980.8), Long's *The Great Succession: Henry James and the Legacy of Hawthorne* (1979.87), and Brodhead's *The School of Hawthorne* (1986.20-23). Numerous studies have focused on other writers: Turgenev, Flaubert, Poe, and Browning. Tintner's *The Book World of Henry James* (1987.122) documents the presence of major and minor writers in James's fiction. Scholars continue to define James's legacy to twentieth-century writers; a small sampling – Edith Wharton, Ernest Hemingway, Flannery O'Connor, and Philip Roth – suggests the range of such studies.

James's stature is such that he casts a shadow far beyond his native and adopted lands; his influence is apparent in the variety of comparative studies as well as in the many countries represented in this volume – Canada, Brazil, the Netherlands, France Italy, Germany, Spain, Romania, the Soviet Union, Japan, and China. This, of course, is hardly surprising: James has always been an international author. The "International Theme" dominates James's fiction, early to late; James first achieved fame over a hundred years ago with "Daisy Miller: A Study" (1878), in which he contrasted American innocence with the chiaroscuro of European experience.

"Daisy Miller," along with several other works, received special attention during their centennials in the late 1970s and early 1980s. Excellent "centennial" essays, surveying the vicissitudes of critical reception, have appeared on the following works: "An International Episode" (1979.155); *Washington Square* (1979.95); "Daisy Miller" (1980.66); *Roderick Hudson* (1981.165); *The Europeans* (1982.56); and *The Portrait of a Lady* (1981.141, 156). Indeed, of all of James's works, *The Portrait of a Lady* has received the most attention during the years 1975 to 1987, including a special issue of the *Henry James Review* [volume 7, nos. 2-3 (Winter-Spring 1986)]. Following *The Portrait* in popularity are the novels of James's major phase – *The Ambassadors, The Wings of the Dove*, and *The Golden Bowl* – along with "The Turn of the Screw." Certain works have been well served by recent theories and approaches: "The Turn of the Screw" and *The Sacred Fount*, by virtue of their ambiguity, have been the focus of epistemological studies, while feminist criticism dominates the scholarship on *The Bostonians*.

Indeed, James's 1886 novel on "the situation of women" attracted particular attention because of its adaptation into film, thus joining the long list of such adaptations. James Ivory's film opened to mixed reviews, although the majority tend to acknowledge that Ivory fails to capture the spirit of James's "very American tale." The film version of *The Bostonians* raises the perennial dilemma of translating literature into a visual medium. Mazella's "artsography," a bibliography of adaptations of James's works (1981.101), documents the many attempts up to 1981 to address that dilemma. The frequency with which James's work has inspired performance adaptations is an irony James surely would have appreciated, given his disastrous reception following the opening of *Guy Domville* – summoned to the stage, James was booed and hissed at by the audience. Leon Edel, in a 1984 *New York Times* article, offers a perceptive analysis of James's "adaptability" to the visual (1984.49).

Clearly, James studies have been advanced in many ways during the thirteen years covered in this volume. This is not to say, however, that the criticism included here is the final word on James. Carlson, for example, rightly calls for a systematic feminist criticism of James (1984.32). Habegger notes that while Edel's biography of James is important, James's life is too large for any one biographer (1987.47); Habegger's essays on Henry James, Sr. (1986.66), Minny Temple (1986.65), and Louisa May Alcott (1985.53) demonstrate that there is ample room for more biographical work on James. Habegger's work, in fact, suggests that many cherished beliefs about James need revision: he portrays the Master, for example, rewriting Minny Temple's letters so that his cousin faithfully mirrors his concept of the tragic heroine.

Strouse's biography of Alice James (1980.138), Maher's biography of Bob and Wilkie James (1986.92), and Feinstein's study of William James (1984.56) also show that scholarship on other members of the James family, the famous and not so famous, illuminates James's life and work in subtle yet significant ways. And finally, a considerable portion of the James canon has yet to receive critical justice, although the criticism included in this volume reflects a growing interest in James's less well-known works. Tintner, for example, uncovers the subtleties in such neglected works as *The Outcry*, while Martin and Ober (1983.123, 124) and Gage (1986.53) on discussing *The Finer Grain* suggest the possibilities for investigating the "architecture" of James's titled sequences. G.K. Hall's *Reference Guides* on James document the tremendous amount of scholarship done on James, yet work much remains.

Jamesians may object to their endeavors being considered a thriving cottage industry, but no one can dispute that James's work – fiction and non-fiction – has occasioned a veritable smorgasbord of scholarship. *Henry James: A Reference Guide, 1975-1987* reveals the richness of the feast.

Principal Works by Henry James

A Passionate Pilgrim, 1875 ("A Passionate Pilgrim," "The Last of the Valerii," "Eugene Pickering," "The Madonna of the Future," "The Romance of Certain Old Clothes," "Madame de Mauves")

Transatlantic Sketches, 1875

Roderick Hudson, 1875

The American, 1877

French Poets and Novelists, 1878

Watch and Ward, 1878

The Europeans, 1878

Daisy Miller, 1878

An International Episode, 1879

The Madonna of the Future, 1879 ("The Madonna of the Future," "Longstaff's Marriage," "Madame de Mauves," "Eugene Pickering," "The Diary of A Man of Fifty," "Benvolio")

Confidence, 1879

Hawthorne, 1879

The Diary of A Man of Fifty, 1880 ("The Diary of a Man of Fifty," "A Bundle of Letters")

Washington Square, 1880

The Portrait of a Lady, 1881

Daisy Miller: A Comedy, 1883

The Siege of London, 1883 ("The Siege of London," "The Pension Beaurepas," "The Point of View")

Portraits of Places, 1883

A Little Tour in France, 1884

Tales of Three Cities, 1884 ("The Impressions of a Cousin," "Lady Barberina," "A New England Winter")

The Author of "Beltraffio", 1885 ("The Author of 'Beltraffio,'" "Pandora," "Georgina's Reasons," "The Path of Duty," "Four Meetings")

Stories Revived, 1885 ("The Author of 'Beltraffio,'" "Pandora," "The Path of Duty," "A Light Man," "A Day of Days," "Georgina's Reasons," "A Passionate Pilgrim," "A Landscape-Painter," "Rose-Agathe," "Poor Richard," "The Last of the Valerii," "Master Eustace," "The Romance of Certain Old Clothes," "A Most Extraordinary Case")

The Bostonians, 1886

The Princess Casamassima, 1886

Partial Portraits, 1888

The Reverberator, 1888

The Aspern Papers, 1888 ("The Aspern Papers," "Louisa Pallant," "The Modern Warning")

A London Life, 1889 ("A London Life," "The Patagonia," "The Liar," "Mrs. Temperly")

The Tragic Muse, 1890

The Lesson of the Master, 1892 ("The Lesson of the Master," "The Marriages," "The Pupil," "Brooksmith," "The Solution," "Sir Edmund Orme")

The Real Thing, 1893 ("The Real Thing," "Sir Dominick Ferrand," "Nona Vincent," "The Chaperone," "Greville Fane")

Picture and Text, 1893

The Private Life, 1893 ("The Private Life," "The Wheel of Time," "Lord Beaupre," "The Visits," "Collaboration," "Owen Wingrave")

Essays in London and Elsewhere, 1893

The Wheel of Time, 1893 ("The Wheel of Time," "Collaboration," "Owen Wingrave")

Theatricals, 1894

Terminations, 1895 ("The Death of the Lion," "The Coxon Fund," "The Middle Years," "The Altar of the Dead")

Theatricals: Second Series, 1895

Embarrassments, 1896 ("The Figure in the Carpet," "Glasses," "The Next Time," "The Way It Came")

The Other House, 1896

The Spoils of Poynton, 1897

What Maisie Knew, 1897

In the Cage, 1898

The Two Magics, 1898 ("The Turn of the Screw," "Covering End")

The Awkward Age, 1899

The Soft Side, 1900 ("The Great Good Place," "Europe," "Paste," "The Real Right Thing," "The Great Condition," "The Tree of Knowledge," "The Abasement of the Northmores," "The Given Case," "John Delavoy," "The Third Person," "Maud-Evelyn," "Miss Gunton of Poughkeepsie")

The Sacred Fount, 1901

The Wings of the Dove, 1902

The Better Sort, 1903 ("Broken Wings," "The Beldonald Holbein," "The Two Faces," "The Tone of Time," "The Special Type," "Mrs. Medwin," "Flickerbridge," "The Story in It," "The Beast in the Jungle," "The Birthplace," "The Papers")

The Ambassadors, 1903

William Wetmore Story and His Friends, 1903

The Golden Bowl, 1904

English Hours, 1905

The American Scene, 1907

The Novels and Tales of Henry James, New York Edition, 1907-1909

Views and Reviews, 1908

Julia Bride, 1909

Italian Hours, 1909

The Finer Grain, 1910 ("The Velvet Glove," "Mora Montravers," "A Round of Visits," "Crapy Cornelia," "The Bench of Desolation")

The Outcry, 1911

A Small Boy and Others, 1913

Notes of a Son and Brother, 1914

Notes on Novelists, 1914

The Ivory Tower, 1917

The Sense of the Past, 1917

The Middle Years, 1917

Gabrielle de Bergerac, 1918

Within the Rim, 1919

Master Eustace, 1920 ("Master Eustace," "Longstaff's Marriage," "Théodolinde," "A Light Man," "Benvolio")

Travelling Companions, 1919 ("Travelling Companions," "The Sweetheart of M. Briseux," "Professor Fargo," "At Isella," "Guest's Confession," "Adina," "De Grey: A Romance")

A Landscape Painter, 1920 ("A Landscape Painter," "Poor Richard," "A Day of Days," "A Most Extraordinary Case")

Writings about Henry James, 1975-1987

1975

1   ALEXANDER, CHARLOTTE. "Henry James and *Hot Corn*." *American Notes & Queries* 14, no. 4 (December):52-53.

Cites the anecdote from *A Small Boy and Others* in which James is not permitted to read *Hot Corn*, a novel by Solon Robinson. Alexander finds James's interest in the incident revealing lack of fulfillment, secretiveness, and voyeurism with which James invests his character.

2   ALLEN, JEANNE THOMAS. "Aspects of Narration in *The Turn of the Screw* and *The Innocents*." Ph.D. dissertation, University of Iowa, 219 pp.

Compares the novella and Jack Clayton's film adaptation, focusing on "aspects of narration" in each. This comparison yields not only new interpretations of each work but suggests a model for examining the relationship between fiction and its translation to film.

See *Dissertation Abstracts International* 37, no. 5 (1976):2846A-2847A.

3   ANDERSON, QUENTIN. "A Master in the Making." *Times Literary Supplement*, no. 3818 (9 May):498-500.

Reviews volume I of James's letters edited by Leon Edel. These letters show that early on James had a clear sense of himself as a

1

writer. Anderson also discusses Edel's biography of James, in which Edel has substituted James's imagination for his character. The letters, in contrast, reflect an "endlessly responsive and responsible man [who] lived the life of dignity, probity, and imaginative generosity."

4   ARMISTEAD, J.M. "Henry James for the Cinematic Mind." *English Record* 26, no. 3 (Summer):27-33.
     Suggests that James could be made more accessible to students by comparing his narrative technique with that of popular or current films and discusses "The Beast in the Jungle," using the "narrator-as-camera" metaphor.

5   AUCHINCLOSS, LOUIS. "Henry James's Literary Use of His American Tour (1904)." *South Atlantic Quarterly* 74, no. 1 (Winter):45-52.
     Discusses James's use of his impressions of America in "A Round of Visits," "Julia Bride," "Crapy Cornelia," "The Jolly Corner," and *The Ivory Tower*, and suggests that in *The American Scene* James was trying out a new, impressionistic method of writing.

6   _____. *Reading Henry James*. Minneapolis: University of Minnesota Press, 181 pp.
     Discusses James's novels, major tales, notebooks, and criticism, assessing his successes and his shortcomings. Auchincloss argues that James was not concerned with consciousness, but with the drama of the "perfect intelligence" and the "finest sensibility" confronted by "lesser intelligences" and "cruder sensibilities."

7   BAMBERG, ROBERT D., ed. *The Portrait of a Lady*. Norton Critical Edition. New York: W.W. Norton, ix, 755 pp.
     Contents include the New York Edition text of the novel and its preface; excerpts from James's *Notebooks*, *Autobiography*, *Italian Hours*, and *Transatlantic Sketches*; contemporary reviews; and reprints of the following:
     F.O. Matthiessen, "The Painter's Sponge and Varnish Bottle" (1944), pp. 577-97;
     Anthony J. Mazzella, "The New Isabel" (n.d.), pp. 597-619;
     Graham Greene, *"The Portrait of a Lady"* (1951), pp. 667-71;

Arnold Kettle, "Henry James: *The Portrait of a Lady*" (1953), pp. 671-89;
Dorothy Van Ghent, "On *The Portrait of a Lady*" (1953), pp. 689-704;
William H. Gass, "The High Brutality of Good Intentions" (1958), pp. 704-13;
Dorothea Krook, "The Portrait of a Lady" (1962), pp. 713-29;
Laurence B. Holland, "The Marriage" (1964), pp. 730-41;
Charles Feidelson, "The Moment of *The Portrait of a Lady*" (1968), pp. 741-51.

8   BELL, MILLICENT. "Fluid Self-Expression." *New Republic* 172, no. 8, issue 3137 (February 22):23-25.
Sketches James's years as an emerging novelist, as revealed in *Henry James Letters I*, edited by Leon Edel. The letters shed light on many aspects of James's life although they do not reveal the "agonies or ecstacies of composition" or ultimate feelings.

9   _____. "Style as Subject: *Washington Square*." *Sewanee Review* 83, no. 1 (Winter):19-38.
Argues that Catherine Sloper's silence reflects a new style of authenticity that triumphs over both the behavior and rhetoric of the other characters in the novel. Likewise, James's discovery of this style signals his artistic freedom from masters and mentors.

10   BENERT, ANNETTE LARSON. "Passion and Perception: A Jungian Reading of Henry James." Ph.D. dissertation, Lehigh University, 365 pp.
Examines the "trials of love," James's primary subject, from the perspective of Jung's theories on personality structure and development. James's early fiction focuses on perceptual and relational difficulties in private life; the work of the eighties explores those difficulties in the public sphere. The work of the nineties focuses on characters "whose perceptions and relationships are severely limited and radically idiosyncratic; *The Ambassadors* resolves the problems of perception and relation by transcending projection to achieve a consciousness fostering individuality."
See *Dissertation Abstracts International* 36, no. 9 (1976):6095A.

1975

11 BIRJE-PATIL, J. *"The Beast in the Jungle* and *Portrait of a Lady."* *Literary Criterion* (University of Mysore, India) 11, no. 4 (Summer):45-52.

Argues that Eliot's poem, *Portrait of a Lady*, is informed by the Jamesian ironies in "The Beast in the Jungle."

12 BLACK, MICHAEL. *"Portrait of a Lady."* In *The Literature of Fidelity.* London: Chatto & Windus, pp. 152-68.

Argues that James's strength lies in "a pecularly witty sort of drawing-room comedy." This novel does not hold up under close scrutiny: "it is an effort by a bystander to give a surmise about things he hasn't really grasped from the inside."

13 BUITENHUIS, PETER. "Exiles at Home and Abroad: Henry Adams and Henry James." *English Studies in Canada* (Toronto) 1, no. 1 (Spring):74-85.

Compares the two men in terms of their experience of a sense of alienation from America and their expression of that alienation in art. Buitenhuis sees Adams's "exile" as deeper and more pessimistic than James's; Adams mourned a lost Eden. In contrast, James's experience was a "well-spring" for his art and enabled him to look to the future with hope.

14 BYERS, PAMELA McLUCAS. "Realism and Convention in Thomas Middleton's City Comedies. The Responsible Narrator: Authorial Presence in Henry James's Late Novels. Bonnie Prince Charles and the Myth of the Highlands: Literature's Remaking of History." Ph.D. dissertation, Rutgers University, 171 pp.

Traces the authorial presence in *The Ambassadors* and *The Golden Bowl*, showing how the Jamesian narrator contributes to the themes of the novels by enabling the reader to participate creatively and to expand consciousness.

See *Dissertation Abstracts International* 36, no. 5 (1975):2838A-2839A.

15 CALVERT, STEVEN LAMONT. "Christian Redemption from Chaos: The Religious Henry James in *The Princess Casamassima*." Ph.D. dissertation, Rutgers University, 183 pp.

Examines the Christian elements in the novel and the means by which the reader participates in Hyacinth Robinson's "religious lesson." James's manipulation of structure and the use of a "double narrative vision" are crucial in involving the reader in the narrative.

See *Dissertation Abstracts International* 36, no. 5 (1975):2839A.

*16 CHAMBERLAIN, V.C. "Techniques and Effects of Realism in the Late Novels of Henry James." Ph.D. dissertation, University of Oxford.

Source: Budd, 1983.32, p. 6, item 27.

17 CHAPIN, HELEN GERACIMOS. "Mythology and American Realism: Studies in Fiction by Henry Adams, Henry James and Kate Chopin." Ph.D. dissertation, Ohio State University, 356 pp.

Finds in the novels of the late nineteenth century–Adams's *Democracy* (1880) and *Esther* (1884), James's *The Princess Casamassima* (1886), and Chopin's *The Awakening* (1899)–realist social documentation alongside mythological literary structures which are focused on the women characters. Chapin argues that realism and mythology are synthesized by naturalism into artistic unity.

See *Dissertation Abstracts International* 36, no. 6 (1975):3646A.

18 CHAPMAN, SARA S. "Stalking the Beast: Egomania and Redemptive Suffering in James's 'Major Phase.'" *Colby Library Quarterly* 11, no. 1 (March):50-66.

Rejects the contention that in his major phase James was detached from the real world, concerned only with technique. In "Beast in the Jungle," "The Jolly Corner," and "The Bench of Desolation," James demonstrates profound and involved humanism and creates tragic heroes whose "fates are affirmative, not disillusioned."

19 COLLINS, MARTHA. "The Center of Consciousness on Stage: Henry James's *Confidence*." *Studies in American Fiction* 3, no. 1 (Spring):39-50.

Approaches the novel as an experiment, in which James combines the center of consciousness of "Daisy Miller" with the dramatic presentation of *The Europeans*. Collins traces the shifts between the two modes, particularly in the rendering of Bernard. The

1975

two narrative techniques are incompletely fused; in subsequent novels James chose either the center or the dramatic method.

20   CONNOLLY, CYRIL. "Edith Wharton and Henry James." In *The Evening Colonnade*. New York: Harcourt Brace Jovanovich, pp. 179-81.
    Sketches the complex relationship between Wharton and James in a review of Bell's *Edith Wharton and Henry James*.
    Reprint of *Sunday Times* (1966) essay.

21   ____. "Henry James." In *The Evening Colonnade*. New York: Harcourt Brace Jovanovich, pp. 175-78.
    Reviews Edel's *Henry James: The Treacherous Years 1895-1900*, "so far his most distinguished volume," which reveals James's "moral and intellectual greatness."
    Reprint of *Sunday Times* (1969) review.

22   ____. "Oscar Wilde and Henry James: An Imaginary Transmogrification." In *The Evening Colonnade*. New York: Harcourt Brace Jovanovich, pp. 171-74.
    Reviews Hyde's *Henry James at Home* and Jullian's *Oscar Wilde* and describes his own meeting with Wilde. Both books present good portraits of the writers.
    Reprint of *Sunday Times* (1969) essay.

23   COSTA, RICHARD HAUER. "Edwardian Intimations of the Shape of Fiction to Come: Mr. Britling/Job Huss as Wellsian Central Intelligences." *English Literature in Transition (1800-1920)* 18:229-42.
    Compares James's and Wells's conception of the novel. James focused on the inward ordering of impressions and experience, as exemplified in *The Ambassadors*. Wells, in contrast, created a hybrid novel that joins the fictional and the reportorial, exemplified by *Mr. Britling* and *The Undying Fire*.

24   COUSINEAU, DIANE LEVINE. "Henry James and Virginia Woolf: A Comparative Study." Ph.D. dissertation, University of California, Davis, 304 pp.

Argues that although James's imaginative vision is dominated by the visual while Woolf's is dominated by the auditory, both "meet in their concern with symbolic form." Cousineau's analysis of *Mrs. Dalloway, To the Lighthouse, The Wings of the Dove*, and *The Golden Bowl* is influenced by the work of Sartre, Poulet, Ricoeur, and Doubrovsky.

See *Dissertation Abstracts International* 36, no. 12, pt. 1 (1976):8044A.

25 CRAIG, DAVID MARTIN. "A Study of Endings of Selected Nineteenth-Century Novels." Ph.D. dissertation, University of Notre Dame, 200 pp.

Examines the mechanisms and meaning of closure in Dickens's *Bleak House*, Eliot's *Daniel Deronda*, Stevenson's *The Master of Ballantrae*, and James's *The Golden Bowl*. James's novel, based on a fairy-tale structure, emphasizes formal closure but undercuts thematic closure. At the end of the novel Maggie does indeed become a fairy-tale princess, but does so only by exploiting the other characters.

See *Dissertation Abstracts International* 36, no. 6 (1975):3675A.

26 CROSBY, PATRICIA LAUER. "Growth to Fulfillment: A Psychological Analysis of Six Heroines of Henry James." Ph.D. dissertation, Miami University, 302 pp.

Analyzes the heroines of *The Portrait of a Lady, What Maisie Knew, The Spoils of Poynton, The Awkward Age, The Wings of the Dove*, and *The Golden Bowl*, using Deutsch's and Horney's typology – narcissism, feminine masochism, and moral masochism – and measuring the personal growth each attains in the course of the novel. By approaching James's work through psychological theories we can gain a better understanding of both James and his art.

See *Dissertation Abstracts International* 36, no. 9 (1976):6096A-6097A.

27 CROWLEY, FRANCIS E. "Henry James' *The Beast in the Jungle* and *The Ambassadors*." *Psychoanalytic Review* 62, no. 1 (Spring):154-63.

Traces similarities between Marcher and Strether but argues that Marcher is the "ironic counterpart of Strether." Marcher is a flat character in comparison to Strether, and May Bartram functions as his "second consciousness."

1975

28   DeLOACH, WILLIAM. "The Influence of William James on the
      Composition of *The American*." *Interpretations: Studies in Language
      and Literature* 7:38-43.
           Notes that Henry "borrowed" from William's 1875 letter on
      conflicting attitudes toward Baudelaire when he composed Christopher
      Newman's letter describing conflicting attitudes toward himself.
      DeLoach suggests that the relationship between the two brothers was
      normal and not neurotic as Edel argues.

29   DORIA, PATRICIA JAMISON. "Narrative Persona in George
      Eliot and Henry James." Ph.D. dissertation, University of Texas,
      Austin, 221 pp.
           Compares chapter 20 of *Middlemarch* and chapter 42 of *The
      Portrait of a Lady* to illuminate each author's handling of narration and
      their attitudes toward the subjectivity of the individual. Doria finds a
      "tension of narrative attitudes" in each work, suggesting the authors'
      awareness of the limitations of human understanding. Eliot strives for a
      "compassionate universal understanding," however, while James's
      interest lies in the potential of the imagination.
           See *Dissertation Abstracts International* 36, no. 10
      (1976):6671A.

30   DUPERRAY, ANNICK. "Henry James et *The Yellow Book*."
      Confluents 1:153-75.
           In French.

31   EDEL, LEON. Introduction to *Henry James Letters, Volume 2:1875-
      1883*. Cambridge: Harvard University Press, Belknap Press, pp. xi-
      xiv.
           Notes that the letters of this period reveal a James freeing
      himself from his family's expectations and building his career as a
      writer.

32   ____. "The Madness of Art." *American Journal of Psychiatry* 132, no.
      10 (October):1005-12.
           Argues that artists deal with depression and loss through their
      art, citing a wide range of artists including James. Edel mentions the
      tale "The Middle Years," one of James's "fables for writers."

33 EUART, PATRICIA MARY. "The Theme of Betrayal in the Fiction of Henry James." Ph.D. dissertation, Brown University, 400 pp.

Argues that the theme of betrayal is central to James's fiction and indeed to his vision of human existence. In coming to terms with the experience of betrayal through his art, James "was asserting the value of his own life."

See *Dissertation Abstracts International* 37, no. 1 (1976):308A.

34 FARRELL, WILLIAM E. "Henry James Is Honored, in a Way." *New York Times* (24 May):56.

Describes the "Lucullan fete" at The Bakery in Chicago, honoring the man who "spawned a still thriving cottage industry in the groves of academe." Topics discussed at the banquet include James's correspondence with Jesse James and the probability that the "latter James" was actually the early Conrad.

35 FAULKNER, PETER. "Henry James and H.G. Wells." In *Humanism in the English Novel.* London: Elek/Pemberton, pp. 71-98.

Argues in the first half of this chapter that James's central concerns are "profoundly humanistic." James's humanism, especially as depicted in *The Golden Bowl*, involves skepticism of dogmas and absolutes and recognition of the complexities of the particular case. The second half of the chapter is devoted to H.G. Wells.

36 FERGUSSON, FRANCIS. "James in the Theater." In *Literary Landmarks: Essays on The Theory and Practice of Literature.* New Brunswick, N.J.: Rutgers University Press, pp. 125-30.

Reviews Edel's *The Complete Plays of Henry James* (1950), praising the volume for making the plays easily accessible.

Reprint of book review, *Partisan Review* 17, no. 6 (July-August 1950).

37 ____. "James's Dramatic Form." In *Literary Landmarks: Essays on the Theory and Practice of Literature.* New Brunswick, N.J.: Rutgers University Press, pp. 48-61.

Suggests that many of James's "dramatic" techniques – the use of picture and scene, a central consciousness, situations as reflectors,

1975

and so on – can illuminate our understanding of Shakespeare, Chekhov, and Ibsen. James's own plays were failures, but his conception of dramatic form can give us the right perspective on the drama of his time as well as of ours.

Reprint of *Kenyon Review* 5, no. 4 (Autumn 1943).

38 FORD, JANE M. "The Father/Daughter/Suitor Triangle in Shakespeare, Dickens, James, Conrad, and Joyce." Ph.D. dissertation, State University of New York, Buffalo, 318 pp.

Argues that there is a connection between the incest theme and the creative process and traces this theme in each artist's work. The treatment of incest follows a pattern over the writer's total career: renunciation in the early work; retention in the middle, and father-manipulated renunciation in the late work. James's works discussed in terms of this pattern include *Watch and Ward, The Portrait of a Lady*, and *The Golden Bowl*.

See *Dissertation Abstracts International* 36, no. 7 (1976):4507A.

39 FRANK, ELLEN EVE. "Promises in Stone: The Architectural Analogy in Walter Pater, Gerard Manley Hopkins, Marcel Proust, Henry James." Ph.D. dissertation, Stanford University, 363 pp.

Examines the use of architecture by these writers, who saw it as analogy for form and style as well as for memory and the mind itself. In chapter 4 Frank discusses James's "house of fiction" and his imaging of the mind and thought process.

See *Dissertation Abstracts International* 36, no. 9 (1976):6074A.

40 FRIEDRICH, OTTO. "A Little Tour with Henry James." *American Scholar* 44, no. 4 (Autumn):643-52.

Compares his own travels through France to those James described in *A Little Tour of France* and wonders what James would have made of twentieth-century France.

41 GALE, ROBERT L. Review of *Henry James Letters I. Nineteenth-Century Fiction* 30, no. 2 (September):221-24.

Praises Edel's prefaces and introduction, and his selection of letters showing James's steady maturation. The volume, however, is flawed by "incomplete annotating, cavalier indexing, and careless copy editing."

See 1976.124.

*42   GERVAIS, D.C. "Gustave Flaubert and Henry James: A Study in
Contrasts." Ph.D. dissertation, University of Edinburgh.
Source: Budd, 1983.32, p. 15, item 66.

43   GILLIE, CHRISTOPHER. "The Early Twentieth-Century Novel:
James, Wells, and Conrad." In *Movements in English Literature,
1900-1940*. Cambridge: Cambridge University Press, pp. 24-31.
    Describes James's predominant theme as the struggle of a
morally sensitive conscience against civilization. This theme is best
expressed in *The Portrait of a Lady* and *The Ambassadors*.

44   GIRLING, HARRY K. "On Editing a Paragraph of *The Princess
Casamassima.*" *Language and Style* 8, no. 4 (Fall):243-63.
    Gives variant readings for the first paragraph in chapter 15
from the manuscript, *The Atlantic Monthly* (January 1886), three early
editions, and the New York Edition in order to show James's "continual
composition by revision" and his refinement of the relations between
signifiers and signified.

45   GOHRBANDT, D. "Aspekte der Heldenfunction in der Romanen
von George Eliot, Henry James und Virginia Woolf" [Aspects of the
function of the hero in the novels of George Eliot, Henry James and
Virginia Woolf]. Ph.D. dissertation, Universität des Saarlandes,
BRD, 519 pp.
    In German.
    Argues that the hero functions as the "main criterion for the
moral seriousness" of these authors' novels.
    See *Dissertation Abstracts International* 37, no. 3
(1977):1/3213C.

46   GOLDBERG, RAQUEL PRADO-TOTARO. "The Artist Fiction
of James, Wharton, and Cather." Ph.D. dissertation, Northwestern
University, 368 pp.
    Examines the "artist fiction" of these authors to determine the
extent to which Wharton and Cather emulated James. Goldberg finds
"striking differences" in style and content in the work of both women

writers and attributes the few resemblances to James to the tradition of the artist tale rather than to discipleship.

See *Dissertation Abstracts International* 36, no. 7 (1976):4475A.

47   GOTTFRIED, MARIANNE HIRSCH. "Confrontation of Cultures: Perception and Communication in the Novels of Henry James, Uwe Johnson and Michel Butor." Ph.D. dissertation, Brown University, 359 pp.

Investigates the experimental elements in six novels – *The Ambassadors, L'Emploi du temps, The Golden Bowl, Mutmassungen über Jakolo, Mobile,* and *Jahrestag* – which "explore the epistemological dimensions of the international theme." Gottfried sees a progression from James's inner, personal response to a foreign culture to Butor's and Johnson's outward-directed approach.

See *Dissertation Abstracts International* 37, no. 1 (1976):296A.

48   GRAHAM, [GEORGE] KENNETH. *Henry James: The Drama of Fulfillment: An Approach to the Novels.* Oxford: Clarendon Press, xvi, 234 pp.

Focuses on James's use of the image of life to suggest wholeness and equilibrium in "Madame de Mauves," "Daisy Miller," *Roderick Hudson,* "The Aspern Papers," *The Tragic Muse, The Spoils of Poynton,* and *The Wings of the Dove.* These works show that James's artistic vision was essentially dramatic, not idealistic, in that it is involved in the "rhythms and contradictions" of experience.

Reprinted in part 1985.78.

49   GRANDEL, HARTMUT. *Henry James in der Deutschen Literaturkritik. Die zeitgenössische Rezeption von 1875 bis 1916* [Henry James in German literary criticism. The contemporary reception from 1875-1916]. Berne: Herbert Lang.

In German.

50   GRENANDER, M.E. "Benjamin Franklin's Glass Armonica and Henry James's 'Jolly Corner.'" *Papers on Language and Literature* 11, no. 4 (Fall):415-17.

Suggests that James's reference to the glass armonica in the second section of the tale may indicate that Brydon induced self-hypnosis. In the eighteenth century, Mesmer used the instrument to play background music during his hypnotic sessions.

*51   GRUBMAN, G. "I.S. Turgenev i Genri Dzheyms" [Ivan Turgenev and Henry James]. *Sever* (Petrozavodsk, USSR) 7:105-11.
       In Russian.
       Source: *Annual Bibliography of English Language and Literature* 50 (1975):494, item 8846.

52   GUNN, GILES B. "From the Ambiguities of James to the Bare Truths of Dreiser." In *F.O. Matthiessen: The Critical Achievement.* Seattle: University of Washington Press, pp. 140-51.
       Describes the writing of *Henry James: The Major Phase* and reiterates Matthiessen's judgments on *The Ambassadors, The Wings of the Dove,* and *The Golden Bowl.* Matthiessen's focus on James as a "'moral romancer'" dominated all of his work on James.

53   GUSTAFSON, JUDITH A. "*The Wings of the Dove*: Or, A Gathering of Pigeons." *Gypsy Scholar* 3, no. 1 (Fall):13-19.
       Suggests that a rigid archetypal reading of Milly Theale results in a "Fair Maiden to end Fair Maidens" when in fact she is James's satire on popular heroines.

54   GVOZDEVA, G.A. "G. Dzheims ob Isskustve Romana" [James on the art of the novel]. *Sbornik Nauchnykh Trudov Moskovskoyo Pedagogicheskogo Institute Inostrannykh Yazykof* 84:299-307.
       In Russian.

55   HADDICK, VERN. "Fear and Growth: Reflections on 'The Beast in the Jungle.'" *Journal of the Otto Rank Association* 9, no. 2 (Winter):38-42.
       Examines James's tale in light of Rank's dyad of fear and growth. Marcher moves toward growth when he recognizes that his fear has turned his life into a retreat before the beast.

56   HALL, WILLIAM F. "Henry James and the Picturesque Mode." *English Studies in Canada* (Toronto) 1, no. 3 (Fall):326-43.

1975

Proposes that "the picturesque" on which includes caricature, melodrama, and the use of art and myth, is a useful concept for the nineteenth-century novel. Hall notes this mode in Hawthorne's *The Blithedale Romance* but focuses more fully on the use of myth in *Roderick Hudson* and melodrama in *The Portrait of a Lady*.

57 HARDY, BARBARA. "Memory and Memories." In *Tellers and Listeners: The Narrative Imagination*. London: Athlone Press, pp. 78-84.

Sees *The Ambassadors* as Strether's quest for a lost past, evoked by the "lemon-coloured volumes." That past is both nourishing and dangerous: Strether discovers the he cannot go back; rather, he must live in the present.

58 HAROLD, BRENT. "Character and Form in Literature and the Visual Arts." *Rendezvous* 10, no. 1 (Fall):1-9.

Argues that character, whether depicted visually or in fiction, exists in two ways: as an illusion of reality or as a model, either cooperative or resistant. Christopher Newman in *The American* is cited as an example of the "model" character who is always resisting form, both author's and other characters'.

59 HARTSOCK, MILDRED E. "Time for Comedy: The Late Novels of Henry James." *English Studies* 56, no. 2 (April):14-28.

Examines comic elements in *The Ambassadors, The Wings of the Dove*, and *The Golden Bowl*. These elements include adjectives and adverbs, apothegms, incongruous juxtapositions, jokes, "heightened cliche," and imagery.

60 HAYES, DENNIS JAMES. "Reliability in James's Fiction of the Dramatic Period." Ph.D. dissertation, Auburn University, 202 pp.

Argues that in the fiction employing third-person narration James "intended his 'heroines' to be admired rather than pitied or censured." Nanda Brookenham, Maisie Farange, and Fleda Vetch are admirable because they renounce material gain for the life of consciousness.

See *Dissertation Abstracts International* 36, no. 2 (1975):888A-889A.

61   HOAG, GERALD. "The Death of the Paper Lion." *Studies in Short Fiction* 12, no. 2 (Spring):163-72.

Sees the narrator of "The Death of the Lion" as unreliable, thus resulting in a greater degree of complexity than attributed to this tale. Hoag focuses on the ironic and comic elements of the tale and calls it James's "open, purgative amusement."

62   HOILE, CHRISTOPHER. "Lambert Strether and the Boaters: Tonio Kröger and the Dancers: Confrontations and Self-Acceptance." *Canadian Review of Comparative Literature/Revue Canadienne de Littérature Comparée* 2, no. 3 (Fall):243-61.

Compares Strether's confrontation with Mme. de Vionnet and Chad with a similar confrontation of Tonio with Hans and Inge to demonstrate that Strether has replaced his illusions with self-knowledge and self-acceptance.

63   HOWARD, RICHARD. "Letters of a Master." *Yale Review* 64, no. 4 (Summer):594-97.

Reviews *Henry James Letters I* and accuses Edel of withholding the letters in which James discusses his physical habits. The level of discourse in such letters would give us a clearer picture of James the writer.

64   HUDSPETH, ROBERT N. "A Hard, Shining Sonnet: The Art of Short Fiction in James's 'Europe.'" *Studies in Short Fiction* 12, no. 4 (Fall):387-95.

Finds that the tale, which James saw as a successful example of his brevity, perfectly expresses the contrast between the narrow life of New England and the rich life of Europe. Despite its compression, "Europe" depicts the deep inner life of its characters.

65   HYDE, H. MONTGOMERY. "Henry James at Home." *Essays by Diverse Hands* 38 (new series). London: Oxford University Press, pp. 58-77.

Describes James's various residences in England, concentrating on Lamb House, and some of the friends who visited him there.

1975

66 HYNES, JOSEPH. "The Transparent Shroud: Henry James and William Story." *American Literature* 46, no. 4 (January):506-27.
Examines James's biography of Story and his motives for writing it. James felt compassion toward him as an early expatriate and as an artist who worked without a clear sense of direction or development and who was beguiled by the richness of Europe. James's attitudes toward Story illuminate his own sense of expatriation.

67 JACOBSON, MARCIA. "Literary Convention and Social Criticism in Henry James's *The Awkward Age*." *Philological Quarterly* 54, no. 3 (Summer):633-46.
Suggests that a comparison of the novel with popular fiction of the nineties shows that James used conventional material to criticize his society. In particular, James was influenced by the "dialogue novels" of the period as well as by the character types of the new woman and the more conservative woman. Read as social criticism, the novel is neither a technical exercise nor psychological analysis, as previously argued.
Reprinted 1983.101 and 1987.44.

68 JEFFREY, DAVID K. "On Henry James." *Scholia Satyrica* 1, no. 2 (Spring):13-18.
Reprints "the most exciting 'find' of recent scholarly adventureship": Mark Twain's "James's Literary Offenses" in which old Mark takes pains to poke fun at Isabell Archer.

69 JONES, GRANVILLE H. *Henry James's Psychology of Experience: Innocence, Responsibility, and Renunciation in the Fiction of Henry James*. De proprietatibus litterararum: Series practica, 79. The Hague: Mouton, xiv, 310 pp.
Examines James's concept of innocence as it affects his characters. In children, the focus is innocence in young adults, innocence is seen in terms of responsibility; and in adults, it is expressed through renunciation. For James innocence is "a continuous moral, philosophical and aesthetic system" that ultimately results in renunciation.

70 KERN, SUSAN JEAN ANDERSON. "Self-Interpretations: The Uses of the Past in Autobiography." Ph.D. dissertation, University of Texas, Austin, 261 pp.

Examines the autobiographies of Henry Adams, Jane Addams, and Henry James, focusing on their analysis of self-identity. In chapter 3, Kerr argues that in his *Autobiography* James identifies the past with the "other" and traces the process by which he can overcome the limitations of time to connect with the sources of his being.

See *Dissertation Abstracts International* 36, no. 2 (1975):889A.

*71   KING, J.M. "Tragedy in the Victorian Novel: Theory and Practice in George Eliot, Thomas Hardy, and Henry James." Ph.D. dissertation, University of Aberdeen.

Source: *Annual Bibliography of English Language and Literature* 50 (1975):470, item 8399.

Revised 1978.58.

72   KIRKPATRICK, JUDITH ANN. "The Artistic Expression of the Psychological Theories of William James in the Writing of Henry James." Ph.D. dissertation, University of Delaware, 171 pp.

Demonstrates that William James's theories of perception and thought processes are reflected in Henry James's fiction and nonfiction. The first four chapters outline these theories and trace their evolution in Henry James's nonfiction; the final chapter focuses on the impact of these theories on *The Wings of the Dove, The Ambassadors*, and *The Golden Bowl*.

See *Dissertation Abstracts International* 36, no. 4 (1975):2207A.

73   KNIGHTS, L[IONEL] C[HARLES]. "Henry James and Human Liberty." *Sewanee Review* 83, no. 1 (Winter):1-18.

Argues that one of James's main concerns was to portray domination in many types of relationships. For James the key to a civilized life was to use the imagination to transcend categorizing people since ready-made judgments lead to coercion and victimization.

Reprinted 1976.108.

74   LABRIE, ROSS. "The Good and the Beautiful in Henry James." *Greyfriar: Siena Studies in Literature* 16:3-15.

Demonstrates that James's central characters have "a discriminating sense of the good and the beautiful" along with an "appetite for fuller awareness" of these qualities – apparent in Isabel Archer and Fleda Vetch. Characters who appreciate either the good or

1975

the beautiful are flawed: Mrs. Wix, who is a moralist; Mrs. Gereth, whose faith is in aestheticism. The Prince and the narrator in "The Aspern Papers" experience a widening of their vision to include both the aesthetic and the moral.

75   LAITINEN, T[UOMO]. "Aspects of Henry James' Style." Ph.D. dissertation, Helsingin Yliopisto (Helsinki University, Finland), 150 pp.

Examines four rhetorical features of James's style to show their function in the fiction. Such features may appear to be contradictory; thus these features must be examined within their contexts.

Revised for publication: 1975.76.

See *Dissertation Abstracts International* 42, no. 3 (1981):6/3063C.

76   LAITINEN, TUOMO. *Aspects of Henry James's Style*. Annales Academiae Scientarium Fennicae, Dissertationes Humanarum Litterarum, 4. Helsinki: Suomalainen Tiedeakatemia.

Traces James's use of exclamation, rhetorical question, emphasis, and hyperbole in *Portrait, The Aspern Papers, The Spoils of Poynton*, and *The Ambassadors*. These rhetorical figures illuminate and differentiate character, thereby showing that James's style, difficult though it may be, is purposeful.

Revision of 1975.75.

77   LANDEIRA, RICARDO LOPEZ. "*Aura, The Aspern Papers*, 'A Rose for Emily': A Literary Relationship." *Journal of Spanish Studies: Twentieth Century* 3:125-43.

Details the many similarities these three works share in the use of imagery, narrative technique, plot structure, and handling of time. Such similarities reflect their "polysemous nature" rather than their interdependence.

78   LANG, HANS-JOACHIM. "The Making of Henry James's 'The American': The Contribution of Four Literatures." *Amerikastudien*, no. 1, 20:55-71.

Argues that the hero in *The House of the Seven Gables* was a model for Christopher Newman. James, however, did not have a complete understanding of Hawthorne's methods, so that the second part of the novel is "literal Gothicism" and "pseudo-Hawthornian."

79   LAY, MARY M. "The Sibling-Protector in Henry James." Ph.D. dissertation, University of New Mexico, 267 pp.
         Traces James's use of the "sibling-protector," who assumes the role of an elder brother or sister to a young dependent charge, beginning with "Gabrielle de Bergerac" to *The Ambassadors*. The sibling-protector generally guides his or her charge to openness to life or to an understanding of reality and, as such, is an essential element in James's exploration of personal growth.
         See *Dissertation Abstracts International* 36, no. 10 (1976):6686A.

80   LEES, FRANCIS NOEL. *"Isabel Clarendon* and Henry James." *Gissing Newsletter*, 11, no. 1 (January):12-14.
         Suggests that the fortune-hunter Vincent Lacour in Gissing's novel was modeled on Morris Townsend in *Washington Square*.

81   McCULLOUGH, JOSEPH B. "Madame Merle: Henry James's 'White Blackbird.'" *Papers on Language and Literature* 11, no. 3 (Summer):312-16.
         Traces the various sources of the name, including de Musset's "Histoire d'un merle blanc" and Ovid's *Metamorphoses*. In addition, McCullough notes that Isabel's connecting Madame Merle with Juno and Niobe should have warned her of Merle's true nature.

82   McINTIRE, MARY BETH. "The Buried Life: A Study of *The Blithedale Romance, The Confidence Man*, and *The Sacred Fount*." Ph.D. dissertation, Rice University, 246 pp.
         Argues that these three novels explore the ways in which the conscious mind maintains its own masquerade and perceives the masquerades of others. In the final chapter McIntire relates James's novel to Hawthorne's and Melville's: Hawthorne's and James's narrators retreat to a solipsistic world "where their conscious idealizing rhetoric is a facade"; in Melville's and James's novels the "other" is masked behind rhetoric and the reader is forced to adopt either/or categories although "truth" is shown to be partial and fragmented.
         See *Dissertation Abstracts International* 36, no. 4 (1975):2183A.

1975

83   MACK, STANLEY THOMAS. "The Narrator in James's 'The Death of the Lion': A Religious Conversation of Sorts." *Thoth: Syracuse University Graduate Studies in English* 16, no. 1:19-25.

Traces the religious imagery in the tale to show that the narrator is converted to the "aesthetic faith" exemplified by Paraday's work.

84   MACKENZIE, MANFRED. "The Lapse and Accumulation of Time in Henry James." In *American Studies Down Under: Pacific Circle 3*. Edited by Norman Harper. University of Queensland Press, pp. 103-10.

Sees "The Middle Years" and "The Pupil" as models of James's sense of time. In the first tale, the artist is granted time to prove himself socially sufficient. When this time extension runs out, the artist is exposed and his artistic claims reveal themselves to be invalid. In the second tale, Mackenzie explores the character's confrontation with his insufficiency, a "time of psychological implosion."

Reprinted in 1976.130.

85   MACNAUGHTON, W.R. "The Narrator in Henry James's *The Sacred Fount*." In *Literature and Ideas in America: Essays in Memory of Harry Hayden Clark*. Edited by Robert Falk. Athens: Ohio University Press, pp. 155-81.

Examines the role and effect of the novel's narrator, focusing on the creation of drama, immediacy, and ambiguity. Suggests that the narrator is a parody of the Jamesian novelist as well as a satirical treatment of the philosopher and the scientist.

86   MEYERS, JEFFREY. "Bronzino, Veronese and *The Wings of the Dove*." In *Painting and the Novel*. New York: Barnes & Noble, pp. 19-30.

Argues that Bronzino's portrait of Lucrezia Panciatichi and Veronese's *The Marriage Feast at Cana* suggest the novel's major themes, reflect the materialism of society, and focus crucial scenes in the novel.

87   MINNICK, THOMAS L. "'The Light of Deepening Experience' in the Major Novels of Henry James." *Rendezvous* 10, no. 2 (Winter):37-51.

Sees James's use of light and dark imagery in *The American,*
The Portrait of a Lady, The Ambassadors, The Wings of the Dove, and
The Golden Bowl reflecting James's transformation from romancer in
the early novels to romantic in the later ones. In the later work James
redefines the concepts of morality and innocence explored in his early
work.

88   MONTEIRO, GEORGE. "'The Items of High Civilization':
     Hawthorne, James, and George Parsons Lathrop." *Nathaniel*
     Hawthorne Journal 1975:146-55.
          Reprints Lathrop's critique of James's *Hawthorne*. Lathrop,
     who wrote *A Study of Hawthorne* (1876), takes James to task for
     describing America as lacking "the items of high civilization." James
     suggested to Tom Perry that Lathrop be "put to bed, & forbidden the
     use of pen and ink."

89   _____. "Washington Friends and National Reviewers: Henry James's
     'Pandora.'" *Research Studies*, 43, no. 1 (March):38-44.
          Argues for a serious assessment of this tale because it contains
     James's reactions to Washington personalities and the Adamses as well
     as his "cat-and-mouse" play with *Daisy Miller*.

90   MOORE, RAYBURN S. "The Epistolary James." *Sewanee Review*
     83, no. 4 (Fall):703-7.
          Reviews the first volume of Edel's *Henry James Letters*, noting
     that the volume gives James's "epistolary greatness" short shrift by
     opting for a general rather than scholarly audience.

91   MORI, MIHOKO. "*Meian to The Golden Bowl*" [Natsume's *Meian*
     and James's *The Golden Bowl*]. *Eigo Seinen* (Tokyo) 121:212-13.
          In Japanese.
          Notes that Soseki Natsume, who had been an admirer of
     William James, read Henry James's *The Golden Bowl* with great
     interest. An examination of *Meian* reveals the influence of James's
     novel on plot, descriptions, and character relationships. See also
     1975.128, 1976.128, and 1976.182.

1975

92   MOSELEY, JAMES G., Jr. *A Complex Inheritance: The Idea of Self-Transcendence in the Theology of Henry James, Sr., and the Novels of Henry James*. Missoula, Mont.: American Academy of Religion and Scholars Press, ix, 169 pp.

Demonstrates that James Senior's theology, particularly his concern with self-transcendence, shaped James's analysis of the growth of the consciousness in his novels and tales. *The Portrait of a Lady* marks James's formulation and criticism of his father's ideas; *What Maisie Knew* and "The Turn of the Screw" probe the successes and failures of self-transcendence; and the three novels of James's major phase present culminations of James's "complex inheritance" from his father. James appropriated his father's belief of the importance of an experience of self-transcendence and focused not on the ethereal but on "actual lives and concrete situations."

Revision of Ph.D. dissertation, University of Chicago, 1973.

93   _____. "Conversion through Vision: Puritanism and Transcendentalism in *The Ambassadors*." *Journal of the American Academy of Religion* 43, no. 3 (September):473-84.

Traces the influences of puritanism and transcendentalism on the novel and shows how James brings these conflicting strains together. Strether moves from a transcendentalism, in which man is good and free, to that of Puritanism, which sees man as sinful and needing regeneration. Yet Strether's "conversion" is based on a transcendentalist vision of human relatedness and on a "truly civilized, harmonious order of human relations."

94   NANCE, WILLIAM L. "Eden, Oedipus, and Rebirth in American Fiction." *Arizona Quarterly* 31, no. 4 (Winter):353-65.

Discusses *The Ambassadors* briefly in connection to the Edenic myth. Strether's visit to the French countryside, where he recognizes Chad and Mme. de Vionnet, is a journey into "the treacherous Eden of the American soil," but he is protected by his age, his aestheticism, and his "Jamesian ethic of renunciation and understanding."

95   NETTELS, ELSA. "Vision and Knowledge in *The Ambassadors* and *Lord Jim*." *English Literature in Transition (1880-1920)* 18, no. 3:181-93.

Discusses similarities and differences between the two novels, focusing on the central consciousness in each–Strether and

Marlow – and the importance of distinguishing between appearance and fact. James depicts a "process of vision" whereby Strether moves from ignorance to understanding. In contrast, Conrad's Marlow experiences "a succession of moments of insight" that are not logically connected.

96 NIEMTZOW, ANNETTE. "Marriage and the New Woman in *The Portrait of a Lady*." *American Literature* 47, no. 3 (November):377-95.
    Attributes James's ideas about the sanctity of marriage and its essential privacy to Henry James, Sr. The novel's open ending, however, shows that James was moving toward modern ideas about marriage. Niemtzow sees the tension between the confinement of marriage and the desire for freedom as a dynamic force in the novel.

97 NORMANN, RALF. "The Concerted Screws of Henry James." *Neuphilologische Mittelungen* (Helsinki) 76, no. 3:317-37.
    Investigates James's technique in creating ambiguity in "The Turn of the Screw," focusing on the careful balance James maintains in presenting two mutually exclusive readings – that the governess's point of view does or does not accurately reflect reality. James creates ambiguity through "touchstone" characters, hints, inevitability of plot, the contradiction between prologue and story, and symbolism.

98 O'CONNOR, DENNIS LAWRENCE. "Henry James and the Language World of Renunciation." Ph.D. dissertation, Cornell University, 152 pp.
    Examines James's language in *The American, Watch and Ward, The Portrait of a Lady*, "The Beast in the Jungle," and "The Figure in the Carpet," applying linguistics and philosophical psychology to understand the renunciatory protagonist's relationship to the world and to the other.
    See *Dissertation Abstracts International* 36, no. 6 (1975):3697A.

99 PAGE, NORMAN. "The Great Tradition Revisited." In *Jane Austen's Achievement*. Edited by Juliet McMaster. New York: Barnes & Noble, pp. 44-63.
    Examines Jane Austen's place in Leavis's "great tradition" and in so doing discusses Austen's influence on the other great novelists designated by Leavis: George Eliot and Henry James. Page finds James's early novels resonant with Austen's subjects, themes, structure,

1975

and diction and argues that James's focus on the heroine, such as in *The Portrait of a Lady*, derives directly from Austen.

100   PARRILL, ANNA S. "Portraits of Ladies." *Tennessee Studies in Literature* 20:92-99.
Compares *The Portrait of a Lady* and Meredith's *The Egoist*, focusing on Isabel Archer and Clara Middleton. Both heroines have "to struggle to retain . . .independence and self-respect in the face of repressive conventions."

101   PAULY, THOMAS H. "Henry James and the Travel Sketch: The Artistry of *Italian Hours*." *Centennial Review* 19, no. 2 (Spring):108-20.
Argues that in the impressionistic travel sketch James found a medium with which he could evoke the "impenetrable mystery" of Italy.

102   ____. "The Literary Sketch in Nineteenth-Century America." *Texas Studies in Language and Literature* 17, no. 2 (Summer):489-503.
Examines Irving's, Hawthorne's, and James's use of the sketch as a "tentative mode of perception" in which the writer could work toward a freedom of expression and understanding. As a result, the sketch is a record of "their own journeys to literary consciousness." Pauly discusses James's *Transatlantic Sketches* and briefly mentions *Italian Hours*.

103   PEARCE, HOWARD. "Henry James's Pastoral Fallacy." *PMLA* 90, no. 5 (October):834-47.
Examines the pastoral worlds created by James's "questing characters" in selected novels and short stories. James uses this "pastoral fallacy" ironically because it reflects the human need to deny death.

104   PETERSON, DALE L. *The Clement Vision: Poetic Realism in Turgenev and James*. Port Washington, N.Y.: Kennikat, 157 pp.
Assesses the impact of Turgenev's realism on Janes's evolution as a novelist, concentrating on the aesthetic, cultural, and temperamental qualities that attracted James to Turgenev and to his idea of realism. Both writers "were temperamentally disposed to

salvage bliss from the banal," and this disposition shaped content – protagonists who are visionaries – and form – the emphasis on dramatiziation. There is a crucial difference between the two writers; however, Turgenev's visionaries are barred from sensual experience while James's renounce it.

105 PURTON, VALERIE. "James's *The Turn of the Screw*, Chapter 9." *Explicator* 34, no. 3 (November):Item 24.
        Sees that the governess's reading of Fielding's *Amelia* indicates her state of mind. The governess identifies with the mother's self-sacrifices and imposes the novel's "moral struggle and extreme emotion" on her surroundings.

106 RAY, LAURA. "Childhood and the English Novel: Two English Girls." *Genre* 8, no. 2 (June):89-106.
        Compares *What Maisie Knew* with *The Young Visitors* by Daisy Ashford, who wrote the novel when nine years old. Both novels are about "the confrontation of perception with convention." Maisie seeks initiation and enlightenment while Ashford's heroine, an "authentic outsider," is obsessed with social form.

107 RICKS, BEATRICE. *Henry James: A Bibliography of Secondary Works*. The Scarecrow Author Bibliographies, no. 24. Metuchen, N.J.: Scarecrow, xxii, 461 pp.
        Lists with some brief annotations scholarship on James up to 1973 and includes contemporary reviews of James's work. The volume is divided into the following sections: biography, criticism of specific works, general criticism, and bibliography.

108 RIHOIT, CATHERINE. "Waiting for Isabel: An Analysis of the Levels of Significance in the First Fifteen Sentences of *The Portrait of a Lady*." In *Studies in English*. Edited by André Joly and Frazer K. Thomas. Lille: Univ. de Lille III, pp. 187-225.
        Analyzes the linguistic elements and structures in the first paragraph of *The Portrait of a Lady* as a way of demonstrating the utility of such analysis in understanding a work of fiction. The analysis of this paragraph reveals that description dominates narration and that the preeminence of combination over selection suggests a focus on the

1975

description of relations. Ambiguity also figures significantly in this novel.

109   RON, MOSHE. "The Subject and the Matter: Interpretations of Henry James and Narrative Theory." Ph.D. dissertation, Yale University, 247 pp.
        Examines, in part 1, "The Real Thing," arguing that there are three phases of interpretation and that meaning is at odds with structure. In part 2, Ron analyzes James's use of the portrait as "exemplary of the structure of mimesis"; and in part 3, Ron discusses Derrida's concept of *citationnalité*.
        See *Dissertation Abstracts International* 36, no. 12 (1979):8062A-8063A.

110   RUTHROF, H.G. "A Note on Henry James's Psychological Realism and the Concept of Brevity." *Studies in Short Fiction* 12, no. 4 (Fall):369-73.
        Describes James's strategies in combining psychological realism, which calls for slow unfolding, with the brevity of the short story. These include innovations in characterization, indirect presentation, drawing a distinction between material calling for anecdotic treatment and that requiring development, and reaching a compromise in the novella.

*111   SAMOKHVALOV, N.I. "Genri Dzheyms i Ernest Kheminguey: Tragediya dobrovol'nogo izgnaniya" [Henry James and Ernest Hemingway: The tragedy of voluntary exile]. *Nauchnye trudy Kubanskogo universiteta* (Krasnodar, USSR) 195:111-18.
        Source: *Annual Bibliography of English Language and Literature* 50 (1975):496, item 8890.

112   SANTANGELO, GENNARO A. "Henry James's 'Maud-Evelyn' and the Web of Consciousness." *Amerikastudien* 20, no. 1:45-54.
        Examines the tale's central intelligence, Lady Emma, to reveal how James joins sensibility and consciousness to convey reality.

113   SARBU, ALADÁR. "Henry James: A pálya és tanulságai" [Henry James: Lessons of a career]. *Filológiai Közlöny* 21:58-78.

In Hungarian.

114   ____. "Some Aspects of the Changing Nature of Twentieth Century English Fiction." In *Studies in English and American*. Vol 2. Edited by Erzsebet Perenyi and Tibor Frank. Budapest: Department of English, L. Eotvos University, pp. 91-119.

Suggests that James's development of the consciousness and his analytical method lay the foundation for the modern novel in which the novelist withdraws from the narrative. James's experimentation with the consciousness as the focus of the narrative prepares the way for the work of Woolf and Joyce.

115   SAVARESE, JOHN EDMUND. "Some Theories of Short Fiction in America in the Nineteenth Century: Poe, Hawthorne and James." Ph.D. dissertation, Princeton University, 415 pp.

Examines the models these writers employed in their short fiction since they lacked a "long tradition of masterpieces" to serve as a pattern for their work. Poe used a mechanical model; Hawthorne, that of an alchemical compound; and James, the pictorial. Savarese concludes by relating James's pictorial model to the New York Edition and Coburn's frontispieces.

See *Dissertation Abstracts International* 37, no. 3 (1976):1555A-1556A.

116   SCHNEIDER, DANIEL J. "The Divided Self in the Fiction of Henry James." *PMLA* 90, no. 3 (May):447-60.

Examines three motifs essential to James's art, reflecting the anxieties of the divided self. These motifs are escape, "seizure by the eye," and quantification; they provide an understanding not only of James's fiction but of his psyche as well.

117   ____. "'A Terrible Mixture in Things': The Symbolism of Henry James." In *Symbolism: The Manichean Vision: A Study in the Art of James, Conrad, Woolf and Stevens*. Lincoln: University of Nebraska Press, pp. 62-117.

Argues that James's symbolism is based on antithesis and the dualism of reality and appearance. Schneider examines the symbolism in *The American*, *The Portrait of a Lady*, and *The Ambassadors*. In *The Ambassadors*, James's use of symbolism is ironic and reflects his effort

1975

to escape partisanship and achieve "perfect detachment" and "perfect freedom."

118   SEBOUHIAN, GEORGE. "The Transcendental Imagination of Merton Densher." *Modern Language Studies* 5, no. 2:35-45.
       Traces Densher's growth in consciousness, attributing that growth to his increasing involvement and affinity with Milly. At the novel's end Densher rejects the material world for the world of consciousness.

119   SERLEN, ELLEN. "The Rage of Caliban: Realism and Romance in the Nineteenth-Century Novel." Ph.D. dissertation, State University of New York, Stony Brook, 275 pp.
       Argues that the fiction of Austen, Emily Brontë, Dickens, Eliot, and James reflects the desire to escape from the radical transformations of nineteenth-century England although the novel has been traditionally associated with realism. In *The Princess Casamassima*, Hyacinth Robinson dies because of his discovery that the ideal is not compatible with the real.
       See *Dissertation Abstracts International* 36, no. 2 (1975):911A.

120   SHARMA, JAGDISH NARAIN. "The Evolution of the International Theme in the Fiction of Henry James." Ph.D. dissertation, Indiana University, 188 pp.
       Traces the development of the international theme throughout James's career, examining his fiction and nonfiction but focusing on *The American, The Portrait of a Lady, The Ambassadors, The Wings of the Dove*, and *The Golden Bowl*. Sharma suggests that this theme disappeared from American literature after James because of changing conditions in America and James's exhaustive treatment of it.
       See *Dissertation Abstracts International* 36, no. 8 (1976):5303A-5304A.

121   SPRINGER, MARY DOYLE. "Henry James, *The Death of the Lion* and the Plot Question." In *Forms of the Modern Novella*. Chicago: University of Chicago Press, pp. 83-87.
       Uses this novella as an example of the "plot of satire" where character is sacrificed to plot.

1975

122 _____ . "An Unexemplary Example in James' *The Pupil*." In *Forms of the Modern Novella*. Chicago: University of Chicago Press, pp. 72-76.
Suggests that the novella is flawed because diffusing of characterization, handling of time, and entering into the consciousness of secondary characters distance the reader from the main characters.

123 SPRINKER, JOHN MICHAEL. "'Questions of Air and Form': Fictional Paradigms in Jane Austen, George Meredith and Henry James." Ph.D. dissertation, Princeton University, 334 pp.
Demonstrates through an analysis of Austen's, Meredith's, and James's novels that each author's choice of form reflects assumptions about the writing process. In his later novels, James "became obsessed with the inherent mendacity of the fictional process" and so wrote the prefaces, which create a world of discourse to counteract the necessary lies of fiction.
See *Dissertation Abstracts International* 37, no. 3 (1976):1535A.

124 STAFFORD, WILLIAM T. "Henry James." In *American Literary Scholarship: An Annual/1973*. Edited by James Woodress. Durham: Duke University Press, pp. 116-34.
Surveys criticism on James published in 1973.

125 _____ . *A Name, Title, and Place Index to the Critical Writings of Henry James*. Englewood, Colo.: Microcard Editions, 270 pp.
Indexes names, titles, and places in James's nonfiction, including books, contributions to books, and contributions to periodicals.

126 STAUBLE, MICHELE. "Henry James als Kritiker Flauberts" [Henry James as a critic of Flaubert]. *Neue Zurcher Zeitung* (Zurich) (25-26 January):61.
In German.

127 STYCZYŃSKA, ADELA. "'The Papers': James' Satire on the Modern Publicity System." *Kwartalnik Neofilologiczny* (Warsaw)22:419-36.
Sees "The Papers" as a continuation of James's criticism of contemporary journalism. The essay concludes with a discussion of

1975

Graham Greene's *The Burnt-Out Case* and Ionesco's *The Leader*, both of which have "thematic links" with James's tale.

128   TANIMOTO, YASUKO. "H. James to Natsume Soseki: Ni Sakka no Ishitsusei" [Henry James and Soseki Natsume: Differences between the two writers]. *Eigo Seinen* (Tokyo) 121:392-93.
In Japanese.
Suggests that as writers Henry James and Natsume Soseki were very different from each other. *The Golden Bowl* was the only book by James that Natsume owned. His reading of the novel was not sympathetic, and he did not like James's style. There is no point then in comparing the works of the two writers, as does Mihoko Mori, 1975.91. See also 1976.146 and 1976.182.

129   TATE, ALLEN. "'The Beast in the Jungle.'" In *Memoirs and Opinions, 1926-1974*. Chicago: Swallow Press, pp. 159-63.
Discusses the structure of the tale's scenes, noting that James does not "render dramatically parts I and II" and that symbolism tends to allegory.
Reprint of *Sewanee Review* 58, no. 1 (1950):5-10.

130   TAYLOR, LINDA JENNINGS. "Henry James and the Critics: The 1880's." Ph.D. dissertation, Brown University, 448 pp.
Examines the contemporary critical response to *The Portrait of a Lady, The Bostonians*, and *The Princess Casamassima* to determine fluctuations in James's reputation and the values and expectations of James's reviewers. Taylor's research revels that James's work was widely known and was reviewed within the context of the major social concerns of the time.
See *Dissertation Abstracts International* 37, no. 1 (1976):319A-320A.

131   ____. "*The Portrait of a Lady* and the Anglo-American Press: An Annotated Checklist, 1880-1886." *Resources for American Literary Study* 5, no. 2 (Autumn):166-98.
Annotates 152 items. These reviews reveal a complex reaction to James's novel; Taylor suggests that a study of contemporary criticism would illuminate James's relation to both the press and his audience.

132   TERRIE, H.L., Jr. "The Varieties of Henry James." *Sewanee Review* 83, no. 4 (Fall):695-703.
        Notes that James often infuses humor into a scene to undercut sentimentality.

133   THOMAS, LLOYD SPENCER. "The Haunts of Language: Superstition and Subterfuge in Henry James's *Stories of the Supernatural*." Ph.D. dissertation, State University of New York, Binghamton, 187 pp.
        Examines the technical devices James used to expose characters' gullibility in seven tales; these devices include the house trope, the monomaniacal guest, nonsense dialogue, religious echo and mimicry, submerged ribaldry, and borrowings from *Commedia Dell'Arte*. Tales discussed are "The Last of the Valerii," "The Ghostly Rental," "The Altar of the Dead," "The Turn of the Screw," "The Great Good Place," "The Beast in the Jungle," and "The Jolly Corner."
        See *Dissertation Abstracts International* 36, no. 3 (1975):1512A.

134   TINTNER, ADELINE R. "*Henry James Letters*." *American Literary Realism, 1870-1910* 8, no. 4 (Autumn):353-59.
        Reviews Edel's *Henry James Letters*, Volumes I and II. These volumes reveal James's early dedication to the life of art and his search for "facts" to become the stuff of his fiction–a search that establishes him as a realist.

135   ____. "Henry James's Salomé and the Arts of the *Fin de Siècle*." *Markham Review* 5 (Fall):5-10.
        Examines the representation of Salomé in the art and literature of the time–particularly in the works of Moreau, Flaubert, Wilde, Strauss, and Beardsley–and shows how James incorporated these various representations in his portrayal of Christina Light. Tintner sees a "strong" symbolist influence on James, especially during the years 1895 to 1905. The essay is illustrated.

136   ____. "Iconic Analogy in 'The Lesson of the Master': Henry James's Legend of Saint George and the Dragon." *Journal of Narrative Technique* 5, no. 2 (May):116-27.

1975

Describes the tale as James's version of the saint's legend, in which Henry St. George, speaking for James, warns of the perils confronting the artist.

137 _____. "The Metamorphoses of Edith Wharton in Henry James's *The Finer Grain*." *Twentieth Century Literature* 21, no. 4 (December):355-79.

Suggests that the tales included in *The Finer Grain* are "fictional analogues" of the relationship between James and Wharton. The five tales of the volume have heroines with many of Wharton's traits and contain many topical references to Wharton's lifestyle, habits, and possessions. Although Wharton never publicly commented on her "portraits," Tintner notes that her fiction contains "hints" of a riposte to *The Finer Grain*.

138 _____. "Sargent in the Fiction of Henry James." *Apollo* 102 (August):128-32.

Traces James's use of and reference to Sargent in the tales and novels written after 1887. James shows his appreciation of Sargent by appropriating him: Sargent influences James's artist figures, and his paintings are frequently alluded to in the fiction. The essay is illustrated with Sargent's works.

Revised 1986.151.

139 TORGOVNICK, MARIANNA. "Novelistic Conclusions: Epilogues in Nineteenth Century Novels." Ph.D. dissertation, Columbia University, 249 pp.

Examines the aesthetic and thematic functions of epilogues to show that epilogues must support and illuminate the novel in order to function as a successful conclusion. Torgovnick discusses James's theories of conclusions, in addition to analyzing the conclusions in his fiction, both quasi-epilogues and "scenic endings."

See *Dissertation Abstracts International* 36, no. 12 (1976):8041A.

140 TUVESON, ERNEST. "'The Jolly Corner': A Fable of Redemption." *Studies in Short Fiction* 12, no. 3 (Summer):271-80.

Sees the tale, influenced by F.W.H. Myers's ideas on the subliminal self, as "one of the most successful depictions of a psychic crisis – from within." Brydon's encounter with his hidden self reflects the problem of the self in the society of the time, making the tale both a parable and critique.

141   UNRUE, DARLENE H. "Henry James's Extraordinary Use of Portraits." *Re/Artes Liberales* 1, no. 2:47-53.

Argues that James's use of portraits is derived from the Gothic romance tradition. The Gothic writers used the "living portrait" as a means of creating suspense and fear; James employs the living portrait to suggest fear elicited by flouting tradition or nature, discovering evil, or anticipating death. Unrue discusses the function of portraits in *The Portrait of a Lady*, "The Jolly Corner," "Owen Wingrave," *The Wings of the Dove*, and *The Sense of the Past*.

142   VEEDER, WILLIAM. *Henry James – The Lessons of the Master: Popular Fiction and Personal Style in the Nineteenth Century*. Chicago: University of Chicago Press, xiii, 287 pp.

Examines James's early novels – from *Watch and Ward* to *The Portrait of a Lady* – to show the influence of the conventions of popular fiction on his style, plot, and characters. Veeder suggests that James's development in these early novels recapitulates that of the Victorian novelist. These novels also introduce concerns and themes that will dominate James's writing career.

143   VENDETTI, JAMES ANTHONY. "A Critical Interpretation of Jack Clayton's Film 'The Innocents.'" Ed.D. dissertation, Columbia University Teachers College, 262 pp.

Examines Clayton's adaptation of "The Turn of the Screw" using the theories of Huss and Silverstein, Richardson, and Durgnat in order to demonstrate the importance of multiple theories in understanding a film.

See *Dissertation Abstracts International* 36, no. 8 (1976):4816A-4817A.

144   VINCEC, SISTER STEPHANIE, C.S.J. "A Variant Edition of Henry James's *The Wings of the Dove*." Ph.D. dissertation, McMaster University, Canada.

1975

> Reprints text of the first edition of the novel (Scribners, 1902) along with a list of substantive variants from the 1902 Constable Edition and the 1909 New York Edition. The introduction to the text discusses the history of the novel; James's comments in letters, notebooks, and the preface; and the effect of the revisions.
>
> See *Dissertation Abstracts International* 36, no. 9 (1976):6106A.

145   VITOUX, PIERRE. "Le Récit dans *The Ambassadors*." *Poétique* 24:460-78.
      In French.

146   WALLACE, RONALD. *Henry James and the Comic Form*. Ann Arbor: University of Michigan Press, 202 pp.
      Demonstrates that James belongs to the tradition of serious high comedy and examines the archetypal elements of comedy in his major novels, beginning with *The American* and concluding with *The Golden Bowl*, in addition to selected tales. Wallace focuses on the characters, plots, theme, and style of these works to show that James's vision is essentially comic in his recognition of human potential and individual limitation.
      Reprint in part: "Gabriel Nash: Henry James's Comic Spirit," *Nineteenth-Century Fiction* 28, no. 2 (1973) 220-24; "Comic Form in *The Ambassadors*," *Genre* 5 (1972) 31-50; "Maggie Verver: Comic Heroine," *Genre* 6 (1973) 404-15.

147   WARD, J.A. "Ambiguities of Henry James." *Sewanee Review* 83, no. 1 (Winter):39-60.
      Describes Jamesian ambiguity as "radical subjectivism" arising out of James's view that the artist must see multiplicity, rather than impose unity.

148   WARD, SUSAN P. "Painting and Europe in *The American*." *American Literature* 46, no. 4 (January):566-73.
      Examines James's use of painting to develop plot and portray characters. Ward concentrates on the opening scene in which Newman looks at Veronese's *The Marriage at Cana* and Murillo's *Madonna*, paintings that foreshadow the novel's conflicts.

149 WATSON, CHARLES N., Jr. "The Comedy of Provincialism: James's 'The Point of View.'" *Southern Humanities Reivew* 9, no. 2 (Spring):173-83.

Approaches James's epistolary tale not as a diatribe against American society and culture but as a "light-hearted" though "intricate comedy of provincialism." The tale shows James's attachment to America, not his aversion to it.

150 WILDS, NANCY G. "Rhetorical Strategy in Early Twentieth-Century Fiction: Studies in Henry James, Ford Madox Ford, and James Joyce." Ph.D. dissertation, University of South Carolina, 201 pp.

Analyzes the stylistic and structural techniques used in "The Beast in the Jungle." *The Good Soldier*, and *A Portrait of the Artist as a Young Man* that enable the reader to make "appropriate responses" to the work. James's tale depends on a triple perspective—the protagonist's consciousness, the views of other characters, and authorial commentary—that, in addition to imagery, foregrounding, and several temporal perspectives, demands continual reorientation on the reader's part.

See *Dissertation Abstracts International* 36, no. 6 (1975):3706A.

151 WILSON, COLIN. "Structure and Technique." In *The Craft of the Novel*. London: Victor Gollancz, pp. 180-85.

Evaluates *The Ambassadors*. While it has a near-perfect structure, it is flawed by James's "tiresome later style" and the vagueness of the credo "Live all you can."

152 WILSON, JAMES D. "The Gospel According to Christopher Newman." *Studies in American Fiction* 3, no. 1 (Spring):83-88.

Argues that in the course of the novel Newman shifts from "evangelist of the American doctrine of success" to high priest of this gospel to demigod, and traces the imagery reflecting this transformation. Newman's ultimate failure shows that the American gospel has no place in Europe.

153 YOSHIDA, YASUO. "*To the Lighthouse* to *The Portrait of a Lady*" [*To the Lighthouse* and *The Portrait of a Lady*]. In *Gengo to Buntai: higashida Chiaki Kyoju Kanreki Kinen Ronbunshu* [Language and

1975

Style: Essays commemorating the sixtieth birthday of Professor Chiaki Higashida.] Osaka: Osaka Kyoiku Tosho, pp. 218-28.
In Japanese.

154   ZLOTNICK, JOAN. "Influence or Coincidence: A Comparative Study of 'The Beast in the Jungle' and 'A Painful Case.'" *Colby Library Quarterly* 11, no. 2 (June):132-35.
Notes that the "remarkable similarities" in the two tales about the "unlived life" suggest that James influenced Joyce.

1976

1   AKIYAMA, MASAYUKI. "A Rapprochement Study of Yasunari Kawabata's *The Sound of the Mountain* and Henry James's *The Ambassadors*." In *Annual Report of Researches*, no. 25. Tokyo: Mishima College, Nihon University, pp. 45-87.
Compares the two novels to show similarities and differences between Japanese and Western treatments of the theme of loss. The discussion includes analyses of attitudes toward nature, life, behavioral patterns, and love – particularly in terms of each novel's hero. In the end, each hero reacts to a sense of loss by attaining "a lofty degree of morality."

2   ALDAZ, ANNA MARIA. "Tiger, Tiger Burning Bright: A Study of Theme and Symbol in Henry James' 'The Beast in the Jungle.'" *ITA Humanidades* (Sao José dos Campos, Brazil) 12:83-85.
Notes that Marcher's connections to the qualities of cold and dark and May's connections to light and fire underscore the thematic dichotomies between the two characters.

3   ANDERSON, CHARLES R. "A Henry James Centenary." *Georgia Review* 30, no. 1 (Spring):34-52.
Notes that 1976 is the centenary of James's debut as "our first international author of distinction" and traces James's development of the international theme in his novels, tales, and travel sketches. James should be honored because he proved in his life and fiction that the American abroad could be cultured and cosmopolitan.

4   ANDERSON, QUENTIN. "Practical and Visionary Americans." *American Scholar* 45 (Summer):405-18.
Discusses briefly James's illustration of the opposition between practical and visionary in Isabel Archer and Maggie Verver.

5   ARMSTRONG, JUDITH. "The Order Broken: The Course of Love." In *The Novel of Adultery*. New York: Barnes & Noble, pp. 119-21.
Suggests that in *The Golden Bowl* Maggie's response to adultery ultimately strengthens her and enables her to repair her damaged relationship with the Prince.

6   ARNAVON, CYRILLE. "Encore *The Ambassadors*." *Etudeo Anglaises* 29:414-23.
In French.
Surveys public reaction to the novel: some readers admire it as a masterpiece while others consider it thin and frivolous. These divergent responses have inspired a large body of criticism about the book.

7   ASHTON, JEAN. "Reflecting Consciousness: Three Approaches to Henry James." *Literature/Film Quarterly* 4, no. 3 (Summer):230-39.
Examines Bogdanovich's *Daisy Miller*, Chabrol's *The Bench of Desolation*, and Rivette's *Céline et Julie vont en bateau* (based on *The Other House*) as different ways of approaching the problems of adapting James's work to film. Bogdanovich's attitude toward James is irreverent; Chabrol focuses on James's subject, Herbert Dodd's consciousness; Rivette captures James's ambiguity by his use of nontraditional techniques.

8   BABIIHA, THADDEO KITASIMBWA. "A Review of Research and Criticism on the James-Hawthorne Relation, 1918-1973." Ph.D. dissertation, Brown University, 673 pp.
Lists and annotates items concerning James's relationship to Hawthorne. Part 1 lists James's writings about Hawthorne; part 2 lists

1976

items examining the general relationship between the two writers; and part 3 lists items examining specific works.

See *Dissertation Abstracts International* 38, no. 6 (1977):3493A.

9   BADGER, REID. "The Character and Myth of Hyacinth: A Key to *The Princess Casamassima.*" *Arizona Quarterly* 32, no. 4 (Winter):316-26.

Examines Hyacinth's character, noting his romanticism and naïveté. Badger discusses the implications of Hyacinth's names and the novel's parallels with the classical myth, and suggests that the mythological connotations illuminate Hyacinth's tragedy and indicate James's assessment of modern society.

10   BAILIE, R.H. "The Creative Evolution of the Fiction of Henry James: A Study of Artistic Development." Ph.D. dissertation, Queen's University of Belfast, United Kingdom, 117 pp.

Argues that James's "imagination aspires to a physical expression in order to resist the physicalization of mental phenomena and of creativity itself." Bailie traces this "paradoxical artistic project" in *The Princess Casamassima, The Sacred Fount,* and *The Golden Bowl.*

See *Dissertation Abstracts International* 37, no. 3 (1977):1/3188C.

11   BASIC, SONJA. "Henry James between Old and New: An Interpretation of *The Wings of the Dove.*" *Studia Romanica et Anglica Zagrebiensis* (Zagreb) 41-42:333-75.

Argues that the novel's problematic nature arises out of James's inability to transform his modernist tendencies into modernist techniques. This is apparent in the conflict between realism and romanticism, particularly in the first half of the novel; in the second half James is able to fuse these two modes by his use of imagery and by his psychological approach. James's way of presenting the mind is largely traditional, but his treatment of imagery in connection with the mind anticipates modernism's "string of associations."

12   BAYM, NINA. "Revision and Thematic Change in *The Portrait of a Lady.*" *Modern Fiction Studies* 22, no. 2 (Summer):183-200.

Compares the 1881 edition with the 1908 revision. The earlier edition reflects the concerns of its time, particularly "the woman question," while the later version focuses on consciousness, James's concern in his later work. Baym also details the changes James made in the portrayal of the novel's characters.

Reprinted 1984.178 and 1987.17.

13 BEAUCHAMP, ANDREA LOUISE ROBERTS. "The Heroine of Our Common Scene: Portrayals of American Women in Four Novels by Edith Wharton and Henry James." Ph.D. dissertation, University of Michigan, 189 pp.

Compares *The Portrait of a Lady* with *The House of Mirth* and *The Golden Bowl* with *The Age of Innocence* to reveal significant differences in Wharton's and James's art. Beauchamp sees differences in each writer's technique and contrasts Wharton's naturalism with James's belief in freedom and individual responsibility.

See *Dissertation Abstracts International* 37, no. 2 (1976):965A.

14 BEIT-HALLALHI, BENJAMIN. "*The Turn of the Screw* and *The Exorcist*: Demoniacal Possession and Childhood Purity." *American Imago* 33, no. 3 (Fall):296-303.

Argues that both novels share the same theme – "the asexual purity of preadolescents" – and that although William Peter Blatty includes pornographic material, his theme is as Victorian and pre-Freudian as James's.

15 BELL, MILLICENT. "Jamesian Being." *Virginia Quarterly Review* 52, no. 1 (Winter):115-32.

Sketches the members of the James family-parents and children-in order to illuminate James's sense of the relation between being and doing. Bell concludes that James both "criticizes and celebrates" the passive personality of his father. In *The Ambassadors*, James shows that one can be an observer and still live fully.

16 BELLRINGER, ALAN W. "*The Ivory Tower*: The Cessation of Concern." *Journal of American Studies* 10, no. 2 (August):241-55.

Connects James's failure to complete *The Ivory Tower* with the First World War. The issues the novel raises – greed, swindling, moral disgust – are serious ones, but they pall in significance in the face of the war's violence and technological inhumanity.

1976

17   BENDER, BERT. "Henry James's Late Lyric Meditations upon the Mysteries of Fate and Self Sacrifice." *Genre* 9, no. 3 (Fall):247-62.

Explains James's late tales – "Owen Wingrave," "The Altar of the Dead," "The Next Time," "Maud Evelyn," "The Beast in the Jungle," and "The Bench of Desolation" – as "tales of the mind in the act of finding," James's meditations upon "his supernatural germ ideas." In particular, Bender focuses on James's use of religious imagery and discusses "The Bench of Desolation" in detail.

18   BERRYMAN, JOHN. "The World of Henry James." In *The Freedom of the Poet*. New York: Farrar, Straus & Geroux, pp. 161-67.

Sees the whole of James's work as the "gradual revelation" of how the "Social Fate" becomes the "Personal Fate" and weighs the merits of first versions of the fiction against those of the New York Edition, arguing that the later version is much richer. Berryman also discusses the shortcomings of Matthiessen's *Henry James: The Major Phase*.

Reprint of *Sewanee Review* 53, no. 2 (Spring 1945):291-97.

19   BERSANI, LEO. "The Jamesian Lie." In *A Future for Astyanax: Character and Desire in Literature*. Boston: Little, Brown & Co., pp. 128-55.

Reprint of *Partisan Review* 36 (Winter 1969):53-79.

20   BLUEFARB, SAM. "The Middle-Aged Man in Contemporary Literature: Bloom to Herzog." *CLA Journal* 20, no. 1 (September):1-13.

Examines the middle-aged men of Joyce, James, Bellow, Dreiser, T.S. Eliot, and Hemingway, seeing a pattern of introspection and retrospection along with the realization of having missed something in life. The section on James focuses on Strether.

21   BRIDEN, E.F. "James's Miss Churm: Another of Eliza's Prototypes?" *Shaw Review* 19, no. 1 (January):17-21.

Notes the "echoes" of James's "The Real Thing" in Pygmalion, particularly in Shaw's depiction of Eliza, but in the other characters as well. Briden also quotes Shaw's review of *Guy Domville* in which he suggests James's fiction is amenable to the stage.

22 BROOKE-ROSE, CHRISTINE. "The Squirm of the True: An Essay in Non-Methodology." *PTL* 1, no. 2 (April):265-94.

Surveys criticism of "The Turn of the Screw" focusing primarily on the "many layers of misreadings" as a way of preparing for her own reading from a semiotic perspective. This perspective will involve respect for the genre and for the "textuality of the text," and a distinction between metalanguage and "the language of the linguistic object examined."

Revised 1981.20. See also Pecora 1985.112.

23 _____. "The Squirm of the True: A Structural Analysis of Henry James's *The Turn of the Screw*." *PTL* 1, no. 3 (October):513-46.

Demonstrates that the tale's structure is based on the mirror, which Lacan associates with the formation of identity. Brooke-Rose then argues that the mirror-structure is linked to the tale's "narrative sentence," typical of myths and folktales, in which an injunction is given, accepted, then transgressed. The narrative sentence or deep structure preserves the ambiguity of the tale, an example of Todorov's "Pure Fantastic," in which events can be explained naturally or supernaturally.

Revised 1981.21. See also Pecora 1985.112.

24 BROOKS, PETER. "Henry James and the Melodrama of Consciousness." In *The Melodramatic Imagination: Balzac, Henry James, Melodrama, and the Mode of Excess*. New Haven: Yale University Press, pp. 153-97, 224-6.

Discusses the various influences on James's "melodramatic imagination," including Balzac and popular French drama, and traces the evolution of James's melodrama from external action in *The American* to the consciousness in the fiction of the major phase. Brooks then examines the function of melodrama in *The Wings of the Dove* as both theme and method.

25 _____. "The Melodramatic Imagination." In *The Melodramatic Imagination: Balzac, Henry James, Melodrama, and the Mode of Excess*. New Haven: Yale University Press, pp. 1-23, 208-9.

Argues that James's melodrama, based on his manichean view of the world, is essentially Balzacian in its "grandiose moral term" even though it is expressed more subtly than Balzac's.

1976

26 BURLUI, IRINA. "Narrative Patterns in Henry James' Short Novels *The Spoils of Poynton* and *What Maisie Knew*." *Analele Ştiinţifice ale Universităţii Iaş* 22:60-63.

Argues that James achieves structural, representational, and psychological narrative intensity by a complex system of events complementing each other by contrast or parallelism; by representing events so that significance is clear to the reader but only gradually so to the characters; and by "conflicts of conscience" involving the characters in a moral and spiritual adventure.

27 BYERS, JOHN R., Jr. "Alice Staverton's Redemption of Spencer Brydon in James' 'The Jolly Corner.'" *South Atlantic Bulletin* 41, no. 2:90-99.

Examines the role of Alice Staverton in the tale, focusing on the hunt motif. She shows Brydon the error of his past selfishness and opens to him a new life.

28 CALDWELL, RACHEL MONK. "Liberation for Women in the Fiction of Henry James." Ph.D. dissertation, Kansas State University, 174 pp.

Traces James's analysis of the position of women throughout his major novels, beginning with *Roderick Hudson* and concluding with *The Golden Bowl*. His early work examines the essential powerlessness of women and links their position to economic factors. By the end of his career, James portrayed women who could take control of their situation without being unfeminine.

See *Dissertation Abstracts International* 37, no. 9 (1977):5823A.

29 CAMPBELL, CHARLES LEO. "The House and the Outsider: Eight Studies in a Narrative Landscape." Ph.D. dissertation, University of Toronto.

Examines the use of the house as an archetype of form in *Beowulf, Clarissa, Frankenstein, Wuthering Heights, The Princess Casamassima, Heart of Darkness, Jacob's Room,* and *Light in August.* Campbell sees the archetype as essentially dialectical because it suggests not only form but that which is excluded from form and thus is related to the connection between the novel and the "real world."

See *Dissertation Abstracts International* 39, no. 4 (1978):2284A.

30 CARR, BARBARA CATHERINE L. "Variations on the Anarchist: Politics Reflected in Fiction." Ph.D. dissertation, Indiana University, 190 pp.

Examines the Bakunin-type anarchist in Turgenev's *Rudin*, Dostoevsky's *The Possessed*, Zola's *Germinal*, James's *The Princess Casamassima*, and Conrad's *Under Western Eyes*. This study focuses on the historical model, the literary transformation of ideology, and characters independent of the model. Although these authors do not subscribe to anarchism, they identify with their anarchist characters and enable the reader to do likewise.

See *Dissertation Abstracts International* 37, no. 8 (1977):5103A.

31 CHASE, JOANNE LOWEY. "Confined Spaces: Limits, 'Fidgets and Starts': The World of James' Late Short Stories." Ph.D. dissertation, Brandeis University, 157 pp.

Assesses strengths and weaknesses of six late tales – "The Bench of Desolation," "Flickerbridge," "Fordham Castle," "Crapy Cornelia," "Mora Montravers," and "A Round of Visits" – by comparing them to earlier masterpieces: "The Beast in the Jungle," "The Altar of the Dead," and *In the Cage*. The later tales depict a world of diminishing expectations and a recognition that human beings can be trapped by "the knowledge of limits."

See *Dissertation Abstracts International* 37, no. 2 (1976):966A.

32 CHURCH, MICHAEL TORRENCE. "The Celibate Ideal: Transformation and the Process of Identity in Henry James's *The Ambassadors*." Ph.D. dissertation, University of Kentucky, 238 pp.

Argues that the novel is dominated by Strether's continual flight from women, thus suggesting that the celibate ideal may be the key to the novel.

See *Dissertation Abstracts International* 38, no. 2 (1977):784A-785A.

33 COLACO, JILL. "Henry James and Mrs. Humphrey Ward: A Misunderstanding." *Notes and Queries* 23, no. 9 (September):408-10.

Suggests that James was mistaken in seeing himself caricatured in Mr. Bellasis, a minor character in *Eleanor*. Mr. Bellasis was in fact modeled on the poet Lamartine.

1976

34   COLLINS, ANGUS PAUL. "Three Apocalyptic Novels: *Our Mutual Friend, The Princess Casamassima, Tender Is the Night.*" Ph.D. dissertation, Indiana University, 317 pp.
Applies the "paradigms of apocalypse" of Raymond Williams and Frank Kermode and argues that the apocalyptic vision occurs in the interaction between aspects of social change and the individual needs of the writer. James's novel is "the climax of a conflict of aesthetic and moral allegiance" and the means by which James could distance himself from social ills.
See *Dissertation Abstracts International* 37, no. 8 (1977):5109A.

35   COLLINS, MARTHA. "The Narrator, the Satellites, and Isabel Archer: Point of View in *The Portrait of a Lady.*" *Studies in the Novel* 8, no. 2 (Summer):142-57.
Describes the multiple points of view in the novel, all of which enable the reader to see Isabel from the inside as well as outside. As a result, the reader experiences Isabel's growth in consciousness as well as the complexity of the character.

36   COMITO, TERRY. Introduction to *The Princess Casamassima.* New York: Thomas Y. Crowell, pp. v-xvii.
Argues that James's concern is for the fate of civilization-even though the novel's subject is a specific society–and for the necessity of a moral code as "a basis for a style" rather than the specific elements of that code.

37   COOLEY, THOMAS. "A Sporting Life: Henry James." In *Educated Lives: The Rise of Modern Autobiography.* Columbus: Ohio State University Press, pp. 101-24.
Argues that James used his autobiography as a means of coming to terms with his failure as a dramatist and of defining his identity as a writer.

38   COY, JAVIER. "A Thematic and Character Approach to Henry James." *Studi Americani* 21-22:109-27.
Argues that James's characters and situations are repetitive and cumulative. Coy isolates two character types–victim and executioner–and four situations: the international theme, the child in an adult world, the artist in an unsympathetic society, and the normal

person in a supernatural world. James's only development can be found in his "'indepth' penetration" of character and situation.

39   CROWLEY, JOHN W. "The Wiles of a 'Witless' Woman: Tina in *The Aspern Papers*." *ESQ* 22, no. 3 (old series no. 84):159-68.
     Argues that Miss Tina is not simple or innocent; rather she is clever, manipulative, and desperate to escape from Julianna's control. The narrator's rejection of her at the end is "poetic justice."

40   CURRY, STEVEN SCOTT. "The Literature of Loss: A Study of Nineteenth-Century English and American Fiction." Ph.D. dissertation, University of California, Davis, 190 pp.
     Examines the experience of loss, focusing on three themes: the qualitative experience of space, the plight of the orphan, and the conflict between the letter and the spirit. Chapter 5 is devoted to James's *The Portrait of a Lady*, which incorporates the three themes and brings the existential crisis of loss to the threshold of the twentieth century.
     See *Dissertation Abstracts International* 37, no. 3 (1976):1529A-1530A.

41   DAVIDSON, CATHY N. "'Circumsexualocution' in Henry James's *Daisy Miller*." *Arizona Quarterly* 32, no. 4 (Winter):353-66.
     Examines the conversations in the tale, underlining the sexual innuendoes they contain. Sex is basic to the tale, but all the characters talk around it, using puns and allusions instead of speaking about it regularly and reducing life's complexities to obsessions and monomanias.

42   DAVIS, SARA deSAUSSURE. "Two Portraits of a Lady: Henry James and T.S. Eliot." *Arizona Quarterly* 32, no. 4 (Winter):367-80.
     Argues that Eliot's "Portrait of a Lady" draws on James's novel for technique and situation but transforms James's material with an ironic reversal. Isabel's plight brings her to self-awareness while Eliot's young man cuts himself off from such awareness.

1976

*43 DELBAERE, JEANNE. "Early Seeds in Jamesian Soil: From *La Vénus d'Ille* to *The Golden Bowl*." *Revue des Langues Vivantes* (Bicentennial Issue):65-79.
    Source: *American Literature* 48, no. 4 (January 1977):621.

44 DENNIS, RODNEY G. Introduction to *The American: The Version of 1877 Revised in Autograph and Typescript for the New York Edition*. Ilkley, Yorkshire: Scholar Press, pp. iii-iv.
    Details the publication and revision history of *The American* and the Houghton Library's acquisition of the autograph manuscript. The manuscript "constitutes the clearest possible record of the ripening of Henry James's artistry."

45 DE ROSE, PETER L. "The Experience of Perception: A Reading of *The Ambassadors*." *Publications of the Arkansas Philological Association* 2, no. 3:1-8.
    Shows that Strether exemplifies James's belief in the primacy of perception as a means of experience. Through the act of seeing, Strether achieves "a profounder intellectual perception and judgment" and is able to cast off preconceived categories. He becomes one of James's artists who experiences life through the imagination.

46 DIEHL, JOANNE FEIT. "'One Life Within Us and Abroad': The Subverted Realist in *The Sacred Fount*." *Journal of Narrative Technique* 6, no. 2 (Spring):92-100.
    Argues that the problem of knowledge comprises both the novel's subject and form in that the reader must reconcile three narrative voices to determine reality. There is no verifiable truth; the novel can only dramatize but not resolve ambiguity.

47 DOLAN, PAUL J. "James: The Aesthetics of Politics." In *Of War and War's Alarms: Fiction and Politics in the Modern World*. New York: Free Press, pp. 70-95.
    Calls *The Princess Casamassima* a "remarkable group portrait of consciousness in and around a political movement." The novel is concerned with the value of aesthetic experience in the social, moral, and political order. Hyacinth must ultimately define his own values and sense of identity; tragically, however, he is torn by his "divided heritage of fine consciousness and limited prospect."

48 DONOGHUE, DENIS. "The American Style of Failure." In *The Sovereign Ghost: Studies in Imagination*. Berkeley: University of California Press, pp. 103-27.

Compares James, Henry Adams, and Allen Tate in their response to the "conditions of failure": the privations and humiliations of life. Tate's is "curial," Adams's "ironic," and James's is "hyperbolic" in that his imagination delights in making the most out of a bleak situation.

Reprinted 1978.31.

49 DOOLING, JOHN JOSEPH. "The Late Victorian Novel of Culture: Walter Pater, Henry James, E.M. Forster." Ph.D. dissertation, University of Pennsylvania, 307 pp.

Argues that the fiction of these writers reflects the ongoing "culture debate" of the early–and mid-Victorian period and that within this debate Pater occupies a central position. The second section of the dissertation focuses on James's reaction to Pater and his own contribution to the debate in *Roderick Hudson, The Portrait of a Lady, The Princess Casamassima, The Ambassadors*, and *The Wings of the Dove*.

See *Dissertation Abstracts International* 37, no. 11 (1977):7140A-7141A.

50 DUHLING, SALLIE RUTH. "Woman in the Tales of Henry James: A Study of His Changing Attitudes toward Europe and America." Ph.D. dissertation, University of Georgia, 159 pp.

Links the change in James's portrayal of American and European women in the tales to his changing attitudes toward American and European culture. Duhling attributes the changes, which include the devaluation of innocence, to James's realization of the importance of manners as "a dictator of action and molder of character."

See *Dissertation Abstracts International* 37, no. 8 (1977):5120A-5121A.

51 DUMITRIU, DANA. *"Ambasadorii" sau despre realismul psihologic* [*The Ambassadors* or on psychological realism]. Bucharest: Cartea Romaneasca, 272 pp.

In Romanian.

1976

52 EAKIN, PAUL JOHN. "Henry James and the New England Con-
    sciousness: *Roderick Hudson, The Europeans, Hawthorne*." In *The
    New England Girl: Cultural Ideals in Hawthorne, Stowe, Howells, and
    James*. Athens: University of Georgia Press, pp. 131-67, 239-41.
        Examines Hawthorne's influence on James's analysis of the
    New England consciousness with its Puritan heritage and his portrayal
    of the American girl. In *Roderick Hudson* James experimented with
    Hawthorne's use of paired heroines: one redemptive; the other
    destructive. In *The Europeans* James broke from Hawthorne with
    Gertrude Wentworth, who combines the "moral seriousness" of the fair
    heroine with the "vitality" of the dark. In *Hawthorne* James creates a
    portrait of the artist who is shaped by New England, focusing on
    Hawthorne's puritan roots and his connection to transcendentalism.

53 ____. "Introduction: History and the Heroines of Fiction." In *The
    New England Girl: Cultural Ideals in Hawthorne, Stowe, Howells, and
    James*. Athens: University of Georgia Press, pp. 3-24.
        Argues that the heroines of Hawthorne, Stowe, Howells, and
    James reflect woman's function as a symbol of cultural ideals in
    nineteenth-century America; in particular, these writers dramatize
    "the essential history of the New England mind" in that century. James's
    linking the American girl with the international theme results in an
    extended metaphor for the "fable of the expatriate American artist."
    Eakin discusses "An International Episode" and "Daisy Miller" as exam-
    ples of James's early treatment of the American girl, focusing on traits
    fully developed in Isabel Archer.

54 ____. "Margaret Fuller, Hawthorne, James, and Sexual Politics."
    South Atlantic Quarterly 75, no. 3 (Summer):323-38.
        Examines Fuller's life, *The Blithedale Romance*, and *The
    Bostonians* as ways to understand the feminist movement and the
    psychology of an individual committed to a cause; traces the influence
    of Fuller on James's creation of Olive Chancellor and Verena Tarrant.

55 ____. "New England in Extremis: *The Bostonians*." In *The New
    England Girl: Cultural Ideals in Hawthorne, Stowe, Howells, and
    James*. Athens: University of Georgia Press, pp. 195-217, 243-45.
        Argues that this novel examines the legacy of transcendentalist
    ideals in contemporary life and issues; that legacy, which includes the
    "romantic cult of friendship," is shown to be in a "final, decadent phase."

The novel also depicts the redemptive power of courtship-as developed by Hawthorne, Stowe, and Howells-as an "empty charade."

56 ____. "The Tragedy of Self-Culture: *The Portrait of a Lady*." In *The New England Girl: Cultural Ideals in Hawthorne, Stowe, Howells, and James*. Athens: University of Georgia Press, pp. 168-94, 241-43.

Details the many ways in which Isabel's character incorporates the ideas and ideals of the transcendentalists. This novel is a critique of that movement, for Isabel's downfall is a result of her self-reliance and inward focus. Isabel, with her "creed of Emersonian individualism," discovers herself to be in "a Hawthornian world of shadows."

57 EDEL, LEON. "The American Artist and His 'Complex Fate.'" In *American Studies Down Under: Pacific Circle 4*. Edited by Norman Harper and Elaine Barry. Victoria, Australia: Australian & New Zealand American Studies Association, pp. 188-203.

Chronicles James's "complex fate" as an expatriate artist. James's vision was always focused on America, even though expatriation was necessary for his survival as an artist. His life and career embodies not only the tension between America and Europe, but also that between the new and the old. *The American Scene* records James's bewilderment at the new America where he found heterogeneity and chaos instead of "organic and health-infusing growth."

58 ____. "Commentary." *Nineteenth-Century Fiction* 31, no. 2 (September):248-51.

Responds to Lohmann's and Arms's criticisms of *Henry James Letters I* (see 1976.124). Edel admits to the justice of some of their points, although he feels the number of errors have been exaggerated. He also questions their motives in publishing "a matter settled months ago" in private correspondence.

59 ____. "Henry James in the Abbey." *Times Literary Supplement* (London), no. 3875 (19 June):741.

Describes James as "a particular symbol of history as well as letters" and "an English hero of whom England shall be proud." This address was given by Edel at the unveiling of the stone commemorating James in Westminster Abbey.

1976

Reprinted 1976.60 and 1979.37.

*60   ____. *Henry James in Westminster Abbey: The Address by Leon Edel*. Honolulu: Petronium Press.
    Source: Cadbury, Laskowski, and Tintner, 1982.24, p. 196.
    Reprint of 1976.59 and 1979.37.

61   ELION, SALLY LLOYD. "The Anguish of Exasperated Taste': Problems of Jamesian Refinement." Ph.D. dissertation, Tufts University, 222 pp.
    Examines the ways in which Jamesian refinement affects character portrayal, audience, execution, narrative technique, and style, focusing on "The Turn of the Screw," *The Awkward Age, In the Cage, The Sacred Fount*, and "The Velvet Glove." Elion argues that "James' exaggerated fear of vulgarity complicated his writing of fiction, and sometimes undermined the realism he so arduously cultivated."
    See *Dissertation Abstracts International* 37, no. 6 (1976):3622A-3623A.

62   FINN, HELENA KANE. "Design of Despair: The Tragic Heroine and the Imagery of Artifice in the Novels by Hawthorne, James, and Wharton." Ph.D. dissertation, St. John's University, 258 pp.
    Argues that in the novels of these authors the failure of their heroines to challenge social constraints is reflected in a change of imagery. Finn sees a pattern moving from the natural through the artificial to the stylized.
    See *Dissertation Abstracts International* 37, no. 9 (1977):5827A.

63   FITZPATRICK, VINCENT. "The Elusive Butterfly's Angry Pursuer: The Jamesian Style, Mencken, and Clear Writing." *Menckeniana* 59 (Fall):13-17.
    Details Mencken's derision of James's style. Mencken's criticism of James reflects his own insistence on clarity in prose.

64   FOGEL, DANIEL MARK. "Extremes and Moderations: The Dialectic of Consciousness in the Later Novels of Henry James." Ph.D. dissertation, Cornell University, 217 pp.

Traces the polarities in *The Portrait of a Lady, The Wings of the Dove, The Awkward Age, The Ambassadors*, and *The Golden Bowl*. Polarity occurs on several levels in these texts: in the Romantic quest for experience and in the stylistic, dramatic, and thematic structures.
        See *Dissertation Abstracts International* 38, no. 10 (1978):6131A-6132A.

65   FOWLER, VIRGINIA CAROL. "The Renunciatory Heroine in Henry James." Ph.D. dissertation, University of Pittsburgh, 181 pp.
        Examines the biographical sources for the renunciatory heroine and traces her evolution in *The American*, "Madame de Mauves," *The Portrait of a Lady, The Wings of the Dove*, and *The Golden Bowl*. These novels suggest that James saw renunciation as a meaningless response to experience and ultimately as a destructive act.
        See *Dissertation Abstracts International* 37, no. 5 (1976):2870A.

66   FRANKLIN, ROSEMARY F. "Military Metaphors and the Organic Structure of Henry James's 'The Aspern Papers.'" *Arizona Quarterly* 32, no. 4 (Winter):327-40.
        Traces the military metaphors that complement the confrontation forming the tale's dramatic structure. Franklin also notes that the tale is closely modeled on the classical dramatic unities; although the tale has the structure of tragedy, it also includes comic elements.

67   FRYER, JUDITH. "The American Princess." In *The Faces of Eve: Women in the Nineteenth Century American Novel*. Oxford: Oxford University Press, pp. 85-142, 266-70.
        Examines James's portrayal of the America princess, who "possesses a unique combination of innocence *and* self-reliance," focusing on Daisy, Isabel, Milly, and Maggie. Fryer discusses these heroines as contrasts to Hawthorne's "pale maiden," embodied in Hilda. Daisy and Milly are close to the "Hawthorne formula" of doomed maidens, while Isabel, James's "most fully developed American Princess," learns through experience a new consciousness and thus becomes open to change. Maggie is the only Princess who can live "happily ever after" but only after she learns to accept the existence of evil.

1976

68 ____. "The Great Mother." In *The Faces of Eve: Women in the Nineteenth-Century American Novel*. Oxford: Oxford University Press, pp. 143-202, 270-72.

Sees Olive Chancellor as exemplifying James's depiction of the controlling, manipulative, possessive mother figure. Fryer distinguishes three types of mothers in James's fiction: the "mother-surrogates" who are similar to Olive and include the Governess, Mrs. Grosse, Mrs. Bread, and Mrs. Wix; the "neglecters" who abdicate their maternal role – Mrs. Moreen, Mrs. Farange, and Mrs. Touchett; and the "real witch-bitches" – Rose Armiger, Madame de Bellegarde, and Madame Merle – who are deliberately destructive.

69 ____. "The New Woman: The Unnatural Lady Reformers of Boston." In *The Faces of Eve: Women in the Nineteenth-Century American Novel*. Oxford: Oxford University Press, pp. 219-33, 273-75.

Examines James's depiction of "new women" in *The Bostonians* – Olive Chancellor, Miss Birdseye, Mrs. Farrinder, and Dr. Prance – arguing that James was unable to see these women as normal. The threat these women pose to James is most apparent in Olive Chancellor, who is portrayed as humorless, impatient, and sexually perverted. The other women are merely sketched, but James also does not take them seriously.

70 FUSSELL, MARY BURTON. "Last Testaments: Writers in Extremis." Ph.D. dissertation, University of California, San Diego.

Sees Melville's *Billy Budd*, James's *The Sense of the Past*, and Fitzgerald's *Tender is the Night* as artistic credos and life summations – all of which are beset by textual problems. Fussell approaches each novel through intuition and detective work in order to arrive at an interpretation, albeit inconclusive.

See *Dissertation Abstracts International* 37, no. 9 (1977):5814A-5815A.

71 GALE, ROBERT L. "An Unpublished Letter from Henry James to F. Marion Crawford." *Revue des Langues Vivantes* (Brussels) 42, No. 2:179-82.

Reprints James's October 28, 1892 letter to Crawford; while the letter is overtly friendly, Gale suggests it may be James's criticism of Crawford.

72 GALLOWAY, DAVID. "Henry James: *Daisy Miller* and the
    International Novel." *Dutch Quarterly Review of Anglo-American
    Letters* 6:304-17.
        Argues that James's treatment of the international theme
    opened English fiction to "the wide range of aesthetic and psychological
    considerations" and was a major contribution to the search for
    American identity.

73 GARGANO, JAMES W. "James's Stories in 'The Story In It.'"
    NMAL: Notes on Modern American Literature 1:Item 2.
        Shows that this tale is a complex examination of the connection
    between life and art.

74 ____. "*Washington Square*: A Study in the Growth of an Inner Self."
    Studies in Short Fiction 13, no. 3 (Summer):355-62.
        Calls Catherine an "early portrait" of the Jamesian protagonist
    who discovers a transforming sense of self; though she lacks the
    psychological depth of James's later protagonists, Gargano suggests
    that her misplaced love may distract the reader from her growth in self-
    knowledge, and details the development of her imagination.
        Reprinted 1987.43.

75 GEARY, EDWARD A. "Morality and Fiction: The Example of
    Henry James." In *"The Need beyond Reason" and Other Essays:
    College of Humanities Centennial Lectures 1975-76.* Edited by Bruce
    B. Clark. Provo: Brigham Young University Press, pp. 105-15.
        Discusses James's moral vision in which art itself becomes a
    moral activity and not simply an instrument of morality. In addition,
    Geary surveys James's fictions – the majority of which pivot on moral
    choice – and categorizes characters in terms of these choices.

76 GERVAIS, DAVID. "James's Reading of *Madame Bovary*." *Cam-
    bridge Quarterly* 7, no. 1:1-26.
        Details James's "creative misreading" of Flaubert's novel and
    suggests it is a result of James's ambivalence toward Flaubert's ideas
    and methods.
        Reprinted in 1978.42.

1976

77   GETZ, THOMAS THEODORE. "Henry James: The Novel as an Act of Self-Consciousness and Conscience." Ph.D. dissertation, University of Iowa, 206 pp.
      Sees James's novels as "integrated *acts* of shaping feeling into an objectified world of character, action, setting, language." Getz judges a selection of James's novels – *The Portrait of a Lady, What Maisie Knew, The Sacred Fount,* and *The Golden Bowl* – by the degree to which James does or does not express his own conscience.
      See *Dissertation Abstracts International* 37, no. 5 (1976):2870A-2871A.

*78   GIBSON, MARY VIRGINIA. "Event and Consciousness in Certain Novels of Henry James and Virginia Woolf." Ph.D. dissertation, University of Chicago.
      Source: Budd, 1983.32, p. 16, item 68.

79   GILL, RICHARD. "Letter from L.P. Hartley." *Journal of Modern Literature* 5, no. 3 (September):529-31.
      Suggests that Hartley, a British novelist "schooled himself in James's symbolism and style" and reprints a letter received from Hartley about James's depiction of English country houses in his fiction.

80   GOETZ, WILLIAM ROBERTSON. "The Apology for Narrative in Balzac, Henry James, and Proust." Ph.D. dissertation, Yale University, 277 pp.
      Examines the various ways these three novelists vindicate their narratives although, in so doing, they reduce the narrative to "some alien mode." In James's case, Goetz traces this conflict in the New York Edition prefaces, which in attempting to account for the narratives become narratives in their own right. Goetz finds "a tension between the text's theoretical claims and its rhetorical procedure" – a tension also apparent in "The Figure in the Carpet."
      See *Dissertation Abstracts International* 37, no. 11 (1977):7119A-7120A.

81   GRELLA, GEORGE. "The Wings of the Falcon and the Maltese Dove." In *A Question of Quality: Popularity and Value in Modern*

Creative Writing. Edited by Louis Filler. Bowling Green, Ohio: Bowling Green University Press, pp. 108-14.

Parallels James's *The Wings of the Dove* and Dashiell Hammet's *The Maltese Falcon*, finding similarities in theme, subject, and technique.

82   GUTWINSKI, WALDEMAR. "Cohesion in James." In *Cohesion in Literary Texts: A Study of Some Grammatical and Lexical Features of English Discourse.* Janua Linguarum: Series minor no. 204. The Hague: Mouton, pp. 83-126.

Applies Halliday's concept of cohesion–the relatedness of clauses and sentences, frequently signaled by anaphora, subordination, and coordination–to the fourth paragraph of chapter 42 of *The Portrait of a Lady.* Analysis shows that James relies primarily on grammatical cohesion and only minimally on lexical cohesion. Anaphora constitute the largest percentage of grammatical items. Gutwinski also examines the cohesion between sentences in the paragraph, noting connections between adjacent sentences and sentences separated from each other. The pattern of cohesive relations in this paragraph is intricate and occurs at various linguistic levels.

83   HABEGGER, ALFRED. "The Autistic Tyrant: Howells' Self-Sacrificial Woman and Jamesian Renunciation." *Novel* 10, no. 1 (Fall):27-39.

Argues that Howells sees marriage as the answer to egotism and autistic withdrawal. His depiction of the self-sacrificing woman as a tyrant comes closer to the truth about the character of such a woman than does James.

84   _____. Introduction to *The Bostonians.* Indianapolis: Bobbs-Merrill Co., pp. ix-xxxv.

Sketches the biographical, cultural, social, and historical background of the novel; describes the three main characters; and briefly discusses the novel's narrative technique. Habegger notes that in this novel James deals with public and social realities and, because of his place on the sidelines of American life, he was uniquely capable of seeing these realities. This edition also contains James's letters commenting on the novel, as well as an annotated bibliography of criticism of the novel.

1976

85　HADDICK, VERN. "Colors in the Carpet." *Gay Literature* 5:19-21.
　　Reviews evidence from James's life and writings that indicate "a gay life experience" and suggests that later in life James came to accept his gay impulses.

86　HALL, RICHARD. "Henry James and the Incest Taboo." *The Advocate*, no. 276 (20 September):49-53.
　　Argues that James "maintained a difficult, emotional and probably incestuous relationship with his brother William," and that this explains James's sexual inactivity. Hall's thesis was later corroborated by Edel, and this article contains "verbatim highlights" from Hall's conversation with Edel. Hall focuses on Edel's failure to be explicit about James's sexuality in his five-volume biography as well as his own personal biases.

87　HALL, SALLIE J. "Henry James and the Bluestockings: Satire and Morality in *The Bostonians*." In *Aeolian Harps: Essays in Literature in Honor of Maurice Browning Cramer*. Edited by Donna G. Fricke and Douglas C. Fricke. Bowling Green, Ohio: Bowling Green University Press, pp. 207-25.
　　Argues that this novel does not prove that James advocates one gender's ascendancy over the other; rather it shows his conviction that both men and women are human beings who are to be treated as ends, not means.

88　HALL, WILLIAM F. "The Meaning of *The Sacred Fount*: 'Its Own Little Law of Composition.'" *Modern Language Quarterly* 37, no. 2 (June):168-78.
　　Focuses on the image of the fount and the painting of *The Man with the Mask* and sees the novel as a comic parable about art as a "human construct," which cannot begin to compare with the "inexhaustible permutations of experience."

*89　HANSON, KATHRYN SCHEFTER. "A Comparative Study of Matthew Arnold and Henry James." Ph.D. dissertation, University of Chicago.
　　Source: Budd, 1983.32, p. 19, item 84.

1976

90 HARDIN, JAMES BUDD. "Henry James and Idealistic Self-Interest." Ph.D. dissertation, Syracuse University, 220 pp.

Examines James's treatment of "major ideas"–beauty, principle, renunciation, dissimulation, love, fate, vision, and self-interest–in the tales written throughout his career. In the majority of tales, the protagonist must reconcile an appetite for life with the need to live according to principle. Fidelity to principle is shown to be consistent with self-interest and the welfare of society.

See *Dissertation Abstracts International* 37, no. 11, (1977):7129A.

91 HELLER, ARNO. "Experiments with the Novel of Maturation: Henry James and Stephen Crane." *Innsbrucker Beiträge zur Kulturwissenschaft*. Sonderheft Bd. 38, AMOE:5-32.

Demonstrates that both authors experimented with the *Bildungsroman*, using contemporary psychological theories and impressionism. *What Maisie Knew* and *The Awkward Age*, with the focus on the consciousness and the dramatic method, respectively, expand the scope of the traditional British novel of maturation while *The Red Badge of Courage*, with its episodic structure, is more closely connected to the American tradition. In both subject and technique, these novels are transitional, preparing the way for the innovative novels of Joyce and Woolf.

92 HOCHMAN, BARUCH. "The Jamesian Situation: World as Spectacle." *University of Denver Quarterly* 11, no. 1 (Spring):48-66.

Discusses James's novels in terms of the essential "Jamesian situation": the struggle for identity in circumstances inimical to the individual. This situation takes the pattern of victim vs. victimizer or child vs. adult, the latter pattern prevalent in James's later work; the international theme is one manifestation of these patterns. Hochman concludes by noting that James's limitation is his treatment of the world as spectacle, which prevents him from mining passional and moral depths.

Revised 1983.92.

93 HOLLY, CAROL THAYER. "Portraits of the Self in Henry James's *Autobiography* and Vladimir Nabokov's *Speak, Memory*." Ph.D. dissertation, Brown University, 288 pp.

1976

Examines James's and Nabokov's understanding of the self and its relation to the past, as well as their views on recreating the past through writing, by a close analysis of their autobiographies.

See *Dissertation Abstracts International* 38, no. 1 (1977):262A-263A.

94   HUBERT, THOMAS. "*The Princess Casamassima*: Ideas against Persons." *Arizona Quarterly* 32, no. 4 (Winter):341-52.

Proposes that the conflict between allegiance to ideology and devotion to persons is central to the novel. James affirms that personal relationships are more valuable than ideology and that such relationships give value to shared beliefs and ideals.

95   HUNKING, ELIZABETH MORSE WALSH, comp. *The Picturesque English of Henry James: A Collection of Quotations*. Philadelphia: Dorrance & Co., 74 pp.

Brief excerpts from James's fiction, nonfiction, and letters.

96   HUNTING, CONSTANCE. "The Identify of Miss Tina in *The Aspern Papers*." *Studies in the Humanities* 5, no. 2:28-31.

Suggests that Miss Tina is the illegitimate daughter of Jeffrey Aspern and Juliana Bordereau's younger sister.

97   INGLIS, TONY. "Reading Late James." In *The Modern English Novel: The Reader, the Writer, and the Work*. Edited by Gabriel Josipovici. New York: Barnes & Novel, pp. 77-94.

Argues that James's late style reflects his recognition of the instability of categories and identities, and of the continual quest for "being and meaning."

98   JACOBSON, JUDITH IRVIN. "The Nature and Placement of Metaphorical Language in Henry James's *The Wings of the Dove*." Ph.D. dissertation, University of Florida, 405 pp.

Examines metaphors in chapters 1, 15, 30, and 38 to "determine the grammatical nature, context, distribution, and function" of the figurative language. Jacobson's analysis shows that James's metaphors often rely on very ordinary language, thus balancing abstract diction and complex sentence structure.

1976

See *Dissertation Abstracts International* 37, no. 10 (1977):6486A.

99 JACOBSON, MARCIA. "Popular Fiction and Henry James's Unpopular *Bostonians*." *Modern Philology* 73, no. 3 (February):264-75.
Examines the ways in which James turned to popular fiction to express unpopular ideas, looking in particular at the "new woman" novel, the lady doctor novel, and the Civil War romance.
Reprinted 1983.101.

100 JAMES, HENRY. "New York: A Spring Impression." *North American Review* 261, no. 2 (Summer):54-8.
Reprints James's sketch that appeared in *The North American Review* in December, 1905.

101 JOHANNSEN, ROBERT RAY. "Romantic Imagery and Realistic Implications in Henry James's Early Novels." Ph.D. dissertation, Arizona State University, 218 pp.
Argues that in James's early novels – *Watch and Ward, Roderick Hudson, The American, The Europeans, Confidence*, and *Washington Square* – imagery and figurative language tend toward the romantic even though the effect is realistic.
See *Dissertation Abstracts International* 37, no. 2 (1976):968A-969A.

102 KADIR, DJELAL. "Another Sense of the Past: Henry James' *The Aspern Papers* and Carlos Fuentes' *Aura*." *Revue de Littérature Comparée* 50, no. 4 (October-December):448-54.
Suggests that, while both writers see the past as immutable and indestructible, there is a fundamental difference between the two. James views the past as "final and irredeemable"; Fuentes' view is cyclical.

103 KASTON, CARREN OSNA. "Fictions of Life in the Novels of Henry James." Ph.D. dissertation, Rutgers University, 350 pp.
Argues that James's renunciatory protagonists – Isabel Archer, Fleda Vetch, Lambert Strether – are "figures of consciousness" who permit others to design their lives and who remain trapped within the

house of fiction. Only Maisie Farange and Maggie Verver are able to escape the "melodrama of manipulation" to create their own lives; ultimately, Maggie uses her own artistry to impose a design on the other characters.

See *Dissertation Abstracts International* 37, no. 6 (1976):3625A.

104 _____. "Houses of Fiction in *What Maisie Knew*." *Criticism* 18, no. 1 (Winter):27-42.

Argues that Maisie grows out of her parents' houses and James's house of fiction and creates her own house of experience. The novel shows that James connected the act of authorship with the process of maturation.

Reprinted 1984.110.

105 KAUL, R.K. "The Jamesian Hero." *Indian Journal of American Studies* 6, nos. 1-2:65-71.

Sketches the Jamesian hero, drawing upon *Roderick Hudson* and the *Autobiography*. This figure is a man of imagination who has a "quick appreciation of beauty."

106 KELLUM, SHARON SMART. "The Art of Self-Incrimination: Studies in Unreliable Narration." Ph.D. dissertation, University of California, Berkeley, 322 pp.

Examines the ways in which an unreliable narrator, who is also a participant, functions in the narrative, focusing on how the narrative enables the reader to judge the narrator. The study begins with James's unreliable narrators in "A Light Man," "The Liar," "The Aspern Papers," "The Patagonia," "The Figure in the Carpet," and *The Sacred Fount*; it also includes analyses of other authors, which demonstrate the range of possibilities with this technique.

See *Dissertation Abstracts International* 38, no. 2 (1977):775A-776A.

107 KHAN, SALAMATULLAH. "The Jamesian View of the American in Europe." In *Studies in American Literature: Essays in Honour of William Mulder*. Edited by Jagdish Chander and Narindar S. Pradhan. Delhi: Oxford University Press, pp. 110-18.

Sees the international theme as a contrast in moral perspectives and in different levels of consciousness. James paid tribute to his countrymen by depicting them placing the moral order above their own needs and desires.

108 KNIGHTS, LIONEL CHARLES. "Henry James and Human Liberty." In *Explorations 3*. Pittsburgh: University of Pittsburgh Press, pp. 24-37.
    Reprint of 1975.73.

109 KONDO, KEIKO. "A Comparative Study of Eliot's Early Poems and James's Work." *Sophia English Studies* 1:53-70.
    Traces the influence of James on Eliot's early work, noting many similarities in each writer's theory of art, impressionism, and use of symbolism. Eliot's later poems, in which he is concerned with the religious and supernatural, depart from James's focus on human society.

110 KRAWITZ, HENRY. "Writers on Painting: A Study of the Theory and Criticism of the Visual Arts in Zola, Wilde, James and Proust and Its Relevance to Their Fiction." Ph.D. dissertation, City University of New York, 655 pp.
    Argues that the art criticism of these writers was most perceptive when it abandoned technical jargon for an intuitive, poetic, psychological, or interdisciplinary approach, and that such *attitudes* are most significant in relating novelists' art criticism to their fiction. James's works discussed here are *The Sacred Fount* and *The Wings of the Dove*.
    See *Dissertation Abstracts International* 37, no. 3 (1976):1531A-1532A.

111 KRIER, WILLIAM J. "The 'Latent Extravagance' of *The Portrait of a Lady*." *Mosaic* 9, no. 3 (Spring):57-65.
    Focuses on Isabel's decision to return to Osmond and why James concludes the novel at this point. Isabel's growth in consciousness ultimately enables her to become the author of her own story; the novel's ambiguous ending is James's recognition of Isabel's emancipation.

1976

112   KRUPNICK, MARK L. "'The Beast in the Jungle' and the Dilemma of Narcissus." *Southern Review* (University of Adelaide) 9, no. 2:113-20.
        Sees masochism permeating the tale's content. James's depiction of masochistic love gives a clue to his art in his "insistence on form and pattern."

113   ____. "*The Golden Bowl*: Henry James's Novel about Nothing." *English Studies* 57, no. 6 (December):533-40.
        Argues that the theme of the novel is the imagination and that James's "towering subjectivity" displaces "the ordinary forms of human relatedness."

114   ____. "Playing with the Silence: Henry James's Poetic of Loss." *Forum* 13, no. 3 (Winter):37-42.
        Argues that James's narrative technique is based on "a loss of the actual and the instinctual" and uses "The Altar of the Dead" as an illustration. The tale questions the value of art as restitution for earthly loss.

115   KUDO, YOSHIMI. "Mizu no Image wo Megutte: *Mill on the Floss* to *The Ambassadors* [The image of water: *The Mill on the Floss* and *The Ambassadors*]. *Eigo Seinen* (Tokyo) 121:439-42.
        In Japanese.
        Demonstrates that the images of water in Eliot's novel are realistic and give coherence to the story; the water images in James's novel are metaphysical and symbolic but become realistic when Strehter discovers Madame de Vionnet with Chad in a boat on the river. The different treatments and uses of the images in each novel suggest artistic differences between the two authors.

116   KUMMINGS, DONALD D. "The Issue of Morality in James's *The Golden Bowl*." *Arizona Quarterly* 32, no. 4 (Winter):381-91.
        Demonstrates that Amerigo and Maggie achieve moral awareness through self awareness. The structure of the novel's books parallels the growth in awareness of these two central characters: in book 1, both Maggie and Amerigo "fall from grace"; in book 2, these characters achieve awareness.

117   LEDGER, MARSHALL. "Ring around *A Christmas Garland.*" In
       *Aeolian Harps: Essays in Literature in Honor of Maurice Browning
       Cramer.* Edited by Donna G. Fricke and Douglas C. Fricke. Bowling
       Green, Ohio: Bowling Green University Press, pp. 227-46.
              Examines "The Mote in the Middle Distance," a parody of
       James, in which Beerbohm demonstrates the depth of his
       understanding of James. The parody succeeds because it is well
       organized and unified and because it is "Beerbohm's own story of his
       relation to James."

118   LEEMING, GLENDA. *Who's Who in Henry James.* New York:
       Taplinger, vii, 120 pp.
              Lists the characters in James's novels and tales and includes a
       brief character sketch of each.

119   LEITCH, THOMAS MICHAEL. "The James Tradition: An Investi-
       gation in Literary History." Ph.D. dissertation, Yale University, 410
       pp.
              Argues that James's indirect strategies of presentation, which
       James connected to his moral vision, became valued for their own sake
       in the work of Conrad, Faulkner, and Joyce. This in turn has resulted in
       "problematical criticism" in which "the critic displaces the author as the
       maker of meaning."
              See *Dissertation Abstracts International* 37, no. 7 (1977):4369A-
       4370A.

120   LEVERENZ, DAVID. "Reflections on Two Henries: James and
       Kissinger." *Soundings* 59, no. 4 (Winter):374-95.
              Finds similarities between Kissinger and James in their
       concern with the "subtleties of international conflict" and a vision of
       world based on a war between good and evil. James's belief in the
       receptive but essentially passive consciousness, however, is a major
       difference from Kissinger's desire for power and manipulation.

121   LEWIS, WYNDAM. "Henry James." In *Enemy Salvoes: Selected
       Literary Criticism.* Edited by C.J. Fox. New York: Barnes & Noble,
       pp. 88-92.

1976

Suggests that James's focus on abstract values and an internalized vision can be explained by the physical and social barrenness of the American scene.

Reprint in part of *Men Without Art* (1934).

122 L'HEUREUX, MAURICE JEAN. "Crosscurrents: Romanticism and Existentialism." Ph.D. dissertation, Saint Louis University, 181 pp.

Demonstrates that both movements are related in revolting against the aesthetic and philosophical formulations of classicism. Similarities are apparent in comparing literature from both movements. Chapter 3 focuses on Hawthorne's "Ethan Brand," James's "The Beast in the Jungle," and Mann's *Doctor Faustus*, in which the protagonists "place their individual drives on a higher plane than the laws of man and God."

See *Dissertation Abstracts International* 37, no. 12 (1977):7743A-7744A.

123 LIBERMAN, TERRI RAE. "The Open Ending in the Later Novels of Henry James." Ph.D. dissertation, Case Western Reserve University, 170 pp.

Examines James's use of the open ending in *The Portrait of a Lady, The Ambassadors, The Wings of the Dove*, and *The Golden Bowl*, finding a tension between "formal resolution" and "thematic irresolution." The world reflected in the open ending is an ambiguous one, and rather than confront it, the protagonist rejects it by choosing renunciation or withdrawal.

See *Dissertation Abstracts International* 37, no. 7 (1977):4370A-4371A.

124 LOHMANN, CHRISTOPH K., and ARMS, GEORGE. "Commentary." *Nineteenth-Century Fiction* 31, no. 2 (September):244-47.

Notes that there are more errors in *Henry James Letters I* than noted by Gale (see 1975.41) and parallels numerous examples from the holograph with Edel's version. The second volume of *Letters* is equally flawed. See Edel's reply, 1976.58.

125 LONG, ROBERT EMMET. "Henry James's Apprenticeship: The Hawthorne Aspect." *American Literature* 48, no. 2 (May):194-216.
   Traces Hawthorne's influence on James's early tales, 1865-1875. James "referred" to Hawthorne in creating character and situation and used Hawthorne to understand the American psyche.
   Reprinted 1979.87.

126 ____. "James's *Roderick Hudson*: The End of the Apprenticeship: Hawthorne and Turgenev." *American Literature* 48, no. 3 (November):312-26.
   Demonstrates that James turned to *The Marble Faun* for his novel's subject and theme but moved from Hawthorne's romantic conception of fiction to the cosmopolitan novel of manners influenced by Turgenev. From Hawthorne James learns how to develop character with "rich suggestiveness"; from Turgenev, James learns a dramatic narrative method.
   Reprinted 1979.87.

127 ____. "Transformations: *The Blithedale Romance* to Howells and James." *American Literature* 47, no. 4 (January):552-71.
   Sees both *The Undiscovered Country* and *The Bostonians* as descendants of Hawthorne's novel and as transitions from the romance to the novel of manners. James deliberately distances himself from Hawthorne's conviction of human isolation by depicting characters who value perception.
   Reprinted 1979.87.

128 LYNA, FRANCISZEK. "The Letters of William James to Wincenty Lutoslawski." *Yale University Library Gazette* 51, no. 1 (July):28-40.
   Mentions William's comment to Lutoslawski on Henry's early fiction. According to William, the early novels are better than his later ones, "'in which he has developed a curious mannerism.'"

129 MACK, STANLEY THOMAS. "Portraits and Portraitists in Hawthorne and James." Ph.D. dissertation, Lehigh University, 134 pp.
   Analyzes Hawthorne's and James's depiction of the artist and their use of the portrait. While both acknowledge that the artist's vision brings power, Hawthorne sees art as corrupting; James sees it as

1976

blessing. Mack finds three distinctive uses of the portrait: as a symbol of the past, as an association, and as a psychic double.

See *Dissertation Abstracts International* 37, no. 11 (1977):7131A-7132A.

130 MACKENZIE, MANFRED. *Communities of Honor and Love in Henry James*. Cambridge: Harvard University Press, vix, 197 pp.

Argues that James's protagonists must overcome their isolation from the strictures of society, physically and psychologically. The protagonist's quest for community is a search for identity, "an ordeal of self-consciousness." The Jamesian hero moves from the "plane of experience" of identity and honor to a higher plane of love, which involves the sacrifice of identity and honor. Mackenzie traces this movement in *The Princess Casamassima, What Maisie Knew*, and *The Golden Bowl*.

Reprinted in part 1985.78; Reprint of *ELH* 39 (March 1972):147-68; *Yale Review* 62 (Spring 1974):347-71; 1975.82.

131 McMURRAY, WILLIAM. "Reality in Henry James's 'The Birthplace.'" *Explicator* 35, no. 1 (Fall):10-11.

Notes that the tale dramatizes James's conviction that art makes life, because the truth about Shakespeare resides within Gedge.

132 MACNAUGHTON, W.R. "Maisie's Grace under Pressure: Some Thoughts on James and Hemingway." *Modern Fiction Studies* 22, no. 2 (Summer):153-64.

Finds similarities in the worlds of *What Maisie Knew* and *The Sun Also Rises*. Both novels depict a moral wasteland where the characters play war games. Maisie and Jake Barnes discover the transforming power of love, although Maisie is successful in living her values while Jake is not.

133 MACNAUGHTON, W.R., AND MARTIN, W.R.. "'The Beldonald Holbein': Another Jamesian Trap for the Unwary." *English Studies in Canada* 2, no. 3 (Fall):299-305.

Sees the tale as an ironic analysis of the "gloved cruelty" of fashionable London society. The authors cite the ironic treatment of Mrs. Munden and the satire directed at the tale's narrator as evidence.

134 MANTHEY, ETHEL VERN. "The Sentimentally Educated Hero: A Comparison of Some Aspects of the Hero of Gustave Flaubert with Two Leading Characters of Henry James." Ph.D. dissertation, Case Western Reserve University, 291 pp.

Compares Hyacinth Robinson and Lambert Strether to the prototype created by Flaubert in Frédéric Moreau, focusing on the hero's educational process and romantic ideal. Manthey discovers similarities in attitudes toward women, the use of determinism, and the need to retreat into passivity.

See *Dissertation Abstracts International* 37, no. 12 (1977):7736A-7737A.

135 MAYER, CHARLES W. "Henry James's 'Indispensable Centre': The Search for Compositional Unity." *Essays in Literature* 3, no. 1 (Spring):97-104.

Describes James's development of the center of consciousness as a means of unifying subject and form, beginning with the "modulated centers" of the early novels to the breakthrough of the focused centers in *The Spoils of Poynton* and *What Maisie Knew.*

136 MAYNARD, REID N. "Autotelism in Henry James's Aesthetic." *Tennessee Studies in Literature* 21:35-42.

Examines autotelism in James's views of the writer's vision, organicism, the "illusion of life," and the intrinsic beauty of art. Maynard suggests that James is not a realist, mimetic, or photographic because for him a work of art "expresses its own beauty and truth" rather than reflects "postulated external absolutes."

137 MELCHIORI, GIORGIO. "James, Joyce e D'Annunzio." In *D'Annunzio e il simbolismo europeo: Atti del Convegno di studio, Gardone Riviera, 14-15-16 sett. 1973* [D'Annunzio and European symbolism: Proceedings of the Gardone Riviera Study Meeting]. Edited by Emilio Mariano. Il filo di Arianna 1. Milan: Il Saggiatore, pp. 299-311.

In Italian.

138 MICHAELS, WALTER BENN. "Writers Reading: James and Eliot." *Modern Language Notes* 91, no. 5 (October):827-49.

1976

Sees James's revisions and prefaces – especially the preface to *The Golden Bowl* – as James's "re-reading" of his work, which calls into question our notion of literary criticism, since any reader can do what James has done. Michaels focuses on "The Turn of the Screw," drawing an analogy between the situations of the governess and the reader. The second half of the essay is devoted to an analysis of T.S. Eliot's 1929 essay on Dante as a model of reading with political implications. James's and Eliot's readings are diametrically opposed, although both affirm "the separate autonomies of reader and text."

139   MILLER, JAMES E., Jr. "Henry James in Reality." *Critical Inquiry* 2, no. 3 (Spring):585-604.
        Argues that James's realism focuses on the middle ground between the perceiver and the perceived, where the observed is shaped by the consciousness of the observer. Miller examines James's metaphor of the window not only as it suggests the relation between fiction and reality, but as it also suggests the relation between fiction and morality. This metaphor shows that James recognized the variety of artistic vision and that the "moral reference" is embedded in the individual consciousness.

140   MOCHI GIOLI, GIOVANNA. "'The Beast in the Jungle' e l'assenza del referente" ['The Beast in the Jungle' and the absence of the referent]. *Paragone* 314:51-76.
        In Italian.

141   MOGEN, DAVID. "Agonies of Innocence: The Governess and Maggie Verver." *American Literary Realism 1870-1910* 9, no. 3 (Summer):231-42.
        Compares Maggie and the governess in their attempt to be saviors: the governess fails; Maggie succeeds. The governess is unable to cope with the ambiguities of evil and is engulfed by hysteria while Maggie, by virtue of her "superior knowledge and experience," discovers the "regenerative power of love."

142   MONTEIRO, GEORGE. "Henry James and Scott Fitzgerald: A Source." *Notes on Contemporary Literature* 6, no. 2 (March):4-6.

1976

Suggests that "Daisy Miller" influences the episode from *Tender is the Night* in which Richard Diver unexpectedly finds Nicole Warren in Switzerland.

143 MOORE, RAYBURN S. "The Strange Irregular Rhythm of Life: James's Late Tales and Constance Woolson." *South Atlantic Bulletin* 41, no. 4 (November):86-93.

   Argues that "The Beast in the Jungle," "The Jolly Corner," and "The Bench of Desolation" – all exploring the theme of "too late" – are James's response to Constance Fenimore Woolson's death.

144 MOORE, ROSEMARY. "The Fate of Love in the Fiction of Henry James: Variations on a Theme Proceeding from an Analysis of the Short Stories." Ph.D. dissertation, University of Adelaide (Australia).

   Traces the fate of the Jamesian hero doomed to frustrated love, focusing on both psychological and environmental determinants. This study examines the "problematical nature" of the hero's consciousness in relation to women, love, and marriage.

   See *Dissertation Abstracts International* 44, no. 1 (1983):170A.

145 MORALES, PETER. "The Novel as Social Theory: Models, Explanation and Values in Henry James and William Dean Howells." *Clio* 5, no. 3 (Spring):331-44.

   Compares *The Bostonians* and *A Hazard of New Fortunes* as explanations of social change, noting that James's approach is Freudian while Howell's is Marxist.

146 MORI, MIHOKO. "'Meian' to *The Golden Bowl*: Saisetsu" ["Meian" and *The Golden Bowl* reconsidered]. *Eigo Seinen* (Tokyo) 122:74-76.
   In Japanese.

   Contrary to Tanimoto (1975.128), it is worthwhile to compare James's *The Golden Bowl* and Natsume's *Meian*. There are differences and similarities; the significance of each needs to be clarified. See also 1976.182.

147 NANCE, WILLIAM L. "'The Beast in the Jungle': Two Versions of Oedipus." *Studies in Short Fiction* 13, no. 4 (Fall):433-40.

1976

Sees the tale operating on two levels: Marcher's consciousness, which abstracts him from reality, and a dream world in which everything in the tale is a projection of Marcher's unconscious. On both levels Marcher has the choice between "heroism or deviance, tragedy or pathology," with deviance and pathology ultimately winning. Nance uses the Oedipus myth, allusions to which he finds in the text, to explore Marcher's failure.

148 _____. "*What Maisie Knew*: The Myth of the Artist." *Studies in the Novel* 8, no. 1 (Spring):88-102.

Focuses on Maisie's trip to France where her knowledge culminates in vision. In addition, Maisie is "initiated into the human community" while at the same time she transcends that community by virtue of her informed and unifying vision.

149 NETTELS, ELSA. "'A Frugal Splendour': Thoreau and James and the Principles of Economy." *Colby Library Quarterly* 12, no. 1 (March):5-13.

Finds similarity in James's and Thoreau's concept of economy as it defines "the processes and the rewards" of their commitment to a life of art. Both reject material wealth, holding that cultivation of the consciousness is deeply rewarding.

150 "1975 Annual Review: Henry James." *Journal of Modern Literature* 5, no. 4:726-33.

Lists criticism published in 1974-1975.

*151 NORRMAN, R.G. "Techniques of Ambiguity in the Fiction of Henry James, with Special Reference to 'In the Cage' and 'The Turn of the Screw.'" Ph.D. dissertation, University of Oxford.

Source: Budd, 1983.32, p. 28, item 127. Revised 1977.80.

152 NOWIK, NANCY ANN. "Melodrama in the Late Novels of Henry James." Ph.D. dissertation, Ohio State University, 232 pp.

Demonstrates that melodramatic elements in *The Sacred Fount, The Ambassadors, The Wings of the Dove,* and *The Golden Bowl* reflect James's "inherently melodramatic" vision of life. Nowik examines melodrama as a movement, traces its influence on James's early work, and focuses on "delayed clarification" and "specification" as melodramatic techniques.

See *Dissertation Abstracts International* 37, no. 2 (1976):972A.

153 PAGE, NORMAN. "The Great Tradition Revisited." In *Jane Austen's Achievement. Papers Delivered at the Jane Austen Bicentennial Conference at the University of Alberta.* Edited by Juliet McMaster. New York: Barnes & Noble, pp. 44-63.

Argues for Austen's place in Leavis's "great tradition" of George Eliot, James, and Conrad and discusses her influence on the major novelists. *The Portrait of a Lady* and other early James novels show James's debt to Austen.

154 PANICHAS, GEORGE A. "The Perspicacious Pilgrim." *Modern Age: A Quarterly Review* 20, no. 2 (Spring):219-21.

Reviews the first volume of Edel's *Henry James Letters*, noting that these letters illuminate the birth and growth of James's artistic consciousness.

Reprinted 1982.113.

155 PERRY, DONNA MARIE. "From Innocence through Experience: A Study of the Romantic Child in Five Nineteenth Century Novels." Ph.D. dissertation, Marquette University, 241 pp.

Traces the development of the child, whose innocence must accommodate worldly experience, in Brontë's *Jane Eyre*, Dickens's *David Copperfield* and *Great Expectations*, Eliot's *The Mill on the Floss*, and James's *What Maisie Knew*. The study is divided between an examination of literary techniques used in exploring the child's consciousness and an analysis of the child-protagonists themselves, who embody "the ambiguities of innocence."

See *Dissertation Abstracts International* 37, no. 6 (1976):3599A.

156 PERSON, LELAND, Jr. "Aesthetic Headaches and European Women in *The Marble Faun* and *The American*." *Studies in American Fiction* 4, no. 1 (Spring):65-79.

Argues that for both Hawthorne (especially in *The Marble Faun*) and the early James, the European woman embodied the "terrifying aspects of Europe" and at the same time the source of "the creation and experience of art." James's novel depicts the encounter between the American and the world of the European woman; Newman's encounter is an immersion in the depths of the self. Newman, however, refuses to learn from the experience.

157 PUTT, S. GORLEY. Introduction to *The Aspern Papers and Other Stories*. Harmondsworth, Middlesex, England: Penguin Books, pp. 7-10.

Notes that in "The Real Thing," "The Papers," and "The Aspern Papers" James is able to create characters who are representative types to point up a moral, but who also have a life of their own.

158 REDDICK, BRYAN. "The Control of Distance in *The Golden Bowl*." *Modern British Literature* 1:46-55.

Discusses the elements distancing the reader from the narrative, which include summaries, scenes from the past, long passages of dialogue with little commentary, imagery, and complex sentence structures.

159 RIHOIT, CATHERINE. "*The Bostonians*: An Investigation of the Female Feature in James's Cosmogony." In *Myth and Ideology in American Culture*. Edited by Régis Durand. Villeneuve-d'Ascq: Univ. de Lille III, pp. 81-110.

Compares positive and negative traits shared by the male and female characters in order to show that James's concern is not the war between the sexes, but "the war between aggressive human beings." James chooses the situation of women as his subject because that situation best fits the structural pattern of the defeat of innocence.

160 ROWE, JOHN CARLOS. *Henry Adams and Henry James: The Emergence of a Modern Consciousness*. Ithaca: Cornell University Press, 254 pp.

Examines the later work of Adams and James in their exploration of the phenomenology of knowing and their sense of the relation between aesthetics and the meaning of history. Both writers "experiment with different forms . . . to give symbolic shape and meaning to a reality and a self," although Adams attempts to construct a historical consciousness while James's response is primarily aesthetic. Both authors acknowledge the individual act of interpretation and the responsibilities implicit in that act. *The American Scene, The Wings of the Dove*, and *The Golden Bowl* are discussed in this study.

161 RUBINSTEIN, ANNETTE T. "Henry James, American Novelist, or Isabel Archer, Emerson's Grand-Daughter." In *Weapons of Criticism: Marxism in America and the Literary Tradition*. Edited by Norman Rudich. Palo Alto, Calif.: Ramparts Press, pp. 311-26.

Locates James within the essentially American tradition of Cooper, Hawthorne, and Melville by virtue of his focus on transcendentalism and the question of individual freedom. *The Portrait of a Lady* is James's experiment to test transcendentalism as a philosophy of life.

162 RUCKER, MARY E. "James's 'The Pupil': The Question of Moral Ambiguity." *Arizona Quarterly* 32, no. 4 (Winter):301-15.

Argues that the tale's theme—"the ambiguous relationship of self and the values by which one sustains relationships between self and others"—is reflected in its technique, which is based on an incongruity between narrative mode and meaning.

163 SACKS, SHELDON. "Novelists as Storytellers." *Modern Philology* 73, no. 4, part 2 (May):S97-S109.

Argues that the importance of "story" as a critical abstraction rests on "the manner in which it is narrated and the appropriateness of its special stylistic density." Sacks looks briefly at Virginia Woolf, Samuel Richardson, Jane Austen, and Henry James, all of whom are great novelists because they are great storytellers.

164 SCHEROR, ELLIOT M. "Intonation and Moral Insight: Reading Henry James Aloud." *Oral English* (LeMoyne College, Syracuse, N.Y.) 1, no. 3:8-13.

Shows that James considered speech and particularly its intonation as essentially moral because speech is the means by which values are transmitted. James's treatment of the speech in *The Wings of the Dove* exemplifies his use of intonation to suggest character and value.

1976

165 SCHNEIDER, DANIEL J. "To the Editor." *PMLA* 91, no. 5 (October):922-23.

Takes issue with Yeazell (1976.207), rejecting her argument that the morality of *The Golden Bowl* is ambiguous and that Maggie inflicts pain. The structure of imagery clearly evaluates each character's morality; while Maggie does inflict pain, she alone has a sense of sin and accepts responsibility for evil. See Yeazell's response 1976.207.

166 _____. "The Unreliable Narrator: James's 'The Aspern Papers' and the Reading of Fiction." *Studies in Short Fiction* 13, no. 1 (Winter):43-49.

Answers Booth's complaint in *The Rhetoric of Fiction* that James's unreliable narrator creates insoluble problems for the reader by demonstrating that Booth did not pay attention to patterns of imagery and character contrasts. Schneider examines these patterns in the tale and concludes that meaning is generally "the product of basic structural oppositions."

167 SCHRIBER, MARY S. "Isabel Archer and Victorian Manners." *Studies in the Novel* 8, no. 4 (Winter):441-57.

Sees James's focus on Isabel's consciousness as a way to subvert the conventional Victorian idea of "lady" as reflection of another. Schriber also details James's juxtaposing Isabel with the novel's female characters to show how she attempts to achieve freedom from the limitations of the role of lady.

168 SEBOUHIAN, GEORGE. "Henry James's Transcendental Imagination." *Essays in Literature* 3, no. 2 (Fall):214-26.

Examines James's transcendentalism, beginning with how James defines it in his nonfiction and concluding with James's use of it in his fiction. For James, the imagination transforms world into self, culminating in a transcendental "vision of being." James's centers of consciousness effect this transcendental transformation who "deal with the world as if it were a mental adventure."

169 SEED, D[AVID]. "Two Contributions to Henry James Bibliography." *Notes and Queries* 23, no. 1 (January):11-12.

Notes two reprints of James's work omitted from Edel's and Laurence's 1961 bibliography: "The Presentation at Court. A Great

1976

Novelist's Vignette of an American Lady Engaged in Conquering Europe" in *Vanity Fair*, December, 1922; and the essay James wrote on Turgenev for *The Atlantic Monthly* that appears in volume I of Hapgood's 1903-1904 edition of *The Novels and Stories of Ivan Turgenieff*.

170   SEED, DAVID. "The Letters of Henry James." *Journal of American Studies* 10, no. 3 (December):383-86.
        Applauds the appearance of Edel's *Henry James Letters*, volumes I and II for the documentary evidence they give of his early literary career. Seed also notes the way in which James's residences affect the style and texture of the letters making them "dramatic reading."

171   SHELDON, PAMELA J. "'The Friends of Friends': Another Twist to 'The Turn of the Screw.'" *Wascana Review* 11, no. 1 (Spring):3-14.
        Compares the two tales, focusing primarily on the similarities in the method of narration in each. The narrator of "The Friends of Friends" and the governess in the 1898 tale "attempt to order her universe by assessing all that happens to her according to the bias of her own madness."

172   SHINN, THELMA J. "The Art of a Verse Novelist: Approaching Robinson's Late Narratives through James's *The Art of the Novel*." *Colby Library Quarterly* 12, no. 2 (June):91-100.
        Argues that E.A. Robinson's poetry incorporates many of James's theories as discussed in the prefaces. Both James and Robinson subordinate style to "dramatic purpose and explore the psychological dimension of character."

173   SPIEGEL, ALAN. "The Development of Cinematographic Form: James, Conrad, Joyce." In *Fiction and the Camera Eye: Visual Consciousness in Film and the Modern Novel*. Charlottesville: University Press of Virginia, pp. 53-68.
        Examines the rhetorical strategy in *What Maisie Knew* to show that in his later work James represents the process of visualization cinematographically instead of scenographically by using "partialized" views of objects. Aspects of objects are seen in isolation, severed from the whole.

1976

174 STAFFORD, WILLIAM T. "Henry James." In *American Literary Scholarship: An Annual/1974*. Edited by James Woodress. Durham: Duke University Press, pp. 87-100.
     Surveys criticism on James published in 1974.

175 STAMBAUGH, SARA. "The Aesthetic Movement and *The Portrait of a Lady*." *Nineteenth-Century Fiction* 30, no. 4 (March):495-510.
     Traces references to the aesthetic movement throughout the novel; the china imagery, for example, reflects the "chinamania" of the period. Stambaugh argues that James sympathized with DuMaurier's criticism of the movement and of Oscar Wilde. James's criticism is apparent in the character of Gilbert Osmond.

176 STEIN, ALLEN F. "Lambert Strether's Circuitous Journey: Motifs of Internalized Quest and Circularity in *The Ambassadors*." *ESQ* 22, no. 4 (old series no. 85):245-53.
     Demonstrates that James applied the conventions of the medieval quest romance to an ordinary, middle-class man. Because of his interior quest, Strether knows himself and can be receptive to "the sensuous possibilities of life."

177 STEPP, WALTER. "*The Turn of the Screw*: If Douglas is Miles . . . ." *Nassau Review* 3, no. 2:76-82.
     Suggests that the role of Douglas, who may be Miles, is to assist the "reader in accepting the governess's legitimacy" and in understanding her "strange journey" from inexperienced youth to wise maturity.

178 STINEBACK, DAVID C. "'Hurried Particles in the Stream': Henry James's *The Bostonians*." In *Shifting World: Social Change and Nostalgia in the American Novel*. Lewisburg, Pa.: Bucknell University Press, pp. 75-86, 180-81.
     Argues that the novel's concern is the "ironic futility of aristocratic illusions in a changing society." Both Olive Chancellor and Basil Ransom are self-deceived about their ability to impose their ideals upon American society.

179 STONE, EDWARD. "Edition Architecture and 'The Turn of the Screw.'" *Studies in Short Fiction* 13, no. 1 (Winter):9-16.
Examines the tale's placement in the New York Edition (in volume 12 with "The Aspern Papers" instead of in volume 17 with the supernatural tales), and concludes that it probably was for reasons of spacing or lack of precise planning.

180 STONE, WILLIAM B. "Idiolect and Ideology: Some Stylistic Aspects of Norris, James, and DuBois." *Style* 10, no. 4 (Fall):405-25.
Shows that an individual's style is the result of social and political orientation and verbal and psychological conditioning. Although *The Pit, The Ambassadors*, and *The Souls of Black Folk,*-all published in 1903 – have the common thread of determinism, the writers' ideological differences are reflected in their style. James's "abstract" style shields "the essentially economic basis of his characters' relationships."

181 TANIMOTO, YASUKO. *"The Golden Bowl* no okeru 'Shiten'" [Point of view in *The Golden Bowl*]. *Eigo Seinen* (Tokyo) 122:324-26.
In Japanese.
Argues that James's point of view in this novel is different from that in the tales of his middle and late periods. Instead of relying on an observer-narrator, James enters the consciousness of the two main characters; the impersonal element within the point of view of these characters is that of the author and enables the story to progress.

182 ____. "Henry James to Natsume Soseki: Ni Sakka no Ishitsusei: Saisetsu" [Differences between James and Natsume reconsidered]. *Eigo Seinen* (Tokyo) 122:486-88.
In Japanese.
Demonstrates that these writers differ greatly in the way they try to convey their own sense of existence in their works. James values sensibility more than intellect; Natsume values intellect more than sensibility. See also 1975.91, 1975.128, and 1976.146.

183 TIMMS, DAVID. "The Governess's Feelings and the Argument from Textual Revision of *The Turn of the Screw*." *Yearbook of English Studies* 6:194-201.

1976

Rejects the idea that James's changes of punctuation–especially the deletion of commas–in the New York Edition of the tale were made to enhance the governess's remarks as "records of feelings." James revises to achieve clarity and grace.

184   TINTNER, ADELINE R. "Arsène Houssaye's 'Capricieuse' and James' 'Capricciosa.'" *Revue de Littératurs Comparée* 50, no. 4 (October-December):478-81.

Notes that James derives his description of the Princess Casamassima as a "capricciosa" from Houssaye's description of the Princess Belgiojoso in *Les Confessions*.

185   ____. "*The Golden Bowl* and Waddesdon Manor." *Apollo* 104 (August):106-13.

Argues that the novel is a tribute to the Baron Ferdinand de Rothschild, his country house, and his collection. The essay includes a portrait of the Baron that is reflected in the description of Adam Verver, photographs of the interior and gardens of Waddesdon Manor, and art objects; it also reprints James's verse to the Baron.

Revised 1986.151; see also Richards, 1983.161.

186   ____. "Henry James at the Movies: Cinematograph and Photograph in 'Crapy Cornelia.'" *Markham Review* 6 (Fall):1-18.

Examines the tale's imagery, drawn from the motion picture of the Corbett-Fitzsimmon prize fight and from contemporary photography. Tintner suggests that James saw film as "random visual experiences" while a photograph was "a tool for the retrieval of an experience or an image." The essay is illustrated with stills of the prize-fight, cartes de visite, and photographs of James.

Revised: 1986.151.

187   ____. "Henry James's Use of *Jane Eyre* in 'The Turn of the Screw.'" *Brontë Society Transactions* 17, no. 1:42-45.

Suggests that James drew on elements from Brontë's life to create the governess and that James may have been inspired by chapter 17 of the novel, in which the Ingrams discuss an affair between a tutor and a governess.

Revised 1987.122.

188 ____. "'High Melancholy and Sweet': James and the Arcadian Tradition." *Colby Library Quarterly* 12, no. 3 (September):109-21.

Argues that James received the Arcadian tradition, which is most apparent in *The Ambassadors*, from Watteau's paintings and Balzac's *Comédie Humaine*. Tintner traces the Arcadian influence throughout James's career, beginning with *The Europeans*, but focuses her discussion in *The Ambassadors*.

Revised 1986.151.

189 ____. "'The Impressions of a Cousin'" Henry James' Transformation of *The Marble Faun*." *Nathaniel Hawthorne Journal*:205-13.

Argues that Hawthorne's novel provided structure and characters for the tale and provides a key for the reader in understanding an otherwise absurd tale. James's tale is problematic, however, because the limitations of space prevent James from fully appropriating his model.

Revised 1987.122.

190 ____. "Isabel's Carriage-Image and Emma's Day Dream." *Modern Fiction Studies* 22, no. 2 (Summer):227-31.

Suggests that Isabel's carriage image is inspired by Emma Bovary's "au gallop de quatre chevaux" and reveals Isabel's romantic vision of life. James reinforces Isabel's romanticism by having her read essays by Ampère *fils*, Mme. Récamier's lover.

Revised 1987.122.

191 ____. "Landmarks of 'The Terrible Town': The New York Scene in Henry James' Last Stories." *Prospects: Annual of American Cultural Studies* 2:399-435.

Argues that James was both fascinated and revolted by the new architecture he found in New York during his 1904 trip. In the stories he wrote as a response to that trip–"The Jolly Corner," "Julia Bride," "Crapy Cornelia," and "A Round of Visits"–James uses that architecture to symbolize the society of New York.

Revised 1986.191.

192 ____. "Poe's 'The Spectacles' and James' 'Glasses.'" *Poe Studies* 9, no. 2 (December):53-54.

1976

Notes the similarities between the two tales.
Revised 1987.122.

193   ____. "A Portrait of the Novelist as a Young Man: The Letters of
Henry James." *Studies in the Novel* 8, no. 1 (Spring):121-28.
Reviews the first two volumes of Edel's *Henry James Letters*,
noting that the letters show that "the structures of James's fiction are
formal renderings of actual experiences."

194   TODD, D.D. "Henry James and the Theory of Literary Realism"
Philosophy and Literature 1, no. 1 (Fall):79-100.
Argues, referring to "The Art of Fiction" and the prefaces that
James was not a comprehensive and consistent literary theoretician. At
best James proposes a general aesthetic of the novel, but Todd finds
that "egregiously defective."
See Lawry 1979.83 for reply.

195   TOMLINSON, THOMAS BRIAN. "'Fits of Spiritual Dread':
George Eliot and Later Novelists." In *The English Middle-Class
Novel*. New York: Barnes & Noble, pp. 114-30.
Discusses the depiction of middle-class life and its involvement
with ordinary existence in George Eliot, Thomas Hardy, Henry James,
and Joseph Conrad. In *The Awkward Age*, James explores the
breakdown of "Victorian middle-class certainties" even though the novel
is based on those certainties. James examines a society much more
limited in scope than does Eliot, but he achieves an "intensity of vision."
He is able to render accurately the consciousness of individuals in that
society.

196   ____. "Henry James: *The Ambassadors*." In *The English Middle-
Class Novel*. New York: Barnes & Noble, pp. 148-65.
Sees the novel as the confrontation of middle-class values with
the values of Europe. While Strether discovers similarities, he also finds
unbridgeable gaps between the two systems of values. In the end,
Strether relies on "American, middle-class honesty of purpose."

197 TREMPER, ELLEN. "Henry James's Altering Ego: An Examination of His Psychological Double in Three Tales." *Texas Quarterly* 19, no. 3 (Autumn):59-75.

Argues that the relationships in "The Aspern Papers," "The Beast in the Jungle," and "The Jolly Corner" reflect James's relationships with Constance Fenimore Woolson, Hendrik Andersen, and Jocelyn Persse. His friendship with Persse liberated James from creating "loveless" characters.

198 UNRUE, DARLENE. "Henry James and the Grotesque." *Arizona Quarterly* 32, no. 4 (Winter):293-300.

Examines James's use of the grotesque character as a means of foreshadowing or revealing. Unrue cites the *"crétin"* in *Roderick Hudson*, the "hag" in *The Wings of the Dove*, Miss Wenham in "Flickerbridge," and Brydon's alter ego in "The Jolly Corner" as examples of this character type, noting that in the later fiction the grotesque functions metaphorically.

199 VANN, BARBARA. "A Psychological Interpretation of *Daisy Miller*." In *A Festschrift for Professor Marguerite Roberts, on the Occasion of Her Retirement from Westhampton College, University of Richmond, Virginia*. Edited by Frieda Elaine Penninger. Richmond: University of Richmond Press, pp. 205-8.

Applies Jung's theories to the tale, arguing that Randolph and Daisy represent two aspects of Winterbourne. Randolph is his open and free spirit, while Daisy is his anima and alter ego. Winterbourne's rejection of Daisy is the "cause" of her death, a death making it impossible for Winterbourne to have a "balanced and complete personality."

200 VINCEC, SISTER STEPHANIE, C.S.J. "'Poor Flopping *Wings'*: The Making of Henry James's *The Wings of the Dove*." *Harvard Library Bulletin* 24, no. 1 (January):60-93.

Details the history of the novel's creation, publication, preface, and revisions in order to explain why the novel does not "project a single coherent picture." Vincec concludes that contrary to "objective criticism," the historical record of a literary work is vital to understanding that work.

1976

201 VISWANATHAN, JACQUELINE. "The Innocent Bystander: The Narrator's Position in Poe's 'The Fall of the House of Usher,' James's 'The Turn of the Screw,' and Butor's *L'Emploi du temps*." *Hebrew University Studies in Literature* 4:27-47.

Argues that Poe's and James's so-called unreliable narrators are actually ambiguous rather than unreliable because they shift from being uninvolved observers to the focus of the narrative. The ambiguity suggested by Poe's narrator and James's governess is more fully developed in the narrator of Butor's novel. Butor's narrator explores individual guilt and responsibility in relation to a whole community, in contrast to Poe's and James's focus on the individual.

*202 WALTON, JAMES. "A Mechanic's Tragedy: Reality in *The Princess Casamassima*." *English Studies Colloquium* (East Meadow, N.Y.)8:1-20.

Source: *MLA International Bibliography* 1 (1976):169, item 9102.

203 WILT, JUDITH. "A Right Issue from the Tight Place: Henry James and Maria Gostrey." *Journal of Narrative Technique* 6, no. 2 (Spring):77-91.

Examines the way the preface of *The Ambassadors* deprives Maria Gostrey of her "human impact" by reducing her to a function, which indicates "the Artist's uneasiness" with his "woman-character." In her conclusion, Wilt suggests that this preface is a continuation of "The Beast in the Jungle."

*204 WIRTH-NESHER, HANA. "Limits of Fiction: A Study of the Novels of Henry James and Virginia Woolf." Ph.D. dissertation, Columbia University.

Source: Budd, 1983.32, p. 41, item 182.

205 WOLF, JACK C. "Henry James and Impressionist Painting." *CEA Critic* 38, no. 3 (March):14-16.

Compares the technique in *The American* to that of French impressionist painting in James's focus on the inner life, his use of numerous phrases that build a sentence, and his creation of the center of consciousness.

1976

206 YEAZELL, RUTH B[ERNARD]. *Language and Knowledge in the Late Novels of Henry James*. Chicago: University of Chicago Press, vii, 143 pp.

Focuses on the language of narrative and dialogue in *The Ambassadors, The Wings of the Dove*, and *The Golden Bowl* to show how the late style shapes characters, the reader's knowledge, and the fictional world of each novel. Yeazell examines the way in which language reflects the ever-widening consciousness, the function of metaphor, the "dialectic of Jamesian talk" that mirrors the consciousness, and the manner in which James compresses "conflicting motives and desires" in Maggie Verver.

Reprinted in part: 1976.208.

207 _____. "Ms. Yeazell Replies." *PMLA* 91, no. 5 (October):923-24.

Responds to Schneider (1976.165), insisting that the imagery does not resolve *The Golden Bowl*'s ambiguous morality.

Reprinted in part 1987.44.

208 _____. "Talking in James." *PMLA* 91, no. 1 (January):66-77.

Examines dialogue in *The Ambassadors, The Wings of the Dove*, and *The Golden Bowl* to show how the characters use talk to create instead of to reveal truth. Talk in these novels create a fluid world, making it difficult "to know where we stand, either morally or epistemologically." See Schneider 1976.165 and Yeazell 1976.207.

Reprinted 1976.206.

1977

1 ALLEN, JEAN THOMAS. "*Turn of the Screw* and *The Innocents*: Two Types of Ambiguity." In *The Classic American Novel and the Movies*. Edited by Gerald Geary and Roger Shatzkin. New York: Ungar, pp. 132-42.

Compares the methods of achieving ambiguity in the tale and in the film, concluding that the film does not produce "the tension of ambiguity."

1977

2   ALTENBERND, LYNN. "A Dispassionate Pilgrim: Henry James's Early Travel in Sketch and Story." *Exploration: Journal of the MLA Special Session on the Literature of Exploration and Travel* 5, no. 1:1-14.

Argues that James's writings of the seventies show that he was not an unreserved idolator of Europe. In the stories of this period James was already examining the international theme.

3   ANDERSON, CHARLES ROBERTS. *Person, Place, and Thing in Henry James's Novels*. Durham: Duke University Press, ix, 308 pp.

Argues that James relies on "objects," which include places as well as things, as a primary means of characterization and that James's characters in turn use such objects as a means of understanding and relating to other characters. Novels discussed include *Roderick Hudson, The American, The Portrait of a Lady, The Princess Casamassima, The Wings of the Dove*, and *The Ambassadors*. In discussing the evolution of James's method of characterization Anderson also considers the influence of nineteenth-century novelists – French, American, and English – as well as the influence of the French literary impressionists on James's technique.

4   ARMSTRONG, NANCY. "Character, Closure, and Impressionist Fiction." *Criticism* 19, no. 4 (Fall):317-37.

Sees literary impressionism as anticipating the "radical reformation of the social function of literature" by rejecting authoritarian readings of the text and opening new interpretive possibilities. Armstrong uses James's "The Turn of the Screw" and Dicken's *Hard Times* as examples.

5   ARMSTRONG, PAUL BRADFORD. "Henry James: Impressionism and Phenomenology." Ph.D. dissertation, Stanford University, 476 pp.

Uses the methods of phenomenology to examine James's epistemology as revealed in *Roderick Hudson, The Portrait of a Lady, What Maisie Knew*, and *The Golden Bowl*. While the primary focus is on James, Armstrong intends this study as an introduction for the American humanist to phenomenology and its relevance to the interpretation of literature.

See *Dissertation Abstracts International* 37, no. 12, pt. 1 (1977):7747A.

6 AUCHINLOSS, LOUIS. "The Late Jamesing of Early James." *Times Literary Supplement*, no. 3906 (21 January):47.

Compares the 1877 and 1907 versions of *The American*. The revisions of the nondialogue passages are improvements; revisions of dialogue, however, diminish Christopher Newman's dramatic force.
Reprinted 1979.3.

7 BABIN, JAMES L. "Henry James's 'Middle Years' in Fiction and Autobiography." *Southern Review*, Louisiana State University 13, no. 3 (July):505-17.

Focuses on the image of "the middle years" in the tale and the way in which James applied that image in his uncompleted autobiography, *The Middle Years*. The "middle years" are those between birth and death, during which what must count is the actual doing, not achieving complete mastery.

8 BANTA, MARTHA. "About America's 'White Terror': James, Poe, Pyncheon, and Others." In *Literature and the Occult: Essays in Comparative Literature*. Edited by Luanne Frank. Arlington: University of Texas at Arlington, pp. 31-53.

Examines the connection between whiteness and the occult in Poe, Melville, and Pyncheon and suggests that in *The Golden Bowl* James too used whiteness to describe Maggie's power to create and to destroy. For James, whiteness is associated with the moral consciousness, which includes the impossible ideal and the possibility of human love.

9 _____. "They Shall Have Faces, Minds, and (One Day) Flesh: Women in Late Nineteenth-Century and Early Twentieth-Century American Literature." In *What Manner of Woman: Essays on English and American Life and Letters*. Edited by Marlene Springer. New York: New York University Press, pp. 235-70.

Traces the portrayal of the American girl as heroine throughout the literature of the period, showing that writers typically granted the heroine intellect and spirit but denied her sensuality and sexuality. James, however, attempted "to join sexual passion, cultural force, and intelligence," but he still maintained, though subtly, a distinction between fine mind and voluptuous body.

1977

10 BARGAINNIER, EARL F. "Browning, James and 'The Private Life.'" *Studies in Short Fiction* 14, no. 2 (Spring):151-58.
Argues against Lind's contention that in "The Private Life" James was writing disguised autobiography [*American Literature* 23 (1951)]:315-22). Rather, the tale is a "conceit" based on Robert Browning and Frederick Leighton, as James had remarked in his note-books.

11 BARR, DAVID BREWSTER. "Character in Henry James: Statement and Narrative Situation in Four Novels." Ph.D. dissertation, University of North Carolina, Chapel Hill, 215 pp.
Argues that between 1881 and 1903 James's verbal presentation of character changed little, but by changing the focus of that presentation and its relation to other elements in the novel James achieved considerable variety in characterization. The four novels considered here are *The Portrait of a Lady, The Bostonians, The Awkward Age,* and *The Ambassadors*.
See *Dissertation Abstracts International* 39, no. 1 (1978):283A-284A.

12 BARRON, ARTHUR. "Scenes from *The Jolly Corner.*" In *The American Short Story*. Edited by Calvin Skaggs. New York: Dell, pp. 116-21.
Film script of the short story.

13 BEAUCHAMP, ANDREA ROBERTS. "'Isabel Archer': A Possible Source for *The Portrait of a Lady.*" *American Literature* 49, no. 2 (May):267-71.
Suggests that Professor Alden's tale, "Isabel Archer," published in *The Ladies' Wreath*, 1848-1849, may have served as a model for James's Isabel, especially because there are many similarities in the two heroines.

14 BIRRELL, T.A. "The Greatness of *The Bostonians.*" *Dutch Quarterly Review of Anglo-American Letters* 7:242-64.
Describes the biographical background of the novel as well as its plot and its structure. Birrell sees the greatness of the novel in its liveliness and its "rich and varied organic texture," never again duplicated in any of James's fiction.

See also Wilkinson 1980.162.

15 BLASING, MUTLU KONUK. "Henry James's Prefaces or the Story of the Stories." In *The Art of Life: Studies in American Autobiographical Literature*. Austin: University of Texas Press, pp. 57-76, 166-68.

Argues that the prefaces are autobiographical in that James looks at his career critically and self-consciously. The prefaces are a "revision" of James's life and epitimize James's credo that art makes life; in them James is both creator and hero of his fiction.

Revised 1979.15.

16 BOLAND, DOROTHY M. "Henry James's 'The Figure in the Carpet'" A Fabric of the East." *Papers on Language and Literature* 13, no. 4 (Fall):424-29.

Sees the tale governed by "karmic law" whereby an individual's life is interwoven with the whole cosmos, and each person must seek a unique path to harmony. The tale's narrator, obsessed with the "figure," loses his connection with transcendant unity.

17 BOVI-GUERRA, PEDRO. "Henry James y Carlos Fuentes: Dos cuentos, paralelos y bifurcaciones." In *Estudios de historia, literatura y arte hispánicos ofrecidos a Rodrigo A. Molina*. Edited by Wayne H. Finke. Madrid: Insula, pp. 71-85.

In Spanish.

*18 BRADBURY, N.A.L. "The Process and the Effect: A Study of the Development of the Novel Form in the Later Work of Henry James." Ph.D. dissertation, University of Oxford.

Source: Budd, 1983.32, p. 4, item 18.

19 BRIGGS, JULIA. "Not Without but Within: The Psychological Ghost Story." In *Night Visitors: The Rise and Fall of the English Ghost Story*. London: Faber & Faber, pp. 142-64.

Traces James's evolution of the ghost story from his early work to "The Turn of the Screw," "the most ambitious and influential of psychological ghost stories," focusing on the ways in which James uses ambiguity to create terror.

1977

20 _____. "A Sense of the Past: Henry James and Vernon Lee." In *Night Visitors: The Rise and Fall of the English Ghost Story*. London: Faber & Faber, pp. 111-23.

Discusses Hawthorne's influence on both writers' connecting the past with ghosts and their use of fantasy elements. Briggs touches upon James's early ghost stories and *The Sense of the Past*.

21 BROOKE-ROSE, CHRISTINE. "Surface Structure in Narrative: The Squirm of the True, Part III." *PTL* 2, no. 3 (October):517-62.

Analyzes the tale's two surface structures, which include the *agencement* or *sjuzet* (the ordering of events) and the actual text (sequence of words) that can be divided into "Author's Metatext" and "Narrator's Metatext." Brooke-Rose suggests that her "semantic grammar" may be applicable to other texts as well.

Revised 1981.22.

22 BURDE, EDGAR J. "*The Ambassadors* and the Double Vision of Henry James." *Essays in Literature* 4, no. 1 (Spring):59-77.

Argues that an opposition between the heroic and the foolish is central to Strether's character and that he is subjected to two irreconcilable points of view: one transcendental, the other worldly. These oppositions are reflected in the novel's method and demand that the reader "see" with both "symbolistic" and "realistic" imagination. This novel marks James's movement from the "disordered ambiguity" of *The Sacred Fount* to a "complex double vision."

23 CARLSON, JERRY W. "*Washington Square* and *The Heiress*: Comparing Artistic Forms" In *The Classic American Novel and the Movies*. Edited by Gerald Geary and Roger Shatzkin. New York: Ungar, pp. 95-104.

Compares the Catherine of the novel, who achieves moral superiority over Sloper and Townsend, with the Catherine of the film, who seeks revenge. The film sacrifices moral complexity and dramatic credibility.

24 CARTER, EVERETT. "Adams and James: Toward the Waste Land." In *The American Idea: The Literary Response to American Optimism*. Chapel Hill: University of North Carolina Press, pp. 242-48.

Examines Adams's and James's loss of faith in America. James's novels are based on the failure of the American ideal and the need to create "a tiny supersensual illusion of freedom" in an evil and tragic world. Carter briefly discusses *The Portrait of a Lady*, *The Wings of the Dove*, and *The Ambassadors*.

25 COCKSHUT, A.O.J. "The Lesbian Theme." In *Man and Woman: A Study of Love and the Novel, 1740-1940*. London: Collins, 192-99.
    Sees *The Bostonians* as "the only novel written in English by a major author which has the lesbian relation as its central subject." James's understanding of the novel's characters enables him to show how "confused and partial" they all are.

26 DAWSON, ANTHONY B. "The Reader and the Measurement of Time in 'The Beast in the Jungle.'" *English Studies in Canada* 3, no. 4 (Winter):458-65.
    Demonstrates how James's use of a complex time scheme and prose style forces the reader to share Marcher's fate of being unable to "grasp the present moment." As a result, the tale underscores what Dawson calls the ambiguity of the reading experience analogous to the writing experience in that, in order to read a work that stresses the importance of life the reader must be detached from life.

27 DAWSON, JAN. "An Interview with Peter Bogdanovich." In *The Classic American Novel and the Movies*. Edited by Gerald Peary and Roger Shatzkin. New York: Ungar, pp. 83-89.
    Bogdanovich discusses how and why he made changes in the characters and notes that he treats *Daisy Miller* as a suspense story.
    Reprint in part: "The Continental Divide: Filming Henry James," *Sight and Sound* 43, no. 1 (Winter 1973/74):14-15.

28 DEAKIN, MOTLEY F. "The Real and Fictive Quest of Henry James." In *Makers of the Twentieth-Century Novel*. Edited by Harry R. Garvin. Lewisburg: Bucknell University Press, pp. 179-91.
    Traces the motifs of the quest and the figure in the shrine, beginning with the travel sketches and concluding with *The Wings of the Dove*. James gradually transforms "the musings of a tourist" into a pattern that provides him with a way to explore the individual psyche.

1977

Reprinted from Bucknell Rev. 14, no. 2 (1966):82-97. Slightly revised to include recent critics.

29   DEAN, SHARON. "James' *The Golden Bowl.*" *Explicator* 35, no. 4 (Summer):8-9.
Sees Charlotte's statement that she and Adam cannot have a child as an indication that he is impotent and as a signal that she is willing to commit adultery.

30   ____. "The Principino and the Ending of James's *The Golden Bowl.*" *American Notes and Queries* 16, no. 3 (November):43-44.
Suggests that Amerigo's taking the Principino at the novel's end shows that James saw parenthood as one of the reasons for the institution of marriage.

31   DIORIO, MARY ANN LUCIA GENOVA. "'Vessels of Experience': A Comparative Study of Women in Selected Novels of Gustave Flaubert and Henry James." Ph.D. dissertation, University of Kansas, 270 pp.
Uses Jung's "feminine principle" to examine the heroines of *Madame Bovary, L'Education sentimentale, The Portrait of a Lady,* and *The Wings of the Dove.* Diorio concludes that both artists have essentially feminine sensibilities.
See *Dissertation Abstracts International* 38, no. 7 (1978):4156A.

32   DUNKLE, JOHN JACOB. "Henry James's *The Aspern Papers*: A Comprehensive Critique." Ph.D. dissertation, St. John's University, 189 pp.
Examines the tale's ambiguity, its revisions, its genre, its place in the James canon, and the characterization of the narrator and Juliana and Tina Bordereau.
See *Dissertation Abstracts International* 38, no. 7(1978):4165A.

33   DUTHIE, ENID L. "Henry James's 'The Turn of the Screw' and Mrs. Gaskell's 'The Old Nurse's Story.'" *Brontë Society Transactions* 17, no. 2:133-37.
Proposes that Gaskell's tale, in which ghosts cause the death of an old woman, influenced James's ghost story. In Gaskell's tale, the

child Rosamond swoons at the sight of the ghost but is saved because her nurse holds her tight.

34   EWELL, BARBARA C. "Parodic Echoes of *The Portrait of a Lady* in Howell's *Indian Summer*." *TSE: Tulane Studies in English* 22:117-31.

Traces the parallels between the two novels and argues that James's novel is essentially tragic while Howells's is comic, seeking to "correct" James's view. Ewell focuses on each heroine's romantic illusions, noting that James renders the tragic implications for Isabel; Howells sees Imogene as fallibly human.

35   FAULKNER, PETER. "Development: [Henry James]." In *Modernism*. London: Methuen & Co., pp. 6-10.

Notes that James's interest in theory and practice is characteristic of modernism. James stressed both the unity and subjectivity of a work of fiction and reconciled the two through the center of consciousness that would create unity without sacrificing complexity.

36   FELMAN, SHOSHANA. "Turning the Screw of Interpretation." *Yale French Studies*, no. 55/56:94-207.

Explores the possibilities and limitations of an "encounter" between literature and psychoanalytic discourse, using "The Turn of the Screw." In her reading of the tale, Felman concentrates not on "what" the story means but "how" it means, and describes how the tale traps the analytical interpretations it invites.

Translated and reprinted 1978.40. Reprinted 1980.51 and 1985.42. See also Pecora 1985.112.

37   FOGEL, DANIEL MARK. "The Jamesian Dialectic in *The Ambassadors*." *Southern Review* (Louisiana State University) 13, no. 3 (July):468-91.

Uses *The Ambassadors* to show that James's fictions have a "dialectic of spiral return" that involves a journey through the antitheses of the starting point, returning to the origin but on a higher plane. The substructure of this movement is based on an array of bipolar elements, which include oxymorons, sentences, and paragraphs. Fogel traces the

1977

"play of oppositions" in many aspects of the novel, ranging from its preface to dialogue.

38   GALE, ROBERT L. "H.J.'s J.H. in 'The Real Thing.'" *Studies in Short Fiction* 14, no. 4 (Fall):396-98.
      Argues that Jack Hawley, friend of the tale's narrator, and John Hay, friend of James, are the reverse of James himself in their criticism and lack of compassion.

39   GILMORE, MICHAEL T. "Henry James: *The Golden Bowl*" In *The Middle Way: Puritanism and Ideology in American Romantic Fiction*. New Brunswick: Rutgers University Press, pp. 195-208.
      Argues that the novel is James's version of the Fall and Redemption and that it chronicles the transformation of Maggie Verver into a puritan saint, who must translate spiritual awakening into wordly action.

40   GREENSTEIN, SUSAN M. "*The Ambassadors*: The Man of Imagination Encaged and Provided For." *Studies in the Novel* 9, no. 2 (Summer):137-53.
      Examines James's link to Strether, particularly in terms of his relationship to America and his fear of having missed life. Greenstein argues that the novel marks a turning point for James in that the novel's "artistry of self-presentation" led to his asserting the primacy of the imagination and reappropriating America.

41   GRINDEA, MIRON, ed. "Letters to the London Library: Edmund Gosse, J.M. Barrie, Henry James, George Moore, T.E. Lawrence, Aldous Huxley." *Adam International Review* 40, nos. 397-400:26-29.
      Reprints James's 5 March 1908 letter to Hagberg Wright of the London Library, discussing the possibility of doing an essay on an unnamed "great man."

*42   HAGGERTY, GEORGE. "Gothic Fiction from Walpole to James: A Study of Formal Development." Ph.D. dissertation, University of California, Berkeley.
      Source: Budd, 1983.32, p. 18, item 81.

43 HALLAB, MARY Y. *"The Turn of the Screw* Squared." *Southern Review* (Louisiana State University) 13, no. 3 (July):492-504.

Traces the fairy tale, mythic, and archetypal patterns in the novella. These patterns, all of which involve a concern with evil, show that the novella was James's way of regressing to childhood in order to resolve the "crisis of depression" he suffered as a result of his failure as a playwright.

44 HALPERIN, JOHN. "Trollope, James, and the International Theme." *Yearbook of English Studies* 7:141-47.

Suggests that Trollope's treatment of the international theme in *The Duke's Children* may have been influenced by "Daisy Miller" and "An International Episode," while *The Portrait of a Lady* may have been influenced by Trollope's novel. Halperin also notes "striking similarities" in the works of the two novelists.

45 HARTSTOCK, MILDRED. "The Most Valuable Thing: James on Death." *Modern Fiction Studies* 22, no. 4 (Winter):507-24.

Examines James's comments on death, ranging from his letters and the essay "Is There a Life After Death?" to his tales and novels. Throughout all of his work, James consistently sees death as a termination, the awareness of which gives fullness to life.

46 _____. "Another Way to Heightened Consciousness." *Humanist* 37, no. 4 (July-August):26-30.

Finds in "The Great Good Place" and Hemingway's "The Big-Two-Hearted River" similar solutions to discovering order and sanity in the chaos of experience and compares Marcher's recognition in "The Beast in the Jungle" with Gabriel's epiphany in Joyce's "The Dead." Literary art offers the reader the possibility of self-renewal and heightened awareness.

47 HOCHMAN, BARUCH. "From *Middlemarch* to *The Portrait of a Lady*: Some Reflections on Henry James and the Traditions of the Novel." *Hebrew University Studies in Literature* 5:102-26.

Argues that in correcting George Eliot's "particularities" James transforms the novel into fable and thus violates its essentially realistic tradition.

1977

48   HOLMBERG, LAWRENCE OSCAR, Jr. "Autobiography and Art: Aesthetic Uses of the Creative Process in the Autobiographies of Henry Adams, Mark Twain, and Henry James." Ph.D. dissertation, University of New Mexico, 178 pp.
     Examines the consciousness of the artist as it manifests itself in these autobiographies, using the theories of Wilhelm Dilthey. Holmberg argues that James's autobiography is shaped by the theme of consciousness as a "critical standard and aesthetic principle."
     See *Dissertation Abstracts International* 38, no. 6 (1977):3500A.

49   HORWITZ, B.D. "The Sense of Desolation in Henry James." *Psychocultural Review* 1, no. 4 (Fall):466-92.
     Argues that many of James's male characters fail to have a sustained relationship with a woman because she represents both a love-object and a threat, and discusses "The Pupil" as an example of this pattern. Horwitz suggests that James projects his complex and ambivalent feelings toward his mother and his brother William onto his male protagonists.

50   HOUSTON, NEAL B. "A Footnote to the Death of Miles." *RE: Artes Liberales* 3, no. 2:25-27.
     Calls the governess the murderess of Miles because she produces the "Valsalva effect"–pressure on the thoracic cavity, which can stop the heart.

51   HUNTLEY, H. ROBERT. "James *The Turn of the Screw*: Its 'Fine Machinery.'" *American Imago* 34, no. 3 (Fall):224-37.
     Suggests that James was experimenting with the *doppelgänger* as a means of addressing problems of form associated with the ghost story. James balances the possibility of genuine apparitions and a neurotic and unreliable narrator to sustain both terror and credibility.

52   HUTCHINSON, STUART. "James's Medal: Options in *The Wings of the Dove*." *Essays in Criticism* 27, no. 4 (October):315-35.
     Argues that the novel is open to many interpretations depending on the perspective of the novel's characters, all of whom are linked by their "various states of dispossession." Moreover, James's sympathetic participation in their inner lives endows this novel and all his later work with humanity.

Reprinted 1983.98.

53 ITAGAKI, KONOMU. *"The Portrait of a Lady* ni okeru seeing no shinko" [The progress of seeing in *The Portrait of a Lady*]. *Eibungaku Kenkyu* (English Literary Society of Japan) 54:83-98.
In Japanese.
Analyzes Isabel in terms of "seeing" as opposed to "feeling" and argues that her refusal of Caspar Goodwood is her final choice of seeing.

*54 JACKSON, KATHERINE ROTHSCHILD. "The Larger Adventure: The Realm of Consciousness in the Fiction of Henry James." Ph.D. dissertation, Harvard University.
Source: Budd, 1983.32, p. 21, item 95.

55 JACOBS, EDWARD CRANEY. "James's 'Amiable Auditress': An Ironic Pun." *Studies in the Novel* 9, no. 3 (Fall):311.
Notes James's 1908 revision of Madame Merle to "amiable auditress" suggests "amiable adultress."

56 JACOBSON, MARCIA. "Convention and Innovations in *The Princess Casamassima." Journal of English and Germanic Philology* 76, no. 2 (April):238-54.
Proposes that contemporary working-class novels, especially those by Besant and Gissing, may have influenced James's novel. James's pessimism, however, forces him to invert the conventional rags-to-riches plot and the optimism of these novels. His lack of political knowledge, however, results in a "disjunction between character and context."
Reprinted 1983.101.

*57 KAPPELER, S.R. "Writing and Reading in Some Works by Henry James." Ph.D. dissertation, University of Cambridge.
Source: *Annual Bibliography of English Language and Literature* 55 (1980):483, item 8957.
Revised 1980.72.

1977

58   KIRSCHKE, JAMES JOSEPH. "Henry James and Impressionism."
      Ph.D. dissertation, Temple University, 392 pp.
           Examines in detail James's impressionism, tracing its source
      from both literature and the visual arts and discussing its impact on
      James's critical theory and narrative techniques.
           See *Dissertation Abstracts International* 38, no. 4 (1977):2112A.

59   KONO, YOSHIO. "Henry James: Ecriture no Tankyusha" [Henry
      James: seeker of ecriture]. In *American Shosetsu no Tenkai*
      [Development of the American novel]. Edited by Katsuji Takamura
      and Iwao Iwamoto. Tokyo: Shohakusha, pp. 123-32.
           In Japanese.
           Sees James as an expatriate whose sole purpose in life was to
      establish his identity through writing.

60   KORENMAN, JOAN S. "Henry James and the Murderous Mind."
      Essays in Literature 4, no. 2 (Fall):198-211.
           Examines the role of the mind in the "Jamesian death" in the
      novels and tales. The majority of these deaths are suicides: the mind
      seeks escape from a psychological blow inflicted by rejection, betrayal,
      or the insensitivity of others.

61   KOTZIN, MICHAEL. "*The American* and *The Newcomes*." *Etudes
      Anglaises* 30, no. 4 (October-December):420-29.
           Argues that Thackeray's novel made a "significant
      contribution" to *The American*, particularly in the characters' names,
      the use of fairy-tale elements, and the portrayal of a defeated hero.

*62   KRENN, HELIENA. "The American Identity in the 'Novels of
      Manners.'" *Fu Jen Studies* (Republic of China) 10:41-57.
           Source: *MLA International Bibliography* Vol. I (1977):137, item
      7308.

63   LABRIE, ROSS. "*The Other House*: A Jamesian Thriller." *North
      Dakota Quarterly* 45, no. 1 (Winter):23-30.
           Argues that *The Other House* deserves attention as a
      psychological thriller. Particularly noteworthy is James's creation of an
      "ambivalent atmosphere" and his "deftness in the art of foreshadowing."

64 LAY, MARY M. "Parallels: Henry James's *The Portrait of a Lady* and Nella Larsen's *Quicksand.*" *CLA Journal* 20, no. 4 (June):475-86.

Compares the two novels, which share many elements except conclusions, in which Helga, Larsen's heroine, fails to shape her destiny while Isabel controls hers. Lay attributes this crucial difference to each author's purpose: we are meant to admire Isabel and to sympathize with Helga.

65 LYCETTE, RONALD L. "Perceptual Touchstones for the Jamesian Artist-Hero." *Studies in Short Fiction* 14, no. 1 (Winter):55-62.

Notes that in "The Real Thing" and "The Middle Years" James combines the artistic and dramatic points of view, which are reflected in the tales' themes. Both tales caution against replacing experience with aesthetic form.

66 McGINTY, SUSAN LINDA. "The Development of the American Heroine in the Short Fiction of Henry James." Ph.D. dissertation, University of Denver, 240 pp.

Traces James's development of the American heroine in seven tales, spanning 1865 to 1908. James refines characterization so that in his later work he can achieve complexity and compression.

See *Dissertation Abstracts International* 38, no. 7 (1978):4143A.

*67 MACKLE, ELLIOTT. "Two Mistakes by Henry James in *The American Scene.*" *American Literary Realism, 1870-1910* 10, no. 2 (Spring):211-12.

Notes that in his chapter on Florida James confuses *The War Trail*, set in Mexico, with *Oceola*, set in Florida. Mackle suggests that James's harsh criticism of the state can be attributed to his impressions shaped by romance and adventure books and to his failure to observe the state's natural landscape.

68 McLUHAN, MARSHALL. "Canada: The Borderline Case." In *The Canadian Imagination: Dimensions of a Literary Culture*. Edited by David Stines. Cambridge: Harvard University Press, pp. 226-48.

Compares the Canadian search for identity to that of the American in the nineteenth century, noting James's conviction that the artist serves a vital role in that search is as valid now as it was then.

1977

69 McMURRAY, WILLIAM. "Reality in James' 'The Great Good Place.'" *Studies in Short Fiction* 14, no. 1 (Winter):82-83.

Notes that in this relatively neglected tale James fuses the inner subjective world with the outer objective world, showing each to be aspects of "a single reality."

70 McNAMARA, PEGGY ANNE. "The Language of Money in the Fiction of Henry James." Ph.D. dissertation, Rice University, 185 pp.

Analyzes the characters' use and misuse of economic language in *The American, The Portrait of a Lady, The Awkward Age,* and in the three major phase novels. McNamara argues that these novels are structured on society's exploitation of the protagonist's ignorance of the exchange system and its economic code.

See *Dissertation Abstracts International* 38, no. 3 (1977):1392A.

*71 MAGILTON. T. "The Spoils of Selfhood: Character and Values in the Fiction of Henry James." Ph.D. dissertation, University of Sheffield.

Source: *Annual Bibliography of English Language and Literature* 55 (1980):484, item 8968.

72 MAINI, DARSHAN SINGH. *Henry James: "The Portrait of a Lady": An Assessment.* Delhi: Oxford University Press, 74 pp.

Examines various elements in the novel, including major characters, the international theme, the depiction of evil, and narrative technique. Isabel's "odyssey" is both personal and archetypal, taking place against the background of an international setting. James's use of the center of consciousness as the narrative mode underpins the novel's concern with primacy of consciousness and the deceptive nature of human reality.

73 MANOLESCU, NICOLAE. "Două femei" [Two women]. *Steaua* 28, no. 8:20.

In Romanian.

74 MARKS, MARGARET LOUISE. "Flannery O'Connor's American Models: Her Work in Relation to That of Hawthorne, James, Faulkner, and West." Ph.D. dissertation, Duke University, 213 pp.

Traces characteristics of the work of these four writers appearing in O'Connor's fiction as well as the extent to which O'Connor adapted these models. Chapter three focuses on her relationship to James, particularly her use of manners to show mystery. See *Dissertation Abstracts International* 38, no. 8 (1978):4830A.

75   MATTHEWS, ROBERT J. "Describing and Interpreting a Work of Art." *Journal of Aesthetics and Art Criticism* 35, no. 1 (Fall):5-14.

Examines the distinction between describing and interpreting, using "The Turn of the Screw" as an example. Matthews distinguishes between the two on their basis as speech acts. Because "the interpreter [is] in a weaker epistemic position vis-à-vis the interpreted object" than one who describes the object, interpretive statements can be neither true nor false.

76   MENIKOFF, BARRY. "A House Divided: A New Reading of *The Bostonians*." *CLA Journal* 20, no. 4 (June):459-74.

Finds that the novel is structured on the well-made play because it is divided into three acts (books), each with three focal scenes. The novel's lack of a definite resolution, however, suggests that literary forms impose artificial neatness upon reality. In addition Menikoff sees the novel as a *psychomachia*, a war between flesh and spirit, and details the martial and religious imagery.

77   MILNE, GORDON. "Henry James." In *The Sense of Society: A History of the American Novel of Manners*. Rutherford, N.J.: Fairleigh Dickinson University Press, pp. 43-70.

Calls James an early master of the novel of manners and surveys his development of the genre. His early international novels and tales set the pattern for his analysis of society, juxtaposing the Old and New World and the "natural and artifical 'nobility.'" His later work continues the international contrast and "offers a more significant analysis of the manners-morals problems lying beneath the surface." Novels discussed in detail include *The American, The Portrait of a Lady, The Wings of the Dove, The Ambassadors*, and *The Golden Bowl*.

78   MONTEIRO, GEORGE. "Henry James and the Lessons of Sordello." *Western Humanities Review* 31, no. 1 (Winter):69-78.

1977

> Argues that James used Browning's poem, "A Light Woman," as the basic material for two tales, "A Light Man" and "The Lesson of the Master."

79 _____. "Innocence and Experience: The Adolescent Child in the Works of Mark Twain, Henry James, and Ernest Hemingway." *Estudos Anglo-Americanos* (Sao Paulo, Brazil) 1:39-57.

> Suggests that Twain's and James's depiction of adolescents as a source of wisdom reflected and developed the romantic idea of the child as father of the man. James used many children as "vehicles of social commentary"; *What Maisie Knew* epitomizes James's treatment of the child. Hemingway, in *In Our Time*, takes up where James leaves off.

80 MONTGOMERY, STEPHEN EDWARD. "The Rhetoric of Pathology: Paradoxical Communication in Henry James's Fiction." Ph.D. dissertation, University of California, San Diego, 150 pp.

> Examines James's use of pathology in terms of characters' behavior and rhetorical strategy in *The Portrait of a Lady, The Bostonians, The Awkward Age, The Ambassadors, The Wings of the Dove*, and *The Sense of the Past*. James traps his characters to force them into pathology, then traps the reader to make that pathology believable.
>
> See *Dissertation Abstracts International* 38, no. 9 (1978):5482A.

81 MOON, HEATH. "Henry James and the English Cult of Nostalgia: The Past Recaptured in the Fiction and Autobiography of Elizabeth Bowen, Sir Osbert Sitwell, and L.P. Hartley." Ph.D. dissertation, University of California, Santa Barbara, 316 pp.

> Demonstrates that two themes of James – "the Oedipal character of nostalgia" and the fondness for the ruling class while recognizing its decadence – serve as models for the fiction and autobiography of these writers. These themes are examined in *The Awkward Age*, "The Turn of the Screw," *The Sacred Fount*, "Crapy Cornelia," and *The Sense of the Past*.
>
> See *Dissertation Abstracts International* 38, no. 10 (1978):6122A-6123A.

82   MORSIANI, GIOVANNI. "Un anarchico fallito" [A failed anarchist]. *Paragone* 324:115-23.
     In Italian.

83   MURPHY, KATHLEEN. "An International Episode." In *The Classic American Novel and the Movies*. Edited by Gerald Peary and Roger Shatzkin. New York: Ungar, pp. 90-94.
     Calls Bogdanovich's *Daisy Miller* a meticulous adaptation of James's tale but suggests that he has too much respect for James because the film is only a "tasteful, sometimes brilliant visualization" of the novella.
     Reprint of *Movietone News*, no. 33 (July 1974):13-16.

84   NASH, CRISTOPHER. "Henry James, Puppetmaster: The Narrative Status of Maria Gostrey, Susan Stringham, and Fanny Assingham as *Ficelles*." *Studies in the Novel* 9, no. 3 (Fall):297-310.
     Analyses James's *ficelle*, noting the epistemological role she plays as well as her "compositional disjunction from the action."

85   NETTELS, ELSA. *James and Conrad*. Athens: University of Georgia Press, xi, 289 pp.
     Discusses the relationship between Conrad and James and their contributions to the development of the novel. Both writers shared a belief in the inner life as an appropriate subject for the novel and experimented with narrative technique to render that inner life. Individual chapters are devoted to individual elements – romance, satire, the grotesque, and tragedy – which James and Conrad combined in their work. Nettels argues that the two writers shaped the conventions of the modern novel by their focus on perception, the relativity of truth, and characters who must define their own world.

86   "1976 Annual Review: Henry James." *Journal of Modern Literature* 6, no. 4:643-47.
     Lists criticism published in 1975-1976.

87   NORRMAN, RALF. "The Intercepted Telegram Plot in Henry James's 'In the Cage.'" *Notes and Queries* 24, no. 5 (October):425-27.

1977

Argues that the telegraphist in this novella, which is an exploration of the limitations of knowledge, exults in her knowledge yet clearly makes many errors in her suppositions. The incident of the intercepted telegram reveals how much she does not know.

88 _____. *Techniques of Ambiguity in the Fiction of Henry James: With Special Reference to "In the Cage" and "The Turn of the Screw."* AAAH (Acta Academiae Aboensis, Ser. A, 54, no. 2). Åbo: Åbo Akademi, 197 pp.

Examines James's use of ambiguity-creating devices, focusing on the incomplete reversals, "blanks" or vague ambiguities, codes and symbols, and misunderstandings. Norrman then discusses *In the Cage* and "The Turn of the Screw" to show how these devices work in the fiction, thus facilitating understanding of James's ambiguity and his "fictional ideolect."

Revision of 1976.151.

89 OKA, SUZUO. "*Meian* to *The Golden Bowl*: Mouhitotsu no Kankei" [The relation of *Meian* and *Golden Bowl*]. *Eigo Seinen* (Tokyo) 123:68-69.

In Japanese.

Notes that similarities can be detected between the works of James and those of Soseki Natsume not only in situation and plot, but also in narrative technique. In *Meian*, Natsume adopts a narrative technique that places equal emphasis on both the observer and the observed, reminiscent of James's middle and late work, including *The Golden Bowl*.

90 OLIVER, CLINTON. "Henry James as a Social Critic." In *Der Englische Soziale Roman Im Neuhzehnten Jahrhundert*. Edited by Konrad Gross. Darmstadt: Wissenschlaftliche Buchgesellschaft, Neuhzehnten Jahrhundert (Wege der Forschung 466), pp. 372-89.

Sees both *The Bostonians* and *The Princess Casamassima* as critiques of society and economic inequalities. One may disagree with James's solution – "art as a primary moralizing force" – but cannot accuse him of being oblivious to social problems.

Reprint of *Antioch Review* 7 (1947):243-58.

91 OTT, JOSEPHINE. "Henry James, critique de Balzac." *L'Année Balzacienne*:273-81.

In French.

Discusses Maurice A. Geracht's "Balzac on 'Le Bénédictin du Réel'" [*L'Année Balzacienne* (1975):289-306], an essay on James and Balzac. James showed respect for Balzac in his criticism throughout his career, as noted by Geracht. Geracht's treatment is poor, however, because he does not consider changes in James's attitudes over the course of his career and because he was using inadequate translations of James's works.

*92 OWEN, A.E. "Theory and Form in the Modern Short Story, with Special Reference to Robert Louis Stevenson, Henry James, and Joseph Conrad." Ph.D. dissertation, London University, Birkbeck College.

Source: *Annual Bibliography of English Language and Literature* 56 (1981):436, item 8014.

93 PAGE, PHILIP. "*The Princess Casamassima*: Suicide and 'The Penetrating Imaginaton.'" *Tennessee Studies in Literature* 22:162-69.

Sees the imagery of "penetrating entrances" as a reflection of James's strategy in developing character and plot as well as an invitation for the reader to share in the novelist's creative act. This last aspect is crucial in understanding the character of Hyacinth Robinson, the novel's "most fundamental mystery."

94 PALMER, JAMES W. "Cinematic Ambiguity: James's *The Turn of the Screw* and Clayton's *The Innocents*." *Literature/Film Quarterly* 5, no. 3 (Summer):198-215.

Focuses on Clayton's creation of ambiguity in his 1962 film version of James's tale. Clayton uses Freudian symbols, the dissolve, and a shifting point of view to convey the atmosphere of the tale.

*95 PANCOST, DAVID WILLIAMS. "Washington Irving's 'Sketch Book' and American Literature to the Rise of Realism: Framed Narrative, the Pictorial Mode, and Irony in the Fiction of Irving, Longfellow, Kennedy, Poe, Hawthorne, Melville, Howells, Twain, James, and Others." Ph.D. dissertation, Duke University.

Source: Budd, 1983.32, p. 29, item 132.

1977

96   PANICHAS, GEORGE A. "The Jamesian Mirror." *Modern Age: A Quarterly Review* 21, no. 2 (Spring):200-3.
      Reviews the second volume of Edel's *Henry James Letters*. The letters of the years 1875 to 1883 reveal James's "moral purposiveness" and dedication to his art as well as his "creative awareness of his life's destiny."
      Reprinted 1982.113.

97   PARRILL, WILLIAM. "Peter Milton, Henry James, and 'The Jolly Corner.'" *Innisfree* 4:16-25.
      Argues that Milton's suite of etchings for "The Jolly Corner" successfully illustrates the tale because he focuses on and juxtaposes motifs rather than on representing incidents from the narrative. As a result, he remains faithful to the text while expanding its meaning.

98   PERSON, LELAND SPENCER, Jr. "Aesthetic Headaches: Images of Women in American Fiction." Ph.D. dissertation, Indiana University, 334 pp.
      Argues that male protagonists have typically denied female characters humanity and identity, stereotyping them either as lifeless or destructive. The "failure of imagination" of these protagonists reflects the failure of American culture in regard to women. A variety of nineteenth-century fiction is discussed, including *Roderick Hudson* and *The American*.
      See *Dissertation Abstracts International* 38, no. 11 (1978):6730A.

99   PHILBIN, ALICE IRENE. "The Literary *Femme Fatale*–A Social Fiction: The Willful Female in the Deterministic Vision of Thomas Hardy and in the Psychological Vision of Henry James." Ph.D. dissertation, Southern Illinois University, Carbondale, 303 pp.
      Examines Hardy's and James's femme fatales within each author's psychosocial milieu and aesthetic vision. The early work of James's and Hardy depend on stereotypical renderings of the femme fatale; in their later work, however, both explore "the complex nature of the socially abused femme fatale."
      See *Dissertation Abstracts International* 38, no. 5 (1977):2815A-2816A.

100   PHILLIPS, KATHY JANETTE. "Self-Conscious Narration in the
        Works of Henry James, Marcel Proust, Gertrude Stein and Alain
        Robbe-Grillet." Ph.D. dissertation, Brown University, 185 pp.
            Examines the "self-conscious devices"-including reticence, plot
        repetition, and internal gloss, in these writers to show a chronological
        development in reflexivity from the nineteenth to twentieth century and
        to argue that ultimately such self-consciousness leads the reader back
        to the larger world even while it celebrates an enclosed world.
            See *Dissertation Abstracts International* 38, no. 12 (1978):7314
        A-7315A.

101   PORAT, ZEPHYRA. "The Madonna and the Cat: Transcendental
        Idealism and Tragic Realism in Henry James's *The Portrait of a
        Lady.*" *Hebrew University Studies in Literature* 5:67-101.
            Attributes Ralph's and Isabel's failure to love to Emersonian
        self-reliance and self-sufficiency. Through the tragic fates of both
        characters, James questions Emerson's faith in the individual
        personality and its ability to transcend the persona society imposes
        upon it.

102   POWERS, LYALL. "Self-Portrait by Henry James." *Michigan
        Alumnus Quarterly Review* 16:113-17.
            Reviews *Henry James Letters I,* edited by Leon Edel. James's
        early letters reflect his concern with his health and his financial
        situation, his response to Europe, and his fondness for Newport.
        Powers finds "the germ of all of James's greatest fiction" present in
        many of these letters.

103   PURDY, STROTHER B. *The Hole in the Fabric: Science,
        Contemporary Literature, and Henry James.* Critical Essays in
        Modern Literature. Pittsburgh: University of Pittsburgh Press, 228
        pp.
            Argues that contemporary literature-particularly the work of
        Beckett, Nabokov, Barth, Vonnegut, Grass, Robbe-Grillet, Ionesco,
        and Borges-is "suspended" between modern scientific theories and a
        literary tradition "faced with the problem of expressing what has never
        been known before." James represents this tradition in his use of the
        supernatural and terror, disoriented time, psychological analysis of the
        erotic, and the concept of nothingness. Works discussed in this study

1977

include "The Turn of the Screw," "The Jolly Corner," *The Sense of the Past, The Awkward Age*, and "The Beast in the Jungle."

104   PUTT, S. GORLEY. "Henry James, Radical Gentleman." *Massachusetts Review* 18, no. 1 (Spring):179-86.
       Argues that James's reputation as an ivory tower intellectual is erroneous because James both satirized and criticized snobbishness, hypocrisy, and greed in his fiction.

105   RIEWALD, J.G. "[Henry James]." In *Beerbohm's Literary Caricatures from Homer to Huxley*. Hamden, Conn.: Archon Press, pp. 224-35.
       Reproduces and briefly annotates four caricatures of James: "Mr. Henry James" (c. 1904); "Mr. Henry James Revisiting America" (1905); "London in November, and Mr. Henry James in London" (1907); and "The Old Pilgrim Comes Home: (1913). The annotation includes a description of the caricature, the occasion of its creation, and Beerbohm's comments on it.

106   RIHOIT, CATHERINE. "L'angle et la différence: L'humor Jamesien, desir de fémininité." *Revue Française d'Etudes Américaines*, 4 (November):72-75.
       In French.

107   RIMMON, SHLOMITH. *The Concept of Ambiguity: The Example of James*. Chicago: University of Chicago Press, xiii, 257 pp.
       Defines ambiguity as the coexistence of conjunction of mutually exclusive elements and distinguishes those elements of narrative and verbal ambiguity. Rimmon then applies the points raised in her discussion of theory to "The Lesson of the Master," "The Figure in the Carpet," "The Turn of the Screw," and *The Sacred Fount*.
       Revision of Ph.D. dissertation, University of London, 1974.
       See also Salmon 1980.123, Williams 1984.225, and Falconer 1987.36. See also Pecora 1985.130.

108   ROSENBLATT, JASON P. "Bridegroom and Bride in 'The Jolly Corner.'" *Studies in Short Fiction* 14, no. 3 (Summer):282-84.

1977

Examines the way in which the parable of the wise and foolish virgins (Matthew 25) is employed in this tale. The parable is reflected in the tale's theme as well as in the structure of "moral opposites."

109   ROUTH, MICHAEL. "Isabel Archer's 'Inconsequence': A Motif Analysis of *The Portrait of a Lady*." *Journal of Narrative Technique* 7, no. 2 (Spring):128-41.
     Argues that Isabel's intellect and spirit are irreconcilable and that this "inconsequence" is a fatal character flaw. In tracing this trait throughout the novel, Routh also looks at the connected motifs of appearance and reality, imagination and theory, convention, and fear. This network of motifs unifies the novel's diverse elements.

110   ROWE, JOHN C[ARLOS]. "The Authority of the Sign in Henry James's *The Sacred Fount*." *Criticism* 19, no. 3 (Summer):223-40.
     Argues that the novel directly addresses the problem of "artistic identity"; that is, the necessity of possessing the imaginative power to recognize the limitations that conventions impose on the individual. The narrator, as a critic of the novel's social world, becomes an artist, "whose imaginative palaces enable him to measure the conventional and determinate meanings that threaten and thus make possible his identity."

111   RUTLEDGE, HARRY C. "Contest and Possession: Classical Imagery in Henry James' *The Golden Bowl*." *The Comparitist: Journal of the Southern Comparative Literature Association* 1:58-64.
     Traces the classical imagery in the novel, much of which has connotations of violence and darkness. Classical images dominate two crucial scenes in the novel: the breaking of the golden bowl, and Charlotte's announcement of the plan to return to America.

112   SALLEE, JONEL CURTIS. "Circles of the Self." Ph.D. dissertation, University of Kentucky, 180 pp.
     Examines the use of the circle metaphor to represent the perceiving self in Whitman's "Song of Myself." James's *The Ambassadors*, Adam's *The Education of Henry Adams*, and Norris's *The Octopus*. Lambert Strether's perceptions solidify and set boundaries to reality (the circumference of the circle) but can break those boundaries once he is able to recognize them as limitations.

1977

See *Dissertation Abstracts International* 38, no. 11 (1978):6730A.

113 SEBOUHIAN, GEORGE. "Adam Verver: Emerson's Poet." *Markham Review* 7 (Fall):39-40.
Argues that Adam is Emerson's "new American," a "seer-poet," noting that James was more receptive to Emerson's transcendentalism during his later years than during his earlier years.

114 SEED, DAVID. "Hyacinth Robinson and the Politics of *The Princess Casamassima*." *Etudes Anglaises* 30, no. 1 (January-March):30-39.
Sees the novel as a transition between realistic action and psychological drama, which explains why Hyacinth's "drama" is unconvincing. James fails to make a connection between Hyacinth's essentially passive idealism and his involvement in political action.

115 SHAW, JEAN BARRETT. "A Native of the James Family." Ph.D. dissertation, University of Louisville, 401 pp.
Examines the interrelationships among the ideas of Henry James Senior, William James, and Henry James and traces those ideas in James's fiction throughout his career, beginning with the early international fiction and concluding with the novels of the major phase.
See *Dissertation Abstracts International* 38, no. 5 (1977):2755A.

116 SHELENY, HARVEY. "Some Aspects of *Brideshead Revisited*: A Comparison with Henry James' *The American*." *Evelyn Waugh Newsletter* 11, no. 2 (Autumn):4-7.
Parallels the two novels, noting the similar families, but focusing on Claire de Cintré and Julia. Claire becomes a nun; Julia becomes nun-like, living a life of chastity and service to others.

117 SHOLLENBERGER, JAMES EDWARD. "'A Box of Fixed Dimensions': Dramatic Structure and the Plays of Henry James." Ph.D. dissertation, Ohio State University, 424 pp.
Argues that James failed as a dramatist because he did not understand the relationship between an audience and stage action; his plays do not contain the necessary internal logic. Examined here are the fifteen plays James wrote during the years 1869 to 1909.

1977

See *Dissertation Abstracts International* 38, no. 8 (1978):4455A.

118 SICKER, PHILIP TIMOTHY. "Beyond the Image: Love and the Quest for Identity in the Fiction of Henry James." Ph.D. dissertation, University of Virginia, 310 pp.

Argues that in James's fiction the characters "continually seek a stable, fully-integrated identity through romantic love" but must progress from idealization of the other to recognition of a kindred spirit. With that recognition only can these characters escape the isolation of consciousness.

See *Dissertation Abstracts International* 39, no. 2 (1978):875A.

119 SKILTON, DAVID. "Late Victorian Choices: James, Wilde, Gissing and Moore." In *The English Novel: Defoe to the Victorians*. New York: Barnes & Noble, pp. 178-91.

Regards James as "the most important technician" of the period, who turned to Balzac and Flaubert for methods of rendering consciousness. James's focus on the individual mind distinguishes him from earlier British novelists and presages the fiction of the twentieth century.

Reprinted 1985.130.

120 SMITH, CARL S. "James's Travels, Travel Writings, and the Development of His Art." *Modern Language Quarterly* 38, no. 4 (December):367-80.

Examines a wide array of nonfiction (essays, letters, autobiography, prefaces, etc.) to show how James's travels trained him as a novelist. Besides providing actual material for his fiction, his travels refined him as a perceptive observer, whose impressions give meaning to that which is observed.

121 SMITH, HENRY NASH. "On Henry James and 'The Jolly Corner.'" In *The American Short Story*. Edited by Calvin Skaggs. New York: Dell, pp. 122-28.

Discusses James's use of the supernatural to convey processes of thought "beyond the resources of ordinary language" and notes Barron's use of sexuality in his film adaptation of the tale as a way of making Brydon's psychological crisis credible.

1977

122 SOMERS, PAUL P., Jr. "Sherwood Anderson's Mastery of Narrative Distance." *Twentieth Century Literature* 23, no. 1 (February):84-93.

Suggests that Anderson's use of narrative distance between the implied author and the narrator in three tales may have been influenced by James's "A Light Man" and "The Aspern Papers."

123 SPENGEMANN, WILLIAM C. "Henry James." In *The Adventurous Muse: The Poetics of American Fiction 1789-1900*. New Haven: Yale University Press, pp. 241-63.

Argues that between *The American* and *The Ambassadors* James shifts from a Romantic narrative, in which travel is justified by a goal representing "some universal truth outside art," to a novel in which travel and art become their own justifications. *The Ambassadors* represents a radical change in American fiction, in that the novel depicts a character whose discovery of art endows him with "aesthetic grace" instead of damning him to "moral perdition."

124 SPILKA, MARK. "Henry James and Walter Besant: 'The Art of Fiction' Controversy." In *Towards a Poetics of Fiction*. Bloomington: Indiana University Press, pp. 190-208.

Details the controversy, beginning with an analysis of Besant's positions and James's responses. James especially took issue with Besant's adherance to rules and categories. Spilka focuses on the revolutionary aspects of James's "The Art of Fiction," including his redefinition of experience in terms of consciousness, his rejection of conventional morality, his coupling of moral and artistic sensibility, and his emphasis on technique instead of content.

125 STAFFORD, WILLIAM T. "Henry James." In *American Literary Scholarship: An Annual/1975*. Edited by James Woodress. Durham: Duke University Press, pp. 115-30.

Surveys criticism published in 1975.

126 STARER, MARILYN MORRIS. "A Review of Criticism on *The Ambassadors* 1903-1972." Ph.D. dissertation, State University of New York, Albany, 117 pp.

Surveys American reviews and scholarly and critical appraisals of the novel within their contemporary context. Individual chapters are devoted to criticism of language, characters, and theme. An annotated bibliography is also included.

See *Dissertation Abstracts International* 38, no. 3 (1977):1396A.

127   STEIN, WILLIAM BYSSHE. "*The Wings of the Dove*: James's Eucharist of *Punch*." *Centennial Review* 21, no. 3 (Summer):236-60.

Argues that *The Wings of the Dove* is a "comedy of social history" whose characters and plot are influenced by humorous magazines of which James was an avid reader. James, consciously and unconsciously, borrows the techniques of nineteenth-century magazine illustrators as a means of satire.

128   STELZIG, EUGENE L. "Henry James and the 'Immensities of Perception': Actors and Victims in *The Portrait of a Lady* and *The Wings of the Dove*." *Southern Humanities Review* 11, no. 3 (Summer):253-65.

Analyzes the "psychological vampirism" in the portraits of ladies as victims. Although Isabel Archer and Millie Theale are surrounded by predatory characters, in the end the two women triumph because they achieve an understanding of the "exploitative nature of human interaction."

129   STOWE, WILLIAM WHITFIELD. "Balzac, James, and the Realistic Novel." Ph.D. dissertation, Yale University, 341 pp.

Examines selected novels of Balzac and James to illuminate techniques of realism, to define a poetics of realism, and to trace Balzac's and James's experimentation with dramatic techniques. Stowe's study shows that "literary sophistication" can be achieved with realism and that realism remains viable within modern experimentation.

See *Dissertation Abstracts Internatinal* 39, no. 3 (1978):2241A-2242A.

130   STYCZYNSKA, ADELA. *The Art of Henry James's Nouvelle: A Study of Theme and Form.* Lódzki, Poland: Uniwersytet Lódzki, 258 pp.

Discusses themes and techniques of James's novellas throughout his career beginning with *A Bundle of Letters* (1879) and concluding with "The Jolly Corner" (1908). James's novellas combine

1977

drama and fiction; their structure is based on the well-made play with chapters corresponding to acts while chacterization is similar to that of the novel. James often experiments with point of view in his novellas; Styczynska notes that "the role of observer – 'reflector' – is of essential importance" as subject and technique. James is a "master and forerunner" of the 20th century novella, and has influenced both fiction and drama.

131   SUTHERLAND, JUDITH CLEVELAND. "At the Edge: Problematic Fictions of Poe, James, and Hawthorne." Ph.D. dissertation, University of Iowa, 165 pp.
    Argues that Poe's *The Narrative of Arthur Gordon Pym*, Hawthorne's *The Marble Fawn*, and James's *The Sacred Fount* are difficult to explicate because each novel is an attempt to define "the special problems inherent in the practice of an American symbolist aesthetic."
    See *Dissertation Abstracts International* 39, no. 1 (1978):289A-290A.

132   TALLMAN, WARREN. "Henry James' Princess." *Open Letter*, 3d Ser., no. 6 (Winter 1976-1977):20-36.
    Focuses on Hyacinth's inability to transcend his blighted life and to attain "absolute inner freedom" that is the prerequisite for "communion" with the princess. Christina thus remains detached from the world of the novel. In his later novels James will create fictional worlds in which his princesses will have "free play and full force."

133   TAYLOR, LINDA J. "Contemporary Critical Response to Henry James's *The Bostonians*: An Annotated Checklist." *Resources for American Literary Study* 7, no. 2 (Autumn):134-51.
    Annotates sixty-two reviews, appearing from 1885 to 1887. Taylor notes that the critical response to the novel was much more favorable than modern critics acknowledge.

134   THOMSON, PATRICIA. "'Dear Old George.'" In *George Sand and the Victorians: Her Influence and Reputation in Nineteenth-Century England*. New York: Columbia University Press, pp. 216-44, 268-70.
    Discusses in detail James's attitudes toward and writings about Sand and summarizes her influence on James's fiction throughout his

career. She was instrumental in James's analyses of emotion and contributed to his understanding of women.

135 TINTNER, ADELINE R. "Autobiography as Fiction: 'The Usurping Consciousness' as Hero of James's Memoirs." *Twentieth Century Literature* 23, no. 2 (May):239-60.

Reads *A Small Boy and Others* and *Notes of a Son and Brother* as autobiographical novels in which the consciousness is hero, and compares them to Proust's *Du côté du chez Swann* and Joyce's *A Portrait of the Artist as a Young Man*. With Proust and James, there is a "spontaneous evolution" in sensibility while Joyce's work bears evidence of the lessons he learned from James.

136 _____. "James and Balzac: *The Bostonians* and 'La Fille aux yeux d'or.'" *Comparative Literature* 29, no. 3 (Summer):241-54.

Traces James's use of Balzac's tale, both in the way he appropriated it and rewrote it. Tintner finds similarities in the basic structure of the two works and suggests that James also wished to criticize the decadent strain in the French novel.

Revised 1987.122.

137 _____. "A Source from *Roderick Hudson* for the Title of *The Custom of the Country*." *NMAL: Notes on Modern American Literature* 1:Item 34.

Suggests that Wharton took her title from Christina Light's remark in *Roderick Hudson* rather than from Fletcher's and Massinger's play.

138 _____. "Why James Quoted Gibbon in 'Glasses.'" *Studies in Short Fiction* 14, no. 3 (Summer):287-88.

Argues that the reference to Gibbon underscores the narrator's "usurping ironic glance."

139 TODOROV, TZVETAN. "The Ghosts of Henry James." In *The Poetics of Prose*. Translated by Richard Howard. Ithaca: Cornell University Press, pp. 179-89.

Surveys James's ghost stories to show the limitations of classifying his oeuvre by genre.

1977

140 ____. "The Secret of Narrative." In *The Poetics of Prose*. Translated by Richard Howard. Ithaca: Cornell University Press, pp. 143-78.

Argues that James's fiction is always based on "the quest for an absolute and absent cause" and uses numerous tales as examples. Todorov examines the variants of the absent – including secrets, ghosts, death, and art – and relates elements within the tale – structure, plot, style, and theme – to the quest for the absent.

See also Williams 1984.225.

141 ____. "The Verbal Age." Translated by Patricia Martin Gibby. *Critical Inquiry* 4, no. 2 (Summer):351-71.

Calls the problem of the relation between reader and text the "nerve center" of *The Awkward Age* and examines the ways in which James uses referential vagueness to explore this problem. Todorov sees the novel as "the perfect fusion of form and content" because the novel itself represents "the obliquity of language and the uncertainty of the world."

142 WARNER, JOHN M. "'In View of Other Matters': The Religious Dimensions of *The Ambassadors*." *Essays in Literature* 4, no. 1 (Spring):78-94.

Shows that at the end of the novel Strether achieves a religious vision of man and not simply a "synthesis of moral and aesthetic values." His renunciation is an act of selflessness; his mode of salvation is as a "disinterested witness to the truth he has arrived at."

143 WILSON, EDMUND. *Letters on Literature and Politics 1912-1972*. Edited by Elena Wilson. New York: Farrar, Straus and Giroux, xxxvii, 768 pp.

Contains many comments on James's work, including letters to Edna Kenton, Morton D. Zabel, and Leon Edel in which Wilson discusses James's ambiguity in "The Turn of the Screw" and *The Sacred Fount*. He also praises Edel's collections of James's nonfiction, *The American Essays of Henry James* and *The Future of the Novel*, noting that "you have really done a service in collecting this stuff."

144 WILSON, RAYMOND J. "Henry James and F. Scott Fitzgerald: Americans Abroad." *Research Studies* 45, no. 2 (June):82-91.

Demonstrates that the similarities in James's and Fitzgerald's depiction of Americans abroad reveal that the expatriate experience is a powerful one, transcending time and circumstance.

145 WINNER, VIOLA HOPKINS. "The American Pictorial Vision: Objects and Ideas in Hawthorne, James, and Hemingway." *Studies in American Fiction* 5, no. 1 (Spring):143-59.

Sees as "uniquely American" these authors' use of pictorial art to develop character and theme and to provide structural unity or spatial order. Winner's discussion of James focuses on *The Ambassadors*, which is influenced and permeated by Impressionism.

146 WOOD, CARL. "Frederick Winterbourne, James's Prisoner of Chillon." *Studies in the Novel* 9, no. 1 (Spring):33-45.

Argues that Byron's poem "The Prisoner of Chillon" is evoked throughout "Daisy Miller" and provides a key to Winterbourne's character. Wood finds a parallel between Bonnivard's desolation and Winterbourne's isolation at the novella's end.

147 YASEEN, M. "An Aspect of *The Ambassadors*." *Aligarh Journal of English Studies* 2:221-30.

Argues that the "polar opposition" between the cultures of New England and Europe is central in this novel and serves the double purpose of social criticism as well as criticism of the Arnoldian sense of life.

148 ZIOLKOWSKI, THEODORE. "Image as Motif: The Haunted Portrait." In *Disenchanted Images: A Literary Iconology*. Princeton: Princeton University Press, pp. 134-40.

Argues that in *The Sense of the Past* James inverts the traditional ghost story by depicting the present haunting the past. James couples two traditional devices—the ghost story and transporting a contemporary into the past—to create an original version of the haunted portrait. In so doing, James plays on his own obsession of being trapped in the past.

1977

149 ____. "Image as Theme: Venus and the Ring." In *Dissenchanted Images: A Literary Iconology*. Princeton: Princeton University Press, pp. 61-65.

Compares "The Last of the Valerii" with Mérimée's "The Venus of Ille," noting the many parallels with Mérimée's tale and the legend of Venus and the king. James "disenchants" the legend by shifting from the supernatural to the psychological.

1978

1 ANAND, MULK RAJ. "A Note on Henry James and the Art of Fiction in India." *Commonwealth Quarterly* 2, no. 7:3-7.

Argues that the Indian novelist, unlike James, cannot be "a dispassionate observer of Fate" but must be "a philosopher committed to life against death."

2 ARMSTRONG, PAUL B. "How Maisie Knows: The Phenomenology of James's Moral Vision." *Texas Studies in Literature and Language* 20, no. 4 (Winter):517-37.

Argues that the novel shows that morality originates from the structure of experience and not from dogma or convention. Maisie is proof of James's recognition that the "moral life" is ambiguous and incomplete and that it must continually evolve out of "the challenges and responsibilities of knowing, freedom, and care."

3 ____. "Knowing in James: A Phenomenological View." *Novel* 12, no. 1 (Fall):5-20.

Explores the meaning of "impression" for James, focusing on its epistemological and phenomenological implications, referring primarily to "The Art of Fiction." Armstrong concludes that the work of both Henry and William James brings phenomenology to "native ground."

4 AUERBACH, NINA. "Beyond the Self: The Spectacle of History and a New Religion." In *Communities of Women: An Idea in Fiction*. Cambridge: Harvard University Press, pp. 115-41.

Examines James's depiction of the female community in *The Bostonians* and his respect for women's demands. In discussing the novel's connecting politics with theatre, Auerbach touches upon *The Princess Casamassima* and *The Tragic Muse*.
Reprinted 1982.3.

5   AZIZ, MAQBOOL. Introduction to *The Tales of Henry James 1870-1874*. Oxford: Clarendon Press, xix-lix.
Describes the editorial problems entailed by the numerous published versions and revisions of James's tales; sketches the textual history and biographical background of the tales written during these years; and argues that in these early tales James articulates "the twin themes of dispossession and crisis of identity" that would dominate his work. Tales included: "Travelling Companions," "A Passionate Pilgrim," "At Isella," "Master Eustace," "Guest's Confession," "The Madonna of the Future," "The Sweetheart of M. Briseux," "The Last of the Valerii," "Mme. de Mauves," "Adina," "Professor Fargo," and "Eugene Pickering."

*6   BALDWIN, A.M. "Memory in Henry James, with Particular Reference to the *Autobiography*, "The Beast in the Jungle," "The Bench of Desolation," *The Ambassadors*," *The Wings of the Dove*." Ph.D. dissertation, University of London, Westfield College.
Source: *Annual Bibliography of English Language and Literature* 55 (1980):481, item 8908.

*7   BARBER, JOHN. "Restoration of King James." *Daily Telegraph* (17 July):10.
Source: *British Humanities Index* 1978, p. 284.

8   BARRETT, PHYLLIS WHITESIDE. "More American Adams: Women Heroes in American Fiction." Ph.D. dissertation, University of Rhode Island, 109 pp.
Argues that many American heroines, including James's Isabel, are part of the tradition of the American Adam rather than of the American Eve.
See *Dissertation Abstracts International* 40, no. 2 (1979):847A-848A.

1978

9   BARRY, PETER. "In Fairness to the Master's Wife: A Re-Interpretation of *The Lesson of the Master*." *Studies in Short Fiction* 15, no. 4 (Fall):385-89.
    Argues that the character of St. George, who is often misread by Overt, shows that while an artist must make choices, he must also take responsibility for them.

10   BARSTOW, JANE MISSNER. "Originality and Conventionality in *The Princess Casamassima*." *Genre* 11, no. 3 (Fall):445-58.
    Traces the interplay of originality and conventionality throughout the novel, especially in the way this dichotomy is present in the patterns of mimicry and acting. Barstow expands this "problematic" of originality and conventionality to embrace the novel itself and ultimately all writing.

11   BENGELS, BARBARA. "The Term of the 'Screw': Key to Imagery in Henry James's 'The Turn of the Screw.'" *Studies in Short Fiction* 15, no. 3 (Summer):323-27.
    Examines the connotations of the image of the screw–the increase of pressure, a boat's propeller, sexual intercourse–and notes that James uses a single image to suggest and unify many diverse strands of imagery.

12   BERKSON, DOROTHY WARREN. "The Ordeal of the American Girl: Female Initiation in Henry James's Fiction." Ph.D. dissertation, University of Illinois, Champaign-Urbana, 202 pp.
    Demonstrates that the American girl is the key to James's moral and social ethic: through her James rejects the myth of the American Adam and the frontier ethic and turns instead to the issue of personal integrity within society. Works examined include "The Last of the Valerii," "Madame de Mauves," "Daisy Miller," *Washington Square, The Portrait of a Lady, The Bostonians, The Wings of the Dove,* and *The Golden Bowl.*
    See *Dissertation Abstracts International* 39, no. 1 (1978):284A.

13   BOGARDUS, RALPH F. "Henry James and the Art of Illustration." *Centennial Review* 22, no. 1 (Winter):77-94.

Studies James's attitudes toward illustrating his work and concludes that in James's view, illustration should complement the text, not interfere with it.

*14   BURLUI, IRINA. "Short Fiction in the Work of Henry James." Ph.D. dissertation, Bucharest University.
Source: Budd, 1983.32, p. 5, item 20.

15   CHARNEY, HANNA. "Variations by Henry James on a Theme of Balzac." *New York Literary Forum* 2:69-75.
Suggests that the idea of absence dominating "The Death of the Lion" can be illuminated by an earlier tale, "The Madonna of the Future," which in turn was inspired by Balzac's "Le Chef d'Oeuvre inconnu."

16   CLARK, SUSAN. "A Note on *The Turn of the Screw*: Death from Natural Causes." *Studies in Short Fiction* 15, no. 1 (Winter):110-12.
Suggests that Miles may have had a heart murmur, resulting in cardiac arrest brought about by physical and emotional overexertion.

17   COHN, DORRIT. *Transparent Minds: Narrative Modes for Presenting Consciousness in Fiction*. Princeton: Princeton University Press, x, 331 pp.
Examines the various kinds of narrative perspectives in the novel. James is mentioned briefly throughout the text, both for his centers of consciousness and for his narrators.

18   COLMER, JOHN. "Political Action and the Crisis of Conscience." In *Coleridge to Catch-22: Images of Society*. New York: St. Martin's, pp. 91-104.
Argues that in *The Princess Casamassima* James examines the conflict between the individual conscience and the need for social reform. In the novel James's "political vision is inseparable from his literary form."

19   _____. "Sex, the Family, and the New Women." In *Coleridge to Catch-22: Images of Society*. New York: St. Martin's, pp. 105-21.

1978

Argues that *The Bostonians* is not about women's emancipation but takes as its central concern the private sacrifices expected by public life. The novel's characters seek publicity and social reform as ways to escape solitude and as substitutes for "normal living."

20 CORSE, SANDRA BAILEY. "The Image of the Novelist in the Critical Works of Henry James." Ph.D. dissertation, Georgia State University, 169 pp.

Examines James's criticism of other novelists, showing that throughout his career he moved from a fairly moralistic view to one that was tolerant and open. Corse divides the criticism according to the novelists' nationality, describing James's judgment of strengths and weakness.

See *Dissertation Abstracts International* 39, no. 8 (1979):4935A-4936A.

21 COSTANZO, WILLIAM VINCENT. "Entangling Metaphors: A Study of the Figurative Language in James and Conrad." Ph.D. dissertation, Columbia University, 214 pp.

Argues that both writers obscure the distinction between literal and figurative language and, in so doing, challenge the assumptions of realism and artistic representation. Works discussed include Conrad's *Lord Jim, Heart of Darkness, An Outcast of the Islands, Nostromo, Victory,* "The Secret Sharer," and *The Shadow-Line*; James's works include "The Beast in the Jungle," *The Ambassadors,* "The Figure in the Carpet," "The Jolly Corner," *The Sacred Fount, The Wings of the Dove,* and *The Sense of the Past.*

See *Dissertation Abstracts International* 39, no. 4 (1978):2285-2286A.

22 CRAWFORD, FRED D., and MORTON, BRUCE. "Hemingway and Brooks: The Mystery of 'Henry's Bicycle.'" *Studies in American Fiction* 6, no. 1 (Spring):106-9.

Explains Bill Gorton's allusion to "Henry's bicycle" in *The Sun Also Rises* as a "jab" at Van Wyck Brooks's suggestion in *The Pilgrimage of Henry James* that an expatriate will pay for his detachment.

23   CROWLEY, J. DONALD, and HOCKS, RICHARD A., eds. *The Wings of the Dove*. Norton Critical Edition. New York: W.W. Norton & Co., viii, 583 pp.

This volume includes the New York Edition of the novel, its preface, textual variants, excerpts from James's *Notebooks*, letters, *Italian Hours, Notes of a Son and Brother*, and "Is There a Life After Death?" The volume also contains reprints of the following criticism:

"Mr. Henry James's New Book," pp. 481-83, reprinted from *Times Literary Supplement* (London), September 1902, p. 263;

William Dean Howells, "Mr. Henry James's Later Work," pp. 483-87, reprinted from *North American Review* 176 (January 1903):126-31;

F.O. Matthiessen, "[James's Masterpiece]," pp. 488-504, reprinted from *Henry James: The Major Phase* (1944), pp. 42-3, 50-2, 55-60, 62-80;

R.P. Blackmur, "[Dramas of the Soil in Action]," pp. 504-7, reprint of Introduction to *The Golden Bowl* (1952), v-x;

Ernest Sandeen, "*The Wings of the Dove* and *The Portrait of a Lady*: A Study of Henry James's Later Phase," pp. 507-20, reprinted from *PMLA* 69 (December 1954):1060-1, 1064-75;

Christof Wegelin, "The Lesson of Spiritual Beauty," pp. 520-29, reprinted from *The Image of Europe in Henry James* (1958), pp. 106-9, 112-15, 117-21;

J.A. Ward, "Social Disintegration in *The Wings of the Dove*," pp. 529-35, reprinted from *Criticism* 2 (Spring 1960):190-95, 198-99, 200-1, 202-3;

Dorothea Krook, "[Milly's and Densher's Ordeal of Consciousness]," pp. 535-51, reprinted from *The Ordeal of Consciousness in Henry James* (1962), pp. 203-15, 221-29;

Sallie Sears, "[Kate Croy and Merton Densher]," pp. 551-63, reprinted from *The Negative Imagination: Form and Perspective in the Novels of Henry James* (1968), pp. 63-74, 90-98;

Laurence B. Holland, pp. 563-73, reprinted from *The Expense of Vision* (1964), pp. 285-91, 298-301, 306-10;

Charles Thomas Samuels, "[A Flawed Hymn to Renunciation]," pp. 574-580, reprinted from *The Ambiguity of Henry James* (1971), pp. 61-65, 66-68, 69-72.

24   DAHL, CURTIS. "The Swiss Cottage's Owner: A Model for J.L. Westgate in James' *An International Episode*." *American Notes and Queries* 17, no. 4 (December):58-60.

1978

Argues that Colonel George T.M. Davis is the model for J.L. Westgate and that the house described in the tale matches Davis's house in Newport, called the Swiss Cottage.

*25   DANIELS, B.J. "A Study of Selected Autobiographical Writings of Henry Adams, Henry James, William Dean Howells and Mark Twain." Ph.D. dissertation, University of London, University College.
           Source: *Annual Bibliography of English Language and Literature* 55 (1980):414, item 7604.

26   DAVIS, SARA deSAUSSURE. "*The Bostonians* Reconsidered." *TSE: Tulane Studies in English* 23:39-60.
           Argues that James's depiction of the women's movement of the nineteenth century is "an allegory of post-war feminism" and that his vision is both provocative and historically valid. DeSaussure focuses on the characters of Verena and Basil, noting that while the portrayal of Basil is inconsistent, James does not sympathize with his views.

27   DEL FATTORE, JOAN "The Hidden Self: A Study of the Shadow Figure in American Short Fiction." Ph.D. dissertation, Pennsylvania State University, 217 pp.
           Examines the shadow figure, an archetypal pattern functioning as a principle of structure, to show that Jungian archetypal analysis can be used to understand the protagonist's experience and to compare different authors' handling of a common pattern. James's "The Beast in the Jungle" and "The Jolly Corner" are included in the works discussed.
           See *Dissertation Abstracts International* 39, 'no. 10 (1979):6127A.

28   DEMILLE, BARBARA MUNN. "The Imperatives of the Imagination: Dickens, James, Conrad, and Wallace Stevens." Ph.D. dissertation, State University of New York, Buffalo, 198 pp.
           Traces the concept of the imagination in these authors, beginning with its Romantic legacy as a means of connecting with the environment but tending also toward solipsism. James differentiates between the selfish and disinterested exercise of the imagination and links it to the effort to understand the moral implications of a situation.

1978

See *Dissertation Abstracts International* 39, no. 9 (1979):5522A-5523A.

29 DONADIO, STEPHEN. *Nietzsche, Henry James, and the Artistic Will*. New York: Oxford University Press, xviii, 347 pp.
    Argues for a connection between Nietzsche's and James's belief in art as a means of creating values and enhancing experience, based on Emerson. Donadio traces Emerson's ideas in the works of Nietzsche and James and shows how they shaped each man's concept of the artist, the nature of reality, and the act of perception.

30 DONALDSON, SCOTT, and MASSA, ANN. "Henry James: Expatriate Extraordinary." In *American Literature: Nineteenth and Early Twentieth Centuries*. New York: Barnes & Noble, pp. 37-46.
    Argues that James's attitude toward Europe and America was ambiguous: he appreciated and depreciated both. Although James needed the "reverberations" of Europe to be an artist, he ultimately affirmed the power of America.

31 DONOGHUE, DENIS. "The American Style of Failure." In *The Sovereign Ghost: Studies in Imagination*. London: Faber and Faber, pp. 103-27.
    Reprint of 1976.48.

32 DURAND, RÉGIS. "*The Turn of the Screw*: le Déni de la fiction." *Etudes Anglaises* 31, no. 1 (January-March):176-87.
    In French.
    Demonstrates that in this tale James uses the device of the "look"–discreet and overt, imagined and real–to situate his story between the dream world and reality. He is thus able to seduce the reader into playing the game set up in the preface and prologue.

33 DYSON, J. PETER. "James' 'The Turn of the Screw.'" *Explicator* 35, no. 3 (Spring):9.
    Traces the governess's use of the image of the beast to prove she knows that she is the source of evil.

1978

34   EDEL, LEON "Portrait of the Artist as an Old Man." *American Scholar* 47 (Winter):52-68.
Sketches Leo Tolstoy, William Butler Yeats, and Henry James in order to understand "some of the human drama and human values in aging." All three men reveal that aging is "a way of crystallizing and summarizing the life of art."
Reprinted 1979.34.

35   ____. "The Two Libraries of Henry James." *University of Chicago Library Society Bulletin* 3, no. 1 (Winter):2-8.
Describes the range of James's library and the dispersal of it after his death. Edel also discusses James's "second library"–those books alluded to in James's fiction. James's libraries embody his conviction that "[i]t is art that *makes* life."
Reprinted 1987.35.

36   EDWARDS, MARY EMILY PARSONS. "I. Henry James and the Woman Novelist: The Double Standard in the Tales and Essays. II. Collaborative Learning: Small, Student-Centered Discussion Groups in the English Classroom." Ph.D. dissertation, University of Virginia, 73 pp.
Argues that James's attitudes toward women writers as well as the role of the woman writer in Victorian society are apparent in his writings about and interactions with various writers, including George Sand, Ouida, Marie Corelli, Vernon Lee, Mrs. Humphrey Ward, and Constance Fenimore Woolson. This study focuses not only on James's essays but on three tales as well: "The Next Time," "Greville Fane," and "The Velvet Glove." While James was a "catalyst for serious women writers," he was also a formidable critic.
See *Dissertation Abstracts International* 40, no. 2 (1979):833A.

37   EGGENSCHWILER, DAVID. "James's 'The Pupil': A Moral Tale without a Moral." *Studies in Short Fiction* 15, no. 4 (Fall):435-44.
Regards Pemberton as crucial to the tale's "moral order," which does not designate guilt or innocence, but which shows "the complexities and dangers of the moral life."

38   FADERMAN, LILLIAN. "Female Same-Sex Relationships in Novels by Longfellow, Holmes, and James." *New England Quarterly* 51, no. 3 (September):309-32.

Examines the treatment of female same-sex relationships in Longfellow's *Kavanaugh*, Holmes's *A Mortal Antipathy*, and James's *The Bostonians*. During the nineteenth century such relationships were seen as normal; twentieth-century pejorative labels – such as perversion, lesbianism, or inversion – are not applicable.

39   FALK, ROBERT. "Henry James's *The American* as a Centennial Novel." In *Essays in Honor of Russel B. Nye*. Edited by Joseph Waldmeir. East Lansing: Michigan State University Press, pp. 31-44.

Argues that this novel is James's response to the centennial because Christopher Newman is "a highly complex assimilation of national legends" and because it reflects James Sr.'s idealism about America as the "New World."

40   FELMAN, SHOSHANA. "Henry James: Folie et interprétation." In *La Folie et La Chose Littéraire*. Paris: Seuil, pp. 239-344.

In French.

Translation and reprint of 1977.36. Also reprinted in English 1980.51 and 1985.42.

41   FETTERLY, JUDITH. "*The Bostonians*: Henry James's Eternal Triangle." In *The Resisting Reader: A Feminist Approach to American Fiction*. Bloomington: Indiana University Press, pp. 101-53.

Focuses on the characters of Basil Ransom and Olive Chancellor as studies in power and powerlessness, respectively. James's fatalism about women's powerlessness is reflected in Verena's fate: to be doomed to find fulfillment in yielding to male domination. Although the story is conventional, James's vision of men and women is not, because his treatment of Olive has "the central elements of a radical feminism."

42   GERVAIS, DAVID. *Flaubert and Henry James: A Study in Contrasts*. London: Macmillan, xiii, 240 pp.

Examines Flaubert's view of tragedy and James's understanding of Flaubert as revealed in his essay on the novelist and in

The Portrait of a Lady. In depicting characters who were unsure whether they were victions of fate or evil, Flaubert achieved tragedy. James's characters take refuge in renunciation, a "pyrrhic moral heroism," and isolate themselves from the world.
Reprint of 1976.76.

43 GILCHRIST, ANDREA LYNN. "Melancholy and Mirth: Realistic and Self-Conscious Modes in Thackeray, Trollope and James." Ph.D. dissertation, Ohio State University, 160 pp.
Demonstrates that realism, which produces the illusion of verisimilitude, and self-consciousness, which draws attention to artifice, can be combined in a text. Gilchrist focuses on techniques that expose and reinforce realism and artifice. In *The Princess Casamassima* James invokes romantic heroism and at the same time portrays Hyacinth Robinson with ironic realism.
See *Dissertation Abstracts International* 39, no. 5 (1978):2952A-2952A.

44 GIRLING, HARRY KNOWLES. "A Toot of the Trumpet against the Scholarly Regiment of Editors (Redefining the Definitive: II)." *Bulletin of Research in the Humanities* 81, no. 3 (Autumn):297-323.
Argues against modern editors regularizing an author's spelling and punctuation and analyzes the changes in the first chapter of various editions of *The Princess Casamassima.*

45 GOETZ, WILLIAM R. "The Allegory of Representation in *The Tragic Muse*." *Journal of Narrative Technique* 8, no. 3 (Fall):151-64.
Sees the novel's subject as representation, which is examined in its three hierarchical levels: politics, painting, and drama. The novel also marks a turning point in James's artistic development, in that it closes his "pictorial phase" and initiates his dramatic experiments of the nineties.

46 GOLDFARB, RUSSELL M., and GOLDFARB, CLARE R. *Spiritualism and Nineteenth-Century Letters.* Rutherford, Madison, Teaneck: Fairleigh Dickinson University Press, pp. 159-60, 163-69.
Notes elements of spiritualism in various early tales, *The Bostonians,* and "The Turn of the Screw." In the tales, spiritualism is

connected with the ghostly and Gothic, while the characters of Verena and the governess are influenced by James's knowledge of mediums.

47 GREEN, ANDRÉ. "The Double and the Absent." Translated by Jacques F. Houis. In *Psychoanalysis, Creativity, and Literature: A French-American Inquiry*. Edited by Alan Roland. New York: Columbia University Press, pp. 271-92.

Argues that the critic, who is also a psychoanalyst, is a "mediator between reader and author, between text as writing and its realization as reading." Green cites *The Ambassadors* as an example of the psychoanalyst's mediation, focusing on a brief mention in the *Notebooks* that Strether had a failed relationship with his son, which is the key to Strether's character.

Reprint of "Le double et l'absent." *Critique* (May 1973).

48 GRIFFITH, THOMAS. "Henry James in Haiti, Where He Never Went." *Atlantic Monthly* 241, no. 5 (May):26, 28.

Sees "Jamesian situations" during a trip to Haiti, where Griffith read *The Golden Bowl*.

49 GUSTAFSON, JUDITH ALMA. "Strategies of Deception: Hawthorne and James and Their Readers." Ph.D. dissertation, Wayne State University, 254 pp.

Argues that Hawthorne and James drew on popular fiction conventions while at the same time they undermined them – thus both authors "double-deal" with their readers' expectations. This double-dealing is further supported by Hawthorne's concern with the subjectivity of perception and James's interest in the bewildered consciousness.

See *Dissertation Abstracts International* 39, no. 3 (1978):1567A.

50 HALLISEY, JEREMIAH JOSEPH. "Provincials in a Wider World: The National Novels of Twain, Adams, Howells, and James." Ph.D. dissertation, Stanford University, 233 pp.

Demonstrates that the novels of these writers – particularly Twain's *The Gilded Age*, Adams's *Democracy*, James's *The Bostonians*, and Howell's *A Modern Instance*, *The Rise of Silas Lapham*, and *A Hazard of New Fortunes* – focus on the experience of regional figures adjusting to an increasingly complex and urbanized America.

1978

See *Dissertation Abstracts International* 39, no. 2 (1978):884A.

51   HARDWIG, MARILYN ROSS. "Henry James's American Males in Europe: *Roderick Hudson, The American, The Ambassadors,* and *The Golden Bowl.*" Ph.D. dissertation, University of Tennessee, 211 pp.

   Links these novels with the issues of James's identity as an American and his perception of the relation between Europe and America. In the first two, James's concern is how well the American male can succeed in Europe; in the later two, how well Europe prepares the American male to return to America.

   See *Dissertation Abstracts International* 39, no. 6 (1978):3580A.

52   HIGGINS, JOANNA A. "The Ambassadorial Motif in *The Ambassadors.*" *Journal of Narrative Technique* 8, no. 3 (Fall):165-75.

   Argues that the ambassadorial motif relates Strether's renunciation to the acceptance of his own limitations. This motif operates at various levels–the level of action, of course, but it also "structures the development of Strether's perceptions" as he discovers the illusory nature of freedom and indeed the world. The ambassadorial motif prompts Higgins to call the novel epistemological in that it explores "the relationship between limited consciousness and the fluctuating boundaries of truth."

53   ISER, WOLFGANG. "Partial Art–Total Interpretation: Henry James, 'The Figure in the Carpet,' In Place of an Introduction." In *The Act of Reading: A Theory of Aesthetic Response.* Baltimore and London: Johns Hopkins University Press, pp. 3-10.

   Argues that this tale suggests that meaning is not something to be extracted from the text but is rather to be experienced. The tale gives an account of two approaches to the text: effect and explanation; Iser suggests that the irreconcilability of the two shows the limitations of the "traditional expository style of interpretation."

   Reprinted 1987.16. See also Williams 1984.225 and Bales 1986.5.

*54   JABLOW, BETSY LYNN. "Illustrated Texts from Dickens to James." Ph.D. dissertation, Stanford University.

   Source: Budd, 1983.32, p. 21, item 94.

1978

55 JONES, O.P. "The Cold World of London in 'The Beast in the Jungle.'" *Studies in American Fiction* 6, no. 2 (Autumn):227-35.
Suggests that James combines both Marcher's inner world and the outer world of London in the image of the beast. Marcher looks to London for a reflection of his "lost identity," but the "greedy world" of London actually reflects Marcher's egotism.

56 JUNGMAN, ROBERT E. "A Mock-Heroic Reference in *The Ambassadors*." *Modern British Literature* 3:79-80.
Suggests that Strether's parody of Caesar's "veni, vidi, vici" sets up a comparison between the two men that works to Strether's disadvantage and shows how James uses allusions to create humor.

57 KERY, LASZLO. "Henry James-kérdések" [Henry James: Problems]. *Filológiai Közlöny* (Budapest) 24:235-50.
In Hungarian.

58 KING, JEANETTE. "Henry James: Freedom and Form – The Tragic Conflict and the Novelists Dilemma." In *Tragedy in the Victorian Novel: Theory and Practice in the Novels of George Eliot, Thomas Hardy and Henry James*. Cambridge: Cambridge University Press, pp. 127-57.
Defines Jamesian tragedy as a sense of wasted life and traces its evolution in *The American, The Portrait of a Lady*, and *The Wings of the Dove*. Tragedy arises out of the main character's conflict between freedom and the need for form, a conflict that mirrors the balance James must achieve between the novel's inclusiveness and the selectivity of art.
Revision of 1975.71.

59 LABATT, BLAIR P. "The Exploring Logic of Henry James." *Cathiers d'études et de recherches victoriennes et édouardiennes* 7:67-81.
Argues that James replaces the "logic" of a didactic system of values with the exploration of the meaning of words. James's rejection of didacticism is a rejection of interpretation and confinement. Words, in contrast, are multifaceted. Labatt examines selected words from *What Maisie Knew, The Awkward Age*, and *The Golden Bowl*.

1978

60 LAVERS, NORMAN. "Art and Reality: The Theme of *The Sacred Fount.*" *Publications of the Arkansas Philological Association* 4, no. 2:37-44.

Argues that because the narrator reiterates many ideas from "The Art of Fiction," the novel is about James's own novel writing and his suspicion that the relationship between himself and the materials he uses for his art may be parasitic.

61 LAWSON, JESSIE EDMINSTER. "The Other Side of the Window: An Essay on Structural Iconography in English and American Fiction." Ph.D. dissertation, University of Missouri-Columbia, 290 pp.

Investigates the symbolic and structural function of the image of the window in nineteenth- and twentieth-century fiction. Lawson argues that the window is an external correlative to the conditions of being, enabling one to see beyond the self but also imposing a barrier between the self and the world. James is discussed in chapters 2 and 4.

See *Dissertation Abstracts International* 40, no. 1 (1979):232A-233A.

62 LESTER, PAULINE. "James's Use of Comedy in 'The Real Thing.'" *Studies in Short Fiction* 15, no. 1 (Winter):33-38.

Traces James's use of the conventions of comedy, as described by Frye, in order to examine the value of artistic representation.

63 McMASTER, R[OWLAND] D. "'An Honorable Emulation of the Author of *The Newcomes*': James and Thackeray." *Nineteenth-Century Fiction* 32, no. 4 (March):399-419.

Proposes that Thackeray's novel was a major literary influence on *Roderick Hudson* and *The American.* There are also many similarities shared by the two writers, including the "ambiguity of facts" and the role of the imagination in shaping the world.

Reprinted 1981.93.

64 MARTIN, ROBERT K. "The 'High Felicity' of Comradeship: A New Reading of *Roderick Hudson.*" *American Literary Realism, 1870-1910* 11, no. 1 (Spring):100-108.

Approaches the novel as the story of Rowland Mallet, who is destroyed by his love for Roderick Hudson. Martin also discusses the influence of *The Blithedale Romance* on the novel, particularly in James's use of the observer-narrator and the "surprise ending."

65 MAURIAC, FRANÇOIS. "James's *The Bostonians.*" In *Transatlantic Mirrors: Essays in Franco-American Literary Relations*. Boston: Twayne, pp. 89-92.
Reprint of 1959 essay. The sexual issues of the novel prompts Mauriac to question whether obsession with sex enriches or impoverishes the novelist. The answer depends on the novelist's mastery of life.

66 MERIVALE, PATRICIA. "The Esthetics of Perversion: Gothic Artifice in Henry James and Witold Gombrowicz." *PMLA* 93, no. 5 (October):992-1002.
Argues that Gombrowicz's *Pornografia* and *Cosmos* and James's "The Turn of the Screw" and *The Sacred Fount* borrow many conventions from the Gothic tradition, but that these novels are "metaphysical detection stories" and "self-reflexive texts." Merivale also discusses the morality of the novels' heroes, who incorporate "innocent" characters into their own texts.

67 MILICIA, JOSEPH. "Henry James's *Winter Tale*: 'The Bench of Desolation.'" *Studies in American Fiction* 6, no. 2 (Autumn):141-56.
Describes the resemblances between Shakespeare's play and James's tale, although the similarities emphasize James's divergence from Shakespeare. Instead of focusing on rebirth and regeneration as does Shakespeare, James is concerned with mental integration, particularly of the masculine and feminine qualities of the mind.

68 MILLER, NANCY K. "Novels of Innocence: Fictions of Loss." *Eighteenth-Century Studies* 11, no. 3 (Spring):325-39.
Links the loss of innocence to the acquisition of knowledge, focusing on *The Portrait of a Lady, La Princesse de Cleves, Manon Lescaut*, and *Clarissa*. Isabel's knowledge gives her mastery, enabling her to "become both the agent and the interpreter of her own fiction."

1978

69   MORRIS, WRIGHT. "Henry James." In *Earthly Delights, Unearthly Adornments: American Writers as Image-Makers*. New York: Harper & Row, pp. 43-50.
Discusses James's responses to America in *The American Scene*. James deplored the lack of consciousness and loss of manners in America.

70   MURPHY, KEVIN. "The Unfixable Text: Bewilderment of Vision in *The Turn of the Screw*." *Texas Studies in Literature and Language* 20, no. 4 (Winter):438-51.
Focuses on James's "strategies of ambiguity": the creation of two tales, duplicitous language, the system of collaboration between characters, and replication of a character's situation in the reader. James forces us to question the act of reading by making an "objective" reading impossible.

71   NARDIN, JANE. "*The Turn of the Screw*: The Victorian Background." *Mosaic* 12, no. 1 (Autumn):131-42.
Reads the tale as an exposure of the destructive nature of Victorian society. Repressive sexual mores and excessive class consciousness are responsible for corrupting the children's innocence and deluding the governess.

72   NETTELS, ELSA. "Henry James and the Art of Biography." *South Atlantic Bulletin* 43, no. 4:107-24.
Examines James's biographies of Hawthorne and Story, his reviews of other biographies, and his "literary portraits" to show that James regarded the biographer as an artist who must be truthful, objective, impartial, yet selective and who must create a complete and balanced picture.

73   ____. "Henry James and the Idea of Race." *English Studies* 59, no. 1 (February):36-47.
Examines the concept of race in the international novels and tales and in *The American Scene* and shows Taine's influence on James's ideas. In the social changes occurring at the turn of the century, James saw race as a determining force but he gave his own characters the power to make choices, to which race contributed but did not control.

74 OBUCHOWSKI, PETER A. "Technique and Meaning in James's *The Turn of the Screw*." *CLA Journal* 21, no. 3 (March):380-89.
Demonstrates that James deliberately avoids the conventional thematic statement because his purpose is to make the reader realize that the events at Bly cannot be verified or explained. To this end, the tale has no center of authority; indeed, the reader must become that center.

75 PANCOST, DAVID W. "Henry James and Julian Hawthorne." *American Literature* 50, no. 3 (November):461-65.
Describes James's meeting with Hawthorne in order to gather information for his book *Hawthorne*. Although each man was critical of the other, the two managed to maintain friendly relations over the years.

76 PATON, WAYNE. "Henry James and Alfred de Musset: A Possible Misattribution." *Long Room* 16/17 (Spring-Autumn):35-36.
Demonstrates that James could not have written a review of *Selections from the Prose and Poetry of Alfred de Musset* (1870) because the reviewer implies having seen a Musset play that was staged at the Comédie Française November 1861 when James was in the United States.

77 PEINOVICH, MICHAEL P., and PATTESON, RICHARD F. "The Cognitive Beast in the Syntactic Jungle: A Study of James's Language." *Language and Style* 11, no. 2 (Spring):82-93.
Examines the beginning of parts I and II of "The Beast in the Jungle" from the perspective of transformational grammar, emphasizing James's use of cognitive verbs. Stylistic features and syntactic elements underscore the story's concern with the individual consciousness in the process of acquiring knowledge and illumination.

78 PEROSA, SERGIO. *Henry James and the Experimental Novel.* Charlottesville: University of Virginia Press, vii, 219 pp.
Argues that the novels of the middle period—from *The Bostonians* (1886) to *The Sacred Fount* (1901)—are essentially experimental, particularly those following James's failed venture as a playwright. The later novels are influenced by his dramatic experience, while those written prior to it bear the imprint of the tenets outlined in

1978

"The Art of Fiction" (1884). Perosa concludes his study with an analysis of James's contribution to *The Whole Family* and his two unfinished novels, *The Ivory Tower* and *The Sense of the Past*. In these final works James returns to the experimentation of his early years, although his focus is on content rather than technique.

79 PRZYBYLOWICZ, DONNA. "The Deconstruction of Time and the Displacement of Desire: The Phenomenological World of the Late Works of Henry James." Ph.D. dissertation, Brandeis University, 343 pp.

Uses the methodologies of Poulet, Derrida, and Lacan to examine those late works preoccupied with time and the past. These concerns are "interwoven with the quest on the part of a central consciousness for knowledge" and are reflected in the narrative structure and style. Throughout these works – which include *The Sacred Fount*, the two unfinished novels, *What Maisie Knew*, "The Beast in the Jungle," "The Jolly Corner," "A Round of Visits," "Crapy Cornelia," *Autobiography*, and *The American Scene* – there is a progression from the "seen" to the process of "seeing."

See *Dissertation Abstracts International* 39, no. 5 (1978):2943A-2944A.

80 RAHV, PHILIP. "The Heiress of All the Ages." In *Essays on Literature and Politics, 1932-1972*. Edited by Arabel J. Porter and Andrew J. Dvosin. New York: Houghton Mifflin, pp. 43-61.

Sketches the evolution of James's American girl, focusing on Mary Garland, Isabel Archer, Milly Theale, and Maggie Verver. James's heiresses are driven "by their need to master the world."

Reprint of *Partisan Review* (May-June 1943) essay.

81 ____. "Henry James and His Cult." In *Essays on Literature and Politics, 1932-1972*. Edited by Arabel J. Porter and Andrew J. Dvosin. New York: Houghton Mifflin, pp. 93-104.

Reviews the fifth volume of Edel's biography of James, criticizing its excessive detail and challenging Edel's assumption of the enduring nature of James's fame. He accuses "James cultists" of reading the Prefaces too literally and of overlooking James's snobbery. He acknowledges James's greatness, but adds that "it is strictly on a national scale that he can be most highly appreciated."

1978

Reprint of *New York Review of Books* (10 February 1972) essay.

*82   RICHARDS, C. "An Approach to Imagery in the Novels of Henry James." Ph.D. dissertation, University of London, Queen Mary College.
     Source: *Annual Bibliography of English Language and Literature* 55 (1980):485, item 8994.

83   ROBINSON, DAVID. "James and Emerson: The Ethical Context of *The Ambassadors*." *Studies in the Novel* 10, no. 4 (Winter):431-46.
     Argues that the novel reflects a conception of morality that is based on the "self-culture" of New England transcendentalism; therefore, James is linked to Emerson by his ideas of the consciousness, as has been argued, but by morality as well.

84   ROMAN, CHRISTINE M. "Henry James and the Surrogate Mothers." *American Transcendental Quarterly* 38 (Spring):193-205.
     Examines Isabel Archer's "surrogate mother" – Mr. and Mrs. Touchett, Ralph Touchett, and Mme. Merle. Isabel moves from learning through them to evaluating them and in this process becomes a mother who can be morally responsible.

85   ROTH, ELLEN SHAMIS. "The Rhetoric of First-Person Point of View in the Novel and Film Forms: A Study of Anthony Burgess' *A Clockwork Orange* and Henry James' *A Turn of the Screw*." Ph.D. dissertation, New York University, 308 pp.
     Compares each work with its film adaptation to show how point of view is established and affects meaning.
     See *Dissertation Abstracts International* 39, no. 8 (1979):4558A.

86   ROTHMEL, STEVEN ZACHARY. "Similarities in the Novelistic Technique of Jane Austen and Henry James." Ph.D. dissertation, University of Utah, 179 pp.
     Argues that Austen and James share many techniques, including point of view, dialogue, ways of revealing mind, setting, and minimal authorial presence. These similarities suggest that Austen had

a strong influence on James and that both writers recognized the importance of technique.

See *Dissertation Abstracts International* 39, no. 10 (1979):6148A-6149A.

87   ROUD, RICHARD. "Turning Points: Ruiz and Truffaut." *Sight & Sound* 47, no. 3 (Summer):163-66.

Discusses Ruiz's *La Vocation Suspendue* and Truffaut's *La Chambre Verte*. Truffaut's film adaptation of "The Altar of the Dead" also borrows some pages from "The Beast in the Jungle" to explore "death-in-life."

88   ROWE, ANNE. "Henry James in Charleston." In *The Enchanted Country: Northern Writers in the South 1865-1910*. Baton Rouge: Louisiana State University Press, pp. 123-38.

Argues that James saw the South as the last holdout of refinement against the vulgarity and commercialism of the age. James's preconceived notions about the South are apparent in *The Bostonians* and were not altered by his visit to Charleston in 1905, as described in *The American Scene*.

89   RUDNICK, LOIS P. "Daisy Miller Revisited: Ernest Hemingway's 'A Canary for One.'" *Massachusetts Studies in English* 7, no. 1:12-19.

Argues that Hemingway's tale, an adaptation of "Daisy Miller," reveals the kinship between the two writers. Both have an uncompromising moral vision, but Hemingway's sense of the world and his use of language stand in stark contrast to James's mythic and linguistic richness.

90   SALMON, RACHEL. "The Typological Mode and Jamesian Poetics." Ph.D. dissertation, Brandeis University, 297 pp.

Argues that Biblical typology illuminates the way meaning is revealed in James's work and suggests that such an approach can be useful in examining ambiguity. Salmon discusses two tales: "The Figure in the Carpet" and "The Beast in the Jungle."

See *Dissertation Abstracts International* 39, no. 6 (1978):3586A-3587A.

91 SAROTTE, GEORGES MICHEL. "Henry James: The Feminine Masochist Syndrome." Translated by Richard Miller. In *Like a Brother, Like a Lover: Male Homosexuality in the American Novel and Theater from Herman Melville to James Baldwin*. Garden City, N.Y.: Anchor Press and Doubleday, pp. 197-211.

Surveys James's childhood, attitude toward women, and his relationships with young men to show his latent homosexuality and suggests that Lambert Strether is a homosexual in search of ideal virility, which is embodied in Chad Newsome.

92 SCHARNHORST, GARY. "*Wuthering Heights* and *The Portrait of a Lady*: A Dynamic Parallel." *Ball State University Forum* 19, no. 1:17-22.

Argues that the many parallels in the two novels in setting, characterization, and theme indicate that Brontë's novel was "a prototype of the international novel" and "a collateral source of ideas for James's novel."

93 SCHEICK, WILLIAM J. "The Fourth Dimension in Wells's Novels of the 1920's." *Criticism* 20, no. 2 (Spring):167-90.

Suggests briefly that Wells's *The Picture of a Lady* (1927) is a reaction against James's *Portrait*: "Wells refuses to provide a nicely framed *portrait*, with an emphasis on completion . . . ; rather he presents a *picture*, the frame of which . . . does not confine or determine the art work . . . ."

94 SCHLIB, JOHN LINCOLN. "Henry James and the Moral Will." Ph.D. dissertation, State University of New York, Binghamton, 247 pp.

Examines James's evaluation of his characters' "moral will" in *The Princess Casamassima, The Spoils of Poynton, What Maisie Knew, The Awkward Age*, and *The Wings of the Dove*. James does not adhere to a rigid code but recognizes "the need for individual action based on close ties to reality and acknowledgement of the perogatives of others." See *Dissertation Abstracts International* 38, no. 8 (1978):4819A.

95 SCHNEIDER, DANIEL J. *The Crystal Cage: Adventure of the Imagination in the Fiction of Henry James*. Lawrence: Regents Press of Kansas, vii, 189 pp.

Argues that James's imagery and indeed his entire body of work derives "from a single imaginative center and a consolidated sense of life." Schneider traces James's concern with freedom and entrapment throughout his career, a concern reflected in imagery, characterization, and plot – the struggle of the free spirit to avoid entrapment. The discussion covers the major fiction as well as James's criticism.

Reprinted in part in 1985.78.

96   SEAMON, ROGER. "Henry James's 'Four Meetings': A Study in Irritability and Condescension." *Studies in Short Fiction* 15, no. 2 (Spring):155-63.

Focuses on the narrator, who embodies the "mutual withholding" typical of the tale's characters, and suggests that his irritation with Carolyn reveals his own self-criticism.

See also Martin 1980.91.

97   SEED, D[AVID]. "The Role of the Narrator in Henry James's Novels 1896-1901." Ph.D. dissertation, University of Hull, United Kingdom.

Argues that James "had no theoretical preference" for objectivity and that in the fiction of this period – *The Awkward Age, In the Cage, What Maisie Knew*, and *The Sacred Fount* – James "retains many of the traditional privileges of the narrator."

See *Dissertation Abstracts International* 38, no. 4 (1978):2/4615C.

98   SEPCIĆ, VIŠNJA. "Henry James's *The Ambassadors* as a Study in Alienation." *Studia Romanica et Anglica Zagrebiensia* 23, no. 1-2:231-72.

Details Strether's responses to his Parisian experience, where he is confronted by a way of life unimaginable in Woollett. He remains isolated because "his great emotional and spiritual adventure takes place primarily in his imagination." At the novel's end, Strether confronts the reality that life has passed him by, but the resilience and courage with which he confronts his pain and loss reveal his inward gain, the reality of an inner imaginative world.

99 SESSOM, SANDRA LEE. "Charlotte in Perspective: A Fuller Reading of *The Golden Bowl*." Ph.D. dissertation, University of Oregon, 223 pp.

Argues that an understanding of Charlotte is crucial to the novel and examines her in relation to the other central characters. Charlotte is "exceedingly complex and reasonably moral" and assists Maggie in saving the marriages.

See *Dissertation Abstracts International* 39, no. 8 (1979):4940A-4941A.

100 SHARMA, J.N. "Two Versions of the New England Moral Consciousness: Henry James's *The Ambassadors*." *Literary Criterion* 13, no. 2:18-26.

Argues that Mrs. Newsome, Chad, and Waymarsh represent the negative aspects of the New England consciousness, based on conventional Puritanism; they embody provinciality, rigidity, self-righteousness, and hypocrisy. Strether, in contrast, develops the positive aspects of the New England consciousness, particularly sensitivity, responsiveness, and moral discrimination.

101 SKLEPOWICH, E.A. "Gilded Bondage: Games and Gamesplaying in *The Awkward Age*." *Essays in Literature* V, no. 2 (Fall):187-93.

Proposes that role of the games in the novel maintains order and creates a social work of art, and traces the literal and metaphoric gamesplaying throughout the novel. The novel puts forward three alternatives: withdrawal, disruption, and participation, but focuses on the third, which offers the possibility of "combining social artifice with moral spontaneity."

102 SMITH, HENRY NASH. "Henry James I: Sows' Ears and Silk Purses." In *Democracy and the Novel: Popular Resistance to Classic American Writers*. New York: Oxford University Press, pp. 128-42, 190-2.

Discusses James's use of "lowbrow" fiction in *Washington Square* and *The Princess Casamassima* and his struggle to succeed as an artist in the face of the demands of a "middlebrow" taste. Smith also examines "Greville Fane" and "The Next Time" as tales in which James explores his predicament.

1978

103   ____. "Henry James II: The Problem of an Audience." In
       *Democracy and the Novel: Popular Resistance to Classic American
       Writers*. New York: Oxford University Press, pp. 143-65, 193-7.
           Surveys James's critical reception from the 1880s to his death.
       During the 1880s James was criticized for being too analytical; during
       the 1890s reviewers were somewhat more receptive, though by no
       means enthusiastic. During the next decade, critics recognized that
       James was transforming the Victorian novel; in the final years of his
       life, his importance was acknowledged although his work did not sell.

104   SNOW, C.P. "Henry James." In *The Realists: Eight Portraits*. New
       York: Charles Scribner's Sons, pp. 256-96.
           Surveys James's life and writing career.

105   SNOW, LOTUS. "Clarissa Dalloway Revisited." *Research Studies* 46,
       no. 3 (September):197-202.
           Compares Woolf's development of Clarissa Dalloway from a
       minor character to the heroine of a novel to James's treatment of
       Christina Light and speculates that, like James, Woolf found that
       Clarissa could not be contained within a single work because she, like
       Christina, was "unrealized, an unexorcised ghost."

106   SNYDER, JOHN. "James's Girl Huck: *What Maisie Knew*."
       American Literary Realism, 1870-1910 11, no. 1 (Spring):109-23.
           Sees Maisie as an "ideal youth" who must transcend the
       conventional, corrupt world of the adults by creating new and humane
       values. Maisie must achieve freedom, but it cannot be the adults'
       libertinism. Because of her love and compassion, Maisie matures.

107   SPIGELMIRE, W. LYNNE. "*Daniel Deronda* and *The Portrait of a
       Lady*: A Revised Estimate of F.R. Leavis' View." Ph.D. dissertation,
       Boston College, 98 pp.
           Refutes Leavis's statement that James's novel is a simplified
       version of Eliot's. Spigelmire finds substantial differences in the
       heroine, the marriage, the husband, the mentor, and the conclusion of
       each novel, indicating a different imaginative vision.
           See *Dissertation Abstracts International* 39, no. 6 (1978):3605A-
       3606A.

108 SPRINGER, MARY DOYLE. *A Rhetoric of Literary Character: Some Women of Henry James*. Chicago: University of Chicago Press, viii, 248 pp.

Examines the function of character in James's fiction, focusing on the heroines of the following works: "The Bench of Desolation," *Washington Square*, "The Turn of the Screw," "The Jolly Corner," "Lady Barbarina," "Benvolio," "The Aspern Papers," and "Madame de Mauves." Springer distinguishes several types of character based on function – main, suppressed, extra, frame, and apologue – and discusses character portrayal, seeing it as a cumulative process.

Reprinted in part 1985.78.

109 STAFFORD, WILLIAM T. "Henry James." In *American Literary Scholarship: An Annual/1976*. Edited by J. Albert Robbins. Durham: Duke University Press, pp. 93-107.

Surveys criticism published in 1976.

110 STERNBERG, MEIR. "Expositional Motivation, Temporal Structure, and Point of View (2): Restricted and Self-Restricted Narration." In *Expositional Modes and Temporal Ordering in Fiction*. Baltimore and London: Johns Hopkins University Press, pp. 276-305, 323-4.

Examines the advantages of James's restricted, omniscient narrative method. These advantages include the creation of heightened interest, economical representation, compositional and thematic unity, control of the reader's distance, and "quasi-mimetic" information distribution.

111 STOCKING, MARION KINGSTON. "Miss Tina and Miss Plin: The Papers behind *The Aspern Papers*." In *The Evidence of the Imagination: Studies of Interactions between Life and Art in English Romantic Literature*. Edited by Donald H. Reiman, Michael C. Jaye, Betty T. Bennett, Doucet Devin Fischer, and Ricki B. Herzfeld. New York: New York University Press, pp. 372-84.

Sketches a portrait of Pauline Clairmont, Clair Clairmont's niece who inspired Miss Tina.

1978

112 STULL, WILLIAM L. "[The Battle of the Century: W.D. Howells, 'Henry James, Jr.,' and the English.]" *American Literary Realism, 1870-1910* 11, no. 2 (Autumn):249-64.

Chronicles the debate resulting from Howell's November 1882 essay and its impact on American literary realism. "Henry James, Jr." forced the British to recognize American fiction and realism; both Howells and James won "independence and self-knowledge."

Note: There is a typographical error in this issue of *ALR*: the title of this essay is transposed with that of the essay that follows it, also by Stull. Thus, pp. 249-64 actually bear the incorrect title: "W.D. Howells' 1899 Lecture Tour: What the Letters Tell."

113 TALBOTT, BARBARA MERLO. "The Material Ideal: Women as Symbols of Success in Selected American Fiction." Ph.D. dissertation, University of Wisconsin, Milwaukee, 203 pp.

Argues that with the conquering of the frontier, woman replaced the land as a token of American idealism, and traces the evolution of the "golden girl" in American fiction. Talbott examines Claire de Cintre, Christina Light, and Maggie Verver, through whom James remade the cult of genteel womanhood.

See *Dissertation Abstracts International* 39, no. 9 (1979):5518A.

114 TATER, MARIA M. "From Science Fiction to Psychoanalysis: Henry James's *Bostonians*, D.H. Lawrence's *Women in Love*, and Thomas Mann's *Mario and the Magician*. In *Spellbound: Studies on Mesmerism and Literature*. Princeton, N.J.: Princeton University Press, pp. 230-71.

Argues that in "Professor Fargo" and *The Bostonians* James replaces Mesmer's animal magnetism with psychological analysis to explain character even though he continued to use metaphors of mesmerism in these works. Both Lawrence and Mann, however, used the tenets of mesmerism to describe and explain attraction and domination.

115 TIMSON, BETH SHAVELY. "'In My Father's House': The Structure of Inheritance in Modern British and American Fiction." Ph.D. dissertation, Vanderbilt University, 221 pp.

Distinguishes two structural patterns related to the house – that of building, which is primarily American, and that of inheriting, primarily British – using the theories of Propp and other formalists.

Timson examines these patterns in a variety of novels, including *The Spoils of Poynton*, discussed as a work that combines both patterns.
See *Dissertation Abstracts International* 39, no. 5 (1978):2934A.

116 TINTNER, ADELINE R. "The Books in the Book: What Henry James' Characters Read and Why." *AB Bookman's Weekly* 61, no. 20 (15 May):3468-94.

Catalogs the references and allusions to books in James's fiction and shows that "there is no accidental allusion or quotation from a book." Books illuminate character and provide the reader with referential analogues. Tintner distinguishes three kinds of books: real books, unidentified books, and books invented by James.
Reprinted 1987.35.

117 ____. "Henry James and Fine Books." *AB Bookman's Weekly* 61, no. 14 (3 April):2406-10.

Shows that James appreciated fine printing and binding and notes the references to bookbinding in James's "library book," *The Princess Casamassima*. James had several friends who were interested in fine books; James himself was concerned with appearance of his published work.

118 ____. "James Corrects Poe: The Appropriation of *Pym* in *The Golden Bowl*." *American Transcendental Quarterly* 37 (Winter):87-91.

Shows how James uses Poe's fantasies and metaphors to reveal the Prince's consciousness. In particular, Poe's "blind white fog" is a metaphor for Amerigo's attempt to understand the Ververs.
Revised 1987.122.

119 ____. "James Writes a Boy's Story: 'The Pupil' and R.L. Stevenson's Adventure Books." *Essays in Literature* 5, no. 1 (Spring):61-73.

Suggests that James used icons from *Kidnapped* and *Treasure Island* as a response to Stevenson's comments in "A Humble Remonstrance" to show that a child's adventure can be an adventure of the consciousness. The essay contains plates of James's comments on the advertisement pages of his copy of *Kidnapped*.
Revised 1987.122.

1978

120 _____. "James's 'The Beldonald Holbein' and Rollins' 'A Burne-Jones Head': A Surprising Parallel." *Colby Library Quarterly* 14, no. 4 (December):183-90.

Finds numerous parallels between Clara Rollins's 1894 tale and James's 1901 tale, suggesting that this is another instance of James rewriting stories that interested him.

121 _____. "Lady into Horse: James's 'Lady Barberina' and *Gulliver's Travels*, Part IV." *Journal of Narrative Technique* 8, no. 2 (Spring):79-96.

Examines the horse metaphors that pervade many aspects of this tale: figures of speech, characters' names, puns, etc. Tintner connects these metaphors to Part IV of *Gulliver's Travels*, the tale's "important literary ancestor," and suggests that Oscar Wilde drew on James's tale for "The Canterville Ghost."

Revised 1987.122.

122 _____. "A Source for Prince Amerigo in *The Golden Bowl*." *NMAL: Notes on Modern American Literature* 2: Item 23.

Demonstrates that James based the character of the Prince on the Marchese Simone de Peruzzi de Medici, who married Edith Story, daughter of William Wetmore Story, the subject of James's biography. Edith had an intense and close relationship with her father, inspiring the novel's triadic relationship of the Prince and the two Ververs.

123 TORGOVNICK, MARIANNA. "James's Sense of an Ending: The Role Played in Its Development by the Popular Conventional Epilogue." *Studies in the Novel* 10, no. 2 (Summer):183-98.

Argues that in his early fiction James uses a "quasi epilogue" reflecting his mockery of the conventional epilogue in "The Art of Fiction." In *The Portrait of a Lady*, James deliberately rejects the conventional epilogue because the novel's focus is character, not plot, while in *The Ambassadors* James creates the "scenic ending" with which he can underscore the novel's meaning.

Reprinted in part 1981.168.

124 TUTTLETON, J[AMES] W. "Propriety and Fine Perception: James's *The Europeans*." *Modern Language Review* 73, no. 3 (July):481-95.

Argues that in this novel James successfully balanced the "folly of 'unsuspectingness'" of the international theme so that he alienated neither Americans nor Europeans. In order to achieve this balance James endowed his characters with cosmopolitanism and adopted a double point of view, sympathizing with the Americans and the Europeans.
Reprinted in part 1985.78.

125   ___, ed. *The American*. Norton Critical Edition. New York: W.W. Norton, x, 496 pp.

Contents include the New York Edition of the novel, its preface, relevant letters and nonfiction by James, contemporary reviews, and reprints of the following:

Edel, Leon. "[A Portrait Rich in National Ambiguities]," pp. 415-26, reprinted from *Henry James: The Conquest of London, 1870-1881* (1962), pp. 245-60;

Cargill, Oscar. "[A Surge of Patriotic Indignation]," pp. 426-41, reprinted from *The Novels of Henry James* (1961), pp. 41-61;

Howe, Irving. "Henry James and the Millionaire," pp. 442-57, reprinted from *Tomorrow* 9 (January 1950): 53-55;

Poirier, Richard. "[The Comedy of Fixed and Free Characters]," pp. 457-62, reprinted from *The Comic Sense of Henry James: A Study of the Early Novels* (1960), pp. 44-50;

Gettmann, Royal A. "Henry James's Revision of *The American*," pp. 462-77, reprinted from *American Literature* 16 (1945): 279-95;

Edel, Leon. "[The Revised Ending of the Play]," pp. 477-92, reprinted from *The Complete Plays of Henry James* (1949), pp. 241-52.

126   VAN HORN, GERALDINE KLOOS. "The Image of the City in the Early Twentieth-Century Novel: Studies of Conrad, James, Woolf, and Joyce." Ph.D. dissertation, Ohio State University, 245 pp.

Argues that sociological studies humanizing the city influenced these novelists' visions of the city. Hyacinth Robinson in *The Princess Casamassima* sees the achievements of mankind as well as "economic horror" in London and Paris; Lambert Strether in *The Ambassadors* attains both a cultural and moral education in Paris.
See *Dissertation Abstracts International* 39, no. 8 (1979):4943A.

127   VIEBROCK, HELMUT. "Die schönen Sachen und die schöne Seele: Ästhetisch-moralische Beobachtungen an James' Roman *Die*

Schätze von Poynton" [The Lovely Things and the Lovely Soul: Moral-Aesthetic Views on James's Novel *The Spoils of Poynton*]. *Nelle Rundschau* 89, no. 4:606-15.
In German.

128 WAGENKNECHT, EDWARD [CHARLES]. *Eve and Henry James: Portraits of Women and Girls in His Fiction*. Norman: University of Oklahoma Press, xi, 217 pp.
Examines the following characters in detail: Daisy Miller, Mme. de Mauves, Isabel Archer, Christina Light, Miriam Rooth, Fleda Vetch, Maisie Farange, Nanda Brookenham, Millie Theale, Kate Croy, Maggie Verver, Charlotte Stant, May Bartram, and Alice Staverton. Wagenknecht discusses character traits and the relationship between character and theme, and surveys and assesses current criticism.
Reprinted in part 1985.78.

129 WATANABE, HISAYOSHI. *Henry James no Gengo: Bungaku no Gengo wo Sasaeru Mono ni Tsuite no Shiron* [Henry James's language: An essay on the language of literature]. Tokyo: Hokuseido, 211 pp.
In Japanese.
Argues that in order to study the language of James's later works, we must also consider the author, the age he lived in, and his relationship to American literature as a whole. James tried to realize himself and to express his vision of the world through language, which is closely related to the view inherent in American literature that language is a medium for asserting one's existence rather than for representing reality.

130 WATT, IAN. "Marlow, Henry James, and 'Heart of Darkness.'" *Nineteenth-Century Fiction* 33, no. 2 (September):159-74.
Examines Conrad's use of Marlow as narrator in the light of James's objections to first person narration. James influenced many aspects of Conrad's work, particularly the use of an open fictional form and the rejection of linear chronology. The two authors differ, however, about the form the central intelligence will take, with Conrad choosing Marlow as a means of embodying "human solidarity."

1978

131 ____. "Le Premier paragraphe des *Ambassadors*: Essai d'explication." *Poétique* 34:172-89.
In French.
Reprint of Watt's 1960 essay, translated into French by Jacques Carré.

132 WHITE, ISABELLE B. "The American Heroine, 1789-1899: Non-Conformity and Death." Ph.D. dissertation, University of Kentucky, 231 pp.
Argues that the heroines of Brown's *The Power of Sympathy* (1789), Rowson's *Charlotte Temple* (1794), Foster's *The Coquette* (1897), Stowe's *Uncle Tom's Cabin* (1852), Hawthorne's *The Blithedale Romance* (1852), James's "Daisy Miller" (1878), Crane's *Maggie: A Girl of the Streets* (1893), and Chopin's *The Awakening* (1899) die because they fail to conform to society's expectation that they be subordinate to men.
See *Dissertation Abstracts International* 40, no. 2 (1979):862A.

133 WOLSTENHOLME, SUSAN. "Possession and Personality: Spiritualism in *The Bostonians*." *American Literature* 49, no. 4 (January):580-91.
Sees the novel's subject as what happens to the individual when society has no firm sense of values. All the characters are aimless, but Verena shows how one can be possessed by the ideas of others because her mind is "utterly vacuous." James's vision of the human condition is devoid of hope.

1979

1 ALLEN, JOHN J. "The Governess and the Ghosts in *The Turn of the Screw*." *Henry James Review* 1, no. 1 (November):73-80.
Argues that the governess is essentially reliable, albeit unaware of all that she reveals, and that the ghosts, therefore, are real.

2 ANDERSON, J.W. "An Interview with Leon Edel on the James Family." *Psychohistory Review* 8:15-22.
Discusses invalidism, Aunt Kate as a model for James's "Kates," the relationship between Henry and William, Edel's own psychological approach to biography, and the relation of biographer to subject.

1979

3   AUCHINCLOSS, LOUIS. "The Late Jamesing of Early James." In
Life, Law, and Letters: Essays and Sketches. New York: Houghton
Mifflin, pp. 91-96.
Reprint of 1977.6.

4   BANTA, MARTHA. *Failure and Success in America: A Literary
Debate*. Princeton: Princeton University Press, 568 pp.
Examines the views of representative American writers from
Emerson to Mailer on what it means to be an American, how
American success is defined, and what strategies are available to cope
with failure. In both his life and his work, James continually needed to
redefine failure as a kind of moral success. Works discussed include
The American, The Ambassadors, The Wings of the Dove, and *The
American Scene*.

5   _____. "James and Stein on 'Being American' and 'Having France.'"
French-American Review 3, no. 3 (Fall):63-84.
Compares James's and Stein's responses to America and
France as expatriates. Both left the United States because they found
the "business mentality" inimical to their art. James had a vivid sense of
the past while Stein was more attuned to the present. James in *The
American Scene* anticipated an America devoid of culture and moral
value; Stein "was content to possess the content of America's large,
empty, flat spaces void of time and identity."

6   BARNETT, LOUISE K. "Jamesian Feminism: Women in *Daily
Miller*." *Studies in Short Fiction* 16, no. 4 (Fall):281-87.
Sees the contrast between what Daisy wants and what the
other female characters have as James's "clearest indictment of a
society restricting its women." Daisy wants to be free and natural in a
society that is rigid and hypocritical.

7   BEATTIE, MUNRO. "Henry James: 'The Voice of Stoicism.'" In
*The Stoic Strain in American Literature: Essays in Honour of Marston
LaFrance*. Edited by Duane J. MacMillan. Toronto: University of
Toronto Press, pp. 63-75.
Shows that James's stoicism arose out of "his own engagements
with adversity" and sketches its impact on his life, his friendships, his

sense of mission as a writer, and his art. Beattie then traces the stoic strain in James's protagonists, including Lambert Strether, Isabel Archer, Fleda Vetch, Kate Cookham, and Maggie Verver.

8   BELLRINGER, ALAN W. *"The Wings of the Dove*: The Main Image." *Modern Language Review* 74, no. 1 (January):12-25.
    Examines in detail the character of Milly Theale, arguing that she was the "crucial emphasis" in the early plan for the novel outlined in the notebooks. The novel is a "record of an abbreviated life and its relations, set in a dense 'continuity of things.'"

*9   BENNETT, MAURICE JOHNNANCE. "The Consciousness of the Artist: Charles Brockden Brown, Nathaniel Hawthorne, and Henry James." Ph.D. dissertation, Harvard University.
    Source: Budd, 1983.32, p. 3, item 10.

10   BEPPU, KEIKO. *The Educated Sensibility in Henry James and Walter Pater*. Tokyo: Shohakusha, v, 241 pp.
    Explores Pater's and James's interest in the "cultivation of the sensibility" as reflected in their fiction. Beppu compares the two authors not to argue for influence but for reciprocal illumination, for both writers saw the artist as the ideal man. James's rendering of the "aesthetic education" in *Roderick Hudson, The Portrait of a Lady, The Ambassadors*, and *The Golden Bowl* shows that "the dialectic of the aesthetic and the moral is resolved in the dynamics of the education of the sensibility"; this dynamic is especially apparent in *The Golden Bowl*.
    Revision of Ph.D. dissertation, University of Michigan, 1973.

11   BIER, JESSE. "Henry James's 'The Jolly Corner': The Writer's Fable and the Deeper Matter." *Arizona Quarterly* 35, no. 4 (Winter):321-34.
    Proposes that Hawthorne and Poe provided a model and antimodel for James's autobiographical tale. Hawthorne influences Brydon's struggle to overcome his disengagement from humanity, while Poe's influence is apparent in the tale's Gothic elements. Hawthorne dominates, however, because James feared Poe's "psychological value" and "artistic power."

1979

12 BLACKALL, JEAN FRANTZ. "Cruikshank's *Oliver* and *The Turn of the Screw*." *American Literature* 51, no. 2 (May):161-78.
Attributes the tale's "fearful confrontations" to James's childhood reading of *Oliver Twist* and Cruikshank's illustrations. The emotional intensity of the tale is a result of James's ability to tap his own childhood years.

13 ____. "Moral Geography in *What Maisie Knew*." *University of Toronto Quarterly* 48, no. 2 (Winter):130-48.
Focuses on Maisie's moral and intellectual maturation and analyzes the symbolic implications of the Boulogne scenes in the novel. Blackall likens this section of the novel to a morality play in which Maisie achieves self-knowledge and assumes responsibility for her own fate.
Reprinted 1987.44.

14 BLAKE, NANCY. "Hystérie, langue et violence: *Les Ailes de la colombe*." In *Le Discours de la violence dans la culture américaine*. Edited by Régis Durand. Lille: Pubs. de l'Univ. de Lille III, pp. 37-47.
In French.

15 BLASING, MUTLU KONUK. "The Story of the Stories: Henry James's Prefaces as Autobiography." In *Approaches to Victorian Autobiography*. Edited by George P. Landow. Athens: Ohio University Press, pp. 311-32.
Revison of 1977.15.

16 BLODGETT, HARRIET. "Verbal Cues in *The Portrait of a Lady*: A Note in Defense of Isabel Archer." *Studies in American Fiction* 7, no. 1 (Spring):27-36.
Examines the "verbal parallelisms," which include phrasing and imagery, to show Isabel's maturation. These parallelisms clearly show James's respect for Isabel; she is, in fact, "James's tribute to the woman who can operate by her ideals."

17 BOCK, DARILYN W. "From Reflective Narrators to James: The Coloring Medium of the Mind." *Modern Philology* 76, no. 3 (February):259-72.

Relates James to the tradition of the Victorian novel and to the experimentation of the twentieth-century novel. The omniscient narrator is the link: James's use of a center of consciousness is a refinement of that point of view. James's interest in the "drama of the troubled consciousness" anticipates twentieth-century experimentalists.

18 BOOTH, WAYNE. "Four Kinds of Reader Misreading: Preconceptions about the Writer and the 'Career-Author': A Lesson by the Master." In *Critical Understanding: The Power and Limits of Pluralism*. Chicago and London: University Press of Chicago, pp. 277-301, 374.

Uses "The Bench of Desolation" and "The Turn of the Screw" to show the important relationship between interpretation and author and takes exception to Edel's portrait of "the howling, embittered James." Booth argues that "our choice of readings implies a choice of 'author.'"

19 BOREN, LYNDA SUE. "A Study of the Relationship of the Philosophical Ideas of Henry James, Senior, and William James to the Later Fiction of Henry James." Ph.D. dissertation, Tulane University, 265 pp.

Argues that James's later work–*What Maisie Knew, The Ambassadors, The Wings of the Dove*, and *The Golden Bowl*–reflects a synthesis of his father's "empirical mysticism" and William James's pragmatism. These novels dramatize Henry James Sr.'s ideas about self and society and William's theories about knowledge and the nature of truth.

See *Dissertation Abstracts International* 40, no. 3 (1979):1465A.

20 BOWEN, ELSIE VAN BUREN. "The Gardens of Henry James." Ph.D. dissertation, Tufts University, 377 pp.

Explores James's use of the garden as a narrative device for authorial commentary without authorial intrusion throughout the fiction and the New York Edition prefaces.

See *Dissertation Abstracts International* 39, no. 12 (1979):7344A-7345A.

1979

21 BRADBURY, NICOLA. "Filming James." *Essays in Criticism*, no. 4 (October):293-301.

Comments on James Ivory's film *The Europeans*, noting that it lacks James's discrimination and that it translates "a peculiarly visual novel into a rather musical film."

22 _____. *Henry James: The Later Novels*. Oxford: Clarendon Press, 228 pp.

Examines the process of reading James's later work in which the reader participates in both the protagonist's experience and the novelist's understanding. Bradbury's discussion covers *The Portrait of a Lady*, the "dramatic" novels of the middle period, the three major late novels, and the two unfinished novels, and focuses on how the interrelationship of author, character, and reader affects the novel's form. Bradbury sees *The Golden Bowl* as James's greatest novel because in it he achieves a balance of "'the process and effect of representation'" by creating an analogy between form and theme: reader and author share the same "interest" as the novel's characters.

23 BURT, DELLA ANN. "The Widening Arc and the Closed Circle: A Study of Problematic Novel Endings." Ph.D. dissertation, Indiana University, 406 pp.

Examines the problematic endings of seven novels: *The Portrait of a Lady*, *Moll Flanders*, *Clarissa*, *Mansfield Park*, *Adam Bede*, *Great Expectations*, and *Native Son*, focusing on the internal elements that prepare the reader for the ending. Structural patterns and themes are crucial in insuring that the ending meets reader expectations.

See *Dissertation Abstracts International* 40, no. 7 (1980):4011A.

24 CASERIO, ROBERT L. "The Story in It: James." In *Plot, Story, and the Novel: From Dickens and Poe to the Modern Period*. Princeton: Princeton University Press, pp. 198-231.

Examines James's use of story, plot, and action, and arguing that in his later novels he shows a "new commitment to story and action." Caserio discusses *The Wings of the Dove* in detail to show James's increased focus on story and action, in contrast to *The American*, *The Portrait of a Lady*, and *The Awkward Age*. Caserio concludes with *The American Scene* to distinguish between story and picture, arguing that James's use of story is a sign of his distance from Hawthornian picture.

Reprinted 1987.15.

25 CLEWS, HETTY JUNE. "The Teller Not the Tale: Studies in the Monologue Novel." Ph.D. dissertation, University of Saskatchewan, Canada.

Explores the monologue novel (a subgenre of first person narration), traces its development, establishes a comparative framework for analyzing this genre, and examines the contemporary use of the genre. "The Turn of the Screw" is seen as an example of "eye witness monologues" that engages the reader by dramatic involvement in events described and by sharing the interpretation of these events.

See *Dissertation Abstracts International* 41, no. 2 (1980):667A.

26 COLEMAN, BASIL. "Staging First Productions, 2." In *The Operas of Benjamin Britten*. Edited by David Herbert. New York: Columbia University Press, pp. 34-43.

Describes the difficulties with casting Miles and Flora and with the numerous sets required for Britten's opera based on "The Turn of the Screw."

27 CULL, FRANCIS CYRIL DUNCAN. "Love and Marriage in the Works of Henry James." D.Litt. dissertation, University of South Africa.

Traces James's ideas about love and marriage in *The Europeans, The Portrait of a Lady, What Maisie Knew, The Wings of the Dove,* and *The Golden Bowl.* Cull suggests that these ideas center on the concepts of "being" and "belonging": characters who allow others to develop most fully are those capable of creating and maintaining relationships.

See *Dissertation Abstracts International* 41, no. 4 (1980):1607A.

28 DAUGHERTY, SARAH B. "James, Renan, and the Religion of Consciousness." *Comparative Literature Studies* 16, no. 4 (December):318-31.

Discusses Renan's influence on James, particularly in shaping the latter's view of consciousness as a means of unifying the multiplicity of experience and observation. In addition, Daugherty suggests that Renan's style, with its "rhetorical balance" and metaphors, gave James a "paradigm" for writing about consciousness.

1979

29 DAVIS, SARA deSAUSSURE. "Feminist Sources in *The Bostonians.*" *American Literature* 50, no. 4 (January):570-87.

Chronicles the women's suffrage movement of the 1880s and shows that James drew upon contemporary affairs for his novel. In particular, the Susan B. Anthony-Anna Dickinson-Whitlaw Reid triangle may have inspired the Olive-Verena-Basil triangle.

30 DEL FATTORE, JOAN. "The 'Other' Spencer Brydon." *Arizona Quarterly* 35, no. 4 (Winter):335-41.

Examines Brydon's inability to achieve genuine self-knowledge. His failure to see himself as he is, not what he thinks he is, is reflected in the two personality pairs in the tale: "Brydon as he is and as he sees himself," and his "might-have-been self, as he imagines it and as it really would have been."

31 DYSON, J. PETER. "Death and Separation in 'Fordham Castle.'" *Studies in Short Fiction* 16, no. 1 (Winter):41-47.

Compares the relevant notebook remarks with the finished tale to show that James was concerned with the consciousness as a "spectator of its own tragedy" and its relation to death.

32 ____. "Romance Elements in Three Late Tales of Henry James: 'Mora Montravers,' 'The Velvet Glove,' and 'The Bench of Desolation.'" *English Studies in Canada* 5, no. 1 (Spring):66-77.

Examines these tales in light of the New York Edition preface to *The American* in which James discusses the romance. Romance is "experience liberated" from the way things happen. In the first tale, Traffle creates a romance while he thinks he is a realist; in the second, romance is a topic within the tale; and in the third, romance elements are exploited in such a way that they become intertwined with reality.

33 EDEL, LEON. Introduction to *The Europeans*. A Facsimile of the Manuscript. New York: Howard Fertig, pp. vii-xiii.

Details the discovery and location of the holograph manuscript as well as its physical condition. Edel calls the novel "a piece of comedy that skates close to cariacature."

34 ____. "Portrait of the Artist as an Old Man." In *Aging, Death, and the Completion of Being*. Edited by David D. Van Tassel. Philadelphia: University of Pennsylvania Press, pp. 193-214.
Reprint of 1978.34.

35 ____. "Westminster Abbey Address." *Henry James Review* 1, no. 1 (November):5-9.
Reprint of 1976.59 and 1976.60. Includes a brief foreword describing the unveiling of the stone commemorating James.

36 EDEL, LEON, and RAY, GORDON N., eds. *Henry James and H.G. Wells: A Record of Their Friendship, Their Debate on the Art of Fiction, and Their Quarrel*. Westport, Conn.: Greenwood, 272 pp.
Reprint of 1958 edition.

37 ELDER, HARRIS JAMES. "From Literature to Cinema: *The American Short Story* Series." Ph.D. dissertation, Oklahoma State University, 158 pp.
Examines the relationship between the short stories and their film adaptation for this television series. In "The Jolly Corner" "the filmmakers solve formidable problems in adapting the interior world of James' story to the screen."
See *Dissertation Abstracts International* 40, no. 8 (1980):4279A.

38 EMPET, CAROL J. "James' *Portrait of a Lady* and Browning's 'My Last Duchess': A Comparison." *DeKalb Literary Arts Journal* 13, nos. 1-2:79-84.
Traces the numerous parallels between the two works, focusing on the many similarities shared by Gilbert Osmond and Count Gismond. Such parallels suggest that James's novel is a variation and extension of the theme of Browning's poem.

39 FERGUSON, SUZANNE. "The Face in the Mirror: Authorial Presence in the Multiple Vision of Third-Person Impressionist Narrative." *Criticism* 21, no. 3 (Summer):230-50.
Uses *The Ambassadors* as an example to show James's intrusions in a narrative, despite his claims to the contrary. James's authorial presence dominates the scene in which Strether discovers

1979

Marie and Chad in the rowboat; the reader in fact is never allowed inside of Strether's consciousness.

*40   FIELD, MARY LEE. "'The Unmitigated "Business Man" Face':
       Portraits of American Business Men by Henry James." *Chu-Shikoku
       Studies in American Literature* (Hiroshima, Japan)15:1-16.
              Source: *MLA International Bibliography*, 1 (1979):192, item
       10017.

 41   FRANK, EVE ELLEN. "Furnished Rooms: 'Objects' and 'Size' in
       James's Fiction." In *Literary Architecture: Essays Toward a Tradition*.
       Berkeley: University of California Press, pp. 195-210.
              Suggests that in James's fiction architecture and furniture
       become images of thought processes because James "identifies
       characters with objects." Space and size thus are crucial concepts in
       James's fiction in that they reflect not only the dimensions of objects
       but of consciousness as well. That James describes his characters and
       his fiction in terms of architecture "suggests that James's art is about art
       itself and that art is conscious consciousness." Frank also notes that
       Alvin Langdon Coburn's photographs for the New York Edition are
       fitting "optical symbols" of James's fiction.

 42   ____. "The House of Fiction." In *Literary Architecture: Essays
       Toward a Tradition*. Berkeley: University of California Press, pp.
       181-6.
              Suggests that this metaphor offers a way to read James's work.
       The windows of the house of fiction are the literary forms shaping the
       subject and the vantage points from which the subject is viewed, while
       the consciousness is the observer at the window.

 43   ____. "Matters of Construction and Adequacy: Architecture and
       Painting." In *Literary Architecture: Essays Toward a Tradition*.
       Berkeley: University of California Press, pp. 211-215.
              Notes that, while James uses other art analogues for his fiction,
       he uses only architectural images to reflect a character's consciousness.
       Painting, for example, can be analogous to the view from the windows
       of the house of fiction; but architecture, which includes the other arts, is
       the appropriate analogue for mind.

44 _____. "The Prefaces: James's Architecture of the Past." In *Literary Architecture: Essays Toward a Tradition.* Berkeley: University of California Press, pp. 171-9.

Analyzes the passage from the preface to *Lady Barbarina and Other Tales* that describes the writing of "The Point of View." The architectural images described in the passage are analogous to James's method; architecture evokes memory, which in turn becomes the source of James's literary art.

45 _____. "Windows of Indirection: James's Narrative Techniques." In *Literary Architecture: Essays Toward a Tradition.* Berkeley: University of California Press, pp. 187-93.

Sees James's indirection – rendering a subject through a character's consciousness – as a reflection of his literary form, techniques, subjects, and his "fear of a participatory life."

46 FRIEDL, HERWIG. "Problemgeschichtliche Überlegungen zum Stellsnwert der Kunst in amerikanischen Kunstlererzählungen" [Reflections on the historic problems of the value of the place of art in American artist narratives]. *Anglia* 97:153-67.

In German.

47 FUNK, RUTH CHRISTY. "Order and Chaos: A Study of Cultural Dialectic in Adams, James, Cather, Glasgow, Warren, and Fitzgerald." Ph.D. dissertation, Syracuse University, 179 pp.

Traces the dialectic of unity and multiplicity, symbolized by Adams's Virgin and the Dynamo, in the work of these authors. Throughout his career, James strove for a balance between the "order of past civilization" and the "chaos of present culture." Novels discussed in the section on James include *The American, The Princess Casamassima,* and *The Ambassadors.*

See *Dissertation Abstracts International* 40, no. 5 (1979):2679A.

48 FURTH, DAVID L. *The Visionary Betrayed: Aesthetic Discontinuity in Henry James's The American Scene.* Cambridge: Harvard University Press, 67 pp.

Argues that in *The American Scene* James recognizes his inability to impose order and coherence on his chaotic impressions of America. James ultimately rejects democracy because it is

1979

indiscriminate in encompassing detail and is thus abhorrent to his sense
of art and the role of the artist.

49 GALE, ROBERT L. "Henry James." In *American Literary
    Scholarship: An Annual/1977*. Edited by James Woodress. Durham:
    Duke University Press, pp. 99-118.
    Surveys criticism published in 1977.

50 GALLOWAY, DAVID. "The Needle and the Thread: Henry James
    and the Concept of Organic Form." In *Englische und amerikanische
    Literaturtheorie: Studien zu ihrer historischen Entwicklung.* Band 2:
    Victorianische Zeit und 20. Jahrhundert. Edited by Rudiger Ahrens
    and Erwin Wolff. Heidelberg: Carl Winter Universitätsverlag, pp.
    266-79.
    Argues that organic form, expressed in the "house of fiction"
metaphor, was central to James's theory and practice of fiction. For
James, a work of art was a projection of the artist's mind in which
ethical and formal concerns were fused in order to produce the
enlargement of experiences.

51 GARGANO, JAMES W. "The 'Look' as a Major Event in James's
    Short Fiction." *Arizona Quarterly* 35, no. 4 (Winter):303-20.
    Surveys the ways in which James uses the glance as visual
discourse and as a special language. Gargano examines the function of
the glance in "Madame de Mauves," "Four Meetings," "The Liar," "The
Real Thing," and "The Beast in the Jungle."

52 GIRGORESCU, DAN. "Un victorian modern" [A modern
    Victorian]. *Contemporanul* (14 September):10.
    In Romanian.

53 GIRGUS, SAM B. "Inner Death and Freedom in Henry James." In
    *The Law of the Heart: Individualism and the Modern Self in
    American Literature*. Austin: University of Texas Press, pp. 84-99,
    164-67.
    Argues that in *The Bostonians* and *The Princess Casamassima*
James explores the victimization of the innocent consciousness by social
and cultural forces while in *What Maisie Knew* James depicts "the
unsuccessful struggle [of the individual self] for life and for love."

54   GOETZ, WILLIAM R. "Criticism and Autobiography in James's Prefaces." *American Literature* 51, no. 3 (November):333-48.

Approaches the prefaces as continuations of the earlier fictions and as "an autobiographical venture" in which James attempts to reappropriate the past. Goetz traces the imagery of the text palimpsest and the house of fiction in order to illuminate the dualism of mimesis, an issue dominating the prefaces. Goetz concludes that the prefaces ultimately blur the distinction between literary and critical texts.

Reprinted 1986.60.

55   GRABLER, STUART MARK. "Symmetry and Ideology: Studies of *The American, The Tragic Muse,* and *The Golden Bowl*." Ph.D. dissertation, State University of New York, Stony Brook, 333 pp.

Traces the relationship between James's use of symmetry and the various ideologies within which James worked throughout his career.

See *Dissertation Abstracts International* 40, no. 6 (1979):3299A.

56   GROVE, JAMES. "The Neglected Dinner in James's *The Wings of the Dove*." *American Notes and Queries* 18, no. 1 (September):5-6.

Examines Mrs. Lowder's second dinner, during which the main characters discuss the absent Milly, and argues that here Densher first shows his ability to appreciate the spiritual dimensions of Milly's innocence.

57   GRUBMAN, G.B. "Amerikanskaja monografija o Turgeneve i Genri Džejmse." *Russkaja Literatura: Istoriko-litaraturnyji Žurnal* (Leningrad, U.S.S.R.) 22, no. 1:211-16.

In Russian.

Reviews American criticism on Turgenev.

58   GRUNES, DENNIS. "The Demonic Child in *The Turn of the Screw*." *Psychocultural Review* 2, no. 4 (Fall):221-39.

Explores the tale within the context of Christian redemption, seeing the demonic child and as an inverted Christ, and also links it to Dickens's depiction of children, Shelley's *Frankenstein*, and Hawthorne's "Rappaccini's Daughter." The child who has fallen from innocence corroborates the Fall and "embodies our sentimental insistence on childhood innocence."

1979

59 HAGGERTY, GEORGE EDGAR. "Gothic Fiction from Walpole to James: A Study of Formal Development." Ph.D. dissertation, University of California, Berkeley, 267 pp.

Argues that Poe's development of the Gothic tale was a response to the difficulty of manipulating Gothic devices to produce certain effects within the novel form. Poe liberates the Gothic from the novel's depth and breadth; Hawthorne and James reintroduce the Gothic to the novel without diminishing the affective potential of the Gothic.

See *Dissertation Abstracts International* 40, no. 7 (1980):4036A.

60 HALL, RICHARD. "An Obscure Hurt: The Sexuality of Henry James: Part I." *New Republic* (28 April):25-31.

Examines the relationship between William and Henry James, suggesting that Henry's "sexual anxiety" might be explained by incestuous feelings for William.

61 _____. "An Obscure Hurt: The Sexuality of Henry James: Part II." *New Republic* (5 May):25-29.

Continues his chronicle of the relationship between William and Henry James, seeing it as "the central emotional experience" of James's life. That relationship explains aspects of James's fiction; for example, Jamesian ambiguity is a device for screening taboo feelings.

62 HARRIS, WENDELL V. "The Sophisticated Tale and the True Short Story." In *British Short Fiction of the Nineteenth Century*. Detroit: Wayne State University Press, pp. 85-89.

Surveys briefly James's development as a short story writer, beginning with his early work, a mixture of "finesse and awkwardness," and concluding with his later work. Harris also distinguishes between James's short fiction, structured on the novella, and his short stories.

63 HEATON, DANIEL H. "The Altered Characterization of Miss Birdseye in Henry James's *The Bostonians*." *American Literature* 50, no. 4 (January):588-603.

Traces the change in Miss Birdseye's character from the negative presentation in the early chapters to a much more favorable portrayal in the later chapters and attributes this change to James's preparation, albeit clumsy, for a more sympathetic treatment of Olive.

64 "Henry James." In *Twentieth-Century Literary Criticism 1900-1960*, vol. 2. Edited by Dedria Bryfonski and Sharon K. Hall. Detroit: Gale, pp. 243-76.

Reprints brief excerpts from the following authors: Joseph Conrad (1905); Ford Madox Hueffer [Ford] (1913); H.G. Wells (1914); Rebecca West (1916); Ezra Pound (1918); T.S. Eliot (1918); H.L. Mencken (1920); Virginia Woolf (1921); E.M. Forster (1927); R.P. Blackmur (1934, 1943, 1951); Stephen Spender (1935); Granville Hicks (1935); Graham Greene (1936); Yvor Winters (1938); F.O. Matthiessen (1944); Gertrude Stein (1947); Edward Sackville-West (1948); F.R. Leavis (1948); René Wellek (1958); Oscar Cargill (1961); Leon Edel (1962, 1964); Dorothea Krook (1962); Hortense Calisher (1967); F.W. Dupee (1974); and Louis Auchincloss (1975).

65 HOLLOWAY, JOHN. "Identity, Inversion, and Density Elements in Narrative: Three Tales by Chekhov, James, and Lawrence." In *Narrative and Structure: Exploratory Essays*. Cambridge: Cambridge University Press, pp. 53-73.

Proposes a system for evaluating episodes in a narrative based on their function, using Chekhov's "A Boring Story," James's "The Lesson of the Master," and Lawrence's "Love Among the Haystacks" as examples.

66 HOLLOWAY, MARCELLA M. "Another Turn to James' *The Turn of the Screw*." *CEA Critic* 41, no. 2 (January):9-17.

Stresses the importance of the total story not just the governess's manuscript. Holloway finds parallels between the introductory material and the manuscript and suggests that the relationship between Douglas and the governess mirrors that between her and the children.

67 HOLMAN, C[LARENCE] HUGH. "The *Bildungsroman*, American Style." In *Windows on the World: Essays on American Social Fiction*. Knoxville: University of Tennessee Press, pp. 168-97.

Argues that there is a special American form of the *Bildungsroman* in which the initiation occurs not through participation but by observation. The discussion includes "Madame de Mauves," "Daisy Miller," and *The Ambassadors*.

1979

68 _____. "'Of Everything the Unexplained and Irresponsible Specimen': Notes on How to Read American Realism." In *Windows on the World: Essays on American Social Fiction*. Knoxville: University of Tennessee Press, pp. 17-26.
  Discusses Turgenev's influence on James's realism, particularly in "the direct representation of life with clarity" and without apparent authorial intrusion.
  Reprint of essay in *Georgia Review* 18 (Fall 1964).

69 _____, comp. "Henry James." In *The American Novel Through Henry James*. 2d ed. Goldentree Bibliographies in Language and Literature. Arlington Heights, Ill.: AHM Publishing Co., pp. 78-96.
  Lists primary texts, bibliographies, biography, and criticism.

70 HOVANEC, EVELYN A. *Henry James and Germany*. Costerus new series vol. 19. Amsterdam: Rodopi, ii, 149 pp.
  Examines James's attitudes toward Germany and Germans, including the source of those attitudes and the effect on his work. Hovanec details all German references in James's nonfiction and fiction and concludes that James generally regarded Germany with discomfort and dislike and recognized parallels between Germany and America.

71 JEFFARES, BO. "The Artist's Tragic Temperament." In *The Artist in Nineteenth Century English Fiction*. Gerrards Cross, Buckinghamshire, England: Colin Smythe, pp. 120-24.
  Details James's portrait of the temperamental artist in *Roderick Hudson*. The tragedy of Roderick Hudson's genius is its volatility and insecurity.

72 JEFFERS, THOMAS L. "Maisie's Moral Sense: Finding Out for Herself." *Nineteenth-Century Fiction* 34, no. 2 (September):154-72.
  Argues that Maisie must discover for herself what constitutes good, and her discovery parallels that of the reader. Although she controls her destiny at the novel's end, it is a destiny "of having to risk moral judgments alone."

73   JILLSON, BARBARA SCHUBELER. "The Narrator-Protagonist and Societal Norms in Selected Modern Novels." Ph.D. dissertation, Case Western Reserve University, 249 pp.

Argues that societal norms provide the reader with a "familiar point of reference" even in those works in which a narrator-protagonist involves the reader in an "unmediated relationship." Jillson cites James's "The Turn of the Screw" as exemplifying this method of analysis because the norms are "well-defined and stable" in this novel.

See *Dissertation Abstracts International* 39, no. 11 (1979):6750A-6751A.

74   JOHNSON, D. BARTON. "A Henry James Parody in *Ada*." *Vladimir Nabokov Research Newsletter*, 3:33-34.

Notes that *Ada*'s Vanvitelli is a parody of Daisy Miller's Giovanelli and that "lettrocalamity" may be a pun on James's style, a "calamity of letters."

75   JOHNSON, JULIE McMASTER. "Death in the Fiction of Henry James: A Formal and Thematic Study." Ph.D. dissertation, Georgia State University, 297 pp.

Details James's many uses of death in the tales and novels. Formal uses include narrative distancing, plot momentum, closure, and metaphor. The thematic use of death is usually related to suicide, with increasing stress on psychological death. Johnson then examines James's ambivalent attitude toward death and its implications for his fiction, particularly in works dealing with relationships between the living and the dead.

See *Dissertation Abstracts International* 41, no. 1 (1980):252A.

76   KANTROW, ALAN M. "Anglican Custom, American Consciousness." *New England Quarterly* 52, no. 3 (September):307-25.

Argues that Puritan and Anglican influences on the nineteenth century American mind can be clearly seen in responses to Catholic Europe and uses *The American* to demonstrate this. In the novel the mysteries of Europe are represented in the image of an impassable wall, while at the same time the European characters strike "sympathetic modes of response" in Newman, suggesting that European customs and manners are part of "the various patrimony of the American mind."

1979

77   KAUFMAN, JULE S. "*The Spoils of Poynton*: In Defense of Fleda
     Vetch." *Arizona Quarterly* 35, no. 4 (Winter):342-56.
          Argues that Fleda Vetch deserves praise, not censure, because
     she possesses greater humanity and sensitivity than Mrs. Gereth, as well
     as integrity, virtue, self-respect, and self-knowledge. Although the novel
     ends in desolation, Fleda in spite of her failure embodies positive values
     James will affirm in his later novels.

78   KIMMEY, JOHN L. "The 'London' Book." *Henry James Review* 1,
     no. 1 (November):61-72.
          Discusses James's plans and notes for a book on London,
     which was to be similar to *The American Scene*. Kimmey chronicles
     James's writings about and responses to London and speculates that
     had James written the book, it would have given an "unequaled view" of
     the city.

79   KIRCHHOFF, FREDERICK. "City as Self: Henry James's Travel
     Sketches of Venice." *Prose Studies 1800-1900* 2:73-87.
          Traces the patterns of disavowal and assimilation in the four
     essays on Venice from *Italian Hours*, arguing that James uses these pat-
     terns to define his identity as a writer.

80   KOZIKOWSKI, STANLEY J. "Unreliable Narration in Henry
     James's 'The Two Faces' and Edith Wharton's 'The Dilettante.'"
     Arizona Quarterly 35, no. 4 (Winter):357-72.
          Compares the two tales, particularly in their use of an
     "observed observer" as a narrator who withholds information. Because
     Wharton places her observer within the action, she achieves the "the-
     matic integrity" that James does not with his more distant observer.
     Kozikowski suggests that Wharton may have written this tale to show
     her independence from James – which, in fact, reflects "The Dilettantes"
     subject.

81   KUDO, YOSHIMI. "Shiten to Ishiki to Kotoba: Henry James no
     The Golden Bowl wo Megutte" [Point of view, consciousness, and
     words: Henry James's *The Golden Bowl*]. *Eigo Seinen* 125:122-24,
     152, 200-2, 250-53.
          In Japanese.

Argues that point of view is the unifying element in James's novels; what is represented as the world is the image of the world reflected in a person's consciousness. James tries to represent this world through words: verbs, abstract nouns, adjectives, pronouns, paraphrases, and articulate images. The problem, however, lies in the fact that the reality created through words is too weak to exist beyond the consciousness represented.

82   LAGRUP, KNUT. "Henry James: En Misantrophisk estet" [Henry James: A misanthropic esthete]. *Horisont: Organ for Svenska Osterbottens literaturvetenskap* (Stockholm) 26, no. 5:6-9.

83   LAWRY, EDWARD G. "To the Editor." *Henry James Review* 1, no. 1 (November):117-21.
        Responds to Todd's (1976.194) portrayal of James as lacking "theoretical competence." Todd discusses James's critical writings stripped of their context and then uses logical analysis to "demolish" their meaning.

84   LEE, BRIAN. *The Novels of Henry James: A Study in Culture and Consciousness*. New York: St. Martin's Press, viv, 123 pp.
        Examines the major works of James's career to demonstrate that the greatness of his art lies in his concern with the individual and the values upon which civilization is based. While acknowledging the influences of others on James, Lee argues that James was essentially original because he responded freely to experience. James's concerns prompted him to focus on the presentation of consciousness, which in turn influenced his fictional technique.

85   LING, AMY. "The Painter in the Lives and Works of Thackeray, Zola, and James." Ph.D. dissertation, New York University, 299 pp.
        Argues that Thackeray's *The Newcomes* and James's *The Tragic Muse* reflect both the awe and suspicion with which the artist has been regarded. Both novels explore the artist's conflict between the demands of art and those of society. Zola, in contrast, does not treat the artist ambivalently in *L'Oeuvre*, which depicts the psychological, emotional, and physical demands of artistic creation.
        See *Dissertation Abstracts International* 40, no. 11 (1980):5853A.

1979

86 LOEB, HELEN MARIE. "Cinderella Displaced and Replaced: Mythic Displacement in 'Tristram and Iseult', *Jane Eyre, Tess of the D'Ubervilles,* and *Turn of the Screw.*" Ph.D. dissertation, University of Wisconsin, Madison, 385 pp.

Argues that two female archetypes – the seductive Eve and the virtuous, nurturing virgin – shape character. "In The Turn of the Screw," the governess is a battleground for the two archetypes; the conflict between the two is never resolved.

See *Dissertation Abstracts International* 40, no. 6 (1979):3318A-3319A.

87 LONG, ROBERT EMMET. *The Great Succession: Henry James and the Legacy of Hawthorne.*" Critical Essays in Modern Literature Series. Pittsburgh: University of Pittsburgh Press, xi, 203 pp.

Traces Hawthorne's influence on James from his early tales to *The Bostonians.* Hawthorne figures importantly in the fiction prior to *Roderick Hudson,* particularly in James's blending of realism and romance. The fiction following *Roderick Hudson* attempted to correct Hawthorne's shortcomings, as outlined in James's *Hawthorne. The Bostonians* is James's "most elaborate restatement of Hawthorne's themes," and although the novel is a culmination of Hawthorne's influence, it does not terminate it. James's relationship to Hawthorne – involving "close kinship and essential conflict, affinity and dissent, agreement and disavowal" – remains throughout James's career.

Reprint of "The Society and the Masks: *The Blithedale Romance* and *The Bostonians,*" *Nineteenth-Century Fiction* 19, no. 2 (September 1964):105-22; "James's *Washington Square*: The Hawthorne Relation," *New England Quarterly* 4 (December 1973):573-90; 1976.125, 126, 127.

88 MacADAM, ALFRED. "La figura en el tapiz: La coincidencia de Cortázar y James." *Inti: Revista de Literatura Hispánica et Luso-Brasilera* 10-11:173-78.

In Portugese.

89 MacANDREW, ELIZABETH. "The Arrival at Consciousness." In *The Gothic Tradition in Fiction.* New York: Columbia University Press, pp. 230-39.

Sees "The Turn of the Screw" as James's restatement of the "innocence-ignorance paradox" – can innocence be safeguarded by ignorance, its greatest danger? – and discusses James's use of Gothic devices.

ignorance, its greatest danger? – and discusses James's use of Gothic devices.

90 McCOLGAN, KRISTIN PRUITT. *Henry James, 1917-1959: A Reference Guide*. Boston: G.K. Hall & Co., xix, 389.

Annotates books, dissertations, and articles on James during the years 1917 to 1959. The annotations are descriptive, not evaluative.

91 MACHANN, VIRGINIA SUE BROWN. "American Perspectives on Women's Initiations: The Mythic and Realistic Coming to Consciousness." Ph.D. dissertation, University of Texas, Austin, 553 pp.

Examines the complex characterization of American heroines arising out of the joining of the initiatory pattern, which stresses the individual, with the depiction of the American woman who has typically been associated with communal concerns. Chapters 3 and 4 are devoted to *The Portrait of a Lady, The Bostonians, The Wings of the Dove*, and *The Golden Bowl* and show James's use of the initiatory pattern to create complexity and ambiguity.

See *Dissertation Abstracts International* 40, no. 3 (1979):1470A.

92 McMAHAN, ELIZABETH. "Sexual Desire and Illusion in *The Bostonians*." *Modern Fiction Studies* 25, no. 2 (Summer):241-51.

Argues that the novel shows that a woman's choice of a husband determines the degree of her freedom. Because Verena (like many women) lacks a sense of identity, she is blinded by hormones and romantic illusion and thus chooses Basil, "a narrow, authoritarian egotist."

93 MAILLOUX, PETER ALDEN. "Paradigms Lost: Studies in the Twentieth-Century Novel." Ph.D. dissertation, University of California, Berkeley, 247 pp.

Argues that although the novel traditionally "cooperates" with its reader by enabling the reader to understand it, the modern novel – exemplified by Joyce's *Ulysses*, James's *The Sacred Fount*, Beckett's *Watt*, and Pynchon's *V.* – deliberately misleads and mystifies the reader. In James's novel, the narrator refuses to give the reader any help in interpreting the narrative. Thus the novel shows that there is no objective truth.

1979

See *Dissertation Abstracts International* 41, no. 2 (1980):669A.

94   MAINI, DARSHAN SINGH. "Love and Sex in Henry James." In
Proceedings of a Symposium on American Literature. Edited by
Marta Sienicka. Seria Filologia Angielska 12, pp. 107-20.
         Argues that James's "sexual imagination" was crucial to his
work and discusses sexuality in terms of James's life and its evolution in
his fiction. Maini also examines James's depiction of women and his use
of sexual imagery.
         Reprinted 1987.79.

95   _____. "*Washington Square*: A Centennial Essay." *Henry James
Review* 1, no. 1 (November):81-101.
         Surveys critical responses to the novel. Criticism has largely
taken its cue from James's disparagement of the novel, although
recently the novel has received more respect. In the second half of the
essay, Maini argues for the novel's importance as a transitional work in
which James completes his lessons from his French masters and begins
to speak with a "clear, new voice."

96   MARKS, PATRICIA. "Culture and Rhetoric in Henry James's 'Poor
Richard' and 'Eugene Pickering.'" *South Atlantic Bulletin* 44, no.
1:61-72.
         Argues that in both tales James shows the protagonist's
understanding and mastery of language as essential to maturity and to
an "adequate world view."

97   MAROTTA, KENNY. "*What Maisie Knew*: The Question of Our
Speech." *ELH* 46, no. 3 (Fall):495-508.
         Contrasts Maisie's use of language with that of the adults,
showing that Maisie's "redemption" lies in her search for fidelity to
language. The novel's narrative method, which demands reader
participation, marks a turning point for James: previous novels showed
the dangers of relying on the narrator's language; the novels after *What
Maisie Knew* reveal the risks such participation entails.

98 MATKOVIĆ, IVAN. "'The Portrait,' 'The Wings' and James's Theory." *Studia Romanica et Anglica Zagrebiensia* 24, nos. 1-2:279-95.

Compares the novels' narrative methods, plot, symbols, and sentence structures and relates them to James's own aesthetic theory. Matković concludes that *The Wings* is a better novel than *The Portrait of a Lady* because of James's achievement of beauty and sublimity, even though those qualities are not James's highest aesthetic values.

99 MAYER, CHARLES W. "Henry James's 'Discriminated Occasion': A Determinant of Form." *Journal of Narrative Technique* 9, no. 3 (Fall):133-46.

Shows that the "discriminated occasion," described in the preface to *The Wings of the Dove*, is the synthesis of picture and scene and the means by which James achieves compostional unity. Mayer examines the central consciousness and the scenic method in *The Wings of the Dove*.

100 _____. "Isabel Archer, Edna Pontellier, and the Romantic Self." *Research Studies* (Pullman, Wash.) 47, no. 2 (June):89-97.

Argues that Isabel and Edna share Emersonian idealism, upon which is based their "American romance of the self." Both heroines must find a relationship between self and the world. Isabel demonstrates how knowledge and experience shapes consciousness and choice; for Edna, knowledge and experience are ineffectual when actions are subject to emotion.

101 _____. "The Triumph of Honor: James and Hemingway." *Arizona Quarterly* 35, no. 4 (Winter):373-91.

Argues that in spite of apparent differences the two authors shared deep affinities. Both have a commitment to craft and a vision of the individual struggling to transcend social roles and expectations; both affirm the power of the individual and the importance of being rather than doing.

102 MAZZENO, LAURENCE W. "Tennyson and Henry James." *Tennyson Research Bulletin* 3, no. 3 (November):111-16.

1979

> Argues that while James criticized Tennyson's works he admired the poet and incorporated elements of *Idylls of the King* in *The Golden Bowl*.

103   MEYERS, JEFFREY. "Velásquez and 'Daisy Miller.'" *Studies in Short Fiction* 16, no. 3 (Summer):171-78.

> Regards Velásquez's painting of Innocent X as the tale's symbolic center because it embodies the ambiguity of the idea of innocence and the distinction between realism and idealism.

104   MIHĂILĂ, RODICA. Introduction to *Ore Petrecute in Anglia* [English Hours]. Bucharest: Sport-Turism, pp. 5-18.

> In Romanian.

105   MILLAR, GAVIN. "Two Worlds." *Listener* (London) 102, no. 2618 (5 July):25-26.

> Notes that Ivory's film adaptation of *The Europeans* lacks the novel's emotional warmth. The novel's "confused mingling" of Europe and America becomes a conflict in the film.

106   MULRAIN, MARY ANN. "British Novels between the Two World Wars with the City of London as Metaphor." Ph.D. dissertation, University of Tulsa, 135 pp.

> Argues that the changing focus of urban novelists reflects changes in British society. James, Conrad, and Greene documented the urban poor who saw revolution as a solution to their plight; Woolf, Waugh, and Harry Green depict a disillusioned middle class who seek escape in social gatherings.
>
> See *Dissertation Abstracts International* 40, no. 11 (1980):5869A.

107   MURPHY, BRENDA. "The Problem of Validity in the Critical Controversy over *The Turn of the Screw*." *Research Studies* (Pullman, Wash.) 47, no. 3 (September):191-201.

> Reviews the lack of consensus of interpreting the tale and attributes it to the conceptual frameworks brought to the text, the impossibility of ascertaining James's intent, but most important, to individual perception and understanding.

108   "1977-1978 Annual Review: Henry James." *Journal of Modern Literature* 7, no. 4:738-42.
    Lists criticism published in 1978-1979.

109   NORRMAN, RALF. "Chiastik inversion: ett monster hos Henry James" [Chiastic inversion: a pattern in Henry James]. In *Pegas och snobollskrig: litteraturvetenskapliga studier tillagnade Sven Linner.* [Pegasus and a battle of snowballs: literary studies in honor of Sven Linner]. Publications of the Research Institute of the Abo Akademi Foundation, no. 44. Abo, Finland: Abo Akademi, pp. 209-25.
    In Finnish.
    Reprinted in 1982.108.

110   ____. "Referential Ambiguity in Pronouns as a Literary Device in Henry James's *The Golden Bowl.*" *Studia Neophilologica* 51, no. 1:31-71.
    Traces the ways in which pronomial ambiguity functions in the novel. These include foreshadowing; reminding reader of the symmetrical relationships; and creating suspense, confusion, and dramatic interest.
    Reprinted in 1982.108.

111   PALLISER, CHARLES. "'A Conscious Prize': Moral and Aesthetic Value in *The Spoils of Poynton.*" *Modern Language Quarterly* 40, no. 1 (March):37-52.
    Argues that James's attitude toward Fleda Vetch is a blend of sympathy for her moral scruples and ironic awareness of her inconsistencies because of her scrupulousness. Fleda's concern with "the internal and psychological sphere" results in her failure to acknowledge "the external world of matter and chance."

112   PASSOW, EMILIE SCHERZ. "Orphans and Aliens: Changing Images of Childhood in Works of Four Victorian Novelists." Ph.D. dissertation, Columbia University, 231 pp.
    Sees the changing depiction of children in the work of Dickens, Emily Brontë, George Eliot, and James as a reaction to a volatile world and a fragmented sense of self. Two patterns are apparent: estrangement and the move from innocence to experience. James's fiction–"The Pupil," *What Maisie Knew*, and "The Turn of the

1979

Screw" – "diminishes the redemptive powers of the child's angle of vision" in the portrayal of neglected children.

See *Dissertation Abstracts International* 40, no. 5 (1979):2698A.

113   PATNODE, DARWIN. "The Quality of Life in *The Ambassadors*." *DeKalb Literary Arts Journal* 13, nos. 1-2:99-108.

Argues that the novel's injunction to "live all you can" does not mean immersion in experience but only spectatorship, especially when experience involves sexuality. Patnode suggests that the novel's reliance upon imagery drawn from the visual arts reinforces Strether's isolation from "present actuality."

114   PATTERSON, RICHARD ALVIN. "Henry James's Fiction on the Twentieth-Century Stage: A Study of Problems in Adaptation and a History of the Critical Response to Dramatizations Produced in London and New York since 1916." Ph.D. dissertation, New York University, 535 pp.

Examines stage adaptations of *The Tragic Muse, Washington Square,* "The Turn of the Screw," *The Portrait of a Lady, The Wings of the Dove, The Reverberator,* and "The Aspern Papers;" in addition, operas: "The Turn of the Screw," "Owen Wingrave," *Washington Square,* and *The Wings of the Dove.* This study assesses the difficulties of adapting James's fiction to the stage, as well as the dramatic elements in the fiction.

See *Dissertation Abstracts International* 40, no. 11 (1980):5860A.

115   PEARCE, ROY HARVEY. "The Cry and the Occasion: 'Chocorua to Its Neighbor.'" *Southern Review* 15, no. 4 (October):777-91.

Argues that Wallace Steven's poem uses James's "topos and iconography" of *The American Scene.* James saw Mount Chocorua as a lesson in history and aesthetics. Pearch traces James's echoes in Stevens and concludes that James is the hero of the poem's third phase.

116   PEROSA, SERGIO. *L'Euro-America di Henry James* [Henry James's Euro-America]. Vicenza: Pozza, 112 pp.

In Italian.

117 PERROT, JEAN. "L'Anamorphose dans les romans de Henry James." *Critique* (Paris) 35, no. 383 (April):334-54.
In French.

118 _____. "Henry James: Stratégie littéraire et constitution de l'image de l'homme de lettres." *Littérature* (Paris, France) 33 (February):37-57.
In French.

119 PETRICK, JOANNE LUCKINO. "Nathaniel Hawthorne, Henry James, and 'The Deeper Psychology.'" Ph.D. dissertation, Ohio State University, 239 pp.
Argues that while both writers were concerned with individual moral responsibility complicated by the social context, James's analysis of "the deeper psychology" is informed by realism and William James's psychological theories and thus is more sophisticated in content and technique than Hawthorne's. James's works discussed here include "The Jolly Corner," "Daisy Miller," "The Beast in the Jungle," "The Author of 'Beltraffio,'" and *The Bostonians*.
See *Dissertation Abstracts International* 40, no. 4 (1979):2065A.

120 PHILLIPS, KATHY J. "Conversion to Text, Initiation to Symbolism, in Mann's *Der Tod in Venedig* and James' *The Ambassadors*." *Canadian Review of Comparative Lit/Revue Canadienne de Littérature Comparée* 6, no. 4 (Fall):376-88.
Traces the use of symbolism in the two works, particularly that related to substitution. The characters' involvement with substitution underscores Mann's and James's focus on art as the double of life.

121 PIPER, MYFANWY. "Writing for Britten." In *The Operas of Benjamin Britten*. Edited by David Herbert. New York: Columbia University Press, pp. 8-21.
Describes the various problems encountered in adapting "The Turn of the Screw," "Owen Wingrave," and "Death in Venice" for opera, particularly in conveying the supernatural in James's tales. Piper wanted to adhere closely to the text; Britten's "sure dramatic instinct" encouraged her to expand it.

1979

122 PROBERT, KENNETH GORDON. "Romance by Intent: A Study of Generic Procedure in *The Blithedale Romance, Moby-Dick, The American,* and *The Great Gatsby.*" Ph.D. dissertation, York University, Canada.

Argues that in all four novels the authors use the norms and themes of the romance to investigate contemporary issues, often relying upon a character who draws attention to the romance elements. James's novel is seen as "an artful manipulation of chivalric and Gothic romance."

See *Dissertation Abstracts International* 40, no. 9 (1980):5040A.

123 PYM, JOHN. "'Where Could I Meet Other Screenwriters?': A Conversation with Ruth Prawer Jhabvala." *Sight & Sound* 48, no. 1 (Winter):15-18.

Discusses Jhabvala's script for *The Europeans.* She had to cut much of the novel's "marvelous Henry James' dialogue" and change the novel's development of plot, which depends on a succession of small scenes.

124 RICHARDS, BERNARD. "James and His Sources: *The Spoils of Poynton.*" *Essays in Criticism* 29, no. 4 (October):302-22.

Identifies the houses Montacute and Fox Warren as models for Poynton and Waterbath, respectively. Although the world of the novel is a fictional one, source studies give us "the palpable constituents" of James's imagination and "windows" into the novel.

125 _____. "The Sources of Henry James's 'The Marriages.'" *Review of English Studies* 30, no. 119 (August):316-22.

Notes that Alice James's remarks on Sir John Rose's proposed marriage to Lady Tweeddale and William James's essay on "The Hidden Self" may have inspired James's tale and may indicate when James wrote it.

126 RON, MOSHE. "A Reading of 'The Real Thing.'" *Yale French Studies* no. 58:190-212.

Describes the conflict in the tale as one between two modes of representation, distinguished by intentionality. Ron also discusses the role of the unreliable narrator, focusing on the relation between the

narrator and the Monarchs, which mirrors the relation between the two pairs of models.
Reprinted 1982.126.

127   RULAND, RICHARD. "Beyond Harsh Inquiry: The Hawthorne of Henry James." *ESQ* 25, no. 2 [old series no. 95]:95-117.
Sees James's *Hawthorne* as central to understanding American culture and art. James discusses the implications of Hawthorne's complaint that America is not congenial to the romance and, in so doing, sheds light on American realism.

128   RYBURN, MAY L. *"Turn of the Screw* and *Amelia*: A Source for Quint?" *Studies in Short Fiction* 16, no. 3 (Summer):235-37.
Notes the similarities between Peter Quint's ghost and Robinson in Fielding's *Amelia* and suggests that Peter Quint is the governess's cleaned-up version of Robinson.

129   SAFRANEK, WILLIAM P. "Longmore in 'Madame de Mauves': The Making of a Pragmatist." *Arizona Quarterly* 35, no. 4 (Winter):293-302.
Sees the tale as a "textbook illustration" of pragmatism. Longmore, the tale's protagonist, moves from idealism, characterized by prescribing conduct for others, being judgmental, and focusing on facts rather than ideals. Safranek details the ways the tale's characters challenge Longmore's idealism.

130   SALZBERG, JOEL. "Mr. Mudge as Redemptive Fate: Juxtaposition in James's *In the Cage*." *Studies in the Novel* 11, no. 1 (Spring):63-76.
Sees Mudge as a foil to the "dubious" values of Mrs. Jordan and Captain Everard. In addition, Salzberg argues that Mudge's task is to "tame the shrew" and save her from her narrow perspective and arrogance.

*131   SANGARI, K. "The Ironic Passion: Henry James and F. Scott Fitzgerald – A Study." Ph.D. dissertation, University of Leeds.
Source: *Annual Bibliography of English Language and Literature* 58 (1983):457, item 8103.

1979

132 SARBU, ALADAR. *Henry James Világa* [Henry James's World]. Budapest: Európa, 269 pp.

133 SCHUG, CHARLES. "Henry James." In *The Romantic Genesis of the Modern Novel*. Pittsburgh: University of Pittsburgh Press, pp. 74-132.

    Examines themes, images, narration, and structure in *The Ambassadors*, *The Wings of the Dove*, and *The Golden Bowl* to show that James's vision of the novel was deliberately romantic and thus forward-looking, because for Schug "the modern novel has a Romantic form."

134 SCURA, DOROTHY McINNIS. *Henry James, 1960-1974: A Reference Guide*. Boston: G.K. Hall & Co., xx, 490 pp.

    Lists books, dissertations, and articles on James published during the years 1960 to 1974 and includes a brief description of each item.

135 SEED, D. "Henry James's Reading of Flaubert." *Comparative Literature Studies* 16, no. 4 (December):307-17.

    Argues that Sainte-Beuve, James's ideal critic, shaped James's early view of Flaubert. James criticized Flaubert's lack of control over technique and excessive sensualism. By the late 1890s, however, influenced by Emile Faguet, James admired Flaubert's work and adopted his "style indirect libre."

136 SHARMA, J.N. *The International Fiction of Henry James*. New Delhi: Macmillan Company of India, 136 pp.

    Analyzes the theme, characterization, and setting of James's great international novels: *The American*, *The Portrait of a Lady*, *The Ambassadors*, *The Wings of the Dove*, and *The Golden Bowl*. Over the course of these novels, James's vision expands from individual manners to the morals of civilization; greater complexity in characterization parallels this broadening vision; and the depiction of setting shifts from representational to impressionistic. Sharma concludes this study by discussing the international theme in the fiction of writers after James, primarily Wharton and Hemingway.

137 SHIPLEY, JEANNE ELIZABETH. "The Authority of Precision: Essays on Henry James and Robert Musil." Ph.D. dissertation, State University of New York, Buffalo, 140 pp.

Argues that *The Portrait of a Lady* reflects the displacement of authority paradigmatic of the modern novel, a displacement associated with the image of the haunted house. Shipley then examines this image in Musil's *Der Mann Ohne Eigenschaften*. Although Musil attempts to restore authority with images of mathematics and precision, such imagery "tends to collapse rather than to support a rhetoric of authority."

See *Dissertation Abstracts International* 39, no. 12 (1979):7335A.

138 SLOMOVITZ, PHILIP. "The Anti-Semitism of Henry James." *Jewish Affairs* 34, no. 12 (December):33, 35.

Recounts Geismar's exposé of James's antiSemitism in *Henry James and The Jacobites*. James's prejudices are apparent in *Roderick Hudson*, *The Awkward Age*, *The Golden Bowl*, and *The American Scene*. Geismar, Slomovitz concludes, "rendered a great service to American culture by exposing the arch-bigot Henry James."

139 SMITH, CARL S. "James's International Fiction: Sources and Evolution." *Centennial Review* 23, no. 4 (Fall):397-422.

Examines the international tales, novels, and travel sketches to demonstrate that James's response to the modern world was a nostalgic return to earlier eras of travel, and to move "his center of interest from the external world to his perception of it."

*140 SPENDER, STEPHEN. "*What Maisie Knew* by Henry James." *Observer Magazine* (12 August):53.
Source: *British Humanities Index* (1979), p. 261.

141 STALLMAN, R.W. "To the Editor." *Henry James Review* 1, no. 1 (November):116.

Recounts a visit with Mr. and Mrs. William James at Chocorua in 1956. Mrs. James showed Stallman the typescript of a BBC program on James, and Stallman wrote two quatrains, included in the letter, based on humorous incidents from the program.

1979

142 STEINHARDT, H. "Il chema Henry James nu Marcel Proust" [He was called Henry James and not Marcel Proust]. *Viata Româneasca* (Budapest) 32, no. 4:59-60.

143 STONE, ALBERT E. "Henry James and Childhood: *The Turn of the Screw*." In *American Character and Culture in a Changing World: Some Twentieth-Century Perspectives*. Edited by John A. Hague. Contributions to American Studies, no. 42. Westport, Conn.: Greenwood Press, pp. 279-92.

　　Demonstrates that, although this tale shares many elements with American fiction about children, it departs from them in its depiction of the limitations of innocence and its criticism of social stratification and religion.

144 STROUT, CUSHING. "Henry James's Dream of the Louvre, 'The Jolly Corner,' and Psychological Interpretation." *Psychohistory Review* 8, no. 1-2:47-52.

　　Shows that psychological criticism must be used with caution in analyzing a work of art, using James's dream of the Louvre and "The Jolly Corner" as an example. Many critics have identified James with Brydon on the basis of that dream; Strout suggests that the dream reflects James's artistic ambition.

　　Reprinted 1983.104.

145 TANIMOTO, YASUKO. "'Shosetsu no Giho' no ichi: James Bungaku no Tenkai ni Okeru" [The place of "The Art of Fiction" in James's literary development]. *Eigo Seinen* (Tokyo) 125:106-8.

　　In Japanese.

　　Suggests that in this essay, published at the turning point in his career, James announces the "freedom of the fiction writer"; he is determined to write artistic fiction in spite of strong pressure from editors and critics.

146 TANNER, TONY. *Henry James I: 1843-1881*. Writers and their Work Series. Essex: Longman for the British Council, 65 pp.

　　Sketches James's life during these years but focuses on the novels of the period as well as *Hawthorne*. Tanner describes the plot, characters, stylistic devices, and themes of these novels. *The Portrait of a Lady* culminates the work of this period and establishes James as a major writer in the United States and in England.

Reprinted 1985.134.

147   ____. *Henry James II: 1882-1898.* Writers and Their Work Series. Essex: Longman for the British Council, 64 pp.

Summarizes the important events but focuses on the novels and novellas of this period. Tanner examines plot, theme, characterization, and style of these works, beginning with *The Bostonians* and concluding with "The Turn of the Screw." During these years James faces several crises in his life–the deaths of his parents and the failure of his plays–and these crises are reflected in the experimental nature of his fiction.

Reprinted 1985.134.

148   TAYLOR, GORDON O. "Chapters of Experience: *The American Scene.*" *Genre* 12, no. 1 (Spring):93-116.

Sees *The American Scene* as an autobiography in which James must resolve questions about his identity as an American and as a writer. The book enabled James "to address American issues as an American" and at the same time to maintain artistic detachment.

Reprinted 1983.197.

149   TEDFORD, BARBARA WILKIE. "Of Libraries and Salmon-Colored Volumes: James's Reading of Turgenev through 1873." *Resources for American Literary Study* 9, no. 1 (Spring):39-49.

Proposes that James started reading Turgenev in the late 1850s because the James family received *Revue des Deux Mondes*, in which Turgenev's work regularly appeared. By 1874, the year of James's essay on Turgenev, James had a long and thorough knowledge of the Russian writer.

150   TELOTTE, J.P. "Language and Perspective in James's *The American.*" *South Atlantic Bulletin* 44, no. 1:27-39.

Demonstrates that in this novel James shows, through Christopher Newman, the limitations of comprehension and the ambiguity of language. At the novel's beginning Newman takes words at face value and reflects his tendency to quantify experience. His dealings with the Bellegardes force him to renounce the words by which he believed he could appropriate reality and to accept the impossibility of fixing reality through its representation.

1979

151 TINTNER, ADELINE R. "Henry James and Gustave Doré."
Markham Review 8 (Winter):21-25.
Traces Doré's influences on James, covering fiction and
nonfiction. Tintner suggests that James was attuned to the "primordial
fears and deep unconscious impulses" of the fairy tales and their
illustrations and also remarks upon the similarities shared by James
and Doré. The illustrations referred to in the essay are also included.
Revised 1986.151.

152 _____. "Henry James and the Symbolist Movement in Art." *Journal
of Modern Literature* 7, no. 3 (September):397-415.
Traces James's use of elements from symbolist art in his tales
and novels. Tintner suggests that James's borrowing of this iconography
is a criticism of the sensualism of the movement. The essay contains
illustrations of the art referred to in the text.
Revised 1986.151.

153 _____. "Hezekiah and *The Wings of the Dove*: The Origin of 'She
Turned her Face to the Wall.'" *NMAL: Notes on Modern American
Literature* 3:Item 22.
Shows that James derived this quote from 2 Kings, 20:2 and
paralleled Milly's death to Hezekiah's. He also used this quotation in
"The Abasement of the Northmores" and in "The Beldonald Holbein."

154 _____. "An Illustrator's Literary Interpretation." *AB Bookman's
Weekly* (26 March):2275, 2278, 2280, 2282.
Analyses John la Farge's illustration heading the original
magazine publication of "The Turn of the Screw." The illustration,
which is included with the essay, captures the dualistic nature of the
governess.

155 _____. "'An International Episode': A Centennial Review of a
Centennial Story." *Henry James Review* 1, no. 1 (November):24-60.
Details the plot, historical background, allusions,
contemporary reception, and current criticism on James's "Centennial"
story, which is "a declaration of independence from the social class
system of England." Tintner appends a contemporary review as well as
a contemporary commentary on "The Art of Fiction" controversy since
in his essay James alludes to this tale.

156   _____. "James' Etonian: A Blend of Literature, Life, and Art." *AB Bookman's Weekly* (19 November):3419-38.

Shows how Bob Bantling in *The Portrait of a Lady* was shaped by George John Whyte-Melville's 1853 novel *Digby Grant: An Autobiography*; by James's acquaintance with Arthur Benson; and by George Frederick Watt's painting *Sir Galahad.*

157   _____. "The Real-Life Holbein in James' Fiction." *AB Bookman's Weekly* (8 January):278-87.

Traces the four "phases" of James's friendship with Isabella Stewart Gardner as they are reflected in his fiction: the first, "A New England Winter"; the second, *The Spoils of Poynton*; the third, "The Beldonald Holbein"; and the fourth, *The Golden Bowl*. The essay includes a reproduction of Holbein's portrait of Lady Butts, from Mrs. Gardner's collection, which James used in "The Beldonald Holbein." Revised 1986.151.

158   _____. "Two Innocents in Rome: Daisy Miller and Innocent the Tenth." *Essays in Literature* 6, no. 1 (Spring):71-78.

Examines James's verbal and visual pun on "innocent" and traces the analogues and differences between Daisy and Innocent the Tenth. Tintner argues that James's use of the portrait "was a step beyond Hawthorne" in coalescing "the formal aspects of language with the dramatic work of art." She also shows that Winterbourne's behavior is as ambiguous as Daisy's.

159   TREADWELL, J.M. "Mrs. Touchett's Three Questions." *American Literature* 50, no. 4 (January):641-44.

Suggests that in chapter 54 Mrs. Touchett's second question, "Do you get on with your husband?" has been inadvertently dropped from the text because Isabel's statement, "It is my husband that doesn't get on with me," is a non sequitur.

160   TRILLING, LIONEL. "Henry James: 'The Pupil.'" In *Prefaces to The Experience of Literature*. New York: Harcourt Brace Jovanovich, pp. 102-6.

Contrasts Morgan's innocence, which derives from his honest view of reality, with the Moreen's deficient sense of reality. Morgan's

1979

death, however, is attributed to Pemberton's "fatally flawed" loyalty and his failure as a moral agent.

161 TROTTER, GARY OWEN. "The Process of Selection in the Art of Henry James." Ph.D. dissertation, State University of New York, Buffalo, 201 pp.

Traces James's "developing consciousness in guiding his intentions toward their realized form in the nouvelle and the novel." Trotter surveys James's career, focusing on *Roderick Hudson, The American,* "Daisy Miller," *The Portrait of a Lady, The Spoils of Poynton,* and *The Ambassadors.* He also draws upon James's notebooks, essays, and letters to supplement his analysis.

See *Dissertation Abstracts International* 40, no. 9 (1980):5060A.

162 WAGGONER, HYATT. "The Presence of Hawthorne." In *The Presence of Hawthorne.* Baton Rouge: Louisiana State University Press, pp. 143-161.

Examines Henry James's, William Faulkner's, and Robert Penn Warren's literary relationship to Hawthorne. Of the three, James's is the clearest and most complex. After reviewing James's "public" statements on Hawthorne in his 1872 review of Hawthorne's notebooks, *Hawthorne* (1979), and the 1904 letter for Hawthorne's centenary, Waggoner suggests that evidence of Hawthorne's kinship and influence is present in James's later works – particularly in James's development of the "deeper psychology," – and his interest in relations between characters and in morality.

163 WARD, J.A. "Henry James and Graham Greene." *Henry James Review* 1, no. 1 (November):10-23.

Compares the two novelists, focusing on *The Wings of the Dove* and *The Heart of the Matter,* particularly in terms of their portrayal of "the world of human sin." Greene is considerably more cynical than James and rejects James's faith that human beings can be "agents of grace."

*164 WATAWUNASHE, JONATHAN. "*Washington Square*: A Novel without a Heroine." *Opus.* University of Salisbury, Zimbabwe, 2d series, 4:36-38.

Source: *Annual Bibliography of English Literature and Language* 54 (1979):446, item 7871.

165 WEINTRAUB, STANLEY. "Lamb House." In *The London Yankees: Portrait of American Writers and Artists in England 1894-1914*. New York: Harcourt Brace Jovanovich, pp. 217-55, 387-88.
Chronicles James's acquisition of Lamb House, his 1904 visit to America, the creation of the New York Edition, and his friendship with Wharton.

166 WERTHEIM, STANLEY. "Images of Exile: *The Portrait of a Lady* and *The Sun Also Rises*." *Hemingway Notes* 5, no. 1:25-27.
Suggests that James's treatment of expatriated Americans in *The Portrait of a Lady* shaped Hemingway's in *The Sun Also Rises*. Mr. Luce is compared to the "overcultivated dilettante" Osmond, whose vulgarity is masked by the veneer of refinement. Jake Barnes is compared to Isabel: both maintain a moral balance and come to terms with traditional patterns of conduct that they can neither fully accept nor reject."

167 WESTBROOK, PERRY D. "American Libertarian Novelists: Henry James." In *Free Will and Determinism in American Literature*. Rutherford: Fairleigh Dickinson University Press, pp. 234-39.
Contrasts Daisy Miller, whom James sees in deterministic terms, with Isabel Archer, who is able to exercise free will.

168 WHELAN, ROBERT E., Jr. "God, Henry James, and 'The Great Good Place.'" *Research Studies* (Pullman, Wash.) 47, no. 4 (December):212-20.
Describes how this short story epitomizes James's religious experience and compares it to James's remarks in his 1910 essay "Is There a Life After Death?"

*169 WHITE, A.H. "The Uses of Obscurity in Meredith, Conrad, and James." Ph.D. dissertation, University of Cambridge.
Source: *Annual Bibliography of English Language and Literature* 56 (1981):438, item 8052.

1979

170 WIRTH-NESHER, HANA. "The Stranger Case of *The Turn of the Screw* and *Heart of Darkness.*" *Studies in Short Fiction* 16, no. 4 (Fall):317-25.

   Compares the two tales with each other and with Stevenson's *The Strange Case of Dr. Jekyll and Mr. Hyde.* All three focus on the problem of good and evil, although the tales of Conrad and James are more terrifying to modern sensibility because evil is portrayed as unidentifiable and as possessing the appearance of good.

171 WITEMEYER, HUGH. *George Eliot and the Visual Arts.* New Haven: Yale University Press, 238 pp.

   Compares James's responses to art to Eliot's throughout text, suggesting that James was more sensitive than Eliot to pictorial art while Eliot responded more to music than did James.

172 WOLFE, CHARLES K. "Victorian Ghost Story Technique: The Case of Henry James." *Romantist* 3:67-72.

   Details James's use of and contribution to the Victorian ghost story, which at the time was beginning to focus on internal rather than external ghosts. Many elements of the genre appealed to James, specifically its amorality and it ambiguity, because they fitted in with his artistic vision. James's use of the genre reflected his interest in point of view, and unreliable narrators contribute to the creation of ambiguity. Wolfe suggests that James proved that the ghost story could be serious art and that it could be opened to psychology. Wolfe discusses, though briefly, all of James's ghost stories.

173 ZABLOTNY, ELAINE. "Henry James and the Demonic Vampire and Madonna." *Psychocultural Review* 3, nos. 3-4 (Summer-Fall):203-24.

   Traces James's use of the figure of woman who appears at first to be Madonna-like, then predatory, and finally Madonna-like again. This figure occurs throughout the fiction, but Zablotny discusses in detail "A Landscape Painter," "DeGrey: A Romance," "Poor Richard," "The Diary of a Man of Fifty," and "The Bench of Desolation."

1980

1 ALEXANDER, CHARLOTTE. "Henry James and *Hot Corn.*" *American Notes and Queries* 19, nos. 3 and 4 (November-December):44-46.

Suggests that James's reminiscence of not being allowed to read Solon Robinson's novel reveals a "lingering sense of deprivation," which Alexander connects to the sexual suggestiveness of the novel's title.

2 ALLEN, JEANNE. "Literary and Cinematic Ambiguity: The Sound of the Turning Screw." In *Purdue University Fifth Annual Conference on Film*. Edited by Maud Walther. West Lafayette, Ind.: Department of Foreign Languages and Literatures, Purdue University, pp. 103-8.

Describes the various levels of ambiguity in the novella, focusing on the way in which linguistic elements contribute to that ambiguity. Clayton's film adaptation, *The Innocents*, must rely on visual devices to create ambiguity – statues, water, and mirrors, for example. Clayton's emphasis, however, is not so much on ambiguity as it is irony, which he creates by "dual visual messages" and the use of music and natural sounds.

3 ANDERSON, LINDA. "Self and Society in H.G. Wells's *Tono-Bungay.*" *Modern Fiction Studies* 26, no. 2 (Summer):199-212.

Examines Wells's novel to show how his concept of fiction departed from that of James's. While James acknowledged that fiction relied on reality, he focused on art as a subjective ordering of that reality. In contrast, Wells saw the novel as primarily referential, commenting on reality.

4 AOKI, TSUGIO. "Kenkyu no genjyo to kadai: Henry James" [Contemporary attitudes to Henry James]. *Eigo Seinen* (Tokyo) 126:168-69.

In Japanese.

Suggests that, on the whole, articles discussing James written by Japanese critics are much too abstract.

1980

5 _____. "Sandaime to shite no Henry James" [Henry James as the third in the James family]. In *Suga Yasuo, Ogoshi Kazuso: Ryo-kyoju Taikan Kinen Ronbunshu* [Essays commemorating the retirement of Professors Suga Yasuo and Ogoshi Kazuoso]. Kyoto: Apollonsha, pp. 853-63.

In Japanese.

Argues that Henry James Senior, a frustrated idealist who squandered the founder James's fortune, offered his novelist son the prototype of the Jamesian character.

6 ASTHANA, RAMA KANT. *Henry James: A Study in the Aesthetics of the Novel*. New Delhi: Associated Publishing House, vii, 130 pp.

Sees James's conception of the novel as constantly evolving and changing throughout his career. Drawing on the notebooks, essays, prefaces, and novels, Asthana traces that evolution and focuses on James's concept and rendering of consciousness. James moves from his belief in reason and form as absolutes to the more relativistic and organic aesthetic of his major phase. Throughout his life, James strove for "a finer and heightened art form" and a more perfect understanding of the complexities of consciousness.

Ph.D. dissertation, Banaras Hindu University, n.d.

7 AUCHARD, JOHN FRANCIS. "Silence in Henry James." Ph.D. dissertation, University of North Carolina, Chapel Hill, 217 pp.

Argues that silence – a metaphor in such early works as *Roderick Hudson, The American*, and *The Portrait of a Lady* – becomes a major dramatic device and a philosophical concern in later works, including *The Spoils of Poynton, The Wings of the Dove*, and *The Golden Bowl*.

See *Dissertation Abstracts International* 41, no. 8 (1981):3577A.

8 BABIIHA, THADDEO K. *The James-Hawthorne Relation: Bibliographical Essays*. Boston: G.K. Hall & Co., xiv, 313 pp.

Contains bibliographical essays on James's discussions of Hawthorne, analyses of the general relationship between James and Hawthorne, and evaluations of the influence Hawthorne's fiction – *The Scarlet Letter, The Blithedale Romance, The Marble Faun*, and other works – has had on James.

9 _____. "A Note on the James and Hawthorne Section in Leary's *Articles on American Literature, 1968-1975.*" *Henry James Review* 1, no. 3 (Spring):267-68.

Points out numerous typographical errors and omissions.

10 BARNETT, LOUISE K. "Displacement of Kin in the Fiction of Henry James." *Criticism* 22, no. 2 (Spring):140-55.

Shows that the family structures in *The Awkward Age, What Maisie Knew, The Portrait of a Lady, Daisy Miller,* and *The Ambassadors* reveal a pattern of unreliability, especially in mother-daughter relationships. The "victims of deprivation" search for surrogates who can never compensate for the failures of the parents.

11 BARRY, P.T. "Physical Descriptions in the International Tales of Henry James." *Orbis Litterarum* 35, no. 1:47-58.

Describes James's system of physical types that consistently reflect the moral and cultural polarities throughout the early international tales.

12 BENERT, ANNETTE LARSON. "The Dark Sources of Love: A Jungian Reading of Two Early James Novels." *University of Hartford Studies in Literature* 12, no. 2:99-123.

Parallels the work of Jung and James focusing on the contrasexual figures of the psyche. Jung holds that men are governed by logos, with eros in the background of the self; women are mirror images of that configuration. Benert examines the principal characters in *Roderick Hudson* to show how they live out the consequences of Jung's scheme.

13 _____. "Public Means and Private Ends: The Psychodynamics of Reform in James's Middle-Period Novels." *Studies in the Novel* 12, no. 4 (Winter):327-43.

Examines James's political vision in *The Princess Casamassima* and *The Bostonians*. James attributes the failure of political reform to the individual's failure in knowledge and in relationships and to the inability of the feminine to correct or mitigate "masculine brutality."

1980

14 BENGELS, BARBARA. "Flights into the Unknown: Structural Similarities in Two Works by H.G. Wells and Henry James." *Extrapolation* 21, no. 4 (Winter):361-66.

Finds similarities shared by "The Turn of the Screw" and *The Time Machine*, particularly in the setting framing the narrative, the creating of credibility, and the central characters.

15 BENT, NANCY PETTENGILL. "Romance and Irony in Henry James's View of Women." Ph.D. dissertation, Syracuse University, 247 pp.

Traces the romance myth of the "divine child," using the work of Jung and Kerenyi, in James's novels and tales, including *The Portrait of a Lady*, "The Pupil," *What Maisie Knew*, *The Awkward Age*, and *The Golden Bowl*. James uses the myth to undercut stereotypical roles of women and to present his own myth of strong women.

See *Dissertation Abstracts International* 42, no. 1 (1981):220A-221A.

16 BEREYZIAT, JEAN. "Ironie, indices et dérobade: 'The Jolly Corner' et la question du sens." *Confluents* 6, no. 2:7-56.

In French.

Argues that the art of irony consists of carefully sowing, sometimes quite subtly, the clues pointing to the irony, then unveiling the true meaning of the ironic event. James's "The Jolly Corner" illustrates this technique.

17 BERKOVE, LAWRENCE. "Henry James and Sir Walter Scott: A 'Virtuous Attachment'?" *Studies in Scottish Literature* 15:43-52.

Traces the phrase "virtuous attachment" in *The Ambassadors* to Scott's 1815 review of Austen's *Emma*, noting that the review contains features anticipating James's novel. Berkove argues for Scott's influence on James who contrasted Scott's moral sensibiity with George Sand's "inability to perceive moral distinctions." Although James criticized Scott, Sand's failure illuminated Scott's success in combining realism and morality.

18 BETSKY-ZWEIG, S. "From Pleached Garden to Jungle and Waste Land: Henry James's Beast." In *Cooper to Philip Roth: Essays on*

American Literature. Edited by J. Bakker and D.R.M. Wilkinson. Costerus new series, vol. 26. Amsterdam: Rodopi, pp. 45-55.

Analyzes the character of May Bartram, focusing on her animal and sphinx-like qualities; May "is both the Beast and its ghost taunting Marcher." Marcher is one of several James characters "who play it safe," asking much of life but giving little in return.

19 BISCHOFF, VOLKER. "The 'New England Conscience,' Thomas Gold Appleton, and Mrs. Vivian." *New England Quarterly* 53, no. 2 (June):222-25.

Traces the phrase "New England conscience," which James used in his 1879 novel *Confidence* to Thomas Gold Appleton's essay "The New England Conscience," in *A Sheaf of Papers*, 1875.
See Sweeney 1981.149.

20 BLACKALL, JEAN FRANTZ. "Literary Allusion as Imaginative Event in *The Awkward Age*." *Modern Fiction Studies* 26, no. 2 (Summer):179-97.

Examines the tangled literary allusions in a passage from the novel. Vanderbank alludes to *Faust, Notre-Dame de Paris*, Page's *Two Prisoners*, Zola's *Paris*, and *Roderick Hudson*. Blackall explains the implications of these references and describes the allusive passage as a mirror for both Vanderbank and the reader, reflecting "possible selves, possible motives, variable denouements."

21 BONARDELLI, GIOVANNI. "A Matter of Trifles." *Estudos Anglo-Americanos* (Sao Paulo, Brazil) 3-4:189-90.

Examines chapter 52 in *The Portrait of a Lady* in which Isabel says good-bye to Pansy at the convent before leaving for England. Isabel is attentive to the ominous details of the setting, thus demonstrating her growth from an unexperienced young lady to a mature woman.

22 BOSE, MITA. "Fictional Conventions in the Novels of Henry James and Edith Wharton." Ph.D. dissertation, Kent State University, 326 pp.

Shows that James's and Wharton's use of contrasting fictional conventions reflect two different kinds of realism. James's mode, "poetic realism," is apparent in *The Portrait of a Lady* and *The*

1980

Ambassadors and focuses on human consciousness. Wharton's "prosaic or literal realism," as seen in *The House of Mirth* and *The Age of Innocence*, is centered on the relationship between the individual and society.

See *Dissertation Abstracts International* 42, no. 1 (1981):212A.

*23 BRENT, JONATHAN. "The Middle World of Walter Pater and Henry James." Ph.D. dissertation, University of Chicago.
Source: Offline Bibliography, BRS Information Technologies, Latham, NY 12110.

24 BRINA, ROBERT RICHARD. "The Larger Ether: A Study of Henry James's Romantic Fiction." Ph.D. dissertation, University of California, Berkeley, 332 pp.
Argues that throughout his work James freed the romance from its limitations and conventions. The romantic, for James, "designate[d] a mode of cognition, an activity by which particular, undisclosed elements may be apprehended." James initially relied on Hawthorne and continued to use Hawthorne's house and garden imagery late in his career. *The Spoils of Poynton* clearly exemplifies the use of these images to explore the romantic quest for "the privileges of vision."
See *Dissertation Abstracts International* 41, no. 7 (1981):3114A-3115A.

25 BRUMM, ANNE-MARIE. "Mouths Biting Empty Air: Ezra Pound's Hugh Selwyn Mauberley and Henry James's Lambert Strether." *Revue de Littérature Comparée* 14, no. 1 (January-March):47-70.
Compares Pound's and James's passive but imaginative heroes, their vision of the artist in society, and their criticism of that society. Both authors capture "the mood of their time and civilization" and their work is still relevant to us, "children – or victims – of the modern age."

26 BUTERY, KAREN ANN. "The Victorian Heroine: A Psychological Study." Ph.D. dissertation: Michigan State University, 396 pp.
Applies Horneyan psychology to the heroines of *Jane Eyre, Daniel Deronda, Jude the Obscure*, and *The Portrait of a Lady* to

illuminate character formation, motivation, and responses to conflicts, and to examine the tension between rhetoric and mimesis.

See *Dissertation Abstracts International* 41, no. 12 (1981):5105A.

27 CHENG, STEPHEN. "The Jamesian Techniques in 'Delirious Mutterings at Midnight.'" *Tamkang Review* 11, no. 1 (Fall):43-64.

Traces James's influence in a novella written by Shui Ching, a modern Taiwanese writer. Shui Ching, who admires James, employs a ficelle, elaborate imagery, limited point of view, and the Jamesian "journey of the mind."

28 CHURCHILL, KENNETH. "The American Novelists in Italy." In *Italy and English Literature, 1764-1930*. New York: Barnes & Noble, pp. 157-61.

Argues that James's first visit to Italy in 1869 awakened in him a desire for "the finest things in life" and the difficulty in attaining them, a theme that dominates James's work. Churchill briefly discusses James's fiction set in Italy: "Travelling Companions," "The Madonna of the Future," "The Last of the Valerri," "Adina," *Roderick Hudson, The Princess Casamassima*, "The Aspern Papers," and *The Wings of the Dove*.

29 COLLISTER, PETER. "Mrs. Humphrey Ward, Vernon Lee, and Henry James." *Review of English Studies* 31, no. 123 (August):315-21.

Details James's and Mrs. Humphrey Ward's disappointment with the actress Mary Anderson, suggesting that *The Tragic Muse* and *Mrs. Bretherton* were inspired by the writers meeting the actress. Collister also notes that Vernon Lee upset both James and Mrs. Humphrey Ward, in the later case because Lee's *Miss Brown* is similar to *Mrs. Bretherton*.

30 COOK, DAVID A., and CORRIGAN, TIMOTHY J. "Narrative Structure in *The Turn of the Screw*: A New Approach to Meaning." *Studies in Short Fiction* 17, no. 1 (Winter):55-65.

Uses a structuralist approach to explain the dynamics of the tale's two levels of reading (what is told and what is deduced). James's use of this dual strategy is deliberate and results in a fiction about the process of fiction.

1980

31   COOK, ELEANOR. "Portraits of Ladies." *Notes and Queries* 27, no. 6 (December):533-34.

   Traces two quoted phrases – "dying fall" and "false note" – in T.S. Eliot's "Portrait of a Lady" to James's *Portrait*. Eliot's lady and young man contrast with Henrietta Stackpole and Ralph Touchett.

32   COSGROVE, WILLIAM, and MATHEES, IRENE. "'To See Life Reflected': Seeing as Living in *The Ambassadors*." *Henry James Review* 1, no. 3 (Spring):204-10.

   Argues that Strether's "seeing" life is a creative, not a voyeuristic, act that indicates Strether's growth as an artist.

33   COWDERY, LAUREN TOZEK. "The 'Nouvelle' of Henry James in Theory and Practice." Ph.D. dissertation, Cornell University, 223 pp.

   Defines James's theory of the novella, drawing on James's critical writings. Individual chapters are then devoted to analyses of four novellas – "Julia Bride," "The Coxon Fund," "Daisy Miller," and "The Birthplace" – that illustrate aspects of the Jamesian novella. James was attracted to the novella by its economy and its ability to accommodate "elaborate arabesques of technique."

   See *Dissertation Abstracts International* 41, no. 3 (1980):1056A. Revised 1986.37.

34   CREE, CHARLES GEORGE. "The Personal and the Theme of the Validity of Authorship in American Fiction." Ph.D. dissertation, Indiana University, 190 pp.

   Traces the use of the pastoral as a means to explore the nature of the creative imagination in Brown, Irving, Hawthorne, and Melville. Although Twain seems to suggest that the pastoral no longer has vitality, Norris and James (in "The Great Good Place") testify to its relevance in twentieth-century literature.

   See *Dissertation Abstracts International* 41, no. 9 (1981):4032A.

35   CROSS, MARY. "Henry James: Fiction as Style." Ph.D. dissertation, Rutgers University, 241 pp.

   Demonstrates that James's style enacts his subject – the growth of the aesthetic and moral sensibility. *The Portrait of a Lady* and *The Ambassadors* exemplify James's uniting content and style.

See *Dissertation Abstracts International* 40, no. 12 (1980):6278A.

36 CROWLEY, FRANK EDWARD. "Identity Themes and Double Consciousness in Henry James, James Joyce and John Fowles: The Myth in the Metaphor." Ph.D. dissertation, State University of New York, Buffalo, 134 pp.

Argues that "the subject matter of James' and Joyce's fiction is really the depiction of states of human consciousness," focusing on these authors' use of metaphor to symbolize "the divided sensibility of the modern mind."

See *Dissertation Abstracts International* 41, no. 8 (1981):3560A.

37 CURTSINGER, E.C. "*The Turn of the Screw* as Writer's Parable." *Studies in the Novel* 12, no. 4 (Winter):344-58.

Demonstrates that the tale "dramatizes the struggle of the writer's creative imagination with the forces of destruction." The governess embodies that imagination; Quint is "anticreation" but is necessary for the governess's act of creation. The writer's imagination "may conceive in purity" but must recognize and participate in "fallen humanity."

Reprinted 1986.39.

38 DAUGHTERTY, SARAH B. "Taine, James, and Balzac: Toward an Aesthetic of Romantic Realism." *Henry James Review* 2, no. 2 (Fall):12-24.

Argues that Taine was instrumental in James's recognition of Balzac's blend of realism and romance. Taine's 1858 essay on Balzac was a "chief source" for James's 1875 essay although James's rejected Taine's praise of Balzac's amorality. In his 1905 essay, however, James was less moralistic in his assessment of Balzac and his critical vocabulary "echoes" Taine's.

39 DEAN, MARTHA BIBBY. "*Washington Square*: Not So Simple As It Seems." *West Virginia University Philological Papers*, series 81, 26, no. 1-2 (August):105-12.

Argues that both irony and the narrator, whose point of view is limited to no one particular character, give the novel complexity and depth. This complexity prevents *Washington Square* from becoming a melodrama.

40 DEAN, SHARON. "Constance Fenimore Woolson and Henry James: The Literary Relationship." *Massachusetts Studies in English* 7, no. 3:1-9.

Traces the "mutual borrowing" of material between James and Woolson with the emphasis on the various ways Woolson influenced James. James uses Woolson's "undeveloped layers" in his own work, as well as drawing upon the ambiguity and the guilt arising from his friendship with her.

41 DENNIS, LARRY R. "Spectres and Spectators in *The Turn of the Screw* and *The Innocents*." In *Purdue University Fifth Annual Conference on Film*." Edited by Maud Walther. West Lafayette, Ind.: Department of Foreign Languages and Literature, Purdue University Press, pp. 96-102.

Parallels James's connection between reading and imagining with Clayton's connection between film viewing and imagining. Dennis focuses on the various means used in the tale and in the film to create suspense and suggest the supernatural.

42 DESMOND, JOHN F. "Flannery O'Connor, Henry James and the International Theme." *Flannery O'Connor Bulletin* 9:3-18.

Argues that while O'Connor was influenced by James's International Theme, her treatment of the theme differs from his in that O'Connor uses the confrontation of cultures to explore aspects of Christian redemption. For O'Connor, Europe represents the "reality of history" as well as the fallen world. The cultural conflict between Europe and America is a means of dramatizing "the dynamic possibilities of the redemptive process."

43 DRYDEN, EDGAR A. "The Image in the Mirror: The Double Economy of James's *Portrait*." *Genre* 13, no. 1 (Spring):31-49.

Examines the implications of the economic metaphor in the novel and its preface and focuses on the "double economy" of the writer who produces and the reader who consumes. The conflict of these incompatible economies is thematized in the novel, which is about what money can and cannot buy.

44   DUPERRAY, ANNICK. "La Bête et le dandy ou la rencontre au coin plaisant." *Confluents* 6, no. 2:105-22.
      In French.

45   DYSON, J. PETER. "Bartolozzi and Henry James's 'Mora Montravers.'" *Henry James Review* 1, no. 3 (Spring):264-66.
      Explains James's allusion to the Italian engraver, whose art was insipid, narrow, and derivative. James uses this reference to illuminate the character of Sidney Traffles.

46   ECKSTEIN, BARBARA JO. "Conventions of Irony in Some American Novels about Art." Ph.D. dissertation, University of Cincinnati, 280 pp.
      Argues that James uses irony in "The Aspern Papers," "The Turn of the Screw," and *What Maisie Knew* to create "a self-reflective art that comments on its own aesthetics." Later novelists, specifically Nabokov and Hawkes, transformed James's conventions of irony to conventions of "art about art." The resulting metafiction redefines aesthetics, and in so doing redefines morality.
      See *Dissertation Abstracts International* 41, no. 3 (1980):1057A.

47   EDEL, LEON. Introduction to *Henry James Letters, Volume 3: 1883-1895*. Cambridge: Harvard University Press, the Belknap Press, xiii-xx.
      Points out that the letters of this period focus on James's relationships, including that with Constance Fenimore Woolson, and foreshadow the "breakdown in his egotism and his opening himself up to homoerotic love."

48   ENGLARO, GRAZIELLA. "Henry James *La panchina dell desolazione*" [Henry James's 'The Bench of Desolation']. *Uomini E Libri* 16, no. 8 (November-December):16.
      In Italian.

49   EVANS, T. JEFF. "F. Scott Fitzgerald and Henry James: The Raw Material of American Innocence." *NMAL: Notes on Modern American Literature* 4:Item 8.

195

1980

Finds a similar sensibility in James's use of "raw" in "Daisy Miller" and Fitzgerald's use of the adjective in *The Great Gatsby*: both authors mourn the inability of "raw" American innocence to transform the world.

50   FABER, M.D. "Henry James: Revolutionary Involvement, the Princess, and the Hero." *American Imago* 37, no. 3 (Fall):245-77.
        Demonstrates that in *The Princess Casamassima* James offers a sound analysis of the psychology of individuals committed to revolutionary movements and discusses the character of Hyacinth Robinson from a psychoanalytic perspective. Faber concludes by suggesting that James, like Hyacinth, was defensive; his work, therefore, can be seen as "screens" that both encounter and avoid subversive actions.

51   FELMAN, SHOSHANA. "Turning the Screw of Interpretation." In *Literature and Psychoanalysis: The Question of Reading: Otherwise*. Edited by Shoshana Felman. Baltimore: Johns Hopkins University Press, pp. 94-207.
        Reprint of 1977.36. Also reprinted 1978.40 (in French), and 1985.42.

52   FINCHAM, GAIL. "'The Alchemy of Art': Henry James's *The Europeans*." *English Studies in Africa* 23, no. 2 (September):83-92.
        Shows that the novel explores the inadequacies of the New England and European worldviews, and achieves a fusion between the two in Felix Young, the artist, a "Bohemian who does not despise the Philistines." Fincham examines the novel's major characters, particularly in terms of their advocacy of morality or aestheticism.

53   FOWLER, VIRGINIA C. "Milly Theale's Malady of Self." *Novel* 14, no. 1 (Fall):57-74.
        Argues that Milly's personality, symbolized by her illness, reflects the psychology of the American girl, particularly her inability to confront life itself and this achieve a sense of identity.
        Reprinted 1984.61.

54 FUSSELL, EDWIN. "The Ontology of *The Turn of the Screw.*" *Journal of Modern Literature* 8, no. 1:118-28.

Argues that the governess has written a novel titled *The Turn of the Screw* and James's novel is about that novel, and analyzes the provenance, form, and style of the governess's novel. James's novel raises the question of why she should be a governess when she can write a novel as good as a man.

55 GALE, ROBERT L. "Henry James." *American Literary Scholarship: An Annual/1978.* Edited by J. Albert Robbins. Durham: Duke University Press, pp. 91-110.

Surveys criticism published in 1978.

56 GALENBECK, SUSAN LYNN CARLSON. "Women, Manners, and Morals: Henry James's Plays and the Comedy of Manners on the Turn-of-the-Century British Stage." Ph.D. dissertation, University of Oregon, 366 pp.

Demonstrates that James's plays depict strong women, capture "the essence of the comedy of manners world," and experiment with elements borrowed from the French well-made play.

See *Dissertation Abstracts International* 41, no. 5 (1980):2103A.

57 GARDNER, HELEN. "Literary Biography." *Modern Language Review* 75, no. 4 (October):xxi-xxxviii.

Discusses the difficulties confronting the literary biographer, given the current critical temper and the artist's tendency to cover his or her tracks. Gardner praises Edel's biography of James, who destroyed many of his private papers but suggests that Edel tends to be reductionary in discussing James's fiction.

Reprinted 1982.55.

58 GARGANO, JAMES W. "James's *The Sacred Fount*: The Phantasmagorical Made Evidential." *Henry James Review* 2, no. 1 (Fall):49-60.

Rejects the judgment of the novel's characters and many critics that the narrator is insane; rather, Gargano argues that the narrator is sane, restrained, and unusually perceptive. The narrator understands the distinction between the phantasmagoric and the evidential, upon which the novel depends, and thus must keep to himself what he

1980

perceives. Gargano thus sees him as yet another of James's characters who practices renunciation.
Reprinted 1987.44.

59 GLASSER, WILLIAM. *"The Turn of the Screw."* In *Essays in Honour of Erwin Stürzl on His Sixtieth Birthday.* Vol. 1. Edited by James Hogg. Salzburg: Inst. fur Englische Aprache & Literatur, Universitat Salzburg, pp. 212-31.
Argues that the controversy regarding the reality of the ghost is resolved if the tale is seen as a romance in which the governess imposes her distorted vision of the world on the reader.

60 GLENN, ELLEN WALKER. "The Androgynous Woman Character in the American Novel." Ph.D. dissertation, University of Colorado, Boulder, 143 pp.
Argues that the potentially androgynous character is unrealized in the realistic novel but possible in the speculative novel. In *The Portrait of a Lady,* James suggests the possibility of androgynous traits within social norms, but depicts the limitations constricting a woman who is intelligent or independent.
See *Dissertation Abstracts International* 41, no. 11 (1981):4713A.

61 GOODMAN, CHARLOTTE. "Henry James, D.H. Lawrence, and the Victimized Child." *Modern Language Studies* 10, no. 1 (Winter):43-51.
Compares Lawrence's "England, My England" and "The Rocking-Horse Winner" with "The Author of 'Beltraffio'" and "The Pupil," respectively. All four tales dramatize the ways family tension damages a young child; this victimized child is central to both James and Lawrence.

62 GRENANDER, M.E. "Henrietta Stackpole and Olive Harper: Emanations of the Great Democracy." *Bulletin of Research in the Humanities* 83, no. 3 (Autumn):406-22.
Suggests that James based Henrietta Stackpole's career abroad on Olive Harper, a notoriously unreliable international correspondent. Stackpole is James's version of what the female correspondent could have become.

63 GRIGG, QUAY. "The Novel in *John Gabriel Borkman*: Henry James's *The Ambassadors*." *Henry James Review* 1, no. 3 (Spring):211-18.

Suggests that Ibsen's play, alluded to in the novel's text, may be a major source for the novel. James borrowed characters and situations from Ibsen. Indeed, James should have followed Ibsen more closely in preparing the reader for Strether's renunciation.

64 HALL, D.A. "A Literature of Synthesis." In *To Keep Moving: Essays 1959-1969*. Geneva, N.Y.: Hobart & William Smith Colleges Press, pp. 19-22.

Argues that James's expatriation enabled him to attain the eclecticism he needed to grow as an artist.

Reprint of 1959 essay.

65 HEWITT, ROSALIE. "Henry James's *The American Scene*: Its Genesis and Its Reception, 1905-1977." *Henry James Review* 1, no. 2 (Winter):179-96.

Recapitulates the book's history and includes an annotated bibliography of criticism 1905 to 1977. Current criticism follows the lead of contemporary criticism by focusing on content, not style.

66 HOCKS, RICHARD A. "*Daisy Miller*, Backward into the Past: A Centennial Essay." *Henry James Review* 1, no. 2 (Winter):164-78.

Reviews critical responses to the tale, ranging from contemporary to current. Hocks also discusses its New York Edition preface, revision, and the transformation of Daisy in subsequent fiction, where the American girl had to struggle for survival in a corrupt world.

67 HUTCHINSON, STUART. "Beyond the Victorians: *The Portrait of a Lady*." In *Reading the Victorian Novel: Detail into Form*. Edited by Ian Gregor. New York: Barnes & Noble, pp. 274-87.

Argues that *The Portrait of a Lady* departs from the didacticism and moral certainties of the Victorian novel because its purpose is to portray Isabel as the author of her own life. While the novel focuses on Isabel's commitment to a life of consciousness, it shows that such a life is "restrictive and self-deceiving."

1980

68   JACOBS, JOHAN UYS. "The Alter Ego: A Study of the Dual Persona of the Artist in the Late Nineteenth and Early Twentieth Century American Novel." Ph.D. dissertation, Columbia University, 457 pp.

Argues that Spencer Brydon and his alter ego provides "a useful metaphor for the development of the American imagination" by representing the European aesthetic tradition and uniquely American "aesthetic premises." Jacobs examines the work of Twain, James, Cather, and Dreiser to show this bifurcation. In *The Bostonians*, "Verena Tarrant turns her back on the realities of American life for a debased notion of romantic and aristocratic form"; her future, James prophesies, is pessimistic.

See *Dissertation Abstracts International* 41, no. 7 (1981):3107A.

69   JEFFERSON, DOUGLAS. Introduction to *What Maisie Knew*. Oxford: Oxford University Press, pp. ix-xxvii.

Discusses Maisie's growth in vision and understanding, and praises James's characterization, which reaches "its highest excellence in this novel." Jefferson also traces the novel's development in James's notebooks and briefly surveys criticism on the novel.

70   JOHNSON, STUART HICKS. "The Stroke of Loss: Writing as Activity and Metaphor in Henry James." Ph.D. dissertation, Boston University, 339 pp.

Explores James's conception of the relation between writer and subject, drawing on "The Turn of the Screw" and "The Third Person" to argue that for James writing is a pursuit of ghosts. In this context, "The Jolly Corner" and *The Sense of the Past* are allegories, showing that the ghosts can turn upon their pursuer. In the remainder of this study, Johnson examines writing as a metaphor for life in *The Wings of the Dove*, *The Ambassadors*, and *The American Scene*.

See *Dissertation Abstracts International* 41, no. 5 (1980):2110A.

*71   JONES, V.M. "The Independent Form: Henry James's Criticism of the Novel." Ph.D. dissertation, Oxford University.

Source: *Annual Bibliography of English Language and Literature* 56 (1981):370, item 6716.

Revised 1985.72.

72   KAPPELER, SUSANNE. *Writing and Reading in Henry James*. New York: Columbia University Press, London: Macmillan Press, xiv, 242 pp.

Explores the relationships among author, critic, and reader in their creation of the text. Because of these complex relationships, a literary text cannot have a definitive reading, so that the focus must be on how meaning is created rather than on what the text means. Kappeler discusses "The Aspern Papers" and *The Sacred Fount* as illustrations of her thesis.

Revision of 1977.57. See also Pecora 1985.112.

73   KASTON, CARREN O. "Emersonian Consciousness and *The Spoils of Poynton*." *ESQ* 26, no. 2 (old series no. 99):88-99.

Argues that James applies Emersonian transcendentalism to the social, not natural, environment. Fleda Vetch shows the dangers of the "selfless self" embodied in Emerson's image of the transparent eyeball.

Reprinted 1984.110.

74   KEMPER, STEVEN EDWARD. "At Odds with Art: The American Writer." Ph.D. dissertation, University of Connecticut, 267 pp.

Examines the American writer's questioning of his art amid the social and cultural context. After sketching Puritan and republican origins of the issue, Kemper focuses on four writers–Hawthorne, Howells, James, and Bellows. Hawthorne separates art from democracy; Howells sees the artist as a businessman; James rejects the belief that the artist is marginal; and Bellows rejects social activity for an inner life.

See *Dissertation Abstracts International* 41, no. 8 (1981):3581A.

75   KIMBALL, SUE L. "To the Editor." *Henry James Review* 1, no. 3 (Spring):274.

Describes her discovery of the James home in Newport, Rhode Island. The house is now used as a funeral home. Kimball includes a photo of the house.

76   KIRBY, DAVE. *America's Hive of Honey, or Foreign Influences on American Fiction through Henry James: Essays and Bibliographies*. Metuchen, N.J., and London: Scarecrow Press, xvii, 214 pp.

1980

Summarizes and evaluates the scholarship on external literary influences on American fiction from Charles Brockden Brown to Henry James. The influences annotated and discussed range from a body of literature, such as the classics, to an individual writer, such as Spenser.

77 KIRK, CAREY H. "*Daisy Miller*: The Reader's Choice." *Studies in Short Fiction* 17, no. 3 (Summer):275-83.

Focuses on James's narrative strategy to engage the reader in adjudicating the character of Daisy and Winterbourne. Kirk calls the tale a "successful *trompe d'oeil*" in which the reader's evaluations are constantly undercut.

78 KNIGHT, EVERETT W. "Chapter IV." In *The Novel as Structure and Praxis from Cervantes to Malraux*. Atlantic Highlands, N.J.: Humanities Press, pp. 80-90.

Argues that James's achievement lies in introducing "taste as a vital criterion while retaining morality in the trivialized form of the diabolical at one extreme and, at the other, a petty, punctilious moralism very close to the conventionalism of which he is alleged to be very critical." Novels discussed include *The Portrait of a Lady*, *The Spoils of Poynton*, and *The Princess Casamassima*.

79 KOLJEVIĆ, SVETOZAR. "The Pitfalls of Perfection in *The Portrait of a Lady*." Translated by Natasha Kolchevska. In *Yugoslav Perspectives on American Literature: An Anthology*. Edited by James L. Thorson. Ann Arbor, Mich.: Ardis, pp. 55-68.

Sees the novel as a romance centering on the conflict between "sensibility and civilization." James's ironic treatment of this romance enables him to overcome the limitations of the "traditional, jagged nineteenth century novel"; thus he is a "pioneer of an architectonic, polyphonic novel of consciousness which works at many levels," because it presupposes a functional relationship between the individual elements of the novel as well as "a multiplicity of meanings for its innumerable internal relationships."

Reprint of "Zamke Savršenstvan u *Portrety Jedne Dame*." *Humor i Mit*. Beograd: Nolit (1968), pp. 165-83. In Serbo-Croatian.

80 KOMODA, JUNZO. "*Neji no Hineri* Hihyo ni tsuite" [Criticism on *The Turn of the Screw*]. In *Suga Yasuo, Ogoshi Kazuso: Ryo-kyoju*

Taikan Kinen Ronbunshu [Essays commemorating the retirement of Professors Yasuo Suga and Kazuso Ogoshi]. Kyoto: Apollonsha, pp. 844-52.

    In Japanese.

    Surveys criticism of the tale up to the 1970s.

    Reprinted in 1981.82.

81   KREISCHER, EDITH "Henry James' 'The Turn of the Screw.'" In *Phantasik in Literatur und Kunst* [Imagination in literature and art]. Edited by Christian W. Thomsen and Jens Malte Fischer. Darmstadt: Wissenschaftliche Buchgesellschaft, pp. 219-36.

    In German.

82   LAY, MARY M. "The Real Beasts: Surrogate Brothers in James's 'The Pupil' and *The Princess Casamassima.*" *American Literary Realism 1870-1910* 13, no. 1 (Spring):73-84.

    Finds similarities in Morgan Moreen and Hyacinth Robinson, who are "disappointed by surrogate brothers and who die in the end. Both works show the dangers of living vicariously, especially when the younger man unquestioningly adopts the older's values.

83   LEVY, LEO B. "*The Golden Bowl* and 'the Voice of Blood.'" *Henry James Review* 1, no. 2 (Winter):154-63.

    Sees the novel as examining the conflicting demands of blood ties and marriage. Maggie matures, yet there is evidence that suggests her tie to Adam has not been weakened. Thus the novel shows that competing relationships cannot be resolved, only brought into balance.

84   _____. "Henry James and the Image of Franklin." *Southern Review* 16, no. 3 (July):552-59.

    Argues that James incorporated Franklin's moral precepts and character into his fiction, autobiography, and *The American Scene.* James's scrupulous pursuit of Franklin's self-control, self-discipline, and self-examination, however, results in unworldliness and isolation, both of which are alien to Franklin.

1980

85   LEWIS, PAUL. "Beyond Mystery: Emergence from Delusion as a Pattern in Gothic Fiction." *Gothic* 2:7-13.
     Focuses on the Gothic villians' moment of insight in which they reject their evil ways. Lewis examines "The Beast in the Jungle" as an exmaple of the successful emergence from destructive egotism.

86   LOBZOESKA, MARIA. "The Tragic Implications of Henry James's Social Novels." In *Aspects of Tragedy in the Twentieth Century English and American Literature*. Edited by Maria Lobzowska. Prace Naukowe Uniwersytetu Slaskiego, 351. Katowice, Poland: Uniwersytet Slaski, pp. 37-46.
     Sees James's "social novels" – especially *The Bostonians, The Princess Casamassima*, and *The Tragic Muse* – as central to his work. In these novels James critiques the genteel tradition; he also explores the artist's moral consciousness as well as his social responsibility to expose the realities masked by the genteel tradition.

87   McFEE, MICHAEL. "The Church Scenes in *The Ambassadors, The American* and *The Wings of the Dove*." *Papers on Language and Literature* 16, no. 3 (Summer):325-28.
     Notes the similarities of the three scenes, particularly the way Strether, Newman, and Densher observe others in the church, and their awareness of "deep estrangement from a source of spiritual comfort for their problems."

88   McKENZIE, LEE SMITH. "Jane Austen, Henry James, and the Family Romance." Ph.D. dissertation, University of Oklahoma, 259 pp.
     Explores similarities in Austen's and James's work, focusing on their treatment of social and cultural changes. In such works as *Pride and Prejudice, Mansfield Park*, "An International Episode," and *The Spoils of Poynton*, both authors depict the fragmentation of society, a retreat from urbanization into family, and the glorification of the home.
     See *Dissertation Abstracts International* 41, no. 10 (1981):4404A.

89   McMURREY, DAVID ALLEN. "The Populist Romance: A Study of Michelet's *Le Peuple* and Selected Novels of Hugo, Zola, James,

and Galdós." Ph.D. dissertation, University of Texas at Austin, 341 pp.

Traces the elements of the populist romance, arguing that the works of Michelet and Hugo represent "the romantic projection of the populist ideal" while Zola and James (in *The Princess Casamassima*) reject the romance for realism. Galdós, however, returns to a "naive romanticism."

See *Dissertation Abstracts International* 41, no. 11 (1981):4706A.

90 MARTIN, TIMOTHY P. "Henry James and Percy Lubbock: From Mimesis to Formalism." *Novel* 14, no. 1 (Fall):20-29.

Outlines the difference between the theories of James and Lubbock. Although they are not "theoretical antagonists," the two have radically diverging views of fiction and of the reading experience. James is a mimetic critic, believing in techniques that increase the illusion of reality and in the "moral quality" of the work; Lubbock is a formalist, concerned primarily with a work's aesthetics.

91 MARTIN, W.R. "The Narrator's 'Retreat' in James's 'Four Meetings.'" *Studies in Short Fiction* 17, no. 4 (Fall):497-99.

Supplements Seamon's reading of the tale (1978.96) by noting the narrator's similarity to the Countess, and agrees with Seamon that the narrator's strong emotion arises out of his refusal to protect himself from self-knowledge.

92 _____ and OBER, WARREN U. "'Crapy Cornelia': James's Self-Vindication?" *Ariel* 11, no. 4 (October):57-68.

Analyzes James's use of the images of fire and the dance to suggest "collaborative intimacy and communication" between the tale's characters but also between James and the reader as well.

93 MASLENNIKOVA, A.A. "Stilisticheskaia funktsiia prilagatel 'nykh v novelle G. Dzheimsa 'Povorot vinta'" [Stylistic functions of adjectives in "The Turn of the Screw"]. *Analiz Stilei zarubeshnoi khudozhestvennoi i nauch-noi literary* (Leningrad University) 2:67-74. In Russian.

1980

94   MAZZELLA, ANTHONY J. "An Answer to the Mystery of *The Turn of the Screw.*" *Studies in Short Fiction* 17, no. 3 (Summer):327-33.
      Approaches the tale as a psychological mystery rather than as a ghost story and so uses the tools of a detective in explaining the tale's anomalies.

*95   MEASHAM, J.D. "Henry James: Adaptations of His Fiction Both by Himself and Others." Ph.D. dissertation, Nottingham University.
      Source: *Annual Bibliography of English Language and Literature* 56 (1981):436, item 8011.

*96   MEYERS, CHARLES JOHN, III. "The Development of the Novellas of Henry James." Ph.D. dissertation, University of Chicago.
      Source: Offline Bibliography, BRS Information Techniques, Latham, NY 12110.

97   MILLER, J. HILLIS. "The Figure in the Carpet." *Poetics Today* 1, no. 3 (Spring):107-18.
      Argues that the tale "mimes . . . unreadability, on the thematic level, on a figurative level, and on the overall organization as text." Miller distinguishes unreadability from ambiguity and "perspectivism" in which each reader derives his or her own meaning from the text. For Miller, the text is unreadable because there is always a figure, a mediating sign, which is both an "obstacle" and a "promise."
      Reprint of 1987.97. See also Rimmon-Kenan 1981.120, Miller 1981.102, Williams 1984.225, and Bloom 1987.16.

98   MILLER, VIVIENNE. "Henry James and the Alienation of the Artist: 'The Lesson of the Master.'" *English Studies in Africa* 23, no. 1 (March):9-20.
      Argues that the tale exemplifies James's "sane" and "balanced" view of the artist, who paradoxically must be detached from life but at the same time must be connected to life, for his art depends on experience. The artist must make sacrifices, but "life" cannot be sacrificed to art.

99   MOON, HEATH. "James's 'A London Life' and the Campbell Divorce Scandal." *American Literary Realism 1870-1910* 13, no. 2 (Autumn):246-58.

Describes the Campbell divorce of 1886 and its aftermath. Although James did not model his characters on the actual participants in the scandal, the tale is part of the scandal's "aftershock," and reflects James's hatred of publicity. Moon treats Laura sympathetically, seeing her as loyal to "a historically circumscribed institution rich in aesthetic associations."

100   NETTELS, ELSA. "Poe and James on the Art of Fiction." *Poe Studies* 13, no. 1 (June):4-8.

Finds similarities in the theories of fiction of Poe and James. Both recognized the importance of the intuitive and the analytical in the creative act, and both insisted on the importance of form to engage the reader's emotions.

101   NORRMAN, RALF. "End-linking as an Intensity-Creating Device in the Dialogue of Henry James's *The Golden Bowl*." *English Studies* 61, no. 3 (June):236-51.

Explores James's use of anadiplosis and rheme to theme intersentence end-linking to create intensity. Such devices require attentiveness in the reader, elevate the subject, endow it with ratiocination, and give dialogue a lifelike sound.

Reprinted 1982.108.

102   O'CONNOR, DENNIS L. "Intimacy and Spectatorship in *The Portrait of a Lady*." *Henry James Review* 1, no. 1 (Fall):25-35.

Examines Isabel's rejection of intimacy with others and her need to be "the sole interpreter of the text of her life." Isabel is typical of the protagonist whose "Jamesian renunciaton permits exploitation and spectatorship" and protects from the risks of intimacy.

103   O'DONNELL, PATRICK. "Between Life and Art: Structures of Realism in the Fiction of Howells and James." *Etudes Anglaises* 33, no. 2 (April-June):142-55.

Sees the fiction of Howells and James reflecting two divergent modes of realism: Howells concentrates on "contiguously related events" while James focuses on the consciousness, using symbols to

1980

explore its relation to the world. O'Donnell uses *A Modern Instance, The Rise of Silas Lapham, The Princess Casamassima,* and *The Ambassadors* to support his argument.

104 OELSCHLEGEL, LAWRENCE EDWARD. "Rhythmic Elements in Three Novels from the Post-Dramatic Period of Henry James: *What Maisie Knew, The Awkward Age* and *The Spoils of Poynston.*" Ph.D. dissertation, University of Maryland, 586 pp.

Argues that James's use of rhythm is guided by function rather than by symmetry: James selected rhythmic devices that tighten structure and create unity. Analyses of narrative rhythm in *What Maisie Knew, The Awkward Age,* and *The Spoils of Poynton* suggest new interpretations of these works.

See *Dissertation Abstracts International* 41, no. 6 (1980):2607A.

105 O'GORMAN, DONAL. "Henry James's Reading of *The Turn of the Screw*: Part I." *Henry James Review* 1, no. 2 (Winter):125-38.

Discusses the tale in light of its New York Edition preface in order to ascertain James's intentions. In part I of a three-part essay O'Gorman focuses on the tale's historical background and its connection with the Christmas season, both of which suggest a theme of reversal – "adult-child, master-servant."

106 _____. "Henry James's Reading of *The Turn of the Screw*: Parts II and III." *Henry James Review* 1, no. 3 (Spring):225-56.

Continues 1980.105. In part II, O'Gorman examines the tale's "prowling spirits," comparing them to the demons described in witchcraft trials; in Part III, O'Gorman focuses on the Devil, arguing that the governess is "possessed." The tale is "an imaginative study of the Devil's pernicious manipulation of human affairs."

*107 OSIPENKOVA, O.I. "Rol'zhivopisi v khudozhestvennoi sisteme G. Dzheimsa" [The role of painting in the artistic system of Henry James]. In *Problemy realizma v zarubezhnoi literature XIX-XX rekov* [Problems of realism in foreign literature of the nineteenth and twentieth century]. Moscow: Moskovskii oblastnoi pedagogicheskii institute im N.K. Krupskoi, pp. 66-77.

In Russian.

Source: *Annual Bibliography of English Language and Literature*, v. 57 (1982):447, item 8143.

108 OTSU, E., BEPPU, K., EBINE, S., and NAMEKATA, A. "Henry James, *The Portrait of a Lady* o Yomu" [Reading Henry James's *The Portrait of a Lady*]. *Eibungaku Kenkyu*. English Literary Society of Japan. 57:324-26.
In Japanese.
Beppu sees Isabel as a "new woman;" Ebine analyzes *The Portrait* as a drama of the self enacted within the framework of the Victorian novel; Namekata discusses the meaning of Isabel's final return to Rome. These papers were part of the symposium at the 52nd annual meeting of the English Literary Society of Japan.

109 OTSU, EIICHIRO. "*Shishatachi* no Aimaisei" [The ambiguity of *The Ambassadors*]. In *Bungaku to America: Ohashi Kenzaburo Kyoju Kanreki Kinen Ronbunshu* [Literature and America: Essays commemorating the sixtieth birthday of Professor Kenzaburo Ohashi]. Vol. 3. Tokyo: Nan'undo, pp. 252-69.
In Japanese.
Analyzes the novel, a tragicomedy of an innocent middle-aged man who awakens to the true meaning of life too late, focusing on point of view and scenic presentation.

110 OTT, JOSEPHINE, trans. "'Honoré de Balzac,' par Henry James, I." *L'Année Balzacienne* 1:245-52.
In French.
See 1981.109 for part II.

111 PANETTA, EILEEN HARRIET. "The Anti-Heroine in the Fiction of Henry James." Ph.D. dissertation, University of Notre Dame, 315 pp.
Examines in detail the "anti-heroines" in *Roderick Hudson, The Europeans, The Portrait of a Lady, The Bostonians, The Princess Casamassima, The Other House, The Wings of the Dove,* and *The Golden Bowl.* While no single pattern emerges, each antiheroine possesses intense vitality from which their "wilfullness" derives. This wilfullness, in turn, makes them ambivalent figures, both admirable and dishonorable.

1980

See *Dissertation Abstracts International* 41, no. 4 (1980):1599A.

112 PETERSON, CARLA L. "Dialogue and Characterization in *The Portrait of a Lady*." *Studies in American Fiction* 8, no. 1 (Spring):13-22.

Examines Isabel's and Osmond's first conversation, noting that although there seems to be a stylistic sameness, differences in language suggest differences in character that will be made explicit in later chapters.

113 POSNOCK, ROSS. "Henry James and the Problem of Robert Browning." Ph.D. dissertation, Johns Hopkins University, 296 pp.

Traces James's relationship to Browning, focusing on Browning's ambiguity as a private poet and as a public gentleman. James exorcised this troubling ambiguity in "The Private Life" and "The Lesson of the Master," thus freeing himself to use Browning in his own art. Posnock details James's "rewriting" of Browning in analyses of *The Wings of the Dove* and *The Golden Bowl*. Ultimately James solves the "problem" of Browning through his art.

See *Dissertation Abstracts International* 41, no. 1 (1980):254A-255A.

114 PUNTER, DAVID. "The Ambivalence of Memory: Henry James and Walter de la Mare." In *The Literature of Terror: A History of Gothic Fictions from 1765 to the Present Day*. London and New York: Longman, pp. 291-313.

Argues that "The Turn of the Screw" and de la Mare's stories are psychologically sophisticated in their connecting fear and self-delusion and in their recognizing the complexity and inaccessibility of the unconscious. While both James and de la Mare use many Gothic elements, the sophistication sets them apart from the Gothic mainstream.

115 QUARTERMAIN, PETER. "'Blocked. Make a Song out of That': Pound's 'E.P. Ode Pour L'Election de son Sepulchre.'" *Kentucky Review* 1, no. 1:32-48.

Argues that Pound rejects the Jamesian consciousness unified by a handed-down criterion; his poem celebrates "an environment of individual and discrete perceptions."

116 RICHARDS, BERNARD. "The Sources of Henry James's 'Mrs. Medwin.'" *Notes and Queries* 27, no. 3 (June):226-30.

Argues that Elizabeth Balch, a minor novelist, was the model for Mamie Cutter; Lady Grantley, whose divorce created a scandal, for Mrs. Medwin; and Robert Temple, Minnie's brother, for Scott Homer.

*117 RIGHELATO, P.J. "'The Personal History . . . of an Imagination': Henry James' Art Seen through His Autobiography." Ph.D. dissertation, Reading University.

Source: *Annual Bibliography of English Language and Literature* 56 (1981):437, item 8019.

118 RIVKIN, JULIA HELEN. "Perspectivism in the Late Novels of Henry James." Ph.D. dissertation, Yale University, 253 pp.

Argues that James's center of consciousness implies multiple visions of the world based on multiple points of view. Although this "perspectivism" is an essentially philosophical position, Rivkin explores its thematic manifestations in *The Ambassadors* and *The Wings of the Dove*.

See *Dissertation Abstracts International* 41, no. 11 (1981):4715A.

119 ROUTH, MICHAEL. "Isabel Archer's Double Exposure: A Repeated Scene in *The Portrait of a Lady*." *Henry James Review* 1, no. 3 (Spring):262-63.

Notes that when Ralph Touchett and Ned Rosier first see Isabel, she is standing in a doorway. This duplication serves the novel's structure: in the first scene Isabel is on the threshold of a life of freedom; in the second, she is trapped by Osmond.

120 ROWE, JOHN CARLOS. "Who'se [sic] Henry James? Further Lessons of the Master." *Henry James Review* 2, no. 1 (Fall):2-11.

Discusses Barthelme's and Graff's critical views of James. Graff criticizes James's insistence on "the groundlessness of all meaning." Barthelme, in contrast, sees James as questioning conventions and subverting "the apparent stability of social truths sustained by secret arts." Rowe concludes that these views demonstrate that the interpretation of literature actively constructs social reality by "questioning its history, threatening its values re-examining its truths."

1980

121   RYAN, JUDITH. "The Vanishing Subject: Empirical Psychology and the Modern Novel." *PMLA* 95, no. 5 (October):857-69.
      Argues that the emphasis of empirical psychology on the intentionality of consciousness shaped James's, Musil's, and Broch's rendering of consciousness in their fiction, while Woolf and Döblin were influenced by the abolishing of the self as a discrete entity. James is a "radical empiricist" in refusing to exclude any aspect of experience, and his work demonstrates that the self is created by the act of perceiving as well as by what it perceives.

122   SAITO, HIKARU. "*Aru Fujin no Shozo* Kaitei ni okeru Hitotsu no Gimon" [on the revision of *The Portrait of a Lady*]. In *Bungaku to America: Ohasi Kenzaburo Kyoju Kanreki Kinen Ronbushnhu* [Literature and America: Essays commemorating the sixtieth birthday of Professor Kenzaburo Ohashi]. Vol. 3. Tokyo: Nan'undo, pp. 240-51.
      In Japanese.
      Argues that James's revision of the novel is not completely successful, particularly in regard to the characters of Osmond and Madame Merle. Their true nature is too obvious in the revision, thus making the story's development unnatural.

123   SALMON, RACHEL. "A Marriage of Opposites: Henry James's 'The Figure in the Carpet' and the Problem of Ambiguity." *ELH* 47, no. 4 (Winter):788-803.
      Rejects Rimmon's discussion of ambiguity in this tale (1977.107), suggesting that the tale is more appropriately seen as a paradox. Ambiguity is present in the tale primarily because of the narrator, but it is there as a means to an end: to convey the paradox that "the figure exists for those capable of seeing it, but not for those who are incapable."
      See also Williams 1984.225.

124   SANTOS, MARIA IRENE RAMALHO de SOUSA. "Isabel's Freedom: Henry James's *The Portrait of a Lady*." *Biblos* 56:503-19.
      Argues that Isabel's return to Osmond at the novel's end is an act of freedom because she accepts her "initially determined, conditioned choice" – her marriage.
      Reprinted 1987.15 and 1987.17.

125 SAVARESE, JOHN E. "Henry James's First Story: A Study of Error." *Studies in Short Fiction* 17, no. 4 (Fall):431-35.

Argues that this tale, dismissed by many, is actually handled with "subtlety and suggestiveness." Savarese examines the tale's characters, all of whom misread each other.

126 SCHLEIFER, RONALD. "The Trap of the Imagination: The Gothic Tradition, Fiction, and *The Turn of the Screw.*" *Criticism* 22, no. 4 (Fall):297-319.

Sees "The Turn of the Screw" as anticipating the transformation of the novel by Kafka, Borges, Dinesen, and Mann; *Dracula* looks backward to the Gothic tradition. While *Dracula* asserts the reality of the numinous, "The Turn of the Screw" shows that the imagination responds to nothing – "to empty letters, to ghosts, to its own unnatural power – the nothing that is not there."

127 SCHNEIDER, DANIEL J. "James's *The Awkward Age*: A Reading and an Evaluation." *Henry James Review* 1, no. 3 (Spring):219-27.

Sees the novel as a tragicomedy exposing the "moral shortcomings" of its characters. It is flawed, however by James's failure to establish the importance and motivation of the characters.

128 SCHOR, NAOMI. "Fiction as Interpretation/Interpretation as Fiction." In *The Reader in the Text: Essays on Audience and Interpretation*. Edited by Susan R. Suleiman and Inge Crosman. Princeton, N.J.: Princeton University Press, pp. 165-82.

Examines the role of the interpreting character in modern fiction. Schor cites the telegraphist in *In the Cage* as an "exemplary interpretant" because she must interpret written signs and encoded messages. In his heroine James links the act of interpretation with the act of imagination.

129 SCHULTZ, ELIZABETH. "'The Pity and the Sanctity and the Terror': The Humanity of the Ghosts in '"The Turn of the Screw."'" *Markham Review* 9 (Summer):67-70.

Demonstrates that the ghosts contribute to the tale's ambiguity because their relationship with each other and with the unknown remain unclear and the exact nature of their wrongdoing remains unspecified.

1980

130 SCRIBNER, MARGO PARKER. "The House of the Imagined
Past: Hawthorne, Dickens, and James." Ph.D. dissertation,
University of Arizona, 200 pp.
　　Examines the use of the house as symbol in Hawthorne's
"Peter Goldthwaite's Treasure," *The House of Seven Gables*, and
"Doctor Grimshaw's Secret"; Dickens's *Bleak House, Great
Expectations*, and *Little Dorrit*; and James's *The Portrait of a Lady*, "The
Jolly Corner," and *The Sense of the Past*. Scribner links the house with
the imagined past, describes the functions of the house as symbol, and
discusses characters' return to and departure from the house as a sign
of growth.
　　See *Dissertation Abstracts International* 41, no. 1 (1980):247A.

131 SEED, DAVID. "James's 'The Lesson of the Master.'" *Explicator* 39,
no. 1 (Fall):9-10.
　　Explains that St. George's references to his work as "*carton-
pierre*," "Lincrusta-Walton," and "brummagaen" are all deprecatory. The
first two refer to building materials used to decorate ceilings and walls,
and the third is a variant of "Birmingham," a "byword for showy or
imitation goods."

132 SHUEY, WILLIAM A., III. "From Renunciation to Rebellion: The
Female in Literature." In *The Evolving Female: Women in
Psychosocial Context*. Edited by Carol Landau Heckerman. New
York: Human Sciences Press, pp. 138-57.
　　Traces the changing concept of renunciation in the heroines of
Dickens, James, Hardy, Lawrence, and Lessing. Shuey argues that
Isabel Archer exemplifies the renunciatory woman of the nineteenth
century. Isabel's renunciation is based not on Christianity but on the
"indissoluability of marriage."

133 SICKER, PHILIP. *Love and the Quest for Identity in the Fiction of
Henry James*. Princeton: Princeton University Press, xv, 196 pp.
　　Traces the evolution of James's idea of romantic love
throughout his career. The early work depicts love as a kind of
infatuation, often with a mental image, while the work of the middle
years focuses on the quest for identity and the essential loneliness of
the individual. In the fiction of his final years, James recognized that
love was a vital part of the human consciousness. In arguing for the

connection between love and identity, Sicker examines the psychological assumptions underlying James's fiction.

134 SIMPSON, LEWIS P. "The Closure of History in a Postsouthern America." In *The Brazen Face of History: Studies in the Literary Consciousness in America*. Baton Rouge: Louisiana State University Press, pp. 270-6.

Notes that James recognized that the novelist and the historian coalesce in the figure of the artist, and saw history as a complex self-consciousness.

135 SMYTH, PAUL ROCKWOOD. "Gothic Influences in Henry James's Major Fiction." Ph.D. dissertation, Michigan State University, 267 pp.

Traces the evolution of James's use of the Gothic in his fiction throughout his career. Beginning with *The American*, Smyth shows James progressed from crude Gothic effects to a sophisticated depiction of evil in *The Golden Bowl*. Other novels examined are *The Portrait of a Lady* and *The Wings of the Dove*.

See *Dissertation Abstracts International* 41, no. 9 (1981):4036A.

136 SOLIMINE, JOSEPH, Jr. "Henry James, William Wetmore Story, and Friend: A Noble Mistake?" *Studies in Browning and His Circle* 8, no. 1 (Spring):57-61.

Attributes Browning's friendship with Story to the poet's ability to see a fellow artist as a human being; James, who was lukewarm toward Story, saw only a flawed artist.

137 STOWELL, H. PETER. *Literary Impressionism, James and Chekhov*. Athens: University of Georgia Press, viii, 277 pp.

Examines James's and Chekhov's similarities and differences, emphasizing their use of literary impressionism, which Stowell argues is a crucial step to modernism in the rejection of realism. Stowell defines the elements of literary impressionism and discusses impressionism in the work of Chekhov and James; James's works examined include *The Portrait of a Lady*, *What Maisie Knew*, *The Sacred Fount*, *The Ambassadors*, and *The Golden Bowl*. For both Chekhov and James, their rejection of realism for impressionism, which acknowledges

1980

individuality of perception and the ambiguity of what is perceived, affected both the form and content of their work.

138 STROUSE, JEAN. "'Peculiar Intense and Interesting Affections.'" In *Alice James: A Biography*. Boston: Houghton Mifflin, pp. 233-52, 346-47.

Chronicles Alice James's relationship with Katharine Loring and suggests that James's "unease" with it is reflected in *The Bostonians*. Strouse attributes the novel's unpopularity to the characters, none of whom are likable, and to James's failure to provide a middle ground between tradition and the "new feminism." Reprinted 1982.140.

139 STROUT, CUSHING. "Psyche, Clio, and the Artist." In *New Directions in Psychohistory: The Adelphi Papers in Honor of Erik H. Erikson*. Edited by Mel Albin. Lexington, Mass.: D.C. Heath & Co., pp. 97-115.

Sees James's life and art exemplifying the biographer's difficulty in distinguishing between author and character. "The Jolly Corner" is James's working out of his complex feelings about America and Europe, but the story is detachable from those feelings. Strout suggests that Edel's assertion that sibling rivalry figures importantly in this tale blurs the distinction between fiction and biography. Revision of 1977 Adelphi Lecture; reprinted 1981.147.

140 SUGA, YASUO. "Drama, America, Henry James." In *Bungaku to America: Ohashi Kenzaburo Kyoju Kanreki Kinen Ronbunshu* [Literature and America: Essays commemorating the sixtieth birthday of Professor Kanzaburo Ohashi]. Vol. 3. Tokyo: Nan'undo, pp. 9-17.

In Japanese.

Surveys the theater of New York, London, and Paris as James saw it, arguing that James's ambivalent attitude toward the theater is a key to his fiction.

141 TANAKA, TAKESHI. "Henry James, *Boston no Hitobito*" [Henry James, *The Bostonians*]. In *Bungaku to America: Ohashi Kenzaburo Kyoju Kanreki Kinen Ronbunshu* [Literature and America: Essays

commemorating the sixtieth birthday of Professor Kenzaburo Ohashi]. Vol. 2. Tokyo: Nan'undo, pp. 127-46.

In Japanese.

Argues that this novel should be reconsidered as a criticism of late nineteenth-century America through the naturalistic presentation of the situation of women.

142 TANNER, TONY. Introduction to *Roderick Hudson*. Oxford: Oxford University Press, ix-xxxviii.

Discusses the novel's ties to Hawthorne's *The Marble Faun* and James's earlier work, as well as the novel's major concerns, including the drama of the observing consciousness, the international theme, and the situation of the American artist in Europe. Tanner also explores the characters of Rowland Mallet, Roderick Hudson, and Christina Light. The various elements in *Roderick Hudson* show that early in his career James was engaged in changing the course of the novel's development.

143 TEDFORD, BARBARA WILKIE. "The Attitudes of Henry James and Ivan Turgenev toward the Russo-Turkish War." *Henry James Review* 1, no. 3 (Spring):257-61.

Reprints James's prose translation of Turgenev's poem "Croquet at Windsor" protesting the brutality of the war. That both authors shared opinions on the struggles for independence in the Balkans contributed to their friendship.

144 TILBY, MICHAEL. "Henry James and Mérimée: A Note of Caution." *Romance Notes* 21, no. 2 (Winter):165-68.

Suggests that P.R. Grover's 1968 article "Mérimée's Influence on Henry James" (*Modern Language Review*, 63:810-7) overstates Mérimée's influence. The extent of influence cannot be determined, but Mérimée's "zealous artistic consciousness" was a "true stimulus" for James.

145 TINTNER, ADELINE R. "Another Germ for 'The Author of Beltraffio': James, Pater and Botticelli's Madonnas." *Journal of Pre-Raphaelite Studies* 1, no. 1:14-20.

Suggests that the character of Mrs. Ambient was inspired by James's responses to Botticelli's Madonna, described in *Transatlantic Sketches* as a mother who would strangle her baby to rescue it from the

future. Tintner also discusses the "Pater elements" apparent in Mark Ambient and in James's impressions of Botticelli.
Revised 1987.122.

146 ____. "Balzac's *La Comédie humaine* in Henry James's *The American*." *Revue de Littérature Comparée*, no. 1 [211] (January-March):101-4.
Sees Balzac's novels as source books on upper class French life for James, who in writing *The American* had not yet gained admission to French society.
Revised 1987.122.

147 ____. "Henry James Writes His Own Blurbs." *AB Bookman's Weekly* 65, no. 20 (19 May):3871-76.
Reprints James's blurb on *The Outcry* and discusses blurbs on other novels of James's. Tintner argues that James insisted on "having a hand" in writing blurbs because the one written for "Julia Bride" was inaccurate.

148 ____. "Jamesian Structures in *The Age of Innocence* and Related Stories." *Twentieth Century Literature* 26, no. 3 (Fall):332-47.
Traces elements in *The Age of Innocence, Old New York*, and "Writing the War Story" that echo James's work. Wharton was influenced by James's early, middle, and late work; Tintner suggests that Wharton made a "conscious effort" to write either a Jamesian novel or a novel worthy of James.

149 ____. "James' *King Lear: The Outcry* and the Art Drain." *AB Bookman's Weekly* 65, no. 5 (4 February):798-828.
Argues that James linked *King Lear* to the theme of the "art drain" in his play and novel because he felt that in selling masterpieces to American collectors the British were giving away their patrimony. Tintner details James's use of Shakespeare and suggests that Edwin Austin Abbey's painting, *King Lear's Daughters*, may have served in part as a model for James.
Revised 1987.122.

150 _____. "'The Papers': Henry James Rewrites *As You Like It*." *Studies in Short Fiction* 17, no. 2 (Spring):165-70.

Shows that seeing the 1903 tale as a reworking of the play illuminates the tale's meaning. Tintner traces James's use of Shakespeare and concludes that recognizing the tale's analogue reveals "the attempt of a great writer to incorporate part of the vision of an even greater one."

Revised 1987.122.

151 _____. "Some Notes for a Study of the Gissing Phase in Henry James's Fiction." *Gissing Newsletter* 16, no. 3 (July):1-15.

Describes the phases of James's use of Gissing: first, after reading *New Grub Street* in 1891, James wrote three tales about "grubbing"; second, James's use of lower class characters in the fiction written during 1898-1900, including *In the Cage*; third, James's return to *New Grub Street* material, 1901-1903; and fourth, a fusion of Gissing and Balzac in the tales of *The Finer Grain* (1910).

152 _____. "Truffaut's *La Chambre vert*: Hommage to Henry James." *Literature/Film Quarterly* 8, no. 2 (Spring):78-83.

Attributes Truffaut's ability to capture James's intentions in "The Altar of the Dead" to a blending of his own predispositions with James's sensibility and outlines the shared "similarities and sympathies" of the two artists.

153 TORGOVNICK, MARIANNA. "Gestural Pattern and Meaning in *The Golden Bowl*." *Twentieth Century Literature* 26, no. 4 (Winter):445-57.

Focuses on the gestural patterns of the novel's final scene in which Maggie accepts a flawed relationship. Torgovnick argues that her approach is a way to "read the late James as he wished to be read" and focuses attention on the true power of any novel – its "representation of human emotions and human dilemmas."

Reprinted in part 1981.167.

154 TOWNSEND, R.C. "The American Male: His Values and His Voids." *Prospects* 5:111-55.

Examines the portrayal of the American man in fiction in light of James's view of the division of the sexes in American society.

1980

Because of that division, men fear women and reject their own feminine qualities. Townsend discusses the fiction of a variety of writers from Melville to Mailer.

155   TURNER, ALDEN R. "The Haunted *Portrait of a Lady*." *Studies in the Novel* 12, no. 3 (Fall):228-38.

Charts the development of Isabel's understanding of the relationship between experience and art and of her consciousness of the transforming power of the artist's imagination. At the novel's end, Isabel has learned that art and life are separate but recognizes "the value of life within form."

156   TUTTLETON, JAMES W. "Rereading *The American*: A Century Since." *Henry James Review* 1, no. 2 (Winter):139-53.

Reviews the critical responses to the novel particularly in its portrayal of a national type and notes the novel's themes and "glittering array" of allusions. Tuttleton also discusses the New York Edition revision and sees the novel as James's unsuccessful attempt to transform the old sentimental romance into a "new realism."

Reprinted 1987.43.

157   VANDERBILT, KERMIT. "'Complicated Music at Short Order' in 'Fordham Castle.'" *Henry James Review* 2, no. 1 (Fall):61-66.

Parallels the structure of the fugue with that of the tale, especially in James's use of motifs that ultimately merge to a "climactic 'key.'" These motifs include an affronting of destiny, a sense of being, and a capacity to give. James gives these motifs "satire inversion" in the tale's protagonist, Abel Taker, while the tale's other characters embody each of the motifs.

158   WALCH, GÜNTER. "'The Private Life': Das Motiv des gedoppelten Menschen in der englischen Literatur der Jahrundertwende" [The Motif of the alter ego in English literature at the turn of the century]. *Zeitschrift fur Anglistik und Amerikanistik* 28, no. 2:101-12.

In German.

159 WATT, IAN. "Marlow and Henry James." In *Conrad in the Nineteenth Century*. London: Chatto & Windus, pp. 200-14.

Argues that James's narrative technique in the fiction of the 1890s influenced Conrad's use of Marlow in *Heart of Darkness*. Marlow's role as both subject and object, however, reflects Conrad's skepticism about understanding character, and thus places Conrad closer to the twentieth century than James.

160 WESSEL, CATHERINE COX. "Culture and Anarchy: The Survival of the Fittest in the Fiction of Henry James." Ph.D. dissertation, Yale University, 303 pp.

Argues that James's vision of human nature was shaped by an Arnoldian faith in cultural traditions and by Darwin's theory of natural selection. James's early work, exemplified by *The Portrait of a Lady*, bears Arnold's imprint; the later work, most notably *The Golden Bowl*, is Darwinian.

See *Dissertation Abstracts International* 41, no. 12 (1981):5103A-5104A.

161 WESTBROOK, WAYNE D. "Stockbrokers to Strikebreakers." In *Wall Street in the American Novel*. New York: New York University Press, pp. 50-57.

Surveys James's portrayal of the businessman in *The American*, *The Reverberator*, "The Jolly Corner," and *The Ivory Tower*. At first James saw the businessman as essentially innocent and Adamic; in *The Ivory Tower*, the characterization is colored by evil.

162 WILKINSON, D.R.M. "A Complete Image: James's *The Bostonians*." In *From Cooper to Philip Roth: Essays on American Literature*. Edited by J. Bakker and D.R.M. Wilkinson. Costerus new series vol. 26. Amsterdam: Rodopi, pp. 34-43.

Agrees with Birrell (1977.14) that James's real focus in the novel is the corrupting influence of abstract causes, and suggests that the conflict between Basil and Olive is personal, for they are both fighting over Verena. Wilkinson also examines the character of Verena and argues that she is much more complex than has been previously acknowledged.

1980

163   WILLIAMS, M.A. "The Drama of Maisie's Vision." *Henry James Review* 2, no. 1 (Fall):36-48.
      Sees the novel as a critique of "established modes of seeing and judging." Maisie's vision matures through her relationship with the other characters and thus Maisie dramatizes "the transforming power of a free and wondering engagement with reality."

164   WILLIS, PATRICIA C. "New York: 'Accessibility to Experience.'" *Marianne Moore Newsletter* 4, no. 1 (Spring):13-14.
      Attributes the poem's final line to the blurb for the English edition of *The Finer Grain* (1910), which quotes James's letter to his publisher.

165   WILSON, FRANKIE, and WESTBROOK, MAX. "Daisy Miller and the Metaphysician." *American Literary Realism 1870-1910* 13, no. 2 (Autumn):270-79.
      Attributes Daisy's "undoing" to her psychological vulnerability as a "creature of inclinations" and Winterbourne's inability to love. The authors also find parallels between Daisy and the Undine myth as described by Irving Massey.

166   WYATT, DAVID. "Modernity and Paternity: James's *The American*." In *Prodigal Sons: A Study in Authorship and Authority*. Baltimore: Johns Hopkins University Press, pp. 1-25.
      Connects the relation between father and son to the relation between the artist and his art, focusing on James's *The American* and its New York revision. James's assertion of authority over his creation is best seen in the novel's revision. In the novel's preface James describes the genesis of the novel occurring in a moment of self-forgetfulness; the revision enabled him to exert his full "paternal" control over his creation. Wyatt also links the novel to James's childhood conflicts, particularly Mary James's domination. Newman cannot consummate a marriage because of James's fear of strong women. Only through his authorship can James reconcile both paternal and maternal roles.

167   ZÉRAFFA, MICHEL, ed. *L'Art de la fiction, Henry James*. Paris: Éditions Klincksieck, 323 pp.
      In French.

168   ZÉRAPHA, MICHEL. "Devant et après Flaubert." *L'Arc* (Aix-en-Provence France) 79:18-21.
         In French.

1981

1   AKIYAMA, MASAYUKI. "The American Image in Kafū Nagai and Henry James." *Comparative Literature Studies* 18, no. 2 (June):95-103.
         Compares Kafū's *A Selected Diary in America and France* with James's *The American Scene*. Kafū was fascinated by American individualism while James felt that individualism was taken to the extreme; both writers were appalled by American materialism.

2   ____. *Henry James Sakuhin Kenkyu: His World, His Thought, His Art* [A study of the works of Henry James]. Tokyo: Nan'undo, 418 pp.
         In Japanese.
         Analyzes James's novels and tales and includes two chapters comparing James and the Novel Prize winner Kawabata.

3   ALLEN, E. "Woman as Signifier in the Novels of Henry James." Ph.D. dissertation, University of Sussex, United Kingdom.
         Explores, using James's novels as examples, "the representation of women and the feminine in the literary text, and the conflicts inherent in the presence of women fundamentally as signs and yet also as people." Allen begins with the phenomenon of the American girl and then traces James's depiction of women in his major works. Allen sees James's rejection of the happy marriage reflecting the conflict inherent in the social existence of women and their individuality and independence.
         See *Dissertation Abstracts International* 45, no. 3 (1984):9/2525C.

4   ALLEN, WALTER. "James." In *The Short Story in English*. New York: Oxford University Press, pp. 42-48.

1981

Calls James "the first and great exponent" of the international theme, as evidenced by "Daisy Miller," "Madame de Mauves," and "Miss Gunton of Poughkeepsie." Allen also mentions "The Real Thing" as one of James's "most deeply disturbing" stories on the artist.

5   ALLISON, JOHN B. *"The Sacred Fount*: James's Literary Joke." *American Transcendental Quarterly* 51 (Summer):183-93.
Argues that the novel's "joke" is on Poe and Hawthorne. Allison details the ways in which James transformed elements borrowed from his predecessors into comedy. The novel reveals the limitations of the imagination when confronted by the "evidential world."

6   BALDINGER, FRIEDRICH. *Vom Faktum sur Fiktion: eine historische und literarische Untersuchung von Henry James' "The Princess Casamassima" und Joseph Conrad's "Under Western Eyes."* Schweizer Anglistische Arbeiten, 103. Bern: Francke, 190 pp.
In German, with English summary.
Examines the ways in which James and Conrad use historial material in their fiction. James's "accurate observation of the social scene" is subordinated to his interest in the psychology of the individual while in Conrad there is a clear and consistent relationship between historical events and characters and the political theme of the novel.

7   BARUCH, ELAINE HOFFMANN. "The Feminine *Bildungsroman*: Education through Marriage." *Massachusetts Review* 22, no. 2 (Summer):335-57.
Discusses a range of novels in which the female protagonist seeks or discovers knowledge through marriage. In *The Portrait of a Lady*, Isabel's marriage, a result of her lack of knowledge, brings her the knowledge of evil.

8   BAXTER, CHARLES. "'Wanting in Taste': *The Sacred Fount* and the Morality of Reading." *Centennial Review* 25, no. 3 (Summer):314-29.
Argues that *The Sacred Fount*, which James called a "consistent joke," raises moral and psychological issues to shame and baffle the reader, and thus is James's "act of aggression in the form of a novel."

9   BAYLEY, JOHN. "Formalist Games and Real Life." *Essays in Criticism* 31, no. 4 (October):271-81.
    Criticizes contemporary theories, particularly structuralism and deconstruction, for reducing literary criticism to a game and divorcing literature from life. Bayley then focuses on Todorov's formalism. Todorov's work on James's tales is "particularly brilliant," although he concentrates on those about a ghost or a secret and ignores the ones exploring society or an individual.

10 BELL, BARBARA CURRIER. "Beyond Irony in Henry James: *The Aspern Papers*." *Studies in the Novel* 13, no. 3 (Fall):282-93.
    Argues that the novella exemplifies James's use of irony as a means of "highlighting an unqualified moral value," not as an end in itself. James treats the Christian story of the Fall with irony to arrive at his own "secular morality," focusing on the search for knowledge without having self-knowledge.

11 BELLRINGER, ALAN W. "Henry James's *The Sense of the Past*: The Backward Vision." *Forum for Modern Language Studies* 17, no. 3 (July):201-16.
    Calls the novel a tale warning against escapism and nostalgia and thus belongs with such works as "The Turn of the Screw" and *The Sacred Fount* by virtue of theme and technique. The novel reveals James's "persistent American modernity."

12 BENNETT, JAMES R. "Plot Repetition: Theme and Variation of Narrative Macro-Episodes." *Papers on Language and Literature* 17, no. 4 (Fall):405-20.
    Examines the reoccurrence of patterns within the "micro-episodes" of the plot whereby theme and character are expanded through variation and repetition. Bennett briefly mentions "The Beast in the Jungle" as a variation of the "five-macro-episode structure" in which five of the six chapters show "'the same act five times.'"

13 BERKSON, DOROTHY. "Tender-Minded Idealism and Erotic Repression in James's 'Madame de Mauves' and 'The Last of the Valerii.'" *Henry James Review* 2, no. 2 (Winter):78-86.
    Argues that both tales are critiques of contemporary sexual attitudes, which are rooted in idealism and the genteel tradition. They

1981

show that the results of such idealism are loneliness and emotional isolation.

14   BERLAND, ALWYN. *Culture and Conduct in the Novels of Henry James*. Cambridge: Cambridge University Press, xi, 231 pp.
      Argues that the idea of civilization as culture is central to James's work and traces the evolution of this idea, drawn from the writings of Matthew Arnold, in *Roderick Hudson*, *The Portrait of a Lady*, *The Bostonians*, *The Princess Casamassima*, *The Tragic Muse*, and *The Ambassadors*. *The Portrait* is discussed in most detail because the novel focuses on civilization through the strategy of the international theme. In the three novels following *The Portrait*, James defends his view of civilization against other views; while in *The Ambassadors* James treats his central theme with complex tone and style.

15   BESSIÈRE, JEAN. "Flaubert, Maupassant et le réalisme américain d'après la critique littéraire de Henry James." In *Flaubert et Maupassant: Ecrivains normands*. Edited by Joseph-Mawrc Bailbé and Jean Pierrot. Pub. de l'Univ. de Rouen, Inst. de Litt. Française, Centre d'Art, Esthétique & Litt. Paris: PU de France, pp. 273-82.
      In French.

16   BLACKALL, JEAN FRANTZ. "The Case for Mrs. Brookenham." *Henry James Review* 2, no. 3 (Spring):155-61.
      Calls Mrs. Brook James's Becky Sharp: she is witty, imaginative, and protean. If the novel is seen as a circus and as a game of wits, she is its heroine.

17   BOISSON, CLAUDE, THOIRON, PHILIPE, and VEYRIRAS, PAUL. "Du son au sens dan 'The Jolly Corner' de Henry James: Analyse d'un texte et esquisse d'une methode." *Confluents* 6, no. 2:57-104.
      In French.

18   BRACHES, ERNST. "De diepe gronden van *The Turn of the Screw*." *Revisor* 8, no. 5 (October):26-39.
      In Dutch.

19 BRITTON, TERRY D. "From Ambivalence to Acquiescence: Studies in Gothic Metaphor." Ph.D. dissertation, University of Oklahoma, 130 pp.

Argues that Dickens, Emily Brontë, and James use Gothic metaphor in their characters' confrontation with the past. Initially Pip, Heathcliff, and Isabel are ambivalent to the past; Gothic structures enable these characters to arrive at acquiescence – and this response is also ultimately experienced by the reader.

See *Dissertation Abstracts International* 41, no. 11 (1982):4829A-4830A.

20 BROOKE-ROSE, CHRISTINE. "*The Turn of the Screw* and its Critics: An Essay in Non-Methodology." In *A Rhetoric of the Unreal: Studies in Narrative and Structure, Especially of the Fantastic.* Cambridge: Cambridge University Press, pp. 128-57.

Revision of 1976.22.

21 _____. "*The Turn of the Screw*: Mirror Structures as Basic Structures." In *A Rhetoric of the Unreal: Studies in Narrative and Structure, Especially of the Fantastic.* Cambridge: Cambridge University Press, pp. 158-87.

Revision of 1976.23.

22 _____. "The Surface Structures in *The Turn of the Screw*." In *A Rhetoric of the Unreal: Studies in Narrative and Structure, Especially of the Fantastic.* Cambridge: Cambridge University Press, pp. 188-229.

Revision of 1977.21.

23 BROWN, CHRISTOPHER. "Poe's 'Masque' and *The Portrait of a Lady*." *Poe Studies* 14, no. 1 (June):6-7.

Proposes Poe's tale as a source for the novel, particularly in depicting Osmond and the Palazzo Roccanera.

24 CARAMELLO, CHARLES. "Performing Self as Performance: James, Joyce, and the Postmodern Turn." *Southern Humanities Review* 15, no. 4 (Fall):301-5.

Compares James's and Joyce's view of the importance of tradition for the artist. James's artist, exemplified in "The Jolly Corner," renovates tradition, while Joyce's artist decomposes it.

25 CARTER, DAVID MICHAEL. "The Development of the Historic Sense in Henry James." Ph.D. dissertation, University of Virginia, 228 pp.

Examines the relationship between the individual and the past in James's fiction and nonfiction, arguing that "James's fictional portrayal of historical influences on character is ... ambivalent." While his characters can be nourished by the past, they can also be harmed by it.

See *Dissertation Abstracts International* 43, no. 5 (1982):1542A.

*26 CICCHETTI, AUDREY HANSSEN. "Henry James and Italy." Ph.D. dissertation, Harvard University.

Source: Offline Bibliography, BRS Information Technologies, Latham, NY 12110.

27 CODY, SUSAN MILNER. "Henry James and James Joyce: A Study in the Continuity of the Modern Novel." Ph.D. dissertation, University of Toronto, Canada.

Argues that James's dramas of consciousness prefigure Joyce's experiments with narrative point of view. Cody examines James's use of the consciousness in *The Ambassadors* and *The Wings of the Dove* as a way to avoid authorial intrusion.

See *Dissertation Abstracts International* 42, no. 9 (1982):3994A.

28 COHEN, PAULA MARANTZ. "Heroinism: The Woman as Vehicle for Values in the Nineteenth-Century Novel from Jane Austen to Henry James." Ph.D. dissertation, Columbia University, 352 pp.

Shows that heroines in nineteenth-century English novels reflect the changing conception of self represented in those novels, using the work of Austen and James as endpoints. In Austen, the heroine is caught in a conflict between her creative imagination and the self-effacing role demanded by society. This conflict dominates the novel up until James, whose heroines remake the social order.

See *Dissertation Abstracts International* 42, no. 1 (1981):222A.

29   CONNAUGHTON, MICHAEL E. "American English and the International Theme in *The Portrait of a Lady.*" *Midwest Quarterly* 22, no. 2 (Winter):137-46.

Analyses James's use of American, Anglo-American, and English dialects to develop character and create the illusion of reality.

30   CONRADI, PETER. "Metaphysical Hostess: The Cult of Personal Relations in the Modern English Novel." *ELH* 48, no. 2 (Summer):427-53.

Examines the character type of the middle-class matron who is "emotionally promiscuous," especially as portrayed in the novels of Iris Murdock, although Conradi also discusses Foster's and Woolf's use of this type. Conradi sees this type prefigured in *The Awkward Age* in the character of Mrs. Brookenham.

31   CRAIG, RANDALL THOMAS. "Reader Response Criticism and Literary Realism of the Late Nineteenth Century." Ph.D. dissertation, University of Wisconsin, Madison, 338 pp.

Argues that writers create readers just as readers create writers. Seeing the text as a bridge between author and reader, Craig examines the gap between real and ideal audiences, strategies and techniques used for closing that gap, and the reader's role in relation to these techniques and strategies. Craig's analysis focuses on Norris's *McTeague*, James's *What Maisie Knew*, Bennett's *The Old Wives' Tale*, and Conrad's *Lord Jim*.

See *Dissertation Abstracts International* 42, no. 3 (1981):1157A.

32   _____. "'Read[ing] the Unspoken into the Spoken': Interpreting *What Maisie Knew.*" *Henry James Review* 2, no. 3 (Spring):204-12.

Traces Maisie's "hermeneutical maturation" and argues that James envisioned similar growth for the reader, who must learn to read and to read into the novel. Both Maisie and the reader must acquire "interpretive and linguistic proficiency"; both must learn to interact with the text to create a dialogue.

33   CROSS, MARY. "Henry James and the Grammar of the Modern." *Henry James Review* 3, no. 1 (Fall):33-43.

Argues that James's emphasis on syntax, word order, and design creates a "literary language" that draws attention to itself and

1981

becomes itself an abstraction. Cross focuses on *The Portrait of a Lady* to show how James's prose becomes a metaphor for the novel's concern with the limitations of language.

34 CULVER, STUART. "Censorship and Intimacy: Awkwardness in *The Awkward Age*." *ELH* 48, no. 2 (Summer):368-86.

Shows how "the awkwardness and obliquity of English speech" is a form of censorship and a "compromise betwen active treatment (taking up) and restraint (letting alone)." Nanda must struggle to define herself in the midst of these shifting strategies.

35 CURTSINGER, E.C., Jr. "Henry James's Farewell in 'The Velvet Glove.'" *Studies in Short Fiction* 18, no. 2 (Spring):163-69.

Rejects reading the tale as a joke on Wharton and suggests that Amy Evans is "the embodied imagination of James's writer."

36 DAUGHERTY, SARAH B. *The Literary Criticism of Henry James*. Athens: Ohio University Press, xiv, 232 pp.

Examines James's literary criticism within its historical context, including the novels he read and the relationships among those novels. A comprehensive study of the criticism and its sources shows that James was widely familiar with the fiction of his time, that he did not set forth rigid technical principles, and that he was more a conservative of the nineteenth century than a prophet of the twentieth. James's criticism illuminates his fiction, particularly the influence of Balzac's realism and Hawthorne's romanticism.

Chapters 1-10 revision of Ph.D. dissertation, University of Pennsylvania, 1973.

*37 DJUKANOVIĆ, BOJKA. "Estetički pogledi Henry Džeymsa" [Aesthetic views on Henry James]. *Spone* (Nikšić, Yugoslavia) 13:75-81.

In Serbo-Croatian.

Source: *Annual Bibliography of English Language and Literature* 54 (1981):434, item 7975.

38 DYSON, J. PETER. "Perfection, Beauty and Suffering in 'The Two Faces.'" *Henry James Review* 2, no. 2 (Winter):116-25.

Analyzes this tale, focusing on characters, theme, and imagery, and discusses its place in the Jamesian canon. The tale's concern with the ambiguity of consciousness – its ability to remedy the deficiencies of nature and its capacity to do evil – is central to James's analysis of the consciousness throughout his career.

39   EDEL, LEON. Introduction to *English Hours*. Oxford: Oxford University Press, vii-xvi.
       Argues that these sketches show three phases of James's response to England. In his early work, James is "the sentimental tourist;" second, he is "an observant stranger"; and third, he is an "insider." As a result, there is a significant autobiographical element in these essays.
       Revised 1981.40.

40   ____. "The Three Travelers in *English Hours*." *Henry James Review* 2, no. 3 (Spring):167-71.
       Revision of 1981.39.

41   EISENSTADT, BEVERLY D. "The Changing Reader: A Study of Three Novels by Henry James." Ph.D. dissertation, Columbia University, 202 pp.
       Demonstrates that *The Tragic Muse, The Awkward Age*, and *The Wings of the Dove* are experiments with narrative techniques designed to demand greater reader participation in texts increasingly indeterminant.
       See *Dissertation Abstracts International* 42, no. 1 (1981):224A.

42   FADERMAN, LILLIAN. "Boston Marriage." In *Surpassing the Love of Men: Romantic Friendship and Love Between Women from the Renaissance to the Present*. New York: William Morrow, pp. 190-96, 446-47.
       Argues that the relationship between Olive and Verena depicted in *The Bostonians* was common in James's day and was not regarded as lesbian, in contrast to current criticism of the novel. James "intended that there be neither heroes nor heroic acts in the ungentle novel." Faderman also notes that James drew on his observation of Alice James and Katharine Loring for this novel's material.

1981

43   FELDMAN, LEONARD MARK. "A Matter of Money: Money and
      the World of the American Novel, 1893-1940." Ph.D. dissertation,
      University of California, Los Angeles, 279 pp.
         Argues that the novels of this period show a movement from
      an ordered, moral world giving way to a world contaminated by money.
      The Golden Bowl, one of the many novels discussed in this study,
      focuses on conflicts arising from the characters' attitudes toward
      money.
         See *Dissertation Abstracts International* 42, no. 8 (1982):3599A-
      3600A.

44   FIELD, MARY LEE. "'Nervous Anglo-Saxon Apprehensions':
      Henry James and the French." *The French-American Review* 5, no. 1
      (Spring):1-13.
         Surveys James's criticism of French fiction, concentrating on
      the change in his definition of vulgarity. Field divides James's attitudes
      into three periods: prior to 1880, James criticized French "uncleanness';
      between 1880 and 1900, James allowed the French writer his donnée;
      and in his later years, James saw vulgarity as "commonness" and love of
      detail.

45   FINCHAM, GAIL. "Fairytale, Mythical and Realistic Elements in
      Henry James's *The Wings of the Dove*." *English Studies in Africa* 24,
      no. 2 (September):95-106.
         Sees Milly Theale as mythic Golden Age Princess, Cinderella,
      Sleeping Beauty, and legendary scapegoat as she grows from innocence
      to knowledge. Fincham charts the "escalation" of fairy tale into
      archetype, noting a parallel movement from the world of the flesh to
      the world of the spirit.

46   FOGEL, DANIEL MARK. *Henry James and the Structure of the
      Romantic Imagination*. Baton Rouge: Louisiana State University
      Press, xiv, 193 pp.
         Argues that James was influenced by the writers of the
      Romantic period and that this influence is apparent in James's use of
      the quest for experience, a bipolar structure for that quest, and the
      synthesis of that bipolarity occurring in a spiral movement – elements
      typical of Romanticism. Fogel traces this "Romantic dialectic of spiral
      return" in *The Awkward Age, The Ambassadors, The Wings of the Dove*,

and *The Golden Bowl* in detail, but also surveys James's entire career in terms of this dialectic.

*47   FREADMAN, R.B. "The Rhetoric of George Eliot's and Henry James's Fiction." Ph.D. dissertation, University of Oxford.
      Source: *Annual Bibliography of English Language and Literature* 58 (1983):432, item 7646.

48   FUJITA, EIICHI. *Sei to Jiyu o Motomete: Henry James no Shosetsu* [Life and freedom in the novels of Henry James]. Osaka: Sogensha, 430 pp.
      In Japanese.
      Examines James's novels and tales in which the innocent youth, the tragic artist, and the cosmopolitan search for life and freedom.

*49   FULLBROOK, K.J. "Henry James and Matthew Arnold: Consciousness, Morality, and the Modern Spirit." Ph.D. dissertation, University of Cambridge.
      Source: *Annual Bibliography of English Language and Literature* 58 (1983):394, item 6969.

50   FUSSELL, EDWIN SILL. "Sympathy in *The Portrait of a Lady* and *The Golden Bowl*." *Henry James Review* 2, no. 3 (Spring):161-66.
      Traces James's sense and use of sympathy, an "all but overwhelming American literary obsession," in these two novels. Fussell notes that James treats Isabel sympathetically, while in *The Golden Bowl*, sympathy has both comic and tragic dimensions.

51   GALE, ROBERT L. "Henry James." In *American Literary Scholarship: An Annual/1979*. Edited by James Woodress. Durham: Duke University Press, pp. 93-113.
      Surveys criticism published in 1979.

52   GASS, WILLIAM H. "Culture, Self, and Style." *Syracuse Scholar* 2, no. 1 (Spring):52-68.

1981

Examines James's use of language in *The Golden Bowl*. His language is "conscious of its own character, as the highest culture must be, if it is ever to be critical of itself"; his sentences are "celebrations of consciousness."
Reprinted 1985.46.

53   GOETZ, WILLIAM. "The 'Frame' of *The Turn of the Screw*: Framing the Reader In." *Studies in Short Fiction* 18, no. 1 (Winter):71-74.
Sees the tale's asymmetrical frame as a "protocol" for reading the tale, in that the text's lack of an epilogue guarantees that the meaning is "undecidable." Ultimately the reader chooses a meaning, but the text will invariably reveal the shortcomings of that meaning.

54   GOLDFARB, CLARE. "An Archetypal Reading of *The Golden Bowl*: Maggie Verver as Questor." *American Literary Realism 1870-1910* 14, no. 1 (Spring):52-61.
Sees Maggie as the archetypal questor who must restore her father to his proper place, American City, where he will transform cultural sterility into fruitfulness. Maggie's successful quest brings her the experience of loss and the knowledge of the ambiguity of human nature.

55   _____. "Matriarchy in the Late Novels of Henry James." *Research Studies* 49, no. 4 (December):231-41.
Traces similarities between Mrs. Lowder in *The Wings of the Dove* and Mrs. Newsome in *The Ambassadors*. Both women are matriarchs who use their power to manipulate and dominate. Maggie Verver, in *The Golden Bowl*, is a matriarch who tempers her power with love.

56   GRAY, PATRICK K. "The Lure of Romance and the Temptation of Feminine Sensibility: Literary Heroines in Selected Popular and 'Serious' American Novels, 1895-1915." Ph.D. dissertation, Emory University, 332 pp.
Traces elements of the romance, including an idealized heroine, a predictable plot, and realistic detail in the fiction of the period to demonstrate that the romance was the means by which the problematic "New Woman" could be assimilated with the culture.

James's *What Maisie Knew* is discussed here, focusing on its dependence on elements borrowed from the conventional romance.
See *Dissertation Abstracts International* 42, no. 5 (1981):2130A.

57 GREENE, GRAHAM. Introduction to *The Portrait of a Lady*. Oxford: Oxford University Press, pp. vii-xiii.
Sees the novel's theme of betrayal as central to James's work and links that theme to Minnie Temple's being betrayed by her body.

58 GREENWALD, ELISSA ANN. "The Hawthorne Aspect: Henry James and American Romance." Ph.D. dissertation, Yale University, 261 pp.
Demonstrates that through his "creative revision" of Hawthorne in the 1879 book and 1904 essay, James constructs a theory of romance compatible with his realism. Romance is "re-presentation" in which the world is transformed by the imagination. Greenwald discusses Hawthorne's and James's theories of romance, relates them to earlier models, and details the romance elements in *The Portrait of a Lady*, *The Bostonians*, and *The Wings of the Dove* in direct comparison to Hawthorne's novels.
See *Dissertation Abstracts International* 42, no. 12 (1982):5121A.

*59 GREGORY, ROBERT DOUGLAS. "Reading as Narcissism: Freud, Twain, James, and Hawthorne." Ph.D. dissertation, University of California, Irvine.
Source: Budd, 1983.32, p. 18, item 79.

60 HAIGHT, GORDON S. "Strether's Chad Newsome: A Reading of James's *The Ambassadors*." In *From Smollett to James: Studies in the Novel and Other Essays Presented to Edgar Johnson*. Edited by Samuel I. Mintz, Alice Chandler, and Christopher Mulvey. Charlottesville: University Press of Virginia, pp. 261-76.
Shows that Strether's vision of Chad is a highly romanticized one.

61 HALPERN, JOSEPH. "Changing Partners in Henry James." *Southern Humanities Review* 15, no. 1 (Winter):53-65.

Uses *The Sacred Fount* as an exemplar of Jamesian narrative, which is grounded in chiasmus and exchange, not linear development.

62 HANLEY, LYNNE T. "The Eagle and the Hen: Edith Wharton and Henry James." *Research Studies* 49, no. 3 (September):143-53.

Describes James's and Wharton's criticisms of each other. James saw Wharton as wasteful, not only in terms of money but of self, time, energy, and emotion, while Wharton accused James of excessive devotion to theory and detachment from life.

63 HARRIS, JANICE H. "Bushes, Bears, and 'The Beast in the Jungle.'" *Studies in Short Fiction* 18, no. 2 (Spring):147-54.

Proposes an alternative reading of the tale based on its language, imagery, and depiction of May. These elements show that Marcher has had a fuller life than has been acknowledged, but also has a poor memory and a lack of self-awareness.

64 HARTSTEIN, ARNOLD MICHAEL. "The Uses of Myth in Four Modern Tragedies: A Discussion of the Relationship between Mythic Content and the Idea of Tragedy in *Moby-Dick, The Princess Casamassima, The Trial*, and *Waiting for Godot*." Ph.D. dissertation, Ohio State University, 132 pp.

Argues that the use of myth in these works ties them to tragedies of the past but at the same time reveals differences between tragedies of the past and of the present. The tragic patterns in James's novels invite the reader to go beyond the political to ponder the riddle of human nature in its social and spiritual dimensions.

See *Dissertation Abstracts International* 42, no. 5 (1981):2128A-2129A.

65 HARVEY, SUSAN ELICIA. "One Fine Ignorance: The Experience of Reading Henry James." Ph.D. dissertation, University of California, Berkeley, 499 pp.

Examines "The Liar," "The Figure in the Carpet," and "The Turn of the Screw" using a reader-response approach to reveal James's manipulative narrative devices. Such an approach results in a re-evaluation of James's use of point of view as well as his moral vision.

See *Dissertation Abstracts International* 43, no. 6 (1982):1972A.

66   HESTON, LILLA A. "The Very Oral Henry James." *Literature in Performance* 1, no. 2 (April):1-12.

Suggests that James's prose must be performed rather than read to be appreciated and to understand the sensibilities of his characters. James's complex syntactic structure and his strategic use of silence express character, emotion, and situation. Heston draws examples from *The Spoils of Poynton* and *The Wings of the Dove*.

67   HILFER, ANTHONY CHANNELL. "Henry James: An Ethics of Intensity." In *The Ethics of Intensity in American Fiction*. Austin: University of Texas Press, pp. 71-102, 186-92.

Examines James's concept of the self in "The Beast in the Jungle" and *The Wings of the Dove*. In both "he judges his characters on the intensity and quality of their responses" to the roles that other characters or situations demand of them. James's characters must choose between self-expansion, which involves "moral spontaneity" and risk-taking, and self-negation, which surrenders identity to the determinations of others.

68   HILL, ROBERT W., Jr. "A Counterclockwise Turn in James's 'The Turn of the Screw.'" *Twentieth Century Literature* 27, no. 1 (Spring):53-71.

Examines in detail the character of Miles and his point of view. Miles falls in with the governess's game of pretending to see ghosts as a way of shutting out others, but the realization that she is out to destroy him kills him.

69   HIRSCH, MARIANNE. "*The Ambassadors*: 'A Drama of Discrimination.'" In *Beyond the Single Vision: Henry James, Michel Butor, Uwe Johnson*. York, S.C.: French Literature Publications, pp. 12-30.

Shows that Strether is able to transcend the limitations of his own vision to achieve a "sublime concensus" of European and American values. He pays a price for this achievement: a "solitary existence."

70   _____. "*The Golden Bowl*: 'That Strange Accepted Finality of Relation.'" In *Beyond the Single Vision: Henry James, Michel Butor, Uwe Johnson*. York, S.C.: French Literature Publications, pp. 57-81.

1981

Sees the international theme as integral to this novel but argues that the resolution of the conflict between the cultures, reflected in the novel's structure, never occurs within the confines of the novel. Rather, the reader must complete the novel's structure and fuse the two parts.

71 _____. "*Passing Time*: 'Ruins of an Unfinished Building.'" In *Beyond the Single Vision: Henry James, Michel Butor, Uwe Johnson*. York, S.C.: French Literature Publications, pp. 31-55.

Compares *The Ambassadors* with Michel Butor's novel. Strether achieves a concensus between two cultures; James's novel "celebrates the primacy of the human imagination." Revel, Butor's protagonist, never experiences a total vision–he becomes an anonymous chronicler of Bleston; Butor's novel focuses not on the individual but on "the city's complex being."

72 HOCKS, RICHARD A., and HARDT, JOHN S. "James Studies 1978-1979: An Analytic Bibliographical Essay." *Henry James Review* 2, no. 2 (Winter):132-52.

Surveys criticism published in 1978 and 1979, including books and articles. On the whole, the criticism of these years focuses on placing Jame in his cultural milieu, but it all too often lacks a sense of the total canon.

73 HOLLOWAY, ANNA REBECCA. "Henry James and the Intellectuals: Relativism and Form in G. Eliot, R. Browning, W. Pater, and H. James." Ph.D. dissertation, Kent State University, 269 pp.

Compares Eliot's *Middlemarch*, Browning's *The Ring and the Book*, and Pater's *Marius the Epicurean* with James's *The Portrait of a Lady, The Wings of the Dove*, and *The Ambassadors*, respectively, to show the conflict between the Victorians' relativism and their intellectual absolutism as well as James's rejection of such absolutism. In addition, while the Victorians base character on social conditions, Jamesian character derives from a developing consciousness.

See *Dissertation Abstracts International* 42, no. 4 (1981):1646A-1647A.

74 HUGHES, CATHERINE BOULTON. "The Detective Form: A Study of Its Sources and Meaning in Late Nineteenth Century Popular Fiction and Works of James and Conrad." Ph.D. dissertation, Brandeis University, 550 pp.

Examines the basic components of the detective genre established by Poe and traces their use in the experimental work of James and Conrad and in the popular fiction of the 1890s. Hughes sees similar concerns in popular fiction and in such novels as *What Maisie Knew*, *The Ambassadors*, *Heart of Darkness*, and *Under Western Eyes*. The loss of the typically tight structure of the genre "reveals the impossibility of maintaining the total rational control of irrational forces so endorsed by the genre."

See *Dissertation Abstracts International* 42, no. 9 (1982):4006A-4007A.

75 IMMELMAN, ELBIE. "Henry James (1843-1916): Master Stylist of the English Novel." *Lantern* (Pretoria) 30, no. 2:80-84.

Summarizes James's life and major concerns, including the international theme and the signficance of creativity.

76 IZZO, DONATELLA. *Henry James*. Florence: Nuovo Italia, 118 pp. In Italian.

77 JENSEN-OSINKI, BARBARA. "The Key to the Palpable Past: A Study of Miss Tina in *The Aspern Papers*." *Henry James Review* 3, no. 1 (Fall):4-10.

Sees Miss Tina as the guardian of the past and of the tightly-knit Venetian social order. Her marriage proposal is an attempt to resolve the conflict between past and present and to invite the narrator to join the Venetian "family."

78 JONES, PETER. "Pragmatism and *The Portrait of a Lady*." *Philosophy and Literature* 5, no. 1 (Spring):49-61.

Traces the "philosophical aspects" of Isabel Archer's character. James depends on a pragmatist method to develop her character, and Jones attributes the ambiguities of the novel to this method.

1981

79   KAUFFMAN, LINDA S. "The Author of Our Woe: Virtue Recorded in *The Turn of the Screw*." *Nineteenth-Century Fiction* 36, no. 2 (September):176-92.

Examines the governess's reading and writing, both manifestations of her imagination. Her reading, especially of *Jane Eyre*, enables her to create a delusional world at Bly. Her writing is an attempt to control reality and the other characters, but it also is a confession of unrequited love. Ultimately the tragedy of the novel is the inability of the characters to "confirm the reality of love."

80   KEYSER, ELIZABETH. "Veils and Masks: *The Blithedale Romance* and *The Sacred Fount*." *Henry James Review* 2, no. 2 (Winter):101-10.

Examines the novels' use of mask imagery, which suggests "the immanence (and imminence) of death." Both narrators are detached from life, content to be observers and thus represent a kind of living death.

81   KIRSCHKE, JAMES J. *Henry James and Impressionism*. Troy, N.Y.: Whitson, xi, 333 pp.

Discusses the origin, history, and techniques of the impressionist painters and their influence on Continental, British, and American literature, which in turn influenced James's theory and practice of fiction. The detached observer, the focus on the intense moment and on the consciousness, the handling of light and color, and the primacy of technique over subject are the features of James's impressionism. Kirschke traces these elements in the tales and novels, beginning with "A Landscape Painter" and concluding with *The Ambassadors*.

Reprint in part of "Henry James's Use of Impressionist Painting Techniques in *The Sacred Fount* and *The Ambassadors*." *Studies in the Twentieth Century* 13 (Spring 1974):83-116.

82   KOMODA, JUNZO. *Henry James 'Neji no Hineri' Ko* [A study of Henry James's "The Turn of the Screw"]. Tokyo: Taimedo, 216 pp.

In Japanese.

Argues that few critical works on this novella provide new perspectives on it as a whole. To gain a new and integrated perspective, we must consider the technical problems inherent in the view that the ghosts are hallucinations and the moral problems inherent in the view that the ghosts are real. Actually, there are three kinds of ghosts in the story: those staged by the children, those that are real people whom the governess mistakes to be ghosts; and those that are the governess's hallucinations. James succeeds in giving seeming coherence to the story by having the governess see these three different kinds as the same.

Reprint of 1980.80.

83   KREYLING, MICHAEL. "Nationalizing the Southern Hero: Adams and James." *Mississippi Quarterly* 34, no. 4 (Fall):383-402.

Focuses on the heroes in *Democracy* and *The Bostonians* to show the "cultural maneuvering" in the North's asserting primacy over the South, using Said's methodology from *Orientalism*. Adams's Ratcliffe is a nationalized Southerner, while Basil Ransom is "the radical and stubborn Other."

84   LAIRD, J.T. "Cracks in Precious Objects: Aestheticism and Humanity in *The Portrait of a Lady*." *American Literature* 52, no. 4 (January):643-48.

Argues that the image of flawed procelain, which links key scenes in chapters 19 and 49, symbolizes Madame Merle's progress from moral sterility to moral values.

85   LEITCH, THOMAS M. "The Editor as Hero: Henry James and the New York Edition." *Henry James Review* 3, no. 1 (Fall):24-32.

Discusses James's selection and revision of works for the New York Edition, noting that James emphasizes the importance of the imagination as a power to transform the world. James presents himself as "his most powerfully imaginative hero"; the legacy of the New York Edition is that "revision displaces vision as the supreme act of the imagination."

86   LESCINSKI, JOAN M. "An Examination of Marriage in Six Novels by Jane Austen and Henry James." Ph.D. dissertation, Brown University, 236 pp.

Demonstrates that both authors deal with similar issues concerning marriage, and both share ideas on the necessary qualifications for a successful marriage. Both value good marriages, although the majority of marriages they depict are failures. Novels discussed here include Austen's *Pride and Prejudice, Persuasion,*

1981

Emma; and James's *The American, The Portrait of a Lady*, and *The Golden Bowl*.
See *Dissertation Abstracts International* 43, no. 2 (1982):452A.

87 LEVY, LEO B. "Consciousness in Three Early Tales of Henry James." *Studies in Short Fiction* 18, no. 4 (Fall):407-12.
Notes that James's protagonists in "A Landscape Painter," "My Friend Bingham," and "Osborne's Revenge" are early versions of the characters trapped by consciousness depicted in such works as "The Aspern Papers," "The Turn of the Screw," and "The Beast in the Jungle."

88 LICHTENBERG, JOSEPH D. "Sweet are the Uses of Adversity: Regression and Style in the Life and Works of Henry James." *Psychoanalytic Inquiry* 1:107-32.
Argues that James's life and art can be understood by two conflicting lines of development: "a remarkable progression in the life of development of narcissism" and "a relative regression in the line of development that leads toward . . . separation and individuation to mature sexual and aggressive functioning." Lichtenberg focuses on two traumatic events – the suicide of Constance Fenimore Woolson and the failure of *Guy Domville* – to show how James's pscyhological development enabled him to overcome severe regression to an ever greater creative output.
Reprinted 1986.87.

89 LIGGERA, J.J. "'She Would Have Appreciated One's Esteem': Peter Bogdanovich's *Daisy Miller*." *Literature/Film Quarterly* 9, no. 1 (Winter):15-21.
Argues that Bogdanovich's film, blending a "Wellesian vocabulary" with a "Jamesian structure" has not received its due from the critics. Liggera praises the film as "gem-like" and calls it "a lovely, imaginative, and yet literal translation" of "Daisy Miller."

90 LOCK, PETER W. "'The Figure in the Carpet': The Text as Riddle and Force." *Nineteenth-Century Fiction* 36, no. 2 (September):157-75.
Sees the tale as "an exercise in production and interpretation." Lock traces the patterns of desire and figure throughout the tale, noting

91 McELROY, JOHN HARMON. "The Mysteries at Bly." *Arizona Quarterly* 37, no. 3 (Autumn):214-36.

Describes the governess as holding her self-respect and respectability above all, so that her account of the events at Bly is based on self-justification. McElroy concludes by noting the tale, with its blend of good and evil, may be outside of the "Christian moral order," but that James is not revising that order because of the combination of circumstance and the governess's character.

92 McMASTER, JULIET. "The Portrait of Isabel Archer." In *The Novel from Sterne to James: Essays on the Relation of Literature to Life*. Edited by Juliet McMaster and Rowland McMaster. New York: Barnes & Noble, pp. 169-87.

Explores Isabel's attraction to suffering and morbidity and attributes it to her vision of herself as a tragic and romantic heroine.

Reprint of *American Literature* 49 (1973):50-66.

93 McMASTER, ROWLAND. "'An Honourable Emulation of the Author of *The Newcomes*': James and Thackeray." In *The Novel from Sterne to James: Essays on the Relation of Literature to Life*. Edited by Juliet McMaster and Rowland McMaster. New York: Barnes & Noble, pp. 147-68.

Reprint of 1978.63.

94 MADDEN, DAVID, and POWERS, RICHARD. "Henry James." In *Writers' Revisions: An Annotated Bibliography of Articles and Books about Writers' Revisions and Their Comments on the Creative Process*. Metuchen, N.J.: Scarecrow Press, pp. 76-83.

Annotates discussions of James's revisions.

95 MALMGREN, CARL. "Henry James's Major Phase: Making Room for the Reader." *Henry James Review* 3, no. 1 (Fall):17-23.

Sees James's later work distinguished by his withdrawal as "Author" to "open interpretive space" for the reader. James dramatizes the consciousness, either through first person narrator as in "The Turn of The Screw" or by omitting a mediating narrator as in *The Awkward Age*. In so doing, James transforms the idea of the author as "a source of ideas and repositor of value."

1981

*96   MANDEL, N.R. "Fairy-Tale and the Fiction of Henry James." Ph.D. dissertation, University of Cambridge.
      Source: *Annual Bibliography of English Language and Literature* 58 (1983):456, item 8080.

97   MARGOLIS, ANNE THRONE. "An International Act: Henry James and the Problem of Audience." Ph.D. dissertation, Yale University, 385 pp.
      Argues that James's fiction was shaped by his interaction with and anticipation of a perceived audience. Margolis shows that during James's middle years, his audience split into those who understood him and those who did not; that James recognized this split; and that James's later work attempts to woo and educate those who did not understand him.
      See *Dissertation Abstracts International* 42, no. 5 (1981):2132A. Revised 1985.91.

98   MARTIN, W.R., and OBER, WARREN U. "Dantesque Patterns in Henry James's 'A Round of Visits.'" *Ariel* 12, no. 4 (October):45-54.
      Traces similarities between James's last tale and Dante's *Inferno*. James's characters attain salvation through the artistic consciousness: the sensitive artist can make his own heaven. The authors suggest that this tale is James's "last testament."

99   MASTRODONNATO, PAOLA GALLI. "Heroines vs. Women: Ideological Confrontation in *Madame Bovary* and *The Portrait of a Lady*." *Gypsy Scholar* 8, no. 1 (Winter):3-18.
      Applies Angenot's concept of isotopia – a "locus of relative ideological cohesion" – to these two novels to show how "interrelated but antagonistic systems of thought and values shape the universe" of Flaubert's and James's novels. For Mastrodonnato, the antagonism occurs between feminist ideology giving center place to a female character and the traditional male dominance. The conflict between these two isotopias transforms the genre of the novel.

100   MAZZELLA, ANTHONY J. "'The Illumination [That] Was All for the Mind': The BBC Video Adaptation of *The Golden Bowl*." *Henry James Review* 2, no. 3 (Spring):213-27.

Calls Pulman's amplification of Bob Assingham's role a stroke of brilliance to encompass visual art and verbal art and shows how Pulman adapted material and used sound to convey the novel's imagery. Mazzella however, finds Pulman's final scene, which departs from the novel, "a strange hybrid."

101 _____. "A Selected Henry James Artsography." *Henry James Review* 3, no. 1 (Fall):44-58.
Lists works adapted from or inspired by James's fiction, and includes dance, opera, film, television, radio, and recordings.

102 MILLER, J. HILLIS. "A Guest in the House: Reply to Shlomith Rimmon-Kenan's Reply." *Poetics Today* 2, no. 1b (Winter):189-91.
Argues that the difference between Rimmon-Kenan's views on ambiguity and his own on unreadability (1980.97) arise out of the difference between the goals of structuralism and of deconstruction. See Rimmon-Kenan 1981.120.

103 MILNE, FRED L. "Atmosphere as Triggering Device in *The Turn of the Screw*." *Studies in Short Fiction* 18, no. 3 (Summer):293-99.
Argues that silence and twilight induce the governess's hallucinations. Milne then traces these atmospheric patterns throughout the tale, showing that they are integral to the plot.

104 "1980-1981 Annual Review: Henry James." *Journal of Modern Literature* 8, no. 3/4:529-34.
Lists criticism published in 1980-81.

105 O'CONNOR, DENNIS. "The Ball." *Henry James Review* 3, no. 1 (Fall):77-78.
Parodies James's prose, inspired by James's remark to Compton Mackenzie.

106 OHI, DEE HANSEN. "The Limits of Revision: Henry James's Rewriting of *Daisy Miller*: A Study." Ph.D. dissertation, University of Denver, 477 pp.

1981

Compares James's revisions of Winterbourne's character. In the earlier version, the influence of Maupassant is apparent; in the New York Edition James attempts to make Winterbourne into a center of consciousness. Winterbourne is, however, inadequate in that role.

See *Dissertation Abstracts International* 42, no. 11 (1982):4824A.

*107 OHTA, RYOKO. "The Window Image of Henry James." *Essays and Studies in British and American Literature* (Tokyo) 27 (Spring):29-74.
Source: *Journal of Modern Literature* 10 (1983):505.

108 OLIVEIRA, CELSO de. "Carlos Fuentes and Henry James: The Sense of the Past." *Arizona Quarterly* 37, no. 3 (Autumn):237-44.
Compares Fuentes' *Aura* with "The Aspern Papers." James's tale served Fuentes as a model, particularly in its contrast of a romantic Byronic world of the past with present-day greed and pettiness. Oliveira holds, however, that the difference between Fuentes and James is "theological" as a way of accounting for *Aura's* "love-death theme."

109 OTT, JOSÉPHINE, trans. "'Honoré de Balzac' par Henry James, II." *L'Année Balzacienne* 2:37-49.
In French.
See 1980.110 for part I.

110 PERROT, JEAN. "Enigme et fiction métalinguistique chez Henry James." *Poétique* 12, no. 45 (February):53-66.
In French.

111 PETRIE, DENNIS W. "Vision of the Artist." In *Ultimately Fiction: Design in Modern American Literary Biography*. West Lafayette: Purdue University Press, pp. 147-77.
Surveys and responds to the major complaints against Edel's biography of James. Although Petrie agrees that a serious flaw is its lack of the scholarly apparatus of footnotes and the citing of specific critics, nevertheless, Edel has given us his portrait of a man of flesh and blood as well as his vision of an artist.

112 PHELAN, JAMES. "Deliberative Acts vs. Grammatical Closure: Stanley Fish and the Language of *The Ambassadors*." In *Worlds from Words: A Theory of Language in Fiction*. Chicago: University of Chicago Press, pp. 15-66.

Uses *The Ambassadors* to reveal the strengths and weaknesses of Fish's reader-response strategy in which the reader constitutes meaning by "deliberative acts." Phelan proposes "grammatical closure," based on syntax and vocabulary, as a way to illuminate the novel's language that enables the reader to share Strether's experience.

113 PILLING, JOHN. "Henry James: *A Small Boy and Others*." In *Autobiography and Imagination: Studies in Self-Scrutiny*. London: Routledge & Kegan Paul, pp. 23-35.

Calls *A Small Boy and Others* a portrait of the history of the imagination in which James is concerned with the relationship between the minutiae of life and the constructions of the imagination and with the movement from specificity to universality. In addition, James's autobiography renders not only his private experience, but "the public experience of a generation."

114 PORTALES, MARCO A. "Strether and Women." *Modern Language Studies* 11, no. 2 (Spring):17-23.

Argues that Strether's relations with women are central to the novel; Maria Gostrey, Mme. de Vionnet, and Jeanne give Strether "the little surprises of life" upon which he thrives.

115 PORTER, CAROLYN. "Henry James: Visionary Being." In *Seeing and Being: The Plight of the Participant Observer in Emerson, James, Adams, and Faulkner*. Middleton, Conn.: Wesleyan, pp. 121-64.

Examines James's development of Emerson's "visionary seer" in a world increasingly reified, beginning with Ralph Touchett in *The Portrait of a Lady* and the narrator in *The Sacred Fount*, but focusing primarily on Maggie Verver in *The Golden Bowl*. Maggie is both visionary seer and "complicit participant" in reification: "her career valorizes the visionary artist's redemptive role" but it "ends by solidifying a world now thoroughly reified."

1981

116   POSNOCK, ROSS. "'The Novel in *The Ring and the Book*': Henry James's Energetic 'Appropriation' of Browning." *Centennial Review* 25, no. 3 (Summer):277-93.

      Shows that in the 1912 essay James does not attempt to rewrite Browning's poem as a novel but praises him for translating the novel's intimacy into the medium of verse.

117   QUEBE, RUTH EVELYN. "*The Bostonians*: Some Historical Sources and Their Implications." *Centennial Review* 25, no. 1 (Winter):80-100.

      Traces contemporary events and figures that either influenced the novel or were incorporated into it. Quebe does mention Reconstruction but focuses on the women's movement.

118   RICHARDS, B.A. "Transformed into Fiction: Henry James and Hardwick House." *Country Life* 170, no. 4393 (29 October):1500, 1503.

      Argues that Gardencourt in *The Portrait of a Lady* was based on Hardwick House, which is the subject of Coburn's frontispiece for the New York Edition of the novel. Richards also finds similarities between the Roses, the occupants of Hardwick House, and the Touchetts.

119   RICHARDS, BERNARD. "Amateurism." *Essays in Criticism* 31, no. 1 (January):61-68.

      Reviews *Henry James's Letters*, I and II, calling them "a disaster." Edel fails to identify people and places and does not adequately cross-reference James's writings. Its index is "slap-dash and perfunctory;" more seriously, "the scale and scope of the edition is misconceived."

120   RIMMON-KENAN, SHLOMITH. "Deconstructive Reflections on Deconstruction: In Reply to Hillis Miller." *Poetics Today* 2, no. 1b (Winter):185-88.

      Replies to Miller's analysis of "The Figure in the Carpet" (1980.97), pointing out that Miller's reading of the text leads to a "see-saw movement" between structuralism and deconstruction. See also Miller 1981.102.

121 ROBINSON, DONITA. "Henry James' Preface to *The Portrait of a Lady*." *Bluegrass Literary Review* 2, no. 2 (Spring-Summer):31-36.
Suggests that the prefaces offer a way to measure James's achievement in the novels and tales. In the preface to *The Portrait*, James focuses on the connection between "the art of writing" and "the experience of life."

122 ROSENZWEIG, PAUL. "'The Illusion of Freedom' in *The Ambassadors*." *Renascence* 33, no. 3 (Spring):143-61.
Contends that Strether's contradictory traits are deliberate and serve the novel's focus on aesthetics and mroality. In the end Strether achieves a complex vision and learns "the value of controlled obfuscation and of the acceptance of selfishness."

123 _____. "James's 'Special-Green Vision': *The Ambassadors* as Pastoral." *Studies in the Novel* 13, no. 4 (Winter):367-87.
Examines James's use of the garden in the novel as setting and metaphor. Rosenzweig argues that the pastoral vision suggested by the garden is crucial to the novel, especially in the way that vision combines the world of art with the world of nature.

124 RUTLEDGE, HARRY C. "Vergil's Dido in Modern Literature." *Classical and Modern Literature* 1, no. 4 (Summer):267-73.
Argues that Dido is the "informing archetype" for Emma Bovary, Milly Theale, and Blanche DuBois and gives these heroines their tragic stature.

125 SALMON, RACHEL. "Naming and Knowing in Henry James's 'The Beast in the Jungle': The Hermeneutics of a Sacred Text." *Orbis Litterarum* 36, no. 4:302-22.
Argues that in this tale James imposes a sacred text, which acknowledges relationship, upon a profane text, which is oriented toward naming. The reader duplicates Marcher's experience of the movement from naming, which draws distinctions, to knowing, which surrenders distinctions.

126 SCHREROR, ELLIOT M. "Exposure in *The Turn of the Screw*." *Modern Philology* 78, no. 3 (February):261-74.

1981

Reads the tale within a Victorian frame of reference, which emphasizes its ghostly and moral elements. In so doing, Schrero traces four different "exposures" in the tale: of Miss Jessel, of the children, of the privileged classes, and of the governess.

127 SCHRIBER, MARY SUZANNE. "Toward Daisy Miller: Cooper's Idea of 'The American Girl.'" *Studies in the Novel* 13, no. 3 (Fall):237-49.

Examines Cooper's American girl, who has many of the qualities developed by James with greater artistry in his American girl. Cooper assigns the American girl the task of nurturing social and cultural values, which Schriber sees as the root of the division of society James described in *The American Scene*.

128 SEED, DAVID. "The Narrator in Henry James's Criticism." *Philological Quarterly* 60, no. 4 (Fall):501-21.

Examines the evolution of James's idea of the proper relationship of author, reader, and fiction in selected critical essays. James rejected the intrusive Victorian narrator, as typified in Trollope's work; but he saw the importance of a narrator in establishing a personal tone in the narrative and in relating the elements of the novel to each other.

129 ____. "Penetrating America: The Method of Henry James's *The American Scene*." *Amerikastudien* 26:340-53.

Argues that in *The American Scene* James's approach is analytical instead of impressionistic as in his earlier travel sketches. The basis of James's analysis is a polarity between city and country, and this polarity influences his response. The passages describing the country are painterly and allusive, while the descriptions of the urban environment, particularly New York, reflect James's bewilderment and alienation.

130 SELTZER, MARK "*The Princess Casamassima*: Realism and the Fantasy of Surveillance." *Nineteenth-Century Fiction* 35, no. 4 (March):506-34.

Finds in the novel a "criminal continuity" among seeing, knowing, and exercising power and focuses on the ways in which the novel's subject and technique reproduce the spy mania of the time.

Seltzer also cites fictional and nonfictional treatments of the London underworld contemporary with the novel, thus giving a context for James's "eccentric contribution to the literature of London exploration." Reprinted 1982.134, 1984.175, and 1987.15.

131 SHAPLAND, ELIZABETH "Duration and Frequency: Prominent Aspects of Time in Henry James' 'The Beast in the Jungle.'" *Papers on Language and Literature* 17, no. 1 (Winter):33-47.

Applies Genette's concepts of duration and frequency to the tale and compares James's use of the iterative and the singulative with Genette's discussion of Proust's technique in *A la recherche du temps perdu*. Genette's structuralist approach offers a way to explain and understand James's ability to create a sense of duration in the tale, and it also illuminates theme.

132 SHURR, WILLIAM H. "Violence and the Political Order." In *Rappaccini's Children: American Writers in a Calvinist World*. Lexington: University of Kentucky, pp. 84-86.

Notes James's early belief that the New England conscience has weakened American culture and suggests that in his final years James saw America as more corrupt than Europe, as evidenced in *The American Scene* and *The Ivory Tower*.

133 SILVER, DANIEL JAY. "Margin and Mystery: The Fate of Intimacy in the Late Novels of Henry James." Ph.D. dissertation, Yale University, 178 pp.

Argues that in the novels of the major phase emotional commitment and the "adventure" of consciousness are linked to "an intimacy of tacitly acknowledge difference" involving repudiation of possession and acceptance of mystery. The last chapter of this study examines this concept of intimacy in the social and cultural contexts of *The American Scene*.

See *Dissertation Abstracts International* 42, no. 12 (1982):5132A.

134 SKLEPOWICH, E.A. "Gossip and Gothicism in *The Sacred Fount*." *Henry James Review* 2, no. 2 (Winter):112-15.

Highlights the many Gothic elements in the novel, which is about "an involved game of gossip and speculation." Beneath the novel's

1981

concern with social reputation is vampirism. In addition, Sklepowich sees both gossip and the Gothic elements as either parodies or approximations of the art of the novelist.

135 SPACKMAN, W.M. "H.J., O.M. (TV)." *New England Review* 4, no. 1 (Autumn):93-96.

Points out the shortcomings of the BBC's version of *The Ambassadors* and *The Golden Bowl* and attributes them to James's failure to write with discipline.

136 SPENGEMANN, WILLIAM. Introduction to *The American*. Harmondsworth, Middlesex, England: Penguin Books, pp. 7-26.

Argues that this novel is central to James's career because with it James changed the static form of the novel to one that can encompass the evolving consciousness of a character.

137 STAFFORD, WILLIAM T. "'The Birthplace': James's Fable for Critics?" In *Books Speaking to Books: A Contextual Approach to American Fiction*. Chapel Hill: University of North Carolina Press, pp. 114-19.

Sees the tale as an argument for maintaining a clear distinction between the artist and the critic.

138 _____. "An 'Easy Ride' for Henry James." In *Books Speaking to Books: A Contextual Approach to American Fiction*. Chapel Hill: University of North Carolina Press, pp. 54-59.

Compares *The American* with *Easy Rider*. In the novel and in the film, the end of the American dream is the same: failure.

139 _____. "'Knower, Doer, and Sayer'–The James Family View of Emerson." In *Books Speaking to Books: A Contextual Approach to American Fiction*. Chapel Hill: University of North Carolina Press, pp. 127-50.

Summarizes his 1953 discussion of the Jameses' views of Emerson and argues for their continued validity. Recent scholarship corroborates and expands his argument that Henry Senior, Henry Junior, and William focused on different aspects of Emerson's ideas.

140 _____. "Milly Theale as America." In *Books Speaking to Books: A Contextual Approach to American Fiction*. Chapel Hill: University of North Carolina Press, pp. 19-22.

Suggests that Milly embodies the dualism of the American ideal: she is "half-Christ-like" and "half-diabolical."

141 _____. "*The Portrait of a Lady*: The Second Hundred Years." *Henry James Review* 2, no. 2 (Winter):91-100.

Surveys selected essays on the novel and focuses on chapters 47 and 48. Isabel's conflicting feelings toward Osmond are explored and Osmond's wittiness is revealed. Stafford sees the controlling tone in this portion of the novel as high comedy.

142 STEELE, ELIZABETH. "A Change of Villains: Hugh Walpole, Henry James, and Arnold Bennett." *Colby Library Quarterly* 17, no. 3 (September):184-92.

Rejects Edel's 1951 thesis that in *The Killer and The Slain* Walpole saw himself as Talbot the killer and James as Tunstall the slain. Steele argues that Bennett is Tunstall, though she admits she has more evidence for James not being Tunstall than she does for Bennett being that character.

143 STERN, FREDERICK C. "The Unified Sensibility: Eliot and James." In *F.O. Matthiessen: Christian Socialist as Critic*. Chapel Hill: University of North Carolina Press, pp. 63-105.

Discusses *Henry James: The Major Phase* in which Matthiessen rejected Van Wyck Brooks's focus on the writer, using instead "the poet's ability to perceive tragedy in life as a central concept in making a value judgment concerning the artist's work." Matthiessen also saw a relationship between T.S. Eliot and James in their use of the objective correlative to reveal their response to their times.

144 STERN, MADELEINE B. "A Lesson for the Master: Henry James and A.K. Loring." *Henry James Review* 2, no. 2 (Winter):87-90.

Identifies Aaron Kimball Loring as the publisher who pirated "A Bundle of Letters."

1981

145 STEWART, J.I.M. "In and Out of the Abyss." *Times Literary Supplement*, no. 4070 (3 April):372.

Reviews the third volume of James's letters edited by Edel. These letters cover a tumultuous time in James's life: his disillusionment with London society, his financial woes, the failure of *Guy Domville*, and Constance Fenimore Woolson's death.

146 STOWE, WILLIAM W. "Interpretation in Fiction: *La Père Goriot* and *The American*." *Texas Studies in Literature and Language* 23, no. 2 (Summer):248-67.

Argues that both novels "depict acts of interpretation in their fictional worlds while giving lessons on their own interpretation and on the art of interpretation in general," and this similarity reveals how James learned the lesson of Balzac. *The American* shows James's discovery that the "melodramatic imagination" is inadequate for both author and character to understand social complexities.

Reprinted in 1983.192.

147 STROUT, CUSHING. "Clio, Psyche, and the Literary Artist." In *The Veracious Imagination: Essays on American History, Literature, and Biography*. Middletown, Conn.: Wesleyan University Press, pp. 264-90.

Reprint of 1980.139.

148 SWEENEY, GERARD M. "The Curious Disappearance of Mrs. Beever: The Ending of *The Other House*." *Journal of Narrative Technique* 11, no. 3 (Fall):216-28.

Calls the novel's ending problematic because "a vicious, calculating, and unrepentant murderess goes free and unpunished," while Mrs. Beever, a figure of authority and traditional values, is banished from the narrative.

149 _____. "Henry James and the 'New England Conscience'–Once Again." *New England Quarterly* 54, no. 2 (June):255-58.

Notes that James used the phrase "New England conscience" earlier than hitherto attributed to him by Bischoff (1980.19) in "A Light Man."

150 SZEGEDY-MASZAK, MIHALY. "Henry James munkas saganak fejlodestorteneti helyerol" [Henry James's career in cultural history]. *Filológiai Közlöny* (Budapest) 27, nos. 1-2:67-73.
    In Hungarian.

151 TADA, TOSHIO. *Irony to Kyokan no Aida: Henry James Sonata* [Between irony and sympathy: Henry James and other writers]. Suita: Kansai Daigaku University Press, 308 pp.
    In Japanese.
    Analyzes *What Maisie Knew* and other novels and stories of James through a close reading of the text, with some chapters on Cooper, Anderson, and others.

152 TANNER, TONY. *Henry James III: 1899-1916.* Writers and Their Work Series. Berkshire, England: Profile Books, 56 pp.
    Sketches James's life and examines the novels of these years, noting theme, plot, characterization, and style. Tanner also briefly discusses James's autobiographical writings. The central paradox of James's life and work, Tanner suggests, is "a desire to have experience without involvement."
    Reprinted 1985.134.

153 TASSEL, JANET Q. "The Sick and the Well: Playing at Life in *Daisy Miller.*" *Studies in the Humanities* (Indiana, Pa.) 8, no. 2 (March):18-20.
    Suggests that James saw Daisy as threatening the social order, citing his "paradoxical use of illness" as evidence. Mrs. Costello, who passes judgment on Daisy, is sickly but lives; Daisy, who rebels against convention, is "vibrantly healthy" but dies.

154 TAYLOR, ANNE ROBINSON. "Henry James: The Penalties of Action." In *Male Novelists and Their Female Voices: Literary Masquerades.* Troy, N.Y.: Whitson, pp. 157-87.
    Argues that in his female characters James could express his wish for power and action in a way he was not able to do through his male characters – the governess in "The Turn of the Screw" is cited as an example. He also punishes his heroines however, by subjecting them "to the destructive forces . . . awaiting anyone who risked a strong forward stride through life."

1981

155   TEMPLETON, WAYNE. "*The Portrait of a Lady*: A Question of Freedom." *English Studies in Canada* 7, no. 3 (Fall):312-28.
        Sees the novel as Isabel's quest for freedom and traces her growth from naïveté and isolation to knowledge and engagement. At the beginning of the novel, Isabel is trapped by her lack of understanding and a network of fears; by its end, she attains self-awareness and freedom, which for Templeton is "a pragmatic encounter with reality."

156   TINTNER, ADELINE R. "The Centennial of 1876 and *The Portrait of a Lady*." *Markham Review* 10 (Fall/Winter):27-29.
        Notes that James's use of 1876, the year Ned Rosier calls on Madame Merle, is an ironic reminder of the freedom Isabel has surrendered in marrying Osmond. Reprinted with this essay is the frontispiece to *A Centennial Call to All Nations*, depicting Columbia draped in the flag, just as Ralph caricatures Isabel.

157   _____. "Euripides Echoed in James' Fiction." *AB Bookman's Weekly* 68, no. 8 (24 August):1011-12, 1014, 1016.
        Suggests *The Bacchae* as a source for "the sacred rage" referred to in *The Ambassadors* and that Teiresias might be a model for Strether.

158   _____. "Henry James and Byron: A Victorian Romantic Relationship." *Byron Journal* 9:52-63.
        Traces James's use of the work of Byron, who fascinated James as both a romantic hero and a creative artist. Tintner sees Byron's influence on works throughout James's career and focuses on his "quest for the Byronic hero," beginning with the references in the early tales and concluding with Byron's reincarnation in Rupert Brooke, in James's preface to Brooke's *Letters from America*, 1916.
        Revised 1987.122.

159   _____. "Henry James as Roth's Ghost Writer." *Midstream* 27, no. 3 (March):48-51.
        Traces Roth's use of two of James's tales in *The Ghost Writer*: the "overt prominence" of "The Middle Years;" and the "covert presence" of "The Author of 'Beltraffio.'"

160 _____. "Henry James's Balzac Connection." *AB Bookman's Weekly* 67, no. 17 (27 April):3219, 3222, 3224, 3226, 3228.

Notes that Louis Leverett, who appears in "A Bundle of Letters" and "A Point of View," and Lambert Strether are based on Balzac's Louis Lambert. The three share similarities, but only Balzac's character can fall in love.

161 _____. "Henry James's Mona Lisas." *Essays in Literature* 8, no. 1 (Spring):105-8.

Traces James's use of *Mona Lisa* in "The Sweetheart of M. Brisseux" and *Confidence.* In the tale this icon suggests the destructive qualities of one of the characters; in the novel, James corrects those destructive characteristics.

Revised 1986.151, 1987.122.

162 _____. "Henry James's *The Outcry* and the Art Drain of 1908-9." *Apollo* (February):110-12.

Suggests that James's 1911 novel was written as a response to the public outcry against the "unprecedented flow" of European art to the United States. James was involved in the "art drain" because of his increasing identification with Britain and because several of his close friends founded the National Art Collections Fund, whose mission was to keep European art in Europe.

Revised 1986.151.

163 _____. "An Interlude in Hell: Henry James's 'A Round of Visits' and *Paradise Lost.*" *NMAL: Notes on Modern American Literature* 5, no. 2 (Spring):Item 12.

Finds parallels in Milton's depiction of Hell in Book One of *Paradise Lost* and James's description of the Waldorf-Astoria in *The American Scene* and of The Pocahontas in "A Round of Visits." Such parallels suggest that "what hell is for James is the reality of New York life."

164 _____. "In the Footsteps of Stendhal: James's 'A Most Extraordinary Case' and *La Chartreuse de Parme.*" *Revue de Littérature Comparée* 55, no. 2 [218] (April-June):232-38.

1981

Sees James's use of Stendhal's novel in his tale as "a trial run for a workable fictional strategy." James "strews clues" throughout his tale to invoke a well-known masterpiece instead of imitating it.

165 _____. "*Roderick Hudson*: A Centennial Reading." *Henry James Review* 2, no. 3 (Spring):172-98.

Surveys the novel's critical reception, and demonstrates that the novel is "a carefully plotted romance of international origin and application" by detailing the various models upon which James drew. Tintner discusses the 1907 revision, which includes a more respectful treatment of America, the "embroidery" of metaphors, and the "third incarnation" of Christina, which is influenced by Salome.

Revised 1987.122.

166 _____. "Vanda de Mergi and Rose Muniment." *Revue de Littérature Comparée* 55, no. 1 [217](January-March):110-12.

Proposes Vanda de Mergi, a young invalid woman in Balzac's novel of conspiracy *L'Envers de l'Histoire Contemporaine*, as the model for Rose Muniment in *The Princess Casamassima*, James's novel of conspiracy.

Revised 1987.122.

167 TORGOVNICK, MARIANNA. "Gesture and the Ending of *The Golden Bowl*." In *Closure in the Novel*. Princeton: Princeton University Press, pp. 143-56, 220-21.

Argues that Maggie's and the Prince's gestures illuminate the novel's apparently ambiguous ending. Maggie submits to the Prince and suppresses her awareness of the Prince's moral flaws.

Reprint in part of 1980.153.

168 _____. "James's Sense of an Ending: The Role Played in its Development by James's Ideas about Nineteenth-Century Endings." In *Closure in the Novel*. Princeton: Princeton University Press, pp. 121-42, 219-20.

Traces James's rejection or manipulation of the traditional epilogue in his early fiction and his development of an ending that forces the reader to reconsider the protagonist's development, especially in *The Portrait of a Lady* and *The Ambassadors*.

Reprint in part of 1978.123.

169 TORSNEY, CHERYL. "Prince Amerigo's Borgia Heritage." *Henry James Review* 2, no. 2 (Winter):126-31.

Suggests that Prince Amerigo's "criminal inheritance" is an important factor in understanding his character.

170 TREMPER, ELLEN. "Henry James's 'The Story in It': A Successful Aesthetic Adventure." *Henry James Review* 3, no. 1 (Fall):11-16.

Argues that the 1902 tale and the 1903 essay "Gabriele D'Annunzio" are companion pieces. In the essay James praised D'Annunzio's evocation of atmosphere and his handling of subject but criticized his inability to render consciousness and his separation of love from life. In the tale James "corrects" D'Annunzio's shortcomings.

171 UNRUE, DARLENE HARBOUR. "The Occult Metaphor as Technique in *The Portrait of a Lady*." *Henry James Review* 2, no. 3 (Spring):199-203.

Examines the occult metaphors in chapter 42, paying particular attention to the way in which those metaphors bridge past and present in Isabel's mind and suggest Isabel's "fearful awareness."

172 VARNER, JEANINE BAKER. "Henry James and Gustave Flaubert: The Creative Relationship." Ph.D. dissertation, University of Tennessee, 146 pp.

Compares Madame Bovary with *The Portrait of a Lady* and *L'Education sentimentale* with *The Princess Casamassima* to show that the critical relationship between these writers stimulated a creative and stylistic relationship.

See *Dissertation Abstracts International* 42, no. 9 (1982):3992A.

173 WADMAN, KAREN L. "*William Wetmore Story and His Friends*: Henry James's Portrait of Robert Browning." *Yearbook of English Studies* 11:210-18.

Argues that Browning is the shaping force of the biography: he is both "touchstone" and "controlling consciousness." Wadman attributes Browning's centrality in the work to Story's happy but boring life and James's admiration for Browning and his condescension to Story.

1981

174   WARE, CHERYL L. "Americans Abroad: Anti-Intellectualism in
       Mark Twain and Henry James." *McNeese Review* 27:50-62.
           Argues that in *The Innocents Abroad* and *The American* the
       authors' anti-intellectualism is apparent in depicting culture as
       feminine, in favoring an egalitarian society over a class-structured one
       and Protestantism over Catholicism, and in believing that business and
       technology will solve all problems. Because both Twain and James were
       products of an anti-intellectual society, they "embodied the very
       conflicts they concerned themselves with in their fiction."

175   WHITE, ALLON. "'The Deterrent Fact': Vulgarity and Obscurity in
       James." In *The Uses of Obscurity: The Fiction of Early Modernism*.
       London: Routledge & Kegan Paul, pp. 130-62, 177-80.
           Explains   James's   use   of   obscurity – as   opposed   to
       ambiguity – as an indication that he was attracted to and repulsed by the
       aesthetically, socially, and sexually vulgar. Especially in the later
       work – *The Sacred Fount, The Ambassadors, The Wings of the Dove*, and
       The Golden Bowl – obscurity is a way to avoid achieving the knowledge
       of "a graspable, unambiguous registration of the object searched out";
       the discovery of a "fact" would make the narrative vulgar.

176   WILSON, R[ICHARD] B[ARTLEY] J[OSEPH]. *Henry James's
       Ultimate Narrative: 'The Golden Bowl.'* St. Lucia: University of
       Queensland Press, xii, 329 pp.
           Begins this in-depth study with a review of criticism, focusing
       on the issues of ambiguity, irony, and morality. Wilson then examines
       the structure of the novel as sketched in its scenario and developed in
       the relationships among the characters. He discusses the development
       of consciousness in the characters both as it reflects and influences
       those relationships, particularly in the novel's final scenes. Wilson
       concludes that this novel, a story "of how the concealed becomes the
       revealed," depicts human problems "more complexly, more variously,
       more penetratingly and more comprehensively than they had hitherto
       been depicted."

177   WINTER, J.L. "The Chronology of James's *Washington Square*."
       Notes and Queries 28, no. 5 (October):426-28.
           Shows that the chronology of the novel's events are confused,
       almost similar to Ptolemaic epicycles and that the main action of the
       novel may be simultaneous with the Civil War.

1981

178 WISEMAN, ADELE. "What Price the Heroine?" *International Journal of Women's Studies* 4, no. 5 (November-December):459-71.

Argues that *The Portrait of a Lady* exemplifies "an ideal of feminine heroism" consonant with the values of James's class, sex, and era and focuses on the strategies by which James brings his characters and readers to that ideal. The novel's characters, particularly the women, act as foils to Isabel to point up her superior, though not exceptional, qualities; Isabel herself is confronted by a limited range of choices and her choices "will show what women are by what a woman can be," but Isabel is too much of a purist for today's women.

179 WOLK, MERLA SAMUELS. "The Safe Place: The Artist Figure in the Novels of Henry James, 1886-1897." Ph.D. dissertation, Wayne State University, 243 pp.

Demonstrates that in *The Bostonians, The Princess Casamassima, The Tragic Muse*, and *What Maisie Knew* the protagonist functions as an artist figure engaged in triangular destructive relationships and ultimately forced to choose between intimacy and art. In the novels of the eighties, the artist is "separated from life's richness," a watcher at the sweet-shop window; in *What Maisie Knew* the artist is within the house of fiction free to exercise the imagination.

See *Dissertation Abstracts International* 42, no. 11 (1982):4836A.

1982

1 ANDERSON, WALTER E. "The Finer Music and the Ass's Bray: Henry James versus American Culture." *Dalhousie Review* 61, no. 4 (Winter):618-30.

Analyzes James's criticisms of the speech and manners of American women in essays he wrote for *Harper's Bazaar* from 1906 to 1907, concluding that these remarks betray "the outraged dignity of a neglected author." Anderson also compares this view of the American woman to that portrayed in *The Bostonians* and finds the novel's "program for male domination" apparent in the essays.

2 ANDERSON IMBERT, ENRIQUE. "Peripecias de una trama de Maupassant (De Paris a Buenos Aires)." *Boletín de la Academia Argentina de Letras* 47, no. 183-84 (January-June):7-20.

In Portuguese.

1982

3   AUERBACH, NINA. *"The Bostonians*: Feminists and the New World." In *American Novelists Revisited: Essays in Feminist Criticism*. Edited by Fritz Fleischmann. Boston: G.K. Hall & Co., pp. 189-208.
        Reprint of 1978.4.

4   BADDER, DAVID. "Aspern." *Sight and Sound* 51, no. 1 (Winter):45.
        Notes that de Gregorio's film adaptation of the tale "preserves the essence of James' moral conundrum."

5   BANTA, MARTHA. "Beyond Post-Modernism: The Sense of History in *The Princess Casamassima*." *Henry James Review* 3, no. 2 (Winter):95-107.
        Discusses the character of Hyacinth Robinson in terms of Jameson's distinction between Identity and Difference, as well as the similarities and differences in James's and Jameson's views of the past, which in turn affect how each regards the future. James's novels recreate life, but they also suggest "the possibilities of living."

6   BASIC, SONJA. "Od realistickog iluzionizma do naratologieje: pripovjedacko glediste ismedju Jamesa i Genetta" [From realistic illusionism to narratology: the notion of 'point of view' in James and Genette]. *Umjetnost rijeci* (Zagreb) 26:213-28.
        In Serbo-Croatian.

7   BELL, MILLICENT. "'Art Makes Life': James's Autobiography." *Revue Française d'Etudes Américaines* 7, no. 14 (May):211-23.
        Describes the method of the *Autobiography*. Impressionistic memories are connected by the nonnarrative and nonsequential consciousness of the mature man who endows meaning and design to seemingly random associations.

8   ____. "Henry James and the Fiction of Autobiography." *Southern Review* 18, no. 3 (July):463-79.
        Examines James's autobiographical writings as fiction, which Bell defines as "a system of order that applies 'discrimination' to the

'inclusion and confusion of life.'" James, therefore, describes his childhood with a view to the destiny he has embraced as a writer.

9 _____. "*The Turn of the Screw* and the *recherche de l'absolu*." *Delta* 15 (November):33-48.

Argues that the tale recounts the governess's need to validate evil in the world and suggests that it is essentially romantic and therefore Manichean. Bell then describes the patterns of duplication and reversal that support the vision of the world as divided and bifurcated.

*10 BICKNELL, M.J. "The Relationship between Form and Theme in Six Novels by Henry James." Ph.D. dissertation, University of London, Queen Mary College.

Source: *Annual Bibliography of English Language and Literature* 58 (1983):453, item 8029.

*11 BLAIN, N.A. "Ideas of 'Life' and Their Moral Force in the Novels of Henry James." Ph.D. dissertation, University of Strathclyde.

Source: *Annual Bibliography of English Language and Literature* 58 (1983):454, item 8030.

12 BLAKE, NANCY. "Le Livre de l'objet: *Les Dépouilles de Poynton*." *Recherches Anglaises et Américaines* 15:83-100.

In French.

13 _____. "'Never Say': L'Art du non-dit dans 'Louisa Pallant.'" *Delta* 15 (November):115-23.

In French.

14 _____. "La Parole impossible: *L'Age difficile* de Henry James." *Delta* 15 (November):63-78.

In French.

1982

15   BLANCHOX, MAURICE. "The Turn of the Screw." Translated by
     Sacha Rabinovitch. In *The Sirens' Song*. London: Harvester Press,
     pp. 79-86.
         Discusses James's use of preliminary *Notebook* sketches as
     first a sign of his "dread of beginning" and later as a confronting of the
     "perfection" of a still indeterminate work.
         Reprint of "The Turn of the Screw" in *Le Livre à Venir*. Paris:
     Gallimard, 1959, pp. 155-64.

16   BLEU, PATRICIA. "Fantastique et revelation dans *The Beast in the
     Jungle*." *Delta* 15 (November):91-102.
         In French.
         Suggests that James creates tension in his work by juxtaposing
     the "fantastic" with "revelation": he creates an enigma inviting further
     investigation, but reveals the secret at the end of the work if at all. A
     common enigma for James – and the one dominating "The Beast in the
     Jungle" – is that of sexuality.

17   BOONE, JOSEPH ALLEN. "Tradition Counter Tradition: Love
     and the Form of Fiction." Ph.D. dissertation, University of
     Wisconsin, 574 pp.
         Examines the depiction of marriage in nineteenth-century
     British and American novels, arguing that the ideal of romantic
     wedlock has been undermined by the open-ended novel, the quest-
     romance, and novels of female community. *The Golden Bowl* is cited as
     an example of the "open-ended novel of 'uneasy wedlock.'"
         See *Dissertation Abstracts International* 43, no. 10
     (1983):3314A.

18   BOREN, LYNDA S. "'Dear Constance', 'Dear Henry': The
     Woolson/James Affair, Fact, Fiction or Fine Art?" *Amerikastudien*
     27:457-66.
         Examines Constance Fenimore Woolson's version of her
     relationship with James as reflected in her notebooks, letters, and
     fiction. Boren suggests that as James withdrew emotionally, Woolson
     "created" a close relationship, even though her bitterness at James's
     retreat is apparent in her writing.

19 BORINSKI, LUDWIG. "Die Entstehung der Moderne bei Henry James" [The rise of the moderns with Henry James]. In *Die amerikanische Literatur in der Weltliteratur: Themen und Aspekte* [American literature in world literature: themes and viewpoints]. Edited by Claus Uhlig and Volker Bischoff. Berlin: Schmidt, pp. 128-42.

   In German.

20 BRAKEL, ARTHUR. "Ambiguity and Enigma in Art: The Case of Henry James and Machado de Assis." *Comparative Literature Studies* 19, no. 4 (Winter):442-49.

   Compares James and his Brazilian contemporary. Although their background and daily life differed, their characters, concerns, and literary criticism have many similarities.

21 BROWN, CLARENCE A. "*The Sacred Fount*: A Study in Art and Value." *Renascence*: 34, no. 2 (Winter):67-80.

   Argues that the novel's fundamental concern focuses on "the process of vision" of the narrator, in whom James's aesthetic and moral values reside.

22 BROWNSTEIN, RACHEL M. "*The Portrait of a Lady*." In *Becoming a Heroine: Reading about Women in Novels*. New York: Viking Press, pp. 239-70, 319-22.

   Argues that the real issue of *The Portrait of a Lady* is Isabel's consciousness, not her marriage. Her actions in the novel, particularly her return to Osmond, are the result of her acceptance of "the history that derived from her attempt to be herself."

   Reprinted 1984.25.

23 BUDD, JOHN. "Philip Roth's Lesson from the Master." *NMAL: Notes on Modern American Literature* 6:Item 21.

   Notes the parallels between *The Ghost Writer* and three of James's tales: "The Middle Years," "The Lesson of the Master," and "The Author of 'Beltraffio.'" Roth emulates, not imitates, James in both form and theme.

24 CADBURY, VIVIAN, and LASKOWSKI, WILLIAM Jr., comps; TINTNER, ADELINE R., annot. "A Bibliography of the Writings

1982

on Henry James by Leon Edel, with Some Annotations." *Henry James Review* 3, no. 3 (Spring):176-99.

Lists Edel's writings from 1930 to 1982. Some items have brief annotations.

25   CARMIGNANI, PAUL. *"The Bostonians* ou la maison divisée." *Delta* 15 (November):49-61.

In French.

Suggests that the self-contradictory and ambiguous style of *The Bostonians* reflects the sociological conflicts of reconstructionist America, the period in which the novel is set.

26   CARROLL, DAVID. "The (Dis)placement of the Eye ("I"): Point of View, Voice, and the Forms of Fiction." In *The Subject in Question: The Languages of Theory and the Strategies of Fiction*. Chicago: University of Chicago Press, pp. 51-66.

Argues that there is a contradiction in James's concept of point of view: on the one hand, point of view determines unity of form; on the other, point of view undermines that unity by suggesting complications, divisions, and interferences.

27   CHRISTMAS, PETER GEORGE. "Public and Private Values: Art, History, and Politics in Dickens, Flaubert, James, and Conrad." Ph.D. dissertation, Stanford University, 429 pp.

Argues that the political, literary, and moral differences between France and England in the second half of the nineteenth century are reflected in the fiction of the period. In *The Princess Casamassima* James initially opposes English moralism and French art, but he comes close to supporting Victorian suspicion of art. In *The Ambassadors*, however, James modifies that opposition and suggests the possibility that art and morality can coexist.

See *Dissertation Abstracts International* 42, no. 11 (1982):4831A.

28   COHEN, PAULA MARANTZ. "Feats of Heroinism in *The Spoils of Poynton*." *Henry James Review* 3, no. 2 (Winter):108-16.

Demonstrates how Fleda Vetch shifts the focus from material objects to the search for freedom. Fleda liberates herself and Mrs. Gereth from things and from roles.

29 COLVILLE, GEORGIANA M.M. "Verena ou la voix détournée: Une Lecture de *The Bostonians*." *Recherches Anglaises et Américaines* 15:69-82.
 In French.

30 CORSE, SANDRA. "From Narrative to Music: Benjamin Britten's *The Turn of the Screw*." *University of Toronto Quarterly* 51, no. 2 (Winter):161-74.
 Details the ways in which Britten's opera reflects and diverges from James's tale. Both works have a complex "layeredness," but in the opera music and text form fluid, overlapping layers.

31 COWDERY, LAUREN T. "Henry James and the 'Transcendent Adventure': The Search for the Self in the Introduction to *The Tempest*." *Henry James Review* 3, no. 2 (Winter):145-53.
 Argues that in this essay James as novelist and critic is "pursuing" his alter ego, Shakespeare, as dramatist and poet.

*32 COY, J. "Los dos Henry James" [The two Henry Jameses]. *Libros* (Madrid) 7 (June):21-23.
 In Spanish.
 Source: *Annual Bibliography of English Language and Literature* 58 (1983):454, item 8035.

33 CRAIG, DAVID M. "The Indeterminacy of the End: Maggie Verver and the Limits of Imagination." *Henry James Review* 3, no. 2 (Winter):133-44.
 Argues that because James has permitted Maggie to write her own text, her uncertainty shapes the novel's indeterminate conclusion. Maggie plots a fairy-tale marriage, but having achieved reunion with the Prince she is confronted with an unknown world of intimacy.

34 CROWE, M. KAREN. "The Tapestry of Henry James's 'The Turn of the Screw.'" *The Nassau Review* 4, no. 3:37-48.
 Examines the function of the frame of the tale as a means of understanding the nature of evil explored in "The Turn of the Screw." Douglas "knows" that evil is relative and that it permeates the story and the world.

1982

*35   CROZIER, J.V. "Making It New: Attitudes towards Time, History, and the European Past in American Literature, with Particular Reference to Hawthorne, James, and Pound." Ph.D. dissertation, University of London, University College.

       Source: *Annual Bibliography of English Language and Literature* 58 (1983):445, item 7878.

36   CURTSINGER, E.C. "James's Writer at the Sacred Fount." *Henry James Review* 3, no. 2 (Winter):117-28.

       Sees *The Sacred Fount* as a parable of the writer and the creative process. The narrator dramatizes the role of the artist while May Server as his muse personifies the imagination. The novel insists that "love is the motivating force of the writer's imagination."

       Reprinted 1986.39.

37   DAUGHERTY, SARAH B. "*The Golden Bowl*: Balzac, James, and the Rhetoric of Power." *Texas Studies in Literature and Language* 24, no. 1 (Spring):68-82.

       Argues that the novel must not be read as moral philosophy. James's invocation of "the example of Balzac" in the novel's preface points to James's "desire to appeal not to his readers' judgment but to their sense of drama." Balzac's influence on this novel is apparent in the intensity with which James renders character and creates drama.

38   DELBANCO, NICHOLAS. "James and Wells." In *Group Portrait: Joseph Conrad, Stephen Crane, Ford Madox Ford, Henry James, and H.G. Wells*. New York: William Morrow & Co., pp. 137-79.

       Chronicles their friendship and quarrel with particular attention to James's offer to collaborate with Wells, Wells's refusal to join the Royal Society of Literature (of which James was a member), and Well's criticism of James.

39   DHAIDAN, ABBAS LAZAM. "Artist and Connoisseur: A Study in Henry James' Use of the Visual Arts." Ph.D. dissertation, University of Toledo, 149 pp.

       Surveys James's autobiography, exhibition reviews, travel sketches, and depiction of artists to show his interest in the dialectic between personal vision and public marketplace confronting the artist.

James's ideas about the artist illuminate his conception of his role as a writer.

See *Dissertation Abstracts International* 43, no. 9 (1983):2996A.

40 DUPERRAY, MAX. "Possession et exorcisme: Aspects du fantasme jamesien dans quelques *ghostly tales*." In *Société des Anglicistes de l'Enseignement Supérieur*. Echanges: Actes du Congrès de Strasbourg. Etudes Anglaises 81. Paris: Didier, pp. 321-32.
    In French.
    Examines the elements of the fantastic in James's tales, including characters shrouded in a mysterious and uncertain past, and James's skill with "non-specification." James creates the fantastic by tying the real to the supernatural. While the tales cannot be strictly classified as fantastic, the value of their fantastic elements should not be underestimated.

41 DURAND-BOGAERT, FABIENNE. "'A Vision of Appearances': Du paraître au même dans *The Wings of the Dove*." *Recherches Anglaises et Américaines* 15:101-9.
    In French.

42 EDEL, LEON. "How I Came to Henry James." *Henry James Review* 3, no. 3 (Spring):160-64.
    Describes his discovery of James, prompted by the suggestion of a professor when Edel was proposing to study James Joyce.

43 _____. "The Question of Exile." In *Asian and Western Writers in Dialogue: New Cultural Identities*. Edited by Guy Amirthanayagan. London: Macmillan, pp. 48-54.
    Calls James the "archetypal exile in American literature" who was never more American than in his portrayal of his countrymen abroad.

44 _____. "Shaping and Telling: The Biographer at Work." *Henry James Review* 3, no. 3 (Spring):165-75.
    Describes the writing of the five-volume biography of James and defends his practice of "extract[ing] from little scraps of evidence the material of drama," giving as example his treatment of James's

1982

relationship with Minnie Temple. Edel stresses the biographer's need to have "imagination of form and structure."

45 _____. "The Terror of the Usual." In *Stuff of Sleep and Dreams: Experiments in Literary Psychology*. New York: Harper & Row, pp. 300-308.

Suggests that James's ghost stories, which rely on the horror imagined beneath the usual and the expected, have their foundation in the "vastations" of Henry James, Sr. and William James, as well as in James's own nightmare confrontation in the Louvre's Galerie d'Apollon.

Reprint of Introduction to Henry James's *Stories of the Supernatural* (1970), pp. v-xiv; also reprinted 1983.57.

46 EDEL, LEON, LAURENCE, DAN H, and RAMBEAU, JAMES. *A Bibliography of Henry James*. Soho Bibliographies 8. 3d ed. rev. Oxford: Clarendon Press, 428 pp.

Revised and updated reprint of 1961 bibliography.

47 FIGUEIREDO, MARIA DO CARMO LANNA. "O 'Unreliable Narrator' em *Dom Casmurro* e *The Aspern Papers*." *Cadernos de Lingüística e Teoria da Literatura* (Universidade Federal de Minas, Brazil) 8 (December):191-202.

In Portuguese with English summary.

Examines the unreliable narrator in the fiction of Machado de Assis and James, showing that this point of view adds complexity to their treatment of universal themes, characterization, and plot.

48 FOGEL, DANIEL MARK. "Leon Edel and James Studies: A Survey and Evaluation." *Henry James Review* 4, no. 1 (Fall):3-30.

Chronicles Edel's life and work and evaluates his major contributions to James scholarship. Fogel concentrates on Edel's edition of the *Letters* and on his biography of James, discussing objections that have been raised about both. Although some objections are justified, Fogel argues that Edel's "energy and his scholarly and artistic integrity" deserve admiration.

49 FRIEDMAN, ALAN W. "Narrative Is to Death as Death is to the Dying: Funerals and Stories." *Mosaic* 15, no. 1 (Winter):650-76.

Surveys the treatment of funerals in a range of literature, beginning with Euripedes' *Trojan Women* and ending with Ford's *The Good Soldier*. Literature, like funerals, "domesticate[s] or socialze[s]" death. Friedman briefly refers to "The Beast in the Jungle."

50 FUNSTON, JUDITH ELLEN. "Henry James's Experiments in Characterization, 1882-1890." Ph.D. dissertation, Michigan State University, 266 pp.

Traces James's shift from using the metaphor of portraiture to that of drama to reflect his method of narration in the novels and tales of this period. In this fiction, James moves from the "painterly" traditional omniscient narrator to the "dramatic" center of consciousness.

See *Dissertation Abstracts International* 43, no. 9 (1983):2992A.

51 GABLER, JANET ANN. "Rhetorical Myth in Henry James's *The Bostonians, The Wings of the Dove*, and *The Golden Bowl*." Ph.D. dissertation, Ohio State University, 321 pp.

Applies George Campbell's theory of moral rhetoric to James's treatment and evaluation of character in these novels. Olive Chancellor, Kate Croy, and Charlotte Verver are "faulty rhetoricians" because they use language to deceive; Merton Densher and Maggie Verver accept their moral responsibility "and thus succeed in the Jamesian world.

See *Dissertation Abstracts International* 43, no. 8 (1983):2678.

52 GALE, ROBERT L. "Henry James." In *American Literary Scholarship: An Annual/1980*. Edited by J. Albert Robbins. Durham: Duke University Press, pp. 103-20.

Surveys criticism published in 1980.

53 _____. "Henry James." In *Dictionary of Literary Biography, Volume 12: American Realists and Naturalists*. Detroit: Gale Research Co., pp. 297-326.

Details James's life and writing, discussing the major works briefly and tracing major themes, concerns, and techniques. The essay lists primary works, biographies, bibliographies, and some secondary

1982

criticism; it also includes photographs, the locations of James's papers, and a reproduction of two autograph pages from the revision of *The Princess Casamassima*.

54   GALENBECK, SUSAN CARLSON. "British Comedy of Manners Distilled: Henry James' Edwardian Plays." *Henry James Review* 4, no. 1 (Fall):61-74.
Focuses on *The High Bid*, James's best play, to show how he blends social criticism and social affirmation in his comedy of manners. James wishes to depict high society preserving its traditions yet adapting to change; Mrs. Gracedew, a typical comedy of manners heroine, "us[es] change to preserve tradition" and "fights to save past, present, and future."

55   GARDNER, H[ELEN]. "Literary Biography." In *In Defense of the Imagination: The Charles Eliot Norton Lectures 1979-1980*. Oxford: Clarendon Press, pp. 165-189.
Reprint of 1980.57. See also Edel 1987.31.

56   GEARY, EDWARD A. "*The Europeans*: A Centennial Essay." *Henry James Review* 4, no. 1 (Fall):31-49.
Discusses critical responses to the novel, beginning with James's own evaluation in a letter to Howells, and notes the novel's two plot lines. The Felix-Gertrude plot is conventional, while the Eugenia-Acton plot anticipates James's later work in its focus on "the controlled shifting consciousness of possibilities."

57   GIRDHARRY, ARNOLD RAMESWAR. "The Geometry of Marriage in Henry James." Ph.D. dissertation, Howard University, 199 pp.
Argues that in *The Portrait of a Lady*, *The Wings of the Dove*, and *The Golden Bowl* the theme of isolation is patterned on geometric structures. An octagon within a circle reflects the relationships among major and minor characters, particularly the tortuous connection of the female protagonist to the other characters. Also, this circular structure mirrors the "en l'air" ending of each novel, in which the artist's unity of vision is "the unity of unresolved vision."
See *Dissertation Abstracts International* 44, no. 1 (1983):168A.

58 GREENSLADE, WILLIAM. "The Power of Advertising: Chad Newsome and the Meaning of Paris in *The Ambassadors*." *ELH* 49, no. 1 (Spring):99-122.

Examines the character of Chad, who embodies the turn-of-the-century advertising man. Chad's "appropriation" of Paris, particularly its cultivation of ambiguity, serves his allegiance to capitalism and publicity.

59 GREGORY, ROBERT. "On Not Going Home: Pound's Reading of James." *Boundary 2* 10, no. 3 (Spring):93-108.

Proposes that Pound saw James "advocating form as a way to mystify the reader and gratify the writer's narcissism." Pound's reading of James involved a "necessary blindness" because James's conviction that the writer was intimately associated with his work threatened Pound's search for an "alternative to the poetics of Solipsism."

60 GRIBBLE, JENNIFER. "Cages." *Critical Review* (Canberra, Australia), no. 24:108-19.

Discusses James's use of the "trapped spectator" and reviews feminist and structuralist perspectives of this figure. While the tale reflects the problem of entrapment developed in James's later novels and can be seen as "a mirror of its own fictitious nature," it celebrates consciousness transforming impressions into knowledge and experience.

61 GUILLEN, J.J. "Presencia textual de Henry James en la novela *The Portrait of a Lady*" [Textual presence of Henry James in *The Portrait of a Lady*]. *Estudios de filologia inglesa* (University of Granada) 10:145-51.

In Spanish.

62 HABEGGER, ALFRED. "The Boy Who Could Not Become a Man." In *Gender, Fantasy, and Realism in the American Novel*. New York: Columbia University Press, pp. 256-73, 356-59.

Argues that James's inability to relate to his peers during his childhood and his troubled relationship with William prevented him from coming to terms with his masculinity. Habegger attributes James's "strange entanglement with Minnie Temple" to his identification with

1982

her; both were "gender outcasts." Only on his deathbed could James assert his dominance by imagining himself Napoleon.

63 _____. "Henry James and W.D. Howells as Sissies." In *Gender, Fantasy, and Realism in the American Novel*. New York: Columbia University Press, pp. 56-65, 316-18.

Argues that both authors saw themselves as misfits in a culture glorifying masculinity and associating literature with femininity. Howells was torn between conforming and heeding his own values while James refused to compromise his values. Habegger attributes Howells's and James's "critical realism" to their alienation and exclusion from a masculinized culture.

64 _____. "'Observing': The View from James's Room in the House of Fiction." In *Gender, Fantasy, and Realism in the American Novel*. New York: Columbia University Press, pp. 274-88, 359-62.

Argues that James was a solipsistic daydreamer, not astute observer. James closed his eyes to an abrasive world and retreated to "fine consciousness," an inner life disassociated from reality; he, therefore, could never truly understand the American character.

65 _____. "The Plot with a Secret." In *Gender, Fantasy, and Realism in the American Novel*. New York: Columbia University Press, pp. 251-55, 355-56.

Suggests that the plot of a man searching for a secret is at the center of James's best work and dramatizes the estrangement of the Jamesian hero from society.

66 _____. "*The Portrait of a Lady*." In *Gender, Fantasy, and Realism in the American Novel*. New York: Columbia University Press, pp. 66-79, 318-20.

Sees the greatness of the novel in James's ability to combine character types and realistic elements as well as in his transformation of a traditional love-interest plot into a psychological study of a woman. Habegger objects to the novel's anti-masculine stance and its "endorsement" of the "self-effacing lady."

67 _____. "Who Made James the Modern American Master and Why?" In *Gender, Fantasy, and Realism in the American Novel*. New York: Columbia University Press, pp. 289-302, 362-64.

Argues that Philip Rahv and Lionel Trilling were largely responsible for James's "canonization" in the 1940s. Both saw *The Bostonians* as evidence of James's social realism although they "exaggerated James's achievement in the novel." Habegger attributes Rahv's and Trilling's revival of James to the failure of their left-wing politics and likens that failure to James's identification with woman's sphere in the face of his own "unachieved manhood."

68 HAVILAND, BEVERLY JOSEPHINE. "The Metaphysics of Self-Consciousness in Balzac and Henry James." Ph.D. dissertation, Princeton University, 462 pp.

Examines the impact of each novelist's metaphysical beliefs on the creation of character. Balzac's fiction reflects an estrangement between self and other; this destructive relation is played out within individual characters as well as in sexual, social, and textual contexts. James explores and rejects this Balzacian opposition in *The Sacred Fount*; in *The Ambassadors* he proposes consciousness as a means of renewing and redeeming life.

See *Dissertation Abstracts International* 42, no. 11 (1982):4820A-4821A.

69 HEWITT, ROSALIE. "Henry James's 'Autumn Impression': The History, the Manuscript, the Howells Relation." *Yale University Library Gazette* 57, no. 1-2 (October):39-51.

Describes the typescript and holograph manuscript in addition to James's dealings with his agent Pinker and *The North American Review*, which published this section of *The American Scene*. Hewitt sees James's addition of a paragraph recalling a stroll with Howells as an expression of loyalty to America and to Howells.

70 HIGGINS, CHARLES. "Photographic Aperture: Coburn's Frontispieces to James's New York Edition." *American Literature* 53, no. 4 (January):661-75.

Describes Coburn as James's "younger alter ego" and his photography as "an ideal medium for [James's] grasping imagination." Higgins discusses many of the frontispieces in relation to the novels,

1982

seeing the photographs as opening symbols and closing echoes in which appearance and reality are fused.

71   HORVATH, BROOKE I. "The Life of Art, the Art of Life: The Ascetic Aesthetics of Defeat in James's *Stories of Writers and Artists.*" *Modern Fiction Studies* 28, no. 1 (Spring):93-107.
        Enumerates and discusses the "artistic presumptions" of James's vanquished artists. These artists do not represent James's aesthetic; rather they "dramatize attitudes opposed to the true artistic sensibility."

72   HOVEY, RICHARD B. "*Washington Square*: James and 'the Deeper Psychology.'" *University of Hartford Studies in Literature* 14, no. 1:1-10.
        Explores the character of Dr. Sloper, whose cruel behavior to Catherine is pathological. Dr. Sloper is narcissistic, sadistic, and masochistic and raises the issue of the connection between emotional pathology and criminality.

73   HUNTER, JEFFERSON. *Edwardian Fiction.* Cambridge: Harvard University Press, xi, 280 pp.
        Examines British fiction of the years 1901 to 1910, focusing on its forms and themes. James is discussed throughout the book as one of a group of writers whose fiction is dominated by the sense of human powerlessness.

74   HUTCHINSON, STUART. "James's *In the Cage*: A New Interpretation." *Studies in Short Fiction* 19, no. 1 (Winter):19-25.
        Argues that the telegraphist is in the cage of her own imagination and thus misreads Mudge. Hutchinson also attributes the telegraphist's entrapment to her fear of sexuality, especially to her loss of virginity.

75   IWASE, SHITSUU. "Geijutsu no Miya o Motomete: *The Golden Bowl* no Adam Verver" [In search of the shrine of art: Adam Verver in *The Golden Bowl*]. *Eigo Seinen* (Tokyo) 128:562-65.
        In Japanese.

Argues that the image of the spider in the novel is a positive one, suggestive of Adam Verver's perseverance in creating his own world by acquiring works of art. He has an eye for the beautiful; for him, collecting art is equivalent to restructuring the world creatively. Verver thinks through poetic images, and what he cultivates by both thinking and collecting is expressed as power – the power of artistic style over life.

76 JACOBS, J.U. "The *Alter Ego*: The Artist as American in 'The Jolly Corner.'" *Theoria* 58 (May):51-60.

Suggests that this tale is a work of art about art in that it epitomizes the paradox of art as a form of death in life and is also a parable of the American artist. Spencer Brydon and his alter ego embody the American man of fact and the European man of fancy, and when each is seen in isolation, they are monstrous.

77 JOHNSON, STUART. "American Marginalia: James's *The American Scene*." *Texas Studies in Literature and Language* 24, no. 1 (Spring):83-101.

Describes the subject of 1907 book as James's attempt to define himself as a writer and the implications of his position as both insider and outsider of the American scene. His journey prompted James to see America as surrounded by a metaphorical margin in whose blankness the writer must seek his subject.

78 JONES, VIVIEN. "James and Trollope." *Review of English Studies* 33, no. 131 (August):278-94.

Proposes that James's essays on Trollope illuminate James's relation to the Victorian tradition and his "innovative critical role at the intersection of realism and modernism." Jones examines comments in letters and essays, focusing on the 1883 essay in *Partial Portraits* as well as on "The Art of Fiction" to trace James's movement from stressing the cognitive function of imagination as a means of creating interest in fiction to valuing formally achieved illusion.

Reprinted 1985.72.

79 KAWIN, BRUCE F. "Frames under Pressure." In *The Mind of the Novel: Reflexive Fiction and the Ineffable*. Princeton: Princeton University Press, pp. 182-86.

1982

Argues that the "point" of "The Turn of the Screw" is to share the governess's uncertainty and clarity with the reader, and describes the various framing devices that underpin the unsettling nature of the tale and the governess's unreliability.

80   KIENIEWICZ, TERESA. *Men, Women, and the Novelist: Fact and Fiction in the American Novel of the 1870s and 1880s.* Washington, D. C.: University Press of America, iv, 171 pp.

Examines a range of novels in order to illuminate the social consciousness and concerns of the period and discusses the position of the novelist in a rapidly changing industrial society. In *The Golden Bowl* James depicts a marriage crisis that is resolved by Maggie's ability to master her "instinctive, elemental reactions" as a woman should and to adhere to social conventions. In *The Bostonians* James addresses the problem of women's emancipation, although he finds Ransom's egotism "more palatable" than Olive's "domineering character." Kieniewicz points out that James was increasingly alienated by the materialism of the society.

81   KIRBY, DAVID. *"The Portrait of a Lady*: 'The Ladies Will Save Us.'" In *The Sun Rises in the Evening: Monism and Quietism in Western Culture*. Metuchen, N.J.: The Scarecrow Press, pp. 76-109, 156-61.

Calls the James novel an "act of consciousness" and notes that Isabel's consciousness holds *The Portrait* together. James's concern with the consciousness is reflected in his use of ambiguity and in various images, particularly those of the medal, the circle, and the house. Isabel finally discovers that her consciousness is the means by which she can attain detachment from Osmond's entrapment; indeed, "James's entire career can be understood as a meditation on detachment."

82   KROOK, DOROTHEA. "Prefigurings of Isabel Archer." *Hebrew University Studies in Literature*:80-98.

Argues that Isabel Archer is prefigured in nine of the tales James wrote during the years 1866 to 1870 and focuses on five:"A Day of Days" (1866), "Gabrielle de Bergerac" (1869), "The Sweetheart of M. Briseux" (1873), "Madame de Mauves" (1874), and "An International Episode" (1878). Krook sees an ascending scale of complexity, ranging from the simple "*ur*-Isabel" of the 1866 tale to the detailed characterization in the 1874 and 1878 tales that together form "an almost complete 'study' for the novel." Tracing the evolution of Isabel Archer reveals James's main concerns with this character and his ability to assimilate the simple into the complex while giving the impression of simplicity.

83   KUBAL, DAVID. "The Urbanity of Henry James." In *The Consoling Intelligence: Responses to Literary Modernism*. Baton Rouge: Louisiana State University Press, pp. 76-91.
    Argues that in Lambert Strether, Milly Theale, and Maggie Verver James shows the necessity of a social awareness and his belief in the individual who grows because of, not in spite of, society.
    Reprint of "Henry James and the Supreme Value," *Arizona Quarterly* 22 (Summer 1966):101-14.

84   LABBE, EVELYNE. "Jungle du temps, jardin de mort" ["The Beast in the Jungle"]. *Recherches Anglaises et Américaines* 15:111-24.
    In French.
    Argues that Marcher spends his life anticipating and avoiding a potentially annihilating event, only to find that the nothingness produced trying to avoid this "beast" is itself the beast.

85   LEAVIS, F.R. "James as Critic." In *The Critic as Philosopher: Essays and Papers by F.R. Leavis*. Edited by G. Singh. London: Chatto & Windus, pp. 109-20.
    Acknowledges James's stature as a theoretician of fiction, particularly his recognition that value judgments cannot be divorced from art.
    Reprint in part of *Henry James: Selected Literary Criticism*, edited by Morris Shapira. Heinemann, 1957.

86   LeFANU, MARK. Introduction to *Washington Square*. Oxford: Oxford University Press, pp. vii-xxvii.
    Sketches the novel's three central characters and praises James's use of wit, comedy, and significant detail. LeFanu argues that this novel best exemplifies James's brevity and drama.

87 LESSER, WENDY CELIA. "The Urban Tradition: Transformations of London as Reflected in Dickens, James, and Conrad." Ph.D. dissertation, University of California, Berkeley, 221 pp.

Parallels the work of these three novelists with the changing London landscape, 1850-1900. Lesser approaches these writers as "masters of the superficial" in that "they understand the ways in which superficial appearances and external judgments ultimately determine the city-dweller's notion of character."

See *Dissertation Abstracts International* 43, no. 8 (1983):2681A.

88 LEWIS, R.W.B. "The Jameses' Irish Roots." *New Republic* nos. 3495-3496 (6-13 January):30-37.

Describes the Irish traits in the James family, focusing on Henry and Alice. Henry tended to Anglicize the Irish elements while Alice felt the "sharpest concern" for Ireland and the Irish.

89 LYONS, RICHARD S. "'In Supreme Command': The Crisis of the Imagination in James's *The American Scene*." *New England Quarterly* 55, no. 4 (December):517-39.

Examines James's imaginative response to America, and relates this dramatic confrontation to James's fiction. Although the imagination has the ability to distort reality, the movement in *The American Scene* as well as in such novels as *The Portrait of a Lady, The Princess Casamassima, The Ambassadors*, and *The Spoils of Poynton* is from escape to confrontation, from detachment to immersion in reality.

90 MACE-TESSLER, MARGARET ANN. "The Scene in Proust and James: A Study of the Narrative Device in *A la recherche* and the Late Novels of Henry James." Ph.D. dissertation, Brandeis University, 244 pp.

Compares Proust's and James's use of the scene, arguing that it is the primary unifying device between thematic and narrative concerns. Both use the scene to introduce characters, present alternative viewpoints, and explore the protagonist's action and growth. While such scenes give conversation a central place, they also reveal the untrustworthy nature of conversation.

See *Dissertation Abstracts International* 43, no. 4 (1982):1739A.

91 McKAY, JANET HOLMGREN. "*The Bostonians*: Unresolved Ambiguity." In *Narration and Discourse in American Realistic Fiction*. Philadelphia: University of Pennsylvania Press, pp. 37-89.

Examines the various methods of discourse in the novel, which include a narrator, directly reported discourse, and indirectly reported discourse, attributing the ambiguity of James's position to the narrator's shifting perspective over the course of the novel. James's experiment with narrative technique fails because his goal of objectivity deprives the reader of sympathy for any one character or idea.

92 MANNING, DALE. "Beyond Colonus: Tragic Vision and Transfigured Imagination in the Late Works of Henry James, William Butler Yeats, and T.S. Eliot." Ph.D. dissertation, Vanderbilt University, 247 pp.

Details the components of the archetypal experience of Oedipus at Colonus as well as the characteristics of the archetypal vision. After discussing the archetype within the contexts of philosophy, psychology, and literary criticism, Manning traces the archetype in the later works of these writers.

See *Dissertation Abstracts International* 43, no. 6 (1982):1968A.

93 MARCO, JOSE MARIA. "Henry James: Evolucion de la conciencia." *Quimera* 16 (February):37-42.

In Spanish.

94 MARTIN, JACKY. "Les Relations enonciatives dans 'Louisa Pallant.'" *Delta* 15 (November):125-32.

In French.

95 MARTIN, W.R., and OBER, WARREN U. "Critical Responsibility in Henry James's 'The Coxon Fund' and 'The Birthplace.'" *English Studies in Canada* 8, no. 1 (March):62-75.

Argues that these two tales depict the responsible critic as one who responds appropriately and appreciatively to the work of art. In "The Coxon Fund" this is shown in the contrast between Ruth and the narrator; in "The Birthplace," Gedge discovers that the real artist lives in the work of art and that the responsible critic must be detached (but never cynical) in order to know the artist and his art.

1982

96   MASSA, ANN. "Henry James (1843-1916)." In *American Literature in Context, IV: 1900-1930*. London: Methuen, pp. 31-44.
Discusses James's alienation from America as reflected in *The American Scene*. James deplored the mediocrity, conformity, and blandness of American culture and saw money as the root of American evil.

*97   MATEI, MIHAI. "Americanii din Anglia şi din Noua Anglie" [Americans from England and New England]. *România Literară* (Budapest) 15 (August):20.
In Romanian.
Source: *Annual Bibliography of English Language and Literature* 57 (1982):446, item 8135.

98   MATHESON, TERENCE J. "Did the Governess Smother Miles? A Note on James's *The Turn of the Screw*." *Studies in Short Fiction* 19, no. 2 (Spring):172-75.
Suggests that Miles dies of asphyxiation, not fright. Matheson catalogs the governess's violent behavior throughout the tale – grabbing, squeezing, shaking Miles – and at the tale's end, pressing him to her heart.

99   MAYER, CHARLES W. "Turgenev and James: Different Versions of the Beast." *Research Studies* (Pullman, Wash.) 50, no. 2 (June):69-78.
Links "The Beast in the Jungle" with Turgenev's story "Knock . . . Knock . . . Knock" (1870). James's and Turgenev's central characters are isolated by supreme egotism, although James's tale differes from Turgenev's in its omission of supernatural intervention, its focus on the protagonist's consciousness, and its concern with the missing of love.

*100   MESSENT, PETER, and PAULIN, TOM eds. Introduction to *Henry James: Selected Tales*. London: Dent, i-xli.
Source: *Annual Bibliography of English Literature and Language* 57 (1982):446, item 8138.

101   MESSICK, JUDITH HASSAN. "Reading as if for Life: The Female Quixote." Ph.D. dissertation, University of California, 234 pp.

Traces the figure of the female Quixote from its beginnings in the eighteenth century to current feminist fiction. Typically, the female Quixote confronts the "learned Doctor" who assumes various manifestations. In *The Portrait of a Lady*, as in *Middlemarch*, the female Quixote honors marital obligations to an older man in spite of a disappointing marriage.

See *Dissertation Abstracts International* 44, no. 1 (1983):166A-167A.

*102   MIGUEZ, MANUAL. "Objects, Images, and the Theatre in Henry James's *The Golden Bowl.*" *Senara: Revista de Filoloxía* 4:239-47.
        Source: *MLA International Bibliography* 1 (1984):199, item 8032.

103   MOCHI, GIOVANNA. *Le 'cose cattive' di Henry James* [Henry James's "Naughty Things"]. Parma: Pratiche Editrice, 105 pp.
        In Italian.

104   MOON, HEATH. "More Royalist Than the King: The Governess, the Telegraphist, and Mrs. Gracedew." *Criticism* 24, no. 1 (Winter):16-35.
        Links "The Turn of the Screw," *In the Cage*, and "Covering End" by virtue of the heroine of each work, who is depicted as loyal to or a savior of the moral and aesthetic culture of the privileged classes. Moon argues that these three works show James's belief that democratization brings about a destruction of the social edifice.

105   MOORE, SUSAN REIBEL. *The Drama of Discrimination in Henry James*. St. Lucia: Unviersity of Queensland Press, xi, 127 pp.
        Examines the protagonist's development of an inclusive vision in *The Europeans, Washington Square, The Portrait of a Lady, The Spoils of Poynton*, and *The Awkward Age*. The Jamesian protagonist must come to terms with other characters and new realities and, in so doing, achieves a heightened awareness. This growth is invariably accompanied by pain.

1982

106　NEWBERRY, FREDERICK. "A Note on the Horror in James's Revision of *Daisy Miller.*" *Henry James Review* 3, no. 3 (Spring):229-32.

　　　Sees James's increased use of the word "horror" in the New York Edition as a way to tighten the tale's structure and to suggest that Winterbourne suspects that Daisy is a "whore."

　　　See also Stafford 1983.190.

107　"1981-1982 Annual Review." *Journal of Modern Literature* 9, nos. 3-4 (December):470-74.

　　　Lists criticism published between 1980 and 1982.

108　NORRMAN, RALF. *The Insecure World of Henry James's Fiction: Intensity and Ambiguity.* London: Macmillan Press, x, 216 pp.

　　　Examines James's use of stylistic devices, including referential ambiguity, end-linking, emphatic affirmation, chiasmus, and the 'finding a formula' formula. The world suggested by these rhetorical strategies is one characterized by uncertainty and insecurity. Although he devotes chapters to each of the devices mentioned, Norrman argues that chiasmus is the most important for the light it sheds not only on James's style, but the content of his work, and the psychology of the man. Norrman's discussion ranges over many of James's works, but *The Golden Bowl* is examined in detail.

　　　Reprints in part 1979.109, 1979.110, and 1980.101.

109　OHSIMA, JIN. *A Unified Sensibility: A Study of Henry James' "The Ambassadors" and Its Scenario.* Tokyo: Hokuseido, iii, 120 pp.

　　　Examines the often diametrical differences between the novel and its scenario. In the novel James developed the theme of consciousness and renunciation and altered the characterization of Chad and Mme. de Viomet. Ohsima attributes these changes to James's understanding of the contrast between European refinement, which is selfish, and American refinement, which encompasses those traits that have been corrupted by capitalism and industrial development.

110　OTTEN, TERRY. "Childhood's End: *The Turn of the Screw* by Henry James." In *After Innocence: Visions of the Fall of Modern Literature.* Pittsburgh: University of Pittsburgh Press, pp. 52-67, 215.

Argues that the tale "portrays the ambiguous state of childhood innocence" in the children and in the governess; indeed, the tale depicts the psychological and metaphysical dimensions of a fall from innocence.

111 OZICK, CYNTHIA. "The Lesson of the Master." *New York Review of Books* 29, no. 13 (12 August):20-21.
      Admits that she mistook the "Master" for the real James and missed James's "essential note." For Ozick, the "Lesson of the Master" is "never to be ravished by the goal" and "never to worship ripe Art or the ripened artist."
      Reprinted 1983.140, 1983.141.
      See also Johnson 1985.71.

112 PANICHAS, GEORGE A. "Henry James and the Paradigms of Character." *Modern Age* 26, no. 1 (Winter):2-7.
      Discusses *Henry James Letters III*, edited by Leon Edel, within a biographical context. Although James was faced with a declining audience for his novels, his failure as a playwright, and the deaths of his brother Garth and his sister Alice, his letters of the period reveal reverence, courage, loyalty, and kindness and thus become standards with which we can judge civilized life.

113 _____. "The Jamesian Mirror." In *The Courage of Judgment: Essays in Criticism, Culture, and Society.* Knoxville: University of Tennessee Press, pp. 211-19.
      Reprint of 1976.154 and 1977.96.

114 PARR, SUSAN RESNECK. "*The Turn of the Screw* (1898) by Henry James." In *The Moral of the Story: Literature, Values, and American Education.* New York and London: Teachers College Press, pp. 69-78.
      Offers a classroom guide to discussing the tale's morals and values, noting that the tale raises questions about the validity of perception and the relationship between perception and judgment.

115 PERROT, JEAN. *Henry James: une écriture enigmatique.* Paris: Aubier-Montaigne, 122 pp.
      In French.

1982

In French. Investigates James's stylistic devices that subtly incorporate a network of literary influences and currents of the Victorian age. Through a carnival-like play of masking without disguising, James captures the essence of a society in his fiction.

116 PETERSON, CARLA L. "Constant's *Adolphe*, James's 'The Beast in the Jungle' and the Quest for the Mother." *Essays in Literature* 9, no. 2 (Fall):224-39.

Compares the two tales on the basis of a shared Romantic quest for identity and authority. In addition both works feature an ambiguous female figure and both reveal the inadequacies of language although both heroes believe language to be the only means of communication.

117 PHELPS, GILBERT. Introduction to *The Europeans*. London: Folio Society, pp. 5-15.

Argues that the novel is an important though neglected part of the James canon, influenced by the "poetic idylls" of Balzac, Sand, and Turgenev. *The Europeans* is a "fruitful variation" of the international theme by placing Europeans in America. James's purpose is not to pass judgment, but to show that his civilized ideal draws upon the best values of both cultures.

118 POIRIER, RICHARD. Foreword to *The Expense of Vision: Essays on the Craft of Henry James*, by Laurence B. Holland. Baltimore: John Hopkins University Press, pp. vii-viii.

Maintains that Holland's approach to the James's novel as a critical text continues to have value and sets a standard for critical studies of James in particular and fiction in general.

119 QUENNELL, PETER. "A Book in My Life." *Spectator* 249, no. 8049 (16 October):27-28.

Attributes the difficulty of reading *The Ambassadors* to James's "oblique approach" to a fairly simple plot.

120 RAMRAS-RAUCH, GILA. "The Governess in *The Turn of the Screw*." In *The Protagonist in Transition: Studies in Modern Fiction*.

European University Studies, series 18 comparative literature, vol. 29. Berne and Francfort: Peter Lang, pp. 75-114.

Calls the novella a distinctly modern work because of its subject—a disrupted family—and narrative technique—a complex, shifting relationship of author, protagonist, and reader. Ramras-Rauch also discusses the ambiguity in the novella, reviewing critical commentary and focusing on the various means James uses to create ambiguity.

121 RENTZ, KATHRYN C. "The Question of James's Influence on Ford's *The Good Soldier*." *English Literature in Transition* 25:104-14, 129-30.

Argues that while Ford begins with a Jamesian situation and Jamesian characters, he informs them with a "pessimistic, ironic vision of life" far removed from a "tidy" and "restrainted" Jamesian world. Ford's plot is also much more complex than any of James's. Ford's differences from James are not so much a critique of "the Master" as they are indications of Ford's own mastery.

122 RICHARD, CLAUDE. "La Romance de Louisa Pallant." *Delta* 15 (November):103-13.

In French.

123 RICHARDS, BERNARD. Introduction to *The Spoils of Poynton*. Oxford: Oxford University Press, pp. vii-xxvi.

Summarizes plot, theme, and characters and sketches the novel's sources and composition.

124 RINGE, DONALD A. "Conclusion." In *American Gothic: Imagination and Reason in Nineteenth-Century Fiction*. Lexington: University Press of Kentucky, pp. 177-89, 207-8.

Sees *The Bostonians* as evidence of the decline of the influence of the Gothic tradition on American fiction. In his tales, however, James was successful in blending the real and the fanciful to achieve psychological subtlety and to create effective Gothic fiction.

125 ROWE, JOHN CARLOS. "The Authority of the Sign in James's *The Sacred Fount*." In *Through the Custom-House: Nineteenth-Century*

1982

American Fiction and Modern Theory. Baltimore: Johns Hopkins University Press, pp. 168-89, 212-14.

Argues that the novel explores artistic identity, narrative authority, and the nature of language—concerns dominating modern critical theory. Rowe discusses these issues within the context of the work of Saussure and Benveniste.

126 _____. "James's Rhetoric of the Eye: Re-Marking the Impression." *Criticism* 24, no. 3 (Summer):233-60.

Returns to the original sense of impressionism—"to press in"—to define it as a crossing of boundaries (past and future, space and time, etc.), and locates in this catechresis the origin of language, the schematizing of differences. Rowe uses James's fiction and nonfiction as a way to investigate impressionism because James understands the consciousness as a "network of signs that requires certain boundaries, necessary forms."

127 _____. "Screwball: The Use and Abuse of Uncertainty in Henry James's *The Turn of the Screw*." *Delta* 15 (November):1-31.

Argues that the tale transforms mastery into "ghostliness," focusing on the uncle's power, whose authority is expressed through repression and censorship. Critical analysis of the hidden dramas, sexual and moral, only serves to mask the uncle's power because it attributes his mastery to another agent.

128 RYAN, JUDITH. "Elective Affinities: Goethe and Henry James." *Goethe Yearbook* 1:153-71.

Argues that *The Golden Bowl* reveals and refines the "mainspring" of *Die Wahlverwandtschaften* (*Elective Affinities*). James enhances the love affairs with "greater psychological and social credibility," but he revokes Goethe's critique of subjectivity.

129 SAMSTAG, SUZANNA M. "Henry James's *The Ambassadors*: 'The Nuance of the Novel.'" *English Studies* (Seoul) 6:109-15.

Examines the use of language to reveal character in the first three chapters of the novel, chapters that establish the basic structure of *The Ambassadors*. In particular, Waymarsh and Maria Gostrey are "two opposing points of reference" for Strether.

130 SCHEIBER, ANDREW JOSEPH. "Unfaithful Accomplices: Form, Theme, and Character in Four Novels of Henry James." Ph.D. dissertation, Michigan State University, 268 pp.

Traces James's awareness of the tension between representation and interpretation, as reflected in characters who function as "surrogate narrators" in *The American, The Portrait of a Lady, The Ambassadors,* and *The Wings of the Dove.* In the first two novels, the aesthetic evaluations of the authorial narrator conflicts with the psychic realities of the protagonists; the surrogate narrator becomes a strategy to overcome this conflict. In the later novels, however, James translates the conflict and its resolution into theme–the contrast between human perception and the "real brutalities" of life.

See *Dissertation Abstracts International* 43, no. 9 (1983):2999A.

131 SCHOENHOLTZ, ANDREW IAN. "The Politics of Knowledge in Nineteenth Century Literature: Keats, Flaubert, Emily Bronte, James, and the Critical Imagination." Ph.D. dissertation, Brown University, 230 pp.

Argues that these writers criticize the "extraordinary desire for totalizing knowledge" of nineteenth-century Western civilization. Chapter four focuses on James's first-person narratives as a critique of the subjective consciousness enacting that knowledge by violating innocence and life.

See *Dissertation Abstracts International* 43, no. 11 (1983):3589A.

132 SEE, FRED G. "Henry James and the Art of Possession." In *American Realism: New Essays.* Edited by Eric J. Sunquist. Baltimore: Johns Hopkins University Press, pp. 119-37.

Regards *The Spoils of Poynton* as the epitome of James's "novels of possession," in which one will struggle to dominate and use another. James uses the theme of possession to represent the transformation of the literary sign to a new mode of signifying realism and to "dramatize a realignment in the whole process of signification" in traditional literary language.

133 SEED, DAVID. "An Early Analogue of *The Europeans*." *American Notes and Queries* 21, nos. 3-4 (November-December):46-47.

Notes that James's 1871 sketch, "Still Waters," published in the *Balloon Post,* anticipates his 1878 novel.

1982

134   SELTZER, MARK. *"The Princess Casamassima*: Realism and the Fantasy of Surveillance." In *American Realism: New Essays*. Edited by Eric J. Sundquist. Baltimore: Johns Hopkins University Press, pp. 95-118.

Reprint of 1981.130; reprinted 1984.175.

135   SHACKELFORD, LYNNE PIPER. "Portrait of an Art Appreciator: Henry James's Art Criticism and Its Pertinence to his Theory and Practice of Fiction." Ph.D. dissertation, University of North Carolina at Chapel Hill, 469 pp.

Traces the development of James's interest in the visual arts and examines James's art criticism, particularly as a means of illuminating his theory of fiction. Shackelford suggests that James insisted on the representation of reality but a representation informed by the creative imagination.

See *Dissertation Abstracts International* 43, no. 5 (1982):1548A.

136   SHUMAKER, CONRAD. "Fathers and Daughters: Nathaniel Hawthorne and Henry James on the Pattern of New England History." Ph.D. dissertation, University of California, Los Angeles, 222 pp.

Relates the nineteenth-century ideal of woman to the Puritan sense of history and examines the influence of both the ideal and the sense of the past in Hawthorne and in James. Both authors use relations between the sexes as a means of understanding America's past. James's works discussed here include *Roderick Hudson, The Europeans, The Bostonians, The Ambassadors*, and *The American Scene.*

See *Dissertation Abstracts International* 43, no. 6 (1982):1975A.

137   SIBLEY, GAY PALMER. "The Cross-Pollination of 'Taste' and Evolutionary Theory in the Development of the British Novel." Ph.D. dissertation, University of Oregon, 289 pp.

Traces the "rhetoric of taste" based on elements of Menippean satire in the development of the novel from Austen to Ford. This rhetoric, the result of the use of an unreliable narrator and language that reveals character – both of which provide no clear interpretation – enables the authors to preserve classical standards of aesthetic sensibility while at the same time reflect new, more democratic standards. Novels discussed include Austen's *Pride and*

1982

Prejudice, Trollope's *Barchester Towers*, Eliot's novels, James's *The Awkward Age, The Sacred Fount,* and *The Golden Bowl,* and Ford's *The Good Soldier.*

See *Dissertation Abstracts International* 43, no. 9 (1983):2999A-3000A.

138 SKLENICKA, CAROL J. "Henry James's Evasion of Ending in *The Golden Bowl." Henry James Review* 4, no. 1 (Fall):50-60.

Sees the novel's lack of a conclusion as a reflection of both Maggie's and the narrator's expanded vision.

139 SMITH, GEOFFREY DAYTON. "The Temple of Analysis: The Behavioral Novel of Henry James." Ph.D. dissertation, Indiana University, 207 pp.

Examines the social behavior in James's novels of manners, showing that this behavior illuminates the central theme of the individual's search for knowledge. There are two benefits to the behavioral approach: it affirms James's prominence as a realist, and it places James's work within the context of contemporary psychological theories.

See *Dissertation Abstracts International* 43, no. 8 (1983):2671A.

140 STROUSE, JEAN. "'Peculiar Intense and Interesting Affections.'" In *Alice James: A Biography.* New York: Bantam Books, pp. 257-78, 376-78.

Reprint of 1980.138.

141 STROUT, CUSHING. "Complementary Portraits: James's *Lady* and Wharton's *Age." Hudson Review* 35, no. 3 (Autumn):405-15.

Sees the novels forming a "diptych": Wharton begins where James left off in that she examines the social context and the male side of the story as well as taking the characters through "to the end of their situation." Although the two writers tell their stories differently, both appreciate renunciation and explore its moral and cultural dimensions.

142 SUNDAHL, DANIEL JAMES. "The High Altar of Henry James: 'The Art of Figuring Synthetically.'" Ph.D. dissertation, University of Utah, 394 pp.

1982

Argues that the quote in the title is a metaphor describing the process in which the germ of an idea results in a novel, including both the arranging and structuring that must occur. This study focuses on the novels written after 1890, tracing James's development of the synthetic method. Sundahl thus demonstrates that for James, "the novel became the equivalent of perceptions provoked by an experience, which had been transformed and delicately adjusted, rather than merely represented."

See *Dissertation Abstracts International* 43, no. 7 (1983):2350A.

143 SUSSMANN, HENRY. "James: Twists of the Governess." In *The Hegelian Aftermath: Readings in Hegel, Kierkegaard, Freud, Proust, and James*. Baltimore: Johns Hopkins University Press, pp. 230-39.

Examines the turnings, doublings, and repetitions in this tale "beyond consistency and logic which . . . appropriate the Hegelian matrix of speculative operations."

144 TAYLOR, LINDA J. *Henry James, 1866-1916: A Reference Guide*. Boston: G.K. Hall & Co., xxvi, 533 pp.

Lists chronologically and annotates published American criticism of James from 1866 to 1916.

145 TAYLOR, MICHAEL J.H. "A Note on the First Narrator of 'The Turn of the Screw.'" *American Literature* 53, no. 4 (January):717-22.

Rejects the idea that the unnamed narrator in the tale's frame is James and suggests that the narrator is "a strangely androgynous figure" in keeping with the tale's ambiguity.

146 TIEDJE, EGON. "Henry James in seiner Zeit: *The Spoils of Poynton* und die gesellschaftliche Wirklichkeit Englands Mitte der neunziger Jahre" [Henry James in his time: *The Spoils of Poynton* and England's social realities in the middle of the nineties]. In *Die amerikanische Literatur in der Weltliteratur: Themen und Aspekte* [American literature in world literature: themes and viewpoints]. Edited by Claus Uhlig and Volker Bischoff. Berlin: Schmidt, pp. 178-95.

In German.

147 TINTNER, ADELINE R. "'Eugene Pickering': Henry James' Shakespearian Burlesque." *AB Bookman's Weekly* 69, no. 13 (29 March):2430, 2432, 2434, 2436, 2438, 2440, 2442.

Demonstrates that James burlesqued *Antony and Cleopatra* and *Romeo and Juliet* in his 1874 tale. James's use of realistic material from his German travels "saves this mixture of two plays shorn of their tragedy and yet not handled farcically."
Revised 1987.122.

148 ____. "'Guest's Confession' and Shakespeare: Henry James's Merchant of New York." *Studies in Short Fiction* 19, no. 1 (Winter):65-69.

Traces James's use of elements from *The Merchant of Venice* in "Guest's Confession," particularly allusions, plot structure, characters, memorable speeches, and theme.
Revised 1987.122.

149 ____. "Henry and William James and Titian's *Torn Glove*." *Iris: Notes in the History of Art* 1 (February):22-24.

Notes that a photograph of William taken when he was twenty-one strongly resembles Titian's portrait. The portrait was regarded by James's contemporaries as "the ideal way for a young man with the world before him to appear." In *The Ambassadors* James connects the portrait with Chad Newsome to suggest Chad's transformation by his European experience.
Revised 1986.151.

150 ____. "Henry James' Debt to George Meredith." *AB Bookman's Weekly* 70, no. 12 (20 September): 1811, 1812, 1814, 1816, 1818, 1820, 1822, 1824-27.

Discusses the similarities between Meredith's *The Egoist* and *The Portrait of a Lady*, focusing on the vigil scenes, the imagery of porcelain, and the portrayal of characters representing the extremes of egotism. In addition, Tintner suggests James turned to Meredith's *Emilia in England* (1864; revised as *Sandra Belloni*, 1886) when he wrote "The Marriages." James's treatment of the material is more realistic than Meredith's.
Revised 1987.122.

1982

151 _____. "Henry James: Figure of the Homosexual Artist in Bruce Elliot's *Village*, a Mass Market Paperback." *Markham Review* 11 (Summer):71-72.

Examines the portrayal of James in the recently published novel, *Village*, showing that the author drew on the final volumes of Edel's biography to depict the James of the 1870s. Tintner also suggests that the authors travesty and caricature James's homosexuality.

152 _____. "Henry James's *Hamlets*: 'A Free Rearrangement.'" *Colby Library Quarterly* 18, no. 3 (September):168-82.

Examines the different uses of Hamlet in "Master Eustace," *The Princess Casamassima*, and *The Ivory Tower*. The tale's characters are based on those of the play; in *The Princess Casamassima* James uses the device of a play-within-a-play to provide an analogy and to foreshadow; in the unfinished novel Gray is a modern version of Hamlet.

Revised 1987.122.

153 _____. "Henry James's 'The Story in It' and Gabriele D'Annunzio." *Modern Fiction Studies* 28, no. 2 (Summer):201-14.

Traces James's use of D'Annunzio's vocabulary, iconography, and attitudes in the 1900 tale. Tintner draws on D'Annunzio's fiction and James's essay on the Italian author to illuminate James's appreciation of D'Annunzio's "sensual approach to experience."

154 _____. "Hiding Behind James: Roth's *Zuckerman Bound*." *Midstream* 28, no. 4 (April):49-53.

Argues that Roth models his novella on "The Jolly Corner" and alludes to "The Figure in the Carpet." In addition, Roth's use of the latter tale reveals that the real figure in the carpet is James's concern with "genital activity."

155 _____. "Pater in *The Portrait of a Lady* and *The Golden Bowl*, Including Some Unpublished Henry James Letters." *Henry James Review* 3, no. 2 (Winter):80-95.

Examines Pater's influence on James's idea of aestheticism and on his fiction. Gilbert Osmond is "the total Paterization of a character" while the tale "Glasses" is based on Arthur Symons's description of Pater in an 1896 essay. Chapter XI of *The Golden Bowl*,

in which Adam Verver describes his philosophy of collecting, is influenced by Pater's belief in art for art's sake. James valued Pater's stress on the value of art, but rejected his "single-minded aestheticism" that taken to its extreme is egotistic and antihumanist.
Revised 1987.122.

156   ____. "Photo Album Sheds Light on James' Book." *AB Bookman's Weekly* 69, no. 22 (31 May):4251, 4254, 4256, 4258-64.
Describes Katherine Loring's photo album, which contains photos James collected when writing *A Little Tour in France*. The order of photographs in the album corresponds to the places discussed in the book; for places that James does not have photographs, his descriptions are vague and focus on the people of the area.

157   TOMASSETTI, ANNA. "Impressioni romane di Henry James" [Henry James's impressions of Rome]. *Studi Romani: Revista Trimestrale dell'Instituto di Studi Romani* 30, no. 1 (January-March):44-58.
In Italian.

158   TORSNEY, CHERYL B. "'The Absent Values, The Palpable Voids': Deconstructing Henry James." Ph.D. dissertation, University of Florida, 229 pp.
Presents deconstructive analyses of *The American, The Spoils of Poynton,* and *The Wings of the Dove* to show that such an approach explains the exclusiveness of the Jamesian text.
See *Dissertation Abstracts International* 43, no. 9 (1983):2994A.

159   VIEILLEDENT, CATHERINE. "*The Wings of the Dove* and the Question of Art." *Delta* 15 (November):79-90.
Examines Milly's central role in the novel and the connection between her and the dove image. At the beginning of the novel, Milly has a frail sense of self, so that she easily falls victim to others' interpretation and exploitation. In confronting the imminence of her death, Millie adopts an "art of living" and accepts her role as dove, a "symbol that celebrates her compliance with the social game, and her preordained role of the giver." In the end, she consciously denies reality, replacing it with "the artistic representation of intense living."

1982

160 VON FRANK, ALBERT J. "James Studies 1980: An Analytical
     Bibliographical Essay." *Henry James Review* 3, no. 3 (Spring):210-28.
     Surveys books and articles published in 1980.

161 WALDMEIR, JOSEPH J. "Miss Tina Did It: A Fresh Look at *The
     Aspern Papers*." *Centennial Review* 26, no. 3 (Summer):256-67.
     Suggests that the conflicting characterization and inconsistent
     motivation in the tale resolve themselves in a "straight" rather than
     "ironic" reading of the text. The narrator is then a "true" innocent;
     Juliana and Tina are unscrupulous and calculating.

162 WARD, J.A. "Silence, Realism, and 'The Great Good Place.'" *Henry
     James Review* 3, no. 2 (Winter):129-32.
     Suggests that while the "Great Good Place" in the tale implies
     a kind of infantile regression and even self-obliteration, it also reflects
     the need for withdrawal from society into silence, a need described by
     both Henry James and Melville.
     Reprinted 1985.160.

163 WATTS, EMILY STIPES. "'The American' and the Artist." In *The
     Businessman in American Literature*. Athens: University of Georgia
     Press, pp. 51-54.
     Suggests that in *The American* James portrays a businessman
     in search of culture. Having found it, however, Newman can no longer
     be a businessman.

164 WEBER, JEAN JACQUES. "Frame Construction and Frame
     Accomodation in a Gricean Analysis of Narrative." *Journal of
     Literary Semantics* 11, no. 2 (October):90-95.
     Applies the Gricean principle of cooperation to the narrator's
     effort in "The Turn of the Screw" to convince the reader that the
     children are in contact with the ghosts. Such an analysis illuminates the
     governess's ideological background. Understanding the governess's
     strategy of "frame accommodation," however, in which she imposes her
     expectations on reality, eliminates much of the tale's ambiguity.

165 WEIMANN, ROBERT. "Realism, Ideology and the Novel in
     America (1886-1896): Changing Perspectives in the Work of Mark

Twain, W.D. Howells, and Henry James." *Zeitschrift für Anglistik und Amerikanistik* 30, no. 3:197-212.

Examines the ways in which Twain, Howells, and James responded to the social and ideological changes in the nineteenth century. These changes forced novelists to reassess the liberal assumptions about culture and society, resulting in "a more highly critical type of realism." In the section of the essay devoted to James, Weimann discusses *The Bostonians* and *The Princess Casamassima*, seeing them as novels in which James questions the ideological assumptions of society. James's questions ultimately result in a reassessment of the content and form of the traditional novel, reflected in *The Tragic Muse*. In this novel James emphasizes the uniqueness and independence of the artist in society.

166   WINKS, ROBIN W. "[The Turn of the Screw]." In *Modus Operandi: An Excursion into Detective Fiction*. Boston: David R. Godine, pp. 13-17.

Reviews possible interpretations of "The Turn of the Screw," and notes that "James writes of those interstices between the watcher-without and the watched, and of how the watched, knowing he is watched, may redefine the relationship between the two."

167   WINNETT, SUSAN BETH. "Terrible Sociability: The Text of Manners in Laclos, Goethe, and Henry James." Ph.D. dissertation, Yale University, 423 pp.

Examines the ways in which the concerns of the novel of manners – customs, mores, rules – enable these writers to write about aspects of experience that "manners" seemingly proscribe. In her discussion of James Winnett argues that the "text of manners" is James's principle of composition in his later work. In *The American Scene* James creates a frame of manners with which he can write about the unwriteable; *The Sacred Fount* is dominated by the inability of the narrator to accommodate his imagination to such a frame; and in *The Golden Bowl* both James and Maggie exploit the "frame of manners" and social conventions to "execute an intention which remains radically private and unsociable."

See *Dissertation Abstracts International* 43, no. 6 (1982):1964A.

168   WOLPERS, THEODOR. "Sujets, Motive und Themen Bei Henry James: Undersuchungen zür siener Literaturkritik und 'The Real

1982

Thing'" [Subjects, motives, and themes of Henry James: Investigations of his literary criticism and The Real Thing]. In *Motive und Themen in Erzählungen des späten 19*. Jahrunderts: Bericht über Kolloquien der Kommission für literaturwissen-schaftliche Motiv- und Themenforschung, 1978-1979, I [Motifs and themes in tales of the late nineteenth century. Report of the meeting of the commission for research into literary motifs and themes]. Göttingen: Vandenhoeck & Ruprecht, pp. 88-141.
In German.

169 WRIGHT, AUSTIN M. "Dynamic Plot: *The Portrait of a Lady*." In *The Formal Principle in the Novel*. Ithaca: Cornell University Press, pp. 195-217.
Concentrates on Isabel's choices, "progressive discriminations," and discoveries throughout the novel to show that the plot can be seen in terms of character growth.

170 YEAZELL, RUTH BERNARD. "Podsnappery, Sexuality, and the English Novel." *Critical Inquiry* 9, no. 2 (December):339-57.
Examines the "double discourse" of the English novel: the novel's evasion of sexuality calls attention to that which it evades. Dickens exposes this duplicity; James also calls attention to "'this immense omission in our fiction,'" but participates in duplicity as well.

171 YOUN, KEE-HAN. "'Madame de Mauves' eui juje" [The theme of Madame de Mauves]. *Journal of English Language and Literature Chung-chong* (Chongju, Korea) 22:23-42.
In Korean.
Source: *Annual Bibliography of English Language and Literature* 59 (1984):434, item 7785.

*172 YOURCENAR, MARGUERITE. "Les Charmes de l'innocence: Une Relecture d'Henry James." *Nouvelle Revue Française* 359 (December):66-73.
In French.

1983

1   ADEGAWA, YUKO. "The Evolving Depiction of Children in the Literature of Henry James." *Bulletin of Daito Bunka University: The Humanities* 21:53-65.

Surveys the children in James's tales and novels, focusing on the adult-child relationship. James's children, for the most part, are struggling to retain and define their individuality in a world of victimizing adults. Adegawa sees a parallel between James's depiction of children and his maturation as an artist.

2   AGNEW, JEAN-CHRISTOPHE. "The Consuming Vision of Henry James." In *The Culture of Consumptions: Critical Essays in American History, 1880-1980.* Edited by Richard Wightman Fox and T.J. Jackson Lears. New York: Pantheon Books, pp. 65-100.

Argues that although James is a critic of American consumer culture, he is "an entrepreneur of observation" whose artistic vision appropriates the world. Agnew traces James's acquisitive vision throughout his work, although he focuses on *The Golden Bowl*, "the first fully achieved literary expression of an American culture of consumption." James's work reveals how deeply the consumer culture has influenced his consciousness.

3   ANDERSON, CHARLES R. "James and Zola: The Question of Naturalism." *Revue de Littérature Comparée* 57, no. 3 (July-September):343-57.

Reviews discussions attempting to prove that James was a naturalist and calls them unconvincing. James's own comments on Zola – an 1880 review of *Nana*, excerpts from letters, and his 1903 essay – show that while James came to admire Zola, he rejected Zola's treatment of detail.

4   ANDERSON, QUENTIN. "Henry James's Cultural Office." *Prospects* 8:197-210.

Argues that the paradox of James's work arises from its appearance of immersion in a social world while at the same time the novels speak to our Emersonian need for individualism and disengagement from that world.

5 ANDERSON, WALTER E. "The Rape of the Eye: A Psychoanalytic Reading of *The Aspern Papers*." *Psychoanalytic Review* 70, no. 1 (Spring):101-19.

Demonstrates that this tale "brings into concentrated focus nearly all the symbols specifically associated with voyeurism in life, literature, and dreams." The tale is a fable of James's own voyeuristic approach to knowledge and experience, and is a product of James's fear of women.

6 ____. "The Visiting Mind: Henry James's Poetics of Seeing." *Psychoanalytic Review* 69, no. 4 (Winter):513-32.

Argues that James substituted imaginative seeing for actual experience and knowledge, which explains why James drew sharp polarities in his fiction between observer and observed. Indeed, James's fiction is "an art of veiling obsessional subjects," and Anderson briefly discusses such subjects in the novels and tales.

7 ANESKO, MICHAEL WALTER. "'Friction with the Market': Henry James and the Profession of Authorship." Ph.D. dissertation, Harvard University, 418 pp.

Explores the complex relationship between the demands of the marketplace and James's imagination. James was acutely aware of the marketplace during the eighties; this concern is reflected in the work of the decade that often depicts a character struggling to reconcile public and private roles.

See *Dissertation Abstracts International* 44, no. 12 (1984):3682A.

8 ____. "'Friction with the Market': The Publication of Henry James's New York Edition." *New England Quarterly* 56, no. 3 (September):354-81.

Argues that market pressures, not the twenty-three volumes of Balzac's *Comédie Humaine*, shaped the New York Edition. Anesko details the changing "architecture" of the edition and chronicles James's dealings with W.C. Brownell, his editor at Scribner's.

Revised 1986.1.

9   AOKI, TSUGIO. "Henry James Enshū: *In the Cage*" [A seminar on Henry James' *In the Cage*]. *Eigo Seinen* (Tokyo) 129:440-42, 498-500, 552-24, 596-98.

In Japanese.

Argues that the point of view adopted in this novel is reminiscent of that in "The Turn of the Screw." Both protagonists are carried away by the power of their imagination. Yet in each work the reader, instead of condemning the protagonist, is made to participate in creating fiction that the fiction itself negates. Although James often seems to treat romantic imagination ironically, the antithesis of romanticism and realism in his works seems to function as a means of preserving romanticism, rather than denying it altogether.

10   ARMSTRONG, PAUL B. "The Hermeneutics of Literary Impressionism: Interpretation and Reality in James, Conrad, and Ford." *Centennial Review* 27, no. 4 (Fall):244-69.

Argues that these three authors inaugurate modern fiction's focus on the process of interpreting or creating reality. Armstrong examines *The Portrait of a Lady* and *The Ambassadors* in terms of questions James raises about the nature of reality and our interpretation of it.

Reprinted 1985.5 and 1987.2.

11   ____. *The Phenomenology of Henry James*. Chapel Hill: University of North Carolina Press, xiii, 242 pp.

Approaches the relation between consciousness and moral vision in James, focusing on *Roderick Hudson*, *The Portrait of a Lady*, *What Maisie Knew*, *The Spoils of Poynton*, and *The Golden Bowl*. Armstrong argues that phenomenology provides a conceptual framework with which to examine that relation and analyzes five aspects of human experience – the "impression," the imagination, freedom, personal relations, and the politics of daily life – drawing on phenomenological theories about consciousness and existence. Applying phenomenological concepts to James's fiction reveals his concentration on human experience; his exploration of the consciousness and the way meaning is created by interpreting experience demonstrates his modernity.

1983

12   BANTA, MARTHA. "Artists, Models, Real Things, and Recognizable Types." *Studies in the Literary Imagination* 16, no. 2 (Fall):7-34.

Examines the use of the type in American art and the fictional depiction of artists during the years 1890 to 1910 as an aspect of the problematic nature of representing reality and the shifting ground between appearance and reality. Banta briefly discusses "The Real Thing," in which kinds of identity are assessed without reference to authenticity.

13   BARBOUR, JOHN D. "Tragedy and Ethical Reflection." *Journal of Religion* 63, no. 1 (January):1-25.

Proposes that "literary tragedy" examines two aspects of "moral significance": virtue resulting in evil, and conflict between different values and between different virtues. Barbour looks at the political novels of Conrad, James, and Warren. Hyacinth Robinson must choose between his allegiance to social justice and his aesthetic sensibility, and he is tempted to do wrong to bring about good.

14   BARNETT, LOUISE K. "Speech in *The Ambassadors*: Woollett and Paris as Linguistic Communities." *Novel* 16, no. 3 (Spring):215-29.

Contrasts the "commercial" language of Woollett with the more adventurous and speculative language of Paris and attributes the failures of communication in the novel to this contrast. In addition, the novel shows that "language has supreme importance in creating the value of experience."

15   BARRETT, DEBORAH JANE BURCH. "The Oblique Heroine: Little Dorrit, Milly Theale, and Caddy Compson." Ph.D. dissertation, Rice University, 255 pp.

Demonstrates that the "oblique heroine," who is indirectly presented in a novel with a dominant male character, serves three functions: illuminates social ills; illustrates the author's belief in limited perceptions; and represents the novelist's ideal.

See *Dissertation Abstracts International* 44, no. 2 (1983):480A-481A.

16   BARRY, PETER. "Citizens of a Lost Country: Kawabata's *The Master of Go* and James's 'The Lesson of the Master.'" *Comparative Literature Studies* 20, no. 1 (Spring):77-93.

Juxtaposes these stories about the relationship between life and art to illuminate the process by which the reader creates a narrative with the guidance of the writer. The "narrative uncertainty" of the two tales demands that the reader suspend belief and accept the narrative as a "surrogate of [the] waking consciousness."

17   BARZUN, JACQUES. "Philosopher as Literary Critic." *Encounter* 60, no. 1 (January):41-44.

Describes William James's reading of and comments on literature, including the fiction of his brother. William's comments on Henry's novels show that William could describe and appreciate a novel even while objecting to its method.

18   BASIĆ, SONJA. "From James's Figures to Genette's *Figures*: Point of View and Narratology." *Revue Française d'Etudes Américaines* 8, no. 17 (May):201-15.

Argues that James influences structuralism and deconstruction particularly in such concepts as unreadability and narrative transmission. The discussion focuses on Genette but covers the work of J. Hillis Miller and Todorov as well.

19   BASS, EBEN E. "Henry James and the Venetian Voice." *Colby Library Quarterly* 19, no. 2 (June):98-108.

Shows that "The Pupil" anticipates *The Wings of the Dove*. Both works, especially the Venetian chapters of the novel, draw figurative language from Psalm 55. Bass focuses on the image of voice, which suggests duplicity, guile, and manipulation.

20   BEAVER, HAROLD. "'The Real Thing' and Unreal Things: Conflicts of Art and Society in Henry James." *Fabula* (Villeneuve d'Ascq) 1 (March):53-69.

Argues that the tale's narrator undermines Wilde's separation of life from art by demonstrating that "qualities predicated of society . . . are in fact a condition of art" and that art does not enjoy a privileged status.

1983

21   BELL, MILLICENT. "'Les Mots ne sont pas la parole': *What Maisie Knew.*" *Revue de Littérature Comparée* 57, no. 3 (July-September):329-42.

Examines the relation between silence and speech, which Bell sees as the central issue of the novel. Maisie's silence in the early chapters is a result of her inability to attach referents to words. As she achieves the knowledge of good and evil, silence is her way of resisting "the language of good" and preserving her freedom.

22   BERRY, NICOLE. "Portraits de demeures: Un Essai Psychanalytique." *Revue de Littérature Comparée* 57, no. 3 (July-September):295-302.

In French.

Argues that James becomes passionately involved in his descriptions of buildings and places. His characters' relationships to these things define their personalities and their relations with others and are thus crucial in understanding their mentality.

23   BERTHOLD, MICHAEL COULSON. "The Idea of 'Too Late' in James's 'The Beast in the Jungle.'" *Henry James Review* 4, no. 2 (Winter):128-39.

Argues that in this tale James breaks with his earlier treatment of the "too late" theme by using it as a central rather than subordinate theme and by focusing on the mourner rather than the mourned. Berthold attributes these shifts to Hawthorne's exploration of the moral aspects of this theme and briefly compares James's treatment with that of Wharton's in *The House of Mirth*.

24   BERTINETTE, ROBERTO. "L'artista di Henry James." In *Le rovine circolari. S.T. Coleridge, E. Brontë, H. James; immagini dell'artista nel XIX secolo* [Circular ruins: S.T. Coleridge, E. Brontë, H. James; images of the artist in the nineteenth century]. Pisa: Editrice Tecnico Scientifica, pp. 91-131.

In Italian.

25   BESSIÈRE, JEAN. "Henry James: Théâtre-roman." *Revue de Littérature Comparée* 57, no. 3 (July-September):315-28.

In French.

26 _____. "L'Illusion du réalisme." *L'Arc* 89:85-90.
In French.

27 BLACKMUR, R.P. *Studies in Henry James*. Edited by Veronica A.
Makowsky. New York: New Directions, 249 pp.
Contents include: Introduction by Veronica A. Makowsky.
Sketches the evolution of Blackmur's work on James, beginning with
the Henry James number of *The Little Review* that suggested the New
Critical approach to James, later developed and refined by Blackmur.
Makowsky then chronicles Blackmur's career-long involvement with
James, tracing his early enthusiasm that later develops into "decreasing
admiration," attributable in part to Blackmur's identification with
James. Makowsky's discussion provides the biographical and
intellectual context for Blackmur's essays that follow.
"The Critical Prefaces of Henry James," pp. 15-44, reprinted
from *Hound and Horn* 7 (1934), 444-77;
"*The Sacred Fount*," pp. 45-68, reprinted from *Kenyon Review* 4
(1942), 328-52;
"In the Country of the Blue," pp. 69-90, reprinted from *Kenyon
Review* 5 (1943), 508-21;
"Henry James," pp. 91-124, reprinted from *Literary History of
the United States*, edited by Robert E. Spiller et al. (1948), pp. 1039-64
in 1974 edition;
"The Loose and Baggy Monsters of Henry James," pp. 125-46,
reprinted from *Accent* 11 (1951), 129-46;
"*The Golden Bowl*," pp. 147-60, reprinted from Introduction to
The Golden Bowl, Grove Press, 1952, pp. v-xxi;
Introductions to the Laurel Henry James Series (1958-1964):
"*The Wings of the Dove*," 161-75, reprinted from 1958, 5-17;
"*The American*," pp. 176-84, reprinted from 1960, 5-13;
"*Washington Square* and *The Europeans*," pp. 185-92, reprinted
from 1959, 5-12;
"*The Portrait of a Lady*," pp. 193-201, reprinted from 1961, 5-
12;
"*The Tragic Muse*," pp. 202-12, reprinted from 1961, 5-15;
"*The Ambassadors*," pp. 213-20, reprinted from 1964, 5-12;
"*The Golden Bowl*," pp. 220-30, reprinted from 1963, 5-13;
"The Spoils of Henry James: A Special Case of the Normal,"
pp. 231-42.
Argues that James focused on the details of life and social
convention to illuminate human nature. His authority, however, is
weakened by his inability to "feel" values as well as to know them.

1983

28   BLAKE, KATHLEEN. "Feminist Self-Postponement in Theory and Literature." In *Love and the Woman Question in Victorian Literature: The Art of Self-Postponement*. Brighton, Sussex, England: The Harvester Press. Totowa, N.J.: Barnes & Noble, pp. 126-31.

Compares *The Portrait of a Lady* and Eliot's *Daniel Deronda* to show how Isabel and Gwendolen fear sexuality and freedom.

29   BLOOMFIELD, SHELLEY COSTA. "The Brief and Crowded Hour: Studies in Narrative Suspense." Ph.D. dissertation, Case Western Reserve University, 189 pp.

Examines the creation and effect of suspense in a narrative. In the fiction of Hawthorne and Melville, suspense evolves from man's attempt to understand a mysterious universe. In James's *The Ambassadors*, however, suspense reveals the mysterious in the commonplace.

See *Dissertation Abstracts International* 44, no. 9 (1984):2765A.

30   BRADBURY, MALCOLM. "Modernity and Modernism: 1900-1912." In *The Modern American Novel*. Oxford: Oxford University Press, pp. 30-36.

Suggests that James's later novels point to modernism in their concern with the problem of knowing what experience is; also in these novels "the apprehensive and the compositional process become analogues." Bradbury sees Wharton as carrying on the work of the early James in her development of the novel of society.

31   BROWN, CLARENCE A. "Structure and Process in *The Wings of the Dove*." *Topic* 37 (Fall):23-34.

Examines the structure of the novel, which is based on the consciousness of several characters. Although Milly is the novel's true center, James's focus on Densher's consciousness shows that "what happens to Densher is . . . the substance of the novel." As a result of his relationship with Milly he is able to transcend selfhood and attains "redemption" – compassion for others.

32   BUDD, JOHN, comp. *Henry James: A Bibliography of Criticism, 1975-1981*. Westport, Conn.: Greenwood Press, 1983, xx, 190 pp.

Covers books, dissertations, theses, articles, and chapters of books published between 1975 to 1981. The items are divided by type; most items are annotated.

33   BUITENHUIS, PETER. "Henry James's 'The Art of Fiction' in Its European Context." *Revue Française d'Études Américaines* 8, no. 17 (May):217-25.

Surveys the influence of Flaubert, Turgenev, and Zola on the essay, which Buitenhuis notes was meant as a rebuttal and not as a theory of fiction. Nevertheless, the essay is important as a serious discussion of fiction, as an attack on the naïveté of the English novel, and as a "declaration of independence for the Anglo-American novel."

34   BURLING, WILLIAM J. "A Test of Character: The James-Daudet Trip to Oxford." *French-American Review* 7:45-51.

Describes Daudet's visit to England in 1895 at a time when James was recovering from the deaths of Constance Fenimore Woolson and Robert Louis Stevenson. James accompanied Daudet to Oxford, and although James did not "revel" in his duties as host, he maintained his composure and geniality in the face of personal crises.

35   BYERS, JOHN R., JR. "Half a Henry James Letter." *American Literary Realism, 1870-1910* 16, no. 1 (Spring):129-31.

Reprints two pages of a four-page letter to George Gissing in 1903. James notes that Well's vision and experience are too simplified, praises Conrad's work, and offers encouragement to Gissing.

36   CAWS, MARY ANN. "Moral-Reading, or Self-Containment with a Flaw." *New Literary History* 15, no. 1 (Autumn):209-15.

Comments on Nussbaum (1983.137), acknowledging James as a "great moralist" but points out that novels are read because we are "bewildered by the rules" and by human suffering. We read and reread James for "reasons of the heart" to discover something more than "strategies of the mind."

37   CLARK, ROBERT. "The Transatlantic Romance of Henry James." *In American Fiction: New Readings.* Edited by Richard Gray. London: Vision Press; Totowa, N.J.: Barnes & Noble, pp. 100-114.

1983

Examines the International Theme in *The American, The Portrait of a Lady*, and *Daisy Miller* as a reflection of the American desire to appropriate European culture.

38 COATES, PAUL. "The Text Against Itself: The Late Henry James: Substitution, Projection, and the Guilty Eye." In *The Realist Fantasy: Fiction and Reality since "Clarissa."* London: Macmillan Press, pp. 130-40, 232.

Sees "The Turn of the Screw" as a "web of substition and exchange" in which the attribution of goodness results in suspicion and evil. Coates links this shift to James's failure to establish his own relationship to the narrative, a failure characteristic of his later tales, most notably "The Beast in the Jungle." James is "unwilling to draw the necessary conclusions from his own complicity with the narrator and unable to develop a form that will connect autobiography with fiction."

39 CONN, PETER. "The Triumph of Reaction: Henry James." In *The Divided Mind: Ideology and Imagination in America, 1898-1917.* Cambridge: Cambridge University Press, pp. 18-48, 320-21.

Sees James's late novels – especially *The Wings of the Dove* and *The Golden Bowl*, as well as *The American Scene* – as evidence of his "despair over modernity" and his conviction that America could never have a meaningful past.

40 CONRAD, JOSEPH. "Letters." In *The Collected Letters of Joseph Conrad, Volume 1: 1861-1897.* Edited by Frederick R. Karl and Laurence Davies. Cambridge: Cambridge University Press, pp. 307, 339, 340, 348, 349, 414, 415.

Reprints letters to and about James. Conrad addresses James as *"cher maître"* and describes himself as a "very humble admirer."

*41 COY, JAVIER. "Henry James, su teoría del arte y el 'arte' de sus críticos" [Henry James, his theory of art and the 'art' of his critics]. *Atlantis* (University of Oviedo, Spain) 5, nos. 1-2:65-82.

In Spanish.

Source: *Annual Bibliography of English Language and Literature* 59 (1984):426, item 7629.

42 CROSS, MARY. "'To Find the Names': *The Ambassadors.*" *Papers on Language and Literature* 19, no. 4 (Fall):402-18.

Describes the novel's movement as based on Strether's search for a language that will accommodate his experience. Cross details Strether's replacement of the rhetoric of Woollett with the suggestive language of Europe. At the novel's end he is the "hero of a text over which he has dominion."

43 _____. "The Syntax of Seeing: Henry James and Paul Cezanne." *French-American Review* 7:34-44.

Finds similarities in method and effect in the work of James and Cezanne. Both artists offer a way of seeing, based on the cumulative shaping of discreet forms and resulting in the transformation of the reader's or viewer's perception. And for both, the medium is as important as the patterns it creates.

44 DEAKIN, MOTLEY. "Two Studies of *Daisy Miller.*" *Henry James Review* 5, no. 1 (Fall):2-28.

In the first part, discusses nineteenth-century associations connected with the settings in the tale and suggests that these associations, particularly the idealization of the individual, illuminate Daisy's character. In the second part, Deakin examines James's treatment of Daisy and Winterbourne, noting that James's contradictory responses to them reveal traits of these characters and their creator.

45 DEAN, SHARON. "The Myopic Narrator in Henry James's 'Glasses.'" *Henry James Review* 4, no. 3 (Spring):191-95.

Sees the tale as an analysis of the limitations of an artistic vision that sacrifices human complexity to beauty.

46 DEBRECZENY, PAUL. "Ivan Turgenev and Henry James: The Function of Social Themes in *Fathers and Sons* and *The Princess Casamassima.*" In *American Contributions to the Ninth International Congress of Slavists, Kiev, September 1983, II: Literature, Poetics, History.* Columbus, Ohio: Slavica, pp. 113-23.

Discusses the major images in each novel in order to compare each writer's integration of political concerns into the aesthetic structure of the novel. Debreczeny focuses on Turgenev's use of eyes,

1983

trees, and frogs; and on James's use of London. He also links Turgenev's and James's interest in the political novel to the "pressures of the age" and to their need to camouflage their emotional concerns.

47   DeLAMOTTE, EUGENIA. "The Power of Pretense: Images of Women as Actresses and Masqueraders in Nineteenth-Century American Fiction." *Studies in American Fiction* 11, no. 2 (Autumn):217-31.
    Argues that Alcott's, Hawthorne's, James's, and Wharton's association of women with acting and masquerade reflects the nineteenth-century connection between women's power and pretense. Woman's "pretense" is a result of her subordinate economic and political position and the cult of domesticity that idealized that position. DeLamotte examines Madame Merle and Isabel Osmond in *The Portrait of a Lady*. Both are victims of the same evil man, but both collaborate in their victimization by self-deception.

48   DOWLING, DAVID, editor. "Henry James, 1843-1916." In *Novelists on Novelists*. London: Macmillan Press, pp. 135-49.
    Excerpts comments on James by Bennett, Conrad, Forster, Hardy, Joyce, Lawrence, Meredith, Thackeray, and Woolf. The chapter on other novelists contains remarks made by James.

49   DUPEE, FREDERICK W. Introduction to *Henry James: Autobiography*. Princeton: Princeton University Press, pp. vii-xiv.
    Suggests that James's *Autobiography* "recounts his discovery of a vocation for writing" and that details are included because they either encouraged or threatened James's development.
    Reprint of 1956 essay.

50   DURAND-BOGAERT, FABIENNE. "Figures et métaphores de la séducion." *L'Arc* 89:65-69.
    In French.

51   DURAS, MARGUERITE. "Le Château de Weatherend–'La Bête dans la jungle.'" *L'Arc* 89:100-2.
    In French.

Discusses her two stage adaptations of "The Beast in the Jungle" (1962 and 1981). In the second, she decided to eliminate the setting change from Weatherend to London so that the castle becomes witness to the time passing between the two central characters. Included are six tableaux describing the setting and stage action for the scenes of the 1981 version.

52 DUYFHUIZEN, BERNARD BOYD. "Difficult Transmissions: The Narrator's Contact with the Reader." Ph.D. dissertation, University of Tulsa, 348 pp.

Applies current narrative theories to works in which the narrative imitates written texts (diaries, letters, manuscripts). "The Turn of the Screw" is discussed as an example of the "extradiegetic narrative of transmission" in which the narrative is presented by a fictional editor.

See *Dissertation Abstracts International* 44, no. 2 (1983):483A.

53 EAKIN, PAUL JOHN. "Henry James and the Autobiographical Act." *Prospects* 8:211-60.

Explores the ways in which writing his autobiography helped James to recover from the financial failure of the New York Edition and William James's death, focusing on the relationship between the autobiographical narrator and the small boy of the narrative. "The autobiographical act" enabled James to revisit the hidden imagination of the boy as a preparation for returning to the creative art of a mature adult.

Reprinted 1985.36.

54 EATON, MARCIA M. "James's Turn of the Speech-Act." *British Journal of Aesthetics* 23, no. 4 (Autumn):333-45.

Argues that speech-act theory, while having limitations, can be useful in literary criticism, and uses the ambiguity of "The Turn of the Screw" as a case in point.

55 EDEL, LEON. "The 'Felt Life' of Henry James." *Revue de Littérature Comparée* 57, no. 3 (July-September):269-73.

Describes James's work as "a constant quest for truths of feeling and motivation" and as "a critique and an analysis."

1983

56   ____. Introduction to *A Little Tour in France*. New York: Straus & Giroux, pp. ix-xix.
     Suggests that James is a model traveler: one who does his "homework" and who travels for "the delights of the senses."

57   ____. "The Terror of the Usual." In *Stuff of Sleep and Dreams: Experiments in Literary Psychology*. New York: Avon Books, pp. 300-308.
     Reprint of 1982.45.

58   EDEL, LEON, and TINTNER, ADELINE R.. "The Library of Henry James, from Inventory, Catalogues, and Library Lists." *Henry James Review* 4, no. 3 (Spring):158-90.
     Lists the contents of James's library, the current location of the volumes, and details the disposition of the library and the compiling of the list.
     Revised 1987.35.

59   ELLMANN, RICHARD. "Henry James among the Aesthetes." *Proceedings of the British Academy* 69:209-28.
     Argues that Pater's *Studies in the History of the Renaissance* was integral in shaping *Roderick Hudson* and James's criticism of aestheticism. Ellmann also discusses James's attitudes toward Oscar Wilde especially in relation to homosexuality.

60   ERMARTH, ELIZABETH DEEDS. "The Example of Henry James." In *Realism and Consensus in the English Novel*. Princeton: Princeton University Press, pp. 257-73.
     Argues that in James's fiction the "consensus" required by realism comes close to breaking down because of James's multiplicity of viewpoints that are constantly struggling "for mental footholds and generalizations." Ermath's discussion focuses on *The Portrait of a Lady*, *The Golden Bowl*, and *The Ambassadors*.

61   ESCH, DEBORAH. "A Jamesian About-Face: Notes on 'The Jolly Corner.'" *ELH* 50, no. 3 (Fall):587-605.
     Examines the implications of the tale's metaphors to show that figurative language, "the narrative's system of written signs," reflects the

tale's concern with the impossibility of fixing or influencing meaning. Brydon does not permit the apparition a life of its own; Miss Staverton accepts it on its own terms and thus serves as an example for the reader.

> Reprinted 1987.15 and 1987.16.

62 FAULKNER, HOWARD. "Text as Pretext in *The Turn of the Screw*." *Studies in Short Fiction* 20, no. 3 (Spring-Summer):87-94.

Sees the governess's reading of her own text as central to the tale, both as a metaphor and as an explanation of the governess's state of mind. The governess attributes supernatural power to the written word and sees the world as her text; she distorts reality, however, instead of explicating it. The reader must succeed where the governess fails.

63 FEINSTEIN, HOWARD M. "A Singular Life: Twinship in the Psychology of William and Henry James." In *Blood Brothers: Siblings as Writers*. Edited by Norman Kiell. New York: International University Press, pp. 301-28.

Traces the relationship between the two brothers, whose various illnesses were attempts to express individuation or identification at crucial junctures. Feinstein examines three of James's early tales – "DeGrey: A Romance," "The Romance of Certain Old Clothes," and "A Light Man" – in which Henry explores his relationship with William.

> Reprinted 1984.56.

64 FERENCZI, AURÉLIEN. "Adapter ou ne pas adapter: Films, télévision, théâtre." *L'Arc* 89:91-96.

In French.

Reviews American, British, and French adaptations of James's texts for the stage, film, and television and explores the validity of the notion that James's work does not lend itself readily to dramatization.

65 FERRARA, RITA. "La figura dello scrittore nei racconti di Henry James" [The figure of the writer in Henry James's tales]. *Il Ponte* 39, nos. 6-9 (30 June -30 September):668-77.

In Italian.

1983

66   FLICK, AREND JOHN. "The Problem of Narrative Reliability in Modern Fiction: James, Conrad, Ford." Ph.D. dissertation, University of California, Berkeley, 322 pp.

Argues that "actualization" – sustaining the illusion of actuality in fiction – and "defamiliarization" – rendering a stale subject unusual – explain the complexities caused by the unreliable narrator in the middle works of Conrad, James, and Ford. Flick examines "The Turn of the Screw" as well as James's narrative theories.

See *Dissertation Abstracts International* 44, no. 8 (1984):2469A.

67   FOGEL, DANIEL MARK. "'The Last Cab' in James 'The Papers' and in *The Secret Agent*: Conrad's Cues from the Master." *Modern Fiction Studies* 29, no. 2 (Summer):227-33.

Describes the influence of James's tale on Conrad's novel and reviews briefly the James-Conrad relationship. Although these are similarities shared by the authors, a "thematic and moral abyss" separates them: Conrad makes James's motifs "unremittingly bleak."

68   FOURNIER, SUZANNE JOAN. "The Nostalgia of Modern Fiction: Loss of Home in George Eliot, Henry James, and William Faulkner." Ph.D. dissertation, University of Notre Dame, 235 pp.

Argues that the work of these authors reflects a preoccupation with "the possibility of returning home – to self, to society, and to an ordered universe." Eliot's novels depict the impact of the loss of tradition and order; James's work portrays the self turning inward to find certitude; Faulkner's characters experience only nostalgia for lost certitude. The fiction of all three show that the certainty and fixed identity traditionally associated with home are no longer possible.

See *Dissertation Abstracts International* 44, no. 6 (1983):1780A-1781A.

69   FOWLER, VIRGINIA C. "Misogynist Stereotypes in *The Princess Casamassima*." *Topic* 37 (Fall):35-42.

Demonstrates that the depiction of women in this novel and their interactions with men suggest "a complex, sometimes glaring and hostile, sometimes subtle and questioning, misogyny." The situation of women, paralleled with that of the lower classes, is that of powerlessness, but the novel seems to show that for some women powerlessness is best.

70 FRYER, JUDITH. "The Other Victoria: 'The Woodhull' and Her Times." *The Old Northwest* 4, no. 3 (September):219-40.
Details the tumultuous career of Victoria Woodhull, who is satirized as Audacia Dangyereyes in Harriet Beecher Stowe's *My Wife and I* and as Nancy Headway in James's "The Siege of London."

71 FUNSTON, JUDITH E. "'All Art Is One': Narrative Techniques in Henry James's *Tragic Muse.*" *Studies in the Novel* 15, no. 4 (Winter):344-55.
Sees the novel as essentially transitional in that James combines the "painterly" mode of omniscient narration with the dramatic mode of the center of consciousness. These two modes explain the problematic nature of the novel; nevertheless, *The Tragic Muse* illuminates James's artistic development.

72 GALE, ROBERT L. "Henry James." In *American Literary Scholarship: An Annual/1981*. Edited by James Woodress. Durham: Duke University Press, pp. 109-25.
Surveys criticism published in 1981.

73 GARDINER, PATRICK. "Professor Nussbaum on *The Golden Bowl.*" *New Literary History* 15, no. 1 (Autumn):179-84.
Comments on Nussbaum (1983.137), disagreeing with her that Maggie has a sense of guilt for her actions.

74 GETZ, THOMAS H. "Henry James: The Novel as Act." *Henry James Review* 4, no. 3 (Spring):207-18.
Sees James's most mature novels – especially *The Portrait of a Lady, The Sacred Fount,* and *The Golden Bowl* – as expressions of feeling, which are dialectical acts because James is both the man who feels and the man who articulates those feelings. *What Maisie Knew* is a failure because James chooses as his focus an inexpressive child, in contrast to the articulate characters of his mature work.

75 GILLON, ADAM. "Conrad and James: A World of Things Beyond the Range of Commonplace Definitions." *Conradiana* 15, no. 1 (Spring):53-64.

1983

Compares James's and Conrad's ideas about the artist's perception and consciousness, drawing from Conrad's *Notes on Life and Letters* and James's "The New Novel." For both writers, "thing" refers to concrete objects possessing a symbolic dimension, hence neither James nor Conrad are conventional realists. Rather, their craft is based on "the *impression* they received and conveyed to the reader."

76 GRAHAM, KENNETH. "Stevenson and Henry James: A Crossing." In *Robert Louis Stevenson*. Edited by Andrew Noble. London: Vision Press; Totowa, N.J.: Barnes & Noble, pp. 23-46.

Compares the concept of art of the two writers, finding similarity in their vision of the interplay of "the stress of the real" and the "shaping, wandering mind."

77 GRANDEL, HARTMUT. "Henry James and Germany." In *American-German Interrelations in the Nineteenth Century*. American Studies, vol. 55. Edited by Christoph Wecker. Munich: Fink, pp. 105-23.

Reviews James's attitudes toward Germany and his critical reception there in the nineteenth century. The critics condemned his unAmericanness and his intellectual narrative method. By the 1950s, however, James's novels, particularly his earlier work, increasingly were regarded as "symbol[s] of cultural unity and solidarity" between America and Europe.

78 GREEN, ANDRÉ. "Le Deuil impossible." *L'Arc* (Aix-en-Provence, France) 89:74-79.

In French.

Suggests that the women in James's life greatly influenced his fiction. In particular, the overwhelming grief caused by the death of his cousin, Minny Temple, drove James to seek escape through his writing.

79 GREGORIO, EDOUARDO de. "Mes papiers d'Aspern." *L'Arc* (Aix-en-Provence, France) 89:97-99.

In French.

Argues that the literary and stylistic difficulties of faithfully rendering James's works on film can be overcome, as demonstrated in Michael Graham's *Les Papiers d'Aspern*.

80 GREGORY, ROBERT. "Henry James and the Art of Execution." *Topic* 37 (Fall):43-48.

Examines the figurative language in "A Round of Visits," showing that the prevalence of death, violence, and revenge supports Freud's view that inspiration is an assault on the boundaries of self and that artistic "execution" is a way of regaining self-mastery.

81 GRIBBLE, JENNIFER. "Introduction." In *The Lady of Shalott in the Victorian Novel*. London: Macmillan Press, pp. 1-43, 205-10.

Discusses the main elements of the image of the Lady of Shalott – the lady, the room, the mirror and the web, and the curse – and identifies them in *The Portrait of a Lady* and "In the Cage."

82 _____. "Portraits of Ladies: *The Wings of the Dove*." In *The Lady of Shalott in the Victorian Novel*. London: Macmillan Press, pp. 154-96, 215-16.

Argues that Millie Theale "of all fictional heroines surely most closely resembles Tennyson's Lady of Shalott" and traces the complex relationship between Millie and Kate, who like Millie – and the Lady – is isolated from reality. Gribble suggests that this novel questions "the Victorian novel's romantic fable" and the human costs demanded by that moral scheme.

83 HALL, RICHARD. "Henry James: Interpreting an Obsessive Memory." *Journal of Homosexuality* 8, nos. 3-4 (Spring-Summer):83-97.

Argues that the "tortured lifetime relationship" between William and Henry was due to "homosexual incest" on Henry's part. Hall suggests that the episode of James's watching for the appearance of a figure in a window, which is repeated throughout the fiction in which the watcher feels betrayed, may have been Henry watching for William, and feeling excluded and betrayed. Hall also discusses Edel's avoidance of homosexual incest in the biography as an indication of the problem of gay criticism and illustrates the "taboos, artifices, and self-deceptions" of literary criticism.

Reprinted 1983.84.

84 _____. "Henry James: Interpreting an Obsessive Memory." In *Literary Visions of Homosexuality*, vol. 6. Research on

1983

Homosexuality 6. Edited by Stuart Kellogg. New York: Haworth Press, pp. 83-97.
Reprint of 1983.83.

85   HARDY, DONALD E. "Conversational Interaction and 'Innocence' in James' *The Ambassadors*." *The Southwest Journal of Linguistics* 6, no. 1 (Spring):16-22.
Applies discourse analysis, particularly the work of H. Paul Grice and Halladay and Hasan, to Strether's conversations. The ambiguity of Strether's conversations is attributable to his character and not to James's style. Strether uses disunity, conversational implicature, and superficial cohesiveness to show that inner growth requires sensitivity to others.

86   HARKINS, JEFFREY PATRICK. "Works of Oscar Wilde and Henry James in and on the Theatre." Ph.D. dissertation, University of Minnesota, 199 pp.
Compares James's and Wilde's plays and drama-criticism in order to illuminate their dramatic theories and practices. Harkins details the influences shaping each playwright's conception of the drama and defines the nature of each's dramatic vision. Harkins attributes James's failure to his inability to produce a viable dramatic theory; Wilde succeeds because he masters the aesthetic issues of theory and practice.
See *Dissertation Abstracts International* 44, no. 3 (1983):611A.

87   "Henry James." In *Twentieth-Century Literary Criticism*. Vol. 11. Edited by Dennis Poupard. Detroit: Gale, pp. 314-49.
Reprints brief excerpts from the following: *North American Review* (1876), Bernard Shaw (1895), William Dean Howells (1903), Edmund Gosse (1920), Percy Lubbock (1921), Van Wyck Brooks (1925), Pelham Edgar (1927), André Gide (1930), Conrad Aiken (1935), Osborn Andreas (1948), Dorothy Van Ghent (1953), Frederick C. Crews (1957), Maxwell Geismar (1963), J.A. Ward (1967), Rudolf R. Kossman (1969), Joyce Carol Oates (1974), Kenneth Graham (1975) Daniel J. Schneider (1978), and Edward Wagenknecht (1983).

88   HERTZ, NEIL. "Dora's Secrets, Freud's Techniques." *Diacritics* 13, no. 1 (Spring):65-76.

Discusses resemblances between James's Maisie and Freud's patient, Dora. James's success with Maisie arises out of his ability to identify Maisie's innocence; Freud's failure with Dora may be attributable to his confusing himself with his "young surrogate." Hertz cautions, however, that the analogy between character and a real patient is easily strained.

89 HEWITT, ROSALIE. "Henry James, the Harpers, and *The American Scene*." *American Literature* 55, no. 1 (March):41-47.
     Attributes the "seriously corrupted text" of the American edition—deletion of numbered chapter divisions and James's running heads, and omission of a section on Florida—to mismanagement and a breakdown in communication between the Harpers and James.

90 HIRSCH, DAVID H. "Henry James and the Seal of Love." *Modern Language Studies* 13, no. 4 (Fall):39-60.
     Argues that the international theme is about love. James's use of allusions from *The Song of Songs* in *The Portrait of a Lady* underpins the novel's theme of the failure of love. In *The Wings of a Dove* James splits the *The Song*'s fusion of bodily and spiritual love into two female protagonists, Kate Croy and Milly Theale.
     Reprinted 1984.93.

91 HIRSH, ALLEN. "*The Europeans*: Henry James, James Ivory, 'And That Nice Mr. Emerson.'" *Literature/Film Quarterly* 11, no. 2 (Spring):112-19.
     Praises Ivory's film because it offers us a glimpse into the America of the 1840s, "a land of fantasy," where New England backwardness, rooted in trancendentalism, is contrasted with European sophistication.

92 HOCHMAN, BARUCH. "The Jamesian Situation: World as Spectacle." In *The Test of Character: From the Victorian Novel to the Modern*. Rutherford: Fairleigh Dickinson University Press, pp. 111-31.
     Revision of 1976.92. The introductory and concluding portions of the essay have been expanded, mainly to relate James to the Victorian tradition and to suggest that James's concern with self-

assertion departs from that tradition epitomized in the work of George Eliot.

93 _____. "On the Shape the Self Takes: Henry James to D.H. Lawrence." In *The Test of Character: From the Victorian Novel to the Modern*. Rutherford: Fairleigh Dickinson University Press, pp. 132-56.

Sees James as a transitional figure in his use of typically Victorian elements that he transforms, thus anticipating the concerns of the modern novelist. Although he briefly discusses the "world" of the novel, Hochman concentrates on James's development of character and identity, against which is contrasted D.H. Lawrence, who "assaults" and "negates" James's conception of the self.

94 HOCKS, RICHARD A. "James Studies 1981: An Analytical Bibliographical Essay." *Henry James Review* 5, no. 1 (Fall):29-59.

Surveys work on James in 1981, covering books and articles.

95 HOLLY, CAROL. "A Drama of Intention in Henry James's *Autobiography*." *Modern Language Studies* 13, no. 4 (Fall):22-31.

Relates James's memory of a moot-court session at Harvard Law School, described in chapter 10 of *Notes of a Son and Brother* to his humiliation on the opening night of *Guy Domville*. James used Rousseau's description of his failure in conducting music of his own composition to link the two memories.

96 _____. "Henry James's Autobiographical Fragment: 'The Turning Point of My Life.'" *Harvard Library Bulletin* 31, no. 1 (Winter):40-51.

Suggests that the fragment links the prefaces with the *Autobiography* and that the autobiographical volumes give a clue about James's turning point: "the discovery that his impressions were 'for' the art of prose fiction."

97 HUH, JOONOK. "Shifting Sexual Roles in Selected American Novels, 1870-1920." Ph.D. dissertation, Indiana University, 173 pp.

Sees the shift in sexual roles in two stages. The first, which is mainly transitional, is reflected in the work of Alcott, Norris, and Chopin, whose heroines subvert male authority. The second stage, apparent in the fiction of Wharton and James, involves assertive heroines and male characters who are "prisoners of a refined self-consciousness."

See *Dissertation Abstracts International* 44, no. 3 (1983):752A.

98 HUTCHINSON, STUART. *Henry James: An American as Modernist*. Critical Studies Series. London: Vision Press, 163 pp.

Argues that throughout his career James was increasingly concerned with creating reality instead of mirroring it, and this concern is apparent in his narrative technique, including the effacement of his authorial presence in the later novels. Novels discussed include *Washington Square, The Portrait of a Lady, The Bostonians, What Maisie Knew, The Ambassadors, The Wings of the Dove*, and *The Golden Bowl*. The chapter on *The Wings of the Dove* is a reprint of 1977.52.

99 IMBERT, HENRI-FRANÇOIS. "Le retour de James." *Revue de Littérature Comparée* 57, no. 3 (July-September):261-67.

In French. Introduces the special issue on James, which includes essays by Edel (1983.55); Perrot (1983.147); Berry (1983.22); Bessière (1983.25); Bell (1983.21); Anderson (1983.3); Perosa (1983.146); Tintner (1983.203); Labia (1983.109); and Miller (1983.127). Topics include biography, psychoanalysis, and the influence of plays and novels on James, emphasizing his relationship to other authors and literary movements.

*100 IRVING, DONALD C. "The Real World and the Made World: The Sociologist's Use of Literary Analogy." *Publications of the Missouri Philological Association* 8:40-44.

Source: *MLA International Bibliography* 1 (1983):200, item 7257.

101 JACOBSON, MARCIA [ANN]. *Henry James and the Mass Market*. University: University of Alabama Press, xii, 189 pp.

Demonstrates that James was sensitive to the demands of the new mass market for fiction, particularly in that the adapted best-selling genres to his own fiction during the eighties and nineties. In *The Bostonians, The Princess Casamassima*, and *The Tragic Muse* James used popular genres to achieve popular success; after his failure in the

1983

theatre, he used conventional forms as a means of social criticism, exemplified in *What Maisie Knew* and *The Awkward Age*.

Reprint in part of 1975.67, 1976.99, 1977.56; reprinted in part 1987.44.

102   JOCHUM, K.P.S. "Henry James's Ambassadors in Paris." *Modern Language Studies* 13, no. 4 (Fall):109-20.

Suggests that combining verifiable and fictitious elements in a novel–as James does in *The Ambassadors*–makes possible a "meaningful discourse" between novelist and reader. Jochum is refuting F.W. Bateson's 1973 claim that the novel's "original sin" is this very combination to persuade suspension of disbelief.

103   JONES, MARJORIE CULLEN. "The Novelist as Biographer: The Truth of Art, the Lies of Biography." Ph.D. dissertation, Northwestern University, 213 pp.

Examines Gaskell's *The Life of Charlotte Brontë*, James's *William Wetmore Story and His Friends*, Forster's *Goldsworthy Lowes Dickinson*, and Woolf's *Roger Fry* to show how these writers used novelistic techniques in these biographies. Each novelist uses standard fictional interests; each discovers something that cannot be revealed; and each is attracted to the information that must be suppressed.

See *Dissertation Abstracts International* 44, no. 11 (1984):3389A.

104   KAGAN-KANS, EVA. "Ivan Turgenev and Henry James: *First Love* and *Daisy Miller*." In *American Contributions to the Ninth International Congress of Slavists, Kiev, September, 1983, ·II: Literature, Poetics, History*. Edited by Paul Debreczeny. Columbus, Ohio: Slavica, pp. 251-65.

Finds similarities in the two writers' attention to the "'significant detail'" and the importance of female characters, but notes contrasting "angles of vision." James recognizes the "possibility of freedom and free will" while Turgenev's view is "inherently pessimistic and essentially Romantic."

105   KENNEDY, ELIZABETH MARIE. "Constance Fenimore Woolson and Henry James: Friendship and Reflections." Ph.D. dissertation, Yale University, 147 pp.

Details Woolson's and James's friendship and its reflection in the work of each writer, including characters, symbols, and themes.
See *Dissertation Abstracts International* 44, no. 9 (1984):2766A-2767A.

106   KERR, HOWARD. "James's Last Early Supernatural Tales: Hawthorne Demagnetized, Poe Depoetized." In *The Haunted Dusk: American Supernatural Fiction, 1820-1920*. Edited by Howard Kerr, John W. Crowley, and Charles L. Crow. Athens: University of Georgia Press, pp. 135-48.
Argues that in "Professor Fargo" James specifically rejects Hawthorne's treatment of the supernatural while in "The Ghostly Rental" he attacks the Gothic poetics of Poe.

107   KOMAR, KATHLEEN L. "Language and Character Delineation in *The Wings of the Dove*." *Twentieth Century Literature* 29, no. 4 (Winter):471-87.
Investigates James's use of language manipulation as a vehicle of characterization for the major characters in the novel. Although James's style is consistent, his use of elements–qualifying phrases, pronominal ambiguity, syntactical inversions–varies with each character. In order to grasp these subtleties of characterization, the reader must "read between the lines."

108   KROOK, DOROTHEA. "Prefigurings in Two Early Stories of Henry James." *Modern Language Studies* 13, no. 4 (Fall):5-21.
Argues that the governess-boy relationship in "Master Eustace" prefigures a similar though more complex relationship in "The Turn of the Screw;" and the "Two Friends/Two Rivals" relationship in "Osborne's Revenge" foreshadows James's development of this pattern throughout his fiction.

109   LABIA, JEAN-JACQUES. "D'une Italie à l'autre: Stendhal in the Carpet." *Revue de Littérature Comparée* 57, no. 3 (July-September):377-93.
In French.
Details Stendhal's influence on the work of James.

1983

110 LAL, MALASHRI. "Hyacinth Robinson's Existential Choice." In *Existentialism in American Literature.* Edited by Ruby Chatterji. Atlantic Highlands, N.J.: Humanities, pp. 110-20.

Argues that Hyacinth's suicide was inevitable given his "existential choice": political idealism or the excellence of art. Lal compares Hyacinth to the Princess, with whom he shares many qualities; the crucial difference, however, is their adherence to their professed principles.

111 LEE, NICHOLAS. "Exposure to European Culture and Self-Discovery for Russians and Americans in the Fiction of Ivan Turgenev and Henry James." In *American Contributions to the Ninth International Congress of Slavists, Kiev, September 1983, II: Literature, Poetics, History.* Edited by Paul Dubreczeny. Columbus, Ohio: Slavica, pp. 267-83.

Compares each writer's treatment of the international theme. James's characters attempt to assimilate the culture of Europe while at the same time preserve their essential Americanness. For Turgenev's characters, "Europe is a set of lessons for taking back to Russia."

*112 LEE, WOO-KUN. "The Real Approach to James's 'The Real Thing.'" *Journal of English Language and Literature* (Kyungpook National University, Taegu, Korea) 2:21-31.

Source: *Annual Bibliography of English Language and Literature* 59 (1984):430, item 7696.

113 LEVINE, PEG ELIZABETH. "The Participant Observer: An American Narrator." Ph.D. dissertation, Ohio State University, 181 pp.

Defines the participant-observer and explores specific traits associated with this narrator, in addition to the ways this narrator affects both the narrative and the reader. This study focuses on Hawthorne's *The Blithedale Romance,* Poe's "The Fall of the House of Usher," Melville's "Bartleby the Scrivener," and James's "Louisa Pallant."

See *Dissertation Abstracts International* 44, no. 4 (1983):1087A.

114 LEVINE, ROBERT T. "A Failure of Reading: *The Aspern Papers* and the Ennobling Force of Literature." *Essays in Arts and Sciences* 12, no. 1 (March):87-98.

Compares the tale's narrator with Jeffrey Aspern to show that the narrator fails as a reader and therefore is not "ennobled" by his understanding of literature.

115 LONG, ROBERT EMMET. *Henry James: The Early Novels*. Twayne United States Authors Series TUSAS 440. Boston: Twayne, 195 pp.

Surveys the early novels, beginning with *Watch and Ward* and concluding with *The Bostonians*. This study includes detailed background information, critical interpretation, sources and influence, discussions of the evolution of the novels and their relationship to each other, and an annotated bibliography of primary and secondary sources. James's early novels are dominated by the international theme and a concern with realism, but above all they celebrate the "consciously lived life."

116 LUBIN, DAVID MARTIN. "Act of Portrayal: Depiction of Character in Works by Thomas Eakins, John Singer Sargent, and Henry James." Ph.D. dissertation, Yale University, 244 pp.

Argues that the conception of character of these three artists was influenced by the economic and political consolidation occurring during the middle of the century; their portraiture is shaped by a "centralization/anti-centralization discourse." Individual chapters examine the operation of this discourse in each artist's work. James's *The Portrait of a Lady* is the subject of one such chapter.

See *Dissertation Abstracts International* 44, no. 9 (1984):2809A.

117 LUCHTING, WOLFGANG A. "Los mecanismos de la ambigüedad: *La juventud en la otra ribera* de Julio Ramón Ribeyro." *Iberomania* 17:131-50.

In Spanish.

118 MacLAINE, DONALD BRENTON. "Absent-Centred Structure in Five Modern Novels: Henry James's *The Princess Casamassima*, Joseph Conrad's *The Secret Agent*, Andrei Bely's *Petersburg*, Joseph

1983

Heller's *Catch-22*, and Thomas Pynchon's *Gravity's Rainbow*." Ph.D dissertation, University of British Columbia.

Identifies the absent center by such devices as indirect narration, anticlimax, and the structuring images of the urban labyrinth or the anarchist explosion. James's novel, which uses these images and the anti-climax, marks the beginning of the "absent-centred structure."

See *Dissertation Abstracts International* 44, no. 5 (1983):1451A.

119   MALTZ, MINNA ANNE HERMAN. "The International Novel: A Study of Its Origins and Emergence as a Genre in Nineteenth Century American Fiction." Ph.D. dissertation, University of Natal (South Africa), 614 pp.

Traces the origins of the international theme, beginning with Irving and continuing through late nineteenth century fiction. Maltz sees James's fiction as the "most accomplished phase of development" and uses it as a basis for evaluating examples of the international theme in Cooper, Hawthorne, Melville, and Howells.

See *Dissertation Abstracts International* 44, no. 4 (1983):1087A.

120   MARSHALL, RICHARD MILTON, Jr. "Henry James and Mark Twain: Public Image versus Literary Reality." Ph.D. dissertation, Purdue University, 175 pp.

Argues that James and Twain are similar in their concern with the International Theme, their celebration of American freshness, and their satirization of American provinciality. Marshall traces these similarities in each writer's major novels and in their nonfiction.

See *Dissertation Abstracts International* 44, no. 9 (1984):2767A.

121   MARTIN, JAY. "Ghostly Rentals, Ghostly Purchases: Haunted Imaginations in James, Twain, and Bellamy." In *The Haunted Dusk: American Supernatural Fiction, 1820-1920*. Edited by Howard Kerr, John W. Crowley, and Charles L. Crow. Athens: University of Georgia Press, pp. 123-31.

Discusses James's, Twain's, and Bellamy's exploration of the unconsciousness. James was slow to focus on the unconscious because of his interest in the consciousness and his dismissal of psychical research. By the late eighties, however, he came to see the unconscious and the consciousness as inseparable. As a result, the unconscious is present in his later work: "Sir Edmund Orme," "The Private Life," "The

Turn of the Screw," "The Great Good Place," "The Jolly Corner," and *The Sense of the Past.*

122   MARTIN, ROBERT K. "James and the 'Ecstatic Vision.'" *Modern Language Studies* 13, no. 4 (Fall):32-38.

Traces James's use of the visionary moment throughout his fiction. These transcendent moments are based in reality and offer insight into human nature.

123   MARTIN, W.R., and OBER, WARREN U. "The Shaping Spirit in James's Last Tales." *English Studies in Canada* 9, no. 3 (September):341-9.

Argue that the first and last tales in *The Finer Grain* – "The Velvet Glove" and "The Bench of Desolation" – are complementary "bookends" to a volume of tales showing the importance of the imagination and art in life. The first tale shows the imagination in power and in action; the last, in abeyance.

124   ____. "'Superior to Oak': The Part of Mora Montravers in James's *The Finer Grain.*" *American Literary Realism, 1870-1910* 16, no. 1 (Spring):121-28.

Show the way in which Mora Montravers, the model and criterion in the tale bearing her name, epitomizes James's "finer grain of accessibility . . . to moving experience." This tale and the others in *The Finer Grain* testify to the power of the imagination.

125   MEDINA, ANGEL. "Edwardian Couples: Aesthetics and Moral Experience in *The Golden Bowl.*" *New Literary History* 15, no. 1 (Autumn):51-71.

Demonstrates that in the novel questions of morality and of identity are intertwined and that the relation between morality and identity is based on "reflectiveness."

126   MEITINGER, SERGE. "Le Cercle du secret." *L'Arc* 89:47-55.
In French.

1983

127 MILLER, JAMES E. "Henry James and the Language of Literature and Criticism." *Revue de Littérature Comparée* 57, no. 3 (July-September):303-13.

   Argues against Todorov's dismissal of James in *The Poetics of Prose*. Todorov quotes James out of context and reduces his work to a formula. Miller focuses on Todorov's discussion of *The Beast in the Jungle* to demonstrate Todorov's misunderstanding of James.

128 MOCHI, GIOVANNA. "Punto di vista e rappresentazione: Riflessioni su una riduzione teatrale de *Aspern Papers* di Henry James" [Point of view and representation: Reflections on a theatrical adaptation of Henry James's "The Aspern Papers"]. *Litterature d'America: Revista Trimestrale* 4, no. 17 (Spring):17-48.

   In Italian.

129 MONTEIRO, GEORGE. "Geography in 'The Siege of London.'" *Henry James Review* 4, no. 2 (Winter):144-45.

   Notes that James corrects the tale's shaky American geography in the New York Edition revision.

130 _____. "'He Do the Police in Different Voices': James's 'The Point of View.'" *Topic* 37 (Fall):3-9.

   Suggests that in this tale no one character is James's spokesman, though there is something of James in each. The form of the tale reflects James's interest in dramatizing a multiplicity of perspectives; its content reflects his ambivalence toward America.

131 _____. "Henry James, Great White Hunter." *Modern Language Studies* 13, no. 4 (Fall):96-108.

   Suggests that Frank R. Stockton's "The Lady, or the Tiger?" and Francis Marion Crawford's *Mr. Isaacs: A Tale of Modern India* may have provided the image of the beast in the jungle for James's tale.

132 MULVEY, CHRISTOPHER. "England: The Aesthetic Landscape." In *Anglo-American Landscapes: Romantic Values in Nineteenth-Century Anglo-American Travel Literature*. New York: Cambridge University Press, pp. 107-22.

Discusses James's response to England, beginning with the "rare emotion" described in "A Passionate Pilgrim" and pervading the essays collected in *English Hours*. While James acknowledged the "ugly things of England," he found elements that were at once foreign and associative and that could energize his imagination.

133 MURPHY, BRENDA. "James's Later Plays: A Reconsideration." *Modern Language Studies* 13, no. 4 (Fall):86-95.
Examines the four plays James wrote during his major phase: *The High Bid, The Outcry, The Other House* and *The Saloon. The High Bid*, a revision of *Summersoft*, reveals Shaw's influence; *The Outcry* is an effective discussion play; *The Other House* bears evidence of Ibsen; and *The Saloon*, the stage adaptation of "Owen Wingrave," employs the new dramatic realism to achieve "a higher aesthetic vision."

134 NALBANTIAN, SUZANNE. "Henry James and the Poetics of Postponement." In *Seeds of Decadence in the Late Nineteenth-Century Novel: A Crisis in Values*. London: Macmillan Press, pp. 37-54, 135-36.
Links James's protagonists who postpone or delay action to the Decadent movement. Nalbantian finds this pattern in *The American, The Portrait of a Lady, The Ambassadors*, and "The Beast in the Jungle."

135 NASSAR, EUGENE PAUL. "Ethical Discontinuity in Henry James's *The Golden Bowl*." In *Essays Critical and Metracritical*. Rutherford: Fairleigh Dickinson University Press, pp. 103-17.
Takes issue with James's withholding evidence of actual adultery between Charlotte and the Prince, calling it a personal failing.

136 "1982-1983 Annual Review: Henry James." *Journal of Modern Literature* 10, nos. 3-4 (November):501-6.
Lists criticism published in 1982-1983.

137 NUSSBAUM, MARTHA CRAVEN. "Flawed Crystals: James's *The Golden Bowl* and Literature as Moral Philosophy." *New Literary History* 15, no. 1 (Autumn):25-50.

1983

Argues that the novel can be seen as a "secular analogue" to the idea of original sin in that it shows human beings as flawed in the search for value. The first half of the novel records Maggie's search for moral perfection; the second half, Maggie's initiation to a fallen world. In addition, the novel acknowledges flawed consciousness, both in its author and its readers.

See also Caws, 1983.36, Gardner 1983.73, Nussbaum 1983.138, Putnam 1983.158, and Wollheim 1983.223.

138 ____. "Reply to Richard Wollheim, Patrick Gardiner, and Hillary Putnam." *New Literary History* 15, no. 1 (Autumn):201-8.

Responds to Wollheim's (1983.223), Gardiner's (1983.73), and Putnam's (1983.158) comments on her essay on *The Golden Bowl* (1983.137).

139 OELSCHLEGEL, LAURENCE E. "Henry James and Meta-metaperspective." *Topic* 37 (Fall):49-50.

Suggests that Maisie's ability to comprehend the perspective of the novel's other characters reveals the complexity of her understanding. Because of her "meta-metaperspective" she can free and separate herself from the "charade" being played out by the other characters.

140 OZICK, CYNTHIA. "The Lesson of the Master." In *Art and Ardor*." New York: Alfred A. Knopf, pp. 291-97.

Reprint of 1982.111, 1983.141.

141 ____. "The Lesson of the Master." In *First Person Singular*. Compiled by Joyce Carol Oates. Princeton: Ontario Review Press, pp. 10-15.

Reprint of 1982.111, 1983.141.

142 PECORA, VINCENT P. "Modernism and the Problem of the Self: Conrad, Joyce, and James." Ph.D. dissertation, Columbia University, 319 pp.

Argues that Conrad's *Heart of Darkness*, Joyce's "The Dead," and James's "The Turn of the Screw" exemplify modernism's "failure of self-consciousness." These narratives explore the mechanisms by which a character preserves a "necessary fiction" of moral behavior.

See *Dissertation Abstracts International* 44, no. 8 (1984):2478A.

143 PEROSA, SERGIO. "Henry James and the Art of Fiction." In *American Theories of the Novel: 1793-1903*. New York: New York University Press, pp. 113-38.

Traces James's theory of fiction, including his early focus on French realism, the "Art of Fiction" debate, the development of a limited point of view, and the use of dramatic elements. James saw the novel offering unlimited possibilities for the capturing, reproducing, and creating of reality. James's views exalted the novel, but they also contributed to its "eventual dissolution from within of its form, function, and role."

144 ____. "Henry James in the Twentieth Century." In *American Theories of the Novel: 1793-1903*. New York: New York University Press, pp. 225-37.

Examines James's mature theory of the novel, based on the prefaces and the essays written after the turn of the century. James believed in the primacy of art and of the imagination, and in the novel's independent and elastic form. James's "valediction" that "art makes life" is his legacy to modern literature.

145 ____. "*Il giro di vite*: Dal racconto di James all'opera di Britten" [*The Turn of the Screw*: From James's tale to Britten's opera]. *Litterature d'America: Revista Trimestrale* 4, no. 17 (Spring):5-16.

In Italian.

146 ____. "James, Tolstoy, and the Novel." *Revue de Littérature Comparée* 57, no. 3 [227] (July-September):359-68.

Examines James's movement from opposition to Tolstoy's novels as "loose, baggy monsters" to an appreciation of them reflecting the richness of life.

147 PERROT, JEAN. "Un Amour de James." *Revue de Littérature Comparée* 57, no. 3 (July-September):275-93.

In French

1983

148 _____. "Un Ecrivain en représentation." *L'Arc* (Aix-en-Provence) 89:22-37.
In French.
Traces the phases in James's personal history in conjunction with the development of his writing, focusing on the play of mirrors that James employed in creating his fiction and his own sense of self. Paradoxically, James's writing, to which he looked for financial support, were nourished by James's image of himself as a writer living only for his art.
See also Saporta 1983.172.

149 PETRY, ALICE HALL. "Jamesian Parody, *Jane Eyre*, and 'The Turn of the Screw.'" *Modern Language Studies* 13, no. 4 (Fall):61-78.
Argues that James undermines the literary tradition of the "plucky English governess" in his tale, which parallels *Jane Eyre* in numerous ways. James's use of Brontë's novel also suggests that the governess is deluded, and that the ghosts do not exist.

*150 PICCINATO, STEFANIA. Introduction to *L'Americano*. Milan: Mondadori, pp. i-liii.
In Italian.
Source: *Annual Bibliography of English Language and Literature* 58 (1983):457, item 8096.

151 POIRIER, RICHARD. "Portrait d'une dame." *L'Arc* 89:38-46.
In French.

152 POOLE, ADRIAN. Introduction to *The Aspern Papers and Other Stories*. Oxford: Oxford University Press, pp. vii-xix.
Suggests that "The Aspern Papers," "The Private Life," "The Middle Years," and "The Death of the Lion" are concerned with "parodies and substitutes and alternatives" for the "intimate and demanding intercourse" of writing and reading.

153 POPOV, NIKOLAJ B. "Klasik na provincialen kontenent" [A classic of a provincial continent]. In *Evropejcite, "portrer na edna dama"* [Europe, *Portrait of a Lady*]. Sofia: Narodna Kultura, pp. 5-19.
In Bulgarian.

154 PRICE, MARTIN. "James: The Logic of Intensity." In *Forms of Life: Character and Moral Imagination in the Novel.* New Haven: Yale University Press, pp. 204-34, 356-57.

Examines James's use of bewilderment in *The Awkward Age* and *The Ambassadors*, arguing that it is central to these novels and to the drama of consciousness. Price sees Vanderbank as tragically divided between two conceptions of life: his own puritanism and his need for rebellion. In Strether, James dramatizes the process whereby accepted beliefs and ideas are questioned and transformed. Thus Price sees James's "intensity" in his depiction of the bewildered consciousness, whether divided against itself or struggling to change and transform itself.

Reprinted 1987.15.

155 PROBERT, K.G. "Christopher Newman and the Artistic American View of Life." *Studies in American Fiction* 11, no. 2 (Autumn):203-15.

Argues that James uses romance and gothic conventions to criticize Newman's "simplistic, manipulative romancing imagination" and his acquisitive, dehumanizing approach to people and things.

156 PROU, SUZANNE. "Le Mal de l'innocence." *L'Arc* (Aix-en-Provence) 89:72-73.

In French.

Suggests that if "The Turn of the Screw" qualifies as a *roman fantastique*, it is due to James's art as a storyteller. The tale's source of horror is not the presence of phantoms but the conflict between adult carnal knowledge and childhood innocence.

157 PURDY, STROTHER B. "To the Editor: Was Henry James Shocked by Pauline Viardot?" *Henry James Review* 5, no. 1 (Fall):78.

Seeks verification that James was shocked by Viardot's gaffe in speaking to one of her servants during dinner.

158 PUTNAM, HILARY. "Taking Rules Seriously—A Response to Martha Nussbaum." *New Literary History* 15, no. 1 (Autumn):193-200.

Disagrees with Nussbaum's "derogatory attitude toward rules and toward the 'Kantian account'" and with her contention that in *The*

1983

Golden Bowl morality is a trade-off between conflicting values. See Nussbaum 1983.137 and 1983.138.

159   REYNOLDS, MARK RIGNEY. "Fatal Facts and Imaginative Needs: Knowledge and Vision in the Fiction of Henry James." Ph.D. dissertation, University of Virginia, 254 pp.
        Argues that James's late style and conception of the novel can be attributed to his concern with the essentially subjective nature of knowledge and the untrustworthy nature of facts.
        See *Dissertation Abstracts International* 45, no. 5 (1984):1400A.

160   RICHARDS, B. "Another Model for Christina Light." *Henry James Review* 5, no. 1 (Fall):60-65.
        Argues that Eleanor Strong served, along with Elena Lowe and other women, as a model for Christina Light.

161   RICHARDS, BERNARD. "Henry James's 'Fawns.'" *Modern Language Studies* 13, no. 4 (Fall):154-68.
        Proposes Surrenden Dering in Kent as the model for Fawns, not the Rothschild palace at Waddesdon, as Tintner (1976.185) suggests. Moreover, the Americans who rented the house, Senator James Donald Cameron and his wife Elizabeth, provided "patterns of social intercourse," and "models of statecraft and diplomacy" for *The Golden Bowl*.

162   _____. "Setting *The Golden Bowl*: Henry James in the Welsh Border Country." *Country Life* 173, no. 4470 (21 April):1022-23.
        Describes James's visit to Pontrilas Court, Herefordshire and suggests that Kentchurch Court, a house in the same district, might have been the inspiration for Matcham in *The Golden Bowl*.

163   RIHOIT, CATHERINE. "Le Fil d'Ariane." *L'Arc* 89:4-17.
        In French.
        Surveys James's major works, arguing that plots can be reduced to cliches; passions and obsessions seem to dissipate upon close analysis. The threads connecting the elusive elements in James's fictions are the substance of his work.

164   ROBSON, W.W. Introduction to *The Portrait of a Lady*. London: Dent, pp. i-xix.
Discusses each of the novel's characters, concluding with a detailed analysis of Isabel Archer. Robson suggests that fear is an important component of Isabel's character: "there is something cautious and theoretical about her" even though the source of her fear remains undefined.

165   ROSENBERG, VICTORIA. "*Washington Square*: 'The Only Good Thing . . . Is the Girl.'" *Dalhousie Review* 63, no. 1 (Spring):54-68.
Argues that Catherine Sloper's "full and moral consciousness" is aptly expressed in the metaphor of the house in Washington Square and that critics, like the novel's characters, have mistaken Catherine as simple, when in fact she is as "strong and solid and dense" as the house.

*166   ROSENBERG, VICTORIA HAMMERLING. "The Journey to 'Intelligent Consciousness' in the Novels of Henry James." Ph.D. dissertation, Dalhousie University, Canada.
Source: Offline Bibliography, BRS Information Technologies, Latham, NY 12100.

167   ROWE, JOHN CARLOS. "What the Thunder Said: James's *Hawthorne* and the American Anxiety of Influence: A Centennial Essay." *Henry James Review* 4, no. 2 (Winter):81-119.
Traces the critical reception of *Hawthorne* from contemporary reviews to Bloom, focusing on the issues of "literary nationality," influence, and tradition. James's book "has been made to play an important role in the general American quest for nationality" in the face of the need for tradition and a desire for originality.

168   SAMSELL, ELLEN CAROL. "American Realists Challenge Conventions, Cliches, and Critics." Ph.D. dissertation, Indiana University, 181 pp.
Shows that the fiction of Crane, Howells, Twain, and James challenged the general culture of nineteenth century America by rejecting traditional character types and formulaic stories to depict everyday people and events. Critics responded to *The Bostonians* with anger, and neglected James's concerns—privacy, individuality, reform, and sexuality.

1983

See *Dissertation Abstracts International* **44**, no. 11 (1984):3384A.

169   SAPORTA, MARC. "L'Avant-Freud." *L'Arc* 89:70-71.
      In French.

170   ____, ed. *Henry James*. Le Revest St. Martin: Le Jas, 108 pp.
      In French.

171   ____. "Et voici Alice." *L'Arc* (Aix-en-Provence) 89:80-84.
      In French.
      Discusses Alice James's chronic ill health and her relationship
to William and Henry. Essay includes two entries from Alice's journal.

172   ____. "Une 'Impénétrable Respectabilité.'" *L'Arc* (Aix-en-Provence)
      89:18-19.
      In French.
      Surveys some of the facts of James's life that may have
contributed to the nervous disorders from which he apparently
suffered. In this preface to Perrot's intellectual portrait of the writer
(see Perrot 1983.148) Saporta notes that biographies of James fail to
explain the neuroses suggested in his writing.

173   SARBU, ALADÁR. "Appearance and Reality in the Later Work of
      Henry James." *John O'Hara Journal* 5, no. 1-2 (Winter):115-22.
      Argues that in *The Ambassadors, The Wings of the Dove,* and
The Golden Bowl the dominant theme is the conflict between
appearance and reality. That theme reflects the conflict between the
moral life and "the social entity"; these novels show that the two are
incompatible.

174   SCHNEIDER, DANIEL J. "The Figure in the Carpet of James's
      Confidence." Henry James Review 4, no. 2 (Winter):120-27.
      Discusses the novel's theme of freedom and enslavement and
James's use of symbols to convey that theme. Schneider sees that the
novel's primary flaw is James's "divided mind:" although he saw tyranny

and aggression, he could not acknowledge "the full ugliness of . . . aggressive egotism."

175   SCHULTZ, ELIZABETH, and YAMAMOTO, FUMIKO. "Ego vs. Relationships in James's *The Golden Bowl* and Sôseki's *Light and Darkness*." *Comparative Literature Studies* 20, no. 1 (Spring):48-65.
      Demonstrates that the fictional worlds of these two contemporaries share many characteristics, including the conflict between past and present. In both novels the writers examine the struggle of husband and wife to attain self-knowledge and sustain love.

176   SCHWARTZ, NINA ELYOT. "Dead Fathers: The Discourses of Modernist Authority." Ph.D. dissertation, University of California, Irvine, 376 pp.
      Draws on semiotic and psychoanalytic theories to argue that "modernist writing represents social authority to be a function of discursive conventions rather than transcendental orders." The fiction of James, Conrad, and Hemingway displaces traditional views of man with determinism thus providing the basis for modernism.
      See *Dissertation Abstracts International* 44, no. 2 (1983):488A.

177   SCOTT, JAMES B. "How the Screw Is Turned: James's *Amusette*." *University of Mississippi Studies in English* 4 (new series):112-31.
      Explains Peter Quint's ghost as Miles dressing in Quint's clothes and playing tricks on the governess and attributes Miles's death to his sudden belief that Quint has returned to punish him.

178   SEIDNER-KEDAR, HELEN. "'Ghosts in the Air of America': Transformation as Theme and Technique in North American Dark Romance." Ph.D. dissertation, University of Toronto.
      Compares Canadian and American dark romance traditions from 1798 to the present, focusing on "transformation." Seidner-Kedar defines transformation as a theme denoting spiritual change and as a technique involving modification of a genre. Transformation and its relation to the romance is analyzed in a number of Canadian and American works, including James's "The Jolly Corner."
      See *Dissertation Abstracts International* 44, no. 10 (1984):3074A.

1983

179 SHAW, VALERIE. "'Artful' Narration: From the Sensation Story to the Scenic Method." In *The Short Story: A Critical Introduction*. London and New York: Longman, pp. 63-81.

Examines the influence of the nineteenth-century French *conte* and the drama on James's short stores, focusing particularly on "The Real Thing." In that tale James perfects the use of the scene that simultaneously typifies characters and reveals changes in relationships between characters.

180 SHERESHEVSKAIA, M.A. "I.S. Turgenev v pis'makh Dzheimsa." *Russkaia Literatura: Istoriko-Literaturnyi Zhurnal* (Leningrad, USSR) 2:133-42.

In Russian.

181 SHIELDS, JOHN C. "*Daisy Miller*: Bogdanovich's Film and James's *Nouvelle*." *Literature/Film Quarterly* 11, no. 2 (Spring):105-11.

Calls Bogdanovich's film a "satiric travesty" of James's novella, and also notes that by shifting the point of view from Winterbourne to himself he creates a "separate and autonomous" work.

182 SIEBERS, TOBIN. "Hesitation, History, and Reading: Henry James's *The Turn of the Screw*." *Texas Studies in Literature and Language* 25, no. 4 (Winter):558-73.

Applies Todorov's concept of hesitation between natural and supernatural explanations of events to James tale. "The Turn of the Screw" thematizes hesitation, but it forces the reader to question not only the opposition between natural and supernatural, but the reading experience itself, subject to changes in "perspective, goals, and signification."

183 SMIT, DAVID. "The Emperor's Later Clothes: An Experiment in Stylistic Theory and the Writing of Henry James." *Iowa Journal of Literary Studies* 4, no. 2:81-90.

Analyzes James's later style, exemplified in *The Ambassadors*, from the perspective of the dualistic theory of language, which holds that "precise expression results from refining a number of options to a single choice but that even a final choice can never exactly reflect reality or a person's state of mind." Smit "revises" several passages from the novel to show that James's meaning could be rendered even if much of his ambiguity is eliminated, thus casting doubt that James's "later idiosyncracies" of style are indeed meaningful.

184 _____. "The Leap of the Beast: The Dramatic Style of Henry James's 'The Beast in the Jungle.'" *Henry James Review* 4, no. 3 (Spring):219-30.

Analyzes the tale's style to show how James uses syntax to create expectations and to resolve suspense. Smit's discussion focuses on conversations within each section of the tale that provide a sense of finality to that section while foreshadowing succeeding sections.

185 SMITH, GEOFFREY D. "How Maisie Knows: The Behavioral Path to Knowledge." *Studies in the Novel* 15, no. 3 (Fall):224-36.

Suggests that Maisie learns from her close observation of behavior in relation to environment and situation and by drawing conclusions from her observations. Her knowledge is greater and sounder than that of the other characters, who rely on "social interaction and verbal deceptions."

186 SMITH, VIRGINIA LLEWELLYN. Introduction to *The Golden Bowl*. Oxford: Oxford University Press, pp. vii-xxxi.

Argues that in this novel James calls into question concepts that form the "solid foundation of the world – love, faith, security." *The Golden Bowl* is the story of Maggie's education, the opening and broadening of her vision, and the transcending of the conventional. Smith also discusses James's use of language and narrative technique in this highly experimental novel.

187 SOKOLIANSKII, M., and TSYBUL'SKAIA, V. "O literature." *Voprosy Literatury* 2:177-210.

In Russian.

188 SOLOMON, PETRE. "Henry James: Lectia maestrului." *România Literăra: Săptăminal de Literatură și Artă Editat de Uniunea Scriitorilor din Republica Socialistu România* 16, no. 31 (August 4):20-21.

In Romania.

1983

189 STAFFORD, WILLIAM T. Note on the Texts in *Novels 1871-1880: Watch and Ward, Roderick Hudson, The American, The European, Confidence*. New York: Library of America, pp. 1269-77.
  Describes the publication history and revisions of these five novels.

190 ____. "To the Editor." *Henry James Review* 4, no. 2 (Winter):80.
  Responds to Newberry (1982.106), citing Lincoln's 1972 discussion of Conrad's use of the horror/whore pun in *Heart of Darkness*. Stafford suggests that James may have borrowed this pun from Conrad.

191 STERN, CAROLYN SIMPSON. "Parties as Reflectors of the Feminine Sensibility: Woolf's *Mrs. Dalloway* Counters James's *The Wings of the Dove*." *Communication Quarterly* 31, no. 2 (Spring):167-73.
  Compares the parties given by Mrs. Dalloway and Milly Theale in the handling of death imagery and as vehicles for communication. Although there are similarities, the crucial differences – James's melodrama and scant detail, Woolf's specificity and manipulation of space to heighten relationship – illuminates "the uniquely feminine elements of women's concerns with communication."

192 STOWE, WILLIAM W. *Balzac, James, and the Realistic Novel*. Princeton: Princeton University Press, xiv, 203 pp.
  Describes Balzac's and James's "systematic realism" as a methodical presentation of a convincing world, using the various systems of this world to structure their texts, so that those texts reproduce the density of experience and force the reader to engage in interpretation. Stowe examines *Le Père Goriot, Illusions Perdues, La Cousine Bette, The American, The Princess Casamassima*, and *The Wings of the Dove*.
  Reprint in part of 1981.146 and 1983.193.

193 ____. "Intelligibility and Entertainment: Balzac and James." *Comparative Literature* 35, no. 1 (Winter):55-69.
  Compares James's and Balzac's "strategies for realism" in *The Awkward Age* and *Une Fille d'Eve*. Both authors created worlds tailored to their fictional aims and engaged the reader's participation in the

fictive world. There is however, a crucial difference between the two writers in terms of content: Balzac focused on the structure of society, while James examined perception and understanding.
Reprinted in 1983.192.

194   STROUT, CUSHING. "Henry James's Dream of the Louvre, 'The Jolly Corner,' and Psychological Interpretation." In *Literature and Psychoanalysis*. Edited by Edith Kruzweil and William Philips. New York: Columbia University Press, pp. 217-31.
Reprint of 1979.144.

195   SUMI, YAEKO. "Jiyū eno Shiren: Henry James—*Aru Fujin no Shozo*" [An ordeal for freedom: *The Portrait of a Lady*]. In *Igirisu Shōsetsu no Joseitachi* [Women in the English novel]. Edited by Yaeko Suni and Naomi Okamura. Tokyo: Keiso Shobo, pp. 169-97.
In Japanese.
Argues that although Isabel makes a fatal mistake in choosing her husband, the way that she confronts her failure and overcomes her predicament must be seen as an achievement of true independence and identity.

196   SWEENEY, GERALD M. "The Deadly Figure in James's Carpet." *Modern Language Studies* 13, no. 4 (Fall):79-85.
Proposes that the theme of "The Figure in the Carpet" concerns artistic questers becoming so obsessed by their search that they lose contact with their own humanity.

197   TAYLOR, GORDON O. "Chapters of Experience: Henry James." In *Studies in Modern American Autobiography*. London: Macmillan Press, pp. 16-40.
Reprint of 1979.148.

198   THOMPSON, PAULA CARLENE. "The Decline of Daisy: Fiction and American Womanhood." Ph.D. dissertation, Ohio State University, 255 pp.
Explores the American girl in the fiction of James, Wharton, Dreiser, and Fitzgerald. Thompson argues that this type, embodied in

1983

Daisy Miller, reflects the "general feeling" of decline in American culture. Daisy's "foibles" become the vices of her successors.

See *Dissertation Abstracts International* 44, no. 9 (1984):2768A-2769A.

199 TIERCE, MIKE. "The Governess's 'White Face of Damnation.'" *American Notes and Queries 21*, no. 9-10 (May-June):137-38.

Suggests that the apparition the governess sees in the glass of the windowpane is her own reflection, which shows that she is "the baffled beast" in "The Turn of the Screw."

200 TINTNER, ADELINE R. "Henry James and Miss Braddon: 'Georgina's Reasons' and the Victorian Sensational Novel." *Essays in Literature* 10, no. 1 (Spring):119-24.

Argues that the tale is not a potboiler but that it is James's "sensation" story using the conventions of the genre as typified in Braddon's fiction. James combines those conventions with his own rigorous standards and draws upon the experimental psychology of the 1880s.

201 _____. "Henry James and the Sleeping Beauty: A Victorian Fantasy on a Fairy-Tale Theme." *Topic* 37 (Fall):10-22.

Examines James's use of the Sleeping Beauty in "Gabrielle de Bergerac," "A Passionate Pilgrim," and "Flickerbridge." In the first two tales, James uses the fairy tale as a metaphor for awakening love, although he gives the Sleeping Beauty a tragic ending. In the third tale, he prevents the Sleeping Beauty from awakening, thus symbolizing his repudiation of women.

202 _____. "Henry James, Orientalist." *Modern Language Studies* 13, no. 4 (Fall):121-53.

Traces the sources and uses of Oriental-images in James's fiction. In his work of the seventies and eighties, James drew from a great diversity of literary and artistic sources. There is an absence of Oriental influence during James's preoccupation with the stage, but in *The Golden Bowl* the writings of Loti and Hunt's painting *The Scapegoat* supply crucial imagery.

203 ____. "Henry James's 'The Pension Beaurepas': 'A Translation into American Terms' of Balzac's *Le Père Goriot.*" *Revue de Littérature Comparée* 57, no. 3 (July-September):369-76.

Traces James's reworking of Balzac's novel in the 1879 tale, noting that James's use of Balzac begins earlier than previously recognized.

Revised 1987.122.

204 ____. "A Jamesian as a Collector." *Professional Rare Bookseller* (Antiquarian Bookseller's Association of America) 6:3-8.

Describes her adventures as a scholar and collector, and the various ways in which each passion ties in with and feeds off the other.

205 ____. "Mothers vs. Daughters in the Fiction of Edith Wharton and Henry James." *AB Bookman's Weekly* 71, no. 23 (6 June):4324-28.

Attributes Wharton's "bad" mothers in part to James's depiction of problematic mother-daughter relationships.

206 ____. "The Museum World of Henry James: The Classical Sculpture Wing." *Trivium* (Dyfed, Wales) 18 (May):87-101.

Examines James's use of classical sculpture as "concrete analogues" in "The Last of the Valerii," *Roderick Hudson*, "The Solution," and "The Tree of Knowledge." The novel and the tales warn of the dangers of using classical sculpture as a model for "lesser talents."

Revised 1986.151.

207 ____. "*Paradise Lost* and *Paradise Regained* in James's *The Wings of the Dove* and *The Golden Bowl.*" *Milton Quarterly* 17, no. 4 (December):125-31.

Reviews James's use of Milton, but concentrates on the similarities of James's two novels to Milton's "twin epics." The structure of *Wings* loosely parallels *Paradise Lost*; the novel's subject concerns temptation and fall; *The Golden Bowl*, modeled on *Paradise Regained*, focuses on regaining a paradise.

Revised 1987.122.

1983

208 _____. "Rudyard Kipling and Wolcott Balestier's Literary Collaboration: A Possible Source for James's 'Collaboration.'" *Henry James Review* 4, no. 2 (Winter):140-43.

Suggests that Kipling's and Balestier's collaboration in *The Naulahka* was the donnée for James's tale, which examines the personal and technical elements of collaboration, especially insofar as two authors can transcend nationality and culture.

209 _____. "A Source for James's 'Maud-Evelyn' in Henry Harland's 'The House of Eulalie.'" *NMAL: Notes on Modern American Literature* 7, no. 2 (Fall):Item 13.

Suggests that in this tale James carries Harland's tale to its logical conclusion. Harland describes grief-stricken parents who build a house for their dead daughter; in James's tale the young man is to pretend to be the daughter's husband.

210 _____. "A Textual Error in *The Spoils of Poynton.*" *Henry James Review* 5, no. 1 (Fall):65.

Notes several errors in a sentence from the New York Edition of the novel and reprints the correct version from the original edition.

211 _____. "An Unpublished Letter of William James." *Manuscripts* 35, no. 2 (Spring):145-48.

Shows that this letter, in which William demonstrates "strong protective feeling" for Henry, calls into question Edel's charge that William resented Henry's success.

212 _____. "W. Somerset Maugham vs. Henry James." *AB Bookman's Weekly* 72, no. 19 (7 November):3092-3120.

Chronicles Maugham's "love-hate" relationship with James, referring to Maugham's criticism of James's work and his use of James's persona and fiction in his own work. Maugham was obsessed with James, whose influence permeates his fiction, but he consistently "[bit] the hand that fed him."

213 TRECHSEL, GISELA BRIGETTE. "The Single Parent in the Fiction of Henry James and Edith Wharton." Ph.D. dissertation, American University, 35 pp.

Examines James's and Wharton's depiction of the single parent in order to illuminate the differences and similarities of the two authors. In each, the single parent reflects changes in society and embodies the conflict resulting when the individual deviates from the norm.

See *Dissertation Abstracts International* 44, no. 2 (1983):491A.

214 WAGENKNECHT, EDWARD. *The Novels of Henry James*. New York: Ungar, vi, 329 pp.

Discusses James's novels from *Watch and Ward* to the unfinished *The Ivory Tower* and *The Sense of the Past*, noting prominent themes, stylistic devices, characters, and plot. A brief biographical sketch is also included. Wagenknecht sees James as "before all else, the novelist of experience imaginatively apprehended."

215 WATTS, EILEEN H. "*The Golden Bowl*: A Theory of Metaphor." *Modern Language Studies* 13, no. 4 (Fall):169-76.

Suggests that metaphor joins reality and experience, resulting in "knowledge by metaphoric implication." *The Golden Bowl* dramatizes metaphor making reality—we know the Prince through the golden bowl.

216 WELLAND, DENNIS. "'Improvised Europeans': Thoughts on an Aspect of Henry James and T.S. Eliot." *Bulletin of the John Rylands University Library of Manchester* 66, no. 1 (Autumn):256-77.

Parallels Adams, James, and Eliot in their attitudes toward America and Europe. All three looked to Europe for a sense of order, rejecting the rush and chaos of the American scene. Yet James and Eliot could only be "improvised" Europeans, because the "nervous self-consciousness" of being an American could never be erased.

217 WESSEL, CATHERINE COX. "Strategies for Survival in James's *The Golden Bowl*." *American Literature* 55, no. 4 (December):576-90.

Examines the novel's animal imagery to show that the characters are involved in a Darwinian struggle for survival. Maggie triumphs because she has power and luck not because her cause is just. The world of the novel, therefore, is neither just nor moral.

1983

218 WESTERVELT, LINDA A. "'The Growing Complexity of Things':
Narrative Technique in *The Portrait of a Lady*." *Journal of Narrative
Technique* 13, no. 2 (Spring):74-85.
Argues that the novel begins as a conventional Victorian novel
but ends as a modern one in that James moves from the opening
chapter's omniscient narrator describing Isabel to the direct
presentation in the vigil chapter.

219 WHITEMAN, BRUCE. "The Henry James Collection at McMaster
University." *Henry James Review* 5, no. 1 (Fall):66-67.
Describes the collection, which contains Simon Nowell-Smith's
extensive collection of James's works.

220 WILLIS, PATRICIA C. "'Tell Me, Tell Me' and Henry James."
Marianne Moore Newsletter 7, nos. 1-2 (Spring-Fall):44-45.
Notes that Moore used passages from William Walsh's 1959
review of James's *Autobiography* in her poem.

*221 WINNER, VIOLA HOPKINS. "The Artist and the Man in 'The
Author of Beltraffio.'" *PMLA* 63:102-8.
Source: Gale (1986.54), p. 128.

222 WOLK, MERLA. "Narration and Nature in *What Maisie Knew*."
Henry James Review 4, no. 3 (Spring):196-206.
Argues that the narrator's relationship to Maisie approximates
that of maternal nurturing. The narrator, "the only reliable guardian of
[Maisie's] interests," creates for her a stable "world of language and
form."

223 WOLLHEIM, RICHARD. "Flawed Crystals: James's *The Golden
Bowl* and the Plausibility of Literature as Moral Philosophy." *New
Literary History* 15, no. 1 (Autumn):185-91.
Disagrees with Nussbaum (1983.137) that the novel can be
read as moral philosophy, although literature is essential to moral
philosophy.
See also Nussbaum 1983.138.

1983

224   ZIEGLER, HEIDE. "James's Central Intelligence and the Deconstruction of Character." *Revue Française d'Etudes Américaines* 8, no. 17 (May):227-38.

Argues that James "deconstructs character by destroying the self as a stable identity in order to reconstruct it in the form of a central intelligence constantly endeavoring to transcend itself"; in so doing James "represents the signifying intention of the text."

1984

1   ADEGAWA, YUKO. "Henry James and His Concept of the Italian Ethos." *Bulletin of Daito Bunka University: The Humanities* 22:95-102.

Surveys James's changing attitudes toward Italy, influenced in part by his relationships with Constance Fenimore Woolson and Hendrick Andersen. In James's later works, Italy expresses the "fusion of sacred and profane love"; in *The Golden Bowl*, the Prince is James's most complete expression of his understanding of Italy.

2   ALLEN, ELIZABETH. *A Woman's Place in the Novels of Henry James*. New York: St. Martin's Press, viii, 223 pp.

Examines James's representation of women in his novels, beginning with *The American* and concluding with *The Golden Bowl*, and in "The Turn of the Screw," "Daisy Miller," and *The Reverberator*. Throughout his fiction, James "attempt[s] to reconcile the contradiction of woman's existence, both as sign and as conscious subject." James's focus on the female consciousness arises out of his exploration of the conflict between sign and self, and Allen's chronological study of his fiction shows that James moves from the American Girl as a sign of consciousness to the woman who "controls how she is seen and what she represents."

Reprinted in part 1987.17.

3   ANDERSON, CHARLES R. Introduction to *The Bostonians*. Harmondsworth, Middlesex, England: Penguin Books, pp. 7-30.

1984

Details the biographical and historical background of the novel, as well as the influence of the French naturalists and Balzac on it. Anderson praises the novel's plot and "the ambiguous nature of the characters" but suggests that James's treatment of Basil Ransom is the novel's major flaw. Anderson also sees this novel as "a satire in the classic tradition" and examines James's use of traditional satiric devices.

4   ANDREWS, TERRY L. "Henry James and Responsible Majesty: Ideals of Authorship in *The Golden Bowl.*" Ph.D. dissertation, Rutgers University, 309 pp.

Argues that this novel is James's greatest because "it is his most compelling both as a realistic novel of individualized characters and social relations, and as a meta-novel of artistic processes." The New York Edition prefaces and "The Lesson of Balzac" (1905) suggest the novel's double nature. Moreover, the novel's preface notes the double nature of the novel's main characters – a double nature that Andrews discusses here.

See *Dissertation Abstracts International* 46, no. 2 (1985):414A-415A.

*5   ARKHIPOV, ANATOLIĬ. "Dva mastera ili tragediia zavisimosti." In *Atti del convegno "Michail Bulgakov": Gargnano del Garda, 17-22 Settembre 1984.* Edited by Eridano Bassarelle and Jitka Křesálková. Milan: Univ. degli Studi di Milano, Instituto di Ling. & Lett. dell'Europa Orientale, pp. 1-17.

Source: *MLA International Bibliography* 1 (1976):171, item 6609.

6   AUCHINCLOSS, LOUIS. *Quotations from Henry James Selected by Louis Auchincloss.* Charlottesville: University Press of Virginia, ix, 167 pp.

Excerpts quotations from James's fiction, criticism, and letters for those "who may find pleasure in a guided browsing in the Master's prose."

7   AUERBACH, JONATHAN. "First Person Singular: Confessional Narrative from Poe to James." Ph.D. dissertation, Johns Hopkins University, 230 pp.

Argues that Poe, Hawthorne, and James use the narrator who is also central character to mock their own confessional impulses. The narrators in "The Aspern Papers," *The Sacred Fount*, and "The Figure in the Carpet" enable James "to define the egocentric imperatives of his craft" without sacrificing the intimacy associated with first-person narrator.

See *Dissertation Abstracts International* 45, no. 3 (1984):847A-848A.

8   AZIZ, MAQBOOL. Introduction to *The Tales of Henry James. Volume III 1875-1879*. Oxford: Clarendon Press, pp. 1-21.

Describes the textual history and biographical background of the tales of this period: "Benvolio," "Crawford's Consistency," "The Ghostly Rental," "Four Meetings," "Theodolinde," "Daisy Miller: A Study," "Longstaff's Marriage," "An International Episode," "The Pension Beaurepas," and "The Diary of a Man of Fifty."

9   BARBOUR, JOHN D. "*The Princess Casamassima* as Tragedy: The Bewilderment of 'A Youth on Whom Nothing Was Lost.'" *Arizona Quarterly* 40, no. 1 (Spring):5-34.

Argues that in this novel James attributes Hyacinth's tragedy to his aesthetic consciousness and his moral sensitivity. These traits, which James clearly admired, are linked to Hyacinth's bewilderment and the events leading to his suicide. Barbour also discusses Hyacinth's stature as a tragic hero and suggests that James saw tragedy as inextricably mixed with life's comedy.

Revised 1984.10.

10   _____. "*The Princess Casamassima* as Tragedy: The Bewilderment of 'A Youth on Whom Nothing Was Lost.'" In *Tragedy as a Critique of Virtue: The Novel and Ethical Reflection*. Chico, Calif.: Scholars Press, pp. 47-67.

Revision of 1984.9.

11   BELL, IAN F.A., ed. Introduction to *Henry James: Fiction as History*. London: Vision Press; Totowa, N.J.: Barnes & Noble, pp. 7-10.

Notes that James deconstructs "the novelistic pretensions of fiction."

1984

12 ____. "Money, History, and Writing in Henry James: Assaying *Washington Square*." In *Henry James: Fiction as History*. London: Vision Press; Totowa, N.J.: Barnes and Noble, pp. 11-48.

Places the novel within the context of the nineteenth-century debate about currency. The novel, influenced by Balzac and Hawthorne, is a critique of a society increasingly concerned with wealth and commodities. Bell relates the indeterminate symbolism of currency to James's concerns in the novel, which are abstractions affecting feeling and behavior. Bell concludes with an analysis of Morris Townsend, who is a victim of the transformation of society and "a paradigm of the conservative resistance to the new."

13 BELL, MILLICENT. "Henry James, Meaning and Unmeaning." *Raritan* 4, no. 2:29-46.

Explores James's "double movement towards and away from the conviction of meaning" throughout his career, discussing novels and short stories. James rejected "traditional systems of meaningfulness"—plot and omniscient narration; but his centers of consciousness enable him to fuse subjectivity and objectivity.

14 ____. "'The Turn of the Screw' and the 'Recherche de L'Absolu.'" In *Henry James: Fiction as History*. Edited by Ian F.A. Bell. London: Vision Press; Totowa, N.J.: Barnes & Noble, pp. 65-81.

Calls the tale a "drama of the self's revelation to itself" and traces the patterns of duplication, reflection, and reversal. Bell attributes the ambiguity of this "moral fable" to the viewpoint in which an assertion can be read as its opposite.

15 BELLRINGER, ALAN W. *The Ambassadors*. London: Allen & Unwin, xv, 189 pp.

Details the novel's genesis, its biographical, social, and historical background, as well as its themes, style, plot, and treatment of the international theme. This volume includes a survey of contemporary and current criticism, in addition to discussions of James's presentation of America and France and his use of Strether to link the two worlds.

16 BENDER, EILEEN T. "'The Question of His Own French': Dialect and Dialectic in *The Ambassadors*." *Henry James Review* 5, no. 2 (Winter):128-34.

Examines the characters' use of French and English to reveal personality traits. Both Chad and Mme. de Vionnet use the languages as masks; Strether's use of language reflects his acceptance of his limitations and his virtues.

17 BENJAMIN, NANCY BERG. "Traditional Enclosed Gardens in Nineteenth-Century American Fiction: The Constriction of Adamic Aspirations." Ph.D. dissertation, University of Houston, 380 pp.

Examines the artificial, enclosed garden (in contrast to R.W.B. Lewis's natural, boundless landscape) in the fiction of Cooper, Hawthorne, and James. In particular, James uses the garden to project a character's psychology and to expose the world as a wilderness. All three writers link their gardens with women, who act as "cicerones to challenge the male isolato's recognized dominance."

See *Dissertation Abstracts International* 45, no. 9 (1985):2873A.

18 BIRD, ALAN. "Suspect Chronology in *The American*." *Notes and Queries* 31, no. 1 (March):70.

Shows that James set the events of the novel at a period during the siege of Paris and the Communard uprising in 1870, making it impossible for Mrs. Tristram to send letters to Newman or attend the theater. Also, Mrs. Tristram (and James, therefore) forgets that Newman has spent six months in California and three months in England.

19 BLAKE, NANCY. "Le Regard de l'autre: Double ou imposture: 'La Bête dans la jungle' de James." *Le Double dans le Romanticisme anglo-américain*. Edited by Christian La Cassagnère. Pubs. de la Faculté des Lettres & Sciences Humaines de l'Univ. de Clermont-Ferrand II 19, pp. 179-89.

In French.

Argues that James develops the theme of the void of the self in "The Beast in the Jungle" through an existential portrayal of the hero's dependence on his reflection in another character and the self-confrontation forced by the loss of this Other. This study of doubling in the relationships of the characters is supported by James's deft use of language to express something without ever saying it.

1984

20   BOGARDUS, RALPH F. *Pictures and Texts: Henry James, A.L. Coburn, and New Ways of Seeing in Literary Culture*. Ann Arbor: UMI Research Press, xv, 249 pp.

Examines the relationship between James's fiction and illustration, focusing on the collaboration between James and Coburn for the New York Edition frontispieces. Bogardus describes Jame's extreme ambivalence to illustrations of his work and his attitudes toward photography within the context of the period, when photography had yet to be accepted as art because it posed the "threat of realism." In his later work, however, James used photographic techniques, particularly the center of consciousness as a camera. The frontispieces of the New York Edition are revolutionary, in that they provide symbols arising out of and complementing the literary text.

This volume includes all the New York Edition frontispieces, other photographs by Coburn, and a selection of contemporary art-photography.

21   BÖKER, UWE. "Wilkie Collins, Henry James und Dr. Carpenters 'Unconscious Celebration'" [Wilkie Collins, Henry James, and Dr. Carpenter's Unconscious Celebration]. *Germanisch-Romanische Monatsschrift* 34, no. 3:323-36.

In German.

22   BRADBURY, NICOLA. "'Nothing that is not there and the nothing that is': The Celebration of Absence in *The Wings of the Dove*." In *Henry James: Fiction as History*. Edited by Ian F.A. Bell. London: Vision Press; Totowa, N.J.: Barnes & Noble, pp. 82-97.

Sees James moving from structuralism in *The Ambassadors* to deconstruction in *The Golden Bowl*, with *The Wings of the Dove* as essentially deconstructive because of Milly's recognition of conflicting intentions and possibilities. Milly is the novel's triumph because she is more powerful in absence than in presence.

23   BRANCH, WATSON. "'The Deeper Psychology': James's Legacy from Hawthorne." *Arizona Quarterly* 40, no. 1 (Spring):67-74.

Suggests that James based the character of Frederick Winterbourne on Giovanni Guasconti of Hawthorne's "Rappacini's Daughter." Just as Guasconti is responsible for the daughter's death, Winterbourne bears moral responsibility for Daisy's death.

24   BROOKS, PETER. Introduction to *The Wings of the Dove*. Oxford: Oxford University Press, pp. vii-xxiii.

Suggests that the primary concern of the novel is the consciousness "engaged in the risky, yet utterly necessary, business of interpretation." Brooks discusses the novel's genesis, sketches its plot, and highlights the novel's melodramatic elements and situations.

25   BROWNSTEIN, RACHEL M. "*The Portrait of a Lady*." In *Becoming a Heroine: Reading About Women in Novels*. Harmondsworth, England: Penguin Books, pp. 239-70, 319-22.

Reprint of 1982.22.

26   BUCKLER, WILLIAM E. "Rereading Henry James Rereading Robert Browning: 'The Novel in *The Ring and the Book*.'" *Henry James Review* 5, no. 2 (Winter):135-45.

Argues that in this essay James's methods mirror Browning's own artistic strategies in *The King and the Book* and that his critical evaluation of the poet still has merit.

27   BUITENHUIS, PETER. "After the Slam of *A Doll's House* Door: Reverberations in the Works of James, Hardy, Ford and Wells." *Mosaic* 17, no. 1 (Winter):83-96.

Discusses the impact of Ibsen's vision of marriage on contemporary British literature and society. James upheld marriage although he depicted it as a prison in *The Portrait of a Lady*. In *The Ambassadors*, however, he recognized that a union could have "a higher, human sanction" than that accorded by law.

28   BUTLER, STEPHEN HENRY. "The Pygmalion Motif and the Crisis of the Creative Process in Modern Fiction." Ph.D. dissertation, Brandeis University, 175 pp.

Argues that the modern writers' attempts to "objectify, animate, and possess their ideal" lead to crisis in which the work of art is regarded ambivalently and in which life and art are confused. James's "The Madonna of the Future" is one of the several works discussed.

See *Dissertation Abstracts International* 45, no. 6 (1984):1743A.

1984

29   CALDER, JENNI. "Cash and the Sex Nexus." In *Sexuality and Victorian Literature*. Tennessee Studies in Literature, edited by Don Richard Cox, vol. 27. Knoxville: University of Tennessee Press, pp. 40-53.

   Discusses Meredith, Gissing, Stevenson, and James on the relation between sex and money. Focusing on *What Maisie Knew* and *The Golden Bowl*, Calder points out that James describes a society in which "the relationship between sex and money was often more intimate than that between men and women."

30   CAMERON, J.M. "History, Realism, and the Work of Henry James." *English Studies in Canada* 10, no. 3 (September):299-316.

   Examines *The Golden Bowl* and *The Wings of the Dove* to show how James uses "solidity of specification" to explore transcendent themes and to achieve tragedy.

31   CARAMELLO, CHARLES. "The Author's Taste, Or, Unturning the Screw." *Dalhousie Review* 64, no. 1 (Spring):36-45.

   Suggests that James was haunted by the tension between mastery, which entails perfection and completion, to life, which entails variation and process. In the New York Edition and in his three "autobiographical reminiscences," James "monumentalizes" himself and at the same time points to the flaws in the monument.

32   CARLSON, SUSAN. "To the Editor." *Henry James Review* 6, no. 4 (Fall):71-74.

   Suggests that although individual works have been examined from the feminist perspective, there is no sense of a "feminist critical community" enriching Jamesian criticism. Carlson discusses *The High Bid* to show how feminist criticism can clarify the choices James makes in depicting characters and using traditional forms. She also includes a bibliography of feminist criticism.

   See also Rowe 1985.125.

33   CERNY, LOTHAR. "Die Wege der Providenz: von Hawthorne zu James" [The paths of fortune: from Hawthorne to James]. In *Anglistentag 1983*. Edited by Jurgen Schlaeger. Giessen, West Germany: Hoffman, pp. 525-42.

   In German.

34 CHAMBERS, ROSS. "Not for the Vulgar? The Question of Readership in 'The Figure in the Carpet.'" In *Story and Situation: Narrative Seduction and the Power of Fiction*. Theory and History of Literature, vol. 12. Minneapolis: University of Minnesota Press, pp. 151-80.

Argues that this tale explores the relationship between critic and text as well as that between critic and lay audience. Chambers discusses many aspects of both relationships, including the issue of power, the role of sexuality and intimacy in the tale, the use of the "reflector" to create uncertainty and unreadability, and the "duality of telling and writing" in the text.

35 CHANG, WANG-ROK. "William James wa Henry James: Pragmatism eui hyangbang eul junksim euro" [Henry James as an pragmatist]. In *Ubo Chang Wang-Rok baska hoegap kinyom nonmyngip* [Essays honoring the sixyieth birthday of Dr. Wang-Rok Chang]. Edited by Ganhang Weewonhoe. Seoul: Tap, pp. 221-66.

In Korean, with English summary.

Demonstrates that James's pragmatism is evident in his life and writing. Many of his recurring themes – the regret for the unlived life and the centrality of growth and experience – are essentially pragmatic. Works discussed include "The Art of Fiction," *The American, The Ambassadors*, "The Turn of the Screw," and "The Jolly Corner."

36 COHEN, PAULA MARANTZ. "*The Golden Bowl*: The 'True' Marriage Realized." In *Portraits of Marriage in Literature*. Edited by Anne C. Hargrove and Maurine Magliocco. Nacomb, Ill.: Essays in Literature, pp. 87-95.

Argues that Maggie's consciousness is animated by love, and at the end of the novel she achieves a moral victory in which personal and social values are brought together.

37 CRAIG, RANDALL. "Reader-Response Criticism and Literary Realism." *Essays in Literature* 11, no. 1 (Spring):113-26.

Examines the problems of applying reader-response criticism to the realistic novel of the nineteenth-century, suggesting that such criticism must expand its scope to include author as well as reader and text. Craig briefly discusses *What Maisie Knew* as an example of James's

1984

concern with his audience as well as with his art: he offers a narrative model for reading activity.

38   CRASNOW, ELLMAN. "James as Janus: Opposition and Economy." In *Henry James: Fiction as History*. Edited by Ian F.A. Bell. London: Vision Press; Totowa, N.J.: Barnes & Noble, pp. 137-155.

Argues that James's non-fiction may be seen as apparent oppositions: impression and expression, passivity and activity, exploitation and conservation. James's *Notebook* scenarios, however, which function as both "pretext" and "metatext," subvert opposition because they are reflexive – James becomes his own reader.

39   CULVER, STUART. "Representing the Author: Henry James, Intellectual Property and the Work of Writing." In *Henry James: Fiction as History*. Edited by Ian F.A. Bell. London: Vision Press; Totowa, N.J.: Barnes & Noble, pp. 114-136.

Discusses the prefaces, which "use the language of financial management to describe the work of composition." The prefaces and the New York Edition show James as an entrepreneur repackaging his work, not as a creator.

40   CULVER, STUART KEITH. "Henry James's New York Edition: The Organic Text and the Mechanics of Publication." Ph.D. dissertation, University of California, Berkeley, 276 pp.

Sees the New York Edition as "a critical representation" of James's career and as an articulation of his authority. Culver examines the New York Edition within the context of the "deluxe edition," discusses James's revisions, and traces James's self-portrait in the prefaces.

See *Dissertation Abstracts International* 46, no. 4 (1985):981A.

41   CURTIS, ANTHONY. Introduction to *The Aspern Papers and The Turn of the Screw*. Harmondsworth, Middlesex, England: Penguin Books, pp. 7-26.

Sees both works as superb examples of the Jamesian tale. Curtis sketches the plot of each, notes some revisions for the New York Edition, and for "The Turn of the Screw" surveys the critical controversy.

42 DAHL, CURTIS. "Lord Lambeth's America: Architecture in James's 'An International Episode.'" *Henry James Review* 5, no. 2 (Winter):80-95.

Details the tale's use of accurate descriptions of New York and Newport, representative architecture of the 1870s, and the symbolic dimension of national architecture – all of which show James to be "a magnificent literary architect." This essay includes illustrations of many of the places and buildings described.

43 D'AQUIN, WILLIAM ARTHUR. "The Politics of Morality: A Study of the Play Element in the Late Novels of Henry James." Ph.D. dissertation, University of Southwestern Louisiana, 204 pp.

Applies the play theories of Huizinga, Caillois, Ehrmann, and Berne to the three novels of the major phase, arguing that such theories illuminate the "thematic dialectics" through which James defines and develops his literary myth. In the early work, play is used to reveal the dialectics of the international theme; in the late work, play reveals how characters create themselves and their world.

See *Dissertation Abstracts International* 46, no. 2 (1985):423A.

44 DEFREN, JUDITH. "The Silent Scream: Patterns of Horror in the Works of Henry James." Ph.D. dissertation, University of Manitoba, Canada.

Argues that horror – a crisis shaking a character's belief in self, others, and society – is central to James's development of character. Defren identifies five patterns of horror: the death of innocence and victimization of the young; the despotism of the family; the well-intentioned destroyer; the betrayal in marriage; and the horror within.

See *Dissertation Abstracts International* 46, no. 1 (1985):151A.

45 DELISSE, LUC. "Le fonds James." *Revue Nouvelle* (Brussels): 11:452-56.

In French.

46 DOTY, KATHLEEN LEILANI. "Fiction into Drama: A Pragmatic Analysis of Dramatic Dialogue in Adaptations." Ph.D. dissertation, University of Washington, 239 pp.

Applies linguistic pragmatics to dialogues in plays that have been adapted from fiction, focusing on questions and answers, deixis

1984

and deictic centering, and conversational implicature. Chapter 3 is devoted to William Archibald's *The Innocents*, adapted from "The Turn of the Screw," in which the playwright transforms thought into actual dialogue.

See *Dissertation Abstracts International* 45, no. 5 (1984):1383A.

47 EDEL, LEON. Introduction to *Henry James Letters Volume 4: 1895-1916*. Cambridge: Harvard University Press, Belknap Press, xiii-xxxi.
Discusses James's sexuality in his personal relationships and his fiction and recounts his friendship with Edith Wharton and with Morton Fullerton. Edel also describes his meetings with Wharton, Fullerton, and Gaillard Lapsley, all of whom offered "a backward glimpse into James's expatriate world."

48 _____. "Walter Berry and the Novelists: Proust, James, and Edith Wharton." *Nineteenth-Century Fiction* 38, no. 4 (March):514-28.
Describes Berry's relationships to James, Proust, and Wharton. Although the majority of the essay is devoted to Wharton, Edel notes that James treated Berry with gently ironic flattery.

49 _____. "Why the Dramatic Arts Embrace Henry James." *New York Times* Section 2, Arts and Leisure (4 March):1, 23.
Attributes the numerous film adaptations of James's novels to "the modernity of his subjects, his singularly accurate psychology, and above all his extraordinary visuality." James invented the "mobile camera" for fiction, and his material exalts the electronic medium rather than catering to it.

50 EDWARDS, LEE R. "'Weddings Be Funerals': Sexuality, Maternity, and Selfhood in *Jude the Obscure, The Awakening*, and *The Portrait of a Lady*." In *Psyche as Hero: Female Heroism and Fictional Form*. Middletown, Conn.: Wesleyan University Press, pp. 104-40.
Discusses the ways in which the traditional marriage plot is altered in these novels so that the heroine has the potential for a wider world of action than did previous heroines. Although Isabel returns to her marriage, she is transformed into a new kind of powerful female figure.

51 ELLIS, JAMES. "The Archaeology of Ancient Rome: Sexual Metaphor in 'The Beast in the Jungle.'" *Henry James Review* 6, no. 1 (Fall):27-31.

Examines the imagery of Rome and of Pompey. Marcher's connection with imperial Rome indicates his grandiose egotism that is doomed to destruction while May's association with Pompey shows her commitment to life and to sexuality. Although at the tale's end Marcher assumes the position of a lover, it is too late: he is a victim of his egotism and his inability to learn from the past.

52 ELLMANN, MAUD. "'The Intimate Difference': Power and Representation in *The Ambassadors*." In *Henry James: Fiction as History*. Edited by Ian F.A. Bell. London: Vision Press; and Totowa, N.J.: Barnes & Noble, pp. 98-113.

Sees the novel as an exploration of political and aesthetic representation in which ambassadors and symbols undermine the power that deputized them.

53 EPSTEIN, JOSEPH. "Henry James: Assailed by the Perception." *New Criterion* 3, no. 3 (November):30-40.

Explores James's sensitivity and sensibility as revealed in Edel's four-volume collection of James's letters. From his early years James was a verbal artist, and throughout his life he evolved a writing style that would reflect the richness and complexity of his mind.

54 ESHUIS, ENNY de BOER. "Reflections on Holland in the Works of Henry James." *Henry James Review* 6, no. 1 (Fall):39-45.

Traces the evolution of James's attitude toward Holland throughout is career in his fiction and nonfiction. In his early work – including *Roderick Hudson, The American*, and *The Europeans* – Holland is seen as a haven but one stifling to the imagination, while in the later work – *The Ambassadors, The Wings of the Dove*, and "Mora Montravers" – Holland becomes a symbol of a tranquil sanctuary.

55 EVANS, JOHN. "Owen Wingrave: A Case for Pacificism." In *The Britten Companion*. Edited by Christopher Palmer. Cambridge: Cambridge University Press, pp. 227-37.

1984

Argues that Britten was attracted to James's tale because he sympathized with James's pacifism. The television opera explores Wingrave's "obsessional" characteristics and Paramore's "sinister nature," and is an uncompromising denunciation of war.

56   FEINSTEIN, HOWARD M. "A Singular Life." In *Becoming William James*. Ithaca: Cornell University Press, pp. 223-35, 361.
      Reprint of 1983.63.

57   _____. "The Use and Abuse of Illness." In *Becoming William James*. Ithaca: Cornell University Press, pp. 182-205, 358-59.
      Discusses the nineteenth century cult of invalidism as a justifiable way of avoiding work, and details William's and Henry's competition to be invalids in order to be sent to Europe to seek a cure.

58   FOGEL, DANIEL MARK. "henry JAMES joyce: The Succession of the Masters." *Journal of Modern Literature* 11, no. 2 (July):199-229.
      Examines James's influence on Joyce, particularly as manifested in *Ulysses*. Joyce's Philip Beaufoy is based on James and the style of "Eumaeus" parodies James's. Fogel traces James's impact on Joyce's early work and concludes that the James figure in *Ulysses* suggests Joyce's "anxiety of influence."

59   _____. "Imaginative Origins: 'Peter Quince at the Clavier' and Henry James." *Wallace Stevens Journal* 8, no. 1 (Spring):22-27.
      Argues that the central trope in Steven's poem may have been suggested by the preface to *The Tempest* (1907), in which James described a "divine musician" improvising at the harpsichord.

60   FOSTER, DENNIS. "Maisie Supposed to Know: Amo(u)ral Analysis." *Henry James Review* 5, no. 3 (Spring):207-16.
      Applies Lacan's paradigm of the relation between self and other to explore Maisie's relation to the adults and the nature of her knowledge.
      See also Rowe 1984.170.

1984

61   FOWLER, VIRGINIA C. *Henry James's American Girl: The Embroidery on the Canvas*. Madison, Wisc.: University of Wisconsin Press, 177 pp.

Traces the growth of the American girl into a mature woman in *The American, The Portrait of a Lady, The Wings of the Dove*, and *The Golden Bowl*, using the developmental theories of Jacques Lacan and R.D. Laing. Fowler also discusses James's analysis of the American girl in *The American Scene*, suggesting that James saw the division of the sexes and the American girl as signs of the problems with American society and culture.

Reprint in part of 1980.53.

62   FREEDMAN, JONATHAN ERNST. "The Quickened Consciousness: Aestheticism in Howells and James." Ph.D. dissertation, Yale University, 470 pp.

Argues that American writers, exemplified by Howells and James, used their encounter with British aestheticism to clarify their own attitudes toward social and moral values of art. James's later work, particularly *The Tragic Muse* and the novels of the major phase, reflect his use of aestheticism as a means to express his own insights.

See *Dissertation Abstracts International* 46, no. 8 (1986):2290A.

63   FREIER, MARY PATRICIA. "'Accessory Invalids' and the 'Central Figure': Illness in the Works of Henry James." Ph.D. dissertation, University of Illinois at Champaign-Urbana, 254 pp.

Demonstrates that while James's depiction of illness in his fiction reflected contemporary medical theories, he did not accept such theories uncritically. Freier also examines James's use of illness as metaphor, as a means of characterization, as a plot device, and as social commentary in such works as *Watch and Ward*, "Daisy Miller," *The Portrait of a Lady*, "The Visits," "The Turn of the Screw," and *The Wings of the Dove*.

See *Dissertation Abstracts International* 45, no. 7 (1985):2101A.

64   FREUNDLIEB, DIETER. "Explaining Interpretation: The Case of Henry James's *The Turn of the Screw*." *Poetics Today* 5, no. 1:79-95.

Argues that understanding interpretation is necessary to explain contradictory interpretations of a text such as James's tale. The concepts of true and false cannot be applied to a literary text in the same way they are applied to an object. Therefore, literary study should

1984

focus not on what a text means, but on how texts are understood and "why certain texts are privileged as literary in our culture."

65   FUNSTON, JUDITH E. "'The Siege of London': James's Dreadful Girl Grown Up." *Arizona Quarterly* 40, no. 1 (Spring):85-96.
    Compares the tale's heroine with Daisy Miller and argues that the differences between the two tales, primarily in narrative technique, show James refining the center of consciousness and moving toward the dramatic presentation of character.

66   _____. "'Xingu': Edith Wharton's Velvet Glove." *Studies in American Fiction* 12, no. 2 (Autumn):227-34.
    Argues that Wharton used this tale to "get back" at James for writing "The Velvet Glove" and to criticize *The Wings of the Dove*.

67   GABLER, JANET A. "The Narrator's Script: James's Complex Narration in *The Bostonians*." *Journal of Narrative Technique* 14, no. 2 (Spring):94-109.
    Demonstrates that the novel's narrative method is carefully controlled and unified by James's use of a narrator to distance himself from an unpopular subject. The "narrator is more engaged with his own drama than with that of his created characters," making this novel one of James's most modern and experimental.

68   GALE, ROBERT L. "Henry James." In *American Literary Scholarship: An Annual/1982*. Edited by J. Albert Robbins. Durham: Duke University Press, pp. 111-26.
    Surveys criticism published in 1982.

69   GARGANO, JAMES W. "'The Patagonia': Henry James at Work." *Arizona Quarterly* 40, no. 1 (Spring):49-65.
    Traces the evolution of this tale from James's notebook entry to finished novella in order to illustrate James's creative process. Special attention is paid to James's development of the narrator and the creation of ancillary characters.

70 GERLACH, JOHN. "Closure in Henry James's Short Fiction." *Journal of Narrative Technique* 14, no. 1 (Winter):60-67.
Suggests that James rejected open-endings for his short stories because of his commitment to "a compressed but fully representational form." James's tales, therefore, are conventional while his novels are innovative.

71 GIRDHARRY, ARNOLD R. "The Circle of Characters in Henry James's *The Portrait of a Lady, The Wings of the Dove*, and *The Golden Bowl.*" *McNeese Review* 30:12-28.
Finds numerous similarities in character and situation in the heroines, heroes, "other" women, confidantes, and minor characters of the three novels. In addition, the novels share a circular pattern centered on marriage.

72 _____. "The Geometry of Marriage in Henry James." *Indian Journal of American Studies* 14, no. 1 (January):119-23.
Examines the "geometric circle of action" in *The Portrait of a Lady, The Wings of the Dove*, and *The Golden Bowl*. The heroines of the three novels search for love and marriage, are tempted and betrayed.

73 GODDEN, RICHARD. "Some Slight Shifts in the Manner of the Novel of Manners." In *Henry James: Fiction as History*. Edited by Ian F.A. Bell. London: Vision Press; Totowa, N.J.: Barnes & Noble, pp. 156-184.
Argues that the novels of James and Fitzgerald reflect a shift in values. James's novels depict the conspicuous leisure and conspicuous consumption typical of an economy that is based on the accumulation of resources; Fitzgerald's novels show an economy based on mass market consumption in which style supplants taste. *The Bostonians*, which Godden discusses in detail, is a harbinger of the shift from accumulation to consumption in its analysis of the relationship between advertising and manners.

74 GOODER, JEAN. "*The Awkward Age*: A Study in Ephemera?" *Cambridge Quarterly* 13, no. 1:21-38.
Rejects the claim that James was divorced from the real world. In *The Awkward Age* James creates a closed, fictional world – but it is

1984

based on James's observation – and reveals the evil of contemporary society.

75 ____. "*The Golden Bowl*, or Ideas of Good and Evil." *Cambridge Quarterly* 13, no. 2:129-46.
    Compares critical commentary on the novel and rejects positive interpretations of its ending. The novel reveals both the power and the danger of the imagination but never resolves this ambiguity.

76 GOODER, R.D. Introduction to *The Bostonians*. Oxford: Oxford University Press, pp. vii-xxxiii.
    Sketches the cultural history of Boston from Puritanism to transcendentalism and suggests that this novel is James's analysis and critique of the consequences of the transcendentalists' optimism.

77 GORDON, H. PAUL. "The Critical Double: Figurative Meaning in Protagoras, James, and Kafka." Ph.D. dissertation, Yale University, 140 pp.
    Examines "the deconstructive pattern of doubling as a model of literary and rhetorical figuration" drawing upon the theories of Aristotle, Richards, Black, Beardsley, Freud, and Jentsch. Gordon then analyzes this pattern in "The Figure in the Carpet," focusing on the figurative references to the figure and on the "chiastic interplay" among the principal characters.
    See *Dissertation Abstracts International* 46, no. 3 (1985):696A.

78 GOSCILO, MARGARET BOZENNA. "The Bastard Hero in the Novel." Ph.D. dissertation, University of Illinois at Champaign-Urbana, 371 pp.
    Argues that the novel is a genre most suited to the "bastard hero" whose alienation matches the novel's "uneasy status outside normative structures." Goscilo contrasts the dynamic heroes of Fielding and Stendhal with Turgenev's and James's passive ones.
    See *Dissertation Abstracts International* 45, no. 7 (1985):2092A.

79 GREENWALD, ELISSA. "The Ruins of Empire: Rereading the Monuments in Hawthorne and James." *CEA Critic* 46, nos. 3-4 (Spring-Summer):48-59.

Demonstrates that Hawthorne's and James's observers appropriate and internalize European ruins as "structures of consciousness." Greenwald focuses on *The Portrait of a Lady* and *The Golden Bowl*. James describes both the transfer of empire and the "tragic sensibility" that accompanies the "inheritance of empire."

80 GREGORY, ROBERT. "Porpoise-iveness with Porpoise: Why Nabokov Called James a Fish." *Henry James Review* 6, no. 1 (Fall):52-59.

Argues that Nabokov attempted to assert his mastery over the text as a rejection of James's surrender of mastery. Nabokov's disclaimers and parodies of James show that James was an influence and a rival. Gregory also sees James's texts as "haunted" by Kantian "purposiveness without a purpose"–that the text provokes unlimited readings even while it gives the illusion of having a "purpose."

81 GRENIER, RICHARD. "*The Bostonians* Inside Out." *Commentary* 78, no. 4 (October):60-65.

Reviews Ivory's film, calling it "one of the most singularly perverse adaptations of classic . . . ever encountered." Ivory turns an antifeminist novel into film depicting Olive's triumph as a feminist.

82 GRIFFIN, SUSAN M. "Seeing Doubles: Reflections of the Self in James's *Sense of the Past*." *Modern Language Quarterly* 45, no. 1 (March):48-60.

Reads the novel as an exploration of knowledge and power, not as James's retreat from the present.

83 ____. "The Selfish Eye: Strether's Principles of Psychology." *American Literature* 56, no. 3 (October):396-409.

Describes James's perceptual psychology as functionalist, so that his observers are actively adjusting to their environment rather than passively receiving it. Strether is always selecting and arranging what he sees. James's active observers refute the claim that James is detached and disengaged from the concerns of real life.

84 GRIGSON, GEOFFREY. Foreword to *A Little Tour in France*. Oxford: Oxford University Press, pp. v-x.

1984

Notes that this book reveals as much about James as it does about France. James is honest in his responses to France; above all, he is urbane "without falseness or condescension."

85   GUILLAUME, ANDRÉ. "The Jamesian Pattern in George Gissing's *New Grub Street.*" *Gissing Newsletter* 20, no. 1 (January):28-33.

Demonstrates that James's *Washington Square* and Gissing's *New Grub Street* possess similarities, including analogous patterns of relationships, sympathetic treatment of the plight of women, and a concern with the "ethics of failure." Such similarities may not be so much a matter of influence as they are indications of the historical development of the novel's technique and subject.

86   GUTIERREZ, DONALD. "The Labyrinth as Myth and Metaphor." *University of Dayton Review* 16, no. 3 (Winter):89-99.

Examines the various meanings of the image of the labyrinth and its use in literature. In "The Jolly Corner" James depicts an internalized labyrinth in Spencer Brydon, who with the assistance of Alice Staverton, his Ariadne, must consolidate his sense of self.

87   HAKIM, ZIAD. "Materialism in the Novels of Howells, James, and Dreiser." Ph.D. dissertation, Southern Illinois University at Carbondale, 144 pp.

Explores the attitudes of James, Howells, and Dreiser to the materialistic values of the post-Civil War period and links literary form to the themes of these authors. James's works discussed here include *The Portrait of a Lady, The Spoils of Poynton, The Wings of the Dove,* and *The Ivory Tower.*

See *Dissertation Abstracts International* 45, no. 8 (1985):2527A.

88   HALTER, PETER. "Is Henry James's 'The Figure in the Carpet' Unreadable?" In *Contemporary Approaches to Narrative.* Edited by Anthony Mortimer. Tübingen, West Germany: Narr, pp. 25-37.

Argues that the tale parallels the quest for understanding a text with the attempt to understand people. Halter focuses on the patterns of relationships in the tale, which suggest that James "shows us we are constantly engaged in reading, deciphering, and interpreting regardless of what we are doing.

89   HENDIN, JOSEPHINE. "What Verena Knew." *New Republic* 3626-3627 (16-23 July):25-29.

Sees the novel as an exploration of the social psychology of desire. Verena, the only character who changes in the novel, loses her sense of identity and her status because of love; Basil is a study of the nature of desire and the mechanisms of seduction.

90   HENDRICKS, SUSAN E. "Henry James as Adapter: *The Portrait of a Lady* and *Can You Forgive Her.*" *Rocky Mountain Review of Language and Literature* 38, nos. 1-2:35-43.

Demonstrates that James drew on Trollope's novel for the major characters in *The Portrait of a Lady* and that James corrects the flaws he saw in Trollope. James transforms Trollope's "pleasant" novel into a "complex study of freedom and responsibility."

91   HERRING, HENRY D. "Constructivist Interpretation: The Value of Cognitive Psychology for Literary Understanding." In *Psychological Perspectives on Literature: Freudian Dissidents and Non-Freudians: A Casebook.* Edited by Joseph Natoli. Hamden, Conn.: Archon, pp. 225-45.

Applies the concepts of cognitive psychology, which examine the relation between thought and action, to literature, using *The Portrait of a Lady* as one of the examples. James gives "incisive cognitive portrayals" of the novel's characters. Herring suggests that a constructivist analysis illuminates Isabel's decision to marry Osmond without having to resort to "tragic fate" as an explanation.

*92   HEYNS, MICHIEL WILLEM. "Unresolved Irony and the Late Novels of Henry James." Ph.D. dissertation, University of Stellenbosch.

Source: *Annual Bibliography of English Language and Literature* 59 (1984):428, item 7667.

93   HIRSCH, DAVID H. "Henry James and the Seal of Love." In *Biblical Patterns in Modern Literature.* Brown Judaic Studies, no. 77. Edited by David H. Hirsch and Nehama Aschkenasy. Chico, Calif.: Scholars Press, pp. 209-26.
Reprint of 1983.90.

1984

94 HOCKS, RICHARD A. and TAYLOR, PAUL. "James Studies 1982: An Analytical Bibliographical Essay." *Henry James Review* 5, no. 3 (Spring):158-86.

Surveys work published on James during 1982, including books and articles.

95 HOWARD, DAVID. "Henry James and 'The Papers.'" In *Henry James: Fiction as History*. Edited by Ian F.A. Bell. London: Vision Pressl; Totowa, N.J.: Barnes & Noble, pp. 49-64.

Examines the tale's three major themes: publicity, religiosity, and violence. Howard sees "The Papers" as an "exuberant representation of a decaying society."

96 HUGHES, CLAIR F. "The Case for Women in Henry James' *The Tragic Muse.*" *Lilium: Journal of Bunkyo Women's College, Hiroshima, Japan* 19:1-10.

Argues that the question of equality of the sexes – social, professional, and political – is central to the novel and examines the characters of Miriam Rooth, Biddy Dormer, and Julia Dallow as facets of this question. Miriam is a "convincing portrait" of a successful professional woman; Biddy in spite of her interest in sculpture chooses the conventional path in marriage; Julia Dallow, the novel's true tragic character, exerts power by influencing others, thus insuring her dependence on those she seeks to control.

97 HUGHSON, LOIS. "History and Biography as Models for Narrative: James's *The Bostonians, The Princess Casamassima*, and *The Tragic Muse.*" *Dickens Studies Annual* 13:261-82.

Argues that in these three novels the mode of biography competes with the mode of history, and that Emersonian consciousness as a structuring agent gives way to action. Unlike Henry Adams, however, in whose late works history triumphs over the individual consciousness, James in his late works reasserts that consciousness as the source of meaning.

98 HUMMA, JOHN B. "James and Fowles: Tradition and Influence." *University of Toronto Quarterly* 54, no. 1 (Fall):79-100.

Demonstrates that James's narrative strategy and "moral foci" anticipate Fowles's fiction, focusing on *The Portrait of a Lady, The*

Ambassadors, The Collector, and *The Magus.* Fowles is part of the "great tradition" of Austen, Eliot, and James by virtue of his vision of morality as necessary for civilization.

99 HYDE, H. MONTGOMERY. "Henry James in His English Home." *Threshold* (Belfast) 34:1-7.
Describes James's acquisition of Lamb House and his domestic staff as well as several anecdotes about James while he lived there.

100 IAN, MARCIA. "The Elaboration of Privacy in *The Wings of the Dove.*" *ELH* 51, no. 1 (Spring):107-36.
Argues that in this novel, self-knowledge precludes knowledge of the other, because the other breaks down boundaries between the self and the world, threatening to annihilate self. Milly surrenders herself to others; Densher experiences the "still communion" within himself and at the end of the novel guards that stillness.

101 INNOCENT, REBECCA MOAKE. "The Frame Tale." Ph.D. dissertation, University of Illinois at Champaign-Urbana, 214 pp.
Examines the effect of the "frame tale" on the narrative in Hardy's "A Few Crusted Characters," James's "The Turn of the Screw," and Barth's "Menelaiad." In James's story, the frame tale contributes ambiguity, forcing the readers to create their own versions of the events at Bly.
See *Dissertation Abstracts International* 45, no. 6 (1984):2087A.

102 JEFFERSON, MARGO. "*The Bostonians* Misses the Boat." *Ms. Magazine* 13, no. 4 (October):33-34.
Sees Ivory's film version of the novel as a failure: although visually handsome, it is socially and psychologically "primitive."

103 JOHNSEN, WILLIAM A. "The Moment of *The American* in *l'Ecriture Judéo-Chrétienne.*" *Henry James Review* 5, no. 3 (Spring):216-20.
Discusses the novel within the context of René Girard's theory of the demythification of sacrificial violence, arguing that Newman turns away from violence and recognizes the sterility of self-sacrifice.

1984

See also Rowe 1984.170.

104   JOHNSON, STUART. "Prelinguistic Consciousness in James's 'Is
       There a Life after Death?'" *Criticism* 26, no. 3 (Summer):245-57.
           Examines James's idea of the transcendent as explored in the
       essay, focusing on the tension between elements of memory and desire.
       This tension runs throughout James's fictions and Johnson traces it in
       "The Altar of the Dead" and "The Great Good Place."

105   JONES, PETER. "Philosophy, Interpretation, and *The Golden
       Bowl*." In *Philosophy and Literature*. Edited by A. Phillips Griffiths.
       Royal Institute of Philosophy Lecture Series, no. 16. Cambridge:
       Cambridge University Press, pp. 211-28.
           Examines the novel's moral dimensions, in which morality
       ought to govern knowledge and action. Maggie rejects Adam's selfish
       and passive mode of being and learns that she must act and take
       responsibility for the consequences of her actions. The novel's moral
       dimension, which arises out of the multiple perspectives of the
       characters, shapes the novel's complex form. Jones concludes by
       suggesting the legitimacy of approaching literature as philosophy;
       James's novel, in its analysis of particular cases, is "one way of doing
       philosophy."

106   JONES, VIVIEN. Introduction to *The Awkward Age*. New York:
       Oxford University Press, pp. vii-xxi.
           Argues that this novel reflects James's interest in the
       contemporary questions raised about women's emancipation,
       education, and sexuality. Jones acknowledges that this is only one
       reading of a highly ambiguous novel.

107   KAEL, PAULINE. "The Woman Question." *The New Yorker* (6
       August):68-72.
           Praises *The Bostonians* as James's most American novel and a
       "marvelous anticipatory look" at modern issues. Ivory's film "is the
       Henry James novel without the revelations"; Vanessa Redgrave's Olive
       is its only redeeming element.

108 KAIRSCHNER, MIMI. "The Traces of Capitalist Patriarchy in the Silences of *The Golden Bowl.*" *Henry James Review* 5, no. 3 (Spring):187-92.

Argues that the silences and lacunae within the text suggest and illuminate Victorian society's patriarchical structures. Kairschner's discussion focuses on Adam Verver as collector and patriarch.

See also Sprinkler 1984.186.

109 KARCHER, CAROLYN L. "Male Vision and Female Revision in James's *The Wings of the Dove* and Wharton's *The House of Mirth.*" *Women's Studies* 10, no. 3:227-44.

Sees James's novel as a "patriarchal attack on female authorship" and as a "patriarchal myth" in which the "monster-woman" is repudiated and the "angel-woman" is enshrined. Wharton's novel is a deliberate rejection of the "patriarchal script" in its exposure of the cultural assumptions confining all women and in its insistence on telling a woman's story from a woman's perspective.

110 KASTON, CARREN. *Imagination and Desire in the Novels of Henry James*. Brunswick, N.J.: Rutgers University Press, xiv, 202 pp.

Examines the theme of renunciation in James's fiction, linking it to the image of the house of fiction in the Prefaces. In renouncing self the protagonist renounces his or her ability to author a fiction. This is apparent in *The American, Washington Square*, and *The Ambassadors* where the protagonists remain in the "parental house of fiction." In *What Maisie Knew, In the Cage*, and *The Golden Bowl* the heroines leave the parental house of fiction to become authors in their own right because they are able to integrate internal and external experience.

Reprint in part of 1976.104, 1980.73; reprinted in part 1987.15.

111 KAUFFMANN, STANLEY. "A Civil War." *New Republic*, no. 3629 (6 August):26-27.

Acknowledges the "perception, taste, and skill" of Ivory's film *The Bostonians* but notes that it fails to capture the novel's "depths and reverberances." Kaufman focuses on the character of Verena, who is not "one of James's better characterizations." Madeline Potter's performance as Verena does nothing to bolster this character.

1984

112   KAZIN, ALFRED. "The James Country." In *An American Procession*. New York: Alfred A. Knopf, pp. 211-34.
      Surveys James's life and work, discussing recurring ideas – the international theme, the loneliness of the artist, the American girl, and moral consciousness. Kazin focuses on *The Portrait of a Lady* and *The Golden Bowl*.

113   KIMBEL, ELLEN. "The American Short Story: 1900-1920." In *The American Short Story 1900-1945: A Critical History*. Edited by Philip Stevick. Boston: Twayne, pp. 35-41.
      Discusses "The Great Good Place," "The Beast in the Jungle," and "The Jolly Corner" briefly. James's early tales dealt with problems of conduct; these later works reflect James's wistful sense of "an experience fraught with possibilities, unpotentiated."

114   KIMMEY, JOHN. "London in *The Portrait of a Lady*." *Henry James Review* 5, no. 2 (Winter):96-99.
      Demonstrates the the novel's three London scenes suggest the conflicting elements of Isabel's character.

115   KIMURA, HARUKO. "Henry James to Margaret Fuller" [Henry James and Margaret Fuller]. *Eigo Seinen* (Tokyo)130:382-84.
      In Japanese.
      Disagrees with Eakin (1976.54) who argues that Isabel Archer and Olive Chancellor were modeled on Margaret Fuller. This seems unlikely because James's comments on Fuller indicate he was not favorably disposed toward her.

116   KUNIHOLM, CAROL CAPRA. "Multiplied Visions: Henry James's *The Better Sort*." Ph.D. dissertation, University of Pennsylvania, 177 pp.
      Examines the complementary, contrasting, and clarifying relationships among the tales in the 1903 collection. These tales focus on "finding a way out of one's own narrow patterns of thought."
      See *Dissertation Abstracts International* 45, no. 6 (1984):1752A.

117 LAIRD, J.T. "Approaches to Fiction: Hardy and Henry James." In *Thomas Hardy Annual No. 2*. Edited by Norman Page. London: Macmillan Press, pp. 41-60.

Attributes the "obtuseness" of James and Hardy in responding to each other's work to their different personalities, backgrounds, and literary theories. Laird focuses on the role of the narrator, morality, realism, and form using *Tess of the d'Urbervilles* and *The Portrait of a Lady* as examples.

118 LANDAU, JOHN. "*The Ambassadors*: The Story of the Story." *Hebrew University Studies in Literature* 12:85-115.

Demonstrates that Strether's unreliability as an ambassador – a representative – "enacts the issues and problems involved in the enterprise of representation." The question of representation pervades many aspects of the novel, including the way characters relate to each other, the analysis of the act of writing, and James's discussion of the novel in the New York Edition preface.

119 LANGLAND, ELIZABETH. "Henry James's Social Aesthetic." In *Society in the Novel*. Chapel Hill: University of North Carolina Press, pp. 114-17.

Suggests that although James inherited George Eliot's "inward" focus on the individual, he did not share her concern for communal values. He emphasized self over community in such novels as *The Ambassadors* and *The Portrait of a Lady*.

*120 LAVIZZARI-RAEUBER, ALEXANDRA. "Künstliche Grenzen. Henry James als Kritiker von George Eliot" [Henry James as a critic of George Eliot]. *Neue Zuricher Zeitung* (27-28 October):67.

In German.

Source: *Annual Bibliography of English Language and Literature* 59 (1984):430, item 7693.

121 LAY, MARY M. "Margaret Drabble's *The Needle's Eye*: Jamesian Perception of Self." *CLA Journal* 28, no. 1 (September):33-45.

Finds numerous parallels between Drabble's novel and *The Ambassadors*, including "fictive worlds" and character portrayal and development.

1984

122   LEE, BRIAN. Introduction to *Washington Square*. Harmondsworth, Middlesex, England: Penguin Books, pp. 7-23.

Sketches the biographical background of this "minor masterpiece of American realism" and the influence of Hawthorne and Balzac on the novel. *Washington Square* is not just a social comedy; ultimately, Catherine Sloper exposes the hidden motives of the other characters.

*123   LEE, WON-YONG. "'The Turn of the Screw': juje eseo bon Miles eui jukum" [The death of Miles in "The Turn of the Screw"]. *Journal of English Language and Literature Chungchong* (Chongju, Korea) 25:19-42.

In Korean.

Source: *Annual Bibliography of English Language and Literature* 59 (1984):430, item 7695.

124   LEE, WOO-KUN. "Henry James eui jakpum e natanan kwanchalja wa 'seeing.'" [The observer and his 'seeing' in Henry James's fiction]. *Journal of Humanities* (Kyungpook National University, Taegu, Korea) 9:81-102.

In Korean with English summary.

Examines the nature of the observer and the evolution of "seeing life" in *Roderick Hudson, The Portrait of a Lady*, and *The Ambassadors*. Both Rowland Mallet and Ralph Touchett are detached observers, living a vicarious life; Lambert Strether is, like James, an active observer and a creative artist for whom observing becomes living.

125   LEEMING, DAVID ADAMS. "Henry James's 'Self-Made Man.'" In *From Rags to Riches: Le Mythe du self-made man*. Edited by Serge Ricard. Aix-en-Provence: Pubs. Univ. de Provence, pp. 71-82.

Sees Christopher Newman as James's self-made man. By denying Newman his fairy-tale princess James transcends the myth by showing that moral growth is more important than material success. Twenty-seven years later in *The Ambassadors* James explores in detail Strether's progress from "the rags of ignorance and moralistic prejudice to the riches of awareness and full exposure to life."

126 LESSER, WENDY. "Peeping through the Apertures: Henry James's Melodramatic Reader." *Southwest Review* 69, no. 3 (Summer):266-77.

Defines melodrama as "a form in which the reader . . . can be both inside and outside the suffering characters" and argues that in James's fiction – particularly in *The Princess Casamassima, The Wings of the Dove*, and "The Beast in the Jungle" – readers and characters participate in melodrama.

127 LEVY, JUDITH. "'The Aspern Papers': A Lacanian Reading." *Hebrew University Studies in Literature* 12:65-84.

Examines the "unarticulated force" in the novella, which governs its form and theme but which is not derived from the characters or events. Although other critics have attempted to explain this hidden core, Levy argues that there is an "unconscious intention" with the text to repeat and displace internally the obscurity and concealment that form the subject of the text.

128 LEWIS, R.W.B. Foreword to *The Art of the Novel: Critical Prefaces by Henry James*. Edited by R.P. Blackmur. New York: Charles Scribner's Sons, pp. Reprint. Boston: Northeastern University Press, pp. vii-xiii.

Describes the provenance of the prefaces, seeing them as an unrivaled "evocation of a creative energy and a shaping power," and briefly sketches Blackmur's career.

129 ____. "The Names of Action: Henry James in the Early 1870's." *Nineteenth-Century Fiction* 38, no. 4 (March):467-91.

Excerpts portions of an "ongoing work," *The Jameses: A Family Narrative*. R.W.B. Lewis describes Henry James's travels in Italy, his reaction to Minny Temple's death, and his writing of *Roderick Hudson*. For Lewis, central to the novel is the conflict between creativity and emotion, which can be traced in James's responses to Italy and Minny.

130 LEWIS, ROGER. "The Child and the Man in Max Beerbohm." *English Literature in Transition* 27, no. 4:296-303.

Argues that Beerbohm rejected and satirized Victorian seriousness. Lewis briefly discusses Beerbohm's caricature of James crouching at a bedroom door, staring at two pairs of shoes. This

1984

caricature, one of Beerbohm's masterpieces, depicts the writer as a trespasser and predator.

131 LIBRACH, RONALD SCOTT. "Phenomenology and Hermeneutics: The Mind's Metaphors for Itself." Ph.D. dissertation, University of Missouri-Columbia, 330 pp.
   Examines the reader's congnitive response to narrative texts using the theories of Husserl, Poulet, Heidegger, and Ingarden. Chapter 2 applies the phenomenological method to James's "The Real Thing."
   See *Dissertation Abstracts International* 45, no. 8 (1985):2515A.

132 LICHTENBERG, JOSEPH D. "The Late Works and Styles of Eugene O'Neill, Henry James, and Ludwig von Beethoven." In *Psychoanalysis: The Vital Issues.* Vol. 1: *Psychoanalysis as an Intellectual Discipline.* Edited by John E. Gedo and George H. Pollock. Emotions and Behavior Monographs, no. 2. New York: International Universities Press, pp. 297-320.
   Finds a similar pattern in the life of these artists in which each man, after a period of success, suffers a trauma, and by drawing on his past and the "aesthetic traditions of his art," evolves a new style. Lichtenberg attributes various aspects of James's late style to his disastrous venture in the theater. These aspects include dramatic elements, idiosyncratic sentence structure and metaphor, the use of symbolism as a unifying device, irony, and suspense.

133 LONG, ROBERT EMMET. "Dramatizing James: *The Bostonians* as a Film." *Henry James Review* 6, no. 1 (Fall):75-78.
   Praises the film as an adaptation, not transcription, of James's novel, noting that the Merchant-Ivory production is "an amalgam of James's characters and insights and Howells' close social realism." Although James's material is difficult to translate into film, this film is a "lesson in imaginative handling."

134 McWHIRTER, DAVID BRUCE. "From Desire to Love: The Late Novels of Henry James." Ph.D dissertation, University of Virginia, 387 pp.
   Argues that the novels of the major phase reflect a radical change in James's conception of love. In his earlier work, James denied

his characters the fulfillment of love. *The Ambassadors* is a culmination of James's commitment to desire in that Strether rejects fulfillment for "a rich imaginative freedom" divorced from reality. *The Wings of the Dove* is a critique of desire: James's use of the multiple consciousness ultimately validates characters' ability to choose based on desire. In *The Golden Bowl*, James transforms desire's "infinite but illusory imaginings" into the limited reality of love.

See *Dissertation Abstracts International* 46, no. 1 (1985):153A.

135 MAID, BARRY M. "*The Ambassadors*: Henry James's Playground in Paris." *Arizona Quarterly* 40, no. 1 (Spring):75-84.

Argues that James depicted Europe and especially Paris as a place where play—as defined by Johan Huizinga—is possible in a way it is not in the United States. Paris offers Strether the personal freedom essential for play.

136 MALTZ, MINNA HERMAN. "The American Vision of Europe in Howell's *Indian Summer* and James's *The Ambassadors*." *Unisa English Studies* (University of South Africa, Pretoria) 22, no. 1:14-16.

Discusses the resemblances and differences in the treatment of the international theme in these novels, suggesting that Howells's was a "seminal influence" on James's. Both novels develop the "too late" theme within the symbolic context of Europe. James's novel, however, is a much more fully realized international novel than Howells's because it dramatizes not only a contrast of manner but the polarity of moral values as well.

137 MARTIN, W.R. "'The Eye of Mr. Ruskin': James's Views on Venetian Artists." *Henry James Review* 5, no. 2 (Winter):107-116.

Traces Ruskin's influence on James's reponses to Venetian paintings. Ruskin was crucial in shaping James's appreciation of various artists—most notably Tintoretto—although in later years James was critical of the writer. Tintoretto came to be an influence in James's art: his use of bold gestures corresponds to James's "profound inner dramas."

138 _____ and OBER, WARREN U. "Henry James and 'Bloodgood.'" *American Notes and Queries* 23, nos. 1-2 (September-October):14-15.

1984

Suggests that James may have based the character of Phil Bloodgood in "A Round of Visits" on Dr. Joseph Colt Bloodgood at Johns Hopkins University Hospital who may have been James's cicerone when he visited the hospital during his last American tour.

139   MAYER, CHARLES W. "Drabble and James: 'A Voyage to Cythera' and 'In the Cage.'" *Studies in Short Fiction* 21, no. 1 (Winter):57-63.

Traces the parallels in theme, character, plot, and narrative method of the two tales. Although Drabble criticizes James's "rarified analyses of the mind," she is committed to the Jamesian approach to consciousness.

140   MAYHEW, PAULA HOOPER. "Narrative Theory: Henry James and H.G. Wells." Ph.D. dissertation, Princeton University, 194 pp.

Compares each writer's "aesthetics of the novel," showing that in spite of his disagreement with James, Wells was influenced by James's narrative theory. Mayhew concludes that although theories of current critics such as Barthes, Genette, Banfield, and Cohn may discount James's and Wells's concerns, these two writers were instrumental in shaping modern narratology.

See *Dissertation Abstracts International* 45, no. 6 (1984):1760A.

141   MELLERS, WILFRID. "Turning the Screw." In *The Britten Companion*. Edited by Christopher Palmer. Cambridge: Cambridge University Press, pp. 144-52.

Shows how Britten's music for the opera parallels James's "poetic vision": Britten's music "reveals the inextricable warp and woof of the natural and supernatural."

142   MIALL, DAVID S. "Designed Horror: James's Vision of Evil in 'The Turn of the Screw.'" *Nineteenth-Century Fiction* 39, no. 3 (December):305-27.

Draws parallels between the Morton apparitions in 1892 and James's tale. Miall argues that James's ghosts are real and are evil, but they are not the agents of evil; the point of the tale is to show that evil lies within the governess and within ourselves. In his discussion Miall draws upon the work of Banta's *Henry James and the Occult* (1972) and Freud's essay, "The Uncanny."

143 MITCHELL, JULIET. *"What Maisie Knew*: Portrait of the Artist as a Young Girl." In *Women: The Longest Revolution*. London: Virago, pp. 171-94.

Reprint of essay from *The Air of Reality: New Essays on Henry James*, edited by John Goode, 1972.

144 MOON, HEATH. "A Freudian Boondoggle: The Case of James's 'The Marriages.'" *Arizona Quarterly* 40, no. 1 (Spring):35-48.

Rejects Freudian interpretations of this tale that hold Adela has a neurotic attachment to her father. Moon argues that "The Marriages" is a critique of British society, in which the vulgar nouveau-riche are rising at the expense of the old, upper class families.

145 MOORE, GEOFFREY. Introduction to *The Portrait of a Lady*. Harmondsworth, Middlesex, England: Penguin Books, pp. 7-38.

Traces the plot in detail, noting the strengths and weaknesses. The first part of the book, which focuses on the international contrast, is overly long and has a "prissy" style; the second part is a romance, marked by tighter prose and James's ambivalence toward Isabel.

146 MOORE, RAYBURN S. "A 'Literary-Gossippy Friendship': Henry James's Letters to Edmund Gosse." *Southern Review* 20, no. 3 (July):570-90.

Reprints a selection of letters to show the range of personal and literary interests James and Gosse shared. The correspondence ranges from the years 1882 to 1915 and reveals James's side of a ripening friendship.

147 NATHAN, RHODA B. "The Farce That Failed: James's *The Spoils of Poynton*." *Journal of Narrative Technique* 14, no. 2 (Spring):110-23.

Suggests that the novel began as a farce and ended as a melodrama but failed to be either. James loses sympathy with Mrs. Gereth part of the way through the book, which may explain the lack of consistency, the use of two genres, and the unambiguous ending.

148 NIGRO, AUGUST J. "Coming of Age in America: The Education of Lambert Strether." In *The Diagonal Line: Separation and*

1984

Reparation in American Literature. Selinsgrove: Susquehanna University Press, pp. 98-106.

Argues that the novel's vision of Strether is an ironic one: although Strether expands his consciousness, he cannot act in accordance with his widened perspective.

149 "1983-1984 Annual Review: Henry James." *Journal of Modern Literature* 11, no. 3-4 (November):458-61.

Lists criticism on James published in 1983-1984.

150 NORDLOH, DAVID J. "First Appearances of Henry James's 'The Real Thing': The McClure Papers as a Bibliographical Resources." *Papers of the Bibliographical Society of America* 78, no. 1:69-71.

Notes that the tale appeared similtanously in eight newspapers in the McClure syndicate. The McClure letterbooks, therefore, can identify publications in newspapers and can provide information on the dissemination of texts.

151 OAKES, RANDY W. "Faces of the Master in Roth's *The Ghost Writer.*" *NMAL: Notes on Modern American Literature* 8 (Autumn):Item 11.

Suggests that the writer Lonoff is Roth's version of Dencombe in James's "The Middle Years."

152 O'CONNOR, LEO F. "Henry James: The Occult in New England." In *Religion in The American Novel.* Lanham, Md: University Press of America, pp. 162-69.

Suggests that *The Bostonians* is James's reaction to the fads in religion following the Civil War. James depicts a war of ideologies in a time of transition.

153 OLNEY, JAMES. "Psychology, Memory, and Autobiography: William and Henry James." *Henry James Review* 6, no. 1 (Fall):46-51.

Argues that there are similarities in William's theory of memory and Henry's depiction of the consciousness in his fiction and autobiography. For both brothers, memory is essentially creative; it "renews and recreates the self and makes it one with all the successive past selves."

154 PAGE, NORMAN, Ed. *Henry James: Interviews and Recollections*. New York: St. Martin's Press, xxii, 158 pp.
   Reprints others' recollections of James, primarily in his later years. The excerpts are arranged by topic rather than chronologically.

155 PARK, CHANG-DO. "Henry James eui gukje sanghwang juje" [The international theme in Henry James's novels]. In *Ubo Chang Wang-Rok baska hoegap kinyom nonmungip* [Essays honoring the sixtieth birthday of Dr. Wang-Rok Chang]. Edited by Ganhang Weewonhoe. Seoul: Tap, pp. 414-24.
   In Korean.

156 PARKER, HERSHEL. "The Authority of the Revised Text and the Disappearance of the Author: What Critics of Henry James Did with Textual Evidence in the Heyday of the New Criticism." In *Flawed Texts and Verbal Icons: Literary Authority in American Fiction*. Evanston: Northwestern, pp. 85-114.
   Surveys the problems created when original editions and author's revisions are ignored, using James scholarship as an example. In so doing Parker exposes the limitations of New Criticism, which has continued to affect work on James.
   Revision in part 1984.157.

157 _____. "Henry James 'In the Wood': Sequence and Significances of His Literary Labors, 1905-1907." *Nineteenth-Century Fiction* 38, no. 4 (March):492-513.
   Revised 1984.156.

158 PELZER, LINDA CLAYCOMB. "Henry James and the Rhetoric of Gesture." Ph.D. dissertation, University of Notre Dame, 227 pp.
   Examines the sources, development, and purpose of James's use of gesture and body-language–a "non-verbal rhetoric." This rhetoric derives from drama; James employs this visual rhetoric to render consciousness, control point of view, and clarify meaning.
   See *Dissertation Abstracts International* 45, no. 6 (1984):1754A.

159 PETRAS, IRINA. "Intensitatea iluziei la Henry James" [Intensity of illusion in Henry James]. *Steaua* 35, no. 5:42.

1984

In Romanian.

160 POWERS, LYALL H. "Henry James and James Baldwin." *Modern Fiction Studies* 30, no. 4 (Winter):651-67.

Traces James's influence on Baldwin, especially as manifested in *Another Country*. Powers notes the many references and echoes in the novel, but argues that James's vision of the "complex fate" of the American artist illuminates Baldwin's work.

161 PREYER, ROBERT O. "Breaking Out: The English Assimilation of Continental Thought in Nineteenth-Century Rome." *Browning Institute Studies* 12:53-72.

Discusses British reponses to Rome, noting that the city "occasions the consciousness of an alternative time sense" where the past shapes the present and the future, creating "an imprisoning narrative pattern of before and after." Preyer briefly mentions both Henry and William James's reponses to Rome.

162 QUINN, ETHEL MARGARET. "Henry James and the Real Thing." Ph.D. dissertation, University of Oregon, 314 pp.

Examines the imagery in *The Portrait of a Lady*, *The Spoils of Poynton*, *The Wings of the Dove*, and *The Golden Bowl*, focusing on the "negative patterns" illustrate the nature of reality implicit in the perceptions of the characters. Quinn's analysis reveals the dynamic power of intention as a catalyst for action.

See *Dissertation Abstracts International* 46, no. 2 (1985):426A.

163 RADIN, VICTORIA. "*The Aspern Papers*." *Plays and Players*, no. 368 (May):27-28.

Reviews Michael Redgrave's adaptation of the tale for the stage, noting that the play does not capture the narrator's irony, the spectator's interest, nor the "battle of wits" between Juliana and Henry Jarvis.

164 RAWLINGS, PETER. Introduction to *Henry James' Shorter Masterpieces*. Vol. 1. Edited by Peter Rawlings. Totowa, N.J.: Barnes & Noble, pp. ix-xxvi.

Discusses James's tales of the 1890s, collected in this volume and its companion, sketching each tale's theme and narrative technique. Tales included in this volume: "Brooksmith," "The Chaperon," "Nona Vincent," "The Middle Years," "The Death of the Lion," and "The Coxon Fund." In these tales, James's focus is on the characters' reflections about events rather than on the events themselves.

165 _____. Introduction to *Henry James' Shorter Masterpieces*. Vol. 2. Edited by Peter Rawlings. Totowa, N.J.: Barnes & Noble, pp. ix-xxiv.
Describes plot, theme, and technique of the tales included in this volume: "The Next Time," "The Figure in the Carpet," "The Way It Came," "John Delavoy," "Paste," and "The Great Good Place." A recurring motif in these stories is retreat and its implications for the characters.

166 REESMAN, JEANNE CAMPBELL. "'Interest' and 'Design': Narrative Epistemology in the Late Novels of Henry James and William Faulkner." Ph.D. dissertation, University of Pennsylvania, 579 pp.
Compares James's and Faulkner's treatment of the problem of knowledge in their late novels: *The Ambassadors, The Golden Bowl, Absalom! Absalom!*, and *Go Down Moses*. In these novels, knowledge is connected to power, freedom, and authority; knowledge is thus related to moral dangers. These novels demand "an hermeneutics of knowledge," not an epistemology, in order to be read.
See *Dissertation Abstracts International* 45, no. 7 (1985):2105A.

167 REYNOLDS, MARK. "Counting the Costs: The Infirmity of Art and *The Golden Bowl*." *Henry James Review* 6, no. 1 (Fall):15-26.
Compares Charlotte's and Maggie's use of art, arguing that in the novel's first book Charlotte imposes her own meaning on appearances, while in the second book Maggie, though manipulating appearances like Charlotte, does so to discover meaning.

168 ROBBINS, BRUCE. "Shooting Off James's Blanks: Theory, Politics, and *The Turn of the Screw*." *Henry James Review* 5, no. 3 (Spring):192-99.
Surveys current critical theory on textual ambiguity, noting it is crucial that "distinctly political criticism" respects the open-endedness

of text and does not claim a final, totalitarian "Truth." Robbins then proposes his own "critical narrative" based on the governess's illusion of her "otherness" from the ghost.

See also Sprinkler 1984.186.

169   ROBSON, W.W. Introduction to *The Golden Bowl*. London: Dent, pp. v-xviii.

Attributes the novel's difficulties to James's late style, elements of which are briefly discussed, and to "the balance of sympathy" – the reader is never sure which character deserves sympathy.

170   ROWE, JOHN CARLOS. "After Freud: Henry James and Psychoanalysis." *Henry James Review* 5, no. 3 (Spring):226-32.

Responds to Johnsen (1984.103), Foster (1984.60), and Winnett (1984.227), acknowledging that these essays "raise fundamental questions about literary function" thus forcing us to question boundaries between disciplines. Rowe suggests, however, that there are formalist tendencies in these antiformalist approaches.

171   _____. *The Theoretical Dimensions of Henry James*. Wisconsin Project on American Writers. Madison: University of Wisconsin Press, xv, 288 pp.

Examines the idea of "author" and its implications for the study and criticism of literature using James as a point of reference. Rowe approaches James and a variety of his works from the perspective of a range of critical theories, including the psychology of influence, reader-response, feminism, Marxism, psychoanalysis, and phenomenology. The discussion covers many of James's works, both fiction and nonfiction; the following receive more extensive treatment: *The Ambassadors, The American Scene*, "The Art of Fiction," "The Aspern Papers," *The Bostonians*, "Greville Fane," *Hawthorne, The Portrait of a Lady*, The New York Edition prefaces, *The Princess Casamassima, The Spoils of Poynton*, and "The Turn of the Screw." Although this study is focused on James, Rowe argues that "the concept of author as a discursive force with social and textual power" is applicable to American literature in general, because the novel has helped to "disguise and idealize the alienation, fragmentation, and isolation so characteristic of modern life."

172   SALE, ROGER. "Henry James." In *Literary Inheritance*. Amherst: University of Massachusetts Press, pp. 155-201.

Discusses James's relation to George Eliot, using *The Portrait of a Lady* and *Daniel Deronda* as comparisons. Eliot's impulse is to be broad, inclusive; James's is to "clos[e] the window on the large world" and to place himself above that world. *The Portrait of a Lady*, particularly its enigmatic ending, was James's criticism of Eliot's conception of the novel and an attempt to master her.

173   SCHEICK, WILLIAM J. "Fictional Structure and Ethics in the Edwardian, Modern and Contemporary Novel." *Philological Quarterly* 62 (Summer):287-311.

Argues that Edwardian novels show a positive correspondence between authorial interest in "fictional architecture" and in authorial concern with ethical matters while modernist fiction tends to dismantle this correspondence. James's novels are at the juncture of Edwardian and modernist fiction because of James's concern with moral values and his "modernist" focus on character rather than on structure.

174   SCHNEIDER, DANIEL J. "James and Conrad: The Psychological Premises." *Henry James Review* 6, no. 4 (Fall):32-38.

Argues that both authors share a similar view that human behavior is motivated by the conflict between passion and morality. This conflict is explored in three themes: needing to maintain an ideal image of self, craving for peace and security, and developing determinism based on naturalism and existential responsibility. Schneider examines these themes in *The Spoils of Poynton, The Golden Bowl, Lord Jim*, and *The Nigger of the Narcissus*.

175   SELTZER, MARK. *Henry James and the Art of Power*. Ithaca: Cornell University Press, 200 pp.

Argues that there is a continuity between art and power in James's fiction, using Foucault's analyses of social discipline and regulation. James's work exemplifies Foucauldian double agency because "the Jamesian aesthetic is elaborated precisely as a way of dissimulating and disavowing the immanence of power in the novel." In this context Seltzer examines *The Princess Casamassima, The Golden Bowl*, and *The American Scene*.

Reprint in part of 1981.130, 1982.134, and 1984.176. Reprint in part 1987.15.

1984

176 _____. "James, Pleasure, Power." *Henry James Review* 5, no. 3 (Spring):199-203.

Argues that literature's disavowal of power underwrites the very power it disavows, and cites James's "the Lesson of Balzac" and *The Golden Bowl* as examples of this "double discourse." Selzer sees the exercise of power in James's aesthetic and in Maggie's manipulation of the other characters.

Reprinted 1984.175.

See also Sprinkler 1984.186.

177 SHARMA, JATINDRA KUMAR. "Response to Alien Culture in Henry James and Raja Rao: Comparative Observations on *The American* and *The Serpent and the Rope*." *Panjab University Research Bulletin (Arts)* 15, no. 1 (April):11-25.

Examines the similarities between these two novels of exile. Both use an international setting, and both attribute failed relationships to individual choices. The protagonist in each novel must seek self-realization and at the same time understand his place in the larger social world.

178 SHELSTON, ALAN, Ed. *Henry James: "Washington Square" and "The Portrait of a Lady": A Casebook*. London: Macmillan Press, 210 pp.

This volume includes "extracts" from James's notebooks, contemporary reviews, and recent criticism:

Alan Shelston, Introduction, pp. 8-21. Highlights critical opinion concerning these two novels during the years covered in this anthology–1880 to 1976. Shelston also suggests that these two novels are in many ways complementary in terms of James's relationship to America, his use of the "portrait," and his development of the American girl.

Q.D. Leavis, "The Father's Tragedy Too," p. 42 from "The Institution of Henry James," *Scrutiny* 15, no. 1 (December 1947):74;

Mary McCarthy, "*The Heiress*: A Dramatisation," pp. 43-44 from "Four Well-Made Plays" (1948) reprinted in *Sights and Spectacles* (1956, 1959), pp. 123-25;

F.W. Dupee, "A Small But Real Triumph," pp. 45-46 from *Henry James* (1951), pp. 63-65;

Richard Poirier, "Melodrama, Irony and the Comic Method," pp. 46-59 from *The Comic Sense of Henry James* (1960), pp. 166-82;

John Lucas, "The Social Context," pp. 59-70 from "*Washington Square*" in *The Air of Reality* (1972), pp. 36-48;

1984

Richard Chase, "Metaphor in *The Portrait*," pp. 125-31 from *The American Novel and Its Tradition* (1957), pp. 120-28;
Leon Edel, "Two Studies in Egotism," pp. 131-40 from *Henry James*, 2 vols. (1977), v. 1, pp. 614-22;
Dorothea Krook, "Two Problems in *The Portrait*," pp. 140-49 from *The Ordeal of Consciousness* (1968), pp. 357-69;
Sister M. Corona Sharp, "Isabel's Confidantes: Henrietta Stackpole and Madame Merle," pp. 150-62 from *The Confidante in Henry James* (1963), pp. 67-82;
Tony Tanner, "The Fearful Self," pp.162-79 from "The Fearful Self: Henry James's *The Portrait of a Lady*," *Critical Quarterly* (Autumn 1965):205-19;
Denis Donoghue, "Isabel's 'Yes' to Life," pp. 179-84 from *The Ordinary Universe* (1968), pp. 70-74;
Nina Baym, "Revision and Thematic Change," pp. 184-202, reprint of 1976.12.

179   SIEBERS, TOBIN. "Literature and Superstition: The Case of 'The Turn of the Screw.'" In *Romantic Fantastic*. Ithaca: Cornell University Press, pp. 50-56.
Describes the patterns of exclusion and difference in the tale, particularly in how the ghosts create an opposition between themselves and the inhabitants at Bly and a secondary opposition between the governess and the children. The focus of the tale is on this secondary opposition; ultimately the reader must choose between "reproduc[ing] the terror of superstition" (and believe in the ghosts) or "conserving the superstitious differences of the story in the metaphors of madness" (and call the governess insane).

180   SMIT, DAVID WILLIAM. "Theories of Style and the Writing of Henry James." Ph.D. dissertation, University of Iowa, 255 pp.
Surveys criticism of James's late style, identifying three basic types – style as identification, style as expression, and style as imitation – and revealing the limitations of each by analyses of sample passages from James. Smit concludes that "only general rationales convincingly account for a style."
See *Dissertation Abstracts International* 45, no. 9 (1985):2888A.

181   SMITH, PETER. "*The Ambassadors*: The History of Morality and Beauty." In *Public and Private Value: Studies in the Nineteenth-Century Novel*. Cambridge: Cambridge University Press, pp. 147-81, 236-37.

1984

Sees this novel as paralleling *The Princess Casamassima* thematically and attributes the success of the later novel to James's discovery that there are differences between the beauty of life and the beauty of art. Smith also argues that *The Ambassadors* reflects James's understanding of his Americanness and its connection with the past, a subject he began to explore in *The Portrait of a Lady*.

182   ____. "*The Princess Casamassima*: James' Address to the Public." In *Public and Private Value: Studies in the Nineteenth-Century Novel*. Cambridge: Cambridge University Press, pp. 121-45, 234-35.

Argues that this novel, more than any other, reveals James's nature as man and writer, particularly in the way James used the work of Dickens, Flaubert, Turgenev, and Balzac. The novel, which both sums up his early work and anticipates his later work, reflects the two irreconcilable strains in James's character: energy and decorousness.

183   SNITOW, ANN B. "The Romances: Comedy, Irony, and Henry James." In *Ford Madox Ford and the Voice of Uncertainty*. Baton Rouge: Louisiana State University, pp. 73-101.

Details James's influence on Ford throughout his fiction but focuses on three of Ford's romances – *The Benefactor, An English Girl*, and *A Call* – as "Jamesian pastiche." In general James offered Ford a "subtle conception of contemporary subject matter" and a "range of attitudes toward social experience." Ultimately, James's influence was far stronger than any other novelist.

184   SOBAL, NANCY LEE. "Curing and Caring: A Literary View of Professional Medical Women." Ph.D. dissertation, 248 pp.

Examines the depiction of women physicians and nurses in nineteenth- and twentieth-century American fiction, focusing on the ways in which such characters reflect the cultural ideal of femininity. James is cited as using, as did other nineteenth-century novelists, the woman physician to explore male-female role reversal.

See *Dissertation Abstracts International* 45, no. 6 (1984):1754A.

185   SOUCHU, LAURENT. "Le Texte à trous: *The Bostonians*." *Revue Française d'Etudes Américaines* 9, no. 20 (May):195-207.

In French.

1984

186 SPRINKLER, MICHAEL. "Historicizing Henry James." *Henry James Review* 5, no. 3 (Spring):203-7.

Responds to Kairschner (1984.108), Seltzer (1984.176), and Robbins (1984.168), noting that literary criticism does not transcend ideology. Sprinkler also suggests that some texts may not be "universalizable and shareable across all social, cultural, and historical boundaries."

187 STANZEL, F.K. "The Zero Grade of Mediacy in the *Notebooks of Henry James*." In *A Theory of Narrative*. Translated by Charlotte Goedsche. Cambridge: Cambridge University Press, pp. 30-37.

Compares the *Notebook* scenario for *The Ambassadors* with the novel, noting that the scenario deals mainly with content, while the mode of narration evolves during the actual process of composition.

188 STEELE, H. MEILI. "Realism and the Drama of Reference in Flaubert's *L'Education sentimentale* and James's *The Golden Bowl*." Ph.D. dissertation, University of North Carolina at Chapel Hill, 239 pp.

Argues that these novels break with realism and present new relationships of language, reference, and ontology. Using the work of Frege, Searle, Ricoeur, and Morot-Sir, Steele examines the creation of space, characters' speech, narratorial authority, and representation of the protagonist's experience.

See *Dissertation Abstracts International* 46, no. 2 (1985):419A.

189 STEIN, ALLEN F. "Henry James: The Early Short Fiction." In *After the Vows Were Spoken: Marriage in American Literary Realism*. Columbus: Ohio State University Press, pp. 55-86.

Sees James's depiction of marriage prior to 1881 colored by melodrama because the early tales are apprentice works and because James saw marriage as a fragile and flawed means of upholding the moral order in a disordered universe. Stein examines "A Tragedy of Error," "My Friend Bingham," "A Problem," "The Last of the Valerii," "Madame de Mauves," and "Crawford's Consistency."

190 ____. "Henry James: The Later Short Fiction." In *After the Vows Were Spoken: Marriage in American Literary Realism*. Columbus: Ohio State University Press, pp. 87-120.

Argues that the tales following *The Portrait of a Lady* are much more subtle than the early tales in the handling of melodramatic

1984

elements and in the depiction of marriage. The later tales focus on the question whether marriage promotes or hinders self-assertion and self-development. Stein discusses "The Author of 'Beltraffio,'" "The Liar," "The Birthplace," "The Lesson of the Master," "Lady Barberina," and "Mora Montravers."

191 _____. "Henry James: The Novels." In *After the Vows Were Spoken: Marriage in American Literary Realism*. Columbus: Ohio State University Press, pp. 121-61.

Examines the marriages depicted in *The Portrait of a Lady, What Maisie Knew, The Awkward Age,* and *The Golden Bowl.* Although James focuses on the negative aspects of marriage, as he does in the tales, he also shows the benefits of marriage, even when marriage causes pain. In *What Maisie Knew* and *The Awkward Age* human weakness subverts marriage; in *The Portrait of a Lady* and *The Golden Bowl,* marriage is a major factor in the heroines' self-discovery and growth.

192 STERNBERG, MEIR. "Spatiotemporal Art and the Other Henry James: The Case of *The Tragic Muse*." *Poetics Today* 5, no. 4:775-830.

Examines the novel's first nine chapters to show how James "substitutes the unities of time and space for the unity of the perceiver." This section of the novel is a "microcosmic foreshadowing" of the characters' shifting relationships, and of the various interactions between time and space, including "foreshadowing across sequence, the play of transition between similarity and plot contiguity, [and] the metamorphosis of analogy."

193 STEWART, J.I.M. "Yours Irrepressibly." *Times Literary Supplement,* no. 4233 (18 May):543.

Reviews the fourth volume of James's letters edited by Edel. These letters are dominated by the "'twaddle of graciousness'" and shed little light on the masterpieces of the period.

194 STOWELL, H. PETER. "Impressionism in James's Late Stories." *Revue de Littérature Comparée* 58, no. 1 [229] (January-March):27-36.

1984

Traces James's literary impressionism in "The Story In It," "Flickerbridge," "The Beast in the Jungle," and "The Birthplace," focusing on the consciousness, the dramatic method, phenomenology, epistemology, and the rendering of atmosphere. These tales show that during 1902 to 1904 James was a "full-fledged impressionist."

195   SUTHERLAND, JUDITH. "James: More than Melody." In *The Problematic Fictions of Poe, James, and Hawthorne*. Columbia: University of Missouri Press, pp. 38-70, 122-23.

Argues that in *The Sacred Fount* James explores the limitations of American transcendentalism and its aesthetic, particularly regarding symbolism, the narrator, and the distancing of the reader from the text. Sutherland also discusses the reflexive nature of the text: "We are continually pulled away from a linear argument and enmeshed in a series of concentric circles of analogy."

196   SZEGEDY-MASZÁK, MIHÁLY. "Henry James, European or American?" In *The Origins and Originality of American Culture*. Edited by Tibor Frank. Budapest: Akadémiai Kiadó, pp. 233-45.

Examines the narrative method and structure in "The Figure in the Carpet"–while the story is linear the narration is circular–and argues that James continually experimented with narration and structure to reject the didactic tradition of the novel and to assimilate a variety of conventions.

197   TAMKIN, LINDA ELLEN. "Heroines in Italy: Studies in the Novels of Ann Radcliffe, George Eliot, Henry James, E.M. Forster, and D.H. Lawrence." Ph.D. dissertation, University of California, Los Angeles, 238 pp.

Argues that for the heroines of these novelists–Emily St. Aubert, Dorothea Brooke, Isabel Archer, Milly Theale, Lucy Honeychurch, and Alvina Houghton–travel enables them to "challenge and redefine their identities" in a culture offering limited options for women. Tamkin finds many similarities among these heroines, including a moral crisis experienced in Italy. Italy thus becomes, for each, a proving ground.

See *Dissertation Abstracts International* 45, no. 8 (1985):2536A.

1984

198   TANIMOTO, YASUKO. "*The Wings of the Dove* to Alice James no Nikki" [*The Wings of the Dove* and the diary of Alice James]. *Eigo Seinen* (Tokyo) 130:70-72.
       In Japanese.
       Suggests that Milly Theale was not solely modeled on Minny Temple, who died in 1870, but also on Alice James, who died in 1892. Alice's diary provided James with the motif for the novel, and the complete edition of the diary, published in 1964, contains many passages reminiscent of those in the novel.

199   TANNER, TONY. Introduction to *The Europeans*. Harmondsworth, Middlesex, England: Penguin Books, pp. 7-29.
       Argues that although contrast is central to the novel, it is not that between Europe and America; rather, it concerns radically different conceptions of life. James's strongest criticism is leveled at the puritanism of the Wentworths, but the Europeanized Americans fail to appreciate the "reticent" virtues of the New Englanders.

200   TELOTTE, J.P. "The Right Way with Reality: James's 'The Real Right Thing.'" *Henry James Review* 6, no. 1 (Fall):8-14.
       Argues that this tale examines the gap between perception and the illusive and uncertain nature of reality. The tale makes clear "the ultimate weakness of all perception that refuses to accept all the limitations of the subjective." "The Real Right Thing" expands the earlier tale "The Real Thing" by exploring the "right" and "wrong" ways of formulating reality.

201   TERRIE, HENRY. Introduction to *Henry James: Tales of Art and Life*. Edited by Henry Terrie. Schenectady: Union College Press, pp. 1-16.
       Sketches the central themes in each of the tales included in this volume – "The Last of the Valerii," "Daisy Miller: A Study," "The Liar," "The Real Thing," "Paste," "The Great Good Place," "The Beast in the Jungle," and "The Jolly Corner" – and appends tales by Maupassant and Mérimée to compare with "Paste."

202   THWAITE, ANN. "Scribbling and Scribbling." In *Edmund Gosse: A Literary Landscape, 1849-1928*. Chicago: University of Chicago Press, pp. 379-82.

Describes James's "intermittent but intimate" relationship with Gosse, including Gosse's visit to James after the failure of *Guy Domville* and James's recounting of his watching one night for a glimpse of an "unapproachable face" briefly illuminated by a lamp.

203   TINTNER, ADELINE R. "Abraham Solomon and Henry James's 'The Birthplace.'" *Journal of Pre-Raphaelite Studies* 4, no. 2 (May):56-61.

Shows that in this tale James uses the "before" and "after" paintings of Abraham Solomon as "pictorial rhetoric" as well as a means of suggesting a lower-middle class atmosphere. The essay contains reproductions of *Waiting for the Verdict* and *Not Guilty*, explicitly invoked in the tale.

Revised 1986.151.

204   ____. "The Disappearing Furniture in Maupassant's 'Qui sait?' and *The Spoils of Poynton*." *Henry James Review* 6, no. 1 (Fall):3-7.

Argues that Maupassant's tale, "Qui Sait?," is a source for James's novel, because there are many parallels between the two works. Maupassant's tale concerns a houseful of disappearing furniture, and the tale's narrator bears many similarities to Mrs. Gereth.

Revised 1987.122.

205   ____. "Ernest and Henry: Hemingway's Lover's Quarrel with James." In *Ernest Hemingway: The Writer in Context*. Edited by James Nagel. Madison: University of Wisconsin Press, pp. 165-78.

Documents Hemingway's love-hate relationship with James as well as James's influence on Hemingway's fiction. In his later work, most notably *The Old Man and the Sea* and *Islands in the Stream*, Hemingway uses themes having a "general kinship" with James's. Hemingway ultimately acknowledges James's stature and influence in his acceptance speech for the Nobel Prize, thus resolving his "lover's quarrel" with James.

206   ____. "Edel's Henry IV." *American Literary Realism, 1870-1910* 17, no. 2 (Autumn):264-76.

Reviews Edel's *Henry James Letters IV*, calling all four volumes the tip of the iceberg because the published letters comprise only one-fifteenth of James's 15,000 letters. Tintner discusses James's

1984

relationships, reading, fiction, and response to the war as reflected in
the published letters, but suggests that the keys to many of James's tales
may be found in the unpublished correspondence.

207 _____. *"False Dawn* and the Irony of Taste–Changes in Art." *Edith
Wharton Newsletter* 1, no. 2 (Fall):1, 3, 8.
    Suggest that James may have told Wharton about Thomas
Jefferson Bryan's gallery of Italian primitives to which he responded
negatively. The gallery may have been the inspiration for Lewis
Raycie's in *False Dawn.*

208 _____. "'The Great Condition': Henry James and Bergsonian Time."
Studies in Short Fiction 21, no. 2 (Spring):111-15.
    Argues that the meaning of the tale hinges on James's intuitive
use of the Bergsonian distinction between the measurement of time and
the duration of time.

209 _____. "A Literary Youth and a Little Woman: Henry James
Reviews Louisa Alcott." In *Critical Essays on Louisa May Alcott.*
Edited by Madeleine B. Stern. Boston: G.K. Hall & Co., pp. 265-69.
    Surveys James's reviews of Alcott's works, noting that while
many of his comments reveal his "priggishness," he "put[s] his finger on
Louisa's peculiar straddling of the two worlds of childhood and
adulthood." Tintner suggests that James's understanding of children
may have come from his reading of Alcott's fiction.

210 _____. "O. Henry and Henry James: The Author of Four Million
Views the Author of Four Hundred." *Markham Review* 13:27-31.
    Details O.Henry's numerous and often humorous references to
James. Tintner suggests that because such references outnumber those
made to any other author, James made a particularly strong impression
on O. Henry.

211 UNRUE, DARLENE. "The Complex Americanism of Henry James
and William Faulkner." In *The Origins and Originality of American
Culture.* Edited by Tibor Frank. Budapest: Akadémiai Kiadó, pp.
247-53.

1984

Finds similarities in James's search for the past in Europe as a way of understanding his American identity and in Faulkner's search for "the aristocratic Southern Past in the defeated Southern Present."

212 VERNON, JOHN. "Labor and Leisure: The Wings of the Dove." In *Money and Fiction: Literary Realism in the Nineteenth and Early Twentieth Centuries*. Ithaca: Cornell University Press, pp. 172-93.

Argues that for James money is "a sign of the life of leisure" haunted by the poverty it excludes. Vernon examines Kate Croy, one of James's fortune-hunters, and links the language of *The Wings of the Dove* to the novel's materiality. The elaborate metaphors and syntax always threaten to break down, just as the rich surfaces mask a sordid reality.

213 VICTOR, DAVID ALLEN. "The Prospering Temptress in Nineteenth-Century American Fiction: Characterization and Literary Realism in the Novels of John W. DeForest and Henry James." Ph.D. dissertation, University of Michigan, 336 pp.

Defines the major traits of the prospering temptress and examines her depiction in de Forest's *Seacliff, Miss Ravenel's Conversion*, and *Playing the Mischief*; and in James's *Roderick Hudson, The Princess Casamassima, The Wings of the Dove*, and *The Golden Bowl*. Victor traces her literary antecedents and argues that she is a distinctly American type.

See *Dissertation Abstracts International* 45, no. 2 (1984):522A.

214 VIDAL, GORE. "Return to *The Golden Bowl*." *New York Review of Books* 30, nos. 21-22 (19 January):8-12.

Describes James's use of the golden bowl to symbolize the flawed marriages and suggests that at the novel's end Charlotte, Amerigo, and Maggie are all trapped in a golden cage, although Maggie is both prisoner and gaoler.

Reprinted 1985.155.

215 VILANEUVA, DARÍO. "*Los Pazos de Ulloa*, el naturalismo y Henry James." *Hispanic Review* 52, no. 2 (Spring):121-39.

In Portuguese.

1984

216 VILLA, VIRGINIA BARRETT. "Vampire Metaphor in Selected Works of Henry James." *Whimsy II (Western Humor and Irony Membership Yearbook)*:19-20.
  Notes that James uses vampire metaphors– involving references to teeth, hands, wings, cloaks, and so forth–to achieve comic and tragic effects in numerous works. The figure of Dracula, for example, suggests the "cloaked brutality of human intercourse."

217 WAGENKNECHT, EDWARD. *The Tales of Henry James*. New York: Ungar, vi, 266 pp.
  Surveys James's tales, focusing on those reprinted in the New York Edition. Each tale is summarized, along with highlights from the relevant preface and a brief sketch of the tale's genesis. The tales not included in the New York Edition are summarized and commented on briefly in an appendix.

218 WARREN, JOYCE W. "The Woman Takes the Center Stage: Henry James." In *The American Narcissus: Individualism and Women in Nineteenth-Century American Fiction*. New Brunswick, N.J.: Rutgers University Press, pp. 231-52, 303-7.
  Discusses James's depiction of complex female characters–most notably Isabel Archer, Christina Light, and Kate Croy–and James's relationships with women, including Alice James, Edith Wharton, and Constance Fenimore Woolson. Warren attributes James's sensitivity to women to his cosmopolitanism and to his questioning of American culture, especially its myth of the strong, heroic, individualistic male.

219 WASSERSTROM, WILLIAM. "Abandoned in Providence: Harriet Beecher Stowe, Howells, and Henry James." In *The Ironies of Progress: Henry Adams and the American Dream*. Carbondale and Edwardsville: Southern Illinios University Press, pp. 51-76, 237-40.
  Argues that *Uncle Tom's Cabin, The Rise of Silas Lapham*, and "The Turn of the Screw" all depict the consequences of "misgovernment" and "misequilibrium," and this misgovernment is reflected in the "mismanagement or mystification of [the] plot." The characters in James's tale have abdicated their roles in the hierarchy of authority or have forfeited trust. James repudiates English equipoise and the American belief in the perfectibility of man.

220 WATKINS, ERIC WALTER. "The Authorial Allusion: A Clue to
the Interpretation of Irony." Ph.D. dissertation, University of
California, San Diego, 191 pp.
  Recommends that Wayne Booth's discussion of allusion in *The
Rhetoric of Irony* be amended to accommodate the role of authorial
allusion in interpreting irony. Three works are discussed: James's "The
Aspern Papers," Conrad's *Heart of Darkness*, and Gide's *Isabelle*.
  See *Dissertation Abstracts International* 45, no. 6 (1984):1745A.

221 WEGELIN, CHRISTOF, Ed. *Tales of Henry James: The Texts of the
Stories; The Author on His Craft; Background and Criticism.* New
York: W.W. Norton & Co., x, 491 pp.
  Contains the following tales: "Daisy Miller: A Study," "An
International Episode," "The Aspern Papers," "The Pupil,"
"Brooksmith," "The Real Thing," "The Middle Years," "The Beast in the
Jungle," and "The Jolly Corner"; and includes relevant selections from
James's notebooks, prefaces, and letters.
  Criticism includes partial reprints of the following:
  David Daiches, "Sensibility and Technique Preface to a
Critique (1943), pp. 419-24;
  Jacques Barzun, "James the Melodramatist" (1943), pp. 424-33;
  F.O. Matthiessen and Kenneth B. Murdock, "[How His Ideas
Came to Him]," in *The Notebooks of Henry James* (1947), pp. 433-35;
  Christof Wegelin, "Revision and Style," (n.d.) pp. 435-42;
  Philip Rahv, "Daisy Miller" (1944), pp. 442-3;
  Carol Ohmann, "Daisy Miller: A Study of Changing Intention"
(1964), pp. 443-52;
  Christof Wegelin, "[An International Episode]" (1958), pp. 452-
55;
  Wayne C. Booth, "'The Purloining of the Aspern Papers' or
'The Evocation of Venice'"? (1961), pp. 455-62;
  Mildred Hartsock, "Unweeded Garden: A View of *The Aspern
Papers*" (1967), pp. 463-70;
  Mildred Hartsock, "[The Pupil]" (1968), pp. 470-72;
  Earle Labor, "James's 'The Real Thing': Three Levels of
Meaning" (1962), pp. 472-75;
  Krishna Baldev Vaid, "The Beast in the Jungle" (1964), pp.
475-81;
  Edwin H. Cady, "[The Beast in the Jungle]" (1971), pp. 481-83;
  Krishna Baldev Vaid, "The Jolly Corner" (1964), pp. 484-87.

1984

222 WESTBROOK, WAYNE W. "Selah Tarrant *à la* Daudet." *Henry James Review* 5, no. 2 (Winter):100-10.

Compares Selah Tarrant with Delobelle from Daudet's *Fromont*, finding numerous similarities. Delobelle serves as a type for Tarrant, especially with his vanity and affectation.

223 WESTERVELT, L.A. "The Individual and the Form: Maggie Verver's Tactics in *The Golden Bowl*." *Renascence* 36, no. 3 (Spring):147-59.

Examines how Maggie uses language – including silence, tone, and ambiguity – to preserve her marriage and family and to create her sense of identity. Her triumph is her ability to trust her version of reality and to resist the reality others attempt to impose on her. Westervelt contrasts Charlotte with Maggie, showing that although she uses Maggie's tactics, she lacks imagination and allows herself to be defined by others.

224 WHELAN, JOHN GRAHAM BRENT. "Reading Fictions: Studies in James and Proust." Ph.D. dissertation, Johns Hopkins University, 308 pp.

Applies the reading models of Frank Kermode and Jean Rousset, particularly regarding the ending, to the work of James and Proust. For James, plot, figurative language, the scene, and perspective open up rather than resolve the text. Proust's use of formal structures also supports "proliferating readings."

See *Dissertation Abstracts International* 45, no. 11 (1985):3342A.

225 WILLIAMS, M.A. "Reading 'The Figure in the Carpet': Henry James and Wolfgang Iser." *English Studies in Africa* 27, no. 2:107-21.

Critiques Iser's reading of the tale (1978.53) noting that while Iser's analysis is "restrictive and inadequate" the tale itself demonstrates Iser's theory of reading. The chief weakness of Iser's reading is the failure to account for the "shifting ironic dimension" of the tale while Iser's notion of "blanks" and "negation" illuminate the text. Williams surveys other readings of the text, including Todorov (1977.140), J. Hillis Miller (1980.97), Shlomith Rimmon-Kenan (1977.107) and Rachel Salmon (1980.123).

226 WILLIAMS, MERVYN. "The Changing Image of Women: The Early James." In *Women in the English Novel, 1800-1900.* London: Macmillan Press, pp. 173-76.

Suggests that James's heroines – Claire de Cintre, Isabel Archer, and Fleda Vetch – are more emancipated than the heroines of previous authors, but they are not completely free. While James did not want women to be slaves, he did want them to keep their "traditional virtues."

227 WINNETT, SUSAN. "*Mise en Crypte*: The Man and the Mask." *Henry James Review* 5, no. 3 (Spring):220-26.

Applies Abraham's and Tovok's idea of *cryptonymie* to the ambiguity of *The Sacred Fount*, particularly in chapter 4 which describes the painting of the man with the mask. The painting is a frame encrypting interpretation, and as such represents ambiguity.

See also Rowe 1984.170.

228 WIRTH-NESHER, HANA. "The Thematics of Interpretation: James's Artist Tales." *Henry James Review* 5, no. 2 (Winter):117-27.

Argues that in his artist tales – "The Author of 'Beltraffio,'" "The Lesson of the Master," and "The Figure in the Carpet" – James uses art as "a metaphor of all human interaction" and uses relationships to examine the nature of art.

229 WOLFF, DONALD ALLEN. "Meditation and Irony: A Study of James's Sense of the Past." Ph.D. dissertation, University of Washington, 332 pp.

Argues that James's sense of the past was based on both cultural and personal history. Throughout his career James searched for a balance between the two, as well as between past and present, and freedom and restraint. Wolff traces James's development of "the past" in his autobiography, *The American Scene, The Awkward Age*, and *The Sense of the Past*. In this last unfinished novel James dramatizes the way the past makes sense of the present.

See *Dissertation Abstracts International* 45, no. 5 (1984):1407A.

230 WRIGHT, NATHALIA. "The American Writer's Search for Identity." *South Atlantic Review* 49:39-55.

1984

>Applies Czeslaw Milosz's statement that "the core of American literature has always been the question, Who am I" to four major novelists–Cooper, Melville, Hawthorne, and James–and four major poets–Poe, Whitman, Dickinson, and Stevens. Wright briefly examines James's international works, including *Roderick Hudson*, "Daisy Miller," *The American, The Portrait of a Lady, The Wings of the Dove*, and *The Golden Bowl*, noting that the memorable characters "triumph morally because of the knowledge they acquire" in Europe. All of the writers see the American as someone who is "acutely and endlessly curious about what it means to be a human being."

231   YOON, KEE-HO. "On Strether's Decision to Leave Paris." *Research Review of Chungbuk National University* (Chongju, Korea) 27:159-70.

>Demonstrates that in Paris Strether's artistic consciousness matures so that he sees not only the truth that is good and beautiful, but also that which is impure and ugly. Strether's discovery of Chad's and Marie's affair initiates him into reality and gives him the courage "to pursue something beyond the human condition," which is the duty of the artist.

1985

1   AKIYAMA, MASAYUKI. "James and Nanboku: A Comparative Study of Supernatural Stories in the West and East." *Comparative Literature Studies* 22, no. 1 (Spring):43-52.

>Compares Nanboku's play *Tōikaidō Yotsuya Kaidan* (1825) with James's "The Romance of Certain Old Clothes," "Sir Edmund Orme," and "The Friends of Friends." Both writers depict ghosts in similar ways, and both see similar reasons for the ghost's return, prompting Akiyama to conclude that these supernatural stories are cautionary tales about the dangers of modern materialism.

2   ALTER, ROBERT. "The Novel and the Sense of the Past." *Salmagundi*, nos. 68-69 (Fall-Winter):91-106.

>Proposes that the novel's narrative freedom gives it a unique relation to both the individual past and the cultural past. A novel such as James's *Portrait of a Lady* gives us special access to a historical past and dramatizes the ways in which consciousness is affected by the "overlapping contexts of culture."

3   ANDERSON, DON. "Can Strether Step into the Same River Twice? *The Ambassadors* as a Meta-Novel." *Sydney Studies in English* 10:61-77.

Argues that the novel is "deeply concerned both aesthetically and morally, with and about the nature (aesthetic and moral) of the human activity of uniting fictions." This concern is located in the growth of Strether's aesthetic awareness, which is inextricably linked to his moral awakening.

4   ARCHER, BARBARA CLARK. "Speech, Manners, and Society in Henry James." Ph.D. dissertation, Columbia University, 257 pp.

Relates James's "The Speech of American Women" and "The Manners of American Women" (1906-1907) to his fiction, showing that such works as "Pandora," "Daisy Miller," *The Bostonians, Washington Square, What Maisie Knew* and *The Awkward Age* contain themes made explicit in the essays. In his fiction and these two essays, James links speech and manners to the social order.

See *Dissertation Abstracts International* 46, no. 8 (1986):2292A.

5   ARMSTRONG, PAUL B. "The Hermeneutics of Literary Impressionism: Interpretation and Reality in James, Conrad, and Ford." In *Poetics of the Elements of the Human Condition: The Sea: From Elemental Stirrings to Symbolic Inspiration, Language, and Life-Significance in Literary Interpretation and Theory.* Edited by Anna-Teresa Tymieniecka. Analecta Husserliana 19. Dordrecht: Reidel, pp. 477-99.

Reprint of 1983.10; reprinted 1987.2. See also Goodson 1985.50.

6   ASSELINEAU, ROGER. "Innocence et experience dans l'oeuvre de Henry James." In *Le Sud et autres points cardinaux.* Edited by Jeanne-Marie Santraud. Paris: Centre de Recherches en Lit. & Civilisation N. Amer., PU de Paris-Sorbonne, pp. 65-74.

In French.

Suggests that James, like his contemporary American novelists, believed in the innocence of youth uncorrupted by the reality of the world. Unlike most of them, however, he argued that to pass from innocence to wisdom one must encounter evil. This dialectic of innocence and experience dominates James's fiction.

1985

7   BAILEY, BRIGITTE GABCKE. "Pictures of Italy: American Aesthetic Response and the Development of the Nineteenth-Century American Travel Sketch." Ph.D. dissertation, Harvard University, 413 pp.

Traces the evolution of the travel sketch in the work of Irving, Cooper, Hawthorne, James, and others. These writers use the sketch as a means of coming to terms with the European scene.

See *Dissertation Abstracts International* 47, no. 1 (1986):175A.

8   BAUER, DALE MARIE. "The Failure of Community: Women and Resistance in Hawthorne's, James's, and Wharton's Novels." Ph.D. dissertation, University of California, Irvine, 282 pp.

Sees *The Blithedale Romance, The Golden Bowl*, and *The House of Mirth* as examples of the "American dialogic novel which celebrates the struggle between social and ideological voices." These novels, Bauer argues, explore relations between the public and the private and in so doing "make intelligible the forms of women's oppression and silence within the discursive strategies proposed as normative in each novel."

See *Dissertation Abstracts International* 46, no. 12 (1986):3718A.

9   BEAVER, HAROLD. "Taking the Organic View." *Times Literary Supplement*, no. 4312 (22 November):1327-28.

Reviews James's literary criticism, published by the Library of America as well as examined in Vivien Jones's *James the Critic* (1985.72). James's criticism reflects his conviction that art, like life, must be organic. Moreover, his belief in the interrelationship of art and morality can still serve as a lesson to twentieth-century critics. Most important, though, James's essays show that criticism, too, can be an art.

10   BELL, IAN F.A. "'This Exchange of Epigrams': Commodity and Style in *Washington Square.*" *Journal of American Studies* 19, no. 1 (April):49-68.

Reads the novel as a critique of rampant materialism and commercialism but also trancendentalism. This critique is realized in Catherine's silence because it "articulates the object of James's disquiet" and "the flawed alternative to it."

11   BELL, MILLICENT. "The Bostonian Story." *Partisan Review* 52, no. 2:109-19.
     Discusses various interpretations, including the recent film version of the novel. The novel is neither romance, tragedy, or fairy tale; it is a comic satire of the division between the sexes.

12   _____. "The Essence of the Master: *Henry James: A Life.*" *New York Times Book Review* (24 November):12.
     Reviews the revision of Edel's biography, suggesting that Edel has not substantially altered his portrait of James and in some instances has weakened his thesis – notably, his treatment of Henry's relationship with William. Bell acknowledges the difficulty of the biographer's task, particularly when the biographer must rely on speculation and imagination.

13   BERSANI, LEO. Foreword to *A World Elsewhere: The Place of Style in American Literature*, by Richard Poirer. Madison: University of Wisconsin Press, pp. ix-xviii.
     Praises Poirer's analysis of *The Ambassadors* because he is receptive to the way style transforms history and language.

14   BISHOP, GEORGE. "Shattered Notions of Mastery: Henry James's 'Glasses.'" *Criticism* 27, no. 4 (Fall):347-62.
     Argues that the tale is concerned with the inability of the author to control the narrative, which is likened to beads on a string in James's notebook and in the tale itself.

15   BISHOP, GEORGE JONATHAN. "When the Master Relents: The Neglected Short Fictions of Henry James." Ph.D. dissertation, State University of New York, Buffalo, 141 pp.
     Analyzes six tales – "A Bundle of Letters," "Glasses," "The Liar," "The Tree of Knowledge," "The Third Person," and "Collaboration" – not generally considered part of the James canon. Bishop's close reading suggests a concept of mastery different from that created by James and perpetuated by critics.
     See *Dissertation Abstracts International* 46, no. 10 (1986):3031A.

1985

16 BLACKALL, JEAN FRANTZ. "Henry and Edith: 'The Velvet Glove' as an 'In' Joke." *Henry James Review* 7, no. 1 (Fall):21-25.
    Examines the significance of the tale's title as it relates to the various novels mentioned in the tale (the tale, for example, involves a novel *The Top of the Tree*; Wharton had recently published *The Fruit of the Tree*). Blackall disputes Edel's and Tintner's reading of the tale as a joke at Wharton's expense, seeing it as a shared and "embellished joke" as well as a reflection of how James assimilated Wharton's devices and used them in his fiction.

17 BLAKE, NANCY. *James, Ecriture et Absence*. Paris: Cistre. 222 pp. In French.

18 BUDD, JOHN. "*The Spoils of Poynton*: The Revisions and the Critics." *Massachusetts Studies in English* 10, no. 1 (Spring):1-11.
    Details the many revisions of *Spoils*, which began as *The Old Things*, a serial published in *The Atlantic Monthly*, April-October 1896. Budd argues that the revisions show James continually creating the novel and that criticism must consider all revisions in order to understand the novel.

19 BUTLER, CHRISTOPHER. Introduction to *The Ambassadors*. Oxford: Oxford University Press, pp. vii-xxi.
    Suggests that in this novel "it is interpretation in all its senses, with which Strether and the reader are primarly concerned," and likens the novel to a series of conversations beginning with a question and containing "carefully graded and artfully deferred answers." Indeed, Strether does not resolve the questions raised in the novel; he arrives at an understanding of himself in relation to the other characters.

20 BYUN, JONG-MIN. "An Overview of Critical Approaches in the Critical Controversy over *The Turn of the Screw*." *Cheju Kyoyuk Taehak* 20 (June):201-10.
    Surveys criticism of the tale. Byun divides the criticism into five "approaches": traditional, formalistic, psychological, mythological and archetypal, and exponential.

21 CARAMELLO, CHARLES. "Reading Gertrude Stein Reading Henry James, or, Eros is Eros is Eros." *Henry James Review* 6, no. 3 (Spring):182-203.

Explores Stein's interpretation of and relation to James, focusing on her autobiographical writings and especially on *Four in America*, a work which advances both Stein's "theoretical program" and an "evolving self-portrait," giving her a central place in American literature. She saw herself as James's successor. Caramello also discusses Stein's aesthetics, especially her concept of "portrait narration" and her sense of tradition, showing her "proximity to James and her distance from her fellow moderns."

22 CARLSON, SUSAN. *Women of Grace: James's Plays and the Comedy of Manners*. Studies in Modern Literature, no. 48. Ann Arbor, Mich.: UMI Research Press, xiii, 185 pp.

Argues that James's plays are stageworthy and "laudible attempts" in the tradition of the British comedy of manners and can hold their own when compared to similar plays written at the turn of the century. Although she details the historical context for these plays, Carlson focuses on James's women characters who have "superior social understanding" and who can enhance social consciousness because of society's double standard.

Revision of Ph.D. dissertation, University of Oregon, 1980.

23 CAWS, MARY ANN. "High Modernist Framing: Framing in the Later James." In *Reading Frames in Modern Fiction*. Princeton: Princeton University Press, pp. 121-206, 281-89.

Traces James's use of framing devices, that highlight and isolate portions of the text from the whole narrative. James moves from such devices based primarily on point of view, which create "pictures," to those primarily psychological, which focus attention on the frame rather than on the picture. The discussion includes *The Sacred Fount,* "The Turn of the Screw," *The Ambassadors, The Wings of the Dove*, and *The Golden Bowl*.

24 CHOI, KYONG DO. "Money and Pragmatic Morality in Henry James." Ph.D. dissertation, University of Nebraska, Lincoln, 172 pp.

Argues that James's ideas about money reflect his "pragmatic morality." *The American* explores the limitations of money when Newman confronts the problems of life; in *The Portrait of a Lady* money becomes a "central force in a relativistic world." *The Ambassadors* links money to a limited moral vision; in *The Golden Bowl* "James examines how one must be intelligent about human life and morality, even in terms of the impact of such a basic necessity as money."

See *Dissertation Abstracts International* 46, no. 12 (1986):3718A-3719A.

25 CLEWS, HETTY. "Eyewitness Monologues." In *The Only Teller: Readings in the Monologue Novel.* Victoria, B.C.: Sono Nis Press, pp. 154-66.

Shows how in "The Turn of the Screw" James, through the governess, forces the reader to "think the evil" and emphasizes "the unseen and the unstable."

26 COHEN, PAULA MARANTZ. "The Shadow of Alice James in Henry James's Family Novels of the Nineties." *American Literary Realism* 18, nos. 1-2 (Spring-Autumn):1-13.

Argues that Alice was the model for Maisie and Nanda and that James's depiction of family dynamics in *What Maisie Knew* and *The Awkward Age* reflects Alice's role in the James family. Cohen sees Alice as the "family scapegoat and receptacle of the symptoms of others" and, although Henry identified with Alice, he was able, unlike Alice, to escape from a destructive family system.

27 COLEMAN, ELIZABETH. "Henry James Criticism: A Case Study in Critical Inquiry." *Nineteenth-Century Fiction* 40, no. 3 (December):327-44.

Argues that James's criticism fails to connect craft with "life," the source of value in fiction. James insists in "The Art of Fiction" that a novel's value comes from representing an illusion of life, a view which Coleman sees as limiting the artist's freedom. Coleman also examines "A Humble Remonstrance" in which R.L. Stevenson describes the ordering of the materials of life as both "meaning" and "methods"; he also grants the artist "the freedom to determine one own's purposes."

28 CROSS, MARY. "The 'Drama of Discrimination': Style as Plot in *The Ambassadors*." *Language and Style* 18, no. 1 (Winter):46-63.

Examines the ways in which complex sentence structures document the expanding world of Strether's imagination. The density of the language, its "planes of tenses," and its rich verbal design force the reader to reorganize habitual perceptions. Cross details the aesthetic and thematic implications of parallelism in the text.

29   DALKE, ANNE FRENCH. "'So Much and So Little Composition':
     The Literary Criticism of Henry James and the Novels of George
     Eliot." *American Transcendental Quarterly* 58 (December):63-72.
         Traces   James's   changing   attitudes   toward   American
     transcendentalism and George Eliot. Early in his career, James
     criticized both the social "thinness" of the Americans' and Eliot's
     preoccupation with society and with detail. By 1885, however, he finds
     that Eliot's fiction lacks "life," and responds positively to Whitman's
     poetry.

30   DAUGHERTY, SARAH B. "Howells Reviews James: The
     Transcendence of Realism." *American Literary Realism* 18, nos. 1-2
     (Spring-Autumn):147-67.
         Argues that Howell's essays on James show that Howells was
     not so much a militant realist as he was a defender of the romance.

31   DAY, WILLIAM P. "The Gothic Themes: Another Turn of the
     Screw." In *In the Circles of Fear and Desire: A Study of Gothic
     Fantasy*. Chicago and London: University of Chicago Press, pp. 114-
     19.
         Notes the influence of *The Mysteries of Udolpho* and *Jane Eyre*
     on the tale and suggests that the Gothic world of the tale triumphs over
     the individual and the values of the nineteenth century.

32   DePROSPO, R.C. "The (Re) Ordering of Nature in the Settings of
     Henry James." *Revue Française d'Études Américaines* 10, no. 26
     (November):373-82.
         Argues that in the settings of his fiction, autobiography, and
     The American Scene, James deconstructs the romantic discourse of
     nature. DeProspo traces James's ambivalence to romanticism in
     Hawthorne, *The Ambassadors*, and *The American Scene*.

1985

33   DONOGHUE, DENIS. "Attitudes toward History: A Preface to *The Sense of the Past.*" *Salmagundi*, no. 68-69 (Fall-Winter):107-24.
     Argues that James was interested in the past only by what could be made of it imaginatively and examines James's unfinished novel to support his argument.

34   DORSEY, LAURENS M. "'Something Like the Old Dream of the Secret of Life': Henry James's Imaginative Vision and Romantic Inheritance, with Special Attention to the Opening Paragraphs of His Preface to *The Spoils of Poynton.*" *Henry James Review* 7, no. 1 (Fall):13-20.
     Demonstrates that James regarded the role of the artistic imagination in essentially romantic terms. The imagination was the "preeminent reality" that could recreate and make permanent the truth of life in the mind in contrast to "the blundering and wasteful life outside the mind."

35   EAGER, GERALD. "A Portrait of Isabel Archer: Correggio's *Virgin Adoring the Christ Child* in Henry James's *The Portrait of a Lady.*" *CEA Critic* 47, no. 4 (Summer):39-50.
     Suggests that the painting illuminates Isabel's character, shining in the "dusky disenchantment" of Europe, and discusses the responses of James's contemporaries to Correggio's work.

36   EAKIN, JOHN PAUL. "Henry James and the Autobiographical Act." In *Fictions in Autobiography: Studies in the Art of Self-Invention*. Princeton: Princeton University Press, pp. 56-125.
     Reprint of 1983.53.

37   EDEL, LEON. "Biography and the Sexual Revolution – Why Curiosity is No Longer Vulgar." *New York Times Book Review* (24 November):13-14.
     Attributes the biographer's freedom to depict the "passional life of his or her subject" to the sexual revolution. All information, however, must be clearly relevant to "the central aim of biography, which is to relate the life lived to the particular achievement." Edel discusses his revision of his biography of James, in which he realized the radical nature of the "biographical revolution."

38   _____. *Henry James: A Life*. New York: Harper & Row, xiv, 740 pp.
One-volume condensed and revised version of Edel's five-volume biography of James, 1953-1972. This revision includes new sources and new material, particularly concerning James's sexuality.

39   EDEL, LEON, and TINTNER, ADELINE R. "The Private Life of Peter Quin(t): Origins of 'The Turn of the Screw.'" *Henry James Review* 7, no. 1 (Fall):2-4.
Details many of the numerous similarities and "echoes" in "The Turn of the Screw" and Tom Taylor's *Temptation*, which James read as a boy. The later tale can be seen as James's rewriting of the "old thriller" "out of his mature imagination."

40   ESCH, DEBORAH LEE. "The Senses of the Past: The Rhetoric of Temporality in Henry James." Ph.D. dissertation, Yale University, 157 pp.
Examines the ways in which *The Portrait of a Lady*, "The Aspern Papers", and "The Jolly Corner" "account for their own rhetorical and temporal complexity." Esch focuses primarily on a second-order, allegorical narrative as the key for understanding the work's rhetoric and temporal structure.
See *Dissertation Abstracts International* 47, no. 4 (1986):1313A-1314A.

41   EVANS, CHRISTINE ANN. "The Darkening Medium: Speech and Silence in the Works of Theodor Fontane, Henry James, and Marcel Proust." Ph.D. dissertation, Harvard University, 231 pp.
Argues that these three writers question the viability of speech as a means of creating relationships and communities. Fontane's characters use speech to control chaotic impulses, but fail; while James does not question the power of speech, he denies it the ability to do good. Proust affirms speech, but only as the best of all evils.
See *Dissertation Abstracts International* 47, no. 1 (1986):170A.

42   FELMAN, SHOSHANA. "Henry James: Madness and the Risks of Practice (Turning the Screw of Interpretation)." In *Writing and Madness (Literature/Philosophy/Psychoanalysis)*. Translated by Martha Noel Evans, the author, and Brian Massumi. Ithaca: Cornell University Press, pp. 141-247.

1985

Reprint of 1977.36, 1978.40 (in French), and 1980.51.

43   FLOWER, DEAN. "Henry James in Northampton: The View from
     Prospect House." *Massachusetts Review* 26, no. 2-3 (Summer-
     Autumn):217-32.
        Describes James's visit to Northampton, Mass. in the fall of
     1864, his use of his memories of that visit in *Roderick Hudson* and *The
     Bostonians*, and his return in May 1905. Photographs of James by
     Katherine McClellan, the Smith College photographer, are included.

44   GABLER, JANET A. "James's Rhetorical Arena: The Metaphor of
     Battle in *The Bostonians*." *Texas Studies in Literature and Language*
     27, no. 3 (Fall):270-83.
        Argues that Olive's rhetoric is unsound while Basil's is sound,
     and concludes that James agrees with Ransom's political views. James,
     however, masks his agreement with a narrator who is "a subtle parody
     of his imagined reader."

45   GALE, ROBERT L. "Henry James." In *American Literary
     Scholarship: An Annual/1983*. Edited by Warren French. Durham:
     Duke University Press, pp. 109-28.
        Surveys criticism published in 1983.

46   GASS, WILLIAM H. "Culture, Self and Style." In *Habitations of the
     Word: Essays*. New York: Simon & Schuster, pp. 185-205.
        Reprint of 1981.52.

47   GERLACH, JOHN. "Converging Closure and the Theory of
     Openness." In *Toward the End: Closure and Structure in American
     Short Story*. University: University of Alabama Press, pp. 74-85.
        Discusses James's endings in his short stories, focusing on
     "Paste," "A Bundle of Letters," "Four Meetings," and "The Altar of the
     Dead." James rejected open endings in favor of a sense of circularity
     that is achieved through repetition.

48   GIRDHARRY, ARNOLD. "Love, Marriage, and Henry James."
     Spectrum (Anna Maria College) 1, no. 1 (Spring-Summer):53-57.

Argues that James's depiction of marriage in *The Portrait of a Lady, The Wings of the Dove*, and *The Golden Bowl* demonstrates his knowledge of love and marriage, particularly concerning the compromises necessary for a workable relationship.

49   GOODER, JEAN. Introduction to *Daisy Miller and Other Stories*. Oxford: Oxford University Press, pp. vii-xxviii.
Suggests that while the international theme is important in "Daisy Miller," "Pandora," "Four Meetings," and "The Patagonia," these stories "dramatize the price of resolving uncertainty" and explore others' complicity in an individual's fate.

50   GOODSON, A.C. "Hermeneutics and History: A Response to Paul Armstrong." In *Poetics of the Elements in the Human Condition: The Sea: From Elemental Stirrings to Symbolic Inspiration, Language, and Life-Significance in Literary Interpretations and Theory*. Edited by Anna-Teresa Tymieniecka. Analecta Husserliana 19. Dordrecht: Reidel, pp. 501-4.
Acknowledges the value of Armstrong's phenomenological approach to James (see Armstrong 1985.5) but suggests that phenomenology cannot account for the power of James's portrayal of "a bourgeois culture *in extremis*." Phenomenology needs to "ground its . . . thematics of understanding in a sense of historical reality."

51   GREINER, DONALD J. *Adultery in the American Novel: Updike, James, and Hawthorne*. Columbia: University of South Carolina Press, 136 pp.
Argues that in his marriage novels Updike blends Hawthorne's exploration of adultery as moral transgression in *The Scarlet Letter* with James's vision of adultery as a disruption of social harmony in *The Golden Bowl*. Greiner discusses James's relationship to Hawthorne, relying primarily on *Hawthorne*. Although his analysis of James focuses on *The Golden Bowl*, Greiner examines the earlier treatment of adultery, "A London Life," in which James was also concerned with the implications of infidelity for society.

52   GRIBBLE, JENNIFER. "Value in *The Golden Bowl*." *Critical Review* (Canberra, Australia), no. 27:50-65.

1985

Examines the golden bowl as a symbol of the ambiguous, even contradictory, values in the novel and as a key to maintaining values amid apparent moral relativism. In the end, Gribble concludes, the golden bowl "holds together a plurality of values that motivate human lives."

53   HABEGGER, ALFRED. "Precocious Incest: First Novels by Louisa May Alcott and Henry James." *Massachusetts Review* 26, no. 2-3 (Summer-Autumn):233-62.

Details the influence of Alcott's novel *Moods* on *Watch and Ward*, arguing that James subverted the "father-daughter incest-fantasy" to a "nice-guys-finish-first daydream."

54   HALPERIN, JOHN. "Elizabeth Bowen and Henry James." *Henry James Review* 7, no. 1 (Fall):45-47.

Notes numerous similarities in the work of the two writers, thereby demonstrating James's influence on Bowen. Among the similarities discussed are style, use of the gesture, the focus on psychological insight, literary impressionism, the international theme, androgyny, and the "cruelty" of innocence.

55   _____. "Trollope, James, and 'The Retribution of Time.'" *Southern Humanities Review* 19, no. 4 (Fall):301-8.

Compares *Washington Square* with Trollope's *Sir Henry Hotspur of Humblethwaite* and concludes that James did not pillage Trollope's work, which focuses on plot. James's concern in his novel is the psychological development of his characters and their dramatic interactions with each other.

56   HARDY, BARBARA. "Henry James: Reflective Passions." In *Forms of Feeling in Victorian Fiction*. London: Peter Owen, pp. 191-215.

Examines James's use of the free indirect style, point of view, imagery, and center of consciousness to represent states of feeling. The discussion focuses on *Roderick Hudson*, *The Portrait of a Lady*, *The Wings of the Dove*, and *The Golden Bowl*.

57 HIGDON, DAVID LEON. "Henry James and Lillian Hellman: An Unnoted Source." *Henry James Review* 6, no. 2 (Winter):134-35.

Notes the similarities between a scene in *The Little Foxes* where Regina Giddens refuses to get her husband's medicine for him and the scene in chapter 22 of *The American* where Madame de Bellegarde withholds the Marquis's medication, contributing to his death. Higdon suggests that James was influential in shaping Hellman's "memories and intentions."

58 HIGDON, DAVID LEON, and BENDER, TODD K. *"A Concordance to Henry James's The American.* New York: Garland, 336 pp.

Includes a verbal index, word frequency table, and field of reference for the New York Edition of *The American.*

59 HOLLY, CAROL. "The British Reception of Henry James's Autobiographies." *American Literature* 57, no. 4 (December):570-87.

Details British critical reception to *A Small Boy and Others* in 1913 and *Notes of a Son and Brother* in 1914. Both volumes were received favorably, and most critics were sensitive to James's aims and style. Of the two volumes, the second was regarded more positively, especially because of James's depiction of family life.

60 HORVATH, BROOKE K. "Henry James, E.D. Hirsch, and Relative Readability: A Note on the Style of *The Turn of the Screw.*" *University of Hartford Studies in Literature* 17, no. 3:12-17.

Applies Hirsch's concept of readability described in *The Philosophy of Composition* to "The Turn of the Screw." James's prose has a high degree of relative readability because he uses the most efficient style to achieve his ends; complex structures and ambiguous pronouns bewilder the reader and make certainty impossible.

61 HOUSTON, NEAL B. "Hemingway: The Obsession with Henry James, 1924-1954." *Rocky Mountain Review of Language and Literature* 39, no. 1:33-46.

Details Hemingway's lifelong and paradoxical obsession with James. While Hemingway acknowledged James's greatness as an artist, he criticized James's sedate life. Houston suggests that Hemingway saw James as "the symbol and antithesis to his own personality and works."

1985

Hemingway's acceptance speech for the Nobel Prize, in which he regrets James's never having received the prize, marks a "cessation of hostilities."

62 HOWARD, PATRICIA, ed. *Benjamin Britten: The Turn of the Screw.* Cambridge Opera Handbooks. Cambridge: Cambridge University Press, xi, 164 pp.
   Contents:
   Jones, Vivien. "Henry James's 'The Turn of the Screw.'" pp. 1-22. Sketches the tale's background, plot, narrative technique, and themes, and surveys its various critical interpretations. Jones notes that the essential ambiguity of the tale makes it particularly resistant to adaptation.
   Howard, Patricia. "Myfanwy Piper's 'The Turn of the Screw': Libretto and Synopsis," pp. 23-62. Argues that both Britten and Piper recognized the essential ambiguity of the tale and retained this element in the music and the libretto. Howard examines the libretto in detail and notes the differences between it and the tale.
   Evans, John. "The Sketches: Chronology and Analysis," pp. 63-71. Describes Britten's composing and revising the score.
   Howard, Patricia. "Structures: An Overall View," pp. 71-90. Details the reciprocal relationship between the opera's musical and dramatic structures.
   Howard, Patricia. "The Climax: Act II scene 8, Miles," pp. 90-101. Shows how the music contributes to the opera's dramatic climax.
   Palmer, Christopher. "The Colour of the Music," pp. 101-25. Examines Britten's orchestration, focusing on how the music both conveys and complements characterization.
   Howard, Patricia. "'The Turn of the Screw' in the Theatre," pp. 126-49. Describes the opera's premiere, critical reception, and performance history. Howard also discusses production options, mainly concerning the handling of the opera's ambiguity and the supernatural elements.

63 HUGHES, CLAIR. "Manners and Morality in *Daisy Miller* and *Washington Square*." *Lilium: Journal of Bunkyo Women's College, Hiroshima, Japan* 20:33-43.
   Shows that Daisy's failure to adhere to the prevailing moral code isolates her from society while Catherine's passionate belief in goodness makes her vulnerable to the machinations of the other characters, although ultimately her independence of mind enables her to triumph. Both works are "Tragedies of Manners" reflecting James's

conviction that manners matter because they are reflection of an immoral code.

64   HUGHSON, LOIS. "From Biography to History: Competing Models for Fiction in James, Howells, and Dos Passos." *CUNY English Forum* 1:329-43.
        Argues that in *The Portrait of a Lady* James uses the model of biography to trace Isabel's education of consciousness; in *The Bostonians* James uses history as a means of explaining the novel's characters and events.

65   IAN, MARCIA. "Consecrated Diplomacy and the Concretion of Self." *Henry James Review* 7, no. 1 (Fall):27-33.
        Traces the "process of epistemological concretion" whereby the Jamesian consciousness achieves self-possession with particular reference to Maggie Verver in *The Golden Bowl*. Throughout the novel Maggie gradually realizes both her separateness and her individuality; these become synonymous with moral responsibility. Her achievement of autonomy however, deprives others of theirs: "she believes herself to be the locus of relationship" for the novel's characters.

66   ICKSTADT, HEINZ. "'The Salt That Saves': Fiction and History in the Late Work of Henry James." In *Mythos und Aufklärung in der amerikanischen Literatur/Myth and Enlightenment in American Literature*. EFG 38. Edited by Dieter Meindl and Frederick W. Horlacher. Erlangen: Universitätsbund Erlangen-Nürnberg, pp. 299-319.
        Examines the interrelationships of art, the present, and history—which for James includes accumulated cultural expression, ongoing process, and symbolic construct—in *The Golden Bowl*, the unfinished novels, the autobiography, and *The American Scene*. In the autobiography James shows that factual history is superseded by the "movement of the mind" creating and remembering.

67   INTONTI, VITTORIA. "Le strutture de simulazione spaziale in *The Wings of the Dove* di Henry James" [Structures of spatial simulation in Henry James's *The Wings of the Dove*]. *Quaderni di Anglistica* 3:79-100.
        In Italian.

1985

*68   IVORY J. "The Trouble with Olive." *Sight and Sound* 54 (Spring):95-100.
       Source: *Humanities Index* 12 (1985-1986):527.

69   JACKSON, WENDELL P. "Theory of the Creative Process in the 'Prefaces' of Henry James." In *Amid Visions and Revisions: Poetry and Criticism on Literature and the Arts*. Edited by Burney J. Hollis. Baltimore: Morgan State University Press, pp. 59-64.
       Notes that according to James, the writer of fiction must be disinterested, open-minded, responsible, and attuned to "fundamental meanings" that underlie the surface appearances.

70   JOHNSON, COURTNEY. "Was There a Real Model for the Portrait in James's *The Sacred Fount*?" *Centennial Review* 28-29, nos. 4-1 (Fall-Winter):105-21.
       Argues that Velásquez's "The Portrait of the Jester Calabazas" is the painting that Leon Edel calls central to the novel's meaning.

71   JOHNSON, STUART. "Germinal James: The Lesson of the Apprentice." *Modern Fiction Studies* 31, no. 2 (Summer):233-47.
       Discusses *Watch and Ward* as a response to Ozick's call to read the early James (1982.111) as a way of returning to a literature that does not differentiate between "life and art, experience and consciousness." Return is impossible, however, because James's revision and ultimate rejection of the "early James" makes this novel the work of the Master.

72   JONES, VIVIEN. *James the Critic*. New York: St. Martin's Press, xiii, 230 pp.
       Examines James's criticism – its sources and influences, its evolution, its themes, and its implications for his fiction. Jones discusses the major essays, including the prefaces, demonstrating that in spite of some ambiguities and contradictions James's criticism forms a coherent poetics of fiction.
       Revision of 1980.72; reprint in part of 1982.78.

73 JURISH, ALICE EILEEN. "And What Is Fate but Love? A Study of Marriage and Passion in the Works of Henry James." Ph.D. dissertation, University of California, Davis, 270 pp.

Argues that James's inability to portray sexuality and physicality is caused by his fear of life; indeed, in his early work love and death are linked. Throughout his life, however, James overcame his fear so that he could unite the physical and the psychological, body and soul. Jurish traces James's struggle with this fear in *The Portrait of a Lady*, "The Beast in the Jungle," *The Ambassadors*, and *The Golden Bowl*.

See *Dissertation Abstracts International* 47, no. 4 (1986):1324A.

74 KEESEY, DOUGLAS. "So Much Life with (So to Speak) So Little Living: The Literary Side of the James-Wells Debate." *Henry James Review* 6, no. 2 (Winter):80-88.

Details the literary aspects of the Wells-James quarrel, contrasting each author's vision of reality, relationship to the reader, and sense of the novel's form. Keesey stresses that each side of the controversy had valid points.

75 KIMBALL, JEAN. "A Classified Subject Index to Henry James's Critical Prefaces to the New York Edition (Collected in *The Art of the Novel*)." *Henry James Review* 6, no. 2 (Winter):89-133.

Indexes subjects in the New York Edition prefaces, organizing the subject into four main categories: allusions, analogies and comparisons, Henry James (divided into novels and tales and personal information), and terms and concepts. The index is keyed to Blackmur's collection of the prefaces in *The Art of the Novel*.

76 KIRKBY, JOAN. "The American Prospero." *Southern Review* (University of Adelaide) 18, no. 1 (March):90-108.

Argues that the use of the figure of Prospero–the artist who imposes order on nature–by Poe, Hawthorne, Melville, and James represents a critique of the American belief in the power of the imagination. Unlike the other authors, James depicts his Prosperos exercising power over the social, not the natural, world. Works mentioned are *The Portrait of a Lady*, *The Sacred Fount*, *The Princess Casamassima*, and *The Golden Bowl*.

1985

77 KNAPP, BETTINA L[IEBOWITZ]. "Henry James: Portraiture and Anima in *The Ambassadors*." In *Word/Image/Psyche*. University: University of Alabama Press, pp. 101-25.

Focuses on Mme. de Vionnet and, to a lesser extent, on her daughter Jeanne as anima figures for Strether and for James because they expand consciousness of "life experience." James's use of portraiture in his work, particularly in rendering Mme. de Vionnet, allows him to express his characters' inner world and to explore new dimensions of his creativity. Knapp, however, also sees James's use of portraiture as his attempt to fix motion.

78 LANE, DENIS, and STEIN, RITA, compc. "Henry James." In *A Library of Literary Criticism: Modern British Literature*. Vol. 5, 2d supplement. New York: Frederick Ungar, pp. 249-54.

Reprints excerpts from the following: Graham, 1975.48; Mackenzie, 1976.130; Schneider, 1978.95; Springer, 1978.108; Tuttleton, 1978.124; Wagenknecht, 1978.128.

79 LEAVIS, Q.D. *Collected Essays. Volume 2: The American Novel and Reflections on the European Novel*. Edited by G. Singh. Cambridge: Cambridge University Press, vii, 280 pp.

Contents:

"Henry James and the Disabilities of the American Novelist in the Nineteenth Century," pp. 108-25. Examines James's difficulties and failures in creating a truly American literature because of his expatriation. For example the speech of his early Americans is lively; the "English," especially of the later novels, is not convincing and idiomatic. James also underwrites the Anglo-American fantasies of the nineteenth century when he should be criticizing them.

"Henry James's Heiress: The Importance of Edith Wharton," pp. 194-208. Reprinted from *Scrutiny* 7, no. 3 (December 1938):261-76. Surveys Wharton's fiction, arguing that she made James's concept of the novel as revealed in *The Portrait of a Lady* and *The Bostonians* into a tradition. Wharton's admiration for James was a "springboard from which to take off as an artist."

"James, Trollope and the American-English Confrontation Theme," pp. 126-50. Argues that James was influenced by Trollope's work far more than James ever acknowledged. Leavis sees this influence most clearly in the Anglo-American marriage theme in "An International Episode," "Lady Barbarina," "The Modern Warning," and "A London Life." Trollope's work forced James to confront "the difficulties and disabilities" of being an American at that time.

418

"A Note on Literary Indebtedness: Dickens, George Eliot, Henry James," pp. 151-57. Reprint of *Hudson Review* 8, no. 3 (Autumn 1955). Compares passages from *Little Dorrit, Middlemarch,* and *The Portrait of a Lady* in which the heroine muses upon the ruins of Rome. Dickens and Eliot achieve poetic drama; James fails to realize Isabel's suffering and resorts to the sentimental and picturesque.

"The Fox is the Novelist's Idea: Henry James and the House Beautiful," pp. 158-76. Traces the theme of "the House Beautiful," an emblem of history and culture, throughout James's fiction. The discussion covers the major novels and some tales, focusing on *The Tragic Muse* and *The Spoils of Poynton.*

"Henry James: The Stories," pp. 177-84. Reprinted from *Scrutiny* 14, no. 3 (Spring 1947), pp. 223-9. Reviews Garnett's anthology of James's stories, faulting it for presenting a very limited, "popular" view of James.

"The Institution of Henry James," pp. 185-93. Reprinted from *Scrutiny* 15, no. 1 (December 1947), pp. 68-74. Reviews Dupee's anthology of criticism on James. Leavis comments briefly on the essays included in the collection.

80   LITTLE, MATTHEW. "Henry James's 'The Art of Fiction': Word, Self, Experience." *Philological Quarterly* 64, no. 2 (Spring):225-38.

Examines Taine's *On Intelligence* to show how James used contemporary psychology in his essay. James's metaphor of the web of consciousness, his ideas about the relationship between perceptions and the perceiver, and his attempt to derive a critical terminology can be traced to Taine.

81   LOEB, MONICA. "Henry James and Joyce Carol Oates: 'The Turn of the Screw' Times Two." *American Studies in Scandinavia* 17, no. 1:1-10.

Compares James's tale with Oates's of the same title from the 1972 collection *Marriages and Infidelities,* finding many parallels in setting, subject, theme, point of view, tone, and style. Oates elaborates many of James's technical and thematic elements and may have even used details from James's life.

82   LUBIN, DAVID M. *"The Portrait of a Lady."* In *Act of Portrayal: Eakins, Sargent, James.* Yale Publications in the History of Art, no. 32. New Haven: Yale University Press, pp. 123-49, 172-5.

1985

Argues that Isabel is a portraitist who typecasts both herself and those around her; it is this tendency that causes her suffering. Although the novel shows the dangers of formalism, it formalizes the characters and encourages the reader to do the same thing.
Reprinted 1987.17.

83   LUCAS, JOHN. "Henry James and *Washington Square*." In *Moderns and Contemporaries: Novelists, Poets, Critics*. Brighton, Sussex: Harvester Press; Totowa, N.J.: Barnes & Noble, pp. 3-26.
Examines James's use of comedy juxtaposed with tragedy, and his "disinterested observation" as a means of creating comedy in the novel.
Reprint of essay in *The Air of Reality: New Essays on Henry James*, Edited by John Goode (1972).

84   McCULLOCH, JEANNE. "The Art of Biography I: 'Leon Edel.'" *Paris Review* (Flushing, N.Y.) 98:156-207.
Recounts Edel's involvement with James's work, his initial interest in James's plays, and the writing of the five-volume biography. Edel also discusses in detail the relation of the biographer to subject and to the biography. For Edel, "the secret of biography resides in finding the link between talent and achievement."

85   MACNAUGHTON, W.R. "In Defense of James's *The Tragic Muse*." *Henry James Review* 7, no. 1 (Fall):5-12.
Argues that *The Tragic Muse* is a "superb piece of realistic long prose fiction" by virtue of its organization, characterization, and dramatization of the conflict between art and society. Macnaughton focuses his discussion on the characters of Gabriel Nash, Peter Sherringham, and Nick Dormer, all of which are highly complex and subtly drawn.

86   MAEKAWA, REIKO. "F.O. Matthiessen: After *American Renaissance*." Ph.D. dissertation, Case Western Reserve University, 298 pp.
Argues that *Henry James: The Major Phase* (1944) and *Theodore Dreiser* (1951) continue the concerns expressed in *American Renaissance* (1941). In the 1944 and 1951 books Matthiessen attempted to unify the dividing strains in American culture: the divergence

between the spiritual life and the socio-material life and between individuality and solidarity.

See *Dissertation Abstracts International* 46, no. 12 (1986):3764A.

87 MAINI, DARSHAN SINGH. "Henry James and the Dream of Fiction." *American Review* (New Delhi) (Winter):71-78.

Attributes James's enduring appeal to his "poetics of the spirit" in which consciousness evolves into conscience. Maini also links James's style, particularly the complex style of the major novels, to his vision of life. Maini concludes with an "imaginative reconstruction" of a typical day in James's life.

Reprinted 1987.79.

88 ____. "The Politics of Henry James." *Henry James Review* 6, no. 3 (Spring):158-71.

Examines James's politics, arguing that although his actual interest in politics was negligible and that he shared the prejudices of his class, he was able through his imagination to understand the psychology of politics and to "penetrate the adversary idea and to empathize." Moreover, while James was on the whole conservative, "suppressed radical and democratic impulses" are apparent in his fiction. Maini discusses *The Bostonians, The Princess Casamassima, The Tragic Muse, English Hours* and *The American Scene.*

Reprinted 1987.79.

89 MANSELL, DARREL. "The Ghost of Language in *The Turn of the Screw*." *Modern Language Quarterly* 46, no. 1 (March):48-63.

Argues that the story is a text describing itself with no reference beyond itself. Words have power in themselves and can "scare up ghosts to haunt the printed page."

*90 MARCHENKO, O.I. "Tipy Abzatsey i ikh stilisticheskaia znachimost' v prose G. Dzheimsa: Na materiale romanov 'Posly,' 'Kryl'ia golubki,' novelly 'Zver' v chasche.'" *Izvestiia Akademii Nauk Turkmenskoi SSR, Seriia Obshchestvennykh Nauk* 3:77-83.

Source: *MLA International Bibliography* 1 (1985):179, item 6886.

1985

91   MARGOLIS, ANNE T[HRONE]. *Henry James and the Problem of Audience: An International Act.* Studies in Modern Literature 49. Ann Arbor: University Microfilms International Research Press, xvii, 249 pp.

Traces James's relationship with the Anglo-American reading public over his career to show that he was concerned with popular success and that this concern influenced his fiction. By the middle of his career, James recognized a "split" in the reading public between those who understood his work and those who did not. In his later work, including the prefaces and the New York Edition, James simultaneously attempted to undercut and join this split.

Revision of 1981.97.

92   MARRONI, FRANCESCO. "Henry James e le possibilita dell'inganno: Una lettura di *The Aspern Papers*" [Henry James and the possibility of deception: A reading of *The Aspern Papers*]. *Auademi di Anglistica* 3:101-19.

In Italian.

93   MARTIN, ROBERT K. "*The Bostonians*: James's Dystopian View of Social Reform." *Mosaic* 18, no. 1 (Winter):107-13.

Sees the novel as a rejection of German idealism and American transcendentalism as reflected in reform movements that threaten the individual's integrity. The novel's stress on the search for self through Verena links it to James's other work.

94   MARTIN, W.R., and OBER, WARREN U. "Hemingway and James: 'A Canary for One' and 'Daisy Miller.'" *Studies in Short Fiction* 22, no. 4 (Fall):469-71.

Note the similarities between the two tales, which suggest that Hemingway drew on James's tale to give his own "structural force and pathos."

95   MEHL, DIETER. "Editing a 'Constantly Revising Author': *The Tales of Henry James* (Oxford) and 'The Works of D.H. Lawrence' (Cambridge)." *Archiv* 222, no. 1:136-43.

Reviews the Oxford edition of James's tales, edited by Maqbool Aziz and the Cambridge edition of D.H. Lawrence's works. In the Oxford edition, Aziz reprints the first version of the tale, while the

1985

Cambridge editors publish the final version. This prompts Mehl to argue that revisions even occuring many years later are part of the creative process.

96   MELCHIORI, BARBARA ARNETT. "Dynamite and Democracy." In *Terrorism in the Late Victorian Novel*. London: Croom Helm, pp. 204-11.
        Argues that in *The Princess Casamassima* James equates socialists with anarchists, as did many novelists of the period.

97   MERCER, CAROLINE G., and WAGENSTEEN, SARAH D. "'Consumption, Heart-Disease, or Whatever': Chlorosis, a Heroine's Illness in *The Wings of the Dove*." *Journal of the History of Medicine and Allied Sciences* 40, no. 3 (July):259-85.
        Argues that Milly died of chlorosis, a disease associated with young women. Mercer and Wagensteen include other literary allusions to the disease, beginning with Shakespeare, as well as a history of diagnosing and treating the disease. The authors also discuss James's relationship with William Wilberforce Baldwin and Sir Andrew Clark, both doctors who treated chlorotic patients.

98   MILLER, KARL. "Mankind and Heaven." In *Doubles: Studies in Literary History*. Oxford: Oxford University Press, pp. 197-208.
        Draws parallels between Dickens's Little Nell and Millie Theale and suggests that *The Wings of the Dove* is concerned with "the old issues of romantic pathos and escape, and of romantic elevation, and enlargement, and diminution." Duality is present in the novel in the "two thieves" and in the antithesis between Kate and Millie, both orphans, who reflect James's two nations.

99   _____. "Queer Fellows." In *Doubles: Studies in Literary History*. Oxford: Oxford University Press, pp. 229-41.
        Examines the romantic and Freudian elements in the tale and suggests that "The Jolly Corner" is charged with James's ambivalence about America and his family. *The Sense of the Past*, James's attempt at a novel-length ghost story, is permeated with similar ambivalence and attributes duality in James's fiction to his divided allegiance to America and Europe.

423

1985

100   MIZRUCHI, SUSAN L[AURA]. "The Politics of Temporality in *The Bostonians*." *Nineteenth-Century Fiction* 40, no. 2 (September):187-215.
      Describes power in the novel as the ability of a character to impose a sense of time and a version of history on another, and examines the attitudes of the principal characters toward time. The narrator manipulates time, often withholding information or foreshadowing events, and thus reveals "a will to power over the reader."

101   ____. "The Power of Historical Knowledge: Narrating the Past in Hawthorne, James, and Dreiser." Ph.D. dissertation, Princeton University, 399 pp.
      Examines the portrayal of characters and narrators reconstructing the past in *The House of the Seven Gables*, *The Bostonians*, *The Wings of the Dove*, and *An American Tragedy*, using the theories of Barthes, Jameson, and White. Mizuchi argues for "a growing awareness both of the relativism of historical knowledge and of the alignment of political power and the powers of historical interpretation, from Hawthorne to Dreiser."
      See *Dissertation Abstracts International* 46, no. 10 (1986):3035A.

102   MOLDSTAD, MARY MARTHA FREW. "Images of Self: The Jamesian Heroine as Reflector of Personal History." Ph.D. dissertation, Kent State University, 278 pp.
      Traces James's identification with the heroines in "Madame de Mauves," "Daisy Miller," *Washington Square*, *The Portrait of a Lady*, *The Bostonians*, *The Princess Casamassima* and *The Wings of the Dove*. Moldstad sees James moving from a confrontation with unfamiliar moral values to participation in intricate human relationships.
      See *Dissertation Abstracts International* 46, no. 6 (1985):1628A.

103   MONTANYE, ELIZABETH ANNE. "Behind the Convention of the Open Ending in Henry James and William Dean Howells." Ph.D. dissertation, Indiana University, 249 pp.
      Compares Howell's and James's use of the open ending to show differences in their realism and in their concept of fiction. James's approach is essentially metaphoric, merging unlike perspectives to reflect life's complexity. His endings are closed rhetorically but open

philosophically. In contrast, Howell's approach is metonymic, showing differences in similar characters and thus affirming the complexity of life. His open endings suggest that life is too complex to be grasped imaginatively.

See *Dissertation Abstracts International* 47, no. 2 (1986):531A.

104 MONTEIRO, GEORGE. "Henry James and Mrs. Roundell's Book." *Notes and Queries* 32, no. 3 (September):365-66.
Identifies the book of Mrs. Charles Roundell (Julia Elizabeth Ann Tollemache) mentioned in a 20 September 1889 letter to E.L. Godkin as *A Visit to the Azores* (1889). James appealed for the book to be published in the United States; he was unsuccessful.

105 NIES, FREDERICK JAMES. "Revision of *The Princess Casamassima*." Ph.D. dissertation, University of South Carolina, 1126 pp.
Details the revisions of chapters 1, 3, 13, 21, 24, 29 of the novel, using the 1885-1886 holograph, the 1885-1886 *Atlantic Monthly* serial, the 1886 British edition, and the 1908 New York Edition. Categories of changes include action, theme, characters, relationship, variation, dialogue, rendering, terseness, and grammar. In the appendices Nies discusses the sources for the novel and its characters.
See *Dissertation Abstracts International* 46, no. 10 (1986):3035A.

106 "1984-1985 Annual Review: Henry James." *Journal of Modern Literature* 12, no. 3-4 (November):499-505.
Lists criticism published in 1984-1985.

107 NOWELL-SMITH, SIMON. *The Legend of the Master, Henry James*. New York: Oxford University Press, x, 213 pp.
Reprint of 1947 compilation of extracts taken from James's letters and others' recollections of him.

108 NUSSBAUM, MARTHA. "'Finely Aware and Richly Responsible': Moral Attention and the Moral Task of Literature." *Journal of Philosophy* 82, no. 10 (October):516-31.

Examines James's analogy drawn between the work of the creative imagination and the work of the moral imagination and argues that "the novel is itself a moral achievement, and the well-lived life is a work of literary art." Nussbaum focuses her discussion on Maggie and James's vision of morality in *The Golden Bowl*.
Revised 1987.97.

109 OLANDER, KAREN A. "The Hawthorne-James Relation: From *The Scarlett Letter* to *The Golden Bowl*." Ph.D. dissertation, University of North Carolina at Chapel Hill, 246 pp.
Argues that Hawthorne exerted an influence on James throughout his career, an influence apparent in James's handling of character, point of view, the occult, and the "moral dramas of consciousness."
See *Dissertation Abstracts International* 47, no. 1 (1985):180A-181A.

110 OLSON, CHRISTOPHER PETER. "Narrational and Temporal Form in the Nineteenth- and Twentieth-Century Novel." Ph.D. dissertation, Northwestern University, 269 pp.
Traces the shifting focus from character and plot to narrational and temporal form, beginning with Eliot and Dickens and concluding with Faulkner and Marquez. Although in many respects James's work is similar to that of Eliot's, his rendering of the counterpoint between Strether's immediate impressions and his recollection of those impressions break from the temporality of the nineteenth century novel.
See *Dissertation Abstracts International* 46, no. 8 (1986):2290-2291A.

111 PALILEO, MARIA CLARISSA. "Native Voices, Foreign Tongues: Colonialism and Form in Philippine Fiction." Ph.D. dissertation, Boston University, 242 pp.
Examines the attempt of the Filipino writers–Jose Rizel, Carlos Bulosan, Manuel Arguilla, and N.V.M. Gonzalez–to come to terms with foreign influence, either through rejection or assimilation. Palileo cites Gonzalez as a writer "dominated" by American culture because his work assimilates James's and Hemingway's techniques.
See *Dissertation Abstracts International* 46, no. 6 (1985):1636A.

112   PECORA, VINCENT P. "Of Games and Governesses." *Perspectives on Contemporary Literature* 11:28-36.
      Reviews the current critical tendency to see "The Turn of the Screw" as a game and laments the loss of significance of the literary work. Critics included are Felman (1977.36), Kappeler (1980.72), Rimmon (1977.107), and Brooke-Rose (1976.22, 23).

113   PENNA, ROSE E.M.D. "La conciencia moral en una novela de H. James." *Letras* (University of Carolica Argentina) 14 (December):67-75.
      In POrtuguese.

114   PEROSA, SERGIO. "*Il giro di vite*: Vicende di un racconto" [*The Turn of the Screw*: Vicissitudes of a tale]. *Ars Majeutica*. Edited by Franco Volpi. Vicenza: Neri Pozza, pp. 113-21.
      In Italian.

115   ____. "What Henry Knew." *New York Times Book Review* (17 February):7-8.
      Reviews the two volumes of James's literary criticism issued by the Library of America. James's wide-ranging criticism reflects his "catholicity and omnivorous taste" and his exploration of the "mysterious sources and the inner workings of fiction."

116   POSNOCK, ROSS. *Henry James and the Problem of Robert Browning*. Athens: University of Georgia Press, xi, 231 pp.
      Examines James's lifelong attempt to come to terms with Browning as man and artist. Posnock discusses the similarities between the two writers, and James's individual works in which James examines the man–"The Private Life" and "The Lesson of the Master"–or shows Browning's influence most clearly–*The Wings of the Dove* and *The Golden Bowl*. Posnock sees James's essay "The Novel in *The Ring and the Book*" as both a tribute to the poet and a resolution of the "problem" by rewriting Browning. Browning's "art of process," finally, "helps James inaugurate the modern novel of consciousness."

1985

117 POWERS, LYALL H. "Thornton Wilder as Literary Cubist: An Acknowledged Debt to Henry James." *Henry James Review* 7, no. 1 (Fall):34-44.

Examines James's influence on Wilder, showing that the dramatic technique in *The Awkward Age* was instrumental in shaping *Theophilus North*. James's use of the dramatic–a "direct showing" of the facets of character rather than an "acting out"–inspired Wilder's "literary cubism," in which the literary work is freed from a chronological sequence to expose different facets of character from several points of view.

118 QUINSAT, GILLES. "L'Enfer de Henry James." *Nouvelle Revue Française* 388 (May):36-52.

In French.

119 REDFORD, BRUCE. "Keeping Story out of History: Henry James's Biographical *tour de force*." *American Literature* 57, no. 2 (May):215-25.

Examines the strategies of "diversion, indirection, and decentralization" in the biography of an artist James saw as mediocre. James depicts Story as a type–actually, the prototype of the expatriate–and employs a digressive narrative structure.

120 ROBERTSON, MICHAEL. "The First 'New Journalism' and American Fiction, 1880-1925: Studies in Howells, James, Crane, Dreiser, and Hemingway." Ph.D. dissertation, Princeton University, 272 pp.

Examines the reciprocal relationship between the rise of the modern newspaper, designed for mass circulation, and the modern novel. In *The Portrait of a Lady* James explores the artist's role in an era of mass publicity.

See *Dissertation Abstracts International* 45, no. 12 (1985):3641A.

121 ROBINSON, DOUGLAS. "The House of Fiction." In *American Apocalypses: The Image of the End of the World in American Literature*. Baltimore: Johns Hopkins University Press, pp. 184-86.

Suggests that in "The Jolly Corner" James proposes a "dialogical community" as a way out of solipsism.

122 RON, MOSHE. "The Art of the Portrait According to James." *Yale French Studies*, no. 69:222-37.

Analyzes "The Liar," focusing on the various implications of the portrait for the tale and for James's view of representation. Ron points out that the portrait in the tale "is not a likeness of the other but a reflection of one's desire in the likeness of the other" and notes that this is close to the core of James's work in that his characteristic hero who in the effort to obtain something possessed by another will portray the other's skeleton in the closet but in so doing betrays his own.

Translated and reprinted 1985.123.

123 _____. "L'Art du portrait selon James." Translated by Ruth Amossy and Nadine Mandel. *Littérature* 57 (February):93-108.

In French. Translation and reprint of 1985.122.

124 ROSS, IAN CAMPBELL. Introduction to *The Europeans*. Oxford: Oxford University Press, vii-xxiii.

Sketches the novel's plot and biographical background and discusses in detail the major characters, especially the Baroness. Ross also suggests that the New England of the novel is identical to the New England described in *Hawthorne* and that the novel criticizes both European and American ways of life but does so by "subtly comic means."

125 ROWE, JOHN CARLOS. "To the Editor." *Henry James Review* 6, no. 2 (Winter):153-54.

Responds to Carlson's letter (1984.32), agreeing with her call for a feminist interpretation of James but stressing the need for a theoretically informed feminist deconstruction of James and indeed of the concept of the novel and of authorship.

126 SABIN, MARGERY. "The Community of Intelligence and the Avant-Garde." *Raritan* 4, no. 3 (Winter):1-25.

Traces the evolution of the concept of intelligence in French and English literary culture and sees Arnold and James as pivotal in developing the English concept. In the prefaces, James argues for the centrality of the novelist's intelligence and the importance of appealing to the reader's intelligence.

1985

127 SCHMITZ, NEIL. "Mark Twain, Henry James, and Jacksonian Dreaming." *Criticism* 27, no. 2 (Spring):155-73.

Argues that in *The Gilded Age* and *Roderick Hudson* Jacksonian style – expansive and optimistic – is demeaned and turned into "tall talk." Twain and James reveal the bankruptcy of the egotism that is the root of the style, although their judgment is colored by "untold anxieties, curious repressions, and a secret dread."

*128 SECOR, ROBERT, and MODDELMOG, DEBRA comps. *Joseph Conrad and American Writers: A Bibliographical Study of Affinities, Influences, and Relations*. Westport, Conn.: Greenwood Press, xxxv, 258 pp.

Source: *American Literature* 58 (1986):149.

*129 SHROYER, THOMAS. "In Search of Divine Gossip: Henry James's Reflections on Letters." *Collection of Articles and Essays* (Seoul) 18:355-60.

Source: *Annual Bibliography of English Language and Literature* 60 (1985):462, item 7509.

130 SKILTON, DAVID. "Late-Victorian Choices: James, Wilde, Gissing, and Moore." In *Defoe to the Victorians: Two Centuries of the English Novel*. New York: Penguin Books, pp. 178-91.

Reprint of 1977.119.

131 SMITH, JOHN WILLIAM. "The Theme of 'Life' in *The Ambassadors* and *The Golden Bowl*: Henry James's Humanistic Salvation Scheme." Ph.D. dissertation, University of Southwestern Louisiana, 283 pp.

Traces the development of this theme in *Roderick Hudson, The American, The Portrait of a Lady, The Ambassadors*, and *The Golden Bowl*. In the early novels, the protagonist is a center of consciousness through which James filters "the materials of a developed awareness." In the later novels, the most significant and unified treatments of "life," James focuses on the consciousness itself.

See *Dissertation Abstracts International* 46, no. 6 (1985):1629A.

132 STAFFORD, WILLIAM T. "Note on the Texts." In *Novels 1881-1886: Washington Square, The Portrait of a Lady, The Bostonians*, vol. 29. New York: Library of America, pp. 1237-42.
   Describes the genesis, publication history, and revisions of these three novels.

133 TALLACK, DOUGLAS. "'The Story of One's Story': A Technique of Authority in Benjamin, Sartre, and the Tales of Henry James." *Cahiers de la Nouvelle* (Angers, France) 5:33-54.
   Discusses the "fictitious recital" that frames a narrative and that establishes the storyteller's authority. Sartre condemns the fictitious recital because it attempts to deny the unpredictability of life and presents the narrative as static. For James and Benjamin, however, "the fictitious recital is a sign of ontological insecurity which exposes both the reification of society by the late nineteenth-century middle-class . . . and the reification of form by Modernism."

134 TANNER, TONY. *Henry James: The Writer and His Work*. Amherst: University of Massachusetts Press, x, 142 pp.
   Reprint of 1979.146, 1979.147, 1981.152.

135 TEYSSANDIER, HUBERT. "De Balzac à James: La Vision de Paris dans *The Ambassadors* (1903)." *Cahiers Victoriens et Edouardiennes de l'Université Paul Valéry* (Montpellier) 21 (April):51-62.
   In French.
   Argues that in *The Ambassadors* James creates a vision of Paris through the perspectives of his characters, their social milieux, and the shift between Paris as a place and as a symbol of civilization. Continuing the tradition of Balzac, James interjects fin-de-siècle irony into his use of Paris as a central concept of the novel.

136 ____. "L'Image de Venise dans *The Wings of the Dove*." In *Home, Sweet Home or Bleak House? Art et littérature a l'époque Victorienne*. Edited by Marie-Claire Hamard. Annales Litts. de l'Univ. de Besançon, 308. Paris: Belles Lettres, pp. 69-82.
   In French.

1985

137 THEROUX, PAUL. Introduction to *What Maisie Knew*. Harmondsworth, Middlesex, England: Penguin Books, pp. 7-19.

Examines the main characters in detail, concentrating on the contrast between them and Maisie, who is compassionate, open, and honest. The characters force her to know "All," and in the end this knowledge of human affairs is the death of her childhood.

Reprinted 1985.138.

138 _____. *"What Maisie Knew."* In *Sunrise with Seamonsters: A Paul Theroux Reader*. Boston: Houghton Mifflin. pp. 335-45.

Reprint of 1985.137.

139 TIMMS, DAVID. "An Unpublished Henry James Letter." *Journal of American Studies* 19, no. 3 (December):415-20.

Reprints a 2 March 1915 letter to Kate Grove, the wife of Archibald Grove, editor of *Macmillan's Magazine*. In the letter James expresses his admiration for the couple's son, Edward, who was fighting in the war.

140 TINTNER, ADELINE R. "'Broken Wings': Henry James' Tribute to a Victorian Novelist." *AB Bookman's Weekly* 75, no. 16 (22 April):3016-28.

Traces James's attitudes toward Mrs. Oliphant and his incorporation of her history and character in "Broken Wings." James admired her capacity for work, her "'cleverness, courage and humanity.'"

141 _____. "Fiction Is the Best Revenge: Portraits of Henry James by Four Women Writers." *Turn-of-the-Century Women* 2, no. 2 (Winter):42-49.

Argues that Vernon Lee, Mrs. Humphrey Ward, Edith Wharton, and Olive Garnett took their revenge on James's criticism and appropriation of their fiction by portraying him in their fiction and by rewriting his fiction.

142 _____. "Henry James and Stark Young: The Correct Version of the Legendary Letter." *American Literature* 57, no. 2 (May):318-21.

Reprints the letter in which James gives Stark Young two reading lists of his novels and notes that Young's apparent interest in James was actually a "failure in understanding."

143 _____. "Henry James and the First World War: The Release from Repression." In *Literature and War: Reflections and Refractions*. Edited by Elizabeth W. Trahan. Monterey, Calif.: Monterey Institute of International Studies, pp. 169-84.

Argues that James's involvement in the First World War, including writing war propaganda, was a result of having resolved his guilt and inhibitions about his inability to participate in the Civil War. This resolution was achieved through the writing of his autobiography. World War I legitimatized James's homoeroticism because it was then acceptable to care for young men. James's appetite for crime stories during this period is also attributable to the war because according to Freud war brings out the primitive instincts in man.

144 _____. "Henry James, *The Scapegoat*, and the William Holman Hunt." *Journal of PreRaphaelite Studies* 6:34-41.

Argues that Hunt's painting, seen by the young James in 1858, is a central image in the second half of *The Golden Bowl*. Maggie, Adam, and Charlotte are connected with this image. Tintner documents James's contact with Hunt, which kept the memory of the painting alive.

145 _____. "Henry James' Two Ways of Seeing." *AB Bookman's Weekly* 75, no. 3 (21 January):363-74.

Suggests that in the 1898 tale "John Delavoy" James distinguishes for the first time between seeing and perceiving. Tintner also enumerates the verbs, metaphors, and puns referring to vision.

146 _____. "Henry James's 'Julia Bride': A Source for Chapter Nine in Edith Wharton's *The Custom of the Country*." *NMAL: Notes on Modern American Literature* 9, no. 3 (Winter). Item 16.

Shows that Wharton used Julia's request to a former fiancé when Undine requests Elmer Moffatt to conceal their past relationship. Wharton's expansion of Julia's situation into a novel reveals how Wharton uses James's work to develop her own ideas.

1985

147 _____. *"The Prague Orgy*: Roth Still Bound to Henry James." *Midstream* 31, no. 10 (December):49-51.

   Demonstrates that the novels in *Zuckerman Bound*, including the epilogue *The Prague Orgy*, are consciously and unconsciously influenced by James.

148 _____. "Roth's 'Pain' and James's 'Obscure Hurt.'" *Midstream* 31, no. 3 (March):58-60.

   Argues that James's *Autobiography* provides the "master plan" for Roth's "autobiography." *The Anatomy Lesson* – the tip-off is Zuckerman's "intolerable and undiagnosable pain." Tintner suggests that Zuckerman's consciousness of James may be the source of the pain.

149 _____. "To the Editor." *Henry James Review* 6, no. 2 (Winter):154-56.

   Describes and quotes a parody of James – his biography written in the Jamesian style – that Tintner found in *Who's "It" in America* (1906) by Charles Eustace Merriman.

150 _____. "The Use of Stupidity as a Narrative Device: The Gullible Teller in James's 'Louisa Pallant.'" *Journal of Narrative Technique* 15, no. 1 (Winter): 70-74.

   Examines the narrator in the tale as an example of the reliable though obtuse narrator who functions in both "The Figure in the Carpet" and *The Sacred Fount*.

151 TORGOVNICK, MARIANNA. "In the Documentary Mode: James, Lawrence, Woolf, and the Visual Arts." In *The Visual Arts, Pictorialism, and the Novel: James, Lawrence, and Woolf*. Princeton: Princeton University Press, pp. 37-69, 229-35.

   Surveys these authors' involvement with the visual arts. Although James used visual art – especially architecture – as a metaphor for his work, he stopped short of Lawrence's and Woolf's experiments with visual art.

152 _____. "Paintbrushes, Chisels, and Red Herrings: Decorative Uses of the Visual Arts and Pictorialism in Selected Novels by James and Earlier Novelists." In *The Visual Arts, Pictorialism, and the Novel:*

James, Lawrence, and Woolf. Princeton: Princeton University Press, pp. 70-106, 235-39.

Examines the use of the visual arts and art metaphors over the course of the history of the novel and in James's *Roderick Hudson* and *The Tragic Muse.* References to art in these two novels and in novels from Fielding to Dickens are "red herrings" because the art is decorative rather than ideological or interpretive. In addition, references to art do not guarantee pictorialism – as illustrated by the early James novels – and illustrations included with the text can often handicap the free function of the reader's imagination.

153 _____. "Perception, Impression, and Knowledge in *The Portrait of a Lady, The Ambassadors,* and *The Golden Bowl.*" In *The Visual Arts, Pictorialism, and the Novel: James, Lawrence, and Woolf.* Princeton: Princeton University Press, pp. 157-91, 243-45.

Traces the evolution of James's use of the visual arts for ideology and his use of pictorialism in these novels. In *The Portrait,* characters' attitudes toward art suggest personality traits; in *The Ambassadors,* the educative value of visual impressions is a major motif; and in *The Golden Bowl,* Maggie's perceptual process is based on what she sees.

154 VEEDER, WILLIAM. "Image as Argument: Henry James and the Style of Criticism." *Henry James Review* 6, no. 3 (Spring):172-81.

Links James's "critical sensibility" with his stylistic development. Veeder stresses that James's position as an expatriate American artist gave him the distance and disinterestedness necessary to the critic. His role as a disinterested critic forced James to develop a style that "multiplies terms" and "elaborates images."

155 VICKERY, JAMES F. "The Fonts of Henry James." Ph.D. dissertation, State University of New York, Buffalo, 190 pp.

Examines James's representation of his heroines from *Watch and Ward* to *The Golden Bowl,* tracing "a progressively insistent materialization" in their depiction, which Vickery sees as the content of Jamesian realism. Vickery also shows that his conclusions about James heroines are confirmed by the analyses of the American woman in *The American Scene.*

See *Dissertation Abstracts International* 46, no. 10 (1986):3037A.

1985

156 VIDAL, GORE. Introduction to *The Golden Bowl*. New York: Penguin Books, p. 7-18.
　　　Reprint of 1984.214.

157 VIELLEDENT, CATHERINE. "L'honnete femme n'a pas de roman': le vulgaire et le romanesque." *Cahiers de la Nouvelle* (Angers, France) 5:79-99.
　　　In French.

158 _____. "Representation and Reproduction: A Reading of Henry James's 'The Real Thing.'" In *Interface: Essays on History, Myth, and Art in American Literature*. Edited by Daniel Royat. Montpellier: Pubs. de la Recherche, Univ. Paul Valéry, pp. 31-49.
　　　Argues that the tale dramatizes the act of interpretation and exemplifies James's concern with reflexivity. The Monarchs show that the artist cannot control his subject; indeed the subject undermines his authority.

159 VINEBERG, STEVE. "The Responsibility of the Adapter: *The Bostonians* on Film." *Arizona Quarterly* 41, no. 3 (Autumn):223-30.
　　　Argues that Ivory's film adaptation turns an "explosively funny" novel into a "solemn costume drama, a graveyard." The only redeeming performance is Vanessa Redgrave, whose rendering of Olive is true to the novel.

160 WAGNER, VERN. "Henry James: Money and Sex." *Sewanee Review* 93, no. 2 (April-June):216-31.
　　　Shows how throughout all periods of his fiction James used money and sex "as the primary impelling forces in human behavior" and draws examples from a wide range of novels and tales, beginning with *The American* and ending with *The Golden Bowl*.

161 WARD, J.A. "Four Fables of Silence: Poe, Melville, James, and Adams." In *American Silences: The Realism of James Agee, Walker Evans, and Edward Hopper*. Baton Rouge: Louisiana State University Press, pp. 27-32.
　　　Reprint of 1982.162.

162 WEBER, HORST. "'The Pleasures of Gentility': Asthetik und Ethik in Henry James' *The Princess Casamassima*" [Aesthetics and Ethics in Henry James's *The Princess Casamassima*]. *Germanisch-Romanische Monatsschrift* 35, no. 4:412-30.
In German.

163 WEISSMAN, JUDITH. "Antique Secrets in Henry James." *Sewanee Review* 93, no. 2 (April-June):196-215.
Suggests that James's and Oscar Wilde's use of antique collecting in their fiction is not just a symbol of a breakdown of the traditional family but an indication of both authors' homosexuality as well.

164 WELLS, SUSAN. "*The Turn of the Screw*, Indeterminacy, and the Dialectics of Possession." In *The Dialectics of Representation*. Baltimore: Johns Hopkins University Press, pp. 80-102.
Examines the levels of indeterminacy in the tale: relations between characters, the narrative frame and the existence of the ghosts. Wells sees the absent uncle's "possession" that refers to ownership or to obsession as central to the tale's indeterminacy. The "indeterminate register" in fact shapes both the tale, including structure, plot, and style, and the reader's response.

165 WILDER, THORNTON. *The Journals of Thornton Wilder 1939-1961*. Edited by Donald Gallup. New Haven: Yale University Press, pp. 58-61, 65-68.
Discusses narrative technique in *The Wings of the Dove*, calling James's use of "centers" a way to avoid omniscience, a "dangerous compromise."

166 WINKGENS, MEINHARD. "Die Bedingungen einer *Ideal Civilization* oder das Aquivalenzystem des Textes: Wirkingsästhetische Überlegungen zu Henry James' 'The Europeans.'" [The demands of an ideal civilization or the equivalence of the text: Reflections on the aesthetic effects on Henry James's *The Europeans*]. *Sprachkunst: Beitrage zur Literaturwissenschraft* 16, no. 2:256-75.
In German.

1985

167   WOLK, MERLA. "The Sweet-Shop Window, the House of Fiction
      and the Jamesian Artist." *American Imago* 42, no. 3 (Fall):269-95.
             Argues that the image of the watcher outside the sweet-shop
      window, which appears in *The Princess Casamassima, What Maisie
      Knew, A Small Boy and Others*, and the Preface to *The Portrait of a
      Lady*, is a vision of the artist. Tracing the use of these images shows the
      evolution of the Jamesian artist from exclusion and deprivation to the
      discovery of a safe place within the house of fiction.

168   WRIGHT, TERENCE. "Rhythm in the Novel." *Modern Language
      Review* 80, no. 1 (January):1-15.
             Examines rhythm as a structuring element in fiction. Wright
      discusses a variety of novels to illustrate the different forms rhythm may
      take, and cites *The Bostonians* as dominated by a rhythm corresponding
      to the thematic motif of "calm" and "unrest."

169   YACOBI, TAMAR. "Hero or Heroine? *Daisy Miller* and the Focus
      of Interest in Narrative." *Style* 19, no. 1 (Spring):1-35.
             Applies Meir Sternberg's theory of the "focus of interest" to
      "Daisy Miller" as a way to determine whether Winterbourne or Daisy is
      the central character. The majority of Sternberg's "indicators" point to
      Winterbourne; indicators that do not, Yacobi suggests, show that this is
      an early, transitional work.

1986

1   ANESKO, MICHAEL. *"Friction with the Market": Henry James and
      the Profession of Authorship*. New York: Oxford University Press, xii,
      258 pp.
             Documents James's continual search for an audience and his
      dealing with many publishers to show how his concern for appealing to
      the "market" shaped his fiction. Although this study concentrates on
      Hawthorne, The Bostonians, The Princess Casamassima, and *The Tragic
      Muse*, Anesko also discusses the creation of the New York Edition.
             Revision in part of 1983.8.

2   ARMSTRONG, PAUL B. "Reading, Representation, and Realism
      in *The Ambassadors*." *Amerikastudien* 31, no. 1 (Summer):111-25.

Argues that although James is a realist, he "challenges the conventions of realism by exposing and exploring their epistemological foundations"; indeed, this exploration becomes the central action in *The Ambassadors*. Both Strether and the reader are forced to question the validity of interpretation. In examining the epistemology of James's "representational practice" Armstrong focuses on "the necessarily partial representation of objects, the authority of the narrator, the temporality of narrative, and the relation between the subjectivity of the reader and the world of the work."

Revised 1987.4.

3 AUCHARD, JOHN. *Silence and Henry James: The Heritage of Symbolism and Decadence*. University Park: Pennsylvania State University Press, 182 pp.

Argues that James's "silences" – as lack of talk and as a structure of negation – reveal his connection with the decadent and symbolist movements. Auchard structures his discussion to reflect the Jamesian thesis and antithesis, pairing *Roderick Hudson* and *The American*, *The Portrait of a Lady* and *The Spoils of Poynton*, *The Wings of the Dove* and *The Golden Bowl*. The role of negation is essentially dialectical in James in its affirmation of vitality and its recognition of chaos and ambiguity.

4 AUERBACH, NINA. "Alluring Vacancies in the Victorian Character." *Kenyon Review* 8, no. 3 (Summer):36-48.

Argues that in *Bleak House, Daniel Deronda*, and *The Portrait of a Lady* "the author's doubts about the integrity of creation are translated into the heroine's horror at the monstrosity of her own existence." As a result, these novels are theatrical in their concern with the spectacle of character. Isabel, for example, "is a tantalizing sequence of picturesque attitudes whom others endow with moral life."

5 BALES, KENT. "Intention and Readers' Responses." *Neohelicon* 13, no. 1:177-94.

Critiques Iser's reading of "The Figure in the Carpet" (Iser 1978.53), arguing that Iser does not examine or even acknowledge his intention in producing his particular reading of the talk; he is blind to the "repertoire of norms" he applies to the text.

1986

6   BAMBROUGH, RENFORD. "Ounces of Example: Henry James, Philosopher." In *Realism in European Literature*. Edited by Nicholas Boyle and Martin Swales. Cambridge: Cambridge University Press, pp. 169-82.
     Argues that James is a realist because of his concern with perception and cognition and with the "middle ground" between the imagination and the actual.

7   BAYLEY, JOHN. Introduction to *The Wings of the Dove*. Harmondsworth, England: Penguin Books, pp. 7-29.
     Discusses the dramatic and melodramatic elements of the novel, and compares it with Shakespeare's *Macbeth* and Dickens' *Our Mutual Friend*. In spite of some shortcomings, the novel "seems to the reader *true*, deep, a mass of complex and authentic creation, querying, wondering, and revealing."

8   BELL, IAN F.A. "A Mere Surface: Wyndham Lewis, Henry James and the 'Latitude' of *Hugh Selwyn Mauberley*." *Paideuma* 15, nos. 2-3 (Fall-Winter):53-71.
     Discusses the Jamesian idea of surface, which rejects "'going behind,'" in terms of Lewis's and Pound's use of it. Surface exposes the "play of power which communication always involves" and ensures the freedom of the reader to "re-compose" and to "imagin[e] alternative worlds."

9   BELL, MILLICENT. "The Critical James." *Sewanee Review* 94, no. 1 (Winter):148-59.
     Reviews *Henry James: Literary Criticism*, edited by Edel and Wilson in the two-volume Library of America edition. Bell notes that James is an "unprescriptive critic" who recognized that each novel must be approached on its own terms.

10 BENDIXEN, ALFRED. Introduction: The Whole Story Behind *The Whole Family*. In *The Whole Family: A Novel by Twelve Authors*. Edited by Alfred Bendixen. York: Ungar, pp. xi-li.
     Chronicles the writing of *The Whole Family*, to which James contributed a chapter, "The Married Son." James was pleased with his contribution but was frustrated when other authors failed to appreciate his work. Bendixen describes the chapter as "a delightfully comic and

thoroughly Jamesean confrontation with the agonies of an aesthetic nature trapped in a materialistic environment."
Reprinted 1986.11.

11 ____. "It Was a Mess! How Henry James and Others Actually Wrote a Novel." *New York Times Book Review* (27 April):3, 28, 29.
Reprint of 1986.10.

12 BENERT, ANNETTE LARSON. "Monsters, Bagmen, and Little Old Ladies: Henry James and the Unmaking of America." *Arizona Quarterly* 42, no. 4 (Winter):331-43.
Finds similar visions of Western civilization in James's *The American Scene* and Max Weber's *The Protestant Ethic and the Spirit of Capitalism*. Both the artist and the scientist see "the danger of a public ethos that narrows all human motivation, all cultural achievement, all social engagement to the rigors of the marketplace."

13 BERKSON, DOROTHY. "Why Does She Marry Osmond? The Education of Isabel Archer." *American Transcendental Quarterly* 60 (June):53-71.
Argues that the special nature of the female *bildungsroman* explains Isabel's decisions to marry Osmond and return to him at the novel's end. Given her innocence, Isabel made a logical choice by marrying Osmond, who offers "nothing" and thus appears to be recognizing her independence. Isabel returns to Rome because of her commitment to Pansy.

14 BERSANI, LEO. "Freud's New World." In *The Freudian Body: Psychoanalysis and Art*. New York: Columbia University Press, pp. 81-106.
Argues that in *The Golden Bowl* Maggie becomes an "unreadable text": the other characters vainly try to interpret her, and she "does nothing but adhere, without the slightest defection into truth, to the decorous life, fed to her by the others, that nothing is wrong with her marriage." Bersani's discussion of this novel prefaces his analysis of Freud's *The Ego and the Id*.

1986

15 BLACKMUR, R[ICHARD] P. "The Critical Prefaces of Henry James." In *Selected Essays of R.P. Blackbur*. Edited by Denis Donoghue. New York: Ecco Press, pp. 249-77.

Surveys the prefaces, "the most eloquent and original piece of literary criticism in existence," describing their main features and identifying recurring themes and subjects in individual prefaces.

Reprint of essay in *The Lion and the Honeycomb* (1955).

16 _____. "Henry James." In *Selected Essays of R.P. Blackmur*. Edited by Denis Donoghue. New York: Ecco Press, pp. 279-310.

Sketches James's life, surveys his major works and themes, and evaluates his place in American literature. James devoted his life to discovering the emotions and motives that lie beneath the surface of life, and this devotion radically shaped James's fiction, forever transforming the novel.

Reprint of essay in *Literary History of the United States*, edited by Robert Spiller (1948).

17 BOONE, JOSEPH A. "Modernist Maneuverings in the Marriage Plot: Breaking Ideologies of Gender in James's *The Golden Bowl*." *PMLA* 101, no. 3 (May):374-88.

Argues that James explores the possibilities and limitations of marriage and of narrative. The novel's ambiguity and open-endedness are James's attempts to "evolve a mode of representation capable of expressing an ambivalent vision of married life beyond the 'happy end' of traditional fictions."

18 BOREN, LYNDA S. "The Performing Self: Psychodrama in Austen, James and Woolf." *Centennial Review* 30, no. 1 (Winter):1-24.

Argues that the fiction of these authors uses dramatic conventions to portray the development of the self; indeed, drama becomes "an analogy for life itself." In "The Turn of the Screw" the governess is an artist who creates her own drama, literally and figuratively.

19 BREWER, DEREK. Introduction to *The Princess Casamassima*. Harmondsworth, England: Penguin Books, pp. 7-30.

Sketches the novel's sources, central characters, structure, and narrative technique, noting that the central interest is on the psychological, moral, and aesthetic.

20   BRODHEAD, RICHARD H. "Henry James: Tradition and the
     Work of Writing." In *The School of Hawthorne*. New York: Oxford
     University Press, pp. 104-20.
         Discusses James's redefinition of the novelist's work as both
     vocation and profession, and his creation of a "fictional canon and of
     fiction as a canon-governed form." Hawthorne is James's "founding
     father" in that he began to establish the legitimacy of the idea of
     authorship.

21   _____. "James in the Beginning." In *The School of Hawthorne*. New
     York: Oxford University Press, pp. 121-39.
         Examines Hawthorne's influence on James's early work. With
     the tales, James is Hawthorne's student; with *Roderick Hudson* he is
     Hawthorne's successor. By 1875, however, James begins to distance
     himself from Hawthorne, which explains the aloofness of his 1879
     Hawthorne. In spite of James's conscious attempts to disavow his
     master, Hawthorne permeates James's imagination; in *The Portrait of a
     Lady*, Hawthorne's influence has "unprecedented force."

22   _____. "James, Realism, and the Politics of Style." In *The School of
     Hawthorne*. New York: Oxford University Press, pp. 140-165.
         Sees James's realism, as manifested in *The Bostonians* and *The
     Princess Casamassima*, as his attempt to create a new tradition for
     himself. Hawthorne's influence is most apparent in *The Bostonians*,
     particularly in the novel's examination of power, and in Christina of *The
     Princess Casamassima*, James's reworking of Zenobia. Hawthorne
     shapes James's political vision, in which the struggle for social change
     arises out of emotional distress, disguising the "pursuit of private
     emotional goals."

23   _____. "Late James: The Lost Art of the Late Style." In *The School
     of Hawthorne*. New York: Oxford University Press, pp. 166-200.
         Argues that James's late style "communicate[s] only when it
     effects an attentive arrest"; the reader must work to understand its
     implied meanings. The late style is derived from James's sense of an
     authorial career and is a reponse to the increased vulgarity of
     contemporary society, both of which Brodhead links to Hawthorne.
     Brodhead focuses on "The Beast in the Jungle" and *The Golden Bowl*;
     the tale "forces a striking account of what Hawthorne's essential work

1986

is" while the novel culminates Hawthorne's lesson to James as a reinvention of the romance.

24   BROWN, CHRISTOPHER. "The Rhetoric of Closure in *What Maisie Knew*." *Style* 20, no. 1 (Spring):58-65.
    Describes the speech of the adults at the novel's end as a parody of closural rhetoric, as defined by Smith and Torgovnick. Maisie's language, in contrast, is effective and mature; unlike the adults, she can bring the novel to a close.

*25 BRUGIERE, B. "A Posthumous Dialog between Henry James and Benjamin Britten on 'The Turn of the Screw.'" *Corps Ecrit* 20:47-61.
    In French.
    (Source: *Arts and Humanities Citation Index* 3 (1987):973.)

26   BUITENHUIS, PETER. "Americans in European Gardens." *Henry James Review* 7, no. 2-3 (Winter-Spring):124-30.
    Argues that James used and developed images and themes from Hawthorne's "Rappaccini's Daughter" in *The Portrait of a Lady*. In examining the garden imagery of the novel, Buitenhuis concludes that James complicates Hawthorne's moral scheme: the novel depicts not simply the destruction of innocence but "the defeat of freedom and opportunity by Americans partly bedazzled by the society, the culture, and the artistic heritage of Europe."

27   BURLESON, DONALD R. "Symmetry in Henry James's 'The Altar of the Dead.'" *Studies in Weird Fiction* 1, no. 1 (Summer):29-32.
    Examines the symmetry of images throughout the tale, which demonstrates that "The Altar of the Dead" is a "superbly crafted work of art" and "an architectural creation" based on the symmetry inherent in the central image of the altar.

28   CESARINI, REMO. "La maschera della medusa" [The Medusa's Mask]. *Belfagor* 41, no. 6 (November 30):605-20.
    In Italian.

29   CHASE, DENNIS. "The Ambiguity of Innocence: *The Turn of the Screw*." *Extrapolation* 27, no. 3 (Fall):197-202.

Attributes much of the tale's supposed ambiguity to the governess's and Miles's innocence and examines the Freudian imagery in the tale.

30   CHAUCHAIX, JACQUELINE, and VERLEY, CLAUDINE. "La Sémiotique de l'espace dans *The Jolly Corner* de Henry James." *La Licorne* 10:17-29.

In French.

31   CHEVIGNY, BELL GALE. "The Edges of Ideology: Margaret Fuller's Centrifugal Evolution." *American Quarterly* 38, no. 2 (Summer):173-201.

Examines the way in which Fuller exposed "American social contradictions" and how her life was reinterpreted after her death. James's *The Bostonians* is a "textualization" of her life, stressing her feminism; *The Portrait of a Lady* rewrites Fuller's attitude toward Italy in that, while Fuller recognizes the contemporary realities of Italy, Isabel Archer is attuned only to the historical Italy.

32   CHILDRESS, RON. "James's *Daisy Miller*." *Explicator* 44, no. 2 (Winter):24-25.

Explores the various meanings of "afraid" in the tale. Winterbourne, whose speech is dotted with "afraid," fears women; Daisy in contrast is fearless.

33   COHEN, PAULA MARANTZ. "Freud's *Dora* and James's *Turn of the Screw*: Two Treatments of the Female 'Case.'" *Criticism* 28, no. 1 (Winter):73-87.

Compares Freud's case history and James's ghost story in the ways in which they raise questions about each genre. Freud's failure with Dora gave him the opportunity to assert his drive for authority by controlling the narrative; James's acknowledgement of ghosts enabled him to expose the limitations of scientific truth.

1986

34   COON, ANNE CHRISTINE. "Widows, Spinsters and Lovers: The
      Controlling Female Figure in the Fiction of Henry James." Ph.D.
      dissertation, State University of New York, Buffalo, 185 pp.
         Examines the role of the controlling female figure in *Roderick
      Hudson*, *The Princess Casamassima*, *The Portrait of a Lady*, *The
      Bostonians*, *The Spoils of Poynton*, and *The Ambassadors*. Coon details
      the many attributes of this figure, explores its functions, and relates it to
      James's family and friends.
         See *Dissertation Abstracts International* 47, no. 4 (1986):1321A.

35   CORSE, SANDRA. "Henry James on Eliot and Sand." *South
      Atlantic Review* 51, no. 1 (January):58-68.
         Details James's critical assessment of George Eliot and
      George Sand. In contrast to his typical treatment of women novelists,
      James respected both novelists for their ability to add positive
      masculine traits to their feminine ones; thus they exemplify James's
      ideal artist, who "envelopes and transforms" experience.

36   COWARD, NANCY POTTS. "Mothers and Sons in the Fiction of
      Mark Twain, William Dean Howells, and Henry James." Ph.D.
      dissertation, University of North Carolina, Chapel Hill, 341 pp.
         Argues that the cult of domesticity, which fostered a close
      bond between mother and son, influenced the life and writings of these
      three writers. Specifically this influence is manifested in a conflict
      between dependence and the need to escape domination. Coward
      suggests that James gave Mary James's undesirable traits to British
      mothers and her desirable ones to American mothers.
         See *Dissertation Abstracts International* 47, no. 5 (1986):1727A.

37   COWDERY, LAUREN T. *The Nouvelle of Henry James in Theory
      and Practice*. Studies in Modern Literature, 47. Ann Arbor:
      University Microfilms International Research Press, ix, 136 pp.
         Examines James's concept of the novella as discussed in the
      prefaces and as practiced in "Daisy Miller," "Julia Bride," "The Coxon
      Fund," and "The Birthplace." Cowdery finds a differentiation between
      anecdote and novella, and between story and subject, although these
      pairs are not polar because the novella subsumes anecdote and story. In
      addition, Cowdery devotes a chapter to James's "fellow writers of the
      nouvelle," which include Bourget, Kipling, and Turgenev, in order to
      illuminate James's theory of the novella.

Revision of 1980.33.

38   COX, JAMES M. "The Memoirs of Henry James: Self-Interest as Autobiography." *Southern Review* 22, no. 2 (April):231-51.
     Discusses *The American Scene* and the *Autobiography*, noting that in the latter work James asserts the primacy and power of consciousness. Cox notes, however, that while James is the "consummate artist" who makes a life of art, he suffers from a narrowness of vision, particularly at the end of his life, which left him unprepared for the horrors of war.

39   CURTSINGER, E.C. *The Muse of Henry James*. Mansfield, Tex.: Latitudes Press, 133 pp.
     Traces Christian metaphors throughout James's fiction, focusing on the blending of classical and Christian tradition in the figure of *"mon bon,"* "the lady of the imagination who merges with the muse who merges with the madonna to bring and receive the message from the gods." Works discussed include "Travelling Companions," "The Madonna of the Future," *Roderick Hudson, The Portrait of a Lady*, "The Author of 'Beltraffio,'" "The Aspern Papers," "The Turn of the Screw," *The Sacred Fount*, and the three novels of the major phase.
     Reprint in part 1980.37 and 1982.36.

40   DAVIS, MARIJANE ROUNTREE. "The Fascination of Knowledge: Imagistic Clues to the Labyrinth of Ambiguity in Henry James's *The Golden Bowl*." Ph.D. dissertation, University of Tennessee, 497 pp.
     Argues that the imagery in the novel gives clues to Maggie's and the reader's quest for knowledge, thus resolving much of the ambiguity long associated with the novel. Davis divides the imagery into seven basic categories: the adventurous, the sensuous, the superficial, the fantastic, the material, the intelligent, and the free.
     See *Dissertation Abstracts International* 47, no. 7 (1987):2583A.

41   DAY, SIMON. "Rooms with a View: The Centenary of Carlyle Mansions, Cheyne Walk." *Country Life* 180, no. 4657 (20 November):1654-5.

1986

Describes James's apartment, where he lived from 1913 to his death in 1916. T.S. Eliot and Ian Fleming were later residents of the same building.

42 DEAN, MISAO. "A Note on *Cousin Cinderella* and *Roderick Hudson*." *Studies in Canadian Literature* 11, no. 1 (Spring):96-98.
Finds similarities between James's novel and Sara Jeannette Duncan's 1908 novel, particularly in the use of the international theme.

43 DeMILLE, BARBARA. "Lambert Strether and the Tiger: Categories, Surfaces and Forms in Nietzsche and Henry James." *South Atlantic Review* 51, no. 1 (January):69-82.
Finds numerous similarities in James's and Nietzsche's view of the relation between art and experience. For both, "the best artist and the highest art consist in the continual formation and renewal of both the artistic perception *and* the form."

44 DiPIERO, W.S. "William James and Henry James." *Triquarterly* 67 (Fall):93-107.
Contrasts William's interest in "formlessness" with Henry's need for order and suggests that the two brothers represent the two divisive forces in the "American poetical character." DiPiero examines these forces in the work of Frost, Lowell, Roethke, and other poets, noting that in spite of this divisiveness there remains an instinct for unity in American poetry.

45 DJWA, SANDRA. "*Ut Pictura Poesis*: The Making of a Lady." *Henry James Review* 7, nos. 2-3 (Winter-Spring):72-85.
Argues that *The Portrait of a Lady* is a critique of Paterian aestheticism that dismisses experience and an embodiment of James's aesthetic, which holds experience to be essential in judging life and art.

46 DUCHARME, MARGARET MARY. "Historical and Political Images in Henry James." Ph.D. dissertation, University of Toronto, Canada.
Argues that James's use of historical and political imagery remains constant throughout his work and that such imagery is crucial in understanding his fiction. And by examining James's letters and non-

fiction, Ducharme shows that James's personal views are in accord with his use of imagery.

See *Dissertation Abstracts International* 47, no. 12 (1987):4395A.

47 DURANTI, FRANCESCA. "Il Sesso degli Angeli' [The gender of angels: Henry James and Hugh Merrow]. *Paragone* 37, no. 440:31-35.

In Italian.

48 EDEL, LEON. "The Myth of America in *The Portrait of a Lady*." *Henry James Review* 7, nos. 2-3 (Winter-Spring):8-17.

Argues that in Isabel James examined the national myth of Emersonian self-reliance. Isabel's tragedy is that she has ignored "the reciprocities of life" and "the delicate balance of societies" because of her self-absorption and her blind belief in freedom and equality. Edel suggests that in Isabel James prophesies our national destiny on the twentieth century.

49 EMERICK, RONALD. "The Love Rectangle in *Roderick Hudson*: Another Look at Christina Light." *Studies in the Novel* 18, no. 4 (Winter):353-66.

Argues that Rowland Mallet influenced Christina's feelings and actions because she loves him and traces the evidence of that love throughout the novel.

50 FISCHER, SANDRA K. "Isabel Archer and the Enclosed Chamber: A Phenomenological Reading." *Henry James Review* 7, nos. 2-3 (Winter-Spring):48-58.

Demonstrates that James's use of house imagery in connection with Isabel shows that "her operative psychological principle . . . is avoidance, non-involvement, and solitude." Her return to Rome brings her full circle from the enclosed room in Albany: Isabel deliberately chooses isolation and entrapment because she fears "the intensity of reality."

51 FOGEL, DANIEL MARK. "Framing James's *Portrait*: An Introduction." *Henry James Review* 7, nos. 2-3 (Winter-Spring):1-6.

1986

Examines the connection between James and Isabel, suggesting that both "succumb to the fascination of the difficult, courting her heroism of exposed positions, and in remarkably similar terms." Isabel is thus bound to James's interest in "the processes of his own imagination."

52 FREADMAN, RICHARD. *Eliot, James, and the Fictional Self: A Study in Character and Narration*. Basingstoke, Hampshire, England: Macmillan Press, x, 285 pp.

Analyzes Eliot's and James's concepts of the novel and characterization. Both novelists are concerned with depicting individuality; Eliot's approach is existential while James's "drifts" toward phenomenology. While both novelists agree on many aspects of the novel, James deviates from Eliot in his use of a less intrusive narrative method, symbol and metaphor to depict character, more unified structure, and less overt moral emphasis. The James novels discussed are *The Portrait of a Lady, The Wings of the Dove*, and *The Golden Bowl*.

53 GAGE, RICHARD PAUL. "Order and Design: Henry James's Titled Story Sequences." Ph.D. dissertation, New York University, 457 pp.

Examines the relationships among the tales within the following volumes: *Terminations* (1895), *Embarrassments* (1896), *The Two Magics* (1898), *The Soft Side* (1900), *The Better Sort* (1903), *The Finer Grain* (1910), and volume 18 of the New York Edition. Gage examines the thematic coherence of these collections within the context of James's critical writings on the importance of order and design.

See *Dissertation Abstracts International* 47, no. 12 (1987):4389A-4390A.

54 GALE, ROBERT L. "Henry James." In *American Literary Scholarship: An Annual/1984*. Edited by J. Albert Robbins. Durham: Duke University Press, pp. 113-31.

Surveys criticism published in 1984.

55 GARGANO, JAMES W. "Imagery as Action in 'The Beast in the Jungle.'" *Arizona Quarterly* 42, no. 4 (Winter):351-67.

Argues that the tale's action arises out of its imagery because Marcher himself is inactive. The imagery includes the seasons, linkage, light, burial, prophetess, Sybil, and sphinx; Gargano traces these images throughout the tale, also noting that James's language reflects the complexity of these intertwined images.

56 GETZ, THOMAS H. "The Self-Portrait in the Portrait: John Ashbury's 'Self-Portrait in a Convex Mirror' and Henry James's 'The Liar.'" *Studies in the Humanities* 13, no. 1 (June):42-51.
Suggests that both works question mimesis as a connection between appearance and reality and stress the importance of the artist's sense of community in avoiding solipsism.

57 GIDE, ANDRÉ. "Henry James." *Yale Review* 75, no. 2 (February):239-41.
In an unsent letter to Charles DuBos, Gide compares James's work to a spider's web and accuses him of a lack of commitment to his narrative: James is detached from his character.
Reprinted from *Yale Review* (Spring 1930).

58 GILMORE, MICHAEL T. "The Commodity World or *The Portrait of a Lady.*" *New England Quarterly* 59, no. 1 (March):51-74.
Defines commodity as the "proprietorship of persons" and traces it in the characters' interactions with each other and in James's relationship to his characters. The novel, a reflection of late nineteenth-century commodity capitalism, is at once a repudiation and corollary of that social order.

59 GILMOUR, ROBIN. "Continuity and Change in the Later Victorian Novel: George Eliot, Meredith, James and Stevenson." In *The Novel in the Victorian Age: A Modern Introduction*. London: Edward Arnold Publishers, pp. 164-74.
Sees James as a link between Meredith's psychological romance and Stevenson's analysis of genres and who was greatly influenced by George Eliot and the tradition of the Victorian novel. *The Portrait of a Lady*, which is discussed in detail, owes much to George Eliot while *The Princess Casamassima* marks James's turning from the Victorian tradition.

1986

60   GOETZ, WILLIAM R. *Henry James and the Darkest Abyss of Romance*. Baton Rouge: Louisiana State University Press, xii, 215 pp.

Examines James's presence as author in his fiction – "The Turn of the Screw," *The Sacred Fount*, and *The Ambassadors* – and in his nonfiction – *Autobiography* and the prefaces. Goetz focuses not on specific biographical elements but on the relationship between James's own sense of identity and his presence in the written text. Goetz's particular interest is the way that relationship affects the narrative method in the fiction and the *Autobiography* as well as the balance James strikes between subjectivity and objectivity.

Reprint in part of 1979.54.

61   GOLOVACHEVA, I.V. "Avtorskii zamysel povesti Genri Dzhamsa *Povorot vinta.*" *Vestnik Leningradskogo Universiteta. Seriia Istorii, Iazyka i Literatury* 2, no. 4 (October):46-50.

In Russian with English abstract.

Demonstrates that James balances both the Gothic and "hallucinatory" elements in "The Turn of the Screw."

62   GREENWALD, ELISSA. "'I and the Abyss': Transcendental Romance in *The Wings of the Dove.*" *Studies in the Novel* 18, no. 2 (Summer):177-92.

Argues that James transcends Hawthorne's romance, particularly that of *The Marble Faun*, by transforming Hawthorne's images into symbols. James can therefore "incarnates the human spirit" in a way Hawthorne could not. Greenwald examines *The Wings of the Dove* in light of James's transformation and sees the novel as an "allegory of the creative imagination."

63   GUNTER, SUSAN ELIZABETH. "The Influence of Turgenev's Heroines on the Women of Henry James's 1880's Novels." Ph.D. dissertation, University of South Carolina, 206 pp.

Parallels Turgenev's heroines with those in *The Portrait of a Lady, The Bostonians, The Princess Casmassima*, and *The Tragic Muse* to show the extent to which the Russian influenced James's depiction of women in his early work.

See *Dissertation Abstracts International* 47, no. 4 (1986):1324A.

1986

64   GUTIERREZ, DONALD. "The Self-Devouring Ego: Henry James'
      The Beast in the Jungle as a Parable of Vanity." *Nassau Review* 5, no.
      2:6-14.
         Examines Marcher's selfishness and blindness. Marcher
exemplifies the dangers of a search for self that is conducted in
isolation.

65   HABEGGER, ALFRED. "Henry James's Rewriting of Minny
      Temple's Letters." *American Literature* 58, no. 2 (May):159-80.
         Compares James's version of the letters, "reprinted" in his
autobiography, with copies of the originals, which Habegger discovered
in 1985 at the Houghton Library. James corrected punctuation, omitted
slang and colloquialisms, and inserted passages of his own. James's
tampering raises questions about his veracity and the authenticity of
other letters included in his autobiography. The essay reprints both the
Houghton Library version and James's version side-by-side for easy
comparison.

66   _____. "The Lessons of the Father: Henry James Sr. on Sexual
      Difference." *Henry James Review* 8, no. 1 (Fall):1-36.
         Details the evolution of James Sr.'s views on marriage,
sexuality, and women, along with the controversy occasioned by his
remarks on the Henry Ward Beecher scandal. These views and the
public outcry shaped Henry James Jr.'s attitudes toward women and
the press, most notably in *The Bostonians*.

67   HALLAB, MARY Y. "Love and Death in *The Sacred Fount*."
      Publications of the Missouri Philological Association 11:27-33.
         Applies Leslie Fiedler's archetypal criticism to the novel,
arguing that vampirism and voyeurism are especially relevant to this
novel. James's depiction of relationships in the novel reflects his
rejection of vampirism as a theory to explain love.

68   HORNE, PHILIP. "The Editing of James's Letters." *Cambridge
      Quarterly* 15, no. 2:126-41.
         Describes Edel's four-volume edition as "essential but
inadequate," criticizing Edel's principles of selection, his unreliability in
editing the actual texts, the scant annotations, and the "omissiveness" of
the index.

1986

69   HUGHES, CLAIR. "Getting and Spending: The Uses of Money in
     the Stories and Novels of Henry James." *Lilium: Journal of Bunkyo
     Women's College, Hiroshima, Japan* 21:31-41.
          Traces the evolution of James's use of wealth in connection
     with character. In his early tales, particularly those with the
     international theme, money is incidental to character, and James treats
     the possession of wealth and the acquisitive nature of the American
     with comedy. In the later novels, especially in *The Wings of the Dove*
     and *The Golden Bowl*, "getting and spending" is an integral part of the
     moral discourse. The knowledge of Milly's fortune corrupts Kate and
     Densher, while in *The Golden Bowl*, monetary transactions and
     acquisitions become metaphors for human relationships.

70   HUSS, ROY. "The Short Story as Case Study: Pathological
     Precociousness in Henry James's 'The Pupil.'" In *The Mindscapes of
     Art: Dimensions of the Psyche in Fiction, Drama, and Film*.
     Rutherford, N.J.: Fairleigh Dickinson University Press, pp. 73-84.
          Explains Morgan's precocity as a result of his parents' public
     image of nurturing him while their irresponsible behavior forces
     Morgan to nurture them, and attributes his moral perception to the
     influence of Zenobie, his nurse, and to Pemberton. Morgan's heart
     failure climaxes "the narcissistic wounding that has assailed his whole
     psychic life" through his parents' inability to fulfill his needs; he has
     been "emotionally orphaned" from the beginning of his life.

71   HYNES, JOSEPH. "The Fading Figure in the Worn Carpet."
     Arizona Quarterly 42, no. 4 (Winter):321-30.
          Sees James along with Saul Bellow, Flannery O'Connor, and
     Walker Percy as "conservative humanists," who search for enduring
     value and reject experience for its own sake. James depicts evil clearly,
     but good only by what it is not, which may account for readers' accusing
     James of emptiness.

72   JOHNSON, WARREN. "*Hyacinth Robinson* or *The Princess
     Casamassima?*" *Texas Studies in Literature and Language* 28, no. 3
     (Fall):296-323.
          Describes James's 1886 novel as two novels – one with a hero,
     the other with a heroine – and focuses on Christina, who "becomes a
     mask for the novelist." Christina's ability to get out of her self mirrors
     the novelist's act of creating character and situation.

73 JORDAN-HENLEY, JENNIFER. "The Art of Architecture in *The Portrait of a Lady.*" *Tennessee Philological Bulletin* 23 (July):75-76.
Demonstrates that architectural imagery in the novel reflects, molds, or traps characters, and traces James's use of architecture in the novel's structure description and characterization. Jordan-Henley also examines the impact of the use of architecture on the reader.

74 JOSEPH, MARY JOHN. "Suicide in Henry James's Fiction." Ph.D. dissertation, Louisiana State University, 294 pp.
Examines James's use of actual and symbolic suicide, linking the act of suicide with contemporary ideas about free will as well as with autobiographical elements.
See *Dissertation Abstracts International* 48, no. 2 (1987):389A.

75 KELLY, EDWARD H. "Trollope's *Barchester Towers.*" *Explicator* 44, no. 2 (Winter):28-29.
Counters James's criticism in *Partial Portraits* of Trollope's use of "ineffective tag names" (e.g., Mr. Quiverful) by noting that James overlooks the name's origin, context, and connotations.

76 KERMODE, FRANK. Introduction to *The Figure in the Carpet and Other Stories*. Harmondsworth, Middlesex, England: Penguin Books, pp. 7-30.
Sketches the plots of the tales included in this volume – "The Author of 'Beltraffio'," "The Lesson of the Master," "The Private Life," "The Middle Years," "The Death of the Lion," "The Next Time," "The Figure in the Carpet," and "John Delavoy" – and examines each tale's connection with James's sense of identity as an artist.

77 KIMMEY, JOHN. "James's London in *The Princess Casamassima.*" *Nineteenth-Century Fiction* 41, no. 1 (June):9-31.
Discusses the way in which the various districts of London described in the novel suggest character and class and amplify theme. James creates rich and varied pictures of the capital and presents it as "a stubborn fact and a projection of the protagonist's complex self."

78 _____. "James's London Tales of the 1880s." *Henry James Review* 8, no. 1 (Fall):37-46.

1986

Argues that in "The Siege of London," "Lady Barbarina," "The Path of Duty," and "A London Life" James's depiction of London mirrors that of DuMaurier's cartoons and that the main characters in all these tales are "candid outsiders." Both aspects foreshadow James's treatment of London in later novels, most notably *The Wings of the Dove*.

79 KITTERMAN, MARY P. EDWARDS. "Henry James and the Artist-Heroine in the Tales of Constance Fenimore Woolson." In *Nineteenth-Century Women Writers of the English-Speaking World*. Contributions in Women's Studies, 69. Westport, Conn.: Greenwood Press, pp. 45-59.

Argues that Woolson's tales about female artist reflect her own complex relationship with James and that James's negative attitude toward women writers affected Woolson's view of herself as an artist.

80 KNAPP, BETTINA L[IEBOWITZ]. "James: 'The Jolly Corner'–The Entrapped Shadow in the Archetypal House." In *Archetype, Architecture, and the Writer*. Bloomington: Indiana University Press, pp. 27-44, 196.

Demonstrates that James uses the archetypal image of the house in his "psychological pilgrimage to the center of being." The house is a metaphor for the unexplored and uncontrollable aspect of Brydon; Brydon's encounter with the house's "former occupant" forces him to a new mode of self-understanding.

81 KNOX, MELISSA. "'Beltraffio': Henry James' Secrecy." *American Imago* 43, no. 3 (Fall):211-27.

Sees the tale as autobiographical in its fascination with secrecy and with self-adoration. Knox attributes James's secrecy to his desire to conceal his homosexuality, but his style–"decorated" and "circumlocutionary"–reveals it.

82 KOPRINCE, SUSAN. "The Clue from *Manfred* in *Daisy Miller*." *Arizona Quarterly* 42, no. 4 (Winter):293-304.

Proposes that Byron's poem sheds light on Winterbourne and traces the parallels between James's and Byron's characters. *Manfred* reveals Winterbourne's shortcomings and foreshadows his "barrenness of spirit."

1986

83 KROOK, DOROTHEA. "Isabel Archer Figures in Some Early Stories of Henry James." *Henry James Review* 7, nos. 2-3 (Winter-Spring):131-39.

Examines the "Isabel figure" in "Poor Richard," "A Most Extraordinary Case," "Travelling Companions," and "Longstaff's Marriage." Such an examination results in a better understanding of Isabel Archer herself, of James's artistic development, and of his creative process. Krook also shows that the Isabel figures anticipate other heroines, particularly Milly Theale.

84 LAWSON, DON S. "Isabel Archer, Beatrice Ambient, and the 'Very Straight Path': Henry James' Heroines Who Make the Wrong Choice." *Tennessee Philological Bulletin* 23 (July):76-77.

Finds similarities in Isabel Archer and Beatrice Ambient and argues that these heroines show the tragic consequences of a narrow view of life.

85 LEEMING, DAVID ADAMS. "An Interview with James Baldwin on Henry James." *Henry James Review* 8, no. 1 (Fall):47-56.

Shows that James's greatest influence on Baldwin is his depiction of the failure of innocence and the myth of freedom. The interview focuses mainly on *The Ambassadors*.

86 LEVIN, HARRY. Introduction to *The Ambassadors*. Harmondsworth, Middlesex, England: Penguin Books, pp. 7-30.

Details the plot and briefly discusses James's style and use of imagery. Levin also examines the evolution of the novel's international theme: in James's early work Europe was associated with corruption; in his later work—particularly in *The Ambassadors* and *The Golden Bowl*—James treats Europe sympathetically and demonstrates a "transvaluation of intercultural values."

87 LICHTENBERG, JOSEPH D. "Sweet Are the Uses of Adversity: Regression and Style in the Life and Works of Henry James." In *Narcissism and the Text: Studies in Literature and the Psychology of Self*. Edited by Lynne Layton and Barbara Ann Schapiro. New York: New York University Press, pp. 213-32.

Reprint of 1981.88.

1986

*88 LORETELLI, ROSAMARIA. "Un altro giro di vite: Attesa e strategie della suspense in The Turn of the Screw di Henry James" [Another turn of the screw: delay and strategies of suspense in "The Turn of the Screw" by Henry James]. In *La performance del testo* ["Performance" in the text]. Edited by Franco Marucci and Adriano Bruttini. Siena: Ticci, pp. 163-73.
    In Italian.

89 LUKACHER, NED. "'Hanging Fire': The Primal Scene of *The Turn of the Screw*." In *Primal Scenes: Literature, Philosophy, Psychoanalysis*. Ithaca: Cornell University Press, pp. 115-32.
    Examines the governess's "process of construction" and the "particularity of [her] vision"; both are intensely self-reflexive in nature. Lukacher also discusses the metaphor of "hanging fire" as a reflection of the tale's "play of concealment and disclosure."
    Reprinted 1987.16.

90 McCORMACK, PEGGY. "The Semiotics of Economic Language in James's Fiction." *American Literature* 58, no. 4 (December):540-56.
    Explores the imagery of economics in James's fiction, focusing on *The Portrait of a Lady* and *The Golden Bowl*. James depicts a society that regards individuals as commodities—the "marriage market," for example. In the fiction, "economic imagery both signifies and provides escape from a world of commodities." James's protagonists use the language of economics to discover their own values.

91 McKEE, PATRICIA. "The Gift of Acceptance: *The Golden Bowl*." In *Heroic Commitment in Richardson, Eliot, and James*. Princeton: Princeton University Press, pp. 270-346.
    Sees acceptance of indeterminacy and difference by characters and readers as crucial to this novel "about belief and love." McKee links the indeterminacy of the novel's content to James's rejection of "the conventional forms of identity and narrative."

92 MAHER, JANE. *Biography of Broken Fortunes: Wilkie and Bob, Brothers of William, Henry, and Alice James*. Hamden, Conn.: Archon Books, xii, 221 pp.
    Focuses on Wilkie and Bob James but describes Henry's relationship with his younger brothers. His devotion remained strong

throughout each brother's life, and James kept in touch with Bob's widow, Mary Alice, William's wife, wrote to James to tell him that the picture he sketched in *Notes of a Son and Brother* did honor to Wilkie and Bob.

93 MAITINO, JOHN ROCCO. "Literary Impressionism in Stephen Crane, Joseph Conrad, and Henry James." Ph.D. dissertation, University of California, Riverside, 255 pp.

Focuses on the reader's experience of impressionist fiction, specifically the strategies that enable the reader to define meaning. Maitino devotes individual chapters to each author, outlining impressionist techniques and relating those techniques to impressionist painting. The study concludes by describing impressionism's influence on modernism.

See *Dissertation Abstracts International* 47, no. 9 (1987):3418A.

94 MANOLESCU, NICOLAE. "Inima si mintea." *Steaua* 37, no. 7 (July):14, 45.

In Romanian.

95 MARCHENKO, O.J. "Kompozitisionno-stilisticheskie osobennosti ésse G. Dzheimsa" [Compositional stylistic peculiarities of H. James's essays]. *Isvestiia Akademii Nauk Turkmenskoi SSR, Seriia Obshchestrennykh Nauk* 1:77-81.

In Russian with English abstract.

Demonstrates that Jame's use of the first person singular is the most characteristic feature of his essays, suggesting James's personal and emotive approach to his subject.

96 MARGERUM, EILEEN GREANEY. "'A Massing of Masterpieces': Henry James's Tales of 1888, Their Composition and Revision." Ph.D. dissertation, Tufts University, 226 pp.

Examines the creation and revision of seven tales written within an eighteen-month period: "The Lesson of the Master," "The Aspern Papers," "Louisa Pallant," "A London Life," "The Patagonia," "The Liar," and "Two Countries" ("A Modern Warning"). Margerum sees a progressive complexity in these tales, both in moral stance and narrative technique. These tales serve as a bridge between James's early and later work.

1986

See *Dissertation Abstracts International* 47, no. 8 (1987):3049A.

97 MARSHALL, SUSAN LOUISE. "'Mitigated Midnight': Henry James and the Limitations of Art." Ph.D. dissertation, University of California, Santa Barbara, 201 pp.

Demonstrates that over the course of his career, James moved from an artistic vision ,imposing moral order, to a vision of life, requiring revision and flexibility. By analyzing the protagonists in *The Portrait of a Lady, The Wings of the Dove, The Ambassadors, The Golden Bowl,* and *The Sense of the Past,* Marshall shows that James failed to reconcile the imaginative realm with that of the real.

See *Dissertation Abstracts International* 48, no. 2 (1987):390A.

98 MARTIN, ROBERT K. "The Sorrows of Young Roderick: Wertherism in *Roderick Hudson.*" *English Studies in Canada* 12, no. 4 (December):387-95.

Traces James's use of *The Sorrows of Young Werther* in this novel, particularly in his concentration on consciousness, the portrayal of Roderick as a doomed genius, and the dangers of the mythology of love. Martin sees the figure of Werther, both "romantic dream" and "ironic commentary," as a guide for James's fiction.

99 MARTIN, W.R., and OBER, WARREN U. Introduction to *The Finer Grain*, vol. 405, Delmar, N.Y.: Scholars' Facsimiles and Reprints, pp. v-xxx.

Suggests that *The Finer Grain* is a "coherent vision" in a way James's other collections of tales are not; this volume is "a testament, James's final salute to the human spirit." These tales–"The Velvet Glove," "Mora Montravers," "A Round of Visits," "Crapy Cornelia," and "The Bench of Desolation"–are difficult, but each in a different way celebrates "the divine yet human faculty of the imagination."

100 _____. "Refurbishing James's 'A Light Man.'" *Arizona Quarterly* 42, no. 4 (Winter):305-14.

Contends that the tale's epigraph from Browning's "A Light Woman" is a red herring and that the tale is actually a version of St. Augustine's *Confessions.*

101 MASSADIER-KENNEY, FRANCOISE. "A Study of Women in Four Realist Writers: Sand, Flaubert, Eliot, and James." Ph.D. dissertation, Kent State University, 185 pp.

Argues that an author's gender does not affect the literary work, using an analysis of description – both physical and psychological – and of narrative structure. Sand's *Indiana*, Flaubert's *Madame Bovary*, Eliot's *Middlemarch*, and James's *The Portrait of a Lady* are used as examples.

See *Dissertation Abstracts International* 47, no. 5 (1986):1721A.

102 MATHEWS, LAURA LENORE. "The Hidden Machinery of Telling: Narrational Technique in Apparently Authorless Novels." Ph.D. dissertation, University of California, Berkeley, 309 pp.

Examines the method of narration in novels that seem "to tell themselves," beginning with a discussion of James's theories and an analysis of *What Maisie Knew, The Wings of the Dove,* and *The Ambassadors*. Mathews then focuses on the different "specialized voices" in Meredith's *The Ordeal of Richard Feverel*, Austen's *Pride and Prejudice*, Faulkner's *As I Lay Dying*, Brontë's *Wuthering Heights*, and Smollett's *The Expedition of Humphrey Clinker*.

See *Dissertation Abstracts International* 47, no. 7 (1987):2597A.

103 MILLIGAN, IAN. "Some Misprints in *The Awkward Age.*" *Notes and Queries* 33, no. 2 (June):177-78.

Notes three misprints in the 1899 edition of the novel subsequently corrected in the 1908 New York Edition: an intrusive 'not' in chapter 15; 'old-mannered' for 'old mannered' in chapter 16; and "I" for he in chapter 36. Also, "inattention" at the end of chapter 35's first paragraph should probably be "attention."

104 MOCHI, GIOVANNA. "Henry James: Le figure dell'autore nelle 'Fables for Critics'" [The author figures in the 'Fables for Critics']. *Revista di Letterature Moderne e Comparte* 39, no. 4:309-25.

In Italian.

105 MOON, MICHAEL. "Sexuality and Visual Terrorism in *The Wings of the Dove.*" *Criticism* 28, no. 4 (Fall):427-43.

Uses the novel as a way to explore connections between sexuality and social systems, such as economics and politics. Moon

1986

locates the power of the novel in its homoeroticism, which is manifested in the dominance of another person by a powerful gaze.

106 MOORE,   GEOFFREY.   Introduction   to   *Daisy   Miller*. Harmondsworth, Middlesex, England: Penguin Books, pp. 7-38.
  Examines the plot in detail and suggests that Daisy "marks the first appearance in literature of the American Princess," the Heiress of all the Ages" and that she is the seed of James's great heroines, Milly Theale and Maggie Verver.

107 _____. Introduction to *Roderick Hudson*. Harmondsworth, Middlesex, England: Penguin Books, pp. 7-32.
  Details the plot and notes that the novel, in some respects a reworking of Hawthorne's *The Marble Faun*, contains many modern characteristics, including its handling of time and its devotion to psychological truth. Moore praises the novel for its youthful, exuberant spirit, suggesting that James "never quite captured again the marvellous force and enthusiasm of this slightly amateurish novel, but ground inexorably towards the style which tends to mar his later achievements."

108 MOTTRAM, ERIC. "'The Infected Air' and 'The Guilt of Inference': Henry James's Short Stories." In *The Nineteenth-Century American Short Story*. Edited by A. Robert Lee. London: Vision Press; New York: Barnes & Noble Books, pp. 164-90.
  Surveys James's tales, focusing on the themes of hidden beasts and encagement. In his tales James examines the darker places of the psyche, the "beasts in the jungle," which imprison and isolate men and women.

109 MURPHY, P.D. "Illumination and Affection in the Parallel Plots of 'The Rich Boy' and 'The Beast in the Jungle.'" *Papers on Language and Literature* 22, no. 4 (Fall):406-16.
  Compares the two tales, concentrating on the "moment-of-crisis" aspect of each, although enumerating other similarities as well. James turns the potential tragedy of this "moment" to farce because Marcher remains narcissistic. Fitzgerald subverts the "moment" not only with the protagonist's failure to change but also with the narrator's inability to learn from that failure.

110 "1985-1986 Annual Review: Henry James." *Journal of Modern Literature* 13, nos. 3-4 (November):489-92.
Lists criticism published in 1985-1986.

111 OAKS, SUSAN JEAN. "Henry James and the Nineteenth-Century Psychology: Empirical Self-Knowledge in *The Bostonians, The Princess Casamassima*, and *The Tragic Muse*." Ph.D. dissertation, New York University, 327 pp.
Argues that these three novels mark a shift in James's vision of the self: instead of depicting the self participating in the world, James's interest becomes "the self defining the world, by first defining itself." Oaks relates William James's psychology to these novels, showing that Henry incorporated William's theories into his fiction.
See *Dissertation Abstracts International* 47, no. 4 (1986):1325A.

112 ORISHIMA, MASASHI. "Nazo-Monogatari no Henry James" [Henry James in his 'enigma' stories]. *Eigo Seinen* (Tokyo) 132:262-66.
In Japanese.
Analyzes Jamesian enigma stories of his "experimental period" – *The Spoils of Poynton, The Sacred Fount*, and "The Aspern Papers" – from a psychoanalytical/deconstructionist perspective.

113 OZICK, CYNTHIA. "A Master's Mind: 'An Unpublished Story Sheds New Light on Henry James's Art and Sexuality.'" *New York Times Magazine* (26 October):52-55.
Suggests that James's unfinished tale, "Hugh Merrow," is a self-portrait in which James begins to acknowledge "his own missed experience" of "biological fruition."

114 PADILLA, ERNEST. "Henry James and the Anxiety of Americanness." Ph.D. dissertation, University of California, San Diego, 174 pp.
Argues that James's international fiction explores the anxiety of national identity and traces the evolution of this anxiety in *The American, The Portrait of a Lady, The Ambassadors*, "The Jolly Corner," and *The Sense of the Past*. Padilla begins with *The American* and *The Portrait* in which the protagonists enrich but not abandon their

1986

Americanness and concludes with protagonists who suffer anxiety because they have lost their American identity.

See *Dissertation Abstracts International* 48, no. 7 (1987):2586A.

115   PERSON, LELAND S., Jr. "Eroticism and Creativity in *The Aspern Papers*." *Literature and Psychology* 32, no. 2:20-31.

Shows that because the narrator cannot accept sexuality–his own, the women's, and Aspern's–he fails in his quest for the poet's "creative energy and vision" as represented by the letters.

116   POIRIER, RICHARD. "The Workshop of His Fiction." *New York Times Book Review* (28 December):10-11.

Reviews *The Complete Notebooks of Henry James*, edited by Leon Edel and Lyall H. Powers. Although this edition reprints pocket diaries, cash accounts, and dictated notes, the actual notebooks remain "the heart of the matter" because they concern themselves with James's creative process.

117   POWERS, LYALL H. "Visions and Revisions: The Past Rewritten." *Henry James Review* 7, nos. 2-3 (Winter-Spring):105-16.

Argues that Lizzie Boott, Clover Adams, and Constance Fenimore Woolson kept James's memories of Minny Temple alive and shaped the New York Edition revision of *The Portrait of a Lady*, particularly the portrayal of Ralph Touchett, the "real" Minny Temple figure. Moreover, James's relationship with Hendrick Andersen revealed the lure and the danger of the erotic, which influenced Isabel's rejection of the erotic for the life of consciousness.

118   PRZYBYLOWICZ, DONNA. *Desire and Repression: The Dialectic of Self and Other in the Late Works of Henry James*. University: University of Alabama Press, vii, 358 pp.

Demonstrates that James's late work explores a sensibility divided between aestheticism and social criticism and that this division is reflected in the "collision" between conventional and experimental narrative techniques, as well as in the rhetoric, which simultaneously works toward knowledge and evades meaning. This study begins with two works of the middle period–*What Maisie Knew* and *The Sacred Fount*–but focuses on the late tales, the unfinished novels, and the autobiography.

Reprinted in part 1987.16.

119 PUTT, S. GORLEY. Introduction to *An International Episode and Other Stories*. Harmondsworth, Middlesex, England: Penguin Books, pp. 7-10.

Notes that the characters in "An International Episode," "The Pension Beaurepas," and "Lady Barberina" are vivid human beings and not national abstractions, even though international contrast is a central theme. Crucial to James's international tales is the degree to which characters cheat or defy social expectations.

120 _____. *A Preface to Henry James*. London: Longman, x, 198 pp.

Sketches James's life and his major works, themes, and techniques. The volume includes "illustrative passages" on selected topics from James's fiction and letters; brief biographies of family members, friends, and contemporary literary figures; and descriptions of James's domestic and social millieus.

121 RENNER, STANLEY. "'Why Can't They Tell You Why?': A Clarifying Echo of *The Turn of the Screw*." *Studies in American Fiction* 14, no. 2 (Autumn):205-13.

Argues that Purdy's and James's tales dramatize the "developmental damage" caused by the Victorian angel of the house; in both tales the male children are victimized by women who perceive themselves as guardians of morality.

122 RENTZ, KATHRYN CURIE. "Ford Madox Ford and the Jamesian Influence." Ph.D. dissertation, University of Illinois at Champaign-Urbana, 348 pp.

Traces James's pervasive and strong influence on Ford's work throughout his career. Rentz demonstrates that Ford's early work was primarily Jamesian pastiche; Ford's experimental work, while innovative, seems to be based on James.

See *Dissertation Abstracts International* 47, no. 7 (1987):2599A.

123 RICHMOND, MARION. "The Early Critical Reception of *The Portrait of a Lady* (1881-1916)." *Henry James Review* 7, nos. 2-3 (Winter-Spring):158-63.

1986

Shows that early critical responses to the novel failed to appreciate James's development of character, although American critics tended to be more favorable than the British critics. The early criticism also demonstrates how Freud and Einstein have shaped our view of human beings and of literature.

124 _____. "Henry James's *The Portrait of a Lady*: A Bibliography of Primary Material and Annotated Criticism." *Henry James Review* 7, nos. 2-3 (Winter-Spring):164-95.

Lists and annotates primary sources and criticism from 1881-1981.

125 RIVKIN, JULIE. "The Logic of Delegation in *The Ambassadors*." *PMLA* 101, no. 5 (October):819-31.

Argues that the "logic of delegation" is not renunciation but displacement similar to Derrida's "logic of the supplement." Displacement also governs the novel's "dual economy," in that the "New England economy of experience as holding in reserve" is replaced with a "Parisian economy of experience as necessitating an expenditure without reserve."

126 ROWE, ANN E. *The Idea of Florida in the American Literary Imagination*. Baton Rouge: Louisiana State University Press, xiv, 159 pp.

Examines the literary response to Florida, beginning with Washington Irving and concluding with Wallace Stevens. James's response to Florida, as described in *The American Scene*, combines enchantment with beauty and disillusionment with "the pushing crowd" and epitomizes James's attitude to America itself.

127 SABISTON, ELIZABETH. "Isabel Archer: The Architecture of Consciousness and the International Theme." *Henry James Review* 7, nos. 2-3 (Winter-Spring):29-47.

Discusses the connections among transcendentalism, the role of women, and architecture in the novel. Architecture reflects the conflict between Isabel's transcendentalism and the materialism of the Europeanized Americans. Isabel is potentially an artist, but as a women does not have an "art" with which to express herself. Thus the novel's ambiguous ending can be attributed to James's denying Isabel a means of expression.

128   SAEKI, YASUKI. "Gekojo, Toshi, Kaiga–*Shisha-tachi* no. Toshizu" [Theater, city, picture: A perspective on *The Ambassadors*]. *Eigo Seinen* (Tokyo) 132:54-58.
      In Japanese.
      Suggests that to read the novel in terms of theater–a metaphor for Paris–leads us to several aspects hidden in the text: acting for another, performative space, reunion, and remembrance.

129   SAVOY, ERIC JAMES. "'Perception at the Pitch of Passion': Henry James, Literary Impressionism, and the Discourse of Optical Registration." Ph.D. dissertation, Queen's University, Kingston, Canada.
      Examines "the differences between realist and impressionist conceptions and representations of perceptual acts." Realism involves a conclusive moral victory based on sight and insight; impressionism, in contrast, focuses on the consciousness struggling to understand the ambiguous appearances of the world. Savoy discusses *The American* as an exmaple of James's early impressionist epistemology and *The Ambassadors* as his mature impressionism.
      See *Dissertation Abstracts International* 47, no. 11 (1987):4086A.

130   SCHARNHORST, GARY. "Henry James and the Reverend William Rounseville Alger." *Henry James Review* 8, no. 1 (Fall):71-75.
      Suggests that James modeled his satiric portraits of Unitarian ministers in *The American* and *The Europeans* on Alger.

131   SCHLOSS, DIETMAR OTTO. "Culture and Criticism in Henry James." Ph.D. dissertation, Northwestern University, 242 pp.
      Argues that James's idea of culture and its relation to consciousness derive from Matthew Arnold, who suggested that the mind acquires knowledge through different cultural perspectives. Schloss approaches *The American Scene* as a work of cultural criticism and as a "rewriting of *Culture and Anarchy*." In addition, Schloss

1986

examines *The American* and *The Ambassadors* as reflections of James's hermeneutics of culture.

See *Dissertation Abstracts International* 47, no. 8 (1987):3051A-3052A.

132 SCHWARZ, DANIEL R. "The Humanistic Heritage of James and Lubbock: The Emergence of an Aesthetic of the Novel." In *The Humanistic Heritage: Critical Theories of the English Novel from James to Hillis Miller*. London: Macmillan Press, pp. 16-40.

Sketches the central ideas of James's literary theory, drawing from his critical essays and the New York Edition prefaces. In many respects, James set the standard for criticism, although his criticism is most valuable in understanding his own fiction. Lubbock codified James's critical tenets and defined James's legacy to modern fiction. James's and Lubbock's criticism focus on the dramatized consciousness as subject, the author's creativity, and the importance of the reader.

133 SECOR, ROBERT. "Henry James and Violet Hunt, the 'Improper Person of Babylon.'" *Journal of Modern Literature* 13, no. 1 (March):3-36.

Chronicles the long friendship between the two, drawing on diaries and the unpublished letters of James and Hunt. James admired her vitality, although he deplored her relations with Ford. Secor suggests that the five tales in *The Finer Grain* reflect aspects of the friendship.

134 SEDGWICK, EVE KOSOFSKY. "The Beast in the Closet: James and the Writing of Homosexual Panic." In *Sex, Politics, and Science in the Nineteenth-Century Novel*. Edited by Ruth Bernard Yeazell. Selected Papers from the English Institute, 1983-84, new series, no. 10. Baltimore: Johns Hopkins University Press, xiv, 195 pp.

Argues that Marcher's "secret" is his homosexuality. The tale mirrors James's relationship with Constance Fenimore Woolson, who forced James to question his own sexuality.

135 SEED, DAVID. "Completing the Picture: Deduction and Creation in Henry James's *The Sacred Fount*." *Etudes Anglaises* 39, no. 3 (July-September):268-80.

Sees the "workings of the imagination" as the novel's focus and the narrator, who observes, analyzes, and manipulates other characters, as a kind of mirror of James. Seed notes that the novel contains elements from a range of genres – detective story, aesthetic parable, and gothic fiction – and suggests that the novel is about the waste of the imagination.

136 _____. "Social Irony and Melodrama in Henry James's *The Other House*." *Durham University Journal* 79, no. 1:71-77.
   Compares *The Tragic Muse* with *The Other House* to show the extent to which James incorporated dramatic techniques, particularly in presenting and developing character, in the later novel. Seed attributes the novel's failure to its attempt to reconcile an "ironic social drama" with Rose Armiger's "tragic intensity."

137 SEIDEL, MICHAEL. "The Lone Exile: James's *The Ambassadors* and *The American Scene*." In *Exile and the Narrative Imagination*. New Haven and London: Yale University Press, pp. 131-63, 222-25.
   Argues that the experience of Europe transforms Strether's sensibility so that he can never truly go back to America – he must remain an exile. In *The American Scene*, James's sense of himself as an exile is apparent.

138 SHARMA, SHRUTI. *Lions in the Path: A Study of George Eliot and Henry James as Theorists of Fiction*. Karnal: Natraj Publishing House, 152 pp.
   Compares Eliot's and James's theories of fiction, arguing that while both novelists shared many ideas on the "art of fiction," James was a much more sophisticated theorist than Eliot although he was deeply influenced by her theory and practice. Sharma discusses the origin of Eliot's theory of fiction; devotes a chapter to James's "The Art of Fiction," and examines James's views on morality in fiction.

139 SHINE, MURIEL G. "In Search of Henry James's Educational Theory: The New Biography as Method." In *Essaying Biography: A Celebration for Leon Edel*. Edited by Gloria Fromm. Honolulu: University of Hawaii Press, pp. 36-58.
   Links James's portrayal of children to his own upbringing and to his ideas of the proper ways to raise children. James's fictional

children are either treated permissively or rejected; his emerging adults must develop awareness of self while confronted with a society lacking a sense of morality. Nanda Brookenham in *The Awkward Age* embodies the "fully and completely developed sensibility" that is the key to James's educational theory.

140   SINYARD, NEIL. "Historian of Fine Consciences: Henry James and the Cinema." In *Filming Literature: The Art of Screen Adaptation*. London: Croom Helm, pp. 25-44.
      Surveys the film adaptations of James's fiction, suggesting that his themes primarily attract such adaptations. His style, tone, and "aesthetic idealism" have not been successfully translated to film.

141   SPECTOR, CHERYL ANN. "Henry James and the Light of Allusion." Ph.D. dissertation, Cornell University, 219 pp.
      Examines James's use of allusion in *Roderick Hudson, The Portrait of a Lady*, and *The Wings of the Dove* to show that it is central to his art and that its use reflects his artistic development.
      See *Dissertation Abstracts International* 47, no. 2 (1986):532A.

142   STAFFORD, WILLIAM T. "The Enigma of Serena Merle." *Henry James Review* 7, nos. 2-3 (Winter-Spring):117-23.
      Explores James's development of Madame Merle, who perhaps baffled James as much she has the readers, in the notebooks and the novel. Stafford details the ways in which Madame Merle and Isabel have parallel destinies and suggests that at the novel's end Isabel becomes "something of a Serena Merle" and Serena Merle becomes "something of an Isabel Archer." He also notes Madame Merle's presence in James's bad heroines.

143   STOEHR, TAYLOR. "Propaganda by the Deed in James." In *Words and Deeds: Essays on the Realistic Imagination*. New York: AMS Press, pp. 59-95.
      Discusses *The Princess Casamassima* as part of a tradition that juxtaposes the political life and the artistic life and which highlights the difference between language and reality—a tradition including Flaubert, Dostoevsky, Turgenev, and Conrad—and which calls into question the assumptions of realism.

144   TELOTTE, J.P. "Children of Horror: The Films of Val Lewton." In *Aspects of Fantasy: Selected Essays from the Second International Conference on the Fantastic in Literature and Film.* Edited by William Coyle. Contributions to Study of Science Fiction and Fantasy, no. 19. Westport, Conn.: Greenwood, pp. 95-106.

Discusses Lewton's films in which children become the source of horror and evil. Telotte sees Lewton's work as a transformation of James's use of children as victims in "The Turn of the Screw," and compares Lewton's and James's skill in creating a tense, ambiguous atmosphere.

145   TINTNER, ADELINE R. "Biography and the Scholar: *The Life of Henry James.*" In *Essaying Biography: A Celebration for Leon Edel.* Edited by Gloria Fromm. Honolulu: University of Hawaii Press, pp. 21-35.

Discusses the differences in the five-volume version of Edel's biography of James and its one-volume revision, noting that the revision reflects Edel's professional and personal growth. Tintner acknowledge's that Edel's *Life,* not James's fiction, has made James known to the American public.

146   ____. "The Charles Dickens Imprint on Henry James." *AB Bookman's Weekly* 78, no. 6 (11 August):453-55.

Traces James's use of *Oliver Twist,* "the beloved novel of James' childhood," in "Julia Bride," particularly in the character of Julia, who is modeled on Nancy Sikes. Both heroines are exploited and destroyed by those around her.

147   ____. "Hogarth's *Marriage à la Mode* and Henry James's 'A London Life': Versions of the English Rococo." *Journal of Pre-Raphaelite Studies* 7, no. 1 (November):69-89.

Details the parallels between Hogarth's paintings for *Marriage à la Mode* and *The Rake's Progress* and James's "A London Life" to show that James explicitly drew upon and "rewrote" Hogarth's work. Tintner also discusses James's lifelong interest in Hogarth. The essay contains reproductions of paintings from both series.
Revised 1987.122.

1986

148   _____. "'In the Dusky, Crowded, Heterogeneous Back-Shop of the Mind': The Iconography of *The Portrait of a Lady*." *Henry James Review* 7, nos. 2-3 (Winter-Spring):140-57.
       Compares the icons in the 1881 and New York Editon of the novel. Icons important in the first edition include porcelain cups, china, carriages, furnishings, and art objects. In the New York Edition, James adds precious and luxurious objects, armor, and objects popular in the twentieth-century. The new icons reflect James's changing tastes and create an Isabel with a new sensibility and a finer consciousness.

149   _____. "James Discovers Jan Vermeer of Delft." *Henry James Review* 8, no. 1 (Fall):57-70.
       Discusses James's appreciation of Vermeer and his use of Vermeer's work in *The Outcry* to reveal crucial aspects of the novel's characters. The essay is illustrated.

150   _____. "James's Legendary Letter to Stark Young Surfaces." *The Southern Quarterly* 24, no. 4 (Summer):8-16.
       Reprints the original of the letter containing James's recommended readings and reveals that the letter was occasioned by a "polite misunderstanding," not Young's interest in James.

151   _____. *The Museum World of Henry James*. Studies in Modern Literature, 56. Ann Arbor: University Microfilms International Research Press, xxviii, 390 pp.
       Traces James's use of art objects and artifacts throughout his fiction, from his early, simplistic "guidebook" handling to the sophisticated images of the final novels. Paintings and sculpture provide James with a way to underline theme or technique. Tintner's book maps James's iconography in a detailed fashion, and includes reproductions of many of the art works to which James refers. This book contains revisions of the following, in addition to much new material: "Maggie's Pagoda: Architectural Follies in *The Golden Bowl*," *Markham Review* 3, no. 6 (May 1973):113-15; "The Elgin Marbles and Titian's 'Bacchus and Ariadne: A Cluster of Keatsian Associations in Henry James," *Notes and Queries* 20 (July 1973):250-2; "Henry James and a Watteau Fan," *Apollo* 99, no. 148 (June 1974):488; 1975.138; 1976.185-186, 188, 191; 1979.151-152, 157; 1981.161-162; 1982.149; 1983.206; 1984.203.

152 ____. "Wharton and James: Some Literary Give and Take." *Edith Wharton Newsletter* 3, no. 1 (Spring):3-5, 8.

Suggests that James and Wharton borrowed elements from each other's work. Tintner shows that Wharton's *The Touchstone* and the tales in *Crucial Instances* are reflected in James's fiction while James's "Broken Wings" and his artist tales are echoed in several of Wharton's stories.

153 TORSNEY, CHERYL B. "The Political Context of *The Portrait of a Lady*." *Henry James Review* 7, nos. 2-3 (Winter-Spring):86-104.

Shows that James's interest in the contemporary controversy over imperialism is reflected in the novel. Isabel and Lord Warburton are associated with "idealistic expansionism," while Osmond and Madame Merle are connected with materialism and imperialism. Moreover, the revision of the novel for the New York Edition reflects James's growing disgust with imperialist politics.

154 VEEDER, WILLIAM, and GRIFFIN, SUSAN M. Introduction to *The Art of Criticism: Henry James on the Theory and Practice of Fiction*. Edited by William Veeder and Susan M. Griffin. Chicago: University of Chicago Press, pp. 1-9.

Outlines James's strong points as a critic, particularly his ability to combine the contemplative and the analytic, the masculine and the feminine, and the scholarly and the worldly; and sketches James's career as critic. The volume itself contains a representative collection of twenty-one essays by James, each followed by a brief commentary placing James's remarks within the context of his career. The editors also provide notes on names, allusions, etc., and list variants to the final versions, reprinted here.

This anthology reprints the following items: "Matthew Arnold's *Essays in Criticism*" (1865); "Sainte-Beuve" (1880, 1904); "*Middlemarch*" (1873); "Honoré de Balzac" (1875, 1878); Selections from *Hawthorne* (1879); "Ivan Turgénieff" (1884, 1888); "The Art of Fiction" (1884, 1888); "Guy de Maupassant" (1888); "Criticism" (1891, 1893); "The Future of the Novel" (1899); New York Edition prefaces for *Roderick Hudson* (1907), *The American* (1907), *The Portrait of a Lady* (1908), *The Awkward Age* (1908), *What Maisie Knew* (1908), *The Aspern Papers* (1908), *The Wings of the Dove* (1909), *The Ambassadors* (1909), *The Golden Bowl* (1909); "Emile Zola" (1903, 1914), and "The Novel in *The Ring and the Book*" (1912, 1914).

1986

155 VITOUX, PIERRE. "El jugeo de la focalizacion." Translated by Reyna Hernandez Romero. *Seminario de Semiotica, Teoría, Análsis* 17 (July-December):137-49.
In Spanish.

156 WEISBUCH, ROBERT. "Henry James and the Treaty of Gardencourt." In *Atlantic Double-Cross: American Literature and British Influence in the Age of Emerson.* Chicago: University of Chicago Press, pp. 275-95, 318-19.
Argues that James was the peacemaker in the American struggle against British influence by thematizing that struggle in novels such as *The Portrait of a Lady* and by presenting himself socially as an Anglo-American writer. Weisbuch examines the American and British elements in *The Portrait*, and suggests that ultimately the novel transcends nationality.

157 WHARTON, EDITH. "Henry James." *Foreign Literatures* 8:77-87.
In Chinese.
Translation of the chapter on James from Wharton's 1934 autobiography *A Backward Glance*.

158 WHITE, ROBERT. "'Love, Marriage, and Divorce': The Matter of Sexuality in *The Portrait of a Lady*." *Henry James Review* 7, nos. 2-3 (Winter-Spring):59-71.
Sketches the Victorian attitudes toward sexuality as well as Henry James Senior's views on marriage in order to reveal the contemporary discourse on sexuality shaping the novel. Contrary to most critics, White shows that James's treatment of Isabel's sexuality was quite frank.

159 WIESENFARTH, JOSEPH. "A Woman in *The Portrait of a Lady*." *Henry James Review* 7, nos. 2-3 (Winter-Spring):18-28.
Argues that the novel traces Isabel's growth from girl to woman who must learn to integrate freedom and knowledge and concern for her marriage. Wiesenfarth isolates three portraits within the novel, each illustrating a phase of Isabel's development: in the first, Isabel represents the myth of freedom; in the second, she represents the myth of concern; in the third, she represents "an integrated life of freedom and concern."

1987

1 ALBERS, CHRISTINA EDNA. "The Guardian Male Figure in Selected Novels of Hawthorne, James, Howells, Cather, and Hemingway." Ph.D. dissertation, University of North Carolina at Chapel Hill, 218 pp.

Traces the evolution of this figure – a hero who woos but fails to win the heroine he loves. James transformed Hawthorne's artistic and detached guardian to one more caring and paternal. Moreover, James's use of the guardian male fits in with his commitment to realism – which included rejection of idealized characters and happy endings – and sensitivity to changing gender roles.

See *Dissertation Abstracts International* 49, no. 8 (1989):2216A.

2 ARMSTRONG, PAUL B. "Bewilderment, Understanding, and Representation." In *The Challenge of Bewilderment: Understanding and Representation in James, Conrad, and Ford*. Ithaca: Cornell University Press, pp. 1-25.

Argues that James, Conrad, and Ford inaugurate modern fiction's concern with the process of interpretation. James's "faith in the real" locates him in the nineteenth century; his questioning of the stability and independence of reality heralds the twentieth. All three novelists are concerned with the dynamics of interpreting and representing reality and with the process of understanding in the reader, who must draw upon personal, everyday experience in order to collaborate with the novelist to create the illusion of reality.

Reprint in part of 1983.10, 1985.5.

3 _____. "Interpretation and Ambiguity in *The Sacred Fount*." In *The Challenge of Bewilderment: Understanding and Representation in James, Conrad, and Ford*. Ithaca: Cornell University Press, pp. 29-62.

Argues that the novel is a radical experiment in interpretation and understanding. Armstrong sees the narrator's excesses as an interpreter as James's questioning the validity of epistemological assumptions as well as exploring the dangers of interpretations – the narrator's attempts to understand others bring him close to solipsism. In addition, the novel's ambiguity "challenge[s] the reader to reflect about the vicissitudes of understanding."

1987

4 ____. "Reality and/or Interpretation in *The Ambassadors*." In *The Challenge of Bewilderment: Understanding and Representation in James, Conrad, and Ford*. Ithaca: Cornell University Press, pp. 63-106.

Suggests that the drama of the novel is not only what Strether knows but how he comes to understand what he knows. Strether embarks on a "quest for certitude," but he discovers the contradiction between reality and interpretation.

Revision of 1986.2.

5 BANTA, MARTHA, ed. *New Essays on "The American."* Cambridge: Cambridge University Press, vii, 172 pp.

Contents include:

Martha Banta, Introduction, pp. 1-42. Discusses the biographical, social, and historical background of the novel and reviews its critical reception. Contemporary criticism focused on James's analysis of the American character; criticism today examines the novel's narrative structure, its realism, and its ties to the romance.

Peter Brooks, "The Turn of *The American*," pp. 43-67. Explains the novel's shift from realism to melodrama and the gothic as a reflection of James's disagreement with the French realists, whose fictions do not appeal to the imagination. James, in contrast, believed in the importance of fully engaging the reader and that melodrama was inherent in the social drama that is the subject of fiction. *The American* shows James to be moving toward the idea of the novel as "an intensified, heightened adventure of reflection or consciousness."

John Carlos Rowe, "The Politics of Innocence in Henry James's *The American*," pp. 69-97. Argues that Newman's innocence is actually ignorance of French history and politics embodied by the Bellegardes. To a certain degree Newman deliberately remains ignorant as a psychological defense to avoid recognizing his own aristocratic pretensions. Newman reveals the dangers of such ignorance; he is a reminder that the "self-reliant American" may repeat "the rigid hierarchies of the European aristocracy."

Carolyn Porter, "Gender and Value in *The American*," pp. 99-129. Attributes the "mystification" of Claire de Cintré's character to her "emblematic status" as "noncommercial, uncontaminated, and incorruptible value." Newman's desire to acquire Clair cannot be satisfied, for in so doing she would then be translated into monetary value. Porter contrasts Claire with Noémie Nioche, who is willing to be purchased.

Mark Seltzer, "Physical Capital: *The American* and the Realist Body," pp. 131-67. Argues that while the novel proposes a distinction between the personal and the commercial, it enacts the interchangeability of these two terms. Seltzer parallels this double discourse with the novel's shifts between realism and romance. The unstable styles of representation reflect and at the same time underwrite "the complicated nexus of bodies and commerce that make up James's account of 'physical capital.'"

6   BASSOFF, BRUCE. "Drifting with Henry James." *Reader* 17 (Spring):44-57.
Recounts his experience teaching *The Sacred Fount*, "The Turn of the Screw," "The Bench of Desolation," and "The Beast in the Jungle," and summarizes the major points of class discussions.

7   BAUER, DALE M., and LAKRITZ, ANDREW. "Language, Class, and Sexuality in Henry James's 'In the Cage.'" *New Orleans Review* 14, no. 3 (Fall):61-69.
Argues that the telegraphist ultimately realizes the poverty of the world she has created from reading romances; the real world is "thing-oriented," not "interpretation-oriented."

8   BAYLEY, JOHN. "Beyond the Great Good Place." *Times Literary Supplement*, no. 4391 (29 May):571-72.
Reviews James's notebooks edited by Edel and Powers. This edition, which includes James's pocket diaries and finances, gives us a new, even intimate, view of the man. The *Notebooks* illuminate James's art, although Murdock and Matthiessen's edition was considerably more useful because of their detailed commentary.

9   BEAVER, HAROLD. "In the Land of Acquisition." *Times Literary Supplement*, no. 4407 (18-24 September):1020-21.
Compares H.G. Well's *The Future in America* (1906) and James's *The American Scene* (1907). Wells praised American progress but deplored mass immigration. James in contrast "bewailed" American materialism, waste, and "immense promiscuity."

1987

10   BENDER, TODD K. *A Concordance to Henry James's "Daisy Miller."* New York: Garland Publishing Co., ix, 159 pp.
Contains the New York Edition of the tale, and tables of low frequency words, high frequency words, and frequency of occurrence for both high and low frequency words.

11   BENERT, ANNETTE LARSON. "Dialogical Discourse in 'The Jolly Corner': The Entrepreneur as Language and Image." *Henry James Review* 8, no. 2 (Winter):116-25.
Examines several elements of the tale, including its point of view, framing dialogue, and imagery to show that in "The Jolly Corner" James depicts his vision of America as a void, a "land of lost possibilities." Benert sees the tale's focus as the dialogue between the intelligible order Brydon wishes to live and the melodramatic order of the ghost, who represents the "psychic blackhole" of America.

*12   BESSIÈRE, JEAN. "Dualité de la nouvelle et du roman: Henry James, Djuna Barnes, Thomas Pynchon." *Palinure* 3 (Spring):28-40.
In French.
Source: Offline Bibliography, BRS Information Technologies, Latham, NY 12110.

13   BISHOP, GEORGE. "Addressing 'A Bundle of Letters': Henry James and the Hazard of Authority." *Henry James Review* 8, no. 2 (Winter):91-103.
Demonstrates that this tale examines the process of learning a language – a system of signification and discourse – and exercising the power and control that language confers.

14   BLEWETT, MARY EDGE. "'The Silver Key': The Familiar Letter in Nineteenth-Century American Literature." Ph.D. dissertation, University of Wisconsin, Milwaukee, 294 pp.
Argues that many of the "familiar letters" of Adams, Howells, and James were carefully crafted literary works, based on eighteenth-century models. In their travel letters and letters to family members, these writers explored the techniques and themes developed in detail in their writing.
See *Dissertation Abstracts International* 48, no. 9 (1988):2336A.

15　BLOOM, HAROLD, ed. *Henry James*. Modern Critical Views. New York: Chelsea, viii, 346 pp.
Contents include:
Harold Bloom, Introduction, pp. 1-14. Suggests that James's fiction is influenced by Emersonian "aspiration and independence." Reprinted 1987.16, and 1987.17;
Francis Fergusson, "James's Idea of Dramatic Form," pp. 15-25, reprint of *Kenyon Review* 5, no. 1 (Autumn 1943);
Richard Poirier, "*The American* and *Washington Square*: The Comic Sense," pp. 27-72, reprinted from *The Comic Sense of Henry James: A Study of the Early Novels* (1967);
Laurence Bedwell Holland, "The Crisis of Transformation: *The Golden Bowl*," pp. 73-94, reprinted from *The Expense of Vision: Essays on the Craft of Henry James* (1964);
Carol Ohmann, "'Daisy Miller': A Study of Changing Intentions," pp. 95-104, reprint of *American Literature* 36, no. 1 (March 1964) and reprinted 1987.16;
Tony Tanner, "The Watcher from the Balcony: *The Ambassadors*," pp. 105-23, reprint of *Critical Quarterly* 8, no. 1 (Spring 1966);
Juliet McMaster, "'The Full Image of a Repetition' in 'The Turn of the Screw,'" pp. 125-30, reprint of *Studies in Short Fiction* 6, no. 4 (Summer 1966);
Elisabeth Hansot, "Imagination and Time in 'The Beast in the Jungle," pp. 131-37, reprint of essay in *Twentieth-Century Interpretations of 'The Turn of the Screw' and Other Tales: A Collection of Critical Essays*. Edited by Jane P. Tomkins (1970);
David Howard, "*The Bostonians*," pp. 139-57, reprint of essay from *The Air of Reality: New Essays on Henry James*. Edited by John Goode (1972);
D.J. Gordon and John Stokes, "The Two Worlds of *The Tragic Muse*: A Holiday in Paris," pp. 159-87, reprint of essay from *The Air of Reality: New Essays on Henry James*. Edited by John Goode (1972);
Robert L. Caserio, "The Story in It: *The Wings of the Dove*," pp. 189-214, reprint of 1979.24;
Martin Price, "James: The Logic of Intensity," pp. 215-34, reprint of 1983.154;
Deborah Esch, "A Jamesian About-Face: Notes on 'The Jolly Corner,'" pp. 235-50, reprint of 1983.61, reprinted 1987.16;
Carren O. Kaston, "Imagination and Desire in *The Spoils of Poynton* and *What Maisie Knew*," pp. 251-75, reprinted from 1984.110;

1987

Mark Seltzer, "*The Princess Casamassima*: Realism and the Fantasy of Surveillance," pp. 277-99, reprint of 1981.130 and from 1984.175;

Maria Irene Ramalho de Sousa Santos, "Isabel's Freedom: *The Portrait of a Lady*," pp. 301-13, reprint of 1980.124 and reprinted 1987.17.

16 _____. *Henry James's "Daisy Miller," "The Turn of the Screw," and Other Tales*. Modern Critical Interpretations. New York: Chelsea, vii, 148 pp.

Contents:

Harold Bloom. Introduction, pp. 1-10. Calls "The Pupil" an "Emersonian parable" of the fate of the American spirit amid the "false values" of Europe. The first portion of the essay is a reprint of the introduction from 1987.15;

Laurence Holland. "The Aspern Papers," pp. 11-23. Reprinted from *The Expense of Vision: Essays on the Craft of Henry James* (1964);

Carol Ohmann. "'Daisy Miller': A Study of Changing Intentions," pp. 25-34. Reprint of *American Literature* 36, no. 1 (March 1964) and reprinted in 1987.15;

Wolfgang Iser. "Partial Art – Total Interpretation," pp. 35-42. Reprinted from 1978.53;

Moshe Ron. "A Reading of 'The Real Thing,'" pp. 43-60. Reprint of 1979.126;

J. Hillis Miller. "'The Figure in the Carpet.'" pp. 61-74. Reprint of 1980.97;

Deborah Esch. "A Jamesian About-Face: Notes on 'The Jolly Corner,'" pp. 75-91. Reprint of 1983.61 and reprinted in 1987.15;

Donna Przybylowicz, "The 'Lost Stuff of Consciousness': The Priority of Futurity and the Deferral of Desire in 'The Beast in the Jungle,'" pp. 93-116. Reprint in part of 1986.118;

Ned Lukacher. "'Hanging Fire': The Primal Scene of *The Turn of the Screw*," pp. 117-32. Reprint of 1986.89.

17 _____. *Henry James's "The Portrait of a Lady*." Modern Critical Interpretations. New York: Chelsea, 171 pp.

Harold Bloom. Introduction, pp. 1-14. Suggests that although *The Portrait* is not an Emersonian novel, Isabel Archer is "Emerson's daughter": her aspirations and her self-reliance are essentially Emersonian. Although her aspirations led her into a disastrous marriage, in the end her salvation lies in the "renewed Emersonian realization that she herself is her own alternative" to Osmond's house of death. The first portion of the essay is a reprint of the Introduction from 1987.15.

Richard Poirier. "Setting the Scene: The Drama and Comedy of Judgment," pp. 15-37. Reprinted from *The Comic Sense of Henry James: A Study of the Early Novels* (1960);

Laurence Bedwell Holland. "Organizing an Ado," pp. 39-69. Reprinted from *The Expense of Vision: Essays on the Craft of Henry James* (1964);

Nina Baym. "Revision and Thematic Change in *The Portrait of a Lady*," pp. 71-86. Reprint of 1976.12.

Elizabeth Allen. "Objects of Value: Isabel and Her Inheritance," pp. 87-97. Reprint in part of 1984.2;

David M. Lubin. "Act of Portrayal," pp. 99-115. Reprint of 1985.82.

Maria Irene Ramalho de Sousa Santos. "Isabel's Freedom: Henry James's *The Portrait of a Lady*," pp. 117-29. Reprint of 1980.124 and 1987.15;

Deborah Esch. "'Understanding Allegories': Reading *The Portrait of a Lady*," pp. 131-53. Examines the novel's connection with portraiture; Isabel's failure as a reader of Osmond, and the novel's "rhetoric of temporality."

18 BLYTHE, RONALD. Introduction to *The Awkward Age*. Harmondsworth, England: Penguin Books, pp. vi-xix.

Sketches the novel's social and biographical background as well as the plot and the traits of the main characters. *The Awkward Age* is "about the desertion of principle, about being young and growing old, and about what happens to young and old alike when they are caught up in one of society's periodic ethical scene-shifts."

19 BOHLMEIJER, ARNO. "The Intruder: Henry James and 'The Turn of the Screw.'" *Encounter* 69, no. 1 (June):41-50.

Sees the novella as "an image of Henry James's nightmarish, personal myth" and compares the novella with James's dream of an intruder using the theories of Jung. The tale recounts "the struggle of the human soul to live with its own evil."

20 BOONE, JOSEPH ALLEN. "*The Golden Bowl*: Maggie's Maneuverings in the Marriage Plot." In *Tradition Counter Tradition: Love and the Form of Fiction*. Chicago: University Press of Chicago, pp. 187-201, 355-57.

1987

Argues that in this novel James used "indeterminate form" to depict "the ambiguous course of marital strife." All the relationships in the novel question the concept of marriage, and the novel's final scene reveals that marriage cannot be a "closed fiction" but is open for interpretation.

21   BOREN, LYNDA S. "Undoing the Mona Lisa: Henry James's Quarrel with da Vinci and Pater." *Mosaic* 20, no. 3 (Summer):95-111.

Argues that James considered Pater's description of the *Mona Lisa* and the imitations it spawned as exemplifying the destructive nature of art when divorced from the humanity of the artist. For James, Michelangelo embodied the vigor and passion of art. Boren traces the dialectical movement between Pater's *Mona Lisa* and Michelangelo's art in *The Portrait of a Lady*, detailing the ways in which Madame Merle is an imitation of the *Mona Lisa* as well as the process by which Isabel is subjected to the tyranny of imitation. Boren concludes by noting the references to art in *The Wings of the Dove* that link it to *The Portrait*.

22   BRADBURY, NICOLA. *An Annotated Critical Bibliography of Henry James*. New York: St. Martin's Press, viii, 142 pp.

Annotates a selection of criticism as a guide to the development of James studies and as a way to organize James criticism into general topics. This bibliography is highly selective, and unlike existing bibliographies on James, it groups criticism into several categories: biography and letters, studies of Henry James and Europe; studies of Henry James and another author or artist, studies of Henry James's criticism; and studies of Henry James.

23   BROYARD, A. "Total Immersion–Henry James and Mineral Waters." *New York Times Book Review* (4 January):10.

Attributes our unwillingness to read James to the patience and importance he gives individuals; such importance "offends our democracy."

24   CAIN, WILLIAM E. "Criticism and Politics: F.O. Matthiessen and the Making of Henry James." *New England Quarterly* 60, no. 2 (June):163-86.

1987

Finds evidence of ambivalence towards James in Matthiessen's work. This ambivalence, Cain argues, reflects Matthiessen's "own fissured allegiances" as literary critic and as socialist. In *Henry James: The Major Phase*, Matthiessen praises James's art but includes "abundant" "small slighting comments." Cain sees the book's strength in Matthiessen's critical attitude and its weakness in Matthiessen's failure to "spell out clearly his sense of the social and political deficiencies of James's art."

25   DANIELS, HOWELL. "Henry James: The Prey of All the Patriotisms." In *The New History of Literature, VIII: American Literature to 1900*. Edited by Marcus Cunliffe. New York: Peter Bendrick Books, pp. 273-96.

Examines James's roles as cultural mediator and commentator as reflected in his writing throughout his career. Ultimately James saw the writer as one who can overcome national prejudices and who can create a "single community of language and manners." The discussion focuses on James's international fiction.

26   DAVIES, DAVID J. "A Comparative Study of London and Paris in the Works of Henry James and Emile Zola with Special Reference to *The Princess Casamassima* and *L'Assommoir*." Ph.D. dissertation, Council for National Academic Awards, United Kingdom, 331 pp.

Examines how James and Zola used London and Paris to indicate social change. James's and Zola's depiction and use of these cities suggests a strong link between the two writers, the importance of James's attention to social detail, and Zola's ability to describe the city poetically.

See *Dissertation Abstracts International* 49, no. 2 (1988):249A.

27   DERRICK, SCOTT S. "Masculine Ease: Men and the Scene of Writing in Nineteenth-Century American Literature." Ph.D. dissertation, University of Pennsylvania, 324 pp.

Examines the idea of masculinity in terms of both the author and his work from historical, biographical, and psychoanalytical perspectives. The chapters on James focus on his concept of "ease" with which he describes relations between men by discussing the *Autobiography, Roderick Hudson, The American*, and *The Ambassadors*.

See *Dissertation Abstracts International* 48, no. 8 (1988):2061A.

1987

28 DONOGHUE, DENIS. "Blackmur on Henry James." In *The Legacy of R.P. Blackmur: Essays, Memoirs, Texts*. Edited by Edward T. Cone, Joseph Frank, and Edmund Keeley. New York: Ecco, pp. 21-43.

Surveys and evaluates Blackmur's work on James. The major portion of this essay details Blackmur's changing interpretation of *The Golden Bowl*, seeing it first as the triumph of good over evil, but finally regarding Maggie as destructive. Blackmur's "wrong" reading results from his misgivings about James; Blackmur distrusted James's confidence in his own art.

29 DORSEY, PETER ANDREW. "The Rhetoric of Conversion in Early Twentieth-Century American Autobiography." Ph.D. dissertation, University of Pennsylvania, 264 pp.

Argues that while American autobiographers examined "the cognitive, social, and aesthetic consequences of any rapturous submission," they linked their illumination to increasing alienation from mainstream America. Writers discussed include Henry Adams, Henry James, Edith Wharton, Ellen Glasgow, Zora Neale Hurston, and Richard Wright.

See *Dissertation Abstracts International* 49, no. 2 (1988):253A.

30 DRUXES, HELGA. "The Feminization of Dr. Faustus: The Quest for Self-Knowledge in the Nineteenth Century." Ph.D. dissertation, Brown University, 158 pp.

Discusses the transference of the Faust myth to the female protagonists in Stendhal's *Lamiel*, Keller's *Der grune Heinrich*, Gautier's *Mademoiselle de Maupin*, and James's *The Portrait of a Lady*, drawing on the theories of Freud, Schor, and Irigary. Druxes sees this feminization occuring in two phases: first, imitation of male quest patterns, then generation of unique quest patterns.

See *Dissertation Abstracts International* 48, no. 4 (1987):919A.

31 EDEL, LEON. "Confessions of a Biographer." In *Psychoanalytic Studies of Biography*. Edited by George Moraitis and George H. Pollock. Emotions and Behavior Monographs, no. 4. Madison, Conn.: International Universities Press, pp. 3-27.

Chronicles his life-long involvement with Henry James and the writing of James's biography and discusses Gardner's criticism of the biography (1982.55). Edel attributes his attachment to James to nostalgia for his own childhood, similar in many ways to James's, and to "the dream of Europe."

32   _____. Introduction: On Selecting Letters. in *Henry James: Selected Letters*. Edited by Leon Edel. Cambridge: The Harvard University Press, Belknap Press, pp. xv-xxvi.

Notes that he chose letters for the light they shed on James as an artist and as a man. Edel also discusses James's friendship with Morton Fullerton as well as Fullerton's relationship with Edith Wharton.

33   _____. Introduction to *The Complete Notebooks of Henry James*. Edited by Leon Edel and Lyall H. Powers. New York: Oxford University Press, ix-xvii.

Describes his discovery of James's notebooks in the "sea chest"; James's habit of note taking, his invocations to his "Good Angel," his transition from writing to dictation, and his social life as reflected in the pocket diaries.

34   _____. "Reply to Dr. Lichtenberg." In *Psychoanalytic Studies in Biography*. Edited by George Moraitis and George H. Pollock. Emotions and Behavior Monographs, no. 4. Madison, Conn.: International Universities Press, Inc., pp. 59-61.

Defends his "timidity" in the first volume of the James biography and suggests that readers derive a sense of "being closer to the truth" in reading psychobiography.

See Lichtenberg 1987.70.

35   EDEL, LEON, and TINTNER, ADELINE R. Comp. and ed. *The Library of Henry James*. Ann Arbor: UMI Research Press, ix, 106 pp.

Contains an inventory of James's library; reprints two essays, Edel 1978.35 and Tintner, 1978.11; and includes photographs of Lamb House and books from James's library.

Revision of 1983.58.

36   FALCONER, GRAHAM. "Flaubert, James and the Problem of Undecidability." *Comparative Literature* 39, no. 1 (Winter):1-18.

1987

Argues for a distinction between James's ambiguity and Flaubert's undecidability and in this context examines "The Aspern Papers" and *L'education sentimentale*. Falconer draws on Rimmon's study of ambiguity (1977.107) and Culler's *Flaubert: The Uses of Uncertainty* (1974).

37   FOSTER, DENNIS A. "Confession and Revenge: James's 'Figure in the Carpet.'" In *Confession and Complicity in Narrative*. New York: Cambridge University Press, pp. 39-51.

Examines the narrator, who finds consolation for his own failure to discover the figure by manipulating the reader. The reader in turn imitates the narrator's "pleasure of usurpation and revenge."

38   FREIER, MARY P. "The Story of 'The Author of "Beltraffio."'" *Studies in Short Fiction* 24, no. 3 (Summer):308-9.

Suggests that Gwendolen has concocted the story that Mrs. Ambient allows Dolcino to die. She fabricates the story to trick the "susceptible and egotistical" narrator.

39   GABLER-HOVER, JANET. "Truth and Deception: The Basis of Judgment in *The Wings of the Dove*." *Texas Studies in Literature and Language* 29, no. 2 (Summer):169-86.

Demonstrates that the moral determinacy of language is a central theme in the novel. The novel examines truth and deception in the ways the characters use language, but it moves beyond this to evaluate the "human impulses" underlying language.

40   GAFFEY, ANNIE ELIZABETH. "'A Period of Quiet Reflection': The Change from Community-Centered to Individual-Centered Life in English Society during the Nineteenth-Century as Reflected in the Novels of Jane Austen, George Eliot, and Henry James." Ph.D. dissertation, University of California, Berkeley, 288 pp.

Demonstrates that the novels of these authors mirror the transformation of English society from the communal to the individual. Austen depicts small, tight-knit communities; Eliot depicts relations among individuals from various communities; James illustrates the individual alienated from community.

See *Dissertation Abstracts International* 48, no. 9 (1988):2331A.

41   GALE, ROBERT L. "Henry James." In *American Literary Scholarship: An Annual/1985*. Edited by J. Albert Robbins. Durham: Duke University Press, pp. 103-22.
     Surveys criticism published in 1985.

42   GARD, ROGER. Introduction to *The Critical Muse: Selected Literary Criticism* by Henry James. Edited by Roger Gard. Harmondsworth, Middlesex, England: Penguin Books, pp. 1-19.
     Attributes James's stature as a critic to his open-mindedness and his defense of the importance of life to art and of art to life. Gard also surveys the "academic ups and downs" of James's criticism. James provokes debate because "of the generous width of his intelligence."

43   GARGANO, JAMES W., ed. *Critical Essays on Henry James: The Early Novels*. Critical Essays on American Literature. Boston: G.K. Hall & Co., ix, 207 pp.
     Reprints contemporary reviews of *Watch and Ward, Roderick Hudson, The American, The Europeans, Confidence, Washington Square, The Portrait of a Lady, The Bostonians, The Princess Casamassima*, and *The Tragic Muse*; and the following twentieth-century essays:
     Richard Poirer, "*Roderick Hudson*," from *The Comic Sense of Henry James*, pp. 71-95, (1967);
     James W. Tuttleton, "Rereading *The American*: A Century Since," pp. 96-116 (1980.156);
     J.A. Ward, "James's *The Europeans* and the Structure of Comedy," pp. 116-28, from *Nineteenth Century Fiction* 19, no. 1 (1964);
     James W. Gargano, "*Washington Square*: A Study in the Growth of an Inner Self," pp. 129-136, (1976.74);
     William H. Gass, "The High Brutality of Good Intentions," pp. 136-144, from *Accent* 18 (1958);
     Leon Edel, "[*The Portrait of a Lady*]," pp. 145-54, from *Henry James: The Conquest of London 1870-1881* (1962);
     Irving Howe, Introduction to *The Bostonians*, pp. 154-169 (1956);
     Oscar Cargill, "*The Princess Casamassima*," pp. 169-183, from *The Novels of Henry James* (1961);
     and the following, written for this volume:
     Adeline R. Tintner, "Miriam as the English Rachel: Gérôme's Portrait of the Tragic Muse," pp. 185-97. Discusses the scene in the greenroom of the Théâtre Française where Miriam rejects Peter and

declares her devotion to the stage. Tintner argues that James's portrayal of Miriam was influenced by Rachel and Gérôme's portrait of her, which is reproduced in the text. Tintner calls this novel a "bravura performance" encompassing the art of "the act, the picture, and the word."

44   ____. *Critical Essays on Henry James: The Later Novels*. Critical Essays on American Literature. Boston: G.K. Hall & Co., ix, 212 pp.

Contents include reprints of contemporary reviews of *The Other House, The Spoils of Poynton, What Maisie Knew, The Awkward Age, The Sacred Fount, The Wings of the Dove, The Ambassadors, The Golden Bowl*, and critical essays by William Dean Howells and Joseph Conrad. It also includes the following essays:

James W. Gargano. Introduction, pp. 1-25. Sketches the biographical context of the novels listed above, and their themes and central characters; and surveys the critical reception of these works.

Richard A. Hocks. "The 'Jourdain' Relationship of Henry to William James in *The Spoils of Poynton*," pp. 67-83. Reprinted from *Henry James and Pragmatistic Thought: A Study in the Relationship Between the Philosophy of William James and the Literary Art of Henry James* (1977), pp. 134-51.

Jean Frantz Blackall, "Moral Geography in *What Maisie Knew*," pp. 84-100. Reprint of 1979.13.

Marcia Jacobson. "*The Awkward Age*," pp. 101-13. Reprint of 1975.67 and in part 1983.101.

James W. Gargano. "James's *The Sacred Fount*: The Phantasmagorical Made Evidential," pp. 113-30. Reprint of 1980.58.

Barton Levi St. Armand. "Lambert Strether's Renaissance: Paterian Resonances in Henry James's *The Ambassadors*," pp. 130-48. Argues that James explores his equivocal attitude toward Pater in the character of Lambert Strether. Strether's failure as an ambassador of moral values and his achievement of aesthetic "success" reflects James's vision of Pater as "Aestheticism's double-agent."

Sallie Sears. "*The Wings of the Dove*," pp. 148-68. Reprinted from *The Negative Imagination* (1968).

Ruth Bernard Yeazell. "The Difficulty of Ending: Maggie Verver in *The Golden Bowl*," pp. 168-90. Reprint of 1976.207, pp. 100-30, 139-40.

Daniel Mark Fogel. "A New Reading of Henry James's 'The Jolly Corner,'" pp. 190-203. Argues that a *Notebook* entry dated 5 February 1895 is in fact the germ of the tale, and suggests the importance of Alice Staverton's role in the tale. Fogel also shows that along with "An International Episode" this is a "centennial" tale containing covert references to 1776 and 1876. The *Notebook* entry and the centennial references suggest that the tale fuses James's "Americano-European legend" with his exploration of "the dark corners and shifting vistas of consciousness."

45   GRANT, WILDA LESLIE. "Women's Search for Identity in Modern Fiction (1881-1927): Self-Definition in Crisis." Ph.D. dissertation, University of Maryland, College Park, 260 pp.

Argues that James, Conrad, Lawrence, and Woolf depicted "a continuous process of women's search for self-definition" with increasing freedom and choice, thus reflecting the contemporary society. Together, these novels – James's *The Portrait of a Lady* and *The Golden Bowl*, Conrad's *Nostromo* and *Victory*, Lawrence's *The Rainbow* and *Women in Love*, and Woolf's *Mrs. Dalloway* and *To the Lighthouse* – present a commentary on the status of women during the years 1881 to 1927.

See *Dissertation Abstracts International* 49, no. 3 (1988):510A.

46   GRIFFIN, SUSAN M. "James's Revisions of 'The Novel in "The Ring and the Book." ' " *Modern Philology* 85, no. 1 (August):57-64.

Details James's revisions of the essay, given as an address to the Royal Society of Literature and later printed in *Quarterly Review*. In the address James focuses on Browning's use of a central consciousness; in the printed version, James stresses "the importance of literary structure in light of contemporary theories of fiction."

47   HABEGGER, ALFRED. "Review Essay – Leon Edel, *Henry James: A Life*." *Henry James Review* 8, no. 3 (Spring):200-8.

Acknowledges Edel's vast knowledge and artistry but details errors and omissions. Habegger points out that telling the story of James's life is a task too large for any one biographer and calls for others to reveal the myriad aspects of James's artistry.

48   HALLAB, MARY Y. "The Governess and the Demon Lover: The Return of a Fairy Tale." *Henry James Review* 8, no. 2 (Winter):104-115.

Traces the parallels in "The Turn of the Screw" and two fairy tales, "The Adventure of Cherry of Zennor" and "The Fairy Widower," focusing particularly on the motifs of the demon lover and the "marriage of death." Hallab sees James's tale as "the story of a whole consciousness," in which masculine and feminine elements are reconciled.

49 HARTMAN, TERESE B. "Conflict, Crisis, and Destruction: The Drama of Self-Assertive Daughters in Henry James." Ph.D. dissertation, State University of New York, Buffalo, 163 pp.
   Identifies three kinds of crises confronting the self-assertive daughter: fortune ("Pandora," "Julia Bride," and "Daisy Miller,"); ideology (*The Spoils of Poynton* and *The Awkward Age*); and paternal possessiveness (*Washington Square, The Outcry,* and *The Golden Bowl*). See *Dissertation Abstracts International* 48, no. 5 (1987):1203A.

50 HELLER, TERRY. "The Master's Trap: James's *The Turn of the Screw*." In *The Delights of Terror: An Aesthetics of the Tale of Terror*. Urbana: University of Illinois Press, pp. 147-68.
   Argues that in this "terror fantasy" the implied reader must love and identify with the governess which means accepting both terror and ambiguity.

51 HOCKS, RICHARD A., HAMER, KAREN R., and BROWN, W. DALE. "James Studies 1983-1984: An Analytic Bibliographic Monograph." *Henry James Review* 8, no. 3 (Spring):155-88.
   First part of a survey of works published on James during the years 1983-1984.

52 HOLBROOK, DAVID. "Authenticity and Sexuality: Henry James's *What Maisie Knew* and *The Awkward Age*." In *The Novel and Authenticity*. London: Vision Press; and Totowa, N.J.: Barnes & Noble, pp. 60-107.
   Contrasts Maisie's authenticity against the adults' inauthenticity—the result of their passion and selfishness—and regards this novel as exemplifying James's moral seriousness. In *The Awkward Age*, however, James's fear of sexuality flaws the novel because in it James wishes to save his heroine from sexuality.

53 HOLLY, CAROL. "'Absolutely Acclaimed': The Cure for Depression in James's Final Phase." *Henry James Review* 8, no. 2 (Winter):126-38.

Demonstrates that to a large degree James's sense of identity was linked to favorable reception of his work. The positive reviews of his autobiography by the British press helped James's overcome his depression over William's death and the failure of the New York Edition.

54 HORNE, PHILIP. "Independent Beauty." *Journal of American Studies* 21, no. 1 (April):87-93.
Reviews the Library of America editions of James's literary criticism, which include American writers, European writers, and the New York Edition prefaces. The essays and reviews reveal the variety, versatility, and the "mobility" of James's intelligence.

55 HOWE, IRVING. "Henry James: The Political Vocation." In *Politics and the Novel*. New York: New American Library, pp. 139-56.
Calls *The Princess Casamassima* a "bewildering mixture of excellence and badness," praising the characters of the Princess and Paul Muniment, but arguing that James did not have "a commanding vision of the political life," and that Hyacinth Robinson is much too passive a hero.
Reprint of 1957 essay.

56 HUTNER, GORDON. "Goodwood's Lie in *The Portrait of a Lady*." *Henry James Review* 8, no. 2 (Winter):142-44.
Sees Goodwood's false claim that Ralph asked him to take care of Isabel as Isabel's ultimate test of self. Her refusal to be seduced shows the magnitude of her growth and her rejection of illusion.

57 IKEDA, MIKIKO. "Areno kara Picturesque e: Poe, Hawthorne, James to 'Riso no Fukei'" [From the wilderness to the picturesque: Poe, Hawthorne, James, and the ideal landscape]. *Eigo Seinen* (Tokyo) 133:114-16.
In Japanese.
Surveys the vogue of the picturesque in mid-nineteenth century America and its influence on Poe, Hawthorne, and James. The Italian landscape, for James, was a "symbol of old world meaning."

1987

58 JARRETT, ROBERT LEE. "Revolutionary Identity and the Literary Past: Intertextuality and Tradition in the American Romance." Ph.D. dissertation, University of California, Riverside, 350 pp.

Traces the attempts of Irving, Cooper, Hawthorne, Melville, James, and Faulkner to create a tradition of the American romance. Jarrett draws on the work of Bloom and Lacan to formulate a psycho-linguistic model for tradition-formation and the structure of literary influence. An analysis of James's *The Sacred Fount*, the focus of chapter 5, reveals James's ambivalence toward his romantic predecessor, Hawthorne.

See *Dissertation Abstracts International* 49, no. 4 (1988):818A.

59 JOHNSON, COURTNEY, Jr. *Henry James and the Evolution of Consciousness: A Study of The Ambassadors*. East Lansing: Michigan State University Press, xvi, 171 pp.

Argues that this novel reflects James's lifelong concern with the consciousness, particularly regarding the transformation of the ordinary consciousness into the extraordinary. This novel offers "the clearest example" of that transformation. In this study Johnson compares William's and Henry's sense of the consciousness, distinguishes between the ordinary and extraordinary, and traces Strether's transformation in detail.

60 JONES, MARNIE. "Telling His Own Story: Henry James's *William Wetmore Story*." *Biography* 10, no. 3 (Summer):241-56.

Sees the biography as a mixture of biography, autobiography, and fiction. James is barely interested in Story; rather, he writes his "own inward history," creating a pattern for his own memoirs.

61 KAI, FUMIO. "Henry James no Shoki Shosetsu: Shizen, Bunmei, Rekishi, Nazo, Yurei" [Henry James's early novels: nature, civilization, history, enigmas, and ghosts]. *Eigo Seinen* (Tokyo) 133:158-62.

In Japanese.

Surveys James's early novels, focusing on how James used the story of Adam and his fall, concentrating on *Roderick Hudson* and *The Portrait of a Lady*.

62 KAUFMAN, MICHAEL EDWARD. "The Forms of Fiction: The Physical Text in the Works of Henry James, Gertrude Stein, William Faulkner, James Joyce, and William Gass." Ph.D. dissertation, University of Illinois at Champaign-Urbana, 200 pp.

Traces the reintroduction of the physical, printed, text into the narrative, beginning with James's *The Golden Bowl* and concluding with Joyce's *Finnegan's Wake* and Gass's *Willie Master's Lonesome Wife*, where the text becomes the narrative.

See *Dissertation Abstracts International* 48, no. 2 (1987):387A-388A.

63 KAVKA, JEROME. "Who is 'The Liar' in Henry James's Short Story? A Comparative Analysis." In *Psychoanalytic Studies in Biography*. Emotions and Behavior Monograph, no. 4. Edited by George Moraitis and George H. Pollock. Madison, Conn.: International Universities Press, pp. 219-61.

Surveys critics of the tale, most of whom condemn Lyon and exonerate Everina, although she too is a liar. Kavka reviews psychoanalytic readings of the tale and attributes the ambiguous portrayal of Everina to James's complex relationship with his mother, who controlled the family with her selflessness. James used his creativity to resolve childhood conflicts and neuroses.

64 KELLOGG, MICHAEL. "The Squirrel's Heartbeat – Some Thoughts on the Later Style of Henry James." *Hudson Review* 40, no. 3 (Autumn):432-36.

Argues that James's "aversion to simplistic assessment" is his greatness and his limitation, for the world of action is dependent on superficialities. Lambert Strether and Maggie Verver are nearly paralyzed by their inability to use "paste-on labels."

65 KEYISHIAN, HARRY. "Cross-Currents of Revenge in James's *The American*." *Modern Language Studies* 17, no. 2 (Spring):3-13.

Attributes the novel's problematic ending to its theme of revenge. Because revenge is an emotional and powerful issue, it can create such a complex response in the reader that the author cannot direct it. While Newman has reconciled his own feelings, the reader's sense of justice has not been satisfied.

1987

66 KROOK, DOROTHEA. "'The Aspern Papers': A Counter-Introduction." In *Essays on English and American Literature and a Sheaf of Poems*. Edited by J. Bakker, J.A. Verleun, J.v.D. Vriesenaerde. Amsterdam: Rodopi, pp. 223-234.

Sees the narrator not as a "moral monster" as Edel depicts him but as "a paradigm of the Jamesian civilized man" who discovers his guilt when he thought he was innocent. The tale is concerned with irreconcilable claims of artistic perfection and human integrity and shows that this conflict confronts the critic and biographer as well as the artist.

67 LEE, ROBIN. "Henry James." In *American Fiction 1865-1940*. London: Longman, pp. 85-107.

Surveys James's life and his major themes and novels, as well as current critical trends, including the work of R.P. Blackmur, John Carlos Rowe, Alfred Habegger, and Elizabeth Allen.

68 LESCINSKI, JOAN, C.S.F. "Heroines under Fire: Rebels in Austen and James." *CEA Critic* 49, nos. 2-4 (Winter-Summer):60-69.

Examines Austen's Elizabeth Bennet and Emma Woodhouse and James's Isabel Archer and Maggie Verver to show that each author was critical of the conventional marriage that demanded a subservient woman. Austen's heroines foreshadow James's more detailed treatment of marriage.

69 LEVINE, PEG. "Henry James's 'Louisa Pallant' and the Participant-Observer Narrator and Responsibility." *Mid-Hudson Language Studies* 10:33-41.

Examines the defense mechanisms and the shortcomings of the tale's "participant-observer narrator" to show that his perceptions are profoundly motivated by self-interest. The narrator rejects responsibility for his own words and actions and thus cannot achieve the involvement with others that is necessary for understanding.

70 LICHTENBERG, JOSEPH D. "Henry James and Leon Edel." In *Psychoanalytic Studies in Biography*. Emotions and Behavior Monographs no. 4. Edited by George Moraitis and George H. Pollock. Madison, Conn.: International Universities Press, Inc., pp. 49-58.

Praises Edel's use of psychoanalytic techniques in his biography of James but notes that Edel often undercuts himself by "making comparisons between his interpretations." Lichtenberg also wonders why readers read an author's biography when the author's fiction is available: "does truth become more capitvating than fiction when we discover the rich truth of an actual person?"

See also Edel 1987.34.

71 ____. "A Memory, a Dream, and a Tale: Connecting Themes in the Creativity of Henry James." In *Psychoanalytic Studies in Biography*. Emotions and Behavior Monographs no. 4. Madison, Conn.: International Universities Press, Inc., pp. 85-109.

Examines James's dream of an adversary in the Galerie d'Apollon as a reflection of his rivalry with William. James's insecurity is reflected in "The Jolly Corner" that incorporates this dream in addition to James's guilt about Constance Fenimore Woolson's suicide. Lichtenberg also analyzes the sexual imagery of James's dream and sees it as a dream of rebirth.

72 LINDBERG-SEYERSTED, BRITA. *Ford Madox Ford and His Relationship to Stephen Crane and Henry James*. Atlantic Highlands, N.J.: Humanities Press International, 123 pp.

Sees the relationship between James and Ford as essentially problematic: Ford greatly admired James, but James seemed to denigrate Ford and was alienated by the scandal with Violet Hunt. The study includes much of the correspondence between the two writers and a discussion of James's influence on Ford's comments on James's work.

73 LITVAK, JOSEPH. "Actress, Monster, Novelist – *The Tragic Muse* as a Novel of Theatricality." *Texas Studies in Literature and Language* 29, no. 2 (Summer):141-68.

Sees the metaphor of the theater in the novel as a "commentary on the . . . situation of the nineteenth-century novelist, in terms of his relation to his art and to the world." Litvak also discusses the character of Miriam, the novel's opaque center, and the complex similarities and differences between her and James.

1987

74 LODGE, DAVID. Introduction to *The Spoils of Poynton*. Harmondsworth, England: Penguin Books, pp. 1-18.

Reviews the major positions of the critical discussion of the novel and argues that evidence from the text is open to double interpretation and that Fleda's character is essentially ambiguous. The text hesitates between alternative meanings; the reader must do the same.

75 LOPES, M. ANGELICA GUIMARAES. "'Estátuas Esculpidas pelo tempo': Imagética como caracterização em *Quincas Borba* e *The Portrait of a Lady*." *Chasqui: Revista de Literature Latinoamericana* (Provo, Utah) 16, no. 1 (February):55-75.

In Portuguese.

76 McCORMACK, PEGGY. "Exchange Economy in Henry James's *The Awkward Age*." *University of Mississippi Studies in English* 5:182-202.

Focuses on James's use of the language and metaphors of economics in this novel to show that such language is an integral part of James's tragic vision. In *The Awkward Age*, as in other novels, James's "protagonist moves from a state of innocence to one of experience as he or she learns the implications of the sexual/economic discourse he or she is forced to encounter."

77 MACHOR, JAMES L. "Urban Pastoralism and Literary Dissent: From 'Brooklyn Ferry' to *The American Scene*." In *Pastoral Cities: Urban Ideals and the Symbolic Landscape of America*. Madison: University of Wisconsin Press, pp. 175-210, 250-55.

Examines responses to urban pastoralism in Whitman, Hawthorne, Dreiser, Wharton, and James. While pastoralism is an ideal to be hoped for, these writers expose the realities contradicting the ideal. In *The American Scene* James shows that the "denial of historical continuity by the entire culture makes achievement of the ideal impossible."

78 MACNAUGHTON, WILLIAM R. *Henry James: The Later Novels*. Twayne's United States Authors Series (TUSAS) 521. Boston: Twayne, 154 pp.

Discusses the genesis, major themes, technique, and criticism of the following novels: *The Princess Casamassima, The Tragic Muse, The Awkward Age, The Ambassadors, The Wings of the Dove,* and *The Golden Bowl,* and offers an original reading of each work. Macnaughton also includes brief biographical sketches of James at the middle and end of his career.

79   MAINI, DARSHAN SINGH. *Henry James: The Indirect Vision.* Studies in Modern Literature, no. 83. Ann Arbor: UMI Research Press, xii, 246 pp.
      Revision of 1973 edition, with the addition of the following reprints: 1979.94; 1985.88; and 1987.80. In addition, the first chapter of this edition incorporates material from 1985.87.

80   _____. "Henry James: The Writer as Critic." *Henry James Review* 8, no. 3 (Spring):189-99.
      Parallels James's fiction and criticism to show that his criticism is a "collateral exercise," sharing the same creative energy and dialectic as his novels. Reprinted 1987.79.

81   MAKOWSKY, VERONICA A. "Blackmur on the Dove's Wings." In *The Legacy of R.P. Blackmur: Essays, Memoirs, Texts.* Edited by Edward T. Cane, Joseph Frank, and Edmund Keeley. New York: Ecco, pp. 63-72.
      Details Blackmur's changing interpretations of the novel and attributes the change to changes in his own life because Blackmur strongly identified with the novel's main characters. Makowsky argues, in fact, that many events in Blackmur's life parallel those in the novel, which he held as his favorite of James's works.

82   MARTIN, W.R., and OBER, WARREN U. "Henry James's 'Traveling Companions': Did the Master Nod?" *Notes & Queries* 34, no. 1 (March):46-47.
      Note that the tale's description of Tintoretto's *Crucifixion* is inaccurate.

83   _____. "James's 'My Friend Bingham' and Coleridge's 'Ancient Mariner.'" *English Language Notes* 25, no. 2 (December):44-48.

1987

Demonstrate that the tale's narrator is a "conflation" of Coleridge's wedding guest and the "Rime's" narrator; the tale exemplifies James's practice of "stealing and keeping."

84 ____. "The Provenience of Henry James's First Tale." *Studies in Short Fiction* 24, no. 1 (Winter):57-8.
     Note that "A Tragedy of Error" is an inversion of the Franklin's Tale in *The Canterbury Tales*.

85 MERIDETH, EUNICE MAE. "Stylistic Gender Patterns in Fiction: A Curricular Concern." Ph.D. dissertation, Iowa State University, 131 pp.
     Analyzes the speech of characters in James's "Daisy Miller", *The Portrait of a Lady*, and *The Bostonians*, and Chopin's *The Awakening*, using a computer program to identify gender patterns. Merideth's hypotheses propose that male speech contains patterns denoting power and strength while female speech denotes politeness and uncertainty. James's work supports both; Chopin's work exhibits variation of the first but support for the second.
     See *Dissertation Abstracts International* 48, no. 7 (1988):1644A.

86 MEYERS, CHERIE KAY BEAIRD. "Aestheticism and the 'Paradox of Progress' in the Work of Henry James, Edith Wharton, and Henry Adams." Ph.D. dissertation, University of Tulsa, 347 pp.
     Examines the influence of British/European Aestheticism on Adams's, James's, and Wharton's depiction of the social changes occurring during the years 1893 to 1913. *The Spoils of Poynton, The Sacred Fount, The Ambassadors*, and *The Golden Bowl* bear the imprint of Pater's "Theoretical Aestheticism," which propounded art for art's sake.
     See *Dissertation Abstracts International* 48, no. 12 (1988):3112A.

87 MILLER, J. HILLIS. "Re-Reading Re-vision: James and Benjamin." In *The Ethics of Reading: Kant, de Man, Eliot, Trollope, James, and Benjamin*. New York: Columbia University Press, pp. 101-27, 133.
     Discusses James's ethics of rereading his own works, drawing upon James's remarks in the New York Edition Preface to *The Golden Bowl*. For James, "to re-read is to be forced by an irresistible necessity

that is not in the text he once wrote and now re-reads, but appears to come from the matter that text represented in a way he now finds inadequate."

88   MILLER, JAMES E., Jr. "The Biographer with the Blue Guitar." In *Psychoanalytic Studies of Biography.* Emotions and Behavior Monographs, no. 4. Edited by George Moraitis and George H. Pollock. Madison, Conn.: International Universities Press, Inc., pp. 29-47.

Sees biography as a literary form in its own right and as a means of illuminating the literary work. Miller cites Edel's *Henry James* as an example of the form in its "Jamesian economy" where all episodes are selected with purpose, discusses the relationship between biography and psychoanalysis – particularly in light of Edel's work – and suggests that biography sheds light on the inner life of the biographer.

89   MITCHELL, LEE CLARK. "The Sustaining Duplicities of *The Wings of the Dove.*" *Texas Studies in Literature and Language* 29, no. 2 (Summer):187-214.

Argues that Kate should not be censured because the narrative's repetitive structure deprives her of free will and therefore responsibility, while it also subverts the reader's approval or disapproval. Mitchell traces the intertwined "mutual deceptions" and concludes that the novel is "so baffling because it questions our forms of interpretation."

90   MONTEIRO, GEORGE. "Henry James and Whitelaw Reid: Some Additional Documents." *Henry James Review* 8, no. 2 (Winter):139-41.

Reprints three letters by Whitelaw Reid, editor of the *Tribune,* that show he was "favorably disposed" to James's work.

91   ____. "Henry James on the Death of Del Hay: A New Letter." *American Literary Realism 1870-1910* 19, no. 3 (Spring):89-90.

Reprints James's letter to John Hay on the death of his oldest child, Del Hay. James describes his memories of the boy.

1987

92   MOON, HEATH. "Is *The Sacred Fount* a Symbolist Novel?" *Comparative Literature* 39, no. 4 (Fall):306-26.

Sees the novel as a hybrid of the novel of manners and symbolism. James's "flirtation" with symbolism was influenced by Gabriele D'Annunzio, whose novel *Le Vergini delle Rocce* (1895) bears many similarities to *The Sacred Fount*. James absorbed the fascination with decay, the mental states and moods of symbolism, but rejected its eroticism, politicizing, and editorializing.

93   MORSE, DAVID. "Henry James: Refusing the Limit." In *American Romanticism Volume 2: From Melville to James: The Enduring Excessive*. Totowa, N.J.: Barnes & Noble, pp. 115-83, 186-87.

Surveys James's novels from *Roderick Hudson* to *The Golden Bowl*, tracing the transcendentalist theme of the individual's struggle to maintain the integrity of the self in a world always threatening to erode that self.

94   MURPHY, JAMES GERALD. "An Analysis of Henry James's Revisions of the First Four Novels of the New York Edition." Ph.D. dissertation, University of Delaware, 212 pp.

Argues that the revisions of *Roderick Hudson, The American, The Portrait of a Lady*, and *The Princess Casamassima* result in an "anomalous" and confusing work. Murphy examines the prefaces to these novels as well, showing that James's stated intentions differed from his original ones and shaped the revisions accordingly.

See *Dissertation Abstracts International* 48, no. 6 (1987):1455A.

95   MYRICK, PATRICIA LYNN. "Gothic Perceptions of the Past in the Nineteenth-Century Novel: Dickens, Hawthorne, Eliot, and James." Ph.D. dissertation, Indiana University, 205 pp.

Argues that these writers used the Gothic "as a means of understanding and articulating their views of the historical past and its relation to the present." In *The Portrait of a Lady* the Gothic suggests a connection between past and present, while in some of his short fictions James uses the Gothic to keep the past uncontaminated by the present or to keep the present open to the past.

See *Dissertation Abstracts International* 49, no. 4 (1988):812A.

96 NIELSON, KATHLEEN BUSWELL. "Comedy in Twentieth Century Fiction: *The Ambassadors, A Passage to India, To the Lighthouse,* and *Surfacing.*" Ph.D. dissertation, Vanderbilt University, 319 pp.

Argues that in these novels comedy is a way of confronting the "chaos of modern experience," and is linked to a central female character who embodies "life force." In *The Ambassadors,* that character is Madame de Vionnet.

See *Dissertation Abstracts International* 48, no. 3 (1987):648A.

97 NUSSBAUM, MARTHA CRAVEN. "Finely Aware and Richly Responsible: Literature and the Moral Imagination." In *Literature and the Question of Philosophy.* Edited by Anthony J. Cascardi. Baltimore: Johns Hopkins University Press, pp. 169-91.

Revision of 1985.108.

98 OLIN-AMMENTORP, JULIE ANDREA. "'This Negotiable World': Money and Marriage in Wharton and James." Ph.D. dissertation, University of Michigan, 167 pp.

Argues that in their novels, Wharton and James portrayed leisure-class marriage as a system using the rhetoric of romantic love to disguise its commercial and exploitative nature. Further, these novels – specifically *The Wings of the Dove, The Golden Bowl, The House of Mirth,* and *The Custom of the Country* – depict a society deeply divided along gender lines.

See *Dissertation Abstracts International* 48, no. 11 (1988):2875A.

99 ORLICH, ILEANA ALEXANDRA. "The Lesson of Balzac: Henry James and the Transatlantic Transit of the Nouvelle." Ph.D. dissertation, Arizona State University, 247 pp.

Demonstrates that the work of Balzac was a dominant influence on James's early work in terms of both style and technique.

See *Dissertation Abstracts International* 48, no. 3 (1987):664A.

*100 PERROT, JEAN. "Henry James: La Nouvelle et le systeme de l'oeuvre." *Palinure* 3 (Spring):14-27.

In French.

1987

Source: Offline Bibliography, BRS Information Technologies, Latham, NY 12110

101   PERSON, LELAND S., Jr. "Strether's 'Penal Form': The Pleasure of Imaginative Surrender." *Papers on Language and Literature* 23, no. 1 (Winter):27-40.

Argues that Strether permits Mme. de Vionnet, Sarah Pocock, and Maria Gostrey to do his imagining for him. Strether's rejection of Maria at the novel's end is in keeping with his inability to participate in experience and his preference for imaginative relationships.

102   PORSDAM, HELLE. "The 'International Theme' Modernized: Henry James' Influence on Ernest Hemingway and F. Scott Fitzgerald." Ph.D. dissertation, Yale University, 231 pp.

Argues that James's treatment of the international theme as a search for personal and national identity shaped Fitzgerald's and Hemingway's use of the theme.

See *Dissertation Abstracts International* 49, no. 4 (1988):857A.

103   POSNOCK, ROSS. "Henry James, Veblen and Adorno: The Crisis of the Modern Self." *Journal of American Studies* 21, no. 1 (April):31-54.

Compares the social criticism of these writers because they "stress the semiological character of manners" and they reveal the repression underlying the veneer of bourgeois respectability. Posnock focuses on the valuation of nonidentity and the polarities within American society as reflected by women and Jews and uses *The American Scene* for the basis of his discussion.

104   ____. "James, Browning, and the Theatrical Self: *The Wings of the Dove* and *In a Balcony*." In *Self, Sign, and Symbol*. Edited by Mark Newman and Michael Payne. Lewisburg: Bucknell University Press, pp. 95-116.

Argues that *The Wings of the Dove* is James's rewriting of Browning's *In a Balcony*; James transforms Browning's poetic drama with a drama of consciousness. Posnock focuses on the "aesthetic impulse" and the "essential theatricality" of Browning's and James's heroines, suggesting that these characters mirror their creators.

105   RECCHIA, EDWARD. "An Eye for an I: Adapting James's *The Turn of the Screw* to the Screen." *Literature/Film Quarterly* 15, no. 1 (January):28-35.
    Demonstrates that in his film adaptation Jack Clayton recreates the tale's ambiguity, "the greatest homage a film adaptor can make" to James.

106   RHEAD, CLIFTON. "Henry James and the Sense of the Past." In *Psychoanalytic Studies in Biography*. Emotions and Behavior Monographs no. 4. Edited by George Moraitis and George H. Pollock. Madison, Conn.: International Universities Press, Inc., pp. 263-78.
    Attributes James's depictions of rivalrous and symbiotic relationships to his relationship with William and suggests that Mary James may have fostered a "sense of ambiguity of self and identity" in the James children.

107   RINGUETTE, DANA JOSEPH. "'These Intenser Lights of Experience': Consciousness and Revision in Henry James." Ph.D. dissertation, University of Washington.
    Argues that "revision for James is a developmental 'principle of growth,' manifested in the relation of consciousness and community." Individual chapters focus on the function of revision in *The Portrait of a Lady*, *What Maisie Knew*, and *The Wings of the Dove*. The study concludes by asserting that revision is an imaginative act, achieving representation that is essentially pragmatic rather than predetermined.
    See *Dissertation Abstracts International* 48, no. 10 (1988):2629A.

108   ROBINSON, GABRIELLE. "Patronage in *The Ambassadors*: A False Position or No Position." *Nineteenth-Century Fiction* 42, no. 2 (September):203-16.
    Argues that this novel depicts a complex series of relationships based on patronage and that, in the course of the novel, Strether does not grow but becomes aware of the all-encompassing nature of the patronage system.

1987

109 ROGERS, HENRY N., III. "Trollope and James: The 'Germ' Within." *SEL: Studies in English Literature, 1500-1900* 27, no. 4 (Autumn):647-62.

Argues for a strong literary relationship between the two writers because they share similar ideas about the creative process. In "The Panjandrum" Trollope depicts how a writer writes a story, and his description bears strong resemblance to James's theories of composition.

110 ROWE, JOHN CARLOS. "The Politics of the Uncanny in Henry James's *The American.*" *Henry James Review* 8, no. 2 (Winter):79-90.

Traces the many elements of doubling in the novel, focusing on Newman and the other characters and on Mozart's *Don Giovanni* and the novel's plot. Newman's failure to recognize himself in the other characters accounts for his experience of strangeness and of the fantastic and explains his psychological innocence.

111 SABIN, MARGERY. "Competition of Intelligence in *The Golden Bowl.*" In *The Dialect of the Tribe: Speech and Community in Modern Fiction.* Oxford: Oxford University Press, pp. 65-105, 297-99.

Examines the characters of Charlotte and Maggie to show how James redefines experience, knowledge, truth, and love. The novel demonstrates that values are corrupted by the real, social world, and that "only isolated acts of mind and language" can preserve them.

112 SABISTON, ELIZABETH JEAN. "Isabel Archer: the Architect of Consciousness." In *The Prison of Womanhood: Four Provincial Heroines in Nineteenth-Century Fiction.* New York: St. Martin's Press, pp. 114-38.

Traces Isabel's connection with architectural imagery to show that throughout the novel she constructs her own "complex architecture" of consciousness and her own fate. James, however, does not permit her "the power of expression," so that at the novel's end she renounces Goodwood's love for "nothing in particular," thus suggesting that James could not imagine "feminine creativity."

113 SCHRIBER, MARY SUZANNE. "Henry James: The Summit of the Male Imagination." In *Gender and the Writer's Imagination: From*

Cooper to Wharton. Lexington: University Press of Kentucky, pp. 117-56, 201-5.

Examines James's analysis and use of the cultural "ideology of women" of his time. Isabel's interest lies in the conflict in her character between her individuality and her conventionality; in *Roderick Hudson* cultural expectations for women are crucial in the characterization of Mary Garland and Christina Light and in Rowland Mallet's response to these women. James is highly critical of the ideology of women: in *The Golden Bowl* he transforms the dark lady and fair heroine stereotypes with the complex characterization of Charlotte Stant and Maggie Verver, while in *The Bostonians* he satirizes the culture that supports the ideology of women. In examining *The Tragic Muse* and its preface, Schriber finds a discrepancy between James's perception of social reality and his imaginative capability in his depiction of Miriam Rooth.

114   SLAUGHTER, CAROLYN OVERTON. "Language as Discourse in Five Modernist American Works." Ph.D. dissertation, University of Arizona, 319 pp.

Examines the nature and function of language, using the work of Heidegger, in exploring literary ambiguity. In her analysis of "The Turn of the Screw," Slaughter suggests that "literality works to indicate, to evoke, to found and maintain as well as to violate or subvert a human order."

See *Dissertation Abstracts International* 49, no. 3 (1988):506a.

115   SMIT, DAVID W. "The Later Styles of Henry James." *Style* 21, no. 1 (Spring):95-106.

Describes a wide variety of styles in James's public and private writing, and in his writing and his speaking (based on "reconstructions"). The essay includes statistical analyses of the differences between James's private and published work.

116   SMITH, GEORGE E., III. "James, Degas, and the Modern View." *Novel* 21, no. 1 (Fall):56-72.

Draws parallels between Degas's paintings and *The Ambassadors*, focusing on the way both James and Degas use the consciousness as observer.

1987

117 SMITH, PAULA VENE. "The Library and the Tea Table: Virginia Woolf and the Fiction of Henry James." Ph.D. dissertation, Cornell University, 221 pp.

Argues that Woolf rewrote the Jamesian canon, questioning the duality of women's position – the codes governing public and private life – as well as the literary tradition that attributes greatness to male writers almost exclusively.

See *Dissertation Abstracts International* 48, no. 10 (1988):2637A-2638A.

118 STEELE, MEILI. "The Drama of Reference in James's *The Golden Bowl.*" *Novel* 21, no. 1 (Fall):73-88.

Applies Gottlob Frege's concept of reference to the dialogues and presentation of character in the novel. Steele shows that the "obscure dialogues" explore "the ontological discontinuity generated by speakers with different referential languages" and examines Maggie's character and consciousness in terms of the "alternative referential languages" that she herself generates. Steele suggests that reference ultimately discloses "the ontological power of language."

119 TANNER, TONY. "Proust, Ruskin, James and *Le Désir de Venise.*" *Journal of American Studies* 21, no. 1 (April):5-29.

Analyzes James's and Proust's visions of Venice, and how Ruskin shaped those visions. For Proust, the idea of Venice evoked pleasure, mystery, ecstasy; its reality was sordid and perverted. For James, who envisioned this city as a woman, Venice was "dazzling" and "iridescent," but it was a "place of death, loss, supersession." Tanner discusses the depiction of Venice in "The Aspern Papers" and *The Wings of the Dove.*

120 TINTNER, ADELINE R. "Adventures in Life and Fiction." *Midstream* 33, no. 6 (June-July):55-56.

Notes James's influence on Philip Roth's *The Counterfile* and *The Prague Orgy.* Tintner suggests that while Roth borrows James's icons, James's art of fiction has enabled Roth to "revolutionize the shape of the novel."

121 ____. "The Art of Rococo Venice in James's Fiction." *AB Bookman's Weekly* 80, no. 12 (21 September):993-1004.

Traces James's "appreciation of Venice in its 18th-century manifestation" throughout his life and his writing, both fiction and nonfiction. The Venetian element is apparent in numerous tales, but dominates "The Aspern Papers." Rococo Venice also figures importantly in *The Sacred Fount, The Wings of the Dove, The Outcry*, and the revision of *The Portrait of a Lady*.

122   ____. *The Book World of Henry James: Appropriating the Classics*. Ann Arbor: University Microfilms International Research Press, xxvi, 412 pp.

Traces in detail James's use of literary works as models for his own fiction and his compulsion to rewrite classics. Tintner argues that James appropriated classics to give his readers signposts, dues, and insights into his own work.

Chapters are devoted to major literary figures – Shakespeare, Milton, and Balzac; to groups – English Romantic Poets; English, American, and European novelists; historians; and the pre-Raphaelites. The greater portion of the book is composed of revisions of articles noted below; chapter 7, "James among the Historians," and chapter 14, "The Monumental Figure of Balzac," contain new material. In chapter 7 Tintner details James's use of DeTocqueville and Gibbon: DeTocqueville contributed to James's development of the international theme while James drew on Gibbon for his treatment of Italy in *The Wings of the Dove* and *The Golden Bowl*. In chapter 14, Tintner sees Rodin's sculpture of Balzac as an analogue to James's evaluation of Balzac as a "monument" of literature. Tintner concludes by declaring that Balzac and Shakespeare were James's two great masters. This volume is illustrated with reproductions of paintings, sculpture, and title pages of books from James's library.

Reprints:

"Balzac's Two Maries and James's *The Ambassadors*," *English Language Notes* 9, no. 4 (June 1972):284-87;

"The Old Things': Balzac's *Le Cure de Tours* and James's *The Spoils of Poynton*," *Nineteenth Century Fiction* 26, no. 4 (March 1972):436-55;

"The Influence of Balzac's *L'Envers de l'histoire contemporaine* on James's 'The Great Good Place,'" *Studies in Short Fiction* 9, no. 4 (Fall 1972):343-51;

"Balzac's 'Madame Firmiani' and James's *The Ambassadors*," *Comparative Literature* 25, no. 2 (Spring 1973):128-35;

"Keats and James and *The Princess Casamassima*," *Nineteenth Century Fiction* 28, no. 2 (September 1973);

1987

"Countess and Scholastica: Henry James's 'L'Allegro' and 'Il Penseroso,'" *Studies in Short Fiction* 11, no. 3 (Summer 1974):267-77; 1976.187, 189-190, 192; 1977.136; 1978.118-119, 121; 1980.145-146, 149-150; 1981.158, 161, 165-166; 1982.147-148, 150, 152, 155; 1983.203, 207; 1984.204; 1986.147; 1987.124-125.

123 _____. "Dear and Venerable Circe: An Unpublished Henry James Letter." *Manuscripts* 39, no. 2 (Spring):156-61.

Reprints a letter to an unknown lady in which James addresses her as Circe and refers to himself as Odysseus. This brief note, accepting an invitation for tea, exemplifies James's appropriating and revising a literary classic. Tintner speculates that Mrs. Kemble may have been the letter's recipient.

124 _____. "Facing the 'Alter Ego': Edgar Allan Poe's Influence on Henry James." *AB Bookman's Weekly* 7, no. 2 (January 12):105-9.

Demonstrates that Poe's "The Fall of the House of Usher" is a chief source for and influence on James's "The Jolly Corner." Tintner explores Poe's influence on James in general, but focuses on the use of doubling in this tale as exemplifying Poe's impact on James.

Revised 1987.122.

125 _____. "Henry James's Professor Fargo and *Don Quixote*: American Realism through a Literary Analogy." *American Literary Realism 1870-1910* 19, no. 3 (Spring):42-51.

Demonstrates that James used *Don Quixote* as an analogue in this 1874 tale that is highly critical of American provincialism. James alluded to *Don Quixote* in various works throughout his career, including the prefaces, often as an analogue for the artist. In this early tale, Cervantes's work enriches James's.

Revised 1987.122.

126 _____. "The Sea of Azof in 'The Turn of the Screw' and Maurice Barres's *Les Déracinés*." *Essays in Literature* 14, no. 1 (Spring):139-43.

Identifies the Sea of Azof (one part of which is fresh, the other too salty to support any life) as an image borrowed from Barres's "gruesome" novel about corrupted students who murder a woman. James uses the novel's "helpless plasticity" of the young and the corrupting atmosphere in his tale.

127 _____. "Thomas Couture's *Romans of the Decadence* and Henry
James's 'The Seige of London.'" *Journal of Pre-Raphaelite and
Aesthetic Studies* 1, no. 1 (Fall):39-47.
Demonstrates that this painting, which depicts a Roman orgy,
shapes the form of James's tale as much as – if not more – than the plays
by Angier and Dumas. The courtesan in the center of the painting
suggests Nancy Headway's place as the tale's focus, while the spectators
at the edge of the picture are echoed in Littlemore and Waterville, the
tale's observers. Tintner also traces many additional parallels between
the painting and the tale.

128 _____ and JANOWITZ, HENRY D. "Inoperable Cancer: An
Alternate Diagnoses for Milly Theale's Illness." *Journal of the History
of Medicine* 42 (January):73-76.
Suggests that because Sir Luke Strett is a surgeon, Milly may
have had inoperable cancer. This is further supported by his advice for
her to enjoy life . . . while she can.

129 VARNADO, S.L. "The Numinous Aesthetic of Henry James." In
Haunted Presence: The Numinous in Gothic Fiction. Tuscaloosa:
University of Alabama Press, pp. 77-94.
Traces James's development of the ghostly tale, focusing on his
juxtaposition of realism with the numinous, "awareness of an objective
spiritual presence." Varnado discusses the various devices James used
in "The Turn of the Screw" – multiple narrative frames, ambience, and
characterization – to create the numinous.

130 VERLEUN, JAN. "Conrad's Modernity and Humanity." In *Essays
on English and American Literature and a Sheaf of Poems*. Edited by
J. Bakker, J.A. Verleun, J.v.d. Vriesenaerde. Amsterdam: Rodopi,
pp. 131-40.
Compares James and Lawrence with Conrad in terms of their
modernity. All three writers could not accept a "soulless universe" and
were convinced of a "spreading corruption" in western culture.
Although these writers share beliefs about the human condition,
Conrad depicts man's predicament most truthfully because he, unlike
James and Lawrence, despairs of any certainties in life.

1987

131   WALSH, KATHLEEN. "Things Must Have a Basis: Verification in
       The Ambassadors, The Wings of the Dove, and *The Golden Bowl."*
       South Atlantic Review 52, no. 2:51-64.
            Argues that Henry James, like William James, saw an
       important connection between reality and impressions, and shows that
       this connection is central to the three major novels. In *The
       Ambassadors,* verification of reality is difficult, but not impossible, and
       the novel charts Strether's movement from false impressions to
       illumination. Densher, in *The Wings of the Dove,* attempts to avoid
       knowledge while Milly is able to transcend hard reality by her
       forgiveness. In *The Golden Bowl,* Maggie uses the "facts" to achieve
       freedom and to create her own reality.

132   WARNER, JOHN M. "Renunciation as Enunciation in James's *The
       Portrait of a Lady."* *Renascence* 39, no. 2 (Winter):354-64.
            Argues that Isabel is a more complex re-working of Claire de
       Cintre, who ultimately achieves an "attunement to reality wider than
       that of self" in spite of Newman's temptation to self-idealization. Isabel
       is tempted by Ralph's romanticization of death and Caspar's love.
       Isabel rejects both to return not to Osmond, but to Rome, with its
       "associations of man with nature, society, *and* the divine." Her return,
       therefore, indicates her awareness of a reality larger than self.

133   WARRINER, ALISON McKEAN. "Adultery in the Novels of Henry
       James." Ph.D. dissertation, University of California, Berkeley, 333
       pp.
            Argues that James's connecting adultery with sexuality and evil
       reflects personal biases, and traces his depiction of adultery in his
       fiction. Warriner begins with the early work, where adultery is
       associated with the international theme and notes that, in much of his
       work, sexuality involves renunciation. In *The Golden Bowl,* however,
       Maggie and Amerigo ultimately achieve a fulfilling sexuality,
       reconciling victim and adulterer.
            See *Dissertation Abstracts International* 48, no. 9 (1988):2340A.

134   WEGELIN, CHRISTOF. "Art and Life in James's 'The Middle
       Years.'" *Modern Fiction Studies* 33, no. 4 (Winter):639-46.
            Shows that in this tale James examines the mystery of artistic
       creation, the core of imagination that cannot be explained or analyzed.
       Wegelin parallels this tale about "the madness of art" with "The Figure

in the Carpet" that also explores the mystery of art. He briefly notes that Philip Roth's *The Ghost Writer* dramatizes "the madness of art" and contains echoes of "The Middle Years."

135   WEGENER, FREDERICK GUSTAV. "Robert Browning and the Literary Apprenticeship of Henry James." Ph.D. dissertation, Harvard University, 187 pp.

Focuses on Browning's influence on James during the years 1864 to 1875. This influence is particularly apparent in three significant tales that are organized around a Browning poem: "The Story of a Masterpiece," "A Light Man," and "The Madonna of the Future."

See *Dissertation Abstracts International* 49, no. 3 (1988):507A.

136   WILT, JUDITH. "Desperately Seeking Verena: A Resistant Reading of *The Bostonians*." *Feminist Studies* 13, no. 2 (Summer):293-316.

Argues that Verena is engaged on the feminist quest for the freedom to choose suffering, although James, fearful of the female artist, ultimately undermines that quest by having Verena "fall" into sexuality.

137   WOLFF, BEVERLY ANNE. "James's Moral Perspective: The Individual Vision in *The Princess Casamassima, The Tragic Muse*, and *The Awkward Age*." Ph.D. dissertation, University of Delaware, 200 pp.

Argues that these three novels show the process by which the individual attains a moral perspective: recognition of one's self, which shapes choices as well as relations with others and with society.

See *Dissertation Abstracts International* 48, no. 8 (1988):2071A.

Subject Index

absence, 1977.140; 1978.15; 1983.118; 1984.22; 1985.17
absolutism, 1981.73
acquiescence, 1981.19
acquisition, 1982.75
Adam, 1987.61
Adam, American, 1978.8, 12
Adams, Clover, 1986.117
Adams, Henry, 1975.13, 70, 89; 1976.48, 160; 1977.24, 48; 1979.47; 1983.216; 1984.97
adaptation, 1980.95; 1981.101; 1983.64; 1984.46
-film, 1975.2, 143; 1976.7; 1977.1, 12, 23, 83, 94; 1978.85, 87; 1979.21, 105, 123; 1980.2, 41, 152; 1981.89; 1982.4; 1983.79, 91, 181; 1984.49, 81, 101, 107, 111, 133; 1985.11, 159; 1986, 140; 1987.105
-opera, 1979.26, 121; 1982.30; 1983.145; 1984.55, 141; 1985.62; 1986.25
-stage, 1979.114; 1983.51, 128, 1984.163
-television, 1977.121; 1979.37; 1981.100, 135

Addams, Jane, 1975.70
Adolphe (Benjamin Constant), 1982.116
Adultery, 1977.29; 1985.51; 1987.133
"The Adventure of Cherry of Zennor," 1987.48
advertising man, 1982.58
aestheticism, 1975.74; 1976.175; 1979.82; 1980.52; 1981.84; 1982.155; 1984.62; 1986.45, 118; 1987.44, 86
aesthetics, 1985.161, 166
The Age of Innocence (Edith Wharton), 1980.22, 148; 1982.141
aging, 1978.34; 1979.34
Alcott, Louisa May, 1983.47; 1984.209; 1985.53
Alden, Professor, 1977.13
alienation, 1983.39; 1984.78
Alger, Reverend William Rounseville, 1986.130
allusion, 1978.56; 1980.20; 1986.141

Densher, Merton, 1975.118;
    1979.56; 1987.131
depression, 1975.32; 1987.53
Les Déracinés (Maurice Barres),
    1987.126
Derrida, Jacques, 1975.109;
    1978.79
desire, 1984.89, 104, 134
detachment, 1982.81, 89; 1986.57
determinism, 1984.174
Deutsch, Helene, 1975.26
development, artistic, 1976.10;
    1979.161
dialect, 1981.29; 1984.16
dialectic, 1977.37; 1979.47; 1983.74
dialogue, 1976.206, 208; 1980.101
Dickens, Charles, 1975.25, 38;
    1979.58; 1982.170; 1984.182;
    1985.79, 98; 1986.146
Dickinson, Anna, 1979.29
didacticism, 1978.59; 1980.67
Dido, 1981.124
difference, 1984.179; 1986.91
Digby Grant (George John Whyte-
    Melville), 1979.156
"The Dilettante" (Edith Wharton),
    1979.80
Dilthey, Wilhelm, 1977.48
disavowal, 1984.175, 176
discontinuity, 1983.135
discourse, 1982.91
-analysis, 1983.85
discrimination, 1981.69; 1982.105
displacement, 1986.125
distance, narrative, 1977.122
distancing, 1976.158; 1984.195
divorce, Campbell, 1980.99
domination, 1975.73
Don Casmurro (Machado de
    Assis), 1982.47
Don Giovanni (Wolfgang
    Mozart), 1987.110

Don Quixote (Miguel de
    Cervantes), 1987.125
doppelgänger, 1977.51. See also
    alter ego, double
Dora (Sigmund Freud), 1986.33
Doré, Gustave, 1979.151
double, 1976.129, 197. See also
    alter ego, doppelgänger
doubling, 1984.77, 175-176;
    1987.110
Doubrovsky, Serge, 1975.24
dove, 1982.159
Drabble, Margaret, 1984.121, 139
drama, 1978.45; 1982.37; 1983.86;
    1986.7
dream, American, 1975.152
Dreiser, Theodore, 1984.87
dualism, 1975.117
Du côté chez Swann (Marcel
    Proust), 1977.135
The Duke's Children (Anthony
    Trollope), 1977.44
DuMaurier, Georges, 1976.175
Duncan, Sara Jeanette, 1986.42
duplication, 1982.9, 143; 1984.14,
    19
Durgnat, Raymond, 1975.143

Easy Rider, 1981.138
economics, 1976.149; 1980.43;
    1986.90; 1987.76
Edel, Leon, 1975.3, 8, 21, 63;
    1976.86; 1978.81; 1979.2;
    1981.111; 1982.42, 44, 48;
    1985.12; 1986.68, 145; 1987.47,
    70, 88
Eden, 1975.94
editing, 1978.44; 1985.95
edition
-Norton critical, 1975.7; 1978.23,
    125
-variant, 1985.144

--"A Day of Days," 1982.82
--"The Death of a Lion," 1975.61,
    83, 121; 1978.15; 1983.152;
    1984.164; 1986.76
--"DeGrey: A Romance,"
    1979.173; 1983.63
--"The Diary of a Man of Fifty,"
    1979.173; 1984.8
--*Embarrassments*, 1986.53
--"Emile Zola," 1983.3
--*English Hours*, 1979.104;
    1981.39-40; 1983.132; 1985.88
--"Eugene Pickering," 1979.96;
    1982.147; 1987.122
--"Europe," 1975.64
--*The Europeans*, 1975.19, 103;
    1976.52, 101, 188; 1978.124;
    1979.21, 27, 33, 105, 123;
    1980.52, 111; 1982.56, 105,
    117, 136; 1983.91; 1984.54,
    199; 1985.124, 165; 1986.130;
    1987.43
--"The Figure in the Carpet,"
    1975.98; 1976.80, 106; 1977.16,
    107; 1978.21, 53, 90; 1980.97,
    123; 1981.65, 90, 120;
    1982.154; 1983.196; 1984.7, 34,
    88, 165, 196, 225, 228;
    1985.150; 1986.5, 76; 1987.16,
    37, 134
--*The Finer Grain*, 1975.137;
    1980.164; 1983.123, 124;
    1986.53, 99, 133
--"Flickerbridge," 1976.31;
    1983.201; 1984.194
--"Fordham Castle," 1976.31;
    1979.30; 1980.157
--"Four Meetings," 1978.96;
    1979.51; 1980.91; 1984.8;
    1985.47, 49
--"The Friends of Friends,"
    1976.171; 1985.1

--*The Future of the Novel*,
    1977.143
--"Gabriele D'Annunzio,"
    1981.170
--"Gabrielle de Bergerac,"
    1975.79; 1982.82; 1983.201
--"Georgina's Reasons," 1983.200
--"The Ghostly Rental," 1975.133;
    1984.8
--"Glasses," 1976.192; 1977.138;
    1983.45; 1985.14, 15; 1987.122
--*The Golden Bowl*, 1975.14, 24-
    26, 35, 38, 47, 59, 72, 74, 87,
    91, 103, 113, 116, 120, 128;
    1976.5, 10, 13, 43, 64, 65, 67,
    77, 103, 113, 116, 123, 130,
    138, 141, 146, 152, 158, 160,
    165, 181-182, 185, 206, 107,
    108; 1977.5, 8, 29, 30, 39, 77,
    89, 111, 113; 1978.12, 48, 51,
    59, 99, 118, 122; 1979.10, 19,
    27, 55, 81, 91, 102, 110, 133,
    136, 138, 157; 1980.7, 15, 83,
    101, 111, 113, 137, 153, 160;
    1981.43, 46, 50, 52, 54-55, 70,
    86, 100, 167, 175, 176;
    1982.17, 33, 37, 51, 57, 75, 80,
    102, 108, 128, 137-138, 155,
    168; 1983.2, 11, 39, 61, 73, 74,
    98, 125, 135, 137, 138, 158,
    161, 162, 173, 175, 202, 207,
    215, 217, 223; 1984.1, 4, 22,
    29, 30, 36, 61, 71, 72, 75, 79,
    105, 108, 110, 112, 134, 162,
    166, 167, 169, 174-176, 188,
    191, 213-214, 223, 230; 1985.8,
    23-24, 48, 51-52, 56, 65-66, 73,
    76, 108-109, 116, 131, 144,
    155-156; 1986.3, 14, 17, 23, 39,
    40, 52, 69, 90-91, 97, 151;
    1987.15, 20, 28, 44-45, 49, 62,
    64, 68, 86, 97, 98, 111, 113,
    122, 131, 133

167, 190; 1977.3, 5, 11, 13, 24,
31, 34, 44, 47, 53, 60, 64, 70,
72, 77, 80, 101, 109, 128;
1978.8, 12, 42, 58, 68, 92-93,
107, 123; 1979.10, 16, 23-24,
27, 38, 91, 98, 136, 137, 161,
166; 1980.7, 10, 15, 21-22, 26,
31, 35, 43, 60, 67, 78-79, 102,
108, 111-112, 119, 122, 124,
130, 132, 155, 160; 1981.7, 14,
19, 23, 29, 33, 50, 57-58, 77,
84, 86, 92, 99, 115, 118, 121,
141, 155, 156, 168, 171, 178;
1982.22, 50, 57, 61, 66, 81, 89,
101, 105, 130, 141, 150, 169;
1983.10, 11, 28, 37, 47, 60, 74,
81, 90, 98, 116, 134, 151, 153,
164, 195, 218; 1984.25, 27, 50,
61, 63, 71, 72, 79, 86, 90-91,
98, 112, 114, 117, 119, 124,
145, 162, 171-172, 178, 181,
191, 197, 230; 1985.2, 24, 35,
40, 48, 56, 64, 73, 76, 79, 82,
102, 120, 131-132, 153, 167;
1986.3-4, 13, 21, 26, 31, 40, 45,
48, 50-52, 56, 58-59, 63, 73, 97,
90, 101, 114, 117, 123-124,
127, 141-142, 148, 153, 156,
158, 159; 1987.15, 17, 21, 30,
43, 45, 56, 61, 68, 75, 85, 94-
95, 107, 112, 121-122, 132
--prefaces, 1975.123; 1976.80, 138,
172, 194; 1977.15, 120;
1978.81; 1979.15, 44, 54;
1981.121; 1983.96, 144;
1984.39, 40, 129, 171; 1985.34,
69, 75; 1986.9, 15, 60, 132,
154; 1987.87
--*The Princess Casamassima*,
1975.10, 15, 17, 44, 79, 119,
130; 1976.9, 10, 29-30, 34, 36,
47, 49, 94, 130, 134, 184, 202;
1977.3, 56, 90, 93, 114, 129,

132; 1978.4, 10, 18, 43-44, 94,
102, 117, 126; 1979.47, 53;
1980.13, 28, 50, 78, 82, 86, 89,
103, 111; 1981.6, 14, 64, 130,
166, 172, 179; 1982.5, 27, 50,
53, 89, 134, 152, 165; 1983.13,
46, 69, 101, 110, 118, 192;
1984.9-10, 97, 126, 171, 175,
181-182, 213; 1985.76, 88, 96,
102, 105, 162, 167; 1986.1, 19,
22, 34, 59, 63, 72, 77, 111, 143;
1987.15, 26, 43, 55, 78, 94,
122, 137
--"The Private Life," 1977.10;
1980.158; 1983.121, 152;
1985.116; 1986.76
--"A Problem," 1984.189
--"Professor Fargo," 1983.106;
1987.125
--"The Pupil," 1975.79, 84, 122;
1976.68, 162; 1977.49; 1978.37,
119; 1979.112, 160; 1980.15,
61, 82; 1983.19; 1984.221;
1986.70; 1987.16, 122
--"The Real Right Thing,"
1984.200
--"The Real Thing," 1975.109;
1976.21, 157; 1977.38, 65;
1978.62; 1979.51, 126; 1981.4;
1983.12, 20, 112, 179;
1984.131, 150, 200-201, 221;
1985.158; 1987.16
--*The Reverberator*, 1980.161;
1984.2
--*Roderick Hudson*, 1975.10, 48,
56, 79; 1976.49, 52, 101, 105,
126, 198; 1977.3, 5, 98, 137;
1978.51, 63, 64; 1979.10, 71,
87, 138, 161; 1980.7, 12, 28,
111, 142; 1981.14, 165;
1982.136; 1983.11, 59, 206;
1984.54, 124, 213, 230;
1985.43, 56, 127, 151; 1986.3,

--"The Turn of the Screw," 1975.2,
10, 92, 97, 103, 105, 133, 143;
1976.14, 22-23, 61, 68, 138,
141, 151, 171, 177, 179, 183,
187, 201; 1977.1, 4, 19, 33, 36,
43, 50-51, 60, 75, 81, 88, 94,
103, 107, 143; 1978.11, 16, 32-
33, 40, 66, 70-71, 74, 85, 108;
1979.1, 12, 16, 25, 26, 58, 66,
73, 86, 89, 107, 112, 121, 128,
143, 154, 170; 1980.2, 14, 30,
37, 41, 46, 54, 59, 70, 80, 81,
93, 94, 105-106, 114, 126, 129;
1981.11, 18, 20-22, 53, 65, 68,
79, 82, 87, 91, 95, 103, 154;
1982.9, 15, 30, 34, 79, 98, 104,
110, 114, 120, 127, 143, 145,
164, 168; 1983.38, 52, 54, 62,
66, 108, 121, 142, 145, 149,
156, 177, 182, 199; 1984.2, 14,
35, 41, 46, 63-64, 101, 123,
141-142, 168, 171, 179, 219;
1985.20, 23, 25, 31, 39, 42, 60,
62, 81, 89, 112, 114, 163-164;
1986.18, 25, 29, 33, 39, 60-61,
88-89, 121, 144; 1987.6, 15-16,
19, 48, 50, 105, 114, 122, 126,
129
--"The Velvet Glove," 1976.61;
1978.36; 1979.32; 1981.35;
1983.123
--"The Visits," 1984.63
--*Washington Square*, 1975.9, 80;
1976.74, 101; 1977.23; 1978.12,
102, 108; 1979.95, 164;
1980.39; 1981.177; 1982.72, 86,
105; 1983.98, 165; 1984.12, 85,
110, 122, 178; 1985.4, 10, 55,
63, 83, 102, 132; 1987.15, 43,
49
--*Watch and Ward*, 1975.38, 98;
1976.101; 1984.63; 1985.53,
71; 1987.43

--"The Way It Came," 1984.165
--*What Maisie Knew*, 1975.10, 26,
60, 74, 92, 106; 1976.26, 68,
77, 91, 103-104, 130, 132, 135,
148, 155, 173; 1977.5, 79;
1978.2, 59, 79, 94, 98, 106;
1979.13, 19, 27, 53, 97, 112,
140; 1980.10, 15, 46, 69, 104,
137, 163; 1981.31-32, 56, 74,
179; 1983.11, 21, 74, 88, 98,
101, 139, 185, 222; 1984.29,
37, 60, 110, 143, 191; 1985.4,
26, 137, 138, 167; 1986.24,
102, 118; 1987.15, 44, 52, 107
--*William Wetmore Story and His
Friends*, 1975.66; 1978.72;
1981.173; 1983.103; 1985.119;
1987.60
--*The Wings of the Dove*, 1975.24,
26, 53, 59, 72, 86-87, 113, 118,
120, 141, 144; 1976.10, 24, 49,
64, 65, 67, 81, 98, 103, 110,
123, 152, 160, 164, 198, 200,
206; 1977.3, 24, 28, 31, 51, 60,
77, 80, 127-129; 1978.6, 12, 21,
23, 58, 94; 1979.4, 8, 14, 19,
24, 27, 56, 91, 98, 99, 133, 136,
153, 163; 1980.7, 28, 70, 87,
111, 113, 118; 1981.27, 41, 45-
46, 55, 58, 66-67, 73, 175;
1982.41, 51, 57, 130, 158-159;
1983.19, 31, 39, 82, 90, 98,
107, 174, 191-192, 207;
1984.22, 24, 30, 54, 61, 63, 66,
71-72, 87, 100, 109, 126, 134,
162, 197-198, 212-213, 205,
230; 1985.24, 48, 56, 67, 97-98,
101-102, 116, 136, 165; 1986.3,
7, 39, 52, 62, 69, 78, 97, 102,
105, 141; 1987.15, 21, 39, 44,
78, 81, 89, 98, 104, 107, 119,
121-122, 128, 131

1984.28, 31, 181; 1985.9, 71,
13
Light and Darkness
(Sosekinatsume), 1983.175
Light, Christina, 1975.135;
1978.105, 113, 128; 1983.160;
1984.218; 1986.72
"A Light Woman" (Robert
Browning), 1977.78; 1986.100
Lincrusta-Walton, 1980.131
linguistics, 1975.108
The Little Foxes (Lillian
Hellman), 1985.57
London, 1978.54, 126; 1979.78;
1981.130; 1982.88; 1984.114;
1986.77, 78; 1987.26
Longmore, 1979.129
look, 1978.32; 1979.51
Lord Jim (Joseph Conrad),
1975.95
Loring, Katharine, 1980.138;
1982.156
loss, 1976.1, 40, 114; 1978.68
love, 1976.130, 132, 141, 144;
1977.8, 118; 1979.27;
1980.133; 1983.90; 1984.36, 90,
134; 1985.48; 1987.111
Lowe, Elena, 1983.160
Lubbock, Percy, 1980.90; 1986.132
Lutoslawski, Wincenty, 1976.128

Madame Bovary (Gustave
Flaubert), 1976.76, 190;
1977.31; 1981.99
Madonna, 1979.178
The Magus (John Fowles), 1984.98
Mallet, Rowland, 1978.64; 1986.49
The Maltese Falcon (Dashiell
Hammett), 1976.81
Manfred (George Gordon, Lord
Byron), 1986.82
Mann, Thomas, 1975.62; 1976.122
manners, 1985.4, 63

-Victorian, 1976.167
manuscript, autograph, 1976.44;
1979.33
A Man with a Torn Glove (Titian),
1982.149
The Man with the Mask, 1976.88;
1984.227
The Marble Faun (Nathaniel
Hawthorne), 1976.156, 189;
1977.131; 1986.62, 107
Marcher, John, 1975.27, 55;
1976.2, 147; 1978.55; 1980.18;
1981.63; 1986.64, 134
marketplace, 1983.7, 8, 101; 1986.1
marriage, 1975.96; 1976.83, 144;
1977.30; 1979.27; 1980.83;
1981.7, 86; 1982.17, 57;
1984.27, 50, 71, 72, 189, 190-
191, 214; 1985.48, 73; 1986.17,
158; 1987.20, 68, 98
-Boston, 1981.42
Marriage a la Mode (William
Hogarth), 1986.147
Marriages and Infidelities (Joyce
Carol Oates), 1985.81
Marxism, 1976.145; 1984.171
masculinity, 1982.62-63; 1987.27
mask, 1981.80
masochism, 1975.26; 1976.112
"The Masque of the Red Death"
(Edgar Allen Poe), 1981.23
masquerade, 1975.85; 1983.47
Massey, Irving, 1980.165
"The Master," 1982.111
The Master of Ballantrae (Robert
Louis Stevenson), 1975.25
The Master of Go (Yasanari
Kawabata), 1983.16
mastery, 1983.80; 1984.31;
1985.14-15
Matcham, 1983.162
materialism, 1984.73, 87; 1985.1,
10; 1986.10-11; 1987.9

matriarchy, 1981.55
Matthiessen, F.O., 1975.52;
    1976.18; 1981.143; 1985.86;
    1987.24
Maugham, W. Somerset, 1983.212
Maupassant, Guy de, 1981.15;
    1982.1; 1984.204
Mauves, Mme. de, 1978.128
meaning, 1983.61; 1984.13
mediation, 1978.47
Medici, Marchese Simone de
    Peruzzi de, 1978.122
Meian (Soseki Natsume), 1975.91,
    128; 1976.146, 182; 1977.89
melodrama, 1975.56; 1976.24-25,
    152; 1984.126, 147; 1986.7,
    136; 1987.5
Melville, Herman, 1975.85;
    1983.119
memoirs, 1987.60
memory, 1978.6; 1984.104, 153
Mencken, H.L., 1976.63
The Merchant of Venice (William
    Shakespeare), 1982.148
Meredith, George, 1975.100;
    1982.150
Mergi, Vanda de, 1981.166
Mérimée, Prosper, 1977.149;
    1980.144
Merle, Madame, 1975.81; 1977.55;
    1986.142
Merriman, Charles Eustace,
    1985.149
mesmerism, 1978.114
meta-metaperspective, 1983.139
metaphor, 1976.98; 1977.112;
    1983.50, 215
-military, 1976.66
-religious, 1975.15, 83; 1976.17;
    1986.39
method
-scenic, 1979.99; 1983.179
-synthetic, 1982.142

Middlemarch (George Eliot),
    1975.29; 1977.47
Miles, 1976.177; 1981.68;
    1983.177; 1984.123
The Mill on the Floss (George
    Eliot), 1976.115
Miller, Daisy, 1976.68; 1978.128;
    1979.167; 1980.165; 1983.198;
    1985.63
Milosz, Czeslaw, 1984.230
Milton, John, 1981.163; 1983.207;
    1987.122
Milton, Peter, 1977.97
mimesis, 1979.54; 1980.90
mirror, 1976.23; 1981.22; 1983.148
misgovernment, 1984.219
misogyny, 1983.69
Miss Brown (Vernon Lee),
    1980.29
A Modern Instance (William Dean
    Howells), 1980.103
modernism, 1976.11; 1977.35;
    1982.19; 1983.30, 98, 12, 176;
    1984.173
"moment-of-crisis," 1986.109
Mona Lisa (Leonardo da Vinci),
    1981.161; 1987.21
money, 1977.70; 1981.43; 1984.12,
    29, 212; 1985.24, 160; 1986.69;
    1987.98
Moods (Louisa May Alcott),
    1985.53
Moore, Marianne, 1980.164;
    1983.220
morality, 1975.74, 87; 1976.75, 87,
    165, 207; 1977.124; 1978.2, 28,
    37, 66, 93, 127; 1979.13, 72;
    1980.78, 176; 1982.27; 1983.36,
    125, 158; 1984.105, 117, 173;
    1987.39, 97
Moreau, Gustave, 1975.135
Moreen, Morgan, 1979.160

"The Prisoner of Chillon" (Geoge
    Gordon, Lord Byron),
    1977.146
process
-creative, 1975.38; 1984.69;
    1985.69
-writing, 1975.123; 1980.70;
    1981.79
progress, 1987.9
Propp, Vladimir, 1978.115
Prospero, 1985.76
Proust, Marcel, 1975.39; 1977.135;
    1979.142; 1982.90; 1984.224;
    1985.41; 1987.119
Psalm 55, 1983.19
psychology, cognitive, 1984.91
psychomachia, 1977.76
publicity, 1984.95
Punch, 1977.127
Purdy, James, 1986.121
Puritanism, 1975.93; 1977.39;
    1978.100; 1979.78; 1984.199
Pygmalion (George Bernard
    Shaw), 1976.21
Pynchon, Thomas, 1987.12

quest, 1977.28; 1981.46, 54;
    1982.116; 1983.55
Quicksand (Nella Larsen),
    1977.64
Quincas Borba (Machado de
    Assis), 1987.75
"Qui Sait?" (Guy de Maupassant),
    1984.204
quixote, female, 1982.101

race, 1978.73
Rachel, 1987.43
Radcliff, Ann, 1985.31
Rahv, Philip, 1982.67
The Rainbow (D.H. Lawrence),
    1987.45

The Rake's Progress (William
    Hogarth), 1986.147
Rank, Otto, 1975.55
Rao, Raja, 1984.177
"Rappaccini's Daughter"
    (Nathaniel Hawthorne),
    1979.58; 1984.23; 1986.26
readability, 1985.60
reader, 1977.141; 1979.93; 1980.72,
    77; 1981.32, 41; 1983.102;
    1984.126; 1987.37
-response, 1981.31, 65, 112;
    1984.37, 171
reading, 1976.138; 1977.26, 57;
    1978.70; 1979.18, 22; 1980.30;
    1981.8, 53, 59; 1983.152;
    1984.88; 1987.23, 87
realism, 1975.16-17, 103, 119;
    1976.11, 101, 136, 139;
    1977.95, 101, 114, 129;
    1978.21, 43, 112; 1979.103,
    127; 1980.22, 89, 103, 137;
    1981.31, 36; 1982.63, 165;
    1983.9, 26, 60, 115, 133, 168,
    192-193; 1984.30, 117, 188;
    1985.155; 1986.2, 6, 129, 143;
    1987.5, 129
-psychological, 1975.110; 1976.51;
    1979.119; 1982.139
reality, 1977.69; 1980.3; 1983.10,
    173; 1984.200, 223; 1985.5;
    1987.4, 131
reception, critical, 1979.64;
    1980.66, 80, 156; 1985.59;
    1987.67
-contemporary, 1975.130-131;
    1977.126, 133; 1978.103;
    1982.144; 1986.123; 1987.43,
    44
-German, 1975.49; 1983.77
-Japanese, 1980.4
recital, fictitious, 1985.133
recollections, 1984.154; 1985.107

541

The Red Badge of Courage
(Stephen Crane), 1976.91
redemption, 1977.39
Redgrave, Michael, 1984.163
reference, 1984.188
refinement, 1976.61; 1978.88
reflexivity, 1985.158
reform, 1978.18-19; 1980.13;
1985.93
regression, 1981.88; 1982.162;
1986.87
Reid, Whitelaw, 1979.29; 1987.90
relativism, 1981.73
reliability, 1975.60
religion, 1979.168; 1984.95, 152
Renan, Ernest, 1979.28
renunciation, 1975.38, 69, 98;
1976.65, 83; 1977.142; 1978.42,
52; 1980.58, 132; 1982.109,
141; 1984.110; 1987.132
repetition, 1985.47; 1987.15
representation, 1978.45; 1979.126,
150; 1982.130, 135; 1984.52,
118; 1986.2; 1987.2, 5
repression, 1982.127; 1987.103
responsibility, 1982.51
revenge, 1987.65
reversal, 1984.14
revision, 1975.44; 1976.12, 181;
1977.6; 1980.122; 1981.94, 106,
165; 1983.129; 1984.40, 156,
157; 1985.18, 95, 105, 132;
1986.96; 1987.17, 46, 94, 107
revolution, 1980.50
The Rhetoric of Irony (Wayne
Booth), 1984.220
rhythm, 1985.168
rhythmic devices, 1980.104
Ribeyro, Julio Ramon, 1983.117
Richardson, Robert, 1975.143
"The Rich Boy" (F. Scott
Fitzgerald), 1986.109
Ricoeur, Paul, 1975.24; 1984.188

The Rime of the Ancient Mariner
(Samuel Taylor Coleridge),
1987.83
The Rise of Silas Lapham
(William Dean Howells),
1980.103
Rivette, Jacques, 1976.7
Robinson, Edgar Arlington,
1976.172
Robinson, Hyacinth, 1975.15;
1976.9, 134; 1977.114, 132;
1980.50; 1982.5; 1983.110;
1986.72; 1987.55
Robinson, Solon, 1975.1; 1980.1
"The Rocking-Horse Winner"
(D.H. Lawrence), 1980.61
Rollins, Clara, 1978.120
roman fantastique, 1983.156
romance, 1975.87, 119; 1976.127;
1977.85; 1979.32, 100, 122,
133; 1980.15, 59, 79, 88-89;
1981.56, 58; 1983.155, 178;
1984.145; 1985.98-99; 1986.23,
62; 1987.5, 7, 58
Romans of the Decadence
(Thomas Couture), 1987.127
romanticism, 1976.11, 101, 122;
1981.36, 46; 1983.9; 1985.32
Rome, 1982.157; 1984.51, 161
Romeo and Juliet (William
Shakespeare), 1982.147
Rooth, Miriam, 1978.128; 1987.43,
73
"A Rose for Emily" (William
Faulkner), 1975.77
Roth, Philip, 1981.159; 1982.23,
154; 1984.151; 1985.147, 148;
1987.120, 134
Rothschild, Baron Ferdinand de,
1976.185
Roundell, Mrs. Charles, 1985.104
Rousset, Jean, 1984.224
Ruiz, 1978.87

"Writing the War Story" (Edith
Wharton), 1980.148
Wuthering Heights (Emile Brontë),
1978.92

"Xingu" (Edith Wharton), 1984.66

The Yellow Book, 1975.30
Young, Stark, 1985.142; 1986.150
The Young Visitors (Daisy
Ashford), 1975.106

Zola, Emile, 1983.3, 33; 1987.26
Zuckerman Bound (Philip Roth),
1982.154; 1985.147

Author Index

Adegawa, Yuko, 1983.1; 1984.1
Agnew, Jean-Christophe, 1983.2
Akiyama, Masayuki, 1976.1;
  1981.1, 2; 1985.1
Albers, Christina Edna, 1987.1
Aldaz, Anna Maria, 1976.2
Alexander, Charlotte, 1975.1;
  1980.1
Allen, E., 1981.3
Allen, Elizabeth, 1984.2; 1987.17
Allen, Jeanne Thomas, 1975.2;
  1977.1; 1980.2
Allen, John J., 1979.1
Allen, Walter, 1981.4
Allison, John B., 1981.5
Altenbernd, Lynn, 1977.2
Alter, Robert, 1985.2
Anand, Mulk Raj, 1978.1
Anderson, Charles R., 1976.3;
  1983.3; 1984.3
Anderson, Charles Roberts,
  1977.3
Anderson, Don, 1985.3
Anderson, J.W., 1979.2
Anderson, Linda, 1980.3
Anderson, Quentin, 1975.3;
  1976.4; 1983.4

Anderson, Walter E., 1982.1;
  1983.5, 6
Anderson Imbert, Enrique, 1982.2
Andrews, Terry L., 1984.4
Anesko, Michael Walter, 1983.7,
  8; 1986.1
Aoki, Tsugio, 1980.4, 5; 1983.9
Archer, Barbara Clark, 1985.4
Arkhipov, Anatolii, 1984.5
Armistead, J.M., 1975.4
Arms, George, 1976.124
Armstrong, Judith, 1976.5
Armstrong, Nancy, 1977.4
Armstrong, Paul Bradford,
  1977.5; 1978.2, 3; 1983.10, 11;
  1985.5; 1986.2; 1987.2, 3, 4
Arnavon, Cyrille, 1976.6
Ashton, Jean, 1976.7
Asselineau, Roger, 1985.6
Asthana, Rama Kant, 1980.6
Auchard, John Francis, 1980.7;
  1986.3
Auchincloss, Louis, 1975.5, 6;
  1977.6; 1979.3; 1984.6
Auerbach, Jonathan, 1984.7
Auerbach, Nina, 1978.4; 1982.3;
  1986.4

Haggerty, George Edgar, 1977.42; 1979.59
Haight, Gordon S., 1981.60
Hakim, Ziad, 1984.87
Hall, D.A., 1980.64
Hall, Richard, 1976.86; 1979.60, 61, 1983.83, 84
Hall, Sallie J., 1976.87
Hall, William F., 1975.56; 1976.88
Hallab, Mary Y., 1977.43; 1986.67; 1987.48
Hallisey, Jeremiah Joseph, 1978.50
Halperin, John, 1977.44; 1985.54, 55
Halpern, Joseph, 1981.61
Halter, Peter, 1984.88
Hamer, Karen R., 1987.51
Hanley, Lynne T., 1981.62
Hanson, Kathryn Schefter, 1976.89
Hansot, Elizabeth, 1987.15
Hardin, James Budd, 1976.90
Hardt, John S., 1981.72
Hardwig, Marilyn Ross, 1978.51
Hardy, Barbara, 1975.57; 1985.56
Hardy, Donald E., 1983.85
Harkins, Jeffrey Patrick, 1983.86
Harold, Brent, 1975.58
Harris, Janice H., 1981.62
Harris, Wendell V., 1979.62
Hartman, Terese B., 1987.49
Hartsock, Mildred E., 1975.59; 1977.45, 46; 1984.221
Hartstein, Arnold Michael, 1981.64
Harvey, Susan Elicia, 1981.65
Haviland, Beverly Josephine, 1982.68
Hayes, Dennis James, 1975.60
Heaton, Daniel H., 1979.63
Heller, Arno, 1976.91
Heller, Terry, 1987.50

Hendin, Josephine, 1984.89
Hendricks, Susan E., 1984.90
Herring, Henry D., 1984.91
Hertz, Neil, 1983.88
Heston, Lilla A., 1981.66
Hewitt, Rosalie, 1980.65; 1982.69; 1983.89
Heyns, Michiel Willem, 1984.92
Higdon, David Leon, 1985.57, 58
Higgins, Charles, 1982.70
Higgins, Joanna A., 1978.52
Hilfer, Anthony Channell, 1981.67
Hill, Robert W., Jr., 1981.68
Hirsch, David H., 1983.90; 1984.93
Hirsch, Marianne, 1981.69, 70, 71
Hirsh, Allen, 1983.91
Hoag, Gerald, 1975.61
Hochman, Baruch, 1976.92; 1977.47; 1983.92, 93
Hocks, Richard A., 1978.23; 1980.66; 1981.72; 1983.94; 1984.94; 1987.44, 51
Hoile, Christopher, 1975.62
Holbrook, David, 1987.52
Holland, Laurence B., 1975.7; 1978.23; 1987.15, 16, 17
Holloway, Anna Rebecca, 1981.73
Holloway, John, 1979.65
Holloway, Marcella M., 1979.66
Holly, Carol Thayer, 1976.93; 1983.95, 96; 1985.59; 1987.53
Holman, C[larence] Hugh, 1979.67, 68, 69
Holmberg, Lawrence Oscar, Jr., 1977.48
Horne, Philip, 1986.68; 1987.54
Horvath, Brooke, 1982.71; 1985.60
Horwitz, B.D., 1977.49
Houston, Neal B., 1977.50; 1985.61
Hovanec, Evelyn A., 1979.70
Hovey, Richard B., 1982.72
Howard, David, 1984.95; 1987.15

Martin, Timothy P., 1980.90
Martin, W.R., 1976.133; 1980.91,
   92; 1981.98; 1982.95;
   1983.123, 124; 1984, 137, 138;
   1985.94; 1986.99, 100; 1987,
   82, 83, 84
Maslennikova, A.A., 1980.93
Massa, Ann, 1978.30; 1982.96
Massadier-Kenney, Francoise,
   1986.101
Mastrodonnato, Paola Galli,
   1981.99
Matei, Mihai, 1982.97
Mathees, Irene, 1980.32
Matheson, Terence J., 1982.98
Mathews, Laura Lenore, 1986.102
Matkovic, Ivan, 1979.98
Matthews, Robert J., 1977.75
Matthiesson, F.O., 1975.7;
   1978.23; 1984.221
Mauriac, Françoise, 1978.65
Mayer, Charles W., 1976.135;
   1979.99, 100, 101; 1982.99;
   1984.139
Mayhew, Paula Hooper, 1984.140
Maynard, Reid N., 1976.136
Mazzella, Anthony J., 1975.7;
   1980.94; 1981.100, 101
Mazzeno, Laurence W., 1979.102
Measham, J.D., 1980.95
Medina, Angel, 1983.125
Mehl, Dieter, 1985.95
Meitzinger, Serge, 1983.126
Melchiori, Barbara Arnett,
   1985.96
Melchiori, Giorgio, 1976.137
Mellers, Wilfrid, 1984.141
Menikoff, Barry, 1977.76
Mercer, Caroline G., 1985.97
Merideth, Eunice Mae, 1987.85
Merivale, Patricia, 1978.66
Messent, Peter, 1982.100
Messick, Judith Hassan, 1982.101

Meyers, Charles John, III, 1980.96
Meyers, Cherie Kay Beaird,
   1987.86
Meyers, Jeffrey, 1975.86; 1979.103
Miall, David S., 1984.142
Michaels, Walter Benn, 1976.138
Miguez, Manual, 1982.102
Mihaila, Rodica, 1979.104
Milicia, Joseph, 1978.67
Millar, Gavin, 1979.105
Miller, J. Hillis, 1980.97; 1981.102;
   1987.16, 87
Miller, James E., 1983.127
Miller, James E., Jr., 1976.139;
   1987.88
Miller, Karl, 1985.98, 99
Miller, Nancy K., 1978.68
Miller, Vivienne, 1980.98
Milligan, Ian, 1986.103
Milne, Fred L., 1981.103
Milne, Gordon, 1977.77
Minnick, Thomas L., 1975.87
Mitchell, Juliet, 1984.143
Mitchell, Lee Clark, 1987.89
Mizruchi, Susan Laura, 1985.100,
   101
Mochi Gioli, Giovanna, 1976.140;
   1982.103; 1983.128; 1986.104
Moddelmog, Debra, 1985.128
Mogen, David, 1976.141
Moldstad, Mary Martha Frew,
   1985.102
Montanye, Elizabeth Anne,
   1985.103
Monteiro, George, 1975.88, 89;
   1976.142; 1977.78, 79;
   1983.129, 130, 131; 1985.104;
   1987.90, 91
Montgomery, Stephen Edward,
   1977.80
Moon, Heath, 1977.81; 1980.99;
   1982.104; 1984.144; 1987.92
Moon, Michael, 1986.105

Moore, Geoffrey, 1984.145; 1986.106, 107
Moore, Rayburn S., 1975.90; 1976.143; 1984.146
Moore, Rosemary, 1976.144
Moore, Susan Reibel, 1982.105
Morales, Peter, 1976.145
Mori, Mihoko, 1975.91; 1976.146
Morris, Wright, 1978.69
Morse, David, 1987.93
Morsiani, Giovanni, 1977.82
Morton, Bruce, 1978.22
Moseley, James G., Jr., 1975.92, 93
Mottram, Eric, 1986.108
Mulrain, Mary Ann, 1979.106
Mulvey, Christopher, 1983.132
Murdock, Kenneth, B., 1984.221
Murphy, Brenda, 1979.107; 1983.133
Murphy, James Gerald, 1987.94
Murphy, Kathleen, 1977.83
Murphy, Kevin, 1978.70
Murphy, P.D., 1986.109
Myrick, Patricia Lynn, 1987.95

Nalbantian, Suzanne, 1983.134
Namekata, A., 1980.108
Nance, William L., 1975.94; 1976.147, 148
Nardin, Jane, 1978.71
Nash, Cristopher, 1977.84
Nassar, Eugene Paul, 1983.135
Nathan, Rhoda B., 1984.147
Nettels, Elsa, 1975.95; 1976.149; 1977.85; 1978.72, 73; 1980.100
Newberry, Frederick, 1982.106
Nielson, Kathleen Buswell, 1987.96
Niemtzow, Annette, 1975.96
Nies, Frederick James, 1985.105
Nigro, August J., 1984.148
Nordloh, David J., 1984.150

Normann, Ralf G., 1975.97; 1976.151; 1977.87, 88; 1979.109, 110; 1980.101; 1982.108
Nowell-Smith, Simon, 1985.107
Nowik, Nancy Ann, 1976.152
Nussbaum, Martha Craven, 1983.137, 138; 1985.108; 1987.97

Oakes, Randy W., 1984.151
Oaks, Susan Jean, 1986.111
Ober, Warren U., 1980.92; 1981.98; 1982.95; 1983.123, 124; 1984.138; 1985.94; 1986.99, 100; 1987.82, 83, 84
Obuchowski, Peter A., 1978.74
O'Connor, Dennis Lawrence, 1975.98; 1980.102; 1981.105
O'Connor, Leo F., 1984.152
O'Donnell, Patrick, 1980.103
Oelschlegel, Lawrence Edward, 1980.104; 1983.139
O'Gorman, Donal, 1980.105, 106
Ohi, Dee Hansen, 1981.106
Ohmann, Carol, 1984.221; 1987.15, 16
Ohsima, Jin, 1982.109
Ohta, Ryoko, 1981.107
Oka, Suzuo, 1977.89
Olander, Karen A., 1985.109
Olin-Ammentorp, Julie Andrea, 1987.98
Oliveira, Celso de, 1981.108
Oliver, Clinton, 1977.90
Olney, James, 1984.153
Olson, Christopher Peter, 1985.110
Orishima, Masashi, 1986.112
Orlich, Ileana Alexandra, 1987.99
Osipenkova, O.I., 1980.107
Otsu, Eiichiro, 1980.108, 109

Shapland, Elizabeth, 1981.131
Sharma, Jagdish Narain, 1975.120;
  1978.100; 1979.136
Sharma, Jatindra Kumar,
  1984.177
Sharma, Shruti, 1986.138
Sharp, Sister M. Corona, 1984.178
Shaw, Jean Barrett, 1977.115
Shaw, Valerie, 1983.179
Sheldon, Pamela J., 1976.171
Sheleny, Harvey, 1977.116
Shelston, Alan, 1984.178
Shereshevskaia, M.A., 1983.180
Shields, John C., 1983.181
Shine, Muriel G., 1986.139
Shinn, Thelma J., 1976.172
Shipley, Jeanne Elizabeth,
  1979.137
Shollenberger, James Edward,
  1977.117
Shroyer, Thomas, 1985.129
Shuey, William A., III, 1980.132
Shumaker, Conrad, 1982.136
Shurr, William H., 1981.132
Sibley, Gay Palmer, 1982.137
Siebers, Tobin, 1983.182; 1984.179
Sicker, Philip Timothy, 1977.118;
  1980.133
Silver, Daniel J., 1981.133
Simpson, Lewis P., 1980.134
Sinyard Neil, 1986.140
Skilton, David, 1977.119; 1985.130
Sklenicka, Carol J., 1982.138
Sklepowich, E.A., 1978.101;
  1981.134
Slaughter, Carolyn Overton,
  1987.114
Slomovitz, Philip, 1979.138
Smit, David William, 1983.183,
  184; 1984.180; 1987.115
Smith, Carl S., 1977.120; 1979.139
Smith, Geoffrey Dayton, 1982.139;
  1983.185

Smith, George E., III, 1987.116
Smith, Henry Nash, 1977.121;
  1978.102, 103
Smith, John William, 1985.131
Smith, Paula Vene, 1987.117
Smith, Peter, 1984.181, 182
Smith, Virginia Llewellyn,
  1983.186
Smyth, Paul Rockwood, 1980.135
Snitow, Ann B., 1984.183
Snow, C.P., 1978.104
Snow, Lotus, 1978.105
Snyder, John, 1978.106
Sobal, Nancy Lee, 1984.184
Sokolianskii, M., 1983.187
Solimine, Joseph, Jr., 1980.136
Solomon, Petre, 1983.188
Somers, Paul P., Jr., 1977.122
Souchu, Laurent, 1984.185
Spackman, W.M., 1981.135
Spector, Cheryl Ann, 1986.141
Spender, Stephen, 1979.140
Spengemann, William C.,
  1977.123; 1981.136
Speigel, Alan, 1976.173
Spigelmire, W. Lynne, 1978.107
Spilka, Mark, 1977.124
Springer, Mary Doyle, 1975.121,
  122; 1978.108; 1985.78
Sprinker, John Michael, 1975.123
Sprinkler, Michael, 1984.186
Stafford, William T., 1975.124,
  125; 1976.174; 1977.125;
  1978.109; 1981.137, 138, 139,
  140, 141; 1983.189, 190;
  1985.132; 1986.142
Stallman, R.W., 1979.141
Stambaugh, Sara, 1976.175
Stanzel, F.K., 1984.187
Starer, Marilyn Morris, 1977.126
Stauble, Michele, 1975.126
Steele, Elizabeth, 1981.142